Agile Data Warehousing for the Enterprise

A Guide for Solution Architects and Project Leaders

Agile Data Warehousing for the Enterprise

A Guide for Solution Architects and Project Leaders

Ralph Hughes, MA, PMP, CSM

AMSTERDAM • BOSTON • HEIDELBERG • LONDON • NEW YORK • OXFORD • PARIS
SAN DIEGO • SAN FRANCISCO • SINGAPORE • SYDNEY • TOKYO

Morgan Kaufmann is an imprint of Elsevier

Acquiring Editor: Steve Elliot
Editorial Project Manager: Lindsay Lawrence
Project Manager: Priya Kumaraguruparan
Cover Designer: Mark Rogers

Morgan Kaufmann is an imprint of Elsevier
225 Wyman Street, Waltham, MA 02451, USA

ISBN: 978-0-12-396464-9

British Library Cataloguing-in-Publication Data
A catalogue record for this book is available from the British Library

Library of Congress Cataloging-in-Publication Data
A catalog record for this book is available from the Library of Congress

For information on all Morgan Kaufmann publications
visit our website at www.mkp.com

Working together
to grow libraries in
developing countries

www.elsevier.com • www.bookaid.org

Advance Praise for *Agile Data Warehousing for the Enterprise*

Agile Data Warehouse for the Enterprise is a must read for any data professional tasked with delivering enterprise reporting and analytics in the nimble, speed-to-value environment that we find ourselves in today. It marries an agile methodology with data warehousing's best practices to create a blueprint for delivering value fast.

— **Nik Green**, Director of Business Intelligence for a multi-billion dollar food retailer

This comprehensive guide provides a solid and complete foundation for agile EDW development including revolutionary new paradigms. I especially like the 'out of the box' thinking, practicality of the techniques, and the research and case studies backing up the validity of the proposed approaches. Recommend reading for all DW/BI technical leaders.

— **Len Silverston**, CEO of Universal Data Models and author of the *Data Model Resource Book* series

Ralph's book goes way beyond just agile programming—it illustrates an iterative approach to the full development life cycle and is particularly relevant to issues of data quality that we focus on at DAMA. The hyper modeling techniques in particular will allow teams to avoid the death trap of producing big, risky application designs up-front before a project's requirements are fully known.

— **Ken Dunn**, President of DAMA's Houston chapter

Ralph's notion of "80/20 specifications" for data warehousing projects really worked, saving our business partners the pain of doing an exhaustive requirements specification up-front. This approach got the team developing the most important features first, letting the product owner fill in details on topics as each one came up later during development.

— **Naveen Thalanki**, Project Manager for a Fortune 500 company

If you're still programming data warehouses by hand, you're wasting 90 percent of your time and money. Ralph's guide for project leaders not only outlines the automated, metadata-driven development we've been practicing for years in the Netherlands, but also links that practice to agile requirements, coding, and quality assurance. It is a unique book, a must read.

— **Ronald Damhof**, DW/BI Consultant to the Dutch Central Bank

The industry has struggled to bring the mechanics and benefits of Agile to the data warehousing and business intelligence communities. Ralph's work in this area is timely and important to assist in driving success within your enterprise and project teams. Following the guidance found in this book will help you deliver value at a rapid pace.

— **Tom Hammergren**, CTO of Cordata Healthcare Innovations and author of *Data Warehousing for Dummies*

Short Contents

1. Solving Enterprise Data Warehousing's "Fundamental Problem"   1

Part I
Summaries of Generic Agile Development Methods

2. Primer on Agile Development Methods   13

3. Introduction to Alternative Iterative Methods   31

Part I References   55

Part II
Review of Fast EDW Coding and Risk Mitigation

4. Essential DW/BI Background and Definitions   59

5. Recap of Agile DW/BI Coding Practices   85

6. Eliminating Risk Through Nested Iterations   109

Part II References   121

Part III
Agile EDW Requirements Management

7. Balancing between Two Extremes   125

8. Redefining the Epic Stack to Enable Value Accounting   151

9. Artifacts for the Generic Requirements Value Chain   169

10. Artifacts for the Enterprise Requirements Value Chain   181

11. Intersecting Value Chains for a Stereoscopic Project Definition   215

Part III References   245

Part IV
Agile EDW Data Engineering

12. Traditional Data Modeling Paradigms and Their Discontents   249

13. Surface Solutions Using Data Virtualization and Big Data   293

14. Agile Integration Layers with Hyper Normalization   329

15. Fully Agile EDW with Hyper Generalization   375

Part IV References   421

Part V
Agile EDW Quality Management Planning

16. Why We Test and What Tests to Run   425

17. Designating Who, When, and
     Where   457

18. Deciding How to Execute the
     Test Cases   477

Part V References   499

Part VI
**Integrating the Pieces of the Agile
EDW Method**

19. The Agile EDW Subrelease Cycle   503

Part VI References   521

Full Contents

List of Figures   xvii
List of Tables   xxiii
Abbreviations   xxv
Foreword   xxvii
Acknowledgments   xxix

1. **Solving Enterprise Data Warehousing's "Fundamental Problem"**

    The Agile Solution in a Nutshell   1
    Five Legs to Stand Upon   3
    The Agile EDW Alternative is Ready to Deploy   5
    Defining a Baseline Method for Agile EDW   5
    Plenty of Motivation to "Go Agile"   7
    Structure of the Presentation Ahead   7

Part I
Summaries of Generic Agile Development Methods

2. **Primer on Agile Development Methods**

    Defining "Agile"   13
    Agile Manifesto Values and Principles   19
    Scrum in a Nutshell   20
      User Stories   21
      Scrum's Five-Step Delivery Iteration   23
    Contributions from Extreme Programming   26
      XP Values and Principles   27

3. **Introduction to Alternative Iterative Methods**

    Lean Software Development   31
      Lean Origins   31
      Lean Methods as a Long-Term Destination   32
      Lean Principles and Tools   33
    Kanban   41
      Quick Sketch of the Kanban Method   41
      Visualizing and Maintaining Continuous Flow   43

      Evidence-Based Service Levels   44
      Comparing Kanban to Scrum   45
    The Hybrid "Scrumban" Approach   47
    Rational Unified Process   49
      RUP Overview   49
      Why Not RUP for DW/BI?   52

Part I References   55

Part II
Review of Fast EDW Coding and Risk Mitigation

4. **Essential DW/BI Background and Definitions**

    Primary Source for DW/BI Standards   60
      Defining Enterprise Data Warehousing   61
    Basic Business Terms   63
    Data and Information Terms   65
    Information Services Terms   66
    Software Engineering Terms   67
    Basic Architectural Concepts   70
      System Architecture   70
      Data Architecture   71
      Reference Architecture   74
      Enterprise Architecture   75
    Architectural Frameworks   76
      Zachman Enterprise Architectural Framework   76
      DAMA Functional Framework   76
      Hammergren DW Planning Matrix   77
    Additional Data Warehousing Concepts   79
    Traditional Project Management Terms   82

5. **Recap of Agile DW/BI Coding Practices**

    Iterative Coding Alone Significantly Improves BI Projects   85
      Yet Data Integration Remains a Challenge   85

New Roles for DW/BI Projects   86
  Project Architect   87
  Data Modeler   88
  Systems Analyst   88
  System Tester   89
  Proxy Product Owner   89
  Scrum Master   90
  Including the New Roles on the Team's
    Whale Chart   90
80/20 Specifications   90
Developer Stories   92
  DW/BI User Stories Hide Much of the
    Data Integration Work   92
  Developer Stories Make DW/BI Work
    More Manageable   93
  Developer Stories Require a Deeper
    Understanding of Value   94
Current Estimates   95
Adding Techniques from Kanban   97
  Pipelined Delivery   98
  Work-in-Progress Limits for Developers   100
  Iteration −1 and 0   100
  Two-Pass Testing   101
Evidence-Based Service Level Agreements   102
Proof that Agile DW/BI Works   104
  Investigating Project Cost Impacts
    in More Detail   106
  Some Myths Prove True   107

6. Eliminating Risk Through Nested
   Iterations

EDW Programs Slip into "231 Swamps"   109
  231 Swamps Derive from a Command
    and Control Strategy   110
Agile's Fundamental Risk Mitigation
  Technique   111
  Agile's General Risk Mitigation Strategy   111
  Eliminating Miscommunication with
    Multiplexed Engineering Phases   113
Agile EDW's Extended Risk Mitigation
  Techniques   114
  Three Types of Risk Threaten EDW
    Programs   114
  Mitigating the Risk of Application
    Coding Concept Errors   116
  Mitigating the Risk of Solution Concept
    Errors   116
  Mitigating the Risk of Business Concept
    Errors   119

Part II References   121

Part III
Agile EDW Requirements Management

7. Balancing between Two Extremes

Building the Case for Effective Requirements
  Management   126
  Developers Often Neglect Requirements
    Work   128
  Motivating Teams to Take Requirements
    Seriously   128
Easy to Overinvest in Requirements
  Management   130
  "Requirements Management" Formally
    Defined   130
  Traditional Projects Employ a Big Spec
    Up Front   130
  Requirements are Inherently Diverse   132
  Business Process Reengineering Can
    Add to the Complexity   135
Reasons Not to Overinvest in Requirement
  Work   136
  Precision at the Expense of Accuracy   137
  Business Partners are Adverse to Traditional
    Requirements Gathering Efforts   138
  Traditional Requirements Management
    Fails More than it Succeeds   139
  The Greatest Failure is Losing Business
    Opportunity   139
Agile's Approach Centers on Balance   141
  Agile Objectives for Requirements
    Management   141
  Knowing when a Backlog is "Good
    Enough"   143
  Enable Regular "Current Estimates"   144
  Keeping the Requirements Management
    Process Agile   144
Two Intersecting Requirements
  Management Value Chains   144
  Salient Differences between GRM
    and ERM   147
Business Analysts Implicit in Two Project
  Lead Roles   149

8. Redefining the Epic Stack
    to Enable Value Accounting

Toward a Robust Epic Decomposition
  Framework   151
  Defining the Backlog Hierarchy's
    Structure   151

Aligning the Epic Stack to the
  Company's Hierarchy   152
Clearly Defining Each Level within the
  Epic Stack   154
Testing Whether Stories are Good Enough   156
Clarifying Everything with Value Accounting   159
The Basics of Value Accounting   160
Value Accounting Makes Developers
  More Effective   161
Value Accounting Mitigates Project Risk   162
Allocating Value Throughout an Epic Tree   163
Identifying the Value of a Project   163
Allocating Value to Epics   164
Allocating Value to Themes and User
  Stories   164
Value Buildups by Environment Provide
  Motivation and Clarity   165

9. Artifacts for the Generic Requirements Value Chain

Beware of Requirements Churn   169
User Modeling/Personas   170
End Users' Hierarchy of Needs   171
Benefits Offered by the BI Hierarchy
  of Needs   173
Mind Maps and Fishbone Diagrams   174
Vision Boxes   176
Vision Statements   176
Product Roadmaps   178

10. Artifacts for the Enterprise Requirements Value Chain

The Generic Value Chain Can Overlook
  Crucial Requirements   181
ERM as a Flexible RM Approach   183
Focusing on Enterprise Aspects of Project
  Requirements   184
Functionality Dimension   184
Polarity Dimension   185
Orientation Dimension   185
Streamlined ERM Templates   186
Uncovering Project Goals with Sponsor's
  Concept Briefing   186
Justification Type   187
Customer Experience Impacts   188
Functional Area Impacts Assessments   188
Value of the Program   188
Program Success Metrics   189

Identifying Project Objectives with
  Stakeholder's Requests   189
Business System Challenges   189
Current Manual Solution   189
Desired Business Solution   190
Volume Requirements and End-User Census 190
Dependent Systems   190
Sketching the Solution with a Vision
  Document   191
Solutions Statements   191
Features and Benefits List   191
Context Diagram   194
Target Business Model   196
High-Level Architectural Diagram   197
Nonfunctional Requirements   197
Segmenting the Project with Subrelease
  Overview   198
Subrelease Identifier   200
Subrelease Scope   200
Business Process Supported   202
Technical Description   207
Nonfunctional Requirements   208
Providing Developer Guidance with
  Module Use Cases   209
Goal   209
Standard Flow of Events   209
Alternative Flow of Events   210
Special Requirements   212
Source-to-Target Mappings as
  Supplemental Specifications   212
Nonfunctional Requirements as
  Supplemental Specifications   212

11. Intersecting Value Chains for a Stereoscopic Project Definition

Intersecting the Two Value Chains   215
Agile EDW's Version of Requirements
  Traceability   215
Addressing Nonfunctional
  Requirements   217
The Proper Problem Domain for
  Agile EDW   217
Agile EDW Supports Broader
  Architectural Activities   219
Supporting the Organization's
  Software Release Cycle   221
Phases Borrowed from Rational Unified
  Process   221
Iterations −1 and 0 Fit into the Inception
  Phase   221

Arriving at a Predevelopment Project
Estimate   223
Managing the Predevelopment Estimate   225
Completing the Release Cycle   226
Techniques for the Elaboration Phase   226
Choosing Developer Stories for the
Elaboration Phase   226
Proving Out Architectures Using a
"Steel Thread"   227
Prioritizing Project Backlogs   228
Managing Incremental Precision   229
A Framework for Visualizing Progressive
Requirements   230
The Freezer, Fridge, Counter Metaphor   230
Effort Levels by Team Roles   232
Visualizing Requirements Management
Demands with Effort Curves   232
Allocating Time for Nonfunctional
Requirements   234
**Conquering Complex Business Rules
with an Embedded Method**   235
Add the Data Cowboy Role   235
Special Skills and Tools for the Data
Cowboy   236
Modified Data Mining Method Can Help   236
Placing Business Rules Discovery and
Analysis into the Effort Curves   238
Interfacing with Project Governance   239
Not Returning to a Waterfall Approach   242

Part III References   245

Part IV
Agile EDW Data Engineering

12. Traditional Data Modeling Paradigms and Their Discontents

EDW at a Crossroads   249
Reviewing the Reference Architecture   249
Standard Normal Forms Lead to Complex
Integration Layers   251
Conformed Dimensions Lead to Complex
Presentation Layers   253
A Peek at the Agile Alternatives   255
Models, Architectures, and Paradigms   257
Data Architecture   257
Data Model   258
Data Modeling Paradigm   259
Normalization Basics   260
Designing Databases to Eliminate
Update Anomalies   260

Example: One Table from First to Fifth
Normal Form   262
Generalization Basics   271
Advantages and Disadvantages of
Generalization   271
Example: Generalizing a Sales Table
for the Party Entity   274
**The Standard Approach and its Data
Modeling Paradigms**   279
**The Traditional Integration Layer as a
Challenged Concept**   281
Involves an Expensive Hidden Layer   281
Results are Difficult to Understand   282
Entails High Maintenance Conversion
Costs   283
**"Straight-To-Star" as a Controversial
Alternative**   286
**Four Change Cases for Appraising a Data
Modeling Paradigm**   286
Change Case 1: Correcting Fourth Normal
Form Errors   287
Change Case 2: Generalizing to the Party
Model   287
Change Case 3: New Trigger Attribute
for a Slowly Changing Dimension   289
Change Case 4: Changing a Fact Table's
Grain   290

13. Surface Solutions Using Data Virtualization and Big Data

Leveraging Shadow It   294
Example of a Five-Step Collaborative
Effort   294
Lessons from the Case History   296
**Faster Value Delivery with Data
Virtualization**   296
Defining Data Virtualization   297
The Basic Use Case   297
DVS Performance Features   299
The Economics of Virtual Solutions   300
DVS Surface Solutions and Progressive
Deployment   302
Comparing DVS Surface Solutions
to the Previous Example   304
Data Virtualization's Value Proposition   305
EDW's Reference Architecture
Becomes Dynamic   306
An Agile Role for Big Data   308
Introducing Big Data Technologies   308
The Need for Big Data Technology   309
The Promise of Schema-On-Read   310
An Introduction to Hadoop   311

Notable Contrasts between SQL and
        MapReduce   314
Making MapReduce Look Like SQL with
        Hive   317
Big Data Is Not Just Hive   324
Using Big Data to Enhance EDW Agility   325

14. Agile Integration Layers with Hyper Normalization

Hyper Normalization Hinges on "Ensemble
        Modeling"   329
    Several Varieties of Hyper Normalization
        Exist   330
Hyper Normalized Data Modeling Concepts   331
    Business Key Entities   333
    Linking Entities   334
    Attribute Entities   335
    Lightly Integrated, Persistent Staging Area 337
    Ensemble Modeling Components
        Allow Light Integration and Agility   339
    An Insert-Only Paradigm   342
    Swedish Variation: Anchor Modeling   343
Reusable ETL Modules Accelerate New
    Development   344
    One ETL Pattern Needed Per Hyper
        Normalized Table Type   345
    Parameter-Driven ETL Module Prototypes   346
    Calling the Reusable ETL Modules   348
    Self-Validating Reusable ETL Modules   350
    Estimate of Comparative Development
        Efforts   352
Common Data Retrieval Challenges
    and Their Solutions   352
    HNF Aids the Leading Edge of the
        Integration Layer Only   353
    Retrieving Data from an HNF Repository
        Doubly Difficult   354
    Solution 0: Focus on Presentation Layer
        Objects   356
    Solution 1: Dummy Attribute Records   356
    Solution 2: Current Record Indicators   356
    Solution 3: Point-in-Time Tables   356
    Solution 4: Table Pruning   358
    Solution 5: Bridging Tables   359
    Solution 6: Retrieval Query Writers   360
    Clearing an Architectural Review   361
Re-Architecting the EDW for Hyper
    Normalization   361
    The Simple Vault Style   362
    The Enhanced Vault Style   363
    The Source Vault Style   364
    The Raw Vault Style   364
    Blending Styles to Achieve Agility   365

Enabling Evolution of Existing EDW
    Components   366
    Change Case 1: Splitting Out Entities   366
    Change Case 2: Upgrading to a
        Party Model   367
HNF-Powered Agile Solutions   368
Evidence of Success   371
    Online Financial Services   372
    The Free University   372

15. Fully Agile EDW with Hyper Generalization

Hyper Generalization Involves a Mix
    of Modeling Strategies   375
    Extreme Generalization   377
    Adding Time-Oriented Object
        Classification   380
    Managing Things and Links with an
        Associative Data Model   381
    Storing Attributes as Name-Value Pairs   384
    Storing Transaction Data in a Lightly
        Dimensionalized Format   385
    Managing Hyper Generalized Data in
        HGF Requires an Automation Tool   386
HGF Enables Model-Driven Development
    and Fast Deliveries   387
    Eliminating Most Logical and Physical
        Data Modeling   387
    Controlling the EDW Design from a
        Business Model Diagram   387
    Driving Design Changes Using a Business
        Model   389
Loading Data into the Hyper Generalized
    Integration Layer   390
    Loading the Dimensional Objects   390
    Loading the Transactional Objects   391
Retrieving Information from a Hyper
    Generalized EDW   392
    HGF Systems Maintain a Performance
        Sublayer   392
    Performance Layer Objects Enable
        Business-Intelligible Data Retrieval   393
Model-Driven Evolution and Fast
    Adaptation   395
    Impact of Model Changes on Existing
        Data   395
    Hyper Generalization Tools Facilitate
        Data Conversions   396
Supporting Derived Elements   397
    Value-Added Loops   397
    Model-Driven Master Data
        Components   398
Addressing Performance Concerns   402

Demonstrating Agility Through Four Change
  Cases   403
    Change Case 1: Upgrading Attributes to
      Entities   403
    Change Case 2: Consolidating Entities
      into the Party Model   406
    Change Case 3: New Trigger for a Slowly
      Changing Dimension   409
    Change Case 4: Increasing the Grain
      of a Fact Table   410
    Recap of Change Case Findings   413
  HGF-Powered Agile Solutions   414
    Easier Backfills for Surface Solutions   415
  Evidence of Success   416
    Case History 1: Model-Driven
      Development in Pharmaceuticals   416
    Case History 2: Hyper Generalized Data
      Warehousing in Specialty Retail   417

Part IV References   421

**Part V
Agile EDW Quality Management
Planning**

16. Why We Test and What Tests to Run

  Why Test?   426
    Testing Keeps Agile Teams from Cutting
      Corners   426
    Testing Keeps Root Cause Analysis
      Manageable   427
    Testing Integrates Teamwork Across the
      Pipeline   428
    Testing Leads to Better Requirements   428
    Testing Makes Real Progress Visible to
      Everyone   428
  An Agile Approach to Quality Assurance   429
    Striving for Balance   429
    Keeping Quality Assurance "Agile"   430
    Extending Test-Led Development Far
      Above Unit Testing   432
  "What to Test?" Answered with Top-Down
    Planning   433
    The Six Dimensions of DW/BI Testing   433
    Preliminary Definitions   435
    Dimension 1: Planning   436
    Dimension 2: System   437
    Dimension 3: Functional   439
    Dimension 4: Polarity   439

    Dimension 5: Time Frame   440
    Dimension 6: Point-of-View   440
  A 2 × 2 Planning Matrix for Top-Down
    Test Selection   441
    A Framework for Assessing a QA Plan's
      Coverage   441
    Linking Test Planning to Requirements
      and Risk Management   443
  "What to Test?" Answered Bottom-Up   444
    Data Warehousing Testing Techniques   444
    Traditional Application Testing
      Techniques   446
    Agile-Specific Test Techniques   449
    An Easy-to-Follow Test Technique
      Matrix for Low-Level Validations   451
    Reusable Test Widgets   452
    Test Cases Roll Forward Along the
      System Dimension   453
    Testing for Convergence   453

**17. Designating Who, When, and
      Where**

  Who Shall Write the Tests?   457
    A Framework for Understanding Who
      Must Do What   458
  When Should Teammates Perform
    Their QA Duties?   463
    Quality Activities Within an Iteration
      Cycle   464
    Quality Duties at the End of a Release
      Cycle   466
  Where Should Teammates Perform
    Their QA Duties?   468
    Distributing Test Activities Across
      Environments   468
    Distributing Test Techniques Across
      Environments   469
  Key Quality Responsibilities by Team Role   470
    Guiding the Team to Self-Organized
      Quality Planning   470
    Suggested Quality Duties by Role   471
  The Overarching Duties of the System
    Tester   473
    Certifying the User Demo's Data   474
  How Many Testers are Needed?   475

**18. Deciding How to Execute the Test
      Cases**

  Good Agile Quality Plans Involve
    Numerous Test Executions   477

Alternatives to Sufficient Testing
Unattractive   480
Facing Up to Test Automation   481
Step 1: Update the Top-Down Plan   482
**Step 2: Start Building the Parameter-Driven
Widgets**   482
Step 3: Plan Out the Test Data Sets   482
Identifying How Many Data Sets are
Required   484
Planning to Create Dozens of Data Sets   485
Planning Storage for Dozens of
Data Sets   487
Planning also for Expected Results   487
**Step 4: Implement the Engine, Whether
Manual or Automated**   487
Defining Test Scenarios   489
**Step 5: Define the Project's Set of Testing
Aspects**   489
**Step 6: Build and Populate the Test Data
Repository**   490
Step 7: Quantify the Testing Objectives   491
Step 8: Begin Creating Test Cases   493
Step 9: Start Up the Engine   493
**Step 10: Visualize Project Progress with
Quality Assurance**   494
Tests Implemented by Environment   494
Connect Top-Down and Bottom-Up
Quality Planning   496
Defects Over Time   496
Current Iteration Burndown Chart   496
Step 11: Document the Team's Success   497

Part V References   499

Part VI
**Integrating the Pieces of the Agile
EDW Method**

19. The Agile EDW Subrelease Cycle

**Making the Release Cycle a
Repeatable Process**   503
Traditional Notions of Data Governance   504
A Life Cycle for Data Governance   505
Data Governance Actions for the EDW
Team   508
Machine-Assisted Data Governance
for the Subrelease Cycle   509
The Agile EDW Subrelease Value Cycle   510
The Fast Requirements Portion of the
Subrelease Cycle   511
The Fast Delivery Portion of the
Subrelease Cycle   512
**Centering the Value Cycle on Data
Governance and Quality**   514
Deepening the Support for Data
Governance   514
Achieving World-Class Quality
Assurance   515
Guiding the Agile EDW Transition   515
The DW/BI Customer's Bill of Rights   516
Toward an Agile EDW Manifesto   518

Part VI References   521

Index   523

List of Figures

Figure 1.1	The negative feedback loop present in most traditionally managed projects.	2
Figure 1.2	The five major components to agile enterprise data warehousing.	4
Figure 1.3	Agile EDW practices switch projects to a positive feedback loop.	4
Figure 1.4	How a team might acquire agile EDW techniques working from the inside out.	8
Figure 2.1	Mind map of generic iterative methods summarized in Chapters 2 and 3.	14
Figure 2.2	A family tree of methods and influences leading to the agile EDW method.	15
Figure 2.3	The traditional waterfall method.	17
Figure 2.4	The Agile manifesto cover page.	17
Figure 2.5	Values and principles of the agile manifesto and Extreme Programming.	18
Figure 2.6	The essence of the Scrum method.	21
Figure 2.7	Typical user story.	22
Figure 2.8	A sample Scrum task board as it would appear in mid-iteration.	24
Figure 2.9	A Scrum burndown chart as it would appear in mid-iteration.	25
Figure 3.1	Lean values, principles, and tools.	33
Figure 3.2	Value-stream analysis of development work for a challenged waterfall project.	34
Figure 3.3	Typical Kanban work board.	42
Figure 3.4	Kanban-style cumulative flow diagram.	43
Figure 3.5	Sample cycle time distribution analysis for a Kanban team.	44
Figure 3.6	Typical stages of "Scrumban"—the transition from Scrum to Kanban.	48
Figure 3.7	Two-tiered Scrumban task board.	48
Figure 3.8	Values and principles of the Rational Unified Process.	50
Figure 3.9	RUP Whale Chart.	51
Figure 3.10	Google Ngram of "Scrum" and "RUP" through 2008.	53
Figure 4.1	Business organizational terms used in this book.	64
Figure 4.2	Business conceptual model.	72
Figure 4.3	Logical data model.	72
Figure 4.4	Physical data model.	73
Figure 4.5	Sample enterprise data warehouse "reference architecture".	75
Figure 4.6	Zachman framework adapted for an enterprise data warehousing program.	77
Figure 4.7	DAMA's framework for data management functions.	78
Figure 4.8	Hammergren's matrix for sequencing DW/BI development work.	79
Figure 5.1	Typical RUP-style whale chart for an agile EDW project.	91
Figure 5.2	Agile EDW user stories result in too many developer stories for one, short Iteration.	92
Figure 5.3	Deriving developer stories from user stories.	94
Figure 5.4	A "current estimate" for an agile data warehousing project.	96
Figure 5.5	Agile data warehousing requires pipelined work specialties.	99
Figure 5.6	Work packages tend to flow diagonally across technical specialties and iterations.	101
Figure 5.7	Cycle time distribution analysis for an agile data warehousing project.	103
Figure 5.8	A current estimate adjusted for observed delivery cycle times.	104
Figure 5.9	Success rates for agile data warehousing teams, by number of agile projects completed, compared to traditional methods.	105
Figure 5.10	Agile's impact upon key performance indicators for data warehousing development projects.	105
Figure 5.11	Agile data warehousing surveys indicate that practitioners have overcome some challenge areas.	107
Figure 6.1	Relative cost of correcting defects grows by 100 between requirements and promotion into production.	112
Figure 6.2	Incremental delivery mitigates risk by increasing the number of product check points.	113
Figure 6.3	The sources of EDW project risk mitigated with three types of iterations.	115
Figure 6.4	Relative timing for the three types of iterations that Agile EDW employs.	118
Figure 7.1	Mind map of topics addressed in Part III.	126
Figure 7.2	Sample EDW requirements expressed at three levels.	127
Figure 7.3	Waterfall-style requirements management.	131
Figure 7.4	Typical requirements work breakdown for a traditional project.	133

Figure 7.5	As-is business process diagram showing a sample work flow requiring re-engineering.	135
Figure 7.6	To-be business process re-engineered to use EDW to communicate between agents.	136
Figure 7.7	Accuracy vs. precision.	137
Figure 7.8	Standard risk analysis.	140
Figure 7.9	Standard analysis adjusted for dollar value of each type of risk.	141
Figure 7.10	Agile EDW's requirements management benefits greatly from intersecting value chains.	146
Figure 7.11	Overall agile EDW requirements management plan.	148
Figure 7.12	Enterprise requirements management roles.	150
Figure 8.1	Big picture – decomposing epics into a backlog of stories.	152
Figure 8.2	Immediate business stakeholder formalizing all levels of stories by linking them to the hierarchy among business stakeholders.	153
Figure 8.3	Primary technique for decomposing user stories into developers stories. Note the 25-to-1 multiplier for this project's user story.	158
Figure 8.4	INVEST and DILBERT'S test.	158
Figure 8.5	Big picture – recompiling modules for perceived value.	160
Figure 8.6	Value build-up charts distinguishing between delivery environments.	166
Figure 9.1	User modeling example.	171
Figure 9.2	Business intelligence user's hierarchy of needs for the example project.	172
Figure 9.3	Mind map & fish bone diagrams.	175
Figure 9.4	Previous mind map re-drawn as a fishbone diagram.	175
Figure 9.5	Front and back of a project vision box.	177
Figure 9.6	Example of a project vision statement.	177
Figure 9.7	Product road map formatted for discussions with product owner.	178
Figure 9.8	Product road map formatted for presentation to conflicting stakeholders.	179
Figure 10.1	Three important dimensions to application requirements.	182
Figure 10.2	Streamlined template for a streamlined *Sponsor's Concept Briefing* (SCB).	187
Figure 10.3	Streamlined template for a streamlined *Stakeholder Request* (SHR).	190
Figure 10.4	Template for a streamlined *Vision Document* (VDoc).	192
Figure 10.5	Sample vision document solution statements.	193
Figure 10.6	Sample vision document solution statements.	193
Figure 10.7	Defining a business solution.	194
Figure 10.8	Sample context diagram for a vision document.	195
Figure 10.9	Sample target business model for a vision document.	196
Figure 10.10	Sample high level architecture diagram for a vision document.	198
Figure 10.11	Target business model for a subrelease overview.	199
Figure 10.12	Subrelease scope drawn on a dimensions of value diagram.	201
Figure 10.13	Subrelease plan summary on a front-end dimensions of value diagram.	201
Figure 10.14	Template for a streamlined Subrelease Overview (SRO)	204
Figure 10.15	Use case model for a subrelease description.	205
Figure 10.16	Venn diagram for a subrelease description.	206
Figure 10.17	Data validation steps for a subrelease description.	206
Figure 10.18	Template for a streamlined *Module Use Case* (MUC).	210
Figure 10.19	Communicating the main flow of events with a level 2 data flow diagram.	211
Figure 10.20	Example of a source-to-target map.	213
Figure 11.1	Tracing requirements between value chains.	216
Figure 11.2	Corporate-level planning functions that generate architectural requirements.	218
Figure 11.3	Typical project release cycle used by large companies.	222
Figure 11.4	Fitting RM artifacts into the pre-development iterations.	223
Figure 11.5	Preparing the pre-development estimate for a new team.	224
Figure 11.6	Requirements management effort curves and timing of artifacts over length of a project (part I).	233
Figure 11.7	Requirements management effort curves and timing of artifacts over length of a project (part II).	234
Figure 11.8	The CRISP-DM process for data mining.	237
Figure 11.9	Interfacing agile EDW RM with project governance.	240
Figure 12.1	Basic EDW reference architecture with data paradigms listed.	250
Figure 12.2	Given the advent of hyper-modeled forms, EDW project leaders now have four data modeling paradigms to choose from.	251
Figure 12.3	Examples of standard normal form data models of increasing complexity.	252
Figure 12.4	Examples of conformed dimensional form models of increasing complexity.	254
Figure 12.5	Example of a hyper normalized data model.	255
Figure 12.6	The main portion of a hyper generalized data model.	256
Figure 12.7	Data architectures, paradigms, and models.	257
Figure 12.8	Business, logical, and physical data models.	259
Figure 12.9	The update anomalies data normalization is designed to prevent.	261
Figure 12.10	Context diagram for the normalization example.	263

Figure 12.11	Sample case's data in its starting arrangement, i.e., zeroth nomal form.	264
Figure 12.12	Impact of a first normal form correction upon sample case's data model.	265
Figure 12.13	Impact of a second normal form correction upon sample case's data model.	266
Figure 12.14	Impact of a third normal form correction upon sample case's data model.	267
Figure 12.15	Impact of a fourth normal form correction upon sample case's data model.	269
Figure 12.16	Impact of a fifth normal form correction upon sample case's data model.	273
Figure 12.17	Level zero data generalization.	275
Figure 12.18	Level one data generalization for the party model.	275
Figure 12.19	Level two data generalization for the party model.	276
Figure 12.20	Data generalization roll-up patterns.	276
Figure 12.21	Level three data generalization for the party model.	277
Figure 12.22	The hub & spoke conception of an enterprise data warehouse.	279
Figure 12.23	A schematic representation of a simple subject area in an EDW presentation layer.	280
Figure 12.24	Standard normal form models are brittle in the face of changing requirements.	283
Figure 12.25	Change Cases #3 and #4 for conformed dimensional form model.	290
Figure 13.1	A surface solution with architectural backfilling that leverages "Shadow IT".	295
Figure 13.2	Basic data integration use case, delivered without data virtualization.	298
Figure 13.3	Basic data integration use case, delivered using a data virtualization server.	298
Figure 13.4	Data virtualization reduces the number of interfaces required for a given set of solutions.	301
Figure 13.5	General surface-solutions delivery pattern with data virtualization.	303
Figure 13.6	Dimensions-of-value analysis for surface solutions with data virtualization.	304
Figure 13.7	Data virtualization's value proposition for agile EDW teams.	306
Figure 13.8	Surface solutions "channels" enabled by data virtualization.	307
Figure 13.9	Notable Apache Hadoop software components.	312
Figure 13.10	Processing pattern for a simple Map/Reduce join operation.	314
Figure 13.11	Sample Map/Reduce code for a simple two-table join.	315
Figure 13.12	Solution architecture for the Facebook Hive data warehousing example.	320
Figure 13.13	Cycle-time analysis for building the components of traditional and big-data DW/BI solutions.	322
Figure 13.14	Cycle-time analysis – cumulative time in learning cycles. Showing how time invested accumulates as learning cycles are repeated.	324
Figure 13.15	Cycle-time analysis – cumulative time in usage cycles. Showing how time invested grows as application is adapted by thousands of end users answering everyday business questions. Rapidly growing cost of HDFS in this scenario should give pause to those considering routing all of an organizations information into a "data lake."	324
Figure 13.16	Big data and traditional RDBMSs are converging.	325
Figure 13.17	A succession of surface solutions leveraging big data.	326
Figure 13.18	EDW reference architecture with surface solutions employing big data technology.	326
Figure 14.1	Ensemble data modeling.	330
Figure 14.2	Family tree of hyper normalized modeling approaches.	331
Figure 14.3	Hyper normalizing a 3NF data model – starting point.	332
Figure 14.4	Structures for the starting model (in 3rd normal form).	333
Figure 14.5	Hyper normalization Step 1 – declare business keys.	334
Figure 14.6	Structures for the hyper normalized model – business keys and their attributes.	335
Figure 14.7	Hyper normalization Step 2 – install many-to-many links between business keys.	336
Figure 14.8	Structures for the hyper normalized model – links and their attributes.	337
Figure 14.9	Hyper normalization Step 3 – split out all attributes to their own tables.	338
Figure 14.10	Hyper normalized model with abbreviated depiction of link and attribute entities.	338
Figure 14.11	Third normal form data warehouses are heavily impacted by new entities.	340
Figure 14.12	Linking tables in a hyper normalized data warehouse insulate existing tables against disruption when new entities are added.	341
Figure 14.13	Data vault model excerpt showing business keys and linking entities with multiple attribute tables.	342
Figure 14.14	Anchor modeled equivalent of the HNF order model.	344
Figure 14.15	Only a few, parm-driven ETL modules are needed to load the bulk of the data warehouse.	346
Figure 14.16	Prototypes for reusable hyper normalized load modules.	347
Figure 14.17	Driver script employing reusable load modules.	348
Figure 14.18	Driver script employing reusable load modules	350
Figure 14.19	Prototypes of reusable test widgets and a driver script calling them.	351
Figure 14.20	SQL query demonstrating the correlated subqueries needed to retrieve information from hyper normalized data warehouses.	355
Figure 14.21	Hyper normalized designs can require many correlated subqueries.	357
Figure 14.22	By using point-in-time tables where needed, we can simplify retrieval queries.	358
Figure 14.23	Data retrieval queries can be (a) simplified through table pruning and (b) generated from DBMS constraints.	359
Figure 14.24	Columns in the resulting bridge table.	360
Figure 14.25	EDW reference architecture adapted for a hyper normalized integration layer.	362
Figure 14.26	Four styles for distributing hyper normalized repositories across the EDW reference architecture.	363

Figure 14.27	Data models for Change Case #1 under hyper normalization.	366
Figure 14.28	Hyper normalized model needed to solve Change Case 2.	368
Figure 14.29	Joins of existing and new tables needed to feed load_link( ) for the Link_Party_Order_Installer table.	369
Figure 14.30	Joins of existing and new tables needed to feed load_link( ) for the Link_Party_Rollup table of dealership relationships.	369
Figure 14.31	Surface solution patterns employing a hyper normalized integration layer.	370
Figure 15.1	Decomposing data into a hyper generalized data store and then projecting it to a star schema.	376
Figure 15.2	Hyper generalizing a HNF data model – starting point.	377
Figure 15.3	Hyper generalization Step 1 – add metadata tables.	378
Figure 15.4	Hyper generalization Step 2 – simplify to one table per function.	378
Figure 15.5	Hyper generalization Step 3 – "shred" attributes into name-value pairs.	379
Figure 15.6	Hyper generalization Step 4 – temporalize thing type relationships.	379
Figure 15.7	Hyper normalization Step 5 – temporalize the remaining entities.	380
Figure 15.8	Business models are machine readable.	382
Figure 15.9	Dimensional objects from the business model translated to records in the associative data model.	382
Figure 15.10	Sample records for things and links in the associative data store.	383
Figure 15.11	Shredding attributes into name-value pairs.	385
Figure 15.12	Pivoting shredded attributes back to their original format.	386
Figure 15.13	Data warehouse business model used for the change cases.	388
Figure 15.14	Example of how graphical model changes impact the associative data store.	389
Figure 15.15	Change Case 1's data transform for dimensions before the business model is updated.	390
Figure 15.16	Starting data transform for the transaction data of Change Case 1.	392
Figure 15.17	Hyper generalized data warehouse automation systems can address the full EDW reference architecture.	393
Figure 15.18	Helper tables allow EDW admins to write queries against business objects.	394
Figure 15.19	Records impacted by flattening the hierarchy between Orders and eSegment	396
Figure 15.20	Steps to updating a hyper generalized EDW's dimensional entities and their data.	397
Figure 15.21	Creating derived columns and master data elements using value-added loops.	398
Figure 15.22	Using the master data management utility of the data warehouse automation tool.	399
Figure 15.23	Sample workflow for master data processing, highlighting the role of the data stewards.	400
Figure 15.24	Master data management front end showing single-record correction screen.	401
Figure 15.25	EDW reference architecture updated to include master data management layers.	402
Figure 15.26	Hyper generalized data warehouse performance benchmarks.	403
Figure 15.27	Business model changes needed to accomplish Change Case 1.	404
Figure 15.28	Data transform needed for Change Case 1 after modifications are made.	405
Figure 15.29	Hyper generalized reporting can successfully span a change in business models	407
Figure 15.30	Business model changes needed to accomplish Change Case 2.	407
Figure 15.31	Pre-loading the Corporate Party objects for customers in Change Case 2.	408
Figure 15.32	Data transform needed for Change Case 2 after modifications are made.	409
Figure 15.33	HGF query writer automatically spans modeling changes. *The data warehouse automation system provides default supertype entity references for customer records that existed before the modeling change.*	410
Figure 15.34	Business model update and resulting reporting for Change Case 4.	411
Figure 15.35	Dimensional data transform changes needed to accomplish Change Case 4.	412
Figure 15.36	Transaction data transform changes needed to accomplish Change Case 4.	413
Figure 15.37	Surface solution patterns employing a hyper generalized integration layer.	415
Figure 16.1	The level-of-effort needed to determine the root-cause of a defect increases exponentially with the number of defects that exist.	427
Figure 16.2	Visualizing quality via the number of tests executing or passing by environment.	429
Figure 16.3	The optimal level of testing is a balance between two types of risks.	430
Figure 16.4	Steps in the test-led development approach.	432
Figure 16.5	Relationships between test terms as used in this book.	435
Figure 16.6	The difference between QC, QA, and QM.	437
Figure 16.7	Relationships between two testing dimensions and physical objects.	438
Figure 16.8	Using the agile 2 × 2 QA planning matrix to visualize a team's choice of test types.	442
Figure 16.9	"Data corners" test technique for models in standard normal form and conformed dimensional form.	445
Figure 16.10	Typical situation requiring a team to use the "expected values" test technique.	447
Figure 16.11	Many unit tests roll forward into the applications integration test suite.	454
Figure 16.12	Overview of an agile QA planning approach.	455
Figure 17.1	V-Model showing quality assurance as the flip side of requirements work.	459
Figure 17.2	V-Model adapted for agile data warehousing and showing the authors and consumers of requirements and specifications.	460
Figure 17.3	Using the 2 × 2 QA planning matrix updated to communicate test writing responsibilities.	461
Figure 17.4	Teams can avoid "over socializing" decisions by employing a "one-up, one-down" validation practice.	463
Figure 17.5	Sequencing QA work within an iteration.	464
Figure 17.6	Quality assurance work linked to the larger project cycles surrounding development iterations.	467

Figure 17.7	The 2 × 2 QA planning matrix updated to show when test cases will run.	468
Figure 17.8	Locating QA work among a data warehouse's execution environments.	468
Figure 17.9	2 × 2 QA planning matrix updated to show where test cases should execute.	470
Figure 18.1	2 × 2 QA planning matrix communicating how team will execute test cases.	481
Figure 18.2	Full regression testing for an EDW requires many data sets.	484
Figure 18.3	Automated testing cycle for a single testing scenario.	489
Figure 18.4	Overview of automated testing by scenario for an EDW.	490
Figure 18.5	Relationship between test case, test assertions, and the data required for each.	492
Figure 18.6	Test case build-up chart for a single iteration.	492
Figure 18.7	Visualizing quality via summary test results by subject area and architectural layer.	493
Figure 18.8	A sample project quality dashboard showing four measures of quality achieved by a development team.	495
Figure 18.9	Supporting quality fulfillment documentation with an automated test engine.	497
Figure 19.1	Enterprise information management includes a business-led data governannce program and an IT-led information management program.	506
Figure 19.2	Agile EDW project start-up aligns well with the data governance cycle.	507
Figure 19.3	Agile EDW subrelease cycle.	510
Figure 19.4	Agile EDW subrelease cycle showing support for data governance.	514
Figure 19.5	Agile EDW subrelease cycle showing support for quality assurance.	516

List of Tables

Table 2.1	Agile Elements by Origin	16
Table 3.1	Some Commonly Cited Advantages of Kanban Over Scrum	46
Table 3.2	Some of the Templates Used with the Rational Unified Process (RUP)	52
Table 4.1	Formal Definitions of Core Data Warehousing Terms	62
Table 4.2	Key Terms and Their Synonyms Used in This Book	63
Table 4.3	Names for Different Groupings of Project Team Members	69
Table 5.1	Areas Where Generic Scrum is Particularly Challenged by Data Integration Work	86
Table 5.2	Factors Having the Greatest Impact for Those Agile DW/BI Practitioners Reporting Increased Costs	106
Table 6.1	Failure Rates for Traditionally Managed Software Development Projects	110
Table 6.2	Examples of Errors by Conceptual Level	115
Table 7.1	Traditional Requirements Analysis Process	132
Table 7.2	Standard Requirements Categories	134
Table 7.3	Comparison of Accuracy and Precision for an Agile Enterprise Data Warehousing Project	138
Table 7.4	Traditional Approaches to Requirements Performed Poorly in the Era Before Agile	139
Table 7.5	Agile Objectives for Requirements Management	145
Table 8.1	Example of How to Codify an Epic Stack for Agile EDW Teams	155
Table 8.2	Sample Epic Tree from the Revenue Assurance Example	157
Table 9.1	Generic Agile RM Techniques	170
Table 10.1	Contrast between Generic and Enterprise Requirements Management Value Chains	183
Table 10.2	Summary of the Artifacts Comprising the Enterprise Value Chain	184
Table 10.3	Fact-Qualifier Matrix for a Subrelease Description	203
Table 11.1	Hierarchy of Enterprise Data Warehouse Planning	220
Table 11.2	Risk Calculation Framework and Example	227
Table 11.3	Progressive Requirements Elaboration Pattern	231
Table 11.4	Steps of the CRISP-DM Process	238
Table 11.5	Assessment of Agile EDW Requirements Management Approach for Agility	243
Table 12.1	History of Data Normalization	262
Table 12.2	Insert Anomaly for the 3NF Sales Channel Table	268
Table 12.3	Sample Case's Tables After 4NF Correction Applied	269
Table 12.4	Records Demonstrating a Fifth-Normal Form Violation	270
Table 12.5	Table Records After 5NF Correction Applied	272
Table 12.6	Realistic Level-of-Effort Per Table for Non-Trivial EDW Re-Engineering Assignments	285
Table 12.7	Summary of Re-Engineering Labor for Four Change Cases when Using a Traditionally Modeled Modeling Paradigm	288
Table 13.1	Comparative Level of Effort for Engineered vs. Declared Objects	302
Table 13.2	Contrast between Surface Solutions Using Shadow IT Versus Data Virtualization Servers	305
Table 13.3	Contrasting the SQL and MapReduce Queries Used for the Two-Table Join Example	317
Table 13.4	Relative Strengths of Data Management Paradigms	318
Table 14.1	Nomenclature Differences between Data Vault and Anchor Modeling Standards	344
Table 14.2	Comparable Conversion Costs Per Table when Employing the Hyper Normalized Data Modeling Paradigm	353
Table 14.3	Hyper Normalization's Impact Upon EDW Re-Engineering Change Cases	367
Table 15.1	Level-of-Effort Estimates for Four Change Cases	406
Table 15.2	Hyper Modeling Approaches Compared	414
Table 16.1	Partial List of Tests Types for EDW Teams to Choose From	434
Table 16.2	Number of Test Packages Needed to Test Everything in Every Way for a Medium-Sized Data Warehouse	435
Table 16.3	Validation Compared to Verification	441
Table 16.4	Simple Tests for a Given Data Warehouse Table	445
Table 16.5	The Combinatorial Reduction Test Case Writing Technique	448
Table 16.6	Combinatorial Reduction Example	449
Table 16.7	QA Planning Grid Showing Test Type by Target Column Type	451
Table 16.8	Sample Function Prototypes for Reusable Test Widgets	452
Table 17.1	Quality Assurance Responsibilities Documented by Roles and by Test Type	462

Table 17.2   Quality Assurance Responsibilities by Key DW/BI Aspect   471
Table 17.3   Key Responsibilities for the Agile EDW System Tester Role   474
Table 17.4   Typical Tester-to-Programmer Ratios for Agile Enterprise Data Warehousing Projects   475
Table 18.1   Estimating the Number of Test Cases Needed for a Modest Level of EDW Testing   478
Table 18.2   Estimating the Number of Low-Level Test Case Executions for Four Subreleases   479
Table 18.3   Sample Source-to-Target Mapping Referencing Reusable Test Widgets   483
Table 18.4   Typical Test Data Sets for Agile EDW Projects   485
Table 18.5   Commonly Employed Testing Aspects   488
Table 18.6   Sample Test Source Data Structure   491

Abbreviations

These abbreviations are employed at times in text and diagrams of this book.

BI   Business Intelligence
CIF   Corporate Information Factory
EA   Enterprise Architecture
EDW   Enterprise Data Warehousing
DAMA   Data Management Association
DBMS   Database Management System
DW/BI   Data warehousing/business intelligence
ERP   Enterprise Resource Planning
IEEE   Institute of Electrical and Electronics Engineers
IT   Information Technology
OID   Object Identifier
OLAP   Online analytical processing (DW/BI applications)
OLTP   Online Transaction Processing (transaction capture applications)
PMO   Project or Program Management Office
RUP   Rational Unified Process
SDLC   Systems Development Lifecycle
SID   Surrogate Identifier
SLA   Service Level Agreement
TDWI   The Data Warehousing Institute
XP   Extreme Programming

DEVELOPMENT TEAM ROLES

DM   Data Modeler
PA   Project Architect
PO   Product Owner
PPO Proxy Product Owner
SA   Systems Analyst
SM   Scrum Master
ST   System Tester

Foreword

When my friend, Ralph Hughes, asked me to write the foreword to his book, I was thrilled. His deep knowledge of the agile methodology plus his long history of building and maintaining business intelligence and data warehouse environments puts him in a unique position to marry these two critical initiatives together.

And so he has done in his latest book, *Agile Data Warehousing for the Enterprise*. The book builds upon the foundation established in his previous books on agile data warehousing by setting forth an unambiguous and thorough body of work defining a reliable set of "best practices" for such undertakings. Why are these necessary? Here is my take on it:

1. To eliminate risk. Best practices mean an agile data warehousing team can determine where gaps or missed opportunities exist in their project activities. These can quickly destabilize forward progress and erode confidence in the overall success of the project.
2. To bridge the gaps in traditional agile methodology for data warehousing. Ralph's book promotes the agile principles useful for fast, rapid *project* development while ensuring the maintainability and long-term *program* aspects of a complicated environment such as data warehousing.
3. To put agile requirements management in a practical light. Generic requirements management and enterprise-capable requirements management are often at odds with each other. Both are mandatory for data warehousing. This book spends significant time explaining these two and how to balance them before continuing the design process.
4. To explain why agile data models are mandatory and how to generate them. Traditional data modeling techniques have their shortcomings. In this book, Ralph described two hyper modeling techniques and why they may be your best alternative to modeling the incredible data complexity found in all mature data warehouses.
5. To engage alternative methods for creating a modern data warehouse environment. These include embracing an organization's "shadow IT" from the business, using data virtualization sensibly, and incorporating big data technologies gracefully.
6. To ensure all development bases are covered. These include mundane activities such as the agile approach to project definition, coding techniques, data engineering, quality assurance and data governance, and appropriate release cycles.

A most complete and thorough "how to" book on agile data warehousing if ever there was one.

Ralph's clear and easy to understand writing style, substantial expertise in this area, and practical examples throughout the book mean the reader will be fully prepared to undertake this complex initiative. Using the book as a guide all but guarantees that the reader will have a much higher success rate in quickly and efficiently creating the most critical components of a fact-based decision-making system.

Claudia Imhoff, Ph.D.
Author of *Corporate Information Factory and
Mastering Data Warehouse Design*

Acknowledgments

Finding a means to quickly deliver and adapt enterprise data warehouses in small increments has been the most difficult professional challenge I have tackled to date. This book took 15 years of experimentation and hard reflection, all of which I could never have accomplished on my own. The people who helped me shape and evaluate the many ideas contained in this book are too numerous to mention, but the contributions of some are so large I must take a moment to acknowledge their input.

Claudia and Dave Imhoff, with the Boulder BI Brain Trust, provided a regular forum with the world's best and most innovative vendors in the enterprise data warehousing industry. These sessions not only supplied me with a steady exposure to the business intelligence industry's current state of the art but also introduced me to many other analysts who offered me many demanding criteria for correct solutions and constantly pointed out where our profession's best practices still need further polishing.

During the years it took to write my three books, Tom Hammergren, who instinctively mastered incremental delivery of data-driven applications long before the word "agile" was coined, supplied me with perennial feedback as the topics for each of my chapters took shape. He also allowed me ample opportunities to learn and employ his *Consensus* software for collaborative requirements management, which I believe provides large organizations one of the best and fastest paths to well-governed data and truly insightful EDW prototypes.

Many other tools enriched my career along the path to publishing, and I thank their creators, such as my brother Lee Hughes, the product manager for Zuzena, who allowed me an in-depth look at what automated testing for data warehouses should look like and a notion of what it takes to distill the requirements of many organization down to a single product flexible enough to solve most of them.

Several professional organizations supplied me with strong communities for vetting new ideas. Almost everyone I met at the Data Management Association provided valuable insights into solving the challenge of incremental data engineering. I thank in particular Michael Brackett, former president of DAMA, who suffered through reading the early drafts of two of my manuscripts. His many books are themselves testaments to hard work and the utmost in professionalism. They set for me a high bar for quality, and his input regarding the content and writing style of my books improved the quality of the final product tremendously.

In this book, the new practices for data engineering represent incredibly iconoclastic material. Readers may not gather from the text how much effort the DW/BI community's thought leaders had to invest, a good percentage of it unpaid, in order to discover, articulate, and codify the new techniques that many of us will undoubtedly rely on in the near future. I would list the contributions of them all at once if it were possible, for each is a star in his or her own right. With his series on *Data Model Resource Books*, Len Silverston brought a lingua franca to the practice of DW/BI data modeling that has given everyone confronting a large data warehouse project a reliable place to start their designs. During the many conversations I had with him, he opened my eyes to the notion of data generalization and how it complements and constrains the practice of data normalization the rest of us obsess over. Daniel Linstedt has invested a large share of his professional life to add data vaulting to our collective toolkits, and anyone who benefits in the future from what I call "hyper normalization" owes him a debt of gratitude for pioneering such a completely new and productive way of building data repositories for decision support systems.

Within the data vaulting community, Tom Breur, Ronald Damhof, and Hans Hultgren graciously shared with me their case histories and discoveries as they pioneered both data vaulting and anchor modeling. They could have stayed silent about the power of hyper normalization, keeping it a trade secret, but instead they have enriched the public domain with their findings so that the rest of us can draw upon those techniques in the many situations where they make sense. Kent Graziano has been a good friend, tirelessly donating his time to the Oracle community that I belonged to for many years and bolstering my thinking on data engineering with candid outlines of real data vaulting projects.

In fact, 20 years ago, he and Bonnie O'Neil inspired me to get up out of my seat at the conferences of the Rocky Mountain Oracle User Group and start presenting, a decision that greatly improved my professional life.

My portfolio of data engineering tools and strategies would not be nearly as complete, however, if I had not been fortunate enough to discuss data warehouse automation at length with the folks at Kalido (now Magnitude Software). John Evans, Darren Peirce, Richard Pinos, and Michael Roberts were incredibly generous with their time, answering the thousands of questions that I had to ask before I understood the simplicity and power of the strategy I have labeled "hyper generalization" in this book. I thank Stephen Pace and Lorita Vannah in particular for reaching out to me at the TDWI conference so many years ago to set off what has been a career-changing series of conversations.

Speaking of TDWI, during the past six years, this organization has provided me with numerous opportunities to repeatedly present my ideas to rooms of 30, 100, sometimes as many as 600 technicians, managers, and executives in the DW/BI industry. No other experience could have so quickly shown me the errors of my crazier ideas and the strength of the good ones I was lucky to have. I thank in particular Paul Kautza, at the time Director of Education at TDWI, for taking a chance on course after course that I authored. I also greatly appreciate David Stodder, TDWI's Director of Research for Business Intelligence, for helping me conduct multiple surveys of the 90,000 members and contacts of TDWI regarding their implementations styles and success rates for agile projects, as experienced by data warehousing departments the world over.

Other colleagues and friends provided inspiration and considerable time in helping make these books become real. Ken Chomic and Sandy Schmidt illustrated with their careers how people who are dedicated to their craft, whether an advanced technology such as in-memory analytics or a complex technique such as project management, can quickly become leaders in their fields. They also proofread the first of my books, when there was no guarantee that the manuscript would ever find its way onto a bookstore shelf. Their time, patience, and insights were a tremendous gift that I will forever appreciate. Moreover, to all of the people kind enough to lend praise quotes, thank you for being such valuable colleagues and for exploring the important topic of this book with me during the past several years.

Knowledge and experience serves no good purpose if it cannot be expressed intelligibly. For that reason, it has been my honor and distinct advantage to work with René Selwyn Hughes, who, as an assiduous student of the English language, proved to be the best copy editor I have ever worked with. My wife, Carole, tolerated me during the periods of obsession and monomania that writing even one book requires. She stoically suffered and supported me as I wrote *three* of them, and she should be nominated for sainthood.

The largest group of kind and generous people that I should acknowledge must unfortunately go only partially identified or even unmentioned by name. Companies these days rarely let their vendors and consultants explicitly reference an organization, the projects undertaken, or the staff members involved. This lamentable practice not only hinders the creation of a solid body of case histories but also prevents me from giving credit to hundreds of teammates who participated in the agile transitions and turnarounds that we performed for their EDW departments. The material in this book would not exist if numerous directors of data warehousing and project leaders in banking, health care, insurance, telecommunications, and discrete manufacturing had not taken the risk of trying a new approach. They gave me and my consulting company the opportunity to prove out this crazy new strategy called "agile." They also provided innumerable suggestions on how to make the process plus its training and metrics far better than I would have formulated on my own. Kind people such as Brian, Lynn, Rob, Chris, Laura, Diane, Xuhui, and Richard, I owe you and your teams a ton of thanks, and although I cannot fully identify you here, I certainly hope you know how much you contributed to the practice of agile data warehousing as it exists today.

—**Ralph Hughes, MA, PMP, CSM**
May 2015

Chapter 1

Solving Enterprise Data Warehousing's "Fundamental Problem"

Let me open this book with an extraordinary claim: After 30 years, we have finally solved the fundamental problem of enterprise data warehousing. This fundamental problem can be stated simply as "In theory, an enterprise data warehouse can be extremely valuable to the sponsoring organization, but in practice one cannot be implemented quickly enough or at a cost that company executives consider reasonable." People like the idea of an enterprise data warehouse (EDW)—a shared repository of standardized and trustworthy information on company events and circumstances, integrated across the many business units within the corporation. What they do not like is that they must wait the better part of a year and invest millions of dollars, only to receive a disappointing small subset of the capabilities they expected. When pursued with a traditional software engineering approach, enterprise data warehouses simply take too long and cost too much to build. With the agile techniques presented in this book, I believe that we have solved that problem.

I have been working in data warehousing since the early 1980s, in roles ranging from extract, transform, and load (ETL) programmer to business intelligence (BI) developer, integration tester, lead designer, project manager, and, more recently, program architect. During the first 15 years of my career, the EDW projects I joined or led were managed using traditional project management techniques. Like many software efforts in that era, these data warehousing projects proved to be so protracted and stressful that they disappointed both the developers and the customers when many of the promised features had to be dropped to meet time and budget constraints. Though my teammates suggested that all large projects naturally experience such challenges, I wondered why we as an industry were not improving our performance as the years went by. Project managers were certainly introducing far more monitoring and control into the methods we employed, but if anything, the project outcomes were getting worse.

I started to see that the EDW development profession had fallen into a negative feedback loop, and that this downward spiral was actually the cause of data warehousing's fundamental problem. As shown in Figure 1.1, this feedback loop begins with the perception that EDW applications are large, complex, and therefore risky to build. We fear failure, so we adopt a plethora of extremely risk-adverse engineering and project management practices that make our developers' task lists considerably longer. The tasks themselves become more difficult to complete due to all the audits and reporting steps that project management requires in order to know that the process is on track. Unfortunately, these longer task lists make the EDW development project even more complex and all that more likely to fail. The higher price tag of the task list and the increasing failure rates heighten the EDW's perceived risk, driving everyone involved into another lap around the fear circle. After a few cycles of this negative feedback, the development process has become so riddled with controls and audits that one wonders how the programmers will be able to get any significant work completed at all.

THE AGILE SOLUTION IN A NUTSHELL

The agile software development movement that started in the early 2000s solved a very similar problem, though it was geared toward the programming of transaction capture systems—that is, non-data warehousing applications. The highlights of the generic agile software development strategy consist of the following:

- Progressive decomposition of requirements to generate a simple list of the programming task
- Co-located, self-organized teams of developers
- Iterative programming techniques that deliver small slices of the application every couple of weeks
- Frequent review of those small slices by one or more members of the end-user community

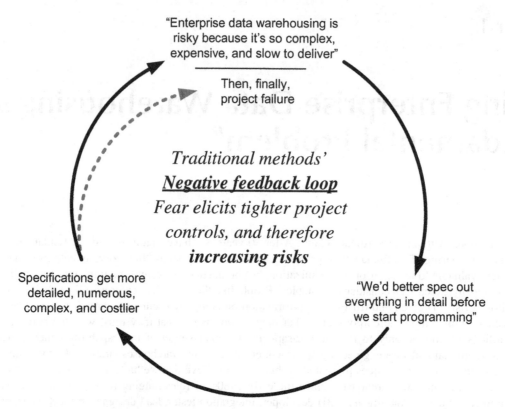

FIGURE 1.1   The negative feedback loop present in most traditionally managed projects.

Many data warehousing teams attempted to utilize this incremental delivery approach, but for a long time they struggled to perform as well as agile developers building transaction-capture systems. This early difficulty was largely due to the fact that data warehouses differ from transaction-capture applications in two crucial ways. First, they have data architectures with two to four times as many layers as transaction systems, often with each layer requiring its own data modeling strategy, a different flavor of data transforms, and even a unique development tool set. It turns out that constructing a data warehouse is like building three to eight separate transaction systems at once.

Second, an EDW's data repositories amass billions if not trillions of records. The initial data load required to put the data warehouse into production usage often runs for many days or weeks. When the warehouse's design must change, the development team can be forced to scrap large portions of the data already captured and repeat the long initial data load. Moreover, if the source for that data is no longer available, the team must then invest hundreds of hours writing, running, and validating conversion scripts that retrofit millions of data records to comply with the warehouse's new design. Evolving an existing data warehouse is like dragging a ball and chain through a swamp.

This double challenge of building and evolving a data warehouse lies at the heart of the fear-drive failure cycle in our profession. Because a single oversight in requirements and design could invalidate months of programming or require weeks of frantic data conversion, data warehousing professionals believed they can not employ agile's iterative and incremental approach. All requirements have to be identified before design work can begin, and the design must be complete and bulletproof before programming can start. Without an incremental delivery strategy, the EDW profession remained mired in the negative feedback loops that agile teams building transaction-capture systems escaped long ago.

The solution to the data warehousing predicament emerged only in the past few years with the advent of incremental data modeling techniques. This new approach to designing a warehouse's data schemas allowed large data repositories to be adapted for new designs after they are initially loaded—without requiring expensive reloads or conversion scripting. These new data modeling techniques worked from the inside out, to make the entirety of agile data warehousing suddenly feasible. Once a team could economically evolve a data warehouse, it was then free to design incrementally, and consequently its analysts could detail requirements a chunk at a time. The big, complete, and perfect specification up-front was no longer necessary. Although a good overall vision for the project is still necessary, by and large data warehousing teams can program and deliver an enterprise business intelligence application one piece at a time. They can readily steer their programming efforts to address many more of their customers' short-term goals, making EDWs far more responsive to business needs—making them, in fact, *agile*. Considerable thought and innovation are still required to adapt all of the software engineering processes besides programming to the peculiarities of data warehousing. However, that remaining work proves to be fairly straightforward now that the "data engineering" component has been solved.

FIVE LEGS TO STAND UPON

In the past 15 years, I have worked with agile teams that have steadily adapted iterative, incremental development techniques to meet the demands of large, data-driven applications such as enterprise data warehouses. These adapted agile practices have certainly accelerated EDW delivery speeds, frequently by a factor of two or three. More importantly, these new agile techniques for EDW have kept the business sponsors and project stakeholders solidly "in the loop," providing frequent reviews of crucial design decisions as each new component is coded. Such frequent business reviews regularly catch misconceptions regarding requirements and design, keeping the development effort intently focused on the features essential for project success and eliminating ill-conceived programming objectives that would have only wasted time and resources. By largely eliminating the risk within large EDW projects, the techniques remove the fear that used to drive us to the specification- and process-heavy project management styles that formerly doomed our applications to failure.

Unfortunately, thousands of data warehousing programs throughout the world still suffer from the waste and frustration forced on them by the fear-driven death spirals. The mission of this book is to illustrate the alternative strategies and techniques that agile enterprise data warehousing teams utilize for building large, data-driven applications. I hope that with the agile EDW approach well documented sponsors, stakeholders, and development team leaders can successfully advocate that their companies switch to an incremental, risk-mitigating approach for their next data warehousing project.

The full practice of agile enterprise data warehousing is a large assembly of principles and techniques. The practitioners of agile enterprise data warehousing derived this collection over many years by borrowing pieces from four different agile methods: Scrum, XP, Kanban, and RUP. We also incorporated a few old-school disciplines from management information science, such as requirements management and quality assurance. By merging these multiple influences and sharing our experiences with each other, our community of DW/BI professionals has arrived at what I consider a baseline approach to enterprise agile data warehousing.

This baseline approach consists of five major elements, as illustrated by the mind map in Figure 1.2. These adapted software engineering discipline represent the five "legs" that the full agile EDW method stands upon:

1. Iterative, incremental application coding (AC) techniques that provide not only faster delivery speeds but also significant risk mitigation
2. Streamlined requirements management (RM) that makes the work of defining a project quick and focused
3. Adaptive data engineering (DE) skills that allow a warehouse's data repository to be built incrementally, then economically revised as requirements change, even after it has been loaded with data
4. Balanced quality assurance (QA) efforts that instill test-led development at all levels of project work
5. Several productivity tools organized into a repeatable "value cycle" (VC) for creating incremental subreleases that amplifies the ability of the other four elements to accelerate deliveries and mitigate risk

This book steps the reader through each of these components and thus serves as a field manual for DW/BI development teams, both those that are just getting started and those that are seeking ways to bring new life to a struggling project. Putting these five legs to work gives even the largest enterprise data warehousing programs incredible traction against the challenges they must conquer—challenges such as uninvolved business partners, incomplete and inconsistent project definitions, rigid data models, and poorly coded application modules. Incorporating these five adapted disciplines allows agile EDW teams to steadily chip away at the unknowns in both business and technical requirements, translate them into lists of actionable development tasks, and steadily deliver a growing collection of user-validated features and performance capabilities.

These agile practices convert the entire EDW development experience into a far more understandable and predictable process for everyone involved, including project sponsors and business stakeholders. The net result is a spiral that operates in the reverse manner of the cycle diagrammed previously. As depicted with Figure 1.3, agile EDW project experiences a positive feedback loop. The desired application is still large and complex, but instead of specifying every last detail of the application before coding begins, the team decomposes the work into small increments that can be easily

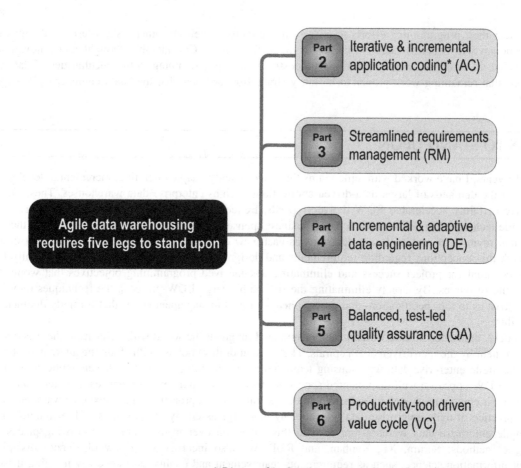

* Discussed in detail in previous book, recapped in Part 2

FIGURE 1.2 The five major components to agile enterprise data warehousing.

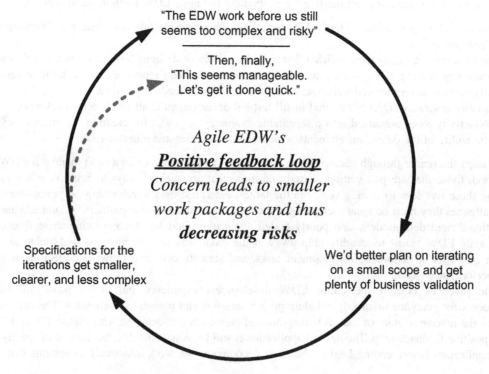

FIGURE 1.3 Agile EDW practices switch projects to a positive feedback loop.

accomplished sequentially. As the team develops the modules for each increment, the business can validate both the new features they offer and how they integrate into an overall system. The enormity of the project transforms into a list of components that both the business and IT readily understand and that can be delivered one after the other without incurring serious risk. With such clarity and low risk, sponsors and project managers can lighten up on the audits and process controls, allowing the programmers to work far more quickly and judging the project's progress by the working modules created.

THE AGILE EDW ALTERNATIVE IS READY TO DEPLOY

This book is designed with two audiences in mind: EDW sponsors and EDW project leaders. By "EDW sponsors," I mean the executives and the representatives of a company department that is funding the development of a data integration application, perhaps with a BI or data analytics front end. These folks on the business side of a project need to realize that an agile alternative to traditional, failure-prone development methods exists. Understanding the nature and advantages of the agile alternative will empower these sponsors to insist that the development teams and project managers who work for them employ an incremental delivery approach.

When referring to "EDW team leaders," I am thinking of the members of the development group other than the programmers who build the data integration and BI components. This group includes roles that go by many names, including solutions architects, project architects, business analysts, data architects, data modelers, systems analysts, technical leads, and system testers. People who fill these roles on a team are usually veteran DW/BI developers and have most likely seen how EDW projects go wrong. Understanding the nature and advantages of the agile EDW method will enable these team leaders to identify methodological problems as they occur within a project and to articulate effective remedies, should they believe that their current project is slipping into a fear-driven death spiral.

For the EDW sponsors, the message in this book can be summarized as a warning:

The project managers working with the information technology (IT) department probably subscribe to an old-fashioned approach to running programming projects. The method they are planning to use to build your enterprise data warehouse has fundamentally misjudged the best way to mitigate the risk of large software development programs. Following their outdated methods, these project managers will lead your development project into a swamp of details and wasted effort from which your data warehousing program will never escape. Because their method is so risky and labor intensive, chances are you will never see half of the EDW features you were promised. Even the minimal data warehouse they will eventually deliver will prove to be impossible to adapt in a business-reasonable timeframe when new user requirements emerge.

To save your program, you must convince IT to employ an iterative delivery method, such as the one presented in this book. By following agile enterprise data warehousing, your development team will be able to provide your company with world-class business intelligence in a fraction of the time, money, and frustration that traditional methods involve. Moreover, you will know throughout the project whether IT is truly achieving your goals. Agile EDW will rapidly provide the business intelligence your company needs to compete and thrive, and it will deliver this capability with far less risk.

For EDW team leaders, the message of this book is an exhortation to see past the ossified software engineering approach that most of us have followed blindly for years:

Try to see the risk of enterprise data warehousing from the project sponsors' point of view, and realize that a delivery schedule measured in years makes no sense for a business analytics development program. Your company has to adopt a faster DW/BI delivery approach in order to compete effectively in the global marketplace and to survive. The risk mitigation strategies presented in this book are strategies rooted in new, agile approaches for requirements management, data modeling, and quality assurance. This combined approach offers a new way to work that delivers DW/BI systems far faster and with more effective safeguards against project failure. When your EDW sponsor says, "IT has got to start delivering faster, better, and cheaper," tell the sponsor that you now have a new, agile method for achieving exactly that goal.

DEFINING A BASELINE METHOD FOR AGILE EDW

As a further purpose for this book, I hope to contribute to the notion of what a "standard method" for agile data warehousing might be. During the past 15 years, the consultants in my company and I have encountered a wide variety of iterative development practices that the people leading those efforts have all called "agile data warehousing," even though many of them were clearly ineffective. To help companies avoid false starts in the future, I believe the community of agile EDW practitioners should settle upon a constellation of practices that they consider generally necessary and sufficient for a reliable incremental EDW development method. Such an outline of a "standard" agile data warehousing method would enable an existing development team to easily spot the gaps and misinterpretations of principles that undermine a team's particular agile implementation. It would also sketch for a company wanting to "go agile" a proper series of steps for such a transformation, since the complete collection of practices is too large and involved for new teams to implement in a single pass.

The agile "methods" available today are not really methods but instead high-level collaboration models. Accordingly, every agile EDW team that I have been asked to coach has derived its own, unique interpretation of iterative development. Variety among agile implementations is a perfectly acceptable result, given that agile principles encourage teams to self-organize and adapt the suggested techniques to meet their particular circumstances. Unfortunately, many of the homegrown implementations I have encountered were incomplete, sometimes grievously so. A good example is a telecommunications firm that invited me to help it because it realized it was practicing "Scrum-But"—regular sprints, as suggested by the Scrum textbooks, *but* without story conferences, task planning, product demonstrations, and iteration retrospectives.

After seeing many incomplete implementations, I realized that companies that desire to adopt a truly effective agile practice need to do far more than just hire a Scrum master or Kanban coach for their projects. In order to succeed, agile developers must certainly master iterative programming techniques, but that achievement will only be the first step in their transformation to a high-performance team. A world-class agile development team must also develop or acquire solid adaptations of the remaining disciplines listed previously. So that teams do not fall into the Scrum-But trap of pursuing large EDW programs with only small fractions of the necessary disciplines in place, those of us who write, speak, and tweet about agile data warehousing could develop a shared notion of what a complete agile EDW implementation includes and thoroughly embed that concept into the advice we provide.

My first two books focused mostly on just one of the five disciplines listed previously—the agile coding practices. They touched lightly on the details of requirements management and quality assurance but left the high-level organization of those disciplines unaddressed. They said little about adaptive data modeling and value-driven release cycles. This current book fills those gaps by describing the adaptations that my colleagues and I have derived for the four disciplines that should surround and support agile programming techniques. Because the agile community is constantly innovating, I am sure that should a standard method for agile EDW someday emerge, it will be significantly broader and better honed than the package of disciplines I have been able to present in my works. But I hope that my books will help the EDW profession to begin deriving a baseline agile method for our craft so that in the future, new teams can quickly arrive at development iterations that reliably achieve 90–95% of their objectives, month in and month out.

Agile concepts are already so numerous and large that even within the space of three books, I believe I have been able to merely sketch the core practices that a DW/BI team would need. For the complete collection of practices, EDW leaders should draw from several other agile data warehousing books, such as *Agile Analytics* by Ken Collier, *Agile Data Warehouse Design* by Lawrence Corr, *Agile Database Techniques* by Scott Ambler, and *Building the Agile Database* by Larry Burns. EDW leaders will benefit also from recommendations found in the seminal works addressing general agile topics, such as *Extreme Programming Explained* by Kent Beck, *Lean Software Development* by Mary and Tom Poppendieck, *Agile Estimating and Planning* by Mike Cohn, and *Scaling Software Agility* by Dean Leffingwell. The wisdom and details that agile EDW team leaders need are already contained in these works. What I have tried to contribute with my work and this book in particular is to sketch in a single place what the overall package of necessary skills looks like and how the pieces can fit together, reinforcing each other and thereby yielding a sold, fault-tolerant, and extremely powerful approach.

Although the body of knowledge for agile EDW is so large that it can be intimidating, EDW leaders should rest assured that it does not all have to be incorporated into a team's practice at once. When my consultants and I start a new agile EDW program from scratch, we ask a customer's DW/BI teams to start with only two of the five disciplines. Most of the teams focus on the agile coding method because it embodies many of the principles and philosophies that must be instilled eventually in all of the disciplines. As a parallel effort, we steer the data architects toward learning agile data modeling techniques so that the design undergirding the EDW program will allow frequent design revisions and incremental learning. Once the team members are fluent in incremental coding practices, we turn their attention to incremental requirements management because this discipline excels at defining small chunks of work that flow perfectly into an iterative programming process.

When the team is ready for another transition step, we typically introduce incremental quality assurance so that the developers start receiving solid feedback on whether their agile requirements and coding are truly effective. We usually reserve the adoption of productivity tools for last so that the team's preferred method determines the tools utilized rather than having the tools dictate how the team will work.

Many people challenge my company for including the notion productivity tools as part of a method, but my colleagues and I have seen the methods of many teams evolve considerably once a tool eliminates hours of work inherent in a key development step. Whereas disciplines one through four listed previously can easily triple a team's delivery pace, employing the tools can offer a second tripling in velocity, so it would be negligent not to give tools a place in the baseline agile data warehousing method. Readers will find that I treat the tools fairly generically in this book, so that the discussion remains firmly focused on how tools must align with a team's preferred development process rather than sinking into a morass of details concerning how developers should employ the tools' many features.

By combining the disciplines outlined in this book, the additional reading I have recommended, and a light consideration of productivity tools, DW/BI team leaders should feel that they have a good baseline description of an agile method that will enable them to both plan the broad arc of an agile transition for their companies and regularly assess where methodological gaps and misinterpretations have hampered a current implementation.

PLENTY OF MOTIVATION TO "GO AGILE"

The motivation to switch a traditional DW/BI department team to iterative techniques is easy to articulate: "Agilizing" a company's approach to requirements, data modeling, and quality can improve by a factor of three an EDW program's delivery speed and development costs. Not coincidentally, agilizing will also drive the defect rate for DW/BI enhancement toward zero, eliminating many risks and greatly increasing customer satisfaction. For teams that add the productivity tools now available, agile practices should allow EDW programs to deliver new business intelligence services with an order of magnitude less labor and time than required by traditional project management and software engineering practices.

I provide evidence for this bold claim in the next few chapters, but first let us consider the impact that a significant acceleration in delivery speed can have for an organization's EDW program. To put it succinctly:

- Business intelligence contributes enormously to the fortunes of the companies we work for.
- Delivering effective business intelligence does not have to be slow, expensive, and prone to failure.
- Agile enterprise data warehousing offers an adaptable path to delivering quality business intelligence in one-tenth the time and cost of traditional software development techniques, greatly reducing the risk inherent in EDW programs.
- Businesses that can reliably build decision support systems to answer crucial business questions in one-tenth the time will be the first companies to seize new business opportunities and will lead their industries' cost curves downward.

This reasoning is why agile data warehousing matters tremendously, and why I have dedicated three books to presenting the approach.

STRUCTURE OF THE PRESENTATION AHEAD

Given the crucial importance of the five legs for agile DW/BI, this book dedicates a set of chapters to each of them in the order listed in the mind map shown previously. Even at an introductory level, discussing methods and techniques that simultaneously affect delivery speed, project cost, and application quality could become an unwieldy presentation. Fortunately, one can understand the multiple components of an agile EDW approach by layering them inside out, much in the pattern by which teams would learn and implement these elements. Figure 1.4 shows this layered approach, and although this drawing depicts risk management as a separate component, in truth all the elements of the method reduce project risk by making EDW development faster, better, and cheaper. For that reason, risk mitigation will serve as a unifying theme that spans all the topics we touch upon.

Part I introduces the agile coding techniques that lie at the heart of agile enterprise data warehousing. The agile coding techniques that my colleagues and I have derived from Scrum and Kanban were covered in detail in my previous two books, so this portion of the text will outline the topic only enough to allow readers who are new to iterative methods to gain a basic familiarity with this foundational material.

Part II begins the discussion of how to employ agile techniques to reduce the risk of BI application projects, both large and small. I summarize the major adaptations to generic agile development methods that DW/BI teams must make to (1) accommodate the added complexity of multilayered data integration applications and (2) pursue the project with teammates who have several non-overlapping technical specialties. Embedded within that presentation are the definitions of the many terms for both traditional and agile development concepts that I employ throughout the remaining chapters. This

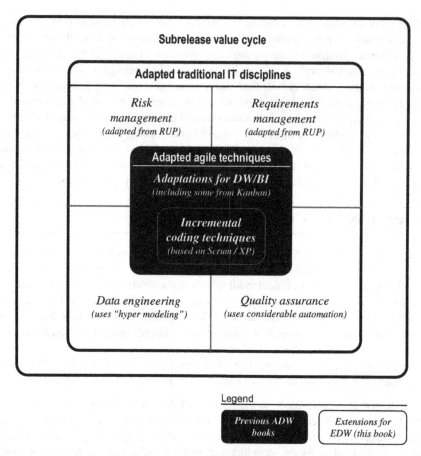

FIGURE 1.4   How a team might acquire agile EDW techniques working from the inside out.

analysis also illustrates how serious conceptual errors originate from three separate levels in DW/BI projects, and it then explains how agile thinking and iterative techniques drive those risks out of the projects that make up an EDW program.

Part III outlines agile EDW's twin approaches to requirements management. First, it discusses the lightweight style for requirements that is utilized by agile teams practicing methods such as Scrum and Kanban. This style serves as a foundation for agile projects and works well for smaller, data mart projects. The text then introduces a flexible, yet far more capable, requirements management system, which my company adapted from an older, more industrial-strength iterative method known as the Rational Unified Process (RUP).

Part IV presents the new concept of "agile data engineering," which incorporates hyper data modeling techniques. These innovative data modeling techniques enable data warehousing teams to start with small data repositories and evolve them later as requirements change, without incurring ruinously expensive re-engineering and data conversion costs. After reviewing the role that data virtualization and big data technology can play in an agile EDW program, the chapters in this part of the book present two styles of hyper modeling: hyper normalization and hyper generalization. Since re-engineering costs represent an enormous portion of the EDW's total cost of development and ownership, these chapters compare the effort needed to re-engineer an EDW data schema using both traditional and hyper modeled design techniques so that readers can appraise hyper modeling's cost-reduction potential for themselves.

Part V focuses on planning an agile quality assurance effort for an enterprise data warehousing program. It first distinguishes between quality management, quality assurance, and quality control and then describes streamlined approaches to all three. It illustrates the effort needed to achieve the extensive progression and regression testing that fast-moving EDW programs absolutely require in order to deliver defect-free applications that delight their end users. This portion of the book also discusses automating the deep execution cycles that full EDW regression testing demands. Automating regression testing allows EDW teams to dedicate far more labor resources to adding new features to the BI applications instead of exhausting themselves by constantly re-validating what they have already built.

Part VI unites the multiple components discussed previously into a single, eight-step value cycle for creating an EDW subrelease. Subreleases form an important part of the agile EDW risk mitigation strategy. The value cycle proposed for each subrelease will not only draw from the new techniques for requirements, design, and quality that are offered in this book but will also illustrate how to support data governance goals and incorporate the latest crop of productivity enhancement tools into a team's iterative delivery approach.

Given the many aspects of agile EDW that are contained in this book, Part VI concludes with short statements that both project sponsors and team leaders might employ to quickly orient everyone who is involved in these enormous projects to the new realities that incremental delivery methods engender. The short statement for the project sponsor manifests as an EDW Customer's Bill of Rights, which distills what executives can expect from their DW/BI development teams now that a comprehensive agile method for data warehousing projects exists. For EDW team leaders, the short orientation statement I offer is an extension of the agile manifesto that includes the additional philosophies teams will need in order to meet the high expectations that the Customer's Bill of Rights will inspire.

Understanding agile techniques and using them to mitigate EDW program risk requires new thinking and ceaseless efforts to control a project's or program's use of time, expenditure of funds, and the quality of its deliverables. However, achieving 10-fold better utilization of company resources is a goal that makes the effort required to learn and implement new ways to work well worth the investment. In the past, the high risk inherent to EDW applications forced DW/BI departments to pursue their projects with extensive specifications up-front, despite the fact that such an approach is slow and prone to failure. This book attempts to clearly articulate the agile alternative so that those decision makers will have both the knowledge and the motivation to make a change for the better.

SUMMARY

Traditional enterprise data warehousing projects easily fall into a negative feedback loop where fear of failure drives companies to instill so many checks and controls on the development process that delivery of value to business stakeholders slows to a crawl. To some extent these process bottlenecks can be corrected by switching to generic incremental programming methods such as Scrum and Kanban once those starter methods have been adapted for the additional complexity that data integration adds to a software development project. In order to deliver at maximum speed and with minimum risk, development teams will also need agile adaptations for the remaining components of the application development life cycle that wrap around the work of programming data transforms and front-end modules. Whereas my earlier books focused upon accelerating the work of programming business intelligence applications, this volume provides detailed guidance for fast and incremental approaches to the three remaining engineering disciplines that every EDW team must master: requirements management, database design, and quality assurance. It also describes how the latest productivity tools for data analytics, such as data virtualization, data warehouse automation, and big data management system, offer teams a new type of application development value cycle that dramatically reduces the amount of labor needed to design, build, and deploy each incremental version of an enterprise data warehouse. By following the suggestions provided in the chapters ahead, EDW project leaders such as solution architects, data modelers, and system testers can accelerate their team's delivery pace by a factor of three. Moreover, by incorporating the new breeds of productivity tools on top of those process improvements, EDW project leaders can triple again their team's delivery speed.

Part I

Summaries of Generic Agile Development Methods

Chapter 2

Primer on Agile Development Methods

Agile enterprise data warehousing (EDW) is a software engineering approach for data analytic systems that borrows from many techniques, old and new. At its core lie agile techniques for general programming that were borrowed from two schools of incremental, iterative development. To make sense of agile programming for data warehousing, the reader will need an overview of the general techniques taken from each of these schools. This chapter provides an introduction to the first school, which consists of methods descending from the agile manifesto, most notably Scrum and Extreme Programming (XP). Chapter 3 provides a quick look at the other school, namely lean software development and Kanban, plus a distant ancestor to all iterative approaches used today, the Rational Unified Process (RUP). The mind map shown in Figure 2.1 illustrates how the presentation of Scrum, XP, lean, Kanban, and RUP is divided between Chapters 2 and 3. For those readers not yet acquainted with iterative and incremental programming techniques, the two chapters in this opening section of the book should serve as primer on the main methods and practices that agile has to offer, providing the background needed to understand the incremental approach to data warehouse development that will be presented later.

Because all of agile EDW's ancestor methods have been well documented in other works, they are only summarized here. A couple of graphics will make these summaries easier to read. First, Figure 2.2 shows the family tree of methods and how they combined into the agile approach to data warehousing/business intelligence (DW/BI) proffered in this book. Second, Table 2.1 lists the primary components employed in agile EDW and documents the ancestor method in which they originated, although the exact origins of some were difficult to uncover completely.

DEFINING "AGILE"

Both traditional and agile approaches largely agree on the major steps and sequencing of activities that comprise disciplined software engineering: system requirements, application requirements, analysis, design, coding, testing, operations, and maintenance. Given the way manufacturing was organized in the mid-20th century, it was easy for project management to think that the work for each step should be finished completely before the development team moved on to the next, as if the project were simply a large automobile making its way along an assembly line. This traditional approach was clearly articulated in 1970 in a paper by TRW's Winston Royce titled "Managing the Development of Large Software Systems." It is often called the "waterfall method" because artifacts for each work step pool up until that step is complete and then cascade down into the next engineering activity, as shown in Figure 2.3. To be fair, Royce and other leading authors at the time were actually warning software developers *against* following this waterfall approach, urging information technology (IT) managers to either prototype heavily before programming or simply plan on throwing away the first version of an application:

> *If the computer program in question is being developed for the first time, arrange matters so that the version finally delivered to the customer for operational deployment is actually the second version insofar as critical design/operations areas are concerned.*
>
> [Royce 1970]

Unfortunately, an approach exactly as depicted in Figure 2.3 was adopted into a 1985 U.S. military standard for systems development and then soon disseminated into the software industry by the military's systems integration contractors [Department of Defense, 1985].

By the mid-1990s, however, a radical alternative to the traditional approach to software development was in the air. The Standish Group had published two versions of its *Chaos Report* survey of 8380, development projects at 365 U.S. companies, revealing that the mainstream approach was failing more often than not to deliver projects on time, on budget, and with all their promised features. The Standish Group's analysis revealed that only projects with very small scopes were achieving anything better than a 50% success rate [Standish Group 1995, 1999]. On a separate front, Japanese

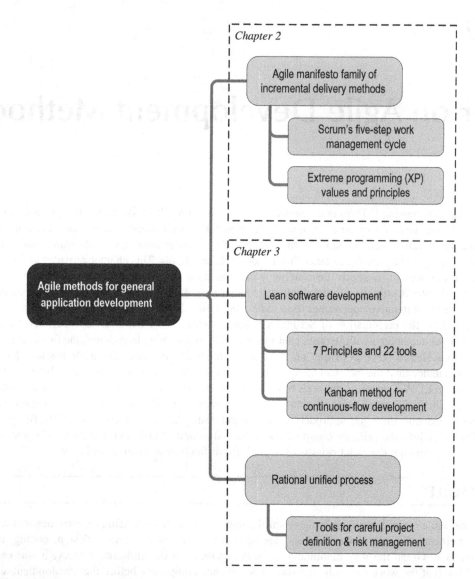

FIGURE 2.1   Mind map of generic iterative methods summarized in Chapters 2 and 3.

manufacturers had recently turned many traditional product engineering concepts on their heads and were decisively outcompeting their U.S. counterparts because they were able to introduce new products across a wide range of industries without having to invest in lengthy product design efforts and large inventories.

As the Japanese business schools began publishing the revolutionary thinking that propelled their manufacturing companies into world dominance, it was natural for U.S. software developers to search for ways to apply those concepts to their world of system design and programming. Moreover, the rise of the Internet and the dot-com boom offered great rewards to those companies that could achieve high speed-to-market and quickly scale up their software systems. The advantages of small work scopes indicated by the Standish Group's *Chaos Reports* naturally led some developers to experiment with incremental and iterative deliveries of software systems. By combining an iterative approach with new Japanese product development techniques, software engineers in a wide range of industries began identifying radically new ways to build applications.

In 2001, 17 thought leaders who had been successfully experimenting and writing about "lightweight programming" techniques met at a ski resort in Snowbird, Utah, to identify the common attributes of their widely varying methods. The result was posted to the web as the "Agile Manifesto" (see http://www.agilemanifesto.org). As listed in Figure 2.4, the cover page of the agile manifesto is a collection of four philosophies for a software development mindset that places the customer first. More than a decade later, the agile software development movement that took root with this manifesto has blossomed into more than a dozen formally defined methods. These many methods exhibit great diversity in techniques, making a single notion of "agile" challenging for many practitioners to define. Still, a solid definition of the

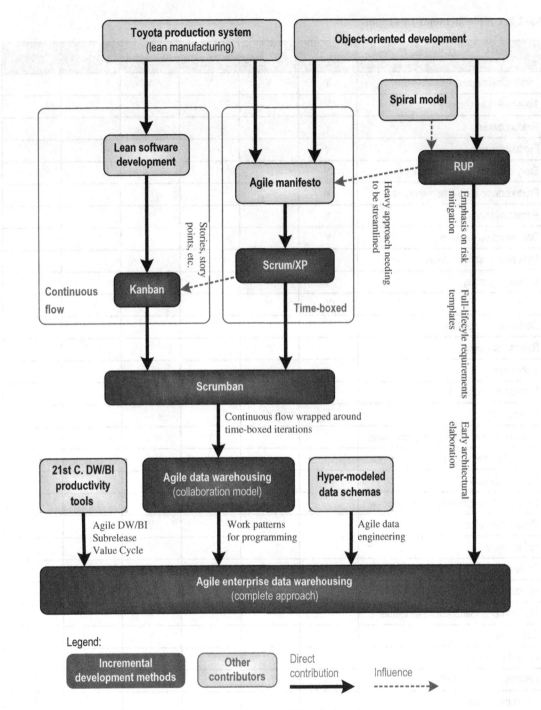

FIGURE 2.2 A family tree of methods and influences leading to the agile EDW method.

word will help people new to this style of software development keep the essential of the iterative approach firmly in focus as they explore the many options available. Moreover, as they become practitioners, a strong definition of the word will allow them to remain true to the concepts that have powered the agile movement's early success.

Many writers today define *agile* as simply any method that adheres to the agile manifesto. This definition is a good first try, but it does not describe succinctly what makes agile different from traditional methods. The authors of the manifesto did provide 12 suggested principles that developers should follow throughout a project. The top half of Figure 2.5 includes these principles, but even though well expressed, this simple list does not provide a capsule summary of "agile" that team leaders can easily keep in mind. If possible to articulate, team leaders could really use a single guiding concept to anchor their thinking as they redesign their group's work habits.

TABLE 2.1 Agile Elements by Origin

Element	Scrum	XP	Kanban	RUP	Standard Proj. Mgt.	DW/BI Adaptations
Iterative development	Y	Y	Y	Y		
Time-boxed iterations	Y					
Product owner	Y					
Product backlog	Y					
Story conferences & task planning	Y					
Product demo days & retrospectives	Y					
Burndown charts	Y					
Daily stand-up meetings	Y					
Task board - status columns	Y					
Backlog grooming	Y					
Velocity	(Y)	Y				
Continuous integration		Y				
Release planning		Y				
Story points		Y				
Test-led development		Y				
User stories		Y				
Continuous flow for supporting disciplines			Y			
Cumulative flow diagram			Y			
SLA calculations			Y			
Task board - engineering phase columns			Y			
Elevate risky elements				Y		
Full life cycle				Y		
Prove out the architecture				Y		
Release cycle				Y		
Requirements management templates				Y		
Use cases				Y		
Current estimates					Y	
Additional leadership roles						Y
Developer stories						Y
Reference architectures						Y

Alistair Cockburn, who participated in drafting the manifesto, offers a definition for agile that is more manageable than a list of 12 principles:

> A system of methods designed to maximize the alignment of the work done by the developers with the direction needed by the business at the time, especially in a context where the business direction changes frequently, ... [where] important facts change, or where we are obliged to adapt to important uncontrolled factors.

[Cockburn 2008]

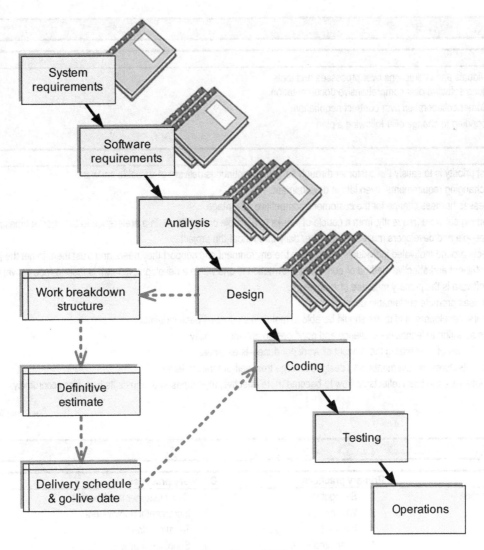

FIGURE 2.3 The traditional waterfall method. *Source: Adapted from [Royce 1970].*

We are uncovering better ways of developing software by doing it and helping others do it.

Through this work we have come to value:

- Individuals and interactions over processes and tools
- Working software over comprehensive documentation
- Customer collaboration over contract negotiation
- Responding to change over following a plan

That is, while there is value in the items on the right, we value the items on the left more.

FIGURE 2.4 The Agile manifesto cover page.

He provides further insight into the notion by describing what a non-agile method is:

One that optimizes toward a different priority [such as seeking] cost efficiency by anticipating, controlling, or eliminating variables so as to eliminate the need for changes and associated costs of changing.

[Cockburn 2008]

Scott Ambler, a methodologies expert who worked for a long time with IBM Rational, describes the non-agile, waterfall approach as one that insists upon creating a "big model up front" before programming can begin [Ambler 2005]. In fact, because it forces a team to sequentially articulate all requirements before design, spell out all design points

Agile manifesto

Philosophies

1 Value individuals and interactions over processes and tools.
2 Value working software over comprehensive documentation.
3 Value customer collaboration over contract negotiation.
4 Value responding to change over following a plan.

Principles

1 Our highest priority is to satisfy the customer through early and continuous delivery of valuable software.
2 Welcome changing requirements, even late in development.
   Agile processes harness change for the customer's competitive advantage.
3 Deliver working software frequently, from a couple of weeks to a couple of months, with a preference to the shorter timescale.
4 Business people and developers must work together daily throughout the project.
5 Build projects around motivated individuals. Give them the environment and support they need, and trust them to get the job done.
6 The most efficient and effective method of conveying information to and within a development team is face-to-face conversation.
7 Working software is the primary measure of progress.
8 Agile processes promote sustainable development.
   The sponsors, developers, and users should be able to maintain a constant pace indefinitely.
9 Continuous attention to technical excellence and good design enhances agility.
10 Simplicity—the art of maximizing the amount of work not done—is essential.
11 The best architectures, requirements, and designs emerge from self-organizing teams.
12 At regular intervals, the team reflects on how to become more effective, then tunes and adjusts its behavior accordingly.

www.agilemanifesto.org

Extreme programming (XP)

Values	Primary practices	Corollary practices
1 Communication	1 Sit together	1 Real customer involvement
2 Simplicity	2 Whole team	2 Incremental deployment
3 Feedback	3 Informative workspace	3 Team continuity
4 Courage	4 Energized work	4 Shrinking teams
5 Respect	5 Pair programming	5 Root-cause analysis
	6 Stories	6 Shared code
Principles	7 Weekly cycle	7 Code and tests
1 Humanity	8 Quarterly cycle	8 Single code base
2 Economics	9 Slack	9 Daily deployment
3 Mutual benefit	10 Ten-minute build	10 Negotiated scope contract
4 Self-similarity	11 Continuous integration	11 Pay-per-use
5 Improvement	12 Test-first programming	
6 Diversity	13 Incremental design	
7 Reflection		
8 Flow		
9 Opportunity		
10 Redundancy		
11 Failure		
12 Quality		
13 Baby steps		
14 Accepted responsibility		

FIGURE 2.5   Values and principles of the agile manifesto and Extreme Programming. *Source: [Beck 1999].*

before coding, and program all modules before system testing, the goal of a waterfall approach actually requires far more than just a big model. It demands multiple "big specifications" up front.

Through his lectures and writings, Ken Collier, another author in the agile DW/BI space, has offered the following definition, which I paraphrase from an opening paragraph of his book on agile analytics:

> *"Agile" is a reserve word meaning a collection of philosophies, practices, behaviors, and techniques that relies on discipline and rigor, but is not heavyweight or overly ceremonious, falling instead in between just enough structure and just enough flexibility.*
>
> [Collier 2011]

After many years of working in this field, a more concise definition emerged from the many agile transition workshops that I have run for companies throughout the world:

> *"Agile" development methods emerge from iterative and incremental practices that constantly deliver quality-assured value to the customer in a manner that steadily mitigates risks within a project and eliminates wasted efforts within the software engineering process.*

Although this definition touches upon the major elements that project leaders need to keep in mind, it is still a bit long-winded. To trim it down to a definition that one can keep in one's back pocket and therefore utilize for daily decision making within a project room, I usually abbreviate the previous notion to the following:

> *Agile is all about constantly delivering value to the customer.*

We can add a quick tag to this statement to highlight agile's contrast with a traditional development approach:

> *Waterfall methods are all about creating a big specification up front.*

These pocket definitions have served the teams I have led very well. In nearly all cases, "constantly delivering value to the customer" has been able to rapidly orient a team toward the true goal of incremental development, enabling it to quickly arrive at the best answers to even the thorniest questions involving perennial challenges such as requirements gathering, application design, work scheduling, scope creep, and system testing.

AGILE MANIFESTO VALUES AND PRINCIPLES

According to surveys of general application development teams, three-fourths of agile data warehousing teams today employ a development process linked to the agile manifesto, making this family of methods the natural place to start in our primer on iterative and incremental development techniques [Hughes & Stodder 2012]. Part of the attraction of this family is certainly the manifesto's clear and compact collection of values and principles as published in 2001.

Many of the agile manifesto thought leaders have emphasized in their writings the power of *values* and *principles* in general. Certainly it is reasonable to think that a group of fast-moving developers, making crucial decisions regarding design and quality under time pressure, would need strong general guidelines to keep their work coherent day after day. The manifesto's values and principles allow teams to move ahead quickly by enabling them to dependably make the right choice without vetting all the alternatives with IT directors or program management.

A *value* is an ideal or quality that a group accepts as a normative criterion for its thinking and behavior. Kent Beck, one of the creators of XP, defines *values* as "the large-scale criteria we use to judge what we see, think, and do" [Beck & Andres 2004]. In the realm of software development, the values espoused by various methods provide an avenue for understanding how they fundamentally differ. As an example, one value integral to waterfall methods, frequently fired at me by traditionally trained project managers, is "all work should be defined in detail before development begins, so that programming can be controlled and measured." When we examine how long it takes to define all the work of a project, this notion seems to elevate command and control goals above placing new software capabilities in end users' hands as early as possible, making one wonder whose needs have determined the pattern of work to be followed—the project manager's or the customer's.

As revealing as they might be, values are too high-level and vague to help much with detailed programming decisions under specific circumstances. *Principles*, however, make up the next level down in normative statements that groups utilize to choose their actions. They contain more domain-specific policy information and come much closer to indicating the practices that a team should follow.

The distinction between values and principles can be easily seen in pages of the agile manifesto's web site. The four values stated on its opening web page are compelling but undeniably too vague to infer any specific practices from. For example, Principle 2's suggestion that teams should "deliver working software frequently, from a couple of weeks to a couple of months" seems far more actionable than the value of "emphasize working software over comprehensive documentation" that we find on the cover page.

Values and principles are very important for agile EDW leaders to keep clear as their teams develop their own implementations of an agile method, because data warehousing places some extreme demands upon the generic iterative methods that require us to bend some of the standard agile practices considerably. Teams that lose sight of the values or principles behind the practices recommended by agile textbooks can easily adapt them in dysfunctional ways. For example, Scrum textbooks specify a practice of demonstrating new features to the business users at the end of each development iteration. This practice is nearly impossible for DW/BI teams pursuing any significant data integration objectives because there is simply too much work required to take a new element from source systems all the way through the extract, transform, and load (ETL) processing and place it on a business intelligence dashboard within two or three short weeks. Many agile data warehousing teams therefore decide that they will still work in iterations but will forget about demonstrating new features at the end of each development cycle. Unfortunately, this adaptation leaves the customers without any sense that progress is being made and denies them the ability to easily redirect the team as business conditions change. More successful agile EDW teams keep the manifesto's Principle 1 in mind and somehow find a way to continuously deliver software to the customer throughout the project. They may have to reinterpret the notion of *working software* to mean landing newly enriched data *closer to* rather than *onto* the end user's dashboard, but at least with every iteration they create a new capability that the end users can validate at the conclusion of every iteration.

SCRUM IN A NUTSHELL

Agile values and principles can be readily seen at work in Scrum, the most popular method in the agile manifesto school. During the early 1990s, Dr. Jeff Sutherland and Ken Schwaber were blending innovative object-oriented programming techniques with concepts that they found in descriptions of the Japanese approach to product development. They called their new approach "Scrum" after the ceremony in a rugby game in which players join together with their arms around their teammates' shoulders in order to get the ball back into play. Sutherland's and Schwaber's experience of building applications with Scrum contributed much to the discussion when they attended the 2001 meeting in Utah that gave rise to the agile manifesto.

Perhaps because it was so well defined at a very early point in agile's history, Scrum has amassed the largest mindshare of all the agile methods, serving as the method for more than half of all agile projects when measured recently [VersionOne 2013]. When my colleagues and I were searching for a formal method to guide our initial incremental delivery approach for data warehousing, we chose Scrum because it appeared to be the easiest method to learn, communicate, track, and customize. These attributes make Scrum a good place for software professionals who are new to iterative development to start learning about the agile software engineering.

Figure 2.6 illustrates the essence of the Scrum approach. First and foremost, Scrum embeds a business partner with the application development team. Naturally, this business partner must understand well the business need for new or enhanced information systems because Scrum teams will take most of their direction from this individual. Because the resulting application will directly reflect the decisions of the business partner, Scrum practitioners call him or her the *product owner*. The team depends on the product owner to decide what features to build into the application and what order to add them. When the product owner reviews the team's deliveries at the end of each development iteration, he or she will also determine whether to accept or reject those modules based on how well they meet the needs of the company. In short, Scrum's notion of a product owner puts the business customer into the project driver's seat. If, upon delivery, the application disappoints the organization that paid for its development due to missing or misconceived features, everyone on the team will have failed, but that failure will have pivoted upon the directions and reviews provided by the team's embedded business partner.

This arrangement makes the product owner one of the team's primary leaders. It is crucial that he work very closely with the developers during the creation of the software. Rather than participating from a distant office and making the developers come to him, Scrum strongly urges the product owner to co-locate in the development room for a good part of every working day so that he can answer the developers' questions about requirements in real time, eye-to-eye. For general software applications, co-locating in the project room also allows the product owner to validate and accept the application components as soon as the developers finish each one. As will be discussed in Part II, this instantaneous review of new modules is difficult to achieve for data warehousing projects because often the data necessary to validate an ETL unit is not available right away. This situation is another example in which the team leaders will have to keep agile values and principles in mind as they improvise on the techniques found in generic Scrum textbooks.

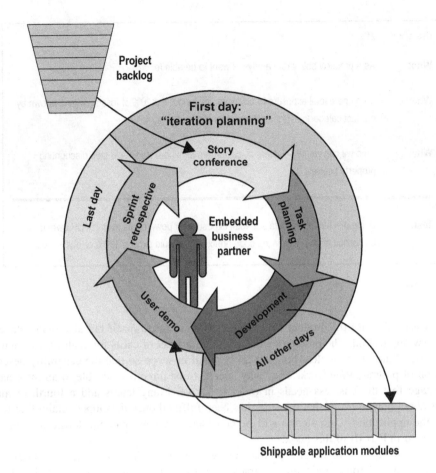

FIGURE 2.6 The essence of the Scrum method.

The only other role for an individual defined by Scrum is "scrum master"—everyone else on the project team is simply a "developer." The Scrum master role is not that of a project manager but is instead that of a facilitator, i.e., someone who knows the Scrum steps and techniques well and can remind the team as needed which steps it should be pursuing on any given day. Because the Scrum master is a facilitator rather than a manager, the role does not require a tremendous amount of time, rarely more than half-time at first and then even less for a mature team. Because this role consumes so little time and requires only a day or two of training, the developers often select one from their own ranks to perform the Scrum master duties.

I have often felt that the word "master" in the name of this role is too strong and improperly suggests that the person in the role should begin dictating actions and controlling the work of the developers. Command and control is counter to the agile principles and often undermines the performance of a team, so I typically suggest to the teams I coach to use either the term *Scrum facilitator* or *Scrum coach* instead.

User Stories

In contrast to the waterfall strategy of a big specification up front, all the agile methods have switched to expressing a project's requirements in very small pieces that are defined continuously throughout a project. Many of these methods, Scrum included, have the product owner express the features he or she wants added to the application by writing a very lightweight artifact known as a "user story."

A typical user story for an insurance policy analysis system is depicted in Figure 2.7. Note that the user story is a short statement that does not describe the feature but instead illustrates how the end users will be able to use the application once the necessary features are in place. A user story is usually a sentence or two, with three key components:

- Who: The stakeholder that the product owner envisions using the application for the given story
- What: The usage or work that this actor will want to accomplish while working with the application
- Why: The value or business benefit the actor and the organization will derive from that usage

```
User story:    213

Who:           As a property policy rate analyst, I want to be able to…

What:          …compare total exposure to policy values for our top 10% of losses, with drilldown by
               product category, customer demographics, and geography…

Why:           …so we can identify clusters of customers for whom we should stop discounting
               property policies.
_____

Test:          Using the June 2014 data set, total exposure for powerboats over 750HP owned by
               unmarried males living in zip code prefix 610* should exceed 130% of policy value
```

FIGURE 2.7   Typical user story.

The "who" is necessary because the product owner represents not just himself but also many stakeholders who will be impacted by the new application. The product owner will author a set of cards for each type of actor that will utilize the application. The "what" needs to be clear but also fairly small in scope so that the capability described can be built during a short iteration of programming work. The "why" needs to be directly traceable to an information capability or a competitive advantage that the business needs in order to thrive. Many teams add a fourth element, "validation," which captures ideas about how to prove that the story has been fulfilled once developers claim that the features needed have been added to the application. User stories will be considered in greater depth during the discussion of requirements management found in Part III of this book.

In the simplest implementations of Scrum, product owners record their user stories on index cards called *story cards*. For teams using an electronic agile project tracking system, these story cards will be stored not on paper cards but, rather, in database records. The team does not pretend that these terse user stories are the project's requirements. Instead, the team considers the story cards to be only a reminder that it needs to have an in-depth conversation with the product owner when the time comes to transform a given user story into working application features.

When kept short as recommended, story cards give the team an extremely effective means of envisioning and managing the project. A collection of 10–20 such story cards often captures the essence of a data mart project. A major data warehouse subject area typically requires 40–80 stories to articulate well. When kept on index cards or printed out from the electronic tracking system, the team can spread out a collection of stories on a large table and quickly reason about the order in which they should be added to the application. The product owner will want to arrange the cards by business priority, but as he or she sorts the cards, the developers can comment on how to sequence them in order to minimize dependencies between the stories and thus lower overall project risk. Such a visual, collaborative planning effort results in a project plan that both business and IT understand and support.

Short story cards also abet keeping project requirements aligned with changing business conditions. If new ideas or needs arise during the project, the product owner can create additional story cards with only a moment's effort per card. In contrast, traditional methods depend upon voluminous requirements specifications documents, which make it difficult for business partners to request new features, causing a project's requirements to steadily grow out of date.

Similarly, story cards can be easily discarded, maintaining a high level of accuracy in an agile project requirement list. If at some point an existing story no longer seems necessary, the product owner simply tears up or deletes the appropriate card. No one will weep over its loss because only a small amount of time had been invested in writing it out in the first place. Waterfall teams, on the other hand, capture requirements in great detail before they start coding, and they must therefore invest many hours into documenting their application's objectives. When the company's situation changes and business partners want to drop requirements, traditional project teams often resist large changes because the analysts rue having to throw away sections of documents they worked so hard to create. All told, story cards can capture business needs quickly and can adapt easily, yielding a far more accurate notion of what a software application should be.

Scrum's Five-Step Delivery Iteration

Once the team arrives at a prioritized collection of user stories, the story cards can be viewed as the list of requested programming work that the product owner is waiting for. Appropriately, agile teams call this list the project's *backlog* of features that the developers owe to the product owner before the project can be considered done. Starting at the top of this backlog and working toward the bottom, the team will steadily transform the user stories into working features using *development iterations* (often called "sprints" by agile developers who practice only Scrum). At times, the team employs other types of iterations, such as those that focus on setting up the programming environment or on polishing a set of modules for promotion into production usage, but the majority of a Scrum team's sprints are development iterations dedicated to programming.

In Scrum, the development iterations will have the same, fixed duration and are thus said to be *time-boxed*. Typically, Scrum teams limit the length of their development iterations to time boxes of 2, 3, or 4 weeks. Figure 2.6 shows five steps that Scrum includes in every development iteration. The first day of each time box is dedicated to *iteration planning*, which involves first a *story conference* and then *task planning*. After that, all but the last day is dedicated to programming. The final day of the iteration's time box is spent (1) reviewing the new features of the application with the product owner in a ceremony called the *user demo* and then (2) reflecting on how the team might improve its policies, practices, and techniques during another ceremony called the *iteration retrospective*. A sketch of each of these steps follows.

Story Conference

Starting at the top of the project backlog, the team discusses at a medium level of detail the requirements implicit in the user stories. The team discusses as many user stories as it thinks it can deliver within the iteration's time box. Many Scrum teams estimate the level of effort required to deliver a given user story using a unit of measure called a "*story point*." Story points are described more fully later, but for the moment we can think of them as a top-down tool for estimating the "size" of a user story—that is, the amount of work it will take to deliver. Story points are derived using pairwise comparisons of the requested work to other modules that the team has already built and remembers quite well.

During a story conference, the teammates will be able to identify approximately the right amount of work for the iteration because they have been tracking how many story points they successfully delivered during previous iterations. In other words, by measuring the number of story points they deliver each iteration, the developers acquire a clear and accurate notion of their team *velocity*.

During the story conference, the team discusses the details of user stories, sizing up each story using story points, until team members have agreed to enough story points to match their delivery velocity. Usually, it will take only a few stories before the team has identified an iteration's worth of work. The handful of story cards selected for development during the time box are transferred from the project backlog onto a candidate *iteration backlog*, and the next step in the Scrum cycle can begin.

Many teams utilize an important variation on the pattern just described. They identify enough stories to match only 80% of their velocity. They reserve the remaining 20% of their bandwidth to work on aspects of the application that the product owner will probably be unable to appreciate, such as writing reusable procedures, building test harnesses, or preparing integration test sets. Because this 20% is often invested in improving the architecture of the applications, teams often call this holdback their "architectural reserve."

Task Planning

Once the story conference has identified a candidate iteration backlog of user stories, the developers will want to double-check that they have identified the right amount of work for one time box. In order to validate their candidate iteration backlog, they decompose each user story from the iteration backlog into the *development tasks* they will need to complete to add the new features with the required capability to the application. In Scrum, all the phases of software engineering are pursued in parallel, so development tasks include not only programming work but also requirements, analysis, design, testing, and documentation—whatever is necessary to achieve new system capabilities with high-quality code.

Starting at the top of the candidate iteration backlog, the teammates estimate the labor hours for each story's required development tasks and maintain a running tally of the work identified for the iteration. When this labor hour total matches the number of work hours they have available during the time box, the developers can declare the iteration backlog filled. They should decline to add any further user stories to the iteration backlog without first removing something from the list. If they did not stop adding stories at this point, they would be implicitly committing to working nights and weekends during the coming few weeks in order to deliver the promised capabilities to the product owner.

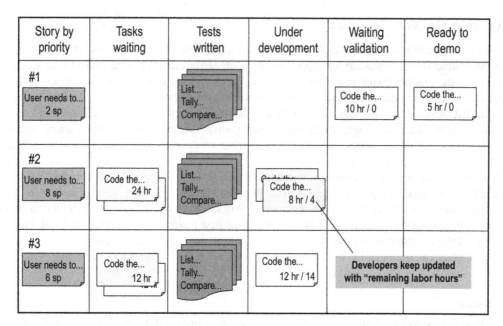

Story by priority	Tasks waiting	Tests written	Under development	Waiting validation	Ready to demo
#1 User needs to... 2 sp		List... Tally.. Compare...		Code the... 10 hr / 0	Code the... 5 hr / 0
#2 User needs to... 8 sp	Code the... 24 hr	List... Tally... Compare...	Code the... 8 hr / 4		
#3 User needs to... 6 sp	Code the... 12 hr	List... Tally... Compare...	Code the... 12 hr / 14	**Developers keep updated with "remaining labor hours"**	

FIGURE 2.8   A sample Scrum task board as it would appear in mid-iteration.

When task planning reveals that the work represented by the candidate iteration backlog does not add up to the available labor hours, the developers give the situation a second look. The discrepancy tells them that something is awry with their estimate of either the story points or the labor hours. To resolve this discrepancy, they alternate between revisiting their story points and their labor hour estimates until they get the two tallies to indicate the same amount of work. Only when the story point and labor hour estimates indicate the same collection of stories for the iteration do the developers make a firm commitment to the product owner as to what features will be added to the application by the end of the iteration.

The collection of stories accepted at the end of task planning becomes the true iteration backlog. Often, a team will identify two or three additional stories that will serve as "stretch goals" for the iteration. The team will work on those items only when some of the stories on the iteration backlog either become stalled due to external events or are completed much more quickly than anyone expected.

Development

After spending a day discussing the iteration's user stories and programming tasks, the developers will understand quite well the work they have committed to complete. Scrum asks them to then spend all but the last of the remaining days in the time box transforming the iteration backlog's user stories into working features that can be placed into production usage the next time a build of the application is promoted into operation. During development, the team will draw upon numerous agile techniques, such as those listed in Table 2.1. Some of the techniques are described later in this book, but readers needing descriptions of the rest can consult my prior two books or textbooks on the methods listed.

To keep the team on track, the Scrum master usually provides the team with a task board, as shown in Figure 2.8. The Scrum master also updates a "burndown chart" that shows the total hours remaining on the uncompleted tasks of the iteration, as depicted in Figure 2.9. The task board is often a paper-based device created with masking tape and index cards tacked to a large area on the wall of the project room. Electronic tracking systems provide a comparable display. The task board has a horizontal swim lane dedicated to each user story on the iteration backlog in which the task cards can travel to the right as developers steadily complete the work represented by the given story. True to the notion of self-organized teams, as advocated by the agile manifesto's principles, when a developer needs work, he scans the task board for the next most important item he is qualified to perform and places his initials on the card to take ownership of it. The task board has columns for each status a task card can experience, such as Task Defined, Tests Written, Under Development, Waiting Validation, Ready to Demonstrate, and Done. Note that this ordering enforces the practice of *test-led development*, as listed in Table 2.1. Test-led development is discussed in detail in Part V of this book.

At the conclusion of each workday, each developer updates her task cards under development by noting the number of hours she believes she will need to complete the work. These updates, along with the original labor estimates on the cards not yet under development, allow the Scrum master to prepare a daily tally of the work still undone. The Scrum

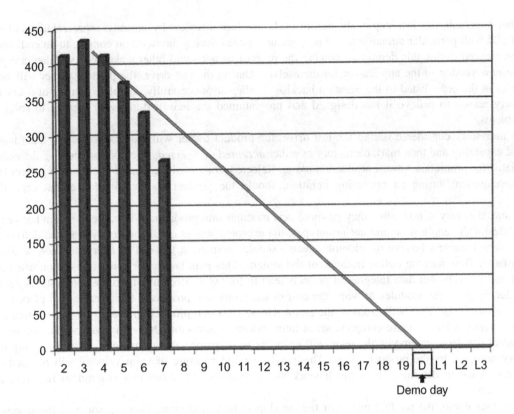

450
400
350
300
250
200
150
100
50
0

2 3 4 5 6 7 8 9 10 11 12 13 14 15 16 17 18 19 D L1 L2 L3

Demo day

FIGURE 2.9   A Scrum burndown chart as it would appear in mid-iteration.

master illustrates the total remaining work for the team by drawing that total on the iteration's burndown chart as a bar for the next workday.

Whereas the task board provides detailed information about the status of an iteration, the burndown chart provides a notion of team progress aggregated across all the developers. As shown in Figure 2.9, the Scrum master can draw a trend line on this burndown chart to reveal whether the team is likely to work off all the tasks by demo day. Used this way, the burndown chart usually provides all the incentive a Scrum team needs to increase its efforts as necessary to meet its commitment to the product owner for the iteration.

User Demo

Scrum teams vary significantly in their use of the fourth step of the Scrum cycle, and the difference in objectives determines whether they should call this step a "user demo" or an "iteration product review." Scrum textbooks provide a baseline concept of a user demo that works well for teams building general software applications or business intelligence front ends. In this concept, the programmers will demonstrate new features to the product owner as they finish coding each module. By the end of the development step, the product owner will be familiar with most of the team's deliverables because he has been accepting or rejecting completed features throughout the iteration. In this case, on the last day of the iteration, the product owner will be able to demonstrate the new features to the business stakeholders of the project, showing them the new version of the application that the programmers have been able to build under his direction. This presentation will provide the team with valuable feedback on its work from the intended end users of the system, making this event appropriately called a "user demo."

As will be discussed in Part II, data integration projects struggle to follow this model. Data for a seamless demonstration will not be available until the team stops programming the data transforms and spends a day or two populating the target tables. In this case, the last day of the iteration will be the first moment the product owner will be able to realistically assess the new features. Typically, product owners prefer to conduct this first review with just the development team present, without a room full of business stakeholders looking on, making this ceremony more of an "iteration product review." Data integration teams still call it a "user demo," but they have clearly changed the notion of *user* to mean just the product owner. Developers still need feedback from a larger collection of business stakeholders, so teams following the iteration product review pattern will have to take extra steps to later demonstrate the new application version to a representative group of end users.

With either approach, this last step of the Scrum cycle involves a review by business representatives of the current application build with particular attention to the new features added during the iteration coming to an end. Module validation is best secured during this demo by allowing the product owner—and other stakeholders if they are present—to test drive the new version of the application for themselves. During the test drive, the product owner will step through the user stories in the order listed in the iteration backlog. If she can successfully complete that set of users stories, the team has every reason to believe it has designed and programmed the new features well enough to solve the target business problems.

For each user story considered during the test drive, the product owner will judge whether the team has delivered the requested capability and then mark each story as either *accepted* or *rejected*. The code supporting the accepted stories can be slated for promotion toward production usage. Rejected stories will be placed back on the project backlog for continued development during an upcoming iteration, should the product owner still desire that capability in the application.

Scrum teams also vary in how often they promote new modules into production. Because the team has been building the real modules of the application and not prototypes, the accepted stories are theoretically ready to deliver to the end users. Many Scrum masters believe development teams should promote at the end of every iteration so that accepted features constantly flow into the online instance of the system. This plan works for some transaction-oriented systems and BI front-end projects, but data integration projects tend to follow a different pattern. When systems get large with many dependencies between modules or when the cost of the promotion process is high, teams will place the accepted stories into a *release pool*. They will promote the entire release pool into production every two to four iterations so that the new online versions have a more complete set of interworking features and the team saves on promotion costs.

At the end of the demo ceremony, the team will calculate its delivery velocity in story points by giving itself credit for each story accepted by the product owner. This newly derived measure of team velocity will be used during the next story conference to determine how much work the developers can reasonably commit to finishing during the upcoming iteration.

During the user demo, the product owner or the developers may find small flaws in some of the stories, either in functionality or in other aspects such as module documentation or performance. If these flaws can be fixed with only a few hours of additional work, the product owner can choose to accept the impacted story with the proviso that these flaws will be corrected within the first few development days of the next iteration. Scrum teams call this collection of quick-fix items the project's *tech debt list*. During planning and development for the next iteration, the Scrum master reminds the developers that they need to work off the items on their tech debt list first before starting on any new features.

Iteration Retrospective

If the team were to start the next iteration immediately upon the conclusion of the user demo step, it might well repeat many of the mistakes made during the prior iteration. To avoid this undesirable outcome, Scrum teams ask the developers to use the last half-day of every iteration to reflect on their effectiveness as a team and to identify new policies and behaviors that will allow the team to deliver more quickly and with higher quality during the next iteration. The Scrum master records the new work patterns that the team agrees to follow but asks the other developers to volunteer to ensure that those policies are honored. If the Scrum master were to himself demand compliance to the new policies, he would become the team's "enforcer" and revert into a project manager, undermining agile's principle of self-organization.

Given the quick sketch of Scrum offered here, it can be seen that this method clearly implements the values and principles listed in the agile manifesto, such as early and continuous delivery, the collaboration of business partners and developers, and continual process improvement. Although Scrum is very popular, it is only one of several agile methods. Other agile methods provide alternative sets of important values, principles, and practices with which teams embarking upon an agile transition should be familiar so that they have the widest possible set of alternatives when they encounter each new challenge.

CONTRIBUTIONS FROM EXTREME PROGRAMMING

The previous summary of Scrum failed to mention that its creators borrowed heavily from another agile approach called Extreme Programming, or simply "XP." XP was created by three of the 17 original authors of the manifesto—Kent Beck, Ron Jeffries, and Ward Cunningham. These thought leaders first described several of the key practices that are integral to Scrum as practiced today, such as user stories and story points. EDW team leaders who want to deepen their understanding of Scrum should acquaint themselves with the origins of these notions, as contained in the writings of the inventors of XP.

XP's focus is on the small team, and it specifies many ways to streamline the programmer tasks required to build working, validated software application. The creators of this method chose the "extreme" moniker because they ask developers to "crank up all the knobs to 10" when it comes to common-sense coding practices such as testing and review—and then leave out everything else [Beck 2001].

Kent Beck, who got Extreme Programming started while building a payroll system for Chrysler during the mid-1990s, illustrates the extremity of his method in his book *Extreme Programming Explained* [Beck 1999]:

- If code reviews are good, we'll review the code all the time (pair programming).
- If testing is good, everybody will test all the time (unit testing), even the customers (functional testing).
- If design is good, we'll make it part of everybody's daily business (refactoring).
- If simplicity is good, we'll always leave the system with the simplest design that supports its current functionality (the simplest thing that could possibly work).
- If architecture is important, everybody will work defining and refining the architecture all the time (metaphor).
- If integration testing is important, then we'll integrate and test several times a day (continuous integration).
- If short iterations are good, we'll make the iterations really, really short—seconds and minutes and hours, not weeks and months and years (the Planning Game).

Scrum clearly incorporates the spirit of many of these principles, although it implements many of the practices within the context of a 2- or 3-week iteration rather than "all the time."

XP was formalized soon after Scrum was introduced, and its programming techniques complemented well Scrum's work-package management patterns. It was no surprise, then, that by the mid-2000s, the two methods were often being taught as one. When most people say they practice Scrum today, they usually mean they are using "Scrum/XP."

Although Scrum borrows heavily from XP, they are not synonymous, and EDW team leaders will be able to guide their teams more clearly if they continue to distinguish the focus of each method. Reflecting upon the outline of Scrum in the previous section, it is clear that Schwaber and Sutherland were focusing on how to marshal work onto a developer's workbench. XP focuses instead on how to actually write the code implicit in each story card. Ken Schwaber, one of the creators of Scrum, once described the collaboration between the two methods as follows:

> *Scrum and extreme programming provide complementary practices and rules. They overlap at ... [iteration] planning.... Both encourage similar values, minimizing otherwise troublesome disconnects between management and developers. Combined, they provide a structure within which a customer can evolve a software product that best meets his or her needs, and can implement quality functionality incrementally to take advantage of business opportunities.*

> [Schwaber & Mar 2002]

Scrum's original omission of programming steps was intentional because its creators were striving for an approach that an organization could drape over its existing engineering practices with the least amount of disruption. This fact suggests that if an existing team's programming practices are already strong, the best agile transition might be to focus most on Scrum's work flow practices and downplay XP's engineering practices. In circumstances in which the team's starting programming practices are weak, then EDW team leaders can be glad that Scrum/XP has engineering patterns already built in.

Readers interested in the distinction between the various agile methods that my colleagues and I have blended as we developed agile data warehousing can refer to Table 2.1. This table lists the component practices by the method that first defined each, as best as I can discern from the agile literature, with the first two columns focusing on Scrum and XP.

XP Values and Principles

In his books, Kent Beck offers a clear list of the values and principles he and his colleagues incorporated into XP and which today undergird Scrum, which in turn lies at the heart of agile data warehousing. Familiarity with these XP principles, then, will allow EDW team leaders to see more deeply into the textbook presentations of agile methods and allow them to be far more innovative as they tailor an iterative method of their own. Indeed, some of the innovations my colleagues and I added to agile data warehousing strike many Scrum masters as heretical. However, we can trace the rationale for all of them to XP values such as *simplicity* and *feedback* or principles such as *economics* and *flow*.

Knowing those aspects of XP inspired and guided us in adapting Scrum when the textbook version of the method did not fit a common DW/BI challenge. All EDW team leaders will need to position themselves to be equally innovative if they wish to cultivate world-class DW/BI teams, so at least one reading of the following principles will be essential to their success. Readers wanting more detailed discussion can consult the works mentioned previously by Cohn, Ambler, and Leffingwell.

XP's Values

Communication: When problems arise in development, someone on the team usually knows the solution. That knowledge needs to move quickly to someone else who has the ability to make a change.

Simplicity: Critics of XP often misinterpret this maxim as suggesting that "all solutions should be simple." The true expression of this concept is that teams should always identify the simplest solution *that could possibly work*. This tenet is XP's version of Occam's razor.

Feedback: In the heat of a development effort, the correct expression of requirements and the best design may be very difficult to obtain. Teams need to establish strong and reliable feedback loops for all their activities so that they can make steady improvements toward a goal rather than staking all effort on a single try.

Courage: All developers must summon the courage to speak the truth, whether the news is good or bad. Working with the truth will allow the team to eventually uncover the best solutions and the project stakeholders to make the necessary difficult decisions, all soon enough to maintain a positive project outcome.

Respect: This value underpins the other four. "If members of a team don't care about each other and what they are doing, ... [or if] members of a team don't care about a project, nothing can save it" [Beck & Andres 2004].

Beck emphasizes that XP's five values need to be deployed as a balanced set, underscoring that any one of them practiced in isolation could lead to rash or counterproductive results that the other values would have helped prevent. The following are examples that he provides:

- Improving communication helps achieve simplicity by eliminating unneeded or deferrable requirements from today's concerns. Working the linkage in reverse, achieving simplicity gives you that much less to communicate about.
- Courage alone is dangerous because doing something without regard for the consequences is not effective teamwork. However, proposing a simple solution when the team has fixated on an overly complex approach is courage mixed with communication, and it is often the one thing that can save a project's budget and timeline.
- Simplicity rarely works well without the feedback that allows a team to measure the quality of a stripped-down approach. "At the same time, the simpler the system, the easier it is to get feedback about it."

Principles

When placed into practice, XP's values quickly point to 14 principles that Beck recommends for guiding programmer work habits in more detail. In order to present them in capsule form, I have paraphrased them considerably in the list that follows and have added my own lessons learned to two of them ("flow" and "failure"). Because Beck's actual treatment of these principles is far more extensive and inspiring than the summaries presented here, folks wishing to practice agile should take a moment to read the original formulations for themselves.

Humanity: People develop software. Methods that neither meet human needs nor honor human limitations cannot succeed for long and thus cannot be considered good business sense.

Economics: Software costs an enormous amount of money to develop. Methods that do not honor the business's need to derive value quickly and avoid unnecessary financial risks will not meet IT's needs for long.

Mutual benefit: Good solutions not only solve problems for IT and the customer at the same time but also balance both parties' present and future needs.

Self-similarity: Software designs turn out to be fractal with similar structures at every level of magnification. Accordingly, practices that perform well at one level of abstraction should be considered at other levels, too. Beck's examples speak of using test-led development not only for coding application units but also for components, subsystems, and entire systems.

Improvement: Rely on steadily improving a team's approach and work product rather than striving for perfection with the first attempt. "Best is the enemy of good enough," and *good enough* places the team in a position to learn fast through feedback.

Diversity: Teams need a variety of skills and attitudes in order to have the multiple perspectives that are needed to see all the problems and pitfalls confronting them.

Reflection: Good teams emerge from regularly considering the quality of their processes, discovering success from the evidence provided by mistakes.

Flow: High performance arises out of small batches that lower risk and allow frequent reflection, so teams should steadily move their processes in the direction of continuous flow. Note that this practice states only a directional preference rather than a required goal. Accordingly, Scrum's preference for structured, time-boxed development is still acceptable as long as the iterations are as short as possible. Judgment will be required to determine if the time box employed is short enough.

Opportunity: Teams need to reinterpret problems as opportunities. When whole-project plans seem impossible to draft, the team can seize the opportunity to switch to iterative, quarterly plans instead. If a single programmer makes too many mistakes, the situation is an opportunity to switch to paired programming. XP's collection of coding practices became robust by innovating around the enduring problems of real people developing software in the face of real adversity.

Redundancy: Teams should strive to solve the difficult problems of fast software delivery in multiple ways. This policy might seem to increase project cost, but the expense of redundant solutions will pale in comparison to the cost of plunging into disaster because all the possibilities were not understood first.

Failure: The fastest way to learn and become a high-performance team is to fail fast, fail cheap, and learn quickly. The applications that emerge from a process replete with tiny failures are the ones that have the best chance of being bulletproof when placed into production.

Quality: Projects do not go faster by accepting lower quality, nor do they go slower by demanding higher quality. Pushing quality higher will meet the customer's overall needs sooner, whereas lowering quality standards often results in later, less predictable deliveries, or applications that are rejected by the end users completely.

Baby steps: "Momentous change taken all at once is dangerous." When confronted with the need for serious innovation, teams should instead identify the smallest change that would move them recognizably in the right direction. Interestingly, this principle suggests a recursive application of iterative and incremental approaches to refining one's iterative and incremental software development method.

Accepted responsibility: Teams will perform better if they treat responsibility as something that can only be willingly accepted by an individual rather than assigned to him or her. Teams should also be very clear on the full set of responsibilities that an individual takes on when he or she accepts a given responsibility. For example, accepting responsibility to code a task also means taking ownership of confirming the details of requirements, design, and testing, not just rushing to churn out 1,000 lines of code.

SUMMARY

The iterative development techniques that we will soon see incorporated into agile data warehousing hail from two separate schools of incremental software engineering: those associated with the agile manifesto and those linked to lean software development. This chapter introduced the agile manifesto school of methods, particularly Scrum and XP. Although teams wanting to get started with agile development can learn just the practices of these methods, knowing the values and principles behind each of them will allow teams to more easily innovate past challenges for which ready-made practices do not exist. Knowing the methods' underlying values and principles will enable EDW team leaders to judge in each case whether the proposed change will still leave the resulting method truly "agile."

Chapter 3

Introduction to Alternative Iterative Methods

Scrum and XP, the methods from the agile manifesto school reviewed in Chapter 2, provide a solid foundation for iterative development in general and for agile data warehousing in particular. The building blocks for adapting agile for enterprise-scale projects will not be complete, however, without some elements from two additional methods and their philosophical underpinnings. The major alternative to the agile manifesto is lean software development, and its showcase method is Kanban. A second alternative to Scrum and XP is the Rational Unified Process (RUP), which actually predates all of the agile methods discussed in this book. The agile enterprise data warehouse (EDW) method presented in this book borrows key elements from both Kanban and RUP. This chapter provides a quick introduction to both so that we can use their concepts later.

LEAN SOFTWARE DEVELOPMENT

The agile manifesto is a wonderfully concise and elegant expression of a novel approach to software development, and the methods associated with it are certainly compelling in theory and successful in practice. Still, I would not want to portray that family of methods as the entirety of the agile movement because that would omit the important contribution that the lean software development school of iterative development has to offer. As depicted previously in Figure 2.2, the lean school shares some of its origins with the agile manifesto group of methods, so understandably many practitioners can borrow easily from both camps. That said, most agile projects draw upon only one school or the other. The practitioners of these two schools seem to speak different languages and for a long time generally ignored one another.

Despite the gap between these two camps, lean is a valuable asset for agile EDW, underpinning some important adaptations we have made to Scrum to answer the challenges posed by multilayered data integration projects. Given that lean software development originates from a closer study of the revolutionary Japanese manufacturing practices of the late 20th century, the literature for this camp also provides many valuable insights as to why the methods from the agile manifesto school work so well in practice. Furthermore, lean practitioners also utilize several tools that the agile manifesto methods have overlooked, and therefore offer some important assets for all agile teams to draw upon. More pointedly, lean principles gave rise to a continuous flow method called Kanban, which agile EDW utilizes in two important ways: (1) better visualization and management of the engineering steps that surround the programming phase of a project and (2) scaling up agile methods to where they can manage large undertakings such as enterprise data warehousing program-level undertakings.

Lean Origins

Whereas Scrum originated from innovations in object-oriented programming with some influence from the Japanese manufacturing revolution, lean software development derived from the reverse process: a close study of Japanese manufacturing, especially the Toyota Production System, which was then applied to software engineering.

The translation of the Toyota production system into the lean application development principles started in the early 2000s with Mary and Tom Poppendieck. Mary had learned about the Toyota production system from 3M, her employer at that time, which was actively researching why the Japanese video cassette manufacturers had suddenly been able to sell their cassettes for half of 3M's production costs [Poppendieck 2004]. Japanese manufacturing prowess had been many decades in the making. Starting in the 1950s, Japanese companies switched to a strategy of increasing profitability and market share by focusing on quality, as advocated by the American statistician Edward Deming, who had found little interest among U.S. companies in his statistical process control techniques [McInnis 2011]. Steady innovation in management attitudes and fabrication techniques culminated in the mid-1970s in the Toyota Production System, as defined by several of Toyota's engineers, including Taiichi Ohno. The approach taken by Ohno and colleagues served as the basis for "lean manufacturing," as popularized by James Womack and Daniel Jones in a series of U.S. books, including *Lean Thinking* [Womack & Jones 2003]. These books are widely cited by lean software development advocates including the Poppendiecks and David Anderson, the creator of the Kanban method.

Womak and Jones provided many examples of how lean manufacturing translated into advance market capabilities, such as when Japanese carmakers were able to bring new vehicle models to market in the late 1980s in 75% less calendar time and nearly half the labor hours as their U.S. competitors. Not surprisingly, U.S. companies began trying to catch up with the Japanese during the early 1990s. Womack and Jones detail how Pratt & Whitney's blade grinding operations for jet engines were able to steadily identify and eliminate both waste and process interruptions using the techniques that Ohno had instilled in the Toyota Production System. With those techniques, Pratt & Whitney was able to rapidly eliminate an $80 million backlog of part shipments and cut its inventory levels and manufacturing costs in half while doubling labor productivity.

Given that both the lean school and the agile manifesto methods were influenced by the Toyota Production System, one would think the two camps would seem very closely aligned. Unfortunately, a minor difference has led to a perceived chasm between the schools in many people's minds. Scrum, the method from the agile manifesto camp with the biggest mindshare, utilizes time-boxed iterations of consistent lengths. Kanban, the most popular lean implementation for software, prefers a continuous flow approach that relies on work-in-progress limits rather than time boxes to control the work. With this seemingly minor difference in approach, the two camps have clearly diverged. Although they still share many of the same concepts, artifacts, and techniques, the two schools began to hold separate conferences and mentioned each other only rarely.

Agile EDW team leaders will benefit tremendously if they can transcend the informal chasm between these two camps and borrow techniques as needed from both lean and Scrum/XP. For example, the lean notion of waste and value streams that is introduced later in this chapter helped my colleagues and I transcend the Scrum/XP's near exclusive focus on programming to see that we needed to apply agile thinking to the full arc of our software engineering process, including requirements and quality assurance. In fact, as agile EDW developers acquire greater agile discipline, they naturally tend to drift away from Scrum's prescribed, time-boxed and ceremonial structure toward the continuous work flow patterns of the lean-based method Kanban. As they draw nearer to Kanban, they spend progressively less time on planning work batches and estimating level of effort, investing that time instead into creating even more new features for their customers and acquiring even greater delivery speed.

Lean Methods as a Long-Term Destination

So why not just start a new agile program with lean principles or using Kanban? As I attempt to illustrate here, the reference works for lean software development can read like the Tao Teh Ching for programmers. They provide a good collection of incredibly insightful maxims but not a clear step-by-step approach to building an application. Kanban fills some of this gap by providing a good collaboration model, offering in particular a much more powerful task board than that employed by Scrum/XP. The fact that Kanban no longer relies on iterations also lets teams deliver software more quickly. But as practitioners who tried to implement Scrum without XP found, a collaboration model is not enough. New agile teams in particular need an iterative collaboration model with clear engineering steps imbedded within it before they will know where to start. In fact, when it comes to many of its details, such as defining small work packets and regularly reviewing a team's process, I have found that Kanban practitioners quietly borrow concepts such as story cards, story points, and retrospectives from Scrum/XP.

My experience of transitioning waterfall-trained programmers into high-performance agile teams has revealed that lean and Kanban requires teams to possess a fairly high level of agile experience and software engineering discipline before they can smoothly switch to the continuous flow model. On the other hand, Scrum/XP, with its more rigid time box, provides sufficiently detailed guidance on what teams should do and when, resulting in far less head scratching for developers who are new to agile. In short, lean and Kanban are fantastic destinations for agile EDW teams when they mature, but Scrum/XP is the approach that lets new teams best follow XP's notion of baby steps.

Scrum, with its five-step, rigidly time-boxed iterations, provides the initial structure needed for teams to acquaint themselves with iterative delivery. Its regular user demos provide a repeated "moment of truth" that guarantees their new work habits can fail only a little bit, wasting at most 2 or 3 weeks of effort. Scrum/XP provides a far easier means for EDW team leaders to get their developers through the agile learning curve with far less confusion and many fewer mistakes. My colleagues and I have obtained good results by starting programmers off with Scrum/XP's structured approach and then gradually refocusing them on the larger principles suggested by lean and Kanban, letting them become steadily more self-organized as the iterations progress.

Because lean and Kanban are crucial, long-term resources for maturing agile teams, the reader will surely benefit from a quick listing of the principles and tools championed by both. Figure 3.1 offers a summary listing of the values

```
┌──────────────────────────────────────────────────────────────────────┐
│ Lean software development                                              │
├──────────────────────────────────────────────────────────────────────┤
│ Principles / tools                                                     │
│                                                                        │
│  1   Eliminate waste                      5  Empower the team          │
│          Tool 1: Seeing waste                    Tool 13: Self-determination │
│          Tool 2: Value stream mapping            Tool 14: Motivation   │
│  2   Amplify learning                            Tool 15: Leadership   │
│          Tool 3: Feedback                        Tool 16: Expertise    │
│          Tool 4: Iterations               6  Build integrity in        │
│          Tool 5: Synchronization                 Tool 17: Perceived integrity │
│          Tool 6: Set-based development            Tool 18: Conceptual integrity │
│  3   Decide as late as possible                  Tool 19: Refactoring  │
│          Tool 7: Options thinking                Tool 20: Testing      │
│          Tool 8: The last responsible moment  7  See the whole         │
│          Tool 9: Making decisions                Tool 21: Measurements │
│  4   Deliver as fast as possible                 Tool 22: Contracts    │
│          Tool 10: Pull systems                                         │
│          Tool 11: Queuing theory                                       │
│          Tool 12: Cost of delay                                        │
└──────────────────────────────────────────────────────────────────────┘
```

FIGURE 3.1   Lean values, principles, and tools. *Source: [Poppendieck 2003].*

tools for lean software development. To provide depth beyond a simple listing, the following section presents capsule summaries of the lean principles and tools that are derived mostly from the Poppendiecks' seminal book *Lean Software Development: An Agile Toolkit* [Poppendieck & Poppendieck 2003]. Following this discussion is an introduction to Kanban so that readers can recognize the concepts when they appear in the presentation of agile EDW later in this book. Even a quick glance at these materials will reveal that there is much explicit and implicit overlap with the philosophies and principles advocated by the authors of the agile manifesto, a fact that will make it easier for team leaders to introduce these concepts when needed by their development teams.

Lean Principles and Tools

The Poppendiecks' *Lean Software Development* book translates the Toyota Production System to application programming by presenting seven key principles with 22 "tools" (practices) distributed within them. This collection begins with a powerful technique for anyone who wants to deliver faster and cheaper—eliminating waste.

Principle 1: Eliminate Waste

While deriving the Toyota Production System, Taiichi Ohno identified the following seven categories of waste, which can be applied to software development with little or no modification:

Waste Found in Manufacturing	As Interpreted for Software Development
Inventory	Partially done work
Extra processing	Large batch reviews, needless or poorly run meetings
Overproduction	Extra features, thrown-away work, building the same thing twice
Transportation	Task switching
Waiting	Time lost in scheduling meetings to answer a question
Motion	Time lost traveling or preparing a presentation to get an answer to a question
Defects	Errors and omissions in requirements design and coding

The first item on the list, inventories, is important. Lean practitioners are adverse to inventories because they represent uncompleted work that can easily become waste should priorities change and the partially finished features are no longer desired for the application. Inventories of incomplete features also become wasted effort when developers struggle to remember where they left off when they later need to resume work on them. In this light, big specifications up front represent a huge inventory for a project, an inventory that will immediately turn into waste when the specified features are descoped. Details for features should be specified just before the necessary modules are programmed, so that the team will be sure that all their careful analysis and design work gets included in the finished system.

The notion of inventory as waste lies behind the lean community's criticisms of time-boxed agile methods such as Scrum. From the lean perspective, Scrum's iteration planning represents an interruption of a team's effort in order to build an inventory—even if it is fairly small—of requirements for the next programming iteration that will only have to be reprocessed when it comes time to actually start programming a given user story. Moreover, without any further controls, Scrum allows work teams to start on all the work tasks at once, which only leads to waste when the developers begin switching between partially completed tasks. As discussed later, lean practitioners prefer to limit the amount of work-in-process so that developers work on only one or two items at a time, thus eliminating task switching and inventories of unprogrammed specifications.

Tool 1: Seeing Waste

Teams should regularly review their current work methods using the seven categories of waste listed previously in order to identify nonproductive aspects of their current engineering process. They should pay particular attention to reducing tracking and control systems because these do not add value to the software under development but instead consume resources so that nonproductive roles such as project managers will know if corrective action is necessary. If teams would instead re-dedicate the tracking and control efforts to just getting more done, the need for corrective action would largely disappear.

Tool 2: Value Stream Mapping

Value stream mapping is a diagrammatic and analysis technique for envisioning a team's current development process. Figure 3.2 displays an example of a value stream map for a data warehousing team when it was following a waterfall process, just before switching to agile. The horizontal dimension of a value stream map shows the movement of work across functional and organizational boundaries. The vertical dimension displays where within each processing phase team resources were invested in development and validation versus being wasted on waiting for the next person to take up the work package.

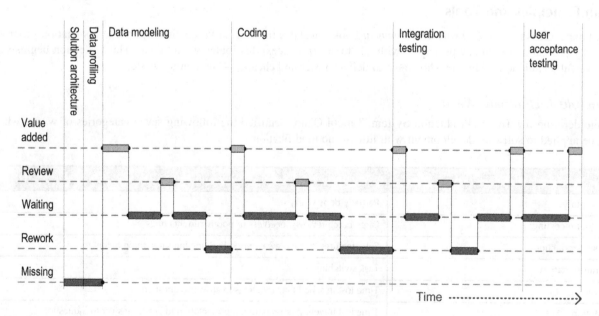

FIGURE 3.2 Value-stream analysis of development work for a challenged waterfall project.

This particular diagram of value stream mapping has been adapted for data warehousing in two ways. First, agile is often criticized for requiring rework to fix coding errors made during hasty programming. To address this concern, my colleagues and I typically add a fourth stratum to our value stream maps to depict rework. As shown in the example, this waterfall team was losing a significant amount of labor time to rework, despite the fact that traditional project management supposedly minimizes coding errors. Second, we add a fifth stratum for work steps that the team realized were missing from their process. We frequently perform assessments of traditionally managed projects before converting them to agile. This stratum allows us to highlight the crucial programming disciplines that every application development effort should include regardless of the method employed and that a data warehousing/business intelligence (DW/BI) team has not yet adopted.

The process portrayed in the sample value stream map above reveals many important clues to why that particular team is struggling to deliver at a reasonable pace. Solution architecture, data profiling, and system testing were all missing from the process. The developers were losing more than half of their cycle time waiting to hand off a package to the next party in the process. Moreover, rework was consuming more than one-third of their resources, despite the fact that the requirements and design for all modules had supposedly been documented thoroughly ahead of time. By offering an overall view of where effort is wasted, value maps enable the team to reason carefully about its current process and identify the most important areas to improve upon next.

Principle 2: Amplify Learning

Lean programming practitioners assert that effective processes are rarely created with a single try. They also believe that no matter how much a particular process has already been tuned, one can always look more closely and find still more wasted effort to eliminate. Because effective work methods need to continually evolve, organizations that focus on learning will improve the fastest.

Tool 3: Feedback

Increasing a team's ability to perceive its effectiveness and adapt the policies controlling its activities is the single most effective way to deal with troubled software development projects and environments. A team should build as many channels for feedback into its process as possible, such as communicating with users via prototypes, proving out design ideas with small portions of actual code, and running tests as soon as code is written. The goal of these efforts is feedback, not perfection.

Faster cycles will generally increase failure rates, and to a point higher failure rates are a desirable outcome. Carefully crafted work that always passes evaluation only confirms the current thinking of a development team and its business sponsors. Avoiding all failure during evaluations consumes tremendous effort and teaches a team very little about where it can improve. To maximize learning, the team should speed up its cycle time until it achieves a reasonable failure rate because failure reveals the misconceptions that always lie hidden within an application's design. Driving these misconceptions to the surface ultimately ensures a project's success.

Tool 4: Iterations

Steady learning through small failures implies many attempts of small scope. In other words, continual learning requires development iterations. Iterations are the universal starting point for all agile development methods because they dramatically increase the feedback over single-pass methods. Whether a project's iterations have a consistent duration or are individually sized to deliver a predetermined increment of features depends on the style of agile that a team employs. All agile methods prefer, however, short durations and correspondingly small scopes in order to increase the number of iterations that can fit within a given calendar time. Frequent iterations greatly increase the number of options and synchronization points that teams can consider throughout the length of a project, giving them more opportunities to resolve requirement and design constraints, thus enabling them to generate better results.

Tool 5: Synchronization

Even with tightly scoped iterations, developers will need to program in multiple, parallel efforts. Hence, they will need to regularly synchronize their efforts to avoid conflicts and miscommunication. For this reason, agile teams have learned to regularly align or "synchronize" their efforts so that they have frequent opportunities to stabilize the overall behavior of the application across its many components. They draw upon several techniques to keep the many, simultaneous efforts coherent, such as daily builds and smoke tests (which prove that an application can simply invoke all its components without crashing).

For the more complex systems, teams often develop the interfaces between modules first—that is, start by programming all the synchronization points—and then backfill functionality for the already integrated components. Another strategy is to program a single-use case from front to back, creating a "steel thread" that exercises all layers of the application's architecture and proving that they all exist and work.

No matter which synchronization strategy a team employs, daily integration of the current build allows the team to keep the application stable and limits the impact of any new defects in design or coding. This effort allows teams to drive out communication and coordination errors early in the project and constrains the impact that coding flaws can have in the later portions of a project when time is growing short.

Tool 6: Set-Based Development

Parallel development of coded units demands managing design and dependencies in detail. When tackling the design of an entire system, developers might think it would be faster to jump straight to a tight specification for each module so that programming can begin sooner. However, such an approach usually leads to wasted effort through suboptimal design because a tight specification for one module forces design constraints on all the other modules in the system, ruling out a large number of feature implementations. By focusing instead on the boundaries rather than the details of a specification for a given module, developers will be able to consider the set of all design choices across all components at once, giving themselves more overall possibilities from which to choose. By narrowing those boundaries gradually, by one module and one reasonable step at a time, the team can consider the ramifications of each design choice on the entire system, allowing the overall best design to emerge from this structured exploration.

Narrowing choices one small step at a time may seem more involved at first. The process may well require more building of multiple prototypes or investigating multiple programming languages and productivity tools before making a final choice. Ultimately, however, this approach demonstrates "going slow in order to go fast." The time invested in steadily narrowing the design choices across all the components of the system typically identifies far better designs. Jumping too fast to a point solution for each module risks ruling out the best design prematurely, and nothing wastes time as much as programming based on a poor design.

Principle 3: Decide as Late as Possible

Lean software development delays committing to design decisions as long as possible because it is easier to change a decision that has not been made. Moreover, development teams should accept the inevitability of change for the business and technology in which they are working and focus on identifying change-tolerant designs, structuring their systems so that they can be readily adapted for the types of changes most likely to occur.

Tool 7: Options Thinking

Both customers and downstream developers should not be asked to make irrevocable decisions until uncertainty is resolved:

> *Delaying irreversible decisions until uncertainty is reduced has economic value. It leads to better decisions, it limits risk, it helps manage complexity, it reduces waste, and it makes customers happy.*
>
> [Poppendieck & Poppendieck 2003, p. 54]

Teams should develop designs based on options that customers can exercise at low cost once they learn more about the software delivered and how it interacts with the business environment into which it is deployed. Options come at a cost, so teams must add them thoughtfully. The best strategy is to actively identify aspects of design that are subject to the greatest uncertainties and that will have major impacts should they be forced to change. Those aspects should be isolated into separate modules and then programmed for flexibility in order to reduce impact of change and thus lower the cost of adaptation.

Tool 8: The Last Responsible Moment

Lean thinking encourages teams to start development when only partial requirements are known—a strategy that calls for developing in short iterations that provide the feedback needed for a team to steadily move toward increasingly solid system designs. So as not to preclude important design decisions, lean teams delay commitments until the last responsible moment—that is, "the moment at which failing to make a decision eliminates an important alternative" [Poppendieck & Poppendieck 2003, p. 57]. The last responsible moment occurs when it becomes clear that if a direction is not taken, a decision will be made by default and probably without the careful consideration required to make a good choice. By waiting until that moment to decide, a team avoids imposing needless constraints on the system that is taking shape.

Lean practices include several techniques that greatly increase a team's ability to delay commitments, including the following:

- Sharing partially complete design information with customers and validators
- Relying on face-to-face collaboration between workers
- Honing the developer's sense of what is critically important within the problem domain
- Continual planning on how to absorb change

Lean theory also recommends several software engineering techniques that originate in object-oriented programming, many of which will greatly assist a full life cycle approach for agile EDW:

- Designing in modules
- Encapsulating variation within modules
- Focusing on interfaces between modules and employing parameter-based invocations
- Trading off performance to achieve greater flexibility
- Emphasizing reuse over repetition of designs and coding
- Avoiding custom tool building
- Abstraction-based designs to maximize the problem domain addressed by each module
- Declarative programming tools such as SQL rather than procedural languages such as C
- Avoiding extra features and deferring future capabilities not absolutely needed now

Tool 9: Making Decisions

Lean practitioners advocate a particular style of decision making that allows teams to simultaneously work fast and avoid major mistakes. This style consists of several problem-solving strategies, including the following:

- Approaching requirements and design breadth-first in order to avoid the uninformed constraints that come with depth-first thinking
- Relying primarily on the intuition, pattern matching skills, and experience of the team's developers
- Employing decomposition and detailed analysis only when teammates have insufficient background to make a decision intuitively
- Articulating in advance and continually evolving a set of values and simple rules for resolving issues, especially rules that emphasize flexibility, robustness, and self-organization

Principle 4: Deliver as Fast as Possible

Lean thinking calls for development teams to deliver as fast as possible in order to mitigate several major risks inherent in software engineering, including the following:

- Amassing a large collection of work-in-process, all of which could be hiding defects
- Seeing a large inventory of requirements and designs grow obsolete when business conditions change
- Falling into engineering processes with long lead times that will require a team to make decisions at an early time point rather than as late as possible

More important, however, is the fact that customers like faster results. Development teams that deliver in shorter cycles give businesses recurring opportunities to learn how new software features can enable them to succeed in a competitive marketplace. To discern ways to achieve a faster deliver pace, lean recommends three tools in particular: pull systems, queuing theory, and proper evaluation of the cost of delays.

Tool 10: Pull-Based Systems

"Thrashing" occurs when developers must move between tasks without completing them, causing them to waste time on multiple restarts and the errors that arise from fractured concentration. Processes that push large bundles of work items onto an engineering team regularly instigate thrashing because they force developers to work on more than an optimal number of items at once. A push-based approach also requires someone to organize, estimate, and prepare the work bundles in advance, which results in an inventory of requirements and design—inventories that risk waste through obsolescence when conditions and plans change.

In contrast, methods that allow developers to pull work onto their workbenches when ready for the next task demonstrate many advantages:

- They avoid plan-driven approaches' habit of "outdriving one's headlights"—that is, trying to plan in detail for situations too far in the future to understand sufficiently today.
- They allow requirements and designs to continue evolving up to the moment development begins, keeping options open and allowing set-based coordination of designs to occur.
- By delaying the moment of commitment, they allow developers to incorporate the current status of the development efforts into their analysis and design, maximizing the impact of feedback.

Perhaps more important, the small batch sizes that arise from pull-based approaches allow teams to greatly localize communication, decision making, and their commitment to success at the "point of attack"—that is, with the developers who must create the software.

Tool 11: Queuing Theory

Customers want short delivery cycle times from their software providers so that they can better compete in the marketplace. Lean encourages teams to incorporate insights from the mathematical study of *queuing theory* to effectively shorten their software engineering cycles. As revealed by queuing theory, delivery cycle times of any system increase exponentially as the utilization rates of the underlying resources approach 100%. Accordingly, lean calls for development teams to stop obsessing about the utilization rates of the individual developers on the teams and to focus instead on the teams' overall throughput:

> Note that it doesn't do any good to increase the utilization of non-bottleneck areas. It doesn't matter how fast you develop software if you can't test it at the same rate. It doesn't matter how fast you develop a system if you don't have the people to deploy it. So, move people to the bottleneck; don't keep piling up work that can't be used immediately.
>
> [Poppendieck & Poppendieck 2003, p. 82]

Instead of utilization, then, teams should focus on the primary factors that determine the typical cycle time for building a module. Queuing theory asserts that the primary determinants of this cycle time are the average size of the work batches and the variation in their size around that mean. Large work items drive utilization and thus cycle times upwards. Work items of variable sizes and characteristics prevent a team from identifying its "sweet spot" of work packages that it can most rapidly deliver en masse. To achieve the fastest throughput, then, teams should steadily reduce batch sizes and define them so that they reliably contain the same amount of work.

Lean coaches also encourage their teams to study and optimize their processes as a whole system. A subset within queuing theory, the theory of constraints, reveals that teams can steadily improve the overall throughput of their processes by identifying and resolving the single biggest bottleneck at a given time and then repeating that effort for the next largest constraint.

Finally, queuing theory advocates developing redundancy among a team's resources so that packages that are surprisingly large or difficult do not absorb the single instance of a given skill and thus block all other work from being completed.

Tool 12: Cost of Delay

Project decisions such as whether to add resources or acquire new tools should be based on the cost of delayed delivery instead of simply the cost of the new assets, which will typically pale in comparison. For example, decisions on software that will affect a company's product offering should consider the impact of a permanent loss of market share and the lower pricing that will result should the development project take longer than necessary. Similarly, decisions for projects designed to improve internal operations should consider the compounded economic value of making the company's functional groups more effective rather than just the cost of implementing the decision.

Principle 5: Empower the Team

When developers are programming quickly, they do not have the time to run every decision up and down the hierarchies that traditional, push-based project management approaches rely on. Moreover, long communication chains tend to distort the situation each time information changes hands on its way to the top of the hierarchy and misinterpret the decision made each time the message is relayed on the way back down.

In the late 20th century, the success of the Toyota Production System and experiments at Microsoft indicated that local decision making greatly improves the quality of the decisions that control a project [Obara & Wilburn 2012,

Chapter 12; Brooks 1995, Chapter 19]. Lean therefore advocates a nontraditional approach to managing programming teams: Focus on overall throughput and learning effectively, and then empower the people who do the work to make the right decisions in designing and executing the delivery process. Empowering the developers on a software project will touch upon four lines of improvement: self-determination, motivation, leadership, and expertise.

Tool 13: Self-Determination

Information technology (IT) managers will unleash hidden potential in their development teams if, rather than telling workers how to do their jobs, they make teammates accountable to each other and then focus on changing the parts of the surrounding system that keep workers from being effective. Each team should design its own work procedures and coordinate work standards with other teams doing similar work. Management's new role should be to coach, train, and clear obstacles for the teams in executing the procedures they design for themselves.

Tool 14: Motivation

Rather than providing teams with a list of tasks, software managers can achieve more by focusing on properly motivating their development teams. First, management needs to create an environment in which team members believe they belong, are considered competent, can safely take risks, and are recognized for making progress. Within such an environment, leadership can create a sense of purpose within a team by providing clear objectives for the project, ensuring that those objectives are achievable, creating for the team access to customers and other subject matter experts, clearing away organizational obstacles, and then charging the team with making its own commitments.

Tool 15: Leadership

Projects need strong leadership within the project room at two levels. First, they need a product champion who provides a compelling vision of the product for the teammates to constantly draw upon. This product champion must intimately understand the organization's need for the new capabilities. Second, they need one or more master developers who can take in customer requirements and articulate a solution, providing guidance on details in those areas in which the other teammates come up short.

Tool 16: Expertise

In order to amplify the impact of the product champion and master developer, companies need to cultivate the expertise of all members of development teams. In order to better disseminate skills, teams should utilize programming practices such as pair programming and design reviews. Managers should encourage developers across teams to form communities of expertise in which they can work and innovate in small groups, regularly circulating their ideas for peer review and widescale adoption. Programming departments can maximize knowledge transfer by arranging for less experienced developers to work for a time with the company's master craftsmen in each technical domain. The knowledge that the less experienced developers gain through this practice should be captured and distilled into development standards that can be widely shared across teams.

Principle 6: Build Integrity in

Lean software developers urge teams to concentrate on the integrity of their results. For these practitioners, "integrity" is an expanded notion of quality that ensures that customer needs are heard and actually incorporated into the functional and performance designs of the software. Integrity also means that all team members thoroughly communicate technical requirements and constraints throughout the development effort so that no oversights or misinterpretations occur. Achieving such results requires effort revolving about four distinct concepts: perceived integrity, conceptual integrity, refactoring, and testing.

Tool 17: Perceived Integrity

Because customers often prove unable to articulate the solution they desire for their business challenges, development teams must assiduously manage requirements throughout the development process. A team can adopt several practices to ensure that its customers will perceive the application as a direct solution to their business problem when delivered:

- Work in close contact with business staff and let them judge the end result
- Utilize a master developer who can bridge the gap between requirements and technical development activities
- Model in a language that both business and IT can understand
- Build out the solution in small increments that each receive in-depth validation from the business community

Tool 18: Conceptual Integrity

A system attains conceptual integrity when its central concepts work together as a smooth, cohesive whole, with a mission-appropriate balance between end-user features and nonfunctional requirements such as maintainability and performance. To achieve conceptual integrity, team members should do the following:

- Stay in constant contact with each other
- Incessantly pursue problem identification and resolution
- Release information in small batches to relevant stakeholders even in a preliminary format
- Ardently cultivate feedback from their peers

Tool 19: Refactoring

Refactoring is the practice of improving the quality of an application's code without affecting its functionality. Good designs for complex systems are not self-evident but instead emerge over time. High-performance teams attain perceived integrity by providing frequent application increments for customer review but then constantly ramp up conceptual integrity by constantly reworking the system's internal quality to achieve a robust and efficient architecture. By focusing on external acceptance first and refactoring second, the team avoids investing effort to achieve technical excellence in features that do not get deployed. For this reason, refactoring should be viewed as a pattern for good, efficient coding and not as rework caused by hurried, undisciplined development.

Tool 20: Testing

High-performance teams leverage frequent testing in multiple ways. First, they write a module's tests before coding in order to communicate how the application should work. Second, they execute tests after coding to confirm that the frequent changes made during small iterations are additive rather than self-canceling in terms of product quality. Third, they use integration testing as a scaffolding to enable reasoning about designs and for validating important design changes throughout the application's development history. Finally, once the application is in production, they use the test collection to document how the system was built. Employed in this way, testing drives and accelerates the process of requirements, design, coding, and maintenance. Test-driven teams achieve speed and responsiveness, thus furthering their ability to delay key decisions until the last responsible moment.

Principle 7: See the Whole

A system is the product of the interactions of all its related parts. As a system grows in complexity, small changes to inputs or design can manifest large, unanticipated consequences, sometimes after considerable delay. In order to anticipate and guard against unintended consequences, lean development cultivates systems-thinking techniques such as the theory of constraints [Goldratt 1990], shifting the burden [Senge 1990, Appendix 2], and the "five whys" [Ohno 1988]. Systems thinking enables a team to envision the likely responses of its software to changing requirements and designs, a capability that the practices of traditional methods (such as extensive documentation, code traces, and change control boards) have proven unable to provide [Poppendieck & Poppendieck 2003, p. 154].

Tool 21: Measurements

Traditional teams attempt to decompose complex processes such as software development into atomic substeps and measure the performance of each. Unfortunately, we rarely have the resources to measure every aspect of a software development process, so we typically choose to measure instead the steps that we can quantify easily. The effect of this practice causes the individuals within that system to shift their attention to optimizing the steps that are measured, introducing distortions to the overall process and harming its overall throughput rather than improving it.

Stepping back, we can see that measuring a handful of component steps is fundamentally misguided. Research by the American mentors of the late 20th-century Japanese manufacturers revealed that only 20% of defects arise from aspects under the direct control of individual workers. The bulk of defects arise from the larger process within which the individuals work. Accordingly, lean teams focus on measuring performance one level up from where they suspect process flaws are occurring so that they stay focused on the system and its overall throughput rather than on less important actions of individuals.

Tool 22: Contracts

Like measurements, the style of the contracts between the parties to a software development project can distort behaviors and impair overall effectiveness. Instead of purely fixed-cost or time-and-materials formats that traditional projects employ, lean encourages managers to include a few, alternative concepts in their contracts with service providers:

- Flexible project scopes
- Sequential delivery of system increments
- Fair sharing of impacts when actual costs deviate significantly in either direction from the project estimates

Adding these notions into a project's contracts allows both customer and vendor to build a relationship based on trust rather than control. Trust greatly increases the flexibility of the relationship and reduces the distraction and cost that contracting can cause, enabling all parties, as an extended team, to respond more quickly and intelligently when business conditions force the customer to update the project's requirements and design.

KANBAN

Taken together, the principles and tools of lean software development summarized above provide only a set of concepts and preferences for software teams to follow. Especially when first starting with incremental delivery, most teams will need far more than such high-level guidance to create for themselves a detailed process for quickly delivering new software. Fortunately, David Anderson pioneered a specific method based on lean concepts during the mid-2000s while managing projects at Microsoft. The resulting method, called Kanban, implements lean's preference for pull-based scheduling in the extreme. Kanban emerged a decade or more after Scrum and has not yet garnered as much attention by agile teams, but it has a growing community of practitioners. Although the Kanban advocates delineate the many distinctions between Scrum and Kanban, the two are not that far apart. In fact, the most successful agile EDW teams find ways to blend the two together as their developers grow more comfortable with agile concepts. For this reason, some familiarity with Kanban is essential for teams wishing to build data warehouses using incremental delivery techniques.

Quick Sketch of the Kanban Method

David Anderson defined Kanban while focusing on two notions of lean thinking that were discussed in the previous section on tools: the theory of constraints and pull-based systems. The theory of constraints led him to devise a work board that highlights the bottlenecks in a team process. He tuned this work board to emphasize the continuous flow so that teams can manage the movement of work to the developers via a small-batch, pull-based control system, doing away with Scrum's structured iterations.

Kanban's primary work management artifact, the work board (or "card board"), reveals much about how the method works. Although there is a great variety in Kanban work boards, Figure 3.3 depicts a typical approach, adapted from Anderson [2010]. This example will quickly introduce the reader to the key elements of the method and the pull-based philosophy that Kanban teams use to organize their work.

On the board are many cards representing work that needs to be done. These small markers are signals, or "kanbans" in Japanese, for which the method is named. Each card represents a small amount of work that the team needs to complete. These small work units could be user stories, as defined by Scrum, but typically they are even smaller—equivalent to what Scrum would call developer tasks. The board has many columns, some of which are organized into column sets. The vertical partitions represent the software engineering process the team currently utilizes. By watching where cards tend to pile up, the team can see the bottlenecks in its system. The team can focus on solving the biggest bottleneck at any given time, as the theory of constraints would instruct it to do.

In order to place cards on the work board, the team must first "groom" the work requested by the customer into appropriately sized tasks. The team places the resulting task cards in the first column to the left, *Groomed Requests*. The team then collectively decides how to advance the cards across the work board. On this board, each task first gets specified and then developed. Next, it is moved into a system integration test environment, and then finally it is staged for promotion into production. This example ends with a *Production* column, where cards for the delivered components sit for 2 weeks while the team monitors the new system build for defects. This last column represents the "warranty period" that the development team offers the organization on its programming. During this warranty period, the developers will directly resolve any defects in the new modules rather than leaving them to the operations team to manage.

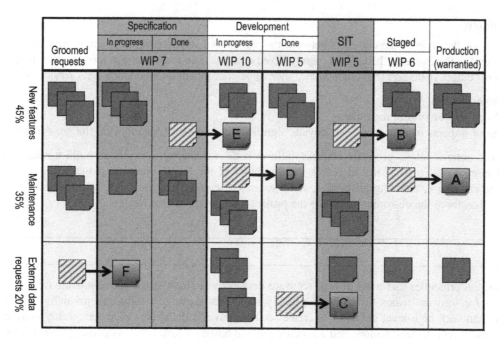

FIGURE 3.3   Typical Kanban work board.

The specification and development processes have two steps each: *In Progress* and *Done*. Each Done column serves as output buffer for its column set, from which the team will pull a card when it needs a work item for an opening in the next column set.

To maintain a steady flow of cards across the work board, Kanban teams place "work-in-progress" (WIP) limits on selected columns or column sets. For our example, the first WIP limit of 7 on *Specification* reminds the team that it will allow itself to keep only seven cards in this column set at any one time. For the Development phase, the team has adopted WIP limits that are more granular: 10 for *Development/In-Progress* and 5 for *Development/Done*. There are no WIP limits in the Production column because the point of the method is to get as many cards as possible into that column. Once the features represented by the cards in the Production column have finished their warranty period, these cards will be removed from the board entirely.

The arrows and letters in Figure 3.3 depict the team's pull-based work management mechanism in action. An update starts on the right side of the board and propagates card movements progressively to the left. The full update depicted in this diagram requires six steps that occur in the following order:

1. The developers have just finished incorporating the newly coded module represented by Card A into the production environment. They move that card into the Production column and will keep it there for the duration of the warranty period.
2. When Card A left the Staged column, it created an open slot within the six-card WIP limit reigning that column. After some discussion, the team decided to finish the testing on Card B so that it could be moved into the Staged column.
3. Card B's movement opened up a slot within system integration testing's (SIT) five-card WIP limit. The team decided to fill this opening with Card C from Development/Done output buffer. The team will now start performing integration testing on the coded module represented by that card.
4. The developers next finished coding for Card D, so it was advanced into the Development/Done column, opening a spot for a new card to enter the Development/In Progress column.
5. The team decided to start coding the module represented by Card E, moving that card ahead one column, creating an opening in the Specification column set.
6. The team decided to fill the Specification column back up to its WIP limit by pulling Card F into the engineering process.

This example makes it clear why agile practitioners call Kanban a "pull-based" or "continuous flow" work management approach. In Scrum, the team took 2 days off every few weeks to prepare a batch of user stories for the next time box. In Kanban, no such interruption takes place. Teammates working on the front columns of the work board continuously define new work. When developers working the rest of the board need something to do, they simply pull a work card forward into the appropriate column set.

In addition to engineering steps running left to right, Kanban boards often have some organization in the vertical dimension as well. The team owning the board in our example employs three swim lanes to help it balance different types of work. Past conversations with the business revealed that, in the current business environment, the team needs to emphasize new features slightly more than improving existing code (maintenance). In addition, the project sponsor has budgeted only one-fifth of the team's bandwidth to meeting ongoing data requests from external parties such as vendors and marketing partners. So they can better visualize their current mix of effort, the developers have designated a separate swim lane for each category of work. Each time they update the board, they will have to consider the total estimated labor for the cards in each swim lane and make sure they have honored the agreed upon distribution between the types of work.

Visualizing and Maintaining Continuous Flow

Figure 3.4 provides an example of the second most important artifact that Kanban teams employ to understand and manage their workflow: the continuous flow diagram (CFD). As the developers complete work and move the appropriate cards across the work board, they maintain a tally of the cards that have landed in each software engineering step, as represented by columns on the work board. If work progresses steadily as planned, the bands on the CFD should trend steadily upward, with the separation between bands equal to the WIP limits the team has set for each column set. When a bottleneck occurs in a particular step of the process, the cards in the column for that step will stop moving. The cards in downstream columns may well keep moving ahead, but the holes that they create as they move will not be filled. If the team continues to prep work, then cards will begin to stack up on the left edge of the board. On the CFD, a plateau will appear for the engineering step where the bottleneck has occurred and for all the upstream engineering that also becomes blocked, much as our example shows for the user acceptance testing (UAT) step in the diagram starting with Week 14.

When a bottleneck occurs, Kanban encourages the developers to "swarm" the problem and get it solved. They should call an impromptu meeting, discuss the likely cause and remedy for the bottleneck, and then spontaneously reallocate their efforts to resolve the challenge. If, for example, system testing is the bottleneck, then developers may very well put down their programming work and all pitch in to validate the work items lingering in the SIT column so that those cards start moving again. Similarly, if the specification step experiences a hold up, testers may redeploy their hours to tasks such as data profiling and business rules documentation so the team can restore the flow of cards on the leading column sets of the work board.

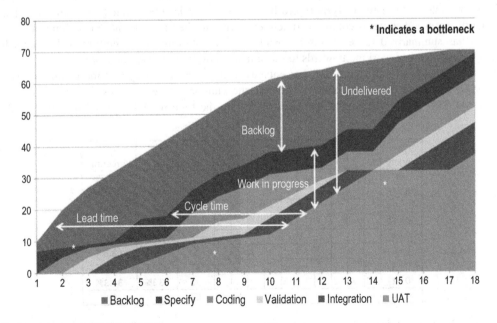

FIGURE 3.4   Kanban-style cumulative flow diagram.

The CFD enables a team to quickly appraise many other aspects of its overall process, including the following:

- The excess of requests over items being developed (the "backlog" arrow in Figure 3.4)
- The amount of time required to transform a request into features reviewable in the UAT environment (the "lead time" arrow)
- The lag in transforming specified work into working code in UAT (the "cycle time" arrow)
- The overall quantity of requested work that the user is still waiting for (the "undelivered" arrow)

The combined effect of the Kanban work board and cumulative flow diagram makes the purpose of the WIP limits readily understandable. Lean software development philosophies encourage teams to minimize multitasking in order to stop losing time switching between tasks. In a perfect world, the WIP limits would be set to 1 on every stage of the board. With that setting, the team would take a card from the groomed requests and swarm upon it. The team would analyze, program, validate, and then promote the software feature represented by the card all in one continuous action. Such single tasking would completely eliminate any time lost to setting aside partially completed development tasks and reloading people's minds with the details involved with other work items.

In the real world, not all tasks will yield to multiple programmers working them at one time. Many tasks are small and linear enough that if two or more developers tried to work them, they would only get in each other's way. If we restricted the team to working just one item at a time, the analyst and testers would fall idle when the coding work began, because they cannot participate in the programming. Moreover, teams get stalled for a short time on many development tasks, such as when they need to clarify a business requirement and their subject matter expert is not immediately available. The whole team would have nothing to do in this situation if the work board's WIP limits were set to 1.

Real-world dynamics therefore require developers to raise the work board's WIP limits slightly above 1 if they are to keep everyone reasonably busy. By loosening up on the WIP limits a little, teams can let developers work in parallel and allow them to stay productive when a task or two gets blocked. Through trial and error, every Kanban team identifies the WIP limits that maximize the throughput of its software development process. Even after they identify an effective set of limits, the developers may have to adjust them later as their own skills and the nature of the work change. The combined objective of Kanban's work board, its WIP limits, and the cumulative flow diagram is to visualize the work flow, spot bottlenecks, and keep the developers single tasking as much as possible.

Evidence-Based Service Levels

A third major artifact employed by Kanban teams enables them to accurately measure their actual cycle times, which they can then share with stakeholders as a basis for realistic service-level agreements. Figure 3.5 shows the calculation for one team. As the project weeks have transpired, this team has recorded the count of work items by the number of days required to complete them. This analysis typically focuses on cycle time—that is, the number of days between pulling a card out of the groomed items column and delivering the finished module into the column for user acceptance testing. The team has summarized these counts by bands of days, starting at the bottom with counts for deliveries requiring 2 days or less and then working upwards to those items requiring 19 days or more.

Easy calculations provide overall tallies and percentages to the right of the cycle time counts by week. The most important portion of this table is the last column showing the cumulative percentages for each band of cycle times. These values start at 33% at the bottom and increase to 95% by the time the tallies reach the 10- to 12-day bracket.

Days worked	\ Project weeks										Count	Tier %	Percentile
	1	2	3	4	5	6	7	8	9	10			
19+											0	0.0%	**100.0%**
16−18	1										1	1.6%	**100.0%**
13−15		1							1		2	3.2%	**98.4%**
10−12	2			1	2	2	1	2		2	12	19.0%	**95.2%**
7−9					3		1		1		5	7.9%	**76.2%**
5−6		1	2	1				1			5	7.9%	**68.3%**
3−4	1	1	2	3		3	3		1	3	17	27.0%	**60.3%**
0−2	2	4	3	2		2		3	2	3	21	33.3%	**33.3%**
Totals	6	7	7	7	5	7	5	6	5	8	63		

FIGURE 3.5 Sample cycle time distribution analysis for a Kanban team.

With this analysis in hand, the team depicted here can reasonably promise its stakeholders that it will deliver on 95% of user requests within 12 days and about two-thirds of them in half that time.

It must be emphasized that the service level commitments generated using this cumulative delivery analyses are *evidence-based*, and thus represent a notable contrast between waterfall and agile project planning. Waterfall methods build estimates based on a work breakdown structures that someone drafts at the beginning of a project before any work has started and often before any programmers have been assigned. Although they represent pure speculation, the delivery dates and project costs derived from these estimates become a rope wrapped around the development team's neck, forcing its teammates to work nights and weekends to make someone else's poorly informed forecast come true. Agile estimates, as demonstrated here for Kanban and later for ADW, are based on actual team performance. Whether they express it as iteration velocity or average cycle time, agile teams simply report real development speeds to their stakeholders, allowing sponsors and project management to calculate completion dates for themselves based on the directly measured facts. Agile teams remeasure their delivery speeds regularly so that stakeholders can keep their predictions updated and their expectations accurate.

Comparing Kanban to Scrum

Kanban clearly reflects its lean development roots in several ways. First, by letting the developers draw cards from the backlog onto their workbench only when they need work to do, Kanban relies on a pull-based scheduling method, true to Tool 10 in the list of lean techniques introduced previously. Scrum, on the other hand, requires a team to take time out from development and define a small batch for the upcoming iteration. Although the developers directly participate in sizing this batch, the commitment they make at the end of the iteration planning day still represents work being pushed upon them, albeit work pushed by the developers themselves.

Second, Kanban's work-in-progress limits reflect a deliberate attempt to maximize throughput by avoiding overload on any one resource, true to the queuing theory of lean Tool 11. Third, the cumulative flow diagram provides the team with constant and timely information on process bottlenecks, creating system feedback as prescribed by lean Tool 3. Because the cumulative flow diagram depicts the overall software delivery process from groomed request to new software modules humming in production, Kanban encourages system-level metrics as stipulated by lean Tool 21, Measurements.

Given that Schwaber and Sutherland introduced Scrum more than 10 years before Anderson published his first book, Kanban advocates consider their method to be a "second-generation" agile method. They cite many advantages they believe it offers over its time-boxed predecessor. Table 3.1 summarizes the most salient points of contrast between the two methods that have come to my attention over the years. Whereas Scrum regularly interrupts development for product demos and iteration planning, Kanban keeps the developers coding, saving between 5% and 20% of a team's project time. Kanban's use of cumulative cycle times and evidence-based forecasting essentially eliminates the need for developers to estimate projects or user stories, again eliminating a distraction that can consume valuable project time.

However, Kanban is not a clearly superior choice for all projects. Teams building large applications with multiple architectural layers often find that the predictable durations of Scrum's iterations gives them a valuable, recurring opportunity to reflect on the project as a whole. The user demo serves as an excuse to pull the many pieces of an application together, essentially forcing teams to run an integration test. Given that data warehouse projects can have programming occurring separately across eight or more data layers at the same time, opportunities to regularly prove that the system integrates provide all stakeholders some welcomed reassurance.

Kanban also performs best when the work can be broken down into small, consistent chunks. For many teams, these work packages are equivalent to what Scrum teams use for their development tasks. When a large development package gets pulled onto the work board, it tends to create a bottleneck all on its own. If two or three oversized tasks sneak onto the board, no amount of adjusting WIP limits can smooth out the process until those tasks have been completed.

Scrum, on the other hand, seems to perform better at the level of user stories, which are much larger than development tasks. Scrum also accommodates user stories that vary in size, as long as the total work for an iteration fits within the team's chosen time box.

For these reasons, the project managers in the consulting company for which I work deploy Scrum and Kanban selectively, especially for large DW/BI programs involving multiple projects. We prefer Kanban for those aspects of a program for which

- there is a lesser degree of unknowns that can create nasty surprises during programming
- work can be reasonably decomposed *a priori* into development tasks, especially using programming patterns

TABLE 3.1 Some Commonly Cited Advantages of Kanban Over Scrum

Topic	
Scrum	Kanban
Work board depicts engineering steps	
Scrum's task board focuses upon status, obscuring where bottlenecks appear.	Kanban's board depicts engineering phases, so inefficiencies in a team's engineering practices become apparent.
Continuous Delivery	
Scrum delivers only at the end of a cycle, forcing customers to wait, even for the most important items.	Kanban works continuously, so that delivery can take place as soon as each component is completed. It can even designate one or two items as "expedited" which causes the team to put aside all other work in order to get those items developed immediately.
Retrospectives	
Scrum teams stop work to review their process, whether there are any outstanding issues or not.	Kanban teams pool up items and hold retrospectives only when it's clearly necessary, thereby minimizing the interruptions to development work.
Multitasking	
Scrum teams often start programming way too many of their task cards at once, forcing upon themselves the waste of multitasking.	Kanban's WIP limits keep a team's multitasking to a minimum, thus eliminate the waste caused by switching between tasks.
Disruptive Transitions	
Scrum forces iterations upon a new team, thus completely disrupting the way they normally do work.	The steps on a Kanban work board match the way the team normally works. WIP limits can be set high and tightened gradually, all requiring less immediate change for an organization.
Resource Flexibility	
Without engineering steps on task board, Scrum requires teams to internalize their work process, making it difficult to changes team personnel.	Because the Kanban work board visualizes how the development should proceed, it is far more tolerant of changing resources, allowing IT to allocate personnel to agile teams as needed.
Work Sizing	
Scrum requires user stories sized so that a few of them can be completed during one time-boxed iteration.	In theory, Kanban allows teams to size work as they see fit. In practice, however, projects flow better with work broken down beyond user stories into many similarly-sized tasks.
Excess Coupling Between Phases	
Scrum over-synchronizes the steps of defining work, coding modules, and validating results, forcing them all to occur within the tight span of one iteration.	Kanban decouples the specification, coding, and validation steps for any given module, allowing each to occur when appropriate. Only the overall flow is constrained in order to minimize multitasking.
Stand-Up Meetings and Scaling	
In Scrum stand-ups, developers focus on the status of work, and therefore end up with long discussions that greatly limit how large a team can grow.	Kanban teams focus only upon the bottlenecks apparent in the work board and cumulative flow diagram, thus a team can process the current state more quickly, allowing teams to scale up.

Advantages expressed from the perspective of a Kanban advocate. (The author considers the notions below worth considering but believes some are overstated.)

- developers will not need to collaborate extensively across disciplines
- the team is well staffed with experienced agile practitioners who instinctively know when special ceremonies such as retrospectives and integration tests need to occur.

In particular, both the business intelligence front-end work and the ongoing maintenance of a data warehouse tend to fit this profile well. With those two categories of work, developers can jump on the requirements, break them down into a big stack of tasks, and let the already disciplined agile programmers start plowing through them without requiring emergency team resynchronization efforts because their teammates instinctively continuously integrate new modules into the application's current build.

In contrast, we prefer Scrum (or the Scrum/Kanban hybrid discussed later) when

- the project involves some serious unknowns or architectural risks
- the team would waste much effort if it tried to break the work into small tasks prematurely

- a more collaborative approach across data warehousing specialties will result in better designs
- the team is new to agile methods.

These conditions occur frequently for the data integration portions of a large DW/BI program, especially when the poor quality of source data threatens to provide a long stream of nasty surprises.

Among lean practitioners, the discussion can take on a "us versus them" tone when they discuss the difference between Kanban and Scrum, which is unnecessary because the two methods agree on so many principles and practices. Kanban still needs to manage requirements once user requests land in the inbox of the development team. The Kanban practitioners I encounter still manage requirements using the user stories, story points, and task cards that Scrum/XP popularized years earlier. When I ask about quality assurance, Kanban advocates endorse test-led development "just like Scrum teams practice." I even hear of Kanban teams temporarily reintroducing time boxes with scripted user demos when their applications are not integrating well. These teams switch back to continuous flow once the system stabilizes and they no longer need regularly scheduled synchronization events.

On the other side, I find many Scrum teams add engineering steps and WIP limits to their task boards as their teams mature. Obviously, much cross-fertilization continues to occur between these two agile camps. They both advocate defining work so that it ties directly to value for the customer first before decomposing into actionable tasks for the programmers. They both support visualizing the work so that teams can self-organize a fast, dependable way to deliver high-quality goods. With another 10 years or so of convergence, the choice for a new agile project may be no longer "Shall we use Scrum or Kanban?" but instead "In which portions of this program should we use time boxes and where should we employ continuous flow?" I believe that orientation is the future of agile DW/BI, so EDW team leaders will do well to be familiar with both Scrum/XP and Kanban now.

THE HYBRID "SCRUMBAN" APPROACH

Interestingly, at approximately the time when the debate between Scrum and Kanban hit its highest boil, a hybrid approach was quietly introduced. With the publication of Corey Ladas' *Scrumban* in 2009, a middle path for agile teams opened up, one in which "Scrum can be a useful scaffold to hold a team together while you erect a more optimized solution in its place" [Ladas 2009]. Indeed, many practitioners find Scrum to be simply easier to explain, train, monitor, and tune in organizations that are completely new to agile thinking, thus making it a better starting point. Yet they want to drop the expensive, time-boxed ceremonies as soon as possible when their teams mature. They simply need a set of waypoints to look for in their journey from Scrum toward lean software development.

Ladas describes Scrumban as a transitional process rather than a method. Teams start with Scrum—for whatever reason—and then steadily move toward Kanban, usually touching upon some predictable milestones along the way. Figure 3.6 depicts these steps in the order that he suggests considering them. The first step can be a carefully defined Scrum process or just a directive such as "See what you can demo to our project sponsor in two weeks." Either way, the new project picks up tremendous value from the simple agile principles that the Scrum imparts upon their teams, including close customer collaboration, co-located teammates, lightweight specifications, and test-led development. Even the task Scrum board provides great benefits in terms of transparency and collaboration because it enables easy, visual control of the process.

As a second step in a Scrumban transition, the agile team should strive to decouple planning and release periods instead of clinging to Scrum's prescription of keeping each planning session linked to one batch of deliverables. Ladas explains that Scrum teams soon realize that there may be a more convenient interval to get people together to plan, and similarly there may be another, more convenient cadence for releasing new versions of the software [Ladas 2009]. Teams taking this step add columns for story preparation to the front of their task board, and columns for system integration at the back, so that they begin to visually manage the software engineering steps that wrap around programming in the same easy manner they manage Scrum task cards. Scrum's original set of columns for task status now lie in the middle under a collective banner labeled "programming," as shown in the sample Scrumban task board depicted in Figure 3.7.

As a third step, Scrum teams will realize that preparing a backlog for the whole project often involves defining stories far in advance of when they are needed or even understandable. As an alternative, teams can work on maintaining just enough stories to keep the team productive. They switch to a buffer of well-defined, actionable stories, letting teams pull work from this buffer whenever they need new items to program. The team leaders monitor this buffer as work is taken from it and start the process of replenishing it with new, well-groomed stories whenever the number in the buffer falls below a particular "order point."

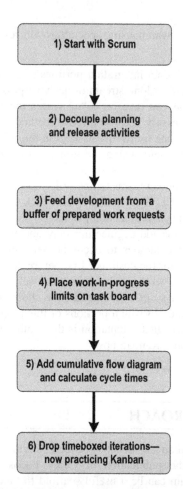

FIGURE 3.6   Typical stages of "Scrumban"—the transition from Scrum to Kanban.

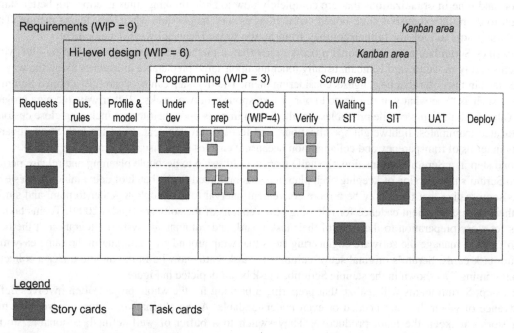

FIGURE 3.7   Two-tiered Scrumban task board.
Note how the work is defined in stories in both the leading and trailing columns, but decomposes into tasks as it enters the coding step in the middle of the process.

Teams making this step often end up with a two-tiered work board that manages work as both stories and tasks, as shown in Figure 3.7. In that example board, the team takes work on as stories, decomposes each of them into tasks for coding, and then reassembles them as stories for validation and deployment. The columns for requests, specification, and design all work with the dark cards, which represent user stories. These stories represent end-user functionality that has been made as atomic as the team's business partners can envision it.

Only when a story card progresses into the development columns do the developers decompose it into tasks so that they can begin managing work that is atomic from a programmer's point of view. After coding and verifying these atomic programming units, the team reassembles the tasks back into user stories as they pull the cards into the columns for SIT. At this point in the development life cycle, such reintegration into user stories makes sense because developers validating and deploying new capabilities must reason and track work in the units of functionality that will be seen by end users. Because the team has finished coding the modules, the programming tasks needed to implement the features articulated by the users stories are now irrelevant details that no longer need to be managed separately.

As a fourth step in the journey in Scrumban, teams usually realize they have far too many tasks in flight during the middle of an iteration. In order to tamp down on the wasted effort caused by that multitasking, teams add WIP limits on the column or column sets of their task board. They begin the process of tuning those WIP limits so that their delivery performance improves as single-tasking begins to take hold.

Most of the WIP limits displayed in Figure 3.7 pertain to the user stories, and some of them span multiple columns. *Requirements*, for example, is envisioned as an end-to-end activity that includes not only requests and business-rule elaboration but also validation by end users that those requirements have been met. Accordingly, the WIP limit of nine stories on *Requirements* applies to all columns from *Requests* to *UAT*. Only the coding step within the *Programming* column set has a WIP limit expressed in tasks (to wit, four items). This limit was obviously designed to keep the programmers from having too many modules checked out and changing at one time.

A fifth milestone in a team's Scrumban evolution is to begin visualizing work with a cumulative flow diagram in order to quote reliable service levels to the team's stakeholders. With this additional practice, the emphasis slowly shifts from the time boxes to honoring and improving upon the quoted cycle time. At this point, Scrum's time box will appear to be a needless vestige from the team's early days, and it can be dropped with little impact on the team's work patterns or performance. The team now begins to demo work whenever the situation at hand seems to demand product owner validation. It conducts retrospectives spontaneously when process improvements need to be made rather than waiting for a magic day when the facilitator tells the team it should reflect on its effectiveness as a team.

Given the five steps outlined previously, an agile team starts with Scrum when it needs a fast introduction to agile development, and then steadily evolves its practices until it arrives at Kanban. The pace of evolution should be appropriate to the team, and the full transition may well take a couple of years. With each evolutionary step, the team's growing discipline and increasingly visual tools allow it to maintain and improve its process while conducting steadily fewer forced ceremonies. Scrumban is the practice of undertaking the next transitional step in this plan only when the team is ready for each one. In fact, some teams may only take a few steps and decide they have the hybrid method they need, whereas others will drive on to eventually switch completely to pure Kanban. Given the availability of a Scrumban path, imposing Kanban upon a new agile team from the start, as some lean practitioner advocate, seems arbitrary and risky. To let developers move toward a leaner approach as they are ready for each step seems more congruous with the agile principle of self-organized teams.

RATIONAL UNIFIED PROCESS

The agile methods of Scrum/XP and lean/Kanban outlined so far provide many of the elements my colleagues and I employed for an early version of agile data warehousing. Even with these three parent methods, however, our method still lacked completely dependable mechanisms for managing the extensive requirements and serious risks that large, enterprise data integration projects entail. To lift the method to where it can address the needs of enterprise data warehousing, we had to borrow a few elements from the granddaddy of all the agile methods—the Rational Unified Process (RUP).

RUP Overview

Rational Unified Process was one of the earliest iterative methods to be widely publicized and was defined a half decade or more before the agile manifesto methods began to appear. What became RUP started with the merging of innovative engineering practices and system modeling techniques created by several luminaries of the object-oriented programming world—Booch, Jacobson, and Rumbaugh [Jacobson & Booch 1999]. In the mid-1990s, these object-oriented practices were consolidated through purchases and hiring by the Rational Software Corporation, where Kruchten began documenting an adaptable approach that would be called the Rational Unified Process [Kruchten 2003]. Rational created a set of engineering tools to facilitate and control the application of the method, and it offered services to help companies adopt both the process and those tools. RUP spread rapidly, with 10,000 companies using it as of 2003, the year Rational was acquired by IBM [Kroll & Kruchten 2003]. Although formal RUP is now a proprietary IBM method, in 2006 the company placed into the public domain a streamlined version of it called OpenUP. There are also several other, public-domain variants of the method available today.

RUP, as offered by IBM, is a very large method that can intimidate many project planners when they first encounter it. Its documentation requires thousands of pages to detail all the roles, processes, and artifacts involved. The method also includes the Unified Modeling Language (UML), a diagramming system that many traditional software engineers find difficult to adapt. IBM also provides a large set of productivity tools such as software modeling systems that can take an application from the idea stage all the way to delivered code [Taft 2013].

RUP and its derivatives represent a very robust and disciplined approach to software engineering. Like the other methods considered previously, RUP offers a set of philosophies, disciplines, and practices that provide the backbone of the method, as listed in Figure 3.8. Perhaps the most important aspect distinguishing it from the other agile methods

Rational unified process

Tenets

1 Iterative
2 Risk-driven

Engineering disciplines

1 Business modeling
2 Requirements
3 Analysis and design
4 Implementation
5 Test
6 Deployment

Supporting disciplines

1 Configuration and change management
2 Project management
3 Environment

Practices

1 **Develop iteratively, with risk as the primary iteration driver**
While it is best to know all requirements in advance, such clarity is usually impossible to achieve.

2 **Manage requirements**
Always keep in mind the requirements set by users.

3 **Employ a component-based architecture**
Breaking down an advanced project is not only suggested but in fact unavoidable. This promotes the ability to test individual components before they are integrated into a larger system. Also, code reuse is a big plus and can be accomplished more easily through the use of object-oriented programming.

4 **Model software visually**
Use diagrams to represent all major components, users, and their interaction. "UML", short for Unified Modeling Language, is one tool that can be used to make this task more feasible.

5 **Continuously verify quality**
Always make testing a major part of the project at any point of time. Testing becomes heavier as the project progresses but should be a constant factor in any software product creation.

6 **Control changes**
Many projects are created by many teams, sometimes in various locations and different platforms may be used. As a result it is essential to make sure that changes made to a system are synchronized and verified constantly.

FIGURE 3.8 Values and principles of the Rational Unified Process. *Source: [Rational 1998].*

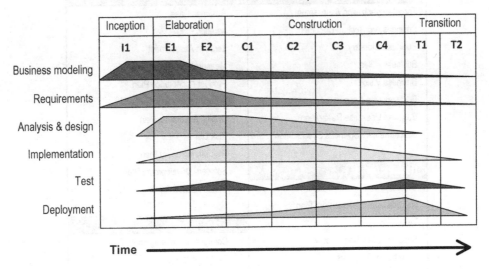

FIGURE 3.9   RUP Whale Chart.

is expressed in its first principle: Develop iteratively, with risk as the primary iteration driver. Outlines for the Scrum, XP, and Kanban methods occasionally mention risk, but RUP employs risk analysis explicitly to sequence the project work stream. As for the remaining RUP practices, they may have seemed heretical when first promoted during the 1990s, but today they are incorporated so deeply into agile development culture that they have been largely covered in the previously discussed material.

RUP projects marshal their resources to eliminate risk, and I believe that this philosophy is the primary benefit that RUP still has to offer methods from both the agile manifesto and lean development schools. Kroll and Kruchten, popular RUP authors, published a book with a section title that sums up RUP's outlook perfectly: "Attack Major Risks Early and Continuously, or They Will Attack You" [Kroll & Kruchten 2003]. To address risk, RUP organizes a product release into four phases: initiation, elaboration, construction, and transition. During *initiation*, project planners set the initial scope and budget for the project. *Construction* is the phase in which the bulk of the application is programmed. In the *transition* phase, responsibility for operations, maintenance, and support of a finished application is transferred to the operations team.

RUP invests most deliberately in mitigating risk in phase 2, *elaboration*. During elaboration, the team identifies where the major risks in requirements, scope, and design of the application could become project-threatening issues. For the remainder of elaboration, the team pursues programming iterations intent on delivering the smallest possible set of functionality that will confirm whether these major risks can be overcome [Aked 2003].

Another notable component of RUP is how it creates a resource planning matrix out of the previously mentioned four phases of a project by intersecting them with nine software engineering disciplines. The result is the famous RUP "whale chart," so named because the shapes on it resembles whales swimming along the ocean surface as shown in Figure 3.9. This chart naturally portrays requirements work preceding design and coding, as one would expect. However, this chart struck an innovative note when first published because, unlike traditional, waterfall methods, it shows requirements and design work continuing throughout the project. Moreover, RUP begins testing far earlier than most traditional methods, and it stipulates that system validation will also be a persistent effort lasting the length of the project.

Finally, RUP assists teams in defining their projects so that risks can be readily identified. It provides a rich set of templates for the many requirements, design, and planning artifacts that it strongly suggests developers create so that they deeply understand the software system they are about to build. These templates are listed in Table 3.2 in roughly the order they occur during a project. A small set of these templates have proven invaluable for bringing disciplined requirements management to agile EDW projects. Five of those templates are considered in depth later in this book.

TABLE 3.2 Some of the Templates Used with the Rational Unified
Process (RUP)

Business Modeling	Management
Target-Organization Assessment	Business Case
Business Architecture Document	Iteration Plan
Business Glossary	Iteration Assessment
Business Rules	Measurement Plan
Business Vision	Product Acceptance Plan
Business Use-Case	Problem Resolution Plan
Business Use-Case Realization	Quality Assurance Plan
Supplementary Business Specification	Risk List
	Risk Management Plan
Requirements	Software Development Plan
Glossary	Status Assessment
Requirements Management Plan	
Vision	**Transition**
Supplementary Specification	Configuration Management Plan
Stakeholder Requests	Deployment Plan
Use-Case	Deployment Bill of Materials
Software Requirements Specification	Deployment Release Notes
	Integration Build Plan
Analysis & Design	
Software Architecture Document	**Environment**
Use-Case Realization	Business Modeling Guidelines
	Design Guidelines
Testing	Development Case
Test Guidelines	Development-Organization Assessment
Iteration or Master Test Plan	Programming Guidelines
Quality Assurance Plan	Use-Case Modeling Guidelines
Test Case	
Test Evaluation Summary	

Compiled from multiple sources including [dbViz 2002] and [University of Houston, Clear
Lake 2002].

Why Not RUP for DW/BI?

Given its position as the first iterative method, the extensive documentation and templates it offers, and its installed base of
tens of thousands of practitioners, one would think RUP would be a popular method for software development programs as
complex and risky as data warehousing. However, in the surveys I conducted in collaboration with The Data Warehousing
Institute, Scrum, Kanban, and their hybrids have proven 20−30 times more popular than RUP, depending on whether a
team was building data integration or data analytic applications [Hughes & Stodder 2012]. Indeed, the Google Ngram
viewer (Figure 3.10) shows that interest in RUP peaked in approximately 2001 and has been on a steady decline since then,
whereas Scrum has been acquiring steadily more attention from those writing books on development methods.

Having worked in both Scrum and RUP environments for some very large companies, I can offer a perspective why
RUP has not held a greater mindshare among agile practitioners. RUP is now proprietary, and the version currently offered
by its vendor is huge and expensive. Project managers and IT directors often find its massive documentation and artifacts
daunting. RUP advocates are quick to mention that RUP is flexible, but flexibility atop a large, opaque process is even
more intimidating. Project planners considering RUP have commented to me that "sure you can adapt the method, but you
better know what you're doing because there are a hundred other moving pieces all connected to the one you're touching."

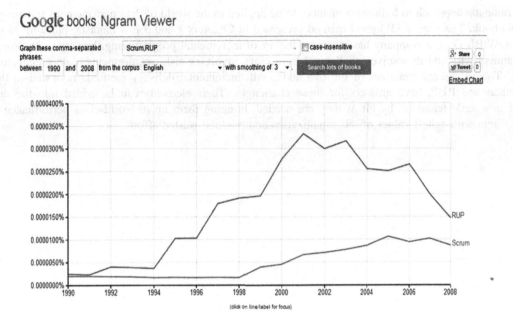

FIGURE 3.10   Google Ngram of "Scrum" and "RUP" through 2008.

The newer, agile methods have many marketing advantages over RUP. They have highly intelligible task boards. They employ user stories that are lightweight and still articulate compelling business value. RUP employs *use cases* that, although they start in summary form, quickly become design heavy with detailed processing steps and alternative flows. The newer agile methods allow a team to model in its preferred language rather than requiring it to switch to UML, and they encourage people to start with paper-based project techniques tools rather than investing in a vendor's complex software suite.

In truth, nothing keeps a company from starting with a small subset of RUP and adding in the more complex pieces as they make sense. That is exactly the spirit behind IBM's OpenUP. Unfortunately for OpenUP advocates, this version of RUP was placed in the public domain long after Scrum, XP, and Kanban were popularized. Scrum in particular defines iterations so that they are immediately understandable, and it offers a facilitator—the Scrum master—who promises to keep things simple and the team moving forward.

We should keep in mind that project planners who are switching to an incremental delivery approach have to choose a method before they understand it completely. In deciding between RUP and agile methods, these planners can either (1) invest time to strip RUP down to where it is something easy to start like Scrum or (2) begin with something easy like Scrum and build it up by borrowing components from RUP. I believe that the agile methods now win more new converts than RUP simply because starting with something that is easy, complete enough, and needing no immediate modification makes sense to more people than field-amputating large portions of a gargantuan method until it's small enough to seem workable.

SUMMARY

The outline of the several methods in Chapters 2 and 3 reveals that the subject of iterative application development methods represents a tremendous amount of material to learn. Given that this large subject cannot be mastered all at once, EDW team leaders should view their agile transition as an extended journey. A company may adopt a particular agile method with the belief that it will suffice for its programming needs, but if it is like most other organizations, its developers will want to evolve that starter method as they learn more about which iterative techniques work and which ones fail in their particular culture, industry, and time point. Accordingly, an organization's software development method must start and grow in much the same way that applications must evolve: iteratively with lots of feedback. Not surprisingly, we can apply agile principles creating an agile software development method, namely take baby steps, iterate, work with just-in-time requirements, hold retrospectives, and steadily improve.

This incremental approach to building a method, to be applied to the world of data management and analytics, is the theme of this book. The Scrum/XP hybrid method presented in Chapters 2 and 3 is a fantastic place to start building a method for DW/BI. Once a company has mastered the art of incremental programming, however, the project team or program planners will find themselves challenged by notions involving risk, requirements, data architecture, quality, and scaling. The values and practices of the two additional, incremental delivery methods reviewed in this chapter, namely Kanban and RUP, have answers for these challenges. Their elements can be added into the development approach of new agile teams bit by bit as they are needed, bringing them up to world-class performance levels in a manner consistent with agile's values of self-organization and minimal wasted effort.

Part I References

Chapter 2

Ambler, S., 2005. Big modeling up front (BMUF) anti-pattern. Agile Modeling (website). <http://www.agilemodeling.com/essays/bmuf.htm> (accessed June 2010).

Beck, K., 1999. Extreme Programming Explained: Embrace Change. Addison-Wesley, Boston.

Beck, K. 2001, March 23. Interview with Kent Beck and Martin Fowler. InformIT (website). <http://www.informit.com/articles/article.aspx?p=20972> (accessed March 2013).

Beck, K., Andres, C., 2004. Extreme Programming Explained: Embrace change, second ed. Addison-Wesley, Boston.

Cockburn, A., 2008, January 2. Quoted in "Defining Agile Methodology." James Bach's Blog. Eastsound, WA: Satisfice, <http://www.satisfice.com/blog/archives/45> (accessed January 2015).

Collier, K., 2001. Agile Analytics. Addison-Wesley, Boston, 2011.

Department of Defense, 1985. Military standard: Defense system, software development, DOD-STD-2167. Washington, DC: Department of Defense. <http://www.everyspec.com> on 2011-09-07T13:00:23 (accessed September 2011).

Hughes, R., Stodder, D., 2012. Accelerating BI/DW value with agile methods: an inside look at trends and best practices. Keynote presentation at The Data Warehousing Institute's September 2012 World Conference, Boston.

Royce, W., 1970, August. Managing the development of large software systems. Proceedings, IEEE WESCON. New York: Institute of Electrical and Electronics Engineers.

Schwaber, K., Mar, K., 2002, March 22. Scrum with XP. InformIT (website). <http://www.informit.com/articles/article.aspx?p=26057&seqNum=3> (accessed January 2015).

The Standish Group International, 1995. The chaos report. <http://www.standishgroup.com> (accessed April 2006).

The Standish Group International, 1999. Chaos: A recipe for success. <http://www.standishgroup.com> (accessed April 2006).

VersionOne Software, 2013. 7th Annual state of agile development survey. <http://www.versionone.com/pdf/7th-Annual-State-of-Agile-Development-Survey.pdf> (accessed January 2015).

Chapter 3

Aked, M., 2003, November 25. Risk reduction with the RUP phase plan. IBM Developer Works (website). <http://www.ibm.com/developerworks/rational/library/1826.html> (accessed April 2014).

Anderson, D., 2010. Kanban: Successful Evolutionary Change for Your Technology Business. Blue Hole Press, Sequim, WA.

Brooks Jr., F.P., 1995. The Mythical Man-Month: Essays on Software Engineering. Addison-Wesley, Boston.

dbViz, 2002. RUP templates. dbViz Project Website (SourceForge). <http://jdbv.sourceforge.net/RUP.html> (accessed September 2013).

Goldratt, E., 1990. What is this Thing Called Theory of Constraints and How Should it be Implemented? North River Press, Great Barrington, MA.

Hughes, R., Stodder, D., 2012. Accelerating BI/DW value with agile methods: an inside look at trends and best practices. Keynote presentation at The Data Warehousing Institute's September 2012 World Conference, Boston.

Jacobson, I., Booch, G., 1999. The Unified Software Development Process. Addison-Wesley, Boston.

Kroll, P., Kruchten, P., 2003. The Rational Unified Process Made Easy: A Practitioner's Guide to the RUP. Addison-Wesley, Boston.

Kruchten, P., 2003. The Rational Unified Process: An introduction, third ed. Addison-Wesley Professional, Boston.

Ladas, C., 2009. Scrumban: Essays on Kanban Systems for Lean Software Development. Modus Cooperandi Press.

McInnis, D., 2011. W. Edwards Deming of Powell, Wyo.: The man who helped shape the world. wyohistory.org (website), Wyoming State Historical Society. <http://www.wyohistory.org/encyclopedia/w-edwards-deming> (accessed January 2015).

Obara, S., Wilburn, D., 2012. Toyota by Toyota: Reflections from the Inside Leaders on the Techniques that Revolutionized the Industry. Productivity Press, Boca Raton, FL.

Ohno, T., 1988. Toyota Production System: Beyond Large-Scale Production. Productivity Press, Boca Raton, FL.

Poppendieck, M., 2004, June 24. An introduction to lean software development. The Lean Mindset (website). <http://www.leanessays.com/2004_06_01_archive.html> (accessed December 2014).

Poppendieck, M., Poppendieck, T., 2003. Lean Software Development: An Agile Toolkit. Addison-Wesley, Boston.

Rational Software, 1998. Rational Unified Process: Best practices for software development teams. <www.ibm.com/developerworks/rational/library/content/03July/1000/1251/1251_bestpractices_TP026B.pdf> (accessed August 2013).

Senge, P., 1990. The Fifth Discipline: The Art & Practice of the Learning Organization. Doubleday, New York.

Taft, D., 2013, April 28. IBM gentrifies rational toolset with UrbanCode. eWeek (website). <http://www.eweek.com/developer/ibm-gentrifies-rational-toolset-with-urbancode> (accessed May 2014).

University of Houston, Clear Lake, 2002. Microsoft Word templates. Rational Unified Process: Overview. University of Houston, Clear Lake (website). <http://sce.uhcl.edu/helm/rationalunifiedprocess/process/templates.htm> (accessed September 2013).

Womack, J.P., Jones, D.T., 2003. Lean Thinking: Banish Waste and Create Wealth in Your Corporation, second ed. Productivity Press, Boca Raton, FL.

Part II

Review of Fast EDW Coding and Risk Mitigation

Chapter 4

Essential DW/BI Background and Definitions

The agile project management techniques described in the previous chapters work well for building software applications in general. Unfortunately, data warehousing teams that have attempted to manage their data integration projects using those generic methods have encountered tremendous difficulties in achieving the desired fast delivery pace. To some extent, the challenge arose from trying to program an application that involves multiple layers of data transformations; however, these teams also discovered that incremental delivery of enterprise data warehouse (EDW) components demands new approaches to the supporting software engineering disciplines of requirements, data modeling, and quality assurance. Before we can explore how to adapt those supporting disciplines, this part of the book fills in two remaining gaps. First, Chapter 4 establishes the vocabulary and concepts for data warehousing and business intelligence that the rest of the book employs. Second, Chapter 5 summarizes the agile programming techniques that were covered in my previous books. Chapter 6 draws upon both of these discussions to illustrate a final preparatory notion—a multi-tiered subrelease cycle that will serve as an agile approach to minimizing the risk of large enterprise data warehousing projects. With that background in place, we will be ready to consider agile versions of the supporting software engineering practices that will allow EDW team leaders to achieve early and continuous delivery of value to their business customers.

As evident in the first few chapters, agile enterprise data warehousing is an enormously broad subject. Defining a baseline approach for this field will touch upon several large topics in software engineering, such as iterative methods, requirements management, data structures, and system validation. Therein lies a tough lexical challenge. Each of these areas has been the focus of hundreds of books by numerous authors, with each of them employing his or her own collection of concepts and vocabulary, which do not all align perfectly. Rather than switching terminologies as I touch upon each information technology (IT) specialty, I employ instead a single set of terms throughout the book, as outlined in this chapter.

Although many readers who have worked in the data warehousing and business intelligence (DW/BI) industry can probably skip much of the details that follow, the major terms of our profession are presented from the ground up so that people transitioning into agile and data warehousing will have an organized introduction to which they can refer in the future. Because I have had to force-fit a few phrases and elevate a couple of jargon words in order to arrive at a single set of terms, even veteran DW/BI professionals might benefit from a quick scan of the following entries:

- Baseline organizational structure (illustrated as part of basic business terms)
- Software engineering environments
- Planning and architectural frameworks
- Reference architectural layers
- Shadow IT
- Topic areas (as opposed to subject areas)

My definitions are admittedly calibrated to private, commercial businesses because most organizations fall within that sector. It is hoped that the definitions provided here will position readers from other sectors to translate these terms to their own particular contexts. Because this book focuses on DW/BI, that sub-industry of IT will determine the definitions used. In the following narrative, I first identify my primary source for definitions from the DW/BI profession and then list the basic terms that those sources employ when describing business users so that we will have a clear means for discussing DW/BI's primary customers. I then address basic notions of IT and conclude by identifying the common data warehousing concepts that underlie the remaining chapters.

PRIMARY SOURCE FOR DW/BI STANDARDS

The basic terms and fundamental concepts of a technical industry can be incredibly difficult to define. Fortunately, data warehousing professionals can draw upon the work of multiple organizations that have already published several glossaries and guides to the concepts and techniques utilized by our industry. The most useful materials are published by the Data Management Association (DAMA) and The Data Warehousing Institute (TDWI).

DAMA is the older of the two organizations. Starting with a single Los Angeles chapter in 1980, this not-for-profit, international association of technical and business professionals has grown to 40 chapters in the United States and another 20 abroad. Dedicated to advancing the concepts and practices of information resource management and data resource management, DAMA provides a forum for vendor-independent analysis and standard definitions to promote the practice of managing information and data as a key enterprise asset [DAMA 2013]. For IT professionals wishing to formally establish their capabilities in the industry, DAMA offers two levels of certification—one for Certified Data Management Professionals (CDMP) and the other for Data Governance and Stewardship Professionals (DGSP).

The other primary association for our industry is TDWI. This organization is a for-profit division of 1105 Media, an integrated business-to-business information and media company that produces more than 10 trade magazines, 40 series of professional conferences, and extensive digital offerings throughout the United States and Europe [TDWI 2013]. Founded in 1995, TDWI is the industry's premier educational and networking organization, currently listing 19 chapters in North America and another 7 overseas. The U.S. national organization of TDWI offers the Certified Business Intelligence Professional (CBIP) certification program in addition to an extensive collection of reference materials, course books, white papers, and blogs to support the professional development of DW/BI practitioners. TDWI also offers five weeklong DW/BI conferences annually within the United States, in addition to other executive summits, seminars, and on-site DW/BI education events.

Importantly, TDWI regularly surveys its considerable list of DW/BI contacts to assess current practices within EDW and use of new technology in the field. I have been privileged to coauthor with TDWI more than one survey focusing on the adoption of agile data warehousing practices. These surveys have revealed that iterative delivery practices have greatly improved the success rates and key performance indicators for those organizations that try them [Hughes & Stodder 2013].

Compared with one another, DAMA appears to be a self-organized network of committees for data professionals interested in understanding and advancing their profession. TDWI serves as a commercially driven forum for the authors and researchers who emerge from the profession, and it provides a dependable series of events that both beginners and seasoned professionals can attend for fast acquisition of standard practices and new ideas. Together, DAMA and TDWI provide a complementary system for deriving and evolving standards for the data management profession.

Regarding the definitions and concepts utilized in this book, both these organizations provide important resources. DAMA offers both a dictionary of data management terms and a guide to the data management body of knowledge (DMBOK) [Earley 2011, Mosley et al. 2009]. The dictionary provides 2000 terms defining a common data management vocabulary for IT professionals, data stewards, and business leaders on more than 40 topics, including finance and accounting, knowledge management, architecture, data modeling, XML, and analytics. Complementing the DAMA dictionary is the *Guide to the Data Management Body of Knowledge*. Written by more than 120 data management practitioners, the DMBOK compiles the industry's commonly accepted principals and best practices. Beyond DW/BI, it addresses other important data management topics, such as governance, architecture, security, and data quality. The DMBOK provides data management and IT professionals, executives, knowledge workers, educators, and researchers with a framework to manage their data and mature their information infrastructure through standard definitions of important data management functions, deliverables, roles, and terminology.

One other source of definitions that deserves mentioning is the *Software Body of Knowledge* published by the Institute of Electrical and Electronics Engineers (IEEE). The IEEE is a not-for-profit professional association dedicated to advancing technological innovation and excellence. Founded in 1963, it currently has approximately 425,000 members, in approximately 160 countries, who provide important guidance and input to international standards-making bodies. IEEE's *Software Engineering Body of Knowledge* (SWEBOK) is in fact an international standard that presents the approaches for developing quality software applications followed by companies and organizations throughout the world.

In the narrative of basic business, IT, and data warehousing terms presented here, I draw mainly upon the DAMA dictionary and DMBOK. Because readers can easily find a reference to those terms by simply searching for an appropriate topic in those documents, I often forego formal citations to that material. Where I draw from TDWI, IEEE, or other sources, I explicitly provide a reference. A few notions discussed in this chapter are based on my own professional experience, and I indicate those terms clearly.

Defining Enterprise Data Warehousing

In Chapter 1, I provided a definition for the word "agile" but left the other components of the term *agile enterprise data warehousing* undefined. It is best to address the data warehousing portion first and then add in the notion of an enterprise.

Achieving clarity on "data warehousing" is a bit of a challenge because industry practitioners tend to use these words loosely, employing many terms to express concepts that are similar but not identical. Adding to the confusion is the closely related term "business intelligence." Many DW/BI professionals will assert that "data warehousing" involves back-end processes that prepare data for analysis, leaving "business intelligence" to signify the data visualizations and other front-end applications employed by end users to actually uncover business insights. This dichotomy certainly aligns with the tool set available from commercial vendors, and we can find formal definitions that support this particular division of labor between the terms. Tools marketed for "data warehousing" seem to support extract, transformation, and loading activities that can all be driven by a company's job scheduler. Indeed, the classic definition of a "data warehouse" is a subject-oriented, integrated, time variant, and nonvolatile collection of detailed and summary data used to *support* strategic decision making within a corporation [Inmon 1995, emphasis mine]. In contrast, vendors advertise "business intelligence" products that enable developers to build end-user interfaces that take data from a warehouse and place it into graphs, pivot tables, and enterprise reporting portals for direct use by a company's business staff. Gartner defines business intelligence to include applications, infrastructure, and tools that *enable access to and analysis of information* to improve and optimize decisions and performance [Gartner 2013].

In practice, however, these terms are often used synonymously. When needing new insights to understand an operational problem, business staff members often say they will get the information from "the data warehouse." When proposing a new means for summarizing information across business units, IT architects and analysts will often state the company needs a better "business intelligence" application. A minority of data management projects do deliver data warehouses without any front-end applications, and at the other end of the spectrum a few business-analysis projects are lucky enough to have a complete source of cleansed and integrated data to start from. For the bulk of projects in the middle, however, investing in a large data-integration project without providing some end-user access would be pointless, and the crucial data analysis applications that the typical company envisions will definitely require some data preparation.

Thus, as actually used in corporations today, data warehousing and business intelligence are joined at the hip. The proper choice in terminology for any given discussion will depend on the emphasis the speaker wishes to make. "DW/BI" is a handy way to speak of both front-end and back-end aspects of an application. The terms "data warehousing" or "data integration" highlight the back-end activities involving extraction, cleansing, transformation, and integration work that a complete DW/BI solution requires. "Business intelligence" indicates that the speaker is thinking more about the front-end application supporting the desired experience that end users will have with the data once it is ready for analysis. However, in the common parlance of our profession, neither "data warehousing" nor "business intelligence" excludes the presence of the other. In this book, I will use these terms with this common overlap in mind.

Table 4.1 provides formal definitions for the terms comprising DW/BI, in addition to definitions for a few of other terms that will be needed in the following chapters, such as "data management" and "data governance." The DW/BI industry employs several other terms that also tend to blend together, such as "information delivery," "data management," and "data analytics." Table 4.2 groups these terms together so that readers will know whether I use them to emphasize the front end, the back end, or the entirety of an information system.

With the terms *agile* and *data warehousing* now clarified, we need to package them together so that the notion of "agile enterprise data warehousing" or "agile EDW" will be clear. Adding the word "enterprise" expands the notion of data warehousing to include the needs of large corporations and even the data management challenges faced by smaller companies as they enter periods of rapid growth. These challenges begin when a company acquires a variety of operational systems, because each one creates a separate pool of information. These multiple data sources invariably have separate owners and distinct stakeholder groups within the company, with each of these groups possessing a unique

TABLE 4.1 Formal Definitions of Core Data Warehousing Terms

Term	
Source	Definition
Business Intelligence	
DAMA	A set of concepts, methods, and processes to improve business decision-making using any information from multiple sources that could affect the business, and applying experiences and assumptions to deliver accurate perspectives of business dynamics [Brackett 2011].
TDWI	Business intelligence (BI) unites data, technology, analytics, and human knowledge to optimize business decisions and ultimately drive an enterprise's success. BI programs usually combine an enterprise data warehouse and a BI platform or tool set to transform data into usable, actionable business information. (http://tdwi.org/portals/)
Data Warehouse	
DAMA	An integrated, centralized decision support database and the related software programs used to collect, cleanse, transform, and store data from a variety of operational sources to support Business Intelligence. A Data Warehouse may also include dependent data marts [DMBOK, pg. 197].
TDWI	1. A subject oriented, integrated, time variant, and non-volatile collection of summary and detailed historical data used to support the strategic decision-making processes for the corporation ("What is a Data Warehouse?" W.H. Inmon, Prism, Volume 1, Number 1, 1995). 2. A copy of transaction data specifically structured for query and analysis (Ralph Kimball, *The Data Warehouse Toolkit*, pg. 310). 3. The foundation for a successful BI program (http://tdwi.org/portals/data-warehousing.aspx).
Data Warehousing	
DAMA	1. The operational extract, cleansing, transformation, and load processes, and associated control processes, that maintain the data contained within a Data Warehouse. 2. The storage of evaluation data for the analysis of trends and patterns in the business [Brackett 2011].
TDWI	1. Data warehousing incorporates data stores and conceptual, logical, and physical models to support business goals and end-user information needs (http://tdwi.org/portals/data-warehousing.aspx). 2. At the highest level, designing a data warehouse involves creating, manipulating, and mapping models. These models are conceptual, logical, and physical (data) representations of the business and end-user information needs. Some models already exist in source systems and must be reverse engineered. Other models, such as those defining the data warehouse, are created from scratch. Creating a data warehouse requires designers to map data between source and target models, capturing the details of the transformation in a metadata repository. Tools that support these various modeling, mapping, and documentation activities are known as data warehouse design tools [TDWI 2011].
Data Integration	
TDWI	Data integration (DI) is a family of techniques and best practices that repurpose data by transforming it as it's moved. ETL (extract, transform, and load) is the most common form of DI found in data warehousing. There are other techniques, including data federation, database replication, data synchronization, and so on. Solutions based on these techniques may be hand coded, based on a vendor's tool, or a mix of both. DI breaks into two broad practice areas. Analytic DI supports business intelligence (BI) and data warehousing (DW), and operational DI is applied outside BI/DW to the migration, consolidation, and synchronization of operational databases, as well as in exchanging data in a business-to-business context [TDWI 2011].
Data Management	
DAMA	The business function that develops and executes plans, policies, practices, and projects that acquire, control, protect, deliver, and enhance the value of data [DMDict].
TDWI	Data management (DM) and information management, a synonym, are broad terms that encompass several data-oriented technical disciplines, such as data integration, data quality, master data management, data architecture, database administration, metadata management, and so on. DM may also include practices that rely heavily on DM, such as business intelligence, data warehousing, and data governance. By extension, enterprise data management (EDM) is a high-level practice that seeks to coordinate DM disciplines, align them with business-oriented goals, and give them consistency and quality through shared data standards and policies for data usage. Synonyms for EDM include unified data management (UDM) and enterprise information management (EIM) [TDWI 2011].
Data Governance	
DAMA	The exercise of authority, control, and shared decision-making (planning, monitoring, and enforcement) over the management of data assets [DMDict].
TDWI	Data governance is usually manifested as an executive-level data governance board, committee, or other organizational structure that creates and enforces policies and procedures for the business use and technical management of data across the organization. Common goals of data governance are to improve data's quality; remediate its inconsistencies; share it broadly; leverage its aggregate for competitive advantage; manage change relative to data usage; and comply with internal and external regulations and standards for data usage. In a nutshell, data governance is an organizational structure that oversees the broad use and usability of data as an enterprise asset [TDWI 2011].

perspective on the company's operations, constraints, and desirable future. These contrasting viewpoints on what the company does and how it should be run frequently affect the foundations of the operational systems that each business group uses, making their data structures and data definitions incompatible and thus requiring DW/BI projects to invest heavily in data harmonization and integration.

Enterprise data warehousing (EDW), then, is the art of integrating information derived from frequently uncooperative stakeholder groups and unaligned data pools into a single information asset that is then used constructively by the general business departments to generate accurate business insights, empowering better business decisions and corporate performance. Some people believe the term EDW means only the back end of an enterprise data analytics system, but I stand with others who employ the expression to signify the full, end-to-end delivery of business insights.

TABLE 4.2 Key Terms and Their Synonyms Used in This Book

Front-End Applications
Business intelligence
Business analytics
Data visualization
Information delivery
Reporting
Dashboarding
User experience (UX)

Back-End Applications
Data warehousing
Data integration
Data transformation
Data management

DW/BI (front-end and back-ends combined)
Data analytics
Decision support systems
Executive information systems
Enterprise data warehousing*
Online analytical processing (OLAP)

* Too big a concept to rule out either front-end or back-end applications; see text.

BASIC BUSINESS TERMS

The chapters that follow discuss gathering business requirements, modeling business entities, and validating that DW/BI applications meet the needs of business users. For this reason, I take a moment to outline the terms used when discussing the customer side of a DW/BI project. Businesses throughout the world are organized in a wide variety of patterns. This section provides a baseline concept to support further discussion of data warehousing customers and beneficiaries. Figure 4.1 places these terms into a more or less "vanilla" organizational structure to provide clarity for the terms defined here.

Enterprise

We should first consider the business definition of "enterprise." Closely following DAMA's definition for this word, I use "enterprise" to mean the integrated set of activities and concerns that an organization employs to define itself based on a self-perceived purpose or point of view. When an IT project is scoped for the enterprise, the term indicates that key activities such as requirements gathering and design cannot myopically focus on a single business unit or an isolated business function. DAMA adds that an enterprise "may be a business, not-for-profit, government agency, or educational institution" [DAMA 2013]. Beyond a large set of purposes, goals, and objectives, *enterprise* also suggests complex sociotechnical systems including people, information, and technologies [Giachetti 2010]. Large IT projects such as DW/BI do well to keep in mind that an enterprise also has governance hierarchies that include an ownership structure and often incurs regulatory oversight even when situated in the for-profit sector. For readability, this book also at times uses the terms "the company," "the corporation," and even "the organization" to indicate that a particular concept or technique must address an enterprise-wide scope.

Business Unit

Large, diversified companies organize themselves into business units in order to segment the management of the company into smaller, organizationally cohesive parts. An example is a national insurance company that has created one business unit for property and casualty products and another unit for life and health policies, with an executive vice president at the helm of each. Although they receive resources and strategic direction from corporate headquarters, business units frequently draft and execute their own competitive plans and maintain their own profit and loss statements. Business units

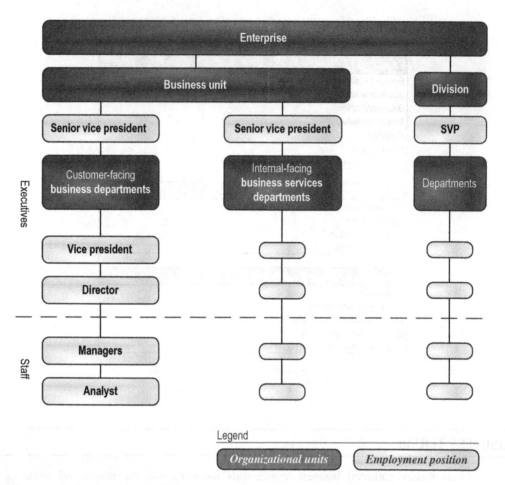

FIGURE 4.1 Business organizational terms used in this book.

are sometimes large enough to have their own internal business services departments, such as marketing, sales, finance, and even IT and project management. Indeed, major corporations can have business units so large and independent that the notions and practices documented in this book for the "enterprise" can frequently apply to them as well. Terms closely related to "business unit" are "subsidiary" and "division," both of which often signify a large business unit associated with a major brand of products within a conglomerate, operating under a separate corporate name and having even greater mission independence. For example, Mack Trucks is a wholly owned subsidiary of Volvo, and Mack de Venezuela C.A. is a division of Mack Trucks that performs final assembly and sales of Mack trucks in South America.

Business Department

A corporation and its major business units contain several functional groupings of staff members, called *departments*. Departments can be *customer-facing*, such as departments of marketing, sales, service, and support. Alternatively, they can be internal *business services departments*, such as departments of finance, accounting, inventory, human resources, and facilities. Many of the customer-facing departments are revenue generating, whereas the business services departments are generally considered cost centers.

Technically, IT and the project management office (PMO) are business services departments, often replicated for each business unit in larger corporations. This book discusses how IT and the PMO can better service their customers, which consist of the company's other business services departments along with the externally facing departments. To keep things clear, then, I use "the business departments" or "the business" to mean all the business departments other than IT and the PMO.

Executive, Director, and Manager

These terms refer to business professionals who possess the authority to manage and make spending decisions within a specified boundary, such as a given business unit or business department. Executives provide leadership to the internal staff members who make up an organization's governance structure. In the nongovernment sectors, "senior executive" refers to an officer of the corporation—that is, a person appointed by the board of directors of a firm, such as a president, chief executive officer, or vice president (VP).

Data warehouses largely support knowledge workers who are organized into hierarchies that report upward to the executives. Accordingly, I use the following general abstraction when discussing the office staffing (from top to bottom) under the aegis of a senior VP: analysts, managers, directors, and VP.

- senior VPs (of various ranks) are responsible for entire business units;
- major business departments, such as "marketing," are managed by VPs, with directors in charge of subspecialties under that department, such as "wholesale marketing"; and
- smaller departments, such as "product management," are overseen by directors, with managers supervising analysts organized by specialty within them, such as "high-speed Internet products."

For easy referencing, the term "staff" refers to the analysts and managers, and "executives" means directors and VPs, as illustrated in Figure 4.1. Because EDW projects typically require millions of dollars to complete, I often assume in this book that the EDW sponsor is a VP of the corporation, although in truth these projects are usually anchored even higher in the organization, such as with a senior or executive VP.

Business Rules

Business rules are the constraints that a company believes should govern the characteristics or behavior of objects or data entities within the enterprise. Business rules describe the desired relationships between the company's physical objects and informational entities. They provide the staff with control points for managing the complexity of activities within the enterprise. For topics pertaining to data quality, business rules describe the constraints that the staff can use to validate the company's information. Business rules also address data characteristics such as optionality, dependencies, valid encodings, and other allowed values.

DATA AND INFORMATION TERMS

Discussions in this book will at times pivot on the distinction between *data* and *information*. "Data" is the more fundamental word and applies to facts in the shape of raw material for an information system. A typical datum is simply the value "42%." Data may be text, numbers, images, or recorded sound, but without greater context, data hold little meaning by themselves.

"Information" is data with context so that it has meaning. To build on our example, "Manufacturer X's 2010 share of the California Blu-Ray DVD recorder market is 42%" provides an idea of how that datum acquires meaning when placed in context. According to the DMBOK entry on "information," some of the context elements that lend data meaning include a business definition, the format in which data is represented, the time frame to which it applies, and the scope of relevance that it has within its designated area of usage.

Understanding data so that it can become information requires "metadata," which is often defined as "data about data." DAMA describes several types of metadata that are discussed later in this book:

- Business: Names and business definition of data elements
- Format: Guidelines on how metadata must be displayed to make sense to the consumer
- Technical: Information regarding how the data is physically stored by the database management system, including field name, data type, length, and precision
- Structural: How atomic-level data items roll up into larger assemblies, such as the way that area code, prefix, and line number combine into a 10-digit phone number

DAMA also lumps several items into "administrative metadata", including the following:

- Data lineage: Where did the facts in a repository come from and how were they validated and combined into their final form within the warehouse?
- Versioning: What point in time or location within a changing series does a given value represent?
- Processing: When was this value acquired or derived?
- Quality: How accurate is the value, even in terms of a plus-or-minus error bar?
- Security: Who owns the information, in terms of both getting bad values corrected and obtaining permission to grant access to another party?

INFORMATION SERVICES TERMS

Information Technology (IT)

IT is typically the department within the enterprise that deals with computer hardware, software applications and systems, the computer-based data of the organizations, and data communications. Companies also name their IT departments as "(management) information services" in the United States or "information, communications, and technology" in the United Kingdom.

For this book, IT for a sizable company can be a large department, with thousands of staff members and often consuming 1% or 2% of corporate revenues. In that capacity, IT must maintain command of a wide range of technologies and the people who understand them. Not surprisingly, the staff for these large IT departments will have formal and very specific training in these technologies, as well as some long-established work processes. Currently, these training and established processes are the "traditional practices" that favor waterfall methods and against which agile will have to compete when a development project team wishes to switch to an incremental delivery approach.

Software and Applications

Software denotes computer programs, including operating systems, utilities, tools, database management systems, and programs for end users. Software supporting one or more related business processes is frequently called a "business application." Software implements the company's business rules in the logic of its applications and therefore imposes semantic meaning on input from humans and devices. Applications purchased ready to operate from the outside are called "commercial, off-the-shelf software" (COTS).

Aside from COTS and "open-source software" (OSS), all other software in the company must be developed in a process often called "computer programming" that many people say results in a "computer program." Unfortunately, "program" is a reserved word for project managers also—a fact that can create much confusion in a book such as this one that discusses software development project management. To avoid this confusion, I generally avoid away from using the term "computer programs" and often refer to software development as "encoding" the company's business rules using a computer language, or more succinctly, "application coding."

End Users

An *end user* is a person or role recognized and authorized to access a particular software application. When important, I will be careful to distinguish between the different roles end users can take, such as knowledge worker, data producer, data consumer, or analyst.

Operational and Analytical Systems

A "system" is an interacting and interdependent group of component items forming a unified whole to achieve a common purpose. A software system consists of multiple software applications. A company's "operational systems" are those systems needed to execute the company's daily commercial transactions and all subsequent data processing needed to complete business obligations. These systems are often called the company's "transaction capture" systems and also "online transaction processing" (OLTP) applications.

The other broad category of software within the company is "analytical systems" or "online analytical processing" (OLAP) applications. The analytical systems are those assemblies of applications that are needed to track and understand the business operations across the enterprise business units and departments, as well as across time. Data warehousing and business intelligence applications fall under this category.

One collection of software that provides much of the information for a company's analytic systems is "accounting systems," which include business applications such as accounts receivable, accounts payable, fixed assets, and general ledger. In larger corporations, a primary source of DW/BI data is also the "enterprise resource planning" (ERP) system, which contains many applications within it, such as materials planning, vendor management, purchasing, and fulfillment, in addition to processes for transferring data to the accounting system.

IT Service Groups

IT departments within most companies organize themselves into service groups for specialties such as desktop technology, application development, networking, infrastructure, information security, and data communications (networking). IT also frequently creates a dedicated service group for each major business system such as billing and ERP.

Companies follow many patterns when it comes to concentrating these IT groups at the corporate level or distributing them across the business units.

DW/BI is often a separate service group that must collaborate with several other IT groups to get the company's analytical applications implemented. One group with which DW/BI must work is the database administrators (DBAs), IT staff who manage the physical aspects of the company's data resources. Another important group for DW/BI is "operations," the team of computer operators that runs applications on data processing equipment in the company's data center, or "machine room." Operations must monitor the automated processing of the data warehouse applications and restore their proper function after they unexpectedly crash.

DW/BI must frequently collaborate also with an enterprise architecture group, a collection of experienced systems and data designers who provide cross-application guidance regarding the company's information strategy, high-level application design, and interdepartmental processing requirements. Because IT service groups such as enterprise architecture, operations, and DBAs must often review and approve the chartering, architecture, detailed designs, and construction of an enterprise data warehouse, the DW/BI service group should make an effort to clearly understand the expectations and requirements that each of these groups will impose.

Shadow IT

Within many large companies, the business units and service departments have become frustrated with the slow pace and high expense of IT's formal application implementation processes. As a consequence, business departments find ways to fund information system development and implementation directly so that IT spending is increasingly occurring outside of the control of the IT department. According to a survey by the Gartner Group, chief marketing officers will be spending more on information systems than on IT by 2017 [Nelson 2013].

"Shadow IT" broadly refers to information processing and application development introduced into an enterprise without IT's assistance. Shadow IT teams often create data marts and even multisubject area data warehouses without coordinating or even informing IT. Often, these projects start innocently enough with power users who begin managing information in spreadsheets and desktop database applications, creating what observers such as TDWI call *spreadmarts* (data marts based on spreadsheets). Over time, these spreadmarts and shadow IT data warehouses grow so large and numerous that they hold a significant and valuable portion of the company's information assets. Shadow IT applications do allow business departments to accomplish their goals faster than IT can support, but on the downside, many uncoordinated development projects waste effort. More important, poor decisions get made when the spreadmarts and isolated data marts provide conflicting and inaccurate business information to executives who must collaborate on a single, company-wide initiative. One advantage to the agile enterprise data warehousing approach promoted by this book is that it includes several mechanisms for incorporating shadow IT groups into the development of the EDW, transforming them into collaborators or "buddy IT" rather than competitors of the corporate IT department.

Competency Centers

According to Gartner, a competency center is an organizational structure used to coordinate IT skills with an enterprise: "Competency centers provide expertise for project or program support, acting both as repositories of knowledge and resource pools for multiple business areas" [Gartner 2013].

Competency centers can range widely in their formality and, for software matters, can be created around topics such as systems engineering, requirements management, configuration or release management, quality assurance, and regulatory compliance. Companies draw upon competency centers to provide a centralized source of expertise to business departments, project teams, and even shadow IT. These centers thus provide an indirect means of standardizing the company's approach to common challenges involving application designs, information analysis, and data integration.

SOFTWARE ENGINEERING TERMS

Software Development Life Cycle (SDLC)

The software development life cycle (SDLC) includes the phases and activities common to software development efforts. Figure 2.3 depicted a traditional, waterfall SDLC. It contains phases (or "steps") for the major development activities of system requirements, software requirements analysis, design, coding, testing, and operations. Rational Unified Process (RUP)'s more recent formulation moves many of these phases to "disciplines" that can be practiced in parallel, leaving the SDLC with phases for only inception, elaboration, construction, and transition. The

RUP phases were introduced in Chapter 2, and fortunately their names do not collide with any of the phases from the traditional approach, so it will be clear from the terminology which SDLC a particular discussion has in mind.

To be thorough, I provide here a quick definition of the traditional SDLC phases, although readers will find a far more careful presentation in the DAMA dictionary and IEEE's SWEBOK [Abran et al. 2005, Earley 2011]. In the following definitions, each phase implicitly includes (1) validating the information provided by the preceding phase and (2) preparing the knowledge needed for the succeeding life cycle step. I have set the goal for each phase as "to the extent appropriate" so that these definitions will be workable for either traditional or agile contexts:

Requirements: Achieving the appropriate level of clarity regarding the user's needs for functional and performance services from the software, in addition to the company's need for integration between applications.

Analysis: Generating the appropriate detail regarding application inputs, processes, outputs, and interfaces. DW/BI projects would include assessing the quality and appropriateness of source data in this step.

Design: Specifying as appropriate the physical characteristics of the application, including major subsystems and their inputs and outputs. This specification will include the application's top-level architecture, including hardware, software, and manual operations. Subsystems are partitioned into one or more design units or modules, and detailed logic specifications are then prepared for each. Design includes clarifying both the nature of an application's user interface at the desktop layer and the structures for the application's data storage.

Coding ("programming"): Translating the detailed specifications produced during the design step into executable systems of software, hardware, and communications. If the software is not acquired, it must be programmed, either at a low level if using a procedural language such as C or at a high level if using a scripting language. The modules or units of the application need to be unit tested, integrated, and retested in a systematic manner. Hardware and communications capabilities must be configured and unit tested also.

Testing: The company assures itself that the application coding is complete and correct and therefore safe to deploy into production usage. Beyond validating the components of a system, testing consists of three major substeps, which are alluded to throughout this book:

1. Integration testing, where the various components of the application are fully assembled to ensure they interact as a coherent system as planned
2. System testing, which validates that the application will perform properly in the machine room as a component of the company's overall IT ecosystem
3. User acceptance testing, during which the user communities examine the running application to ensure that it meets functional and performance requirements

Testing will need to be performed in two styles, which are also mentioned in the following chapters:

1. Progression testing: Confirming that a development team has delivered *new* modules that are complete and correct
2. Regression testing: Confirming that the features previously delivered have not been adversely impacted by any new programming.

Operations: The system is available for business users as envisioned during the requirements phase. Often, IT professionals refer to the transition of applications to an operational status as "promotion into production usage," so we often refer to a new application's ultimate destination as simply "production."

Developers and Programmers

Reflecting on the software development life cycle, one can see that providing a new application for end users requires far more than just encoding a design into a software language. A software project will need business experts, architects, analysts, and data modelers to identify requirements and draft the application's design, as well as testers to validate everyone's work. This book describes many ways for different combinations of these individuals to interact. To make those discussions clear, Table 4.3 outlines the grouping of team members I have in mind. Some readers may be surprised that the system testers are included among the team leaders. As discussed later in this book, agile data warehousing expands the duties of this role so that a team's system tester provides all other teammates with a strong sense of direction and an opinion as to when the the team's quality assurance work is sufficiently completed.

Software Engineering

According to the Association for Computing Machinery (ACM), software engineering is concerned with developing and maintaining software systems that behave reliably and efficiently, are affordable to develop and maintain, and satisfy all the requirements that customers have defined for them [ACM 2006]. IEEE defines software engineering more succinctly as

TABLE 4.3 Names for Different Groupings of Project Team Members

Term	Meaning
Programmers	Project members coding in a computer language or configuring a DW/BI tool to transform a design into a software application.
Product Owner	The embedded business staff member who works daily with the agile development team, providing it with requirements and validating results. Considered part of the team, in fact part of the team leadership.
Team Leaders	Project members who provide the requirements, guidances, and designs that programmers will code into an application. Includes the product owner and IT roles such as solution architect, IT analyst, data modeler, and application designer, plus the system tester who validates the application once coded.
Developers	Project members performing technical work to create the application, i.e., the team's technical leaders and programmers. This term excludes teammates who are business staff members, for whom the developers are working.
Subject Matter Experts	Project members from the business staff that provide business requirements to the developers. For agile projects, this group includes the business person embedded with the agile team (the "product owner") and other business experts who work with the developers, sometimes intermittently.
Development Team	All project members working extensively to create an application design or programming the application's components. Usually excludes subject matter experts and even staff in supporting IT service groups unless the members of this latter group are regularly spending large portions of their time with the project team.
Stakeholders	Individuals outside the team and perhaps outside the company who can affect or will be affected by the outcome of the project.
Close Stakeholders	Business staff who actively work with the development team to identify requirements and validate IT's deliverables. For agile teams, exclude the product owner, who is involved with the team far more than the people falling into this category.

"a systematic, disciplined, quantifiable approach to the development, operation, and maintenance of software." In this book, I use the term to emphasize that DW/BI application development is more than programming—that it requires purposeful, well-sequenced, and skillful efforts in the realms of requirements, analysis, design, coding, and testing. Throughout my years in DW/BI, I have found that when "programmers" make the effort to acquire "software engineering skills," they often transform themselves from journeyman developers into technical leads and even software architects. For this reason, software engineering should also mean "executing the company's software development life cycle with discipline."

Units and Components

The software engineering discipline provides a careful notion of how the elements of a software application should be assembled. From the bottom up, programmers build units and then components and configuration items. They then assemble configuration items together into systems. The distinction between these divisions of a system is often imprecise and context based, but software engineering instructs us to at least try to define these notions for each application with care because they each require a different form of collaboration and validation.

Units can be more precisely described as the most atomic collection of application code that can be designed, programmed, and managed as a whole, usually by one programmer at a time. Units are often the processes included on the lowest level of a data flow diagram and are frequently managed individually using one text file, resulting in one source code repository object.

Components are the first-level assemblies of coding units, typically still small enough to be managed and worked on by a single programmer but large enough to be commonly referenced and reused by others within the development team.

Configuration items are collections of components that have attained enough size and scope of impact that usually multiple programmers are involved in their design, coding, and management. Configuration items are also the highest level items that the team places on its list of the pieces that should be integrated together into a new version of the application, which must be promoted into the testing and later the production environments.

Module serves as a convenient collective noun for all the above and thus means an application component that performs a specific role in the system being developed.

Configuration Management and Application Builds

As applications grow larger, development teams need to exercise *configuration management*—that is, a set of activities for defining how the many pieces of an application fit together into an executable whole and for controlling that assembly process. Each time the application is assembled with a given version of the pieces, that particular combination is considered a unique "application build" and given a "build number." Configuration management typically relies on a "version control" utility that holds a copy of each instance of the application modules plus the metadata needed to identify each one. Version control enables the team to (1) know exactly which instances of the modules compose a given build and (2) perfectly assemble any arbitrary build of the application by drawing the right module instances from the version control repository.

Environments

In general, *environments* are the conditions surrounding data, such as databases, data formats, servers, network, and any other components that affect the data. DW/BI departments typically maintain a set of named environments that closely align with the major steps in the SDLC that they follow. Creating, validating, and deploying an application requires steadily "promoting" a given application from one environment to the next, as will be clear in the following ordered list of environments that I employ for the discussions in this book:

Sandbox: A workspace into which a developer can copy the necessary portions of an application in order to perform unit and component programming.

Development (DEV): An environment in which the developers can assemble and test run a build of the application.

System Integration Test (SIT): An environment to which the team's system testers can promote a given build for independent validation. When a build passes SIT testing, the team can optionally decide to begin the process of releasing it to end users. With this decision, the build becomes a "release candidate."

User Acceptance Testing (ACC): An environment to which the team will promote a release candidate for thorough validation by representatives from the end-user community.

Production (PROD): The environment in which the application will run in order to provide information services to the end users. When placed in PROD, the build is considered a "release" and given a version number.

BASIC ARCHITECTURAL CONCEPTS

In software engineering, *architecture* is a high-level design process that yields an organized arrangement of components intended to optimize the function, performance, feasibility, cost, and usability of a complex application. Data warehouses require architectural reasoning at many levels, including systems, data, and enterprise perspectives. This section names and defines these many levels, as they will be frequently utilized in the chapters that follow.

System Architecture

Software applications for the enterprise must constructively participate in the company's overall data processing ecosystem. An application's *system architecture* defines the technical niche that an application will occupy in that ecosystem and the behavior required of it by the surrounding applications. For drafting system architectures, my company has enjoyed reliable success by following an international standard called the Reference Model for Open Distributed Processing (RM-ODP), which defines the scope and high-level structural organization that an application's systems architectural description should communicate. RM-ODP defines five essential viewpoints for modeling systems architecture that provide a solid, stereoscopic perspective on a proposed application [Malveau & Mowbray 2003]. These five viewpoints reliably guide teams in drafting easily intelligible architectural descriptions with full breadth and an appropriate level of detail, leaving little possibility for any serious gaps in the development team's analysis. RM-ODP specifies that these five viewpoints be addressed, but it does not specify the particular format or conclusions each viewpoint should take. In practice, development teams document these viewpoints using their preferred set of diagrams and written artifacts, although it pays for companies to standardize on the format for architectural descriptions so that the resulting documents are comparable between applications.

RM-ODP's five viewpoints are as follows:

Enterprise viewpoint: A business model of the application, which will allow IT to validate its understanding and intentions with the end users.

Information viewpoint: A model of the information of existing and planned data assets and how these assets are processed and manipulated.

Computational viewpoint: A plan for partitioning the application into software configuration items and components that are capable of supporting data processing, including the necessary distribution of components across the company's telecommunications network. This viewpoint should also address components that are developed versus those that will be acquired and configured. The computation view allows all stakeholders to understand and validate the complexity of the proposed application and thus judge the design's impact on important nonfunctional requirements, such as manageability, extensibility, and adaptability.

Engineering viewpoint: The distributed processing plan for the application, including coordination of its components, given the way in which they will be physically separated as documented in the computational viewpoint. For data warehousing in particular, this viewpoint includes the acquisition of data from source systems, whether it be via direct data connections, messaging, or file transfers. It also addresses how the warehouse will communicate outwardly to other systems that need status messages or data extracts of their own.

Technology viewpoint: A mapping between all objects identified in the other viewpoints and the standards and technologies available. This viewpoint focuses on the specifications for a system's hardware and enabling software, such as operating systems, data communication utilities, and data storage subsystems. Data conversion libraries and low-level source data translators such as XSLT packages would be included in this architectural viewpoint as well.

Data Architecture

The data warehousing community typically refers to RM-ODP's information viewpoint as an application's "data architecture." Both DAMA and TDWI offer extensive guidance on how project teams should derive and articulate a data architecture. Because these recommendations are explored in depth when we discuss agile data engineering, only the major components are identified here. A warehouse's data architecture is the result of activities related to identifying, naming, defining, structuring, and documenting the application as a data resource. It also includes specifying how the integrity, accuracy, and effectiveness of the application's information will be ensured, especially when that information is integrated from sources spread throughout the many business units and departments of the enterprise. With good data architecture, the warehouse's design and construction will be business driven, based on real-world subjects perceived by the enterprise, so that it contains information that is easily identifiable, readily available, high quality, and consistent across the company's organizational boundaries [Brackett 2005].

Development teams record the intended and actual structure of a data warehouse's information repository by maintaining multiple *data models* within the application's data architectural description. These models incorporate diagrams and textual information. The diagrams have varying formats depending on whether they express a business conceptual, logical, or physical viewpoint.

Business Conceptual Model

IT frequently needs to communicate an application's requirements and design concepts to business partners who have no technical training. Business conceptual models are a good place to start given that they are a depiction of only the business-visible elements within a subject area, displaying the business-intelligible entities known to exist and the relationships between them. Details concerning the entities' attributes are omitted completely, making this model an easy first step toward understanding the high-level contents and purposes of any data collection. As an example, Figure 4.2 provides an excerpt from a business conceptual model.

Conceptual models that focus on business concepts are frequently called "business conceptual models" or simply "business model," the term I will usually employ. While interacting with sponsors, end users, and other business stakeholders in the early phases of a project, data warehousing development teams rely on business models to validate their understanding about business requirements and to communicate their high-level plans for a DW/BI application. They often build business models for the source systems that will supply a warehouse with data and build another set for the "target" data repository—that is, for the proposed data warehouse as it will appear to the business user.

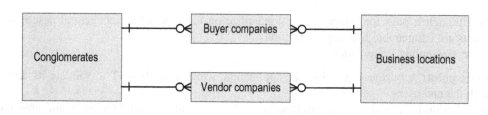

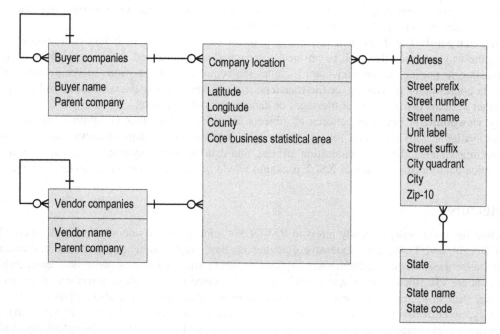

FIGURE 4.2   Business conceptual model.

FIGURE 4.3   Logical data model.

Logical Data Model

Whereas business models provide a high-level view of a data collection's contents, *logical* models express greater detail about how that collection is structured for a more technical audience. After using business models to establish the important entities for which an application must plan, development teams use a **logical data model** (LDM) to document in detail how data should appear to the end users and applications that must work with the information it contains. The purpose of an LDM is to document the logic that governs the information within a data resource, focusing on what data items it contains, what those elements mean, and how they can be used. Like business models, LDMs provide business-centric descriptions of entities and the relationships between them, but they also describe the entities' attributes and the data integrity rules controlling the information stored within them. Figure 4.3 reveals a logical model that might be derived from the business model excerpt shown previously. For clarity, it only names the attributes, but some logical models document data types and lengths as well.

LDMs abstract out any notion of how the data is actually structured within its repository, leaving that topic to the next model type. For DW/BI, LDMs provide an implementation-independent and application-neutral depiction of either the sources from which the warehouse will pull information or the target repository within which it will store data.

Physical Data Model

Often, the reality of how the data is physically stored on disk is vastly different from how the database management system will make it appear to the end users when accessed. DBAs frequently reconceptualize the entities and attributes for efficiency, performance, and manageability before they create the actual storage structures for the data. They also rename the entities and their attributes to meet their own set of standards. Whereas logical models communicate *what* a data resource contains, a physical data model (PDM) documents technical details regarding *how* that information is physically arranged and constrained within the actual structures of its repository. Instead of entities, attributes, and rules, a PDM documents tables, columns, and constraints. Figure 4.4 contains an example of how the data depicted

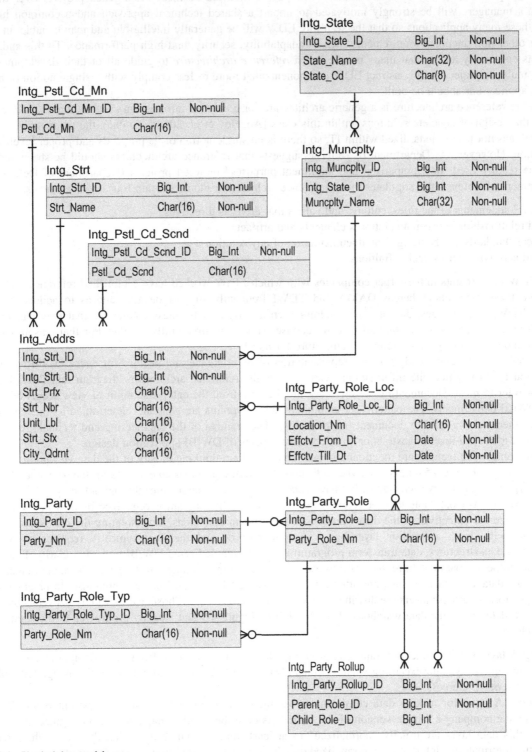

FIGURE 4.4   Physical data model.

in the previous LDM might appear in a physical data model, after the data's entities have been consolidated by the physical data designer into tables.

Reference Architecture

The DW/BI department of any sizable company will pursue multiple business intelligence projects over time. The department's managers will be strongly motivated to impart a shared technical approach and a common high-level design on these many applications so that the resulting EDW will be generally intelligible and maintainable, in addition to meeting other nonfunctional requirements such as adaptability, security, and high performance. To this end, DW/BI departments commonly adopt what many people call a *reference architecture* to guide all of their development teams so that the multiple projects will construct EDW components that more or less comply with a single notion of how data warehouse applications should be built.

A software reference architecture is a generic architecture for a class of information systems that is used as a foundation for the design of concrete solutions within this class [Angelov et al. 2012]. To date, the meaning of "reference architecture" has not been standardized within IT, so there is no single notion of its purposes and proper levels of detail or abstraction. However, the Department of Defense suggests that reference architectures should be structured so that they can be readily used for "comparison and alignment purposes" between projects [Department of Defense 2010]. The Department of Defense also stipulates that a reference architecture should contain four major elements:

- High-level statements of the rules, culture, and values that drive its directives
- Desired relationships between a solution's elements and artifacts
- Technical standards for the design and documentation of any solution
- Standard acronyms, terms, and definitions

Most EDW departments in the larger companies with which I have worked have established reference architectures that achieve these elements. Whereas DAMA and TDWI frequently suggest design patterns to address commonly encountered DW/BI challenges, data analysts address such a variety of business challenges that they cannot issue a single high-level design and claim that all data warehouses should be structurally similar. For that reason, each company needs to devise on its own a reference architecture for its EDW.

Conceivably, a company could draft one representation of its reference architecture for every ODP-RM viewpoint listed previously. In practice, the informational viewpoint is the reference architecture diagram that DW/BI development teams refer to most. Documenting the reference architecture from the enterprise point of view seems out of scope for most DW/BI departments. The patterns for computational viewpoints are generally determined by the data architecture and are therefore wasteful to document independently. The features of the engineering and technology viewpoints affect items at too low a level of abstraction to affect most aspects of DW/BI application design.

When reference architectures are mentioned in later chapters, I am thinking mostly of the data viewpoint and assume the one illustrated in Figure 4.5 unless otherwise indicated. This figure provides an example for the data side of an EDW, as is fairly typical of the many such standards I have encountered at large companies throughout the years, although certainly many variations exist. Note that the reference architecture in the diagram is organized by *abstraction layers* that compartmentalize the objectives of the data warehouse into separate data areas, thus isolating the issues that each layer must contend with. Each abstraction layer has a specific purpose and therefore typically requires its own mini-environment of data structures, data transform programming, and even dedicated DW/BI tools. For clarity, I have placed what appears to be a separate data repository into each layer shown in this diagram. Because abstraction layers tend to have their own database schemas, they are often referred to as the "data layers" of the warehouse. In practice, how the physical repositories for these layers are distributed or combined across DW/BI hosts varies widely between companies.

In general, data enters the data warehouse from the left of Figure 4.5 and steadily progresses to the right, layer by layer, as follows:

- Landing: A layer where extract programs can place raw data taken or received from a source application.
- Data cleansing: A layer for executing whatever data cleansing can be achieved before data is integrated with information from other sources.
- Integration: A layer for making data consistent across the organizational boundaries of the enterprise. This layer represents the company's "single version of the truth." As described in the chapters on data engineering, the structures of this data layer are usually "normalized" to at least third normal form, which drives out the redundancy within the information. Unfortunately, normalized data is very difficult for end-user staff to work with.

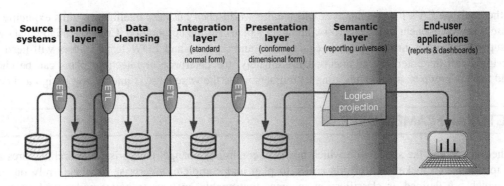

FIGURE 4.5 Sample enterprise data warehouse "reference architecture".

- Presentation: A layer for "de-normalizing" and reorganizing data so that end-user staff members can readily understand it and bring it into their business analyses. Although reorganized for business user purposes, DW/BI departments want this layer to reflect a single approach to the company's information, so data in the presentation layer cannot always be made application specific.
- Semantics: A layer allowing presentation data to be re-projected to better support specific end-user applications. Objects in these re-projections often receive considerable grooming and renaming so that end users will readily understand the "semantics" (meaning) of the information it provides. This layer is typically composed of virtual rather than persisted data resources (see Chapter 13).
- End-user BI applications: The collection of business intelligence applications that visualize data warehouse information for business analysis. Like the semantic layer, this portion of the reference architecture can include many virtual data resources as well as analytical applications that are widely distributed across end-user desktops and mobile devices.

Enterprise Architecture

Although the complexity of a data warehouse tempts one to plan solely within the boundaries of his or her current project, the needs of the enterprise will soon impinge on a project so narrowly defined. Data analytics projects are so expensive and their potential value so great that large corporations must inevitably manage them as a strategic asset, one that serves many parties across the company's organizational boundaries and integrates with many other applications in order to leverage existing analytic applications. For this reason, EDW team leaders need to plan on collaborating with the company's enterprise architects, who inevitably must approve of many data warehousing requirements and design elements.

Enterprise architecture (EA) is a discipline with a much larger scope than data warehousing. EA provides strategic plans for standardizing, integrating, and optimizing the company's overall processes for delivering goods and services to customers. The enterprise architects of a company maintain a list of prioritized, aligned initiatives and road maps defining the present and future of the company:

> *[EA presents] business and IT leaders with signature-ready recommendations for adjusting policies and projects to achieve target business outcomes ... [and] steer[s] decision making toward the evolution of the [desired] future state architecture.*
>
> [Gartner 2013]

An EA is typically a large body of work, with many company-wide specifications with which teams building both manual and automated systems within the organization must align. Its artifacts include as-is and to-be versions of the following [Earley 2001]:

- Business goals for the company
- Organizational business architecture
- Comprehensive business process model
- Information value chains
- Corporate data models
- Data integration standards
- Application component architecture
- Standard infrastructure technologies

Many of the goals on EA's list of initiatives will require world-class business intelligence, thus explicitly making the data warehouse a key component in the enterprise architect's plans for the corporation. Consequentially, data warehousing teams must support EA goals in their project requirements and designs, and EDW team leaders will need to vet their high-level designs with the enterprise architects. Unfortunately, the enterprise architectural plans can be challenging to support should the EA group be actively updating its artifacts while the warehouse is undergoing design and construction.

ARCHITECTURAL FRAMEWORKS

Because of their scope and the speed with which business conditions change, enterprise data architectures are difficult to draft and maintain. To make such efforts easier to plan and complete, enterprise architects rely on *architectural frameworks*, which are defined as classification schemes that enable analysts to better understand an area of study. Frameworks often include a repeatable analytical approach with recommendations on how to use the classification tool effectively. Although their scope is only a subset of EA, DW/BI programs face many of the same planning issues as EA, and thus architectural frameworks represent a valuable tool set that EDW team leaders should be ready to use, both for their own projects and for communicating with enterprise architects.

Three frameworks that data warehouse teams will find particularly useful are the Zachman EA framework, the DAMA functional framework, and the Hammergren planning framework.

Zachman Enterprise Architectural Framework

When formalizing his approach to enterprise architecture in the late 1960s, John Zachman created an analytical matrix by intersecting the six fundamental interrogatives (who, what, when, where, why, and how) with the five levels of modeling regularly employed for computer system design: context, concepts, logical, physical, and detailed specification.

As can be seen from Figure 4.6, this framework enumerates a rich set of artifacts for fully describing an existing or a desired information system within an enterprise computing environment [Sessions 2007].

For enterprise data warehousing projects, I have employed the earlier 2001 version of the framework where the "what" column translated to data concepts [Zachman 2011].

The bottom half of the figure shows a streamlined version of this older framework, which my project teams have used to great effect as we planned out the multi-departmental aspects of our data warehousing applications.

Consider, for example, how Cell C1R2 calls for the team leaders to consider "what" (entities) from the perspective of all relevant data owners throughout the organization.

To achieve this objective, they will have to examine multiple sources and many consumers when identifying business entities to include in the application's architecture, eventually organizing the important data items into a business conceptual model and documenting the relationships between them.

Later in the project, the data definition catalog specified in Cell C1R5 will require them to revisit key components of "what" at the specification level, prompting these team leads to translate the business conceptual model into entity names and definitions acceptable to all the stakeholder business groups.

Similarly, the business process model called for in Cell C2R2 will guide them into considering the "how" (processes) as it will manifest at the conceptual level, so the EDW team will have to think through the ways the data warehouse should connect to the company's wider ecosystem of operational systems, even coordinating these plans with the other DW/BI application teams.

By forcing systems planners to look across the organization from many viewpoints and at several different levels of detail, this framework leads to reliably comprehensive designs.

My adapted version of the framework is surely not as powerful or as complete as the current offering from Zachman International, but it works well for DW/BI solution architects, keeping them from overlooking any important system requirements as they elaborate upon the enterprise nature of their data warehousing applications.

DAMA Functional Framework

The DAMA functional framework offers a comprehensive and widely accepted approach to planning a company's data management function and a standard set of activities for completing that plan [Mosley et al. 2009, p. 12]. Whereas the Zachman framework's intent is to generate a series of models describing how a general application will fit within the enterprise information ecosystem, the DAMA framework focuses more narrowly on planning the implementation of

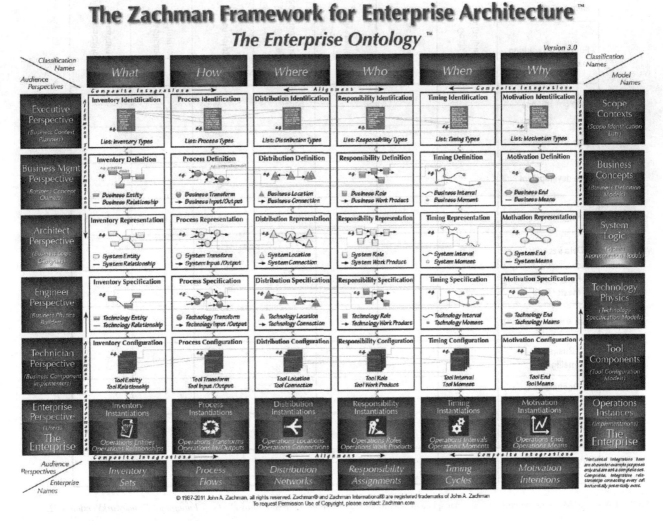

FIGURE 4.6   Zachman framework adapted for an enterprise data warehousing program. *Adapted from the Zachman Framework, 2001 version, as presented in [DMDict] and [Session 2007].*

data management systems in particular. Figure 4.7 illustrates how this framework intersects a particular model of an organizational environment (the columns) with a list of common data management functions (the rows). For example, to complete the planning goals stipulated by the shaded portion of this grid, one would have to articulate roles and responsibilities and also the technologies that the DW/BI department will use (columns D and E) for managing data security, master data, and the data warehouse itself (rows 5–7).

As with the Zachman approach, only a subset of the framework will apply strongly to any given DW/BI project. However, DW/BI teams protect themselves from serious oversights by considering the entire planning grid, at least at a high level, during their initial project planning. They also benefit greatly by occasionally reviewing it throughout a project as a dependable way to detect whether their project has changed significantly, necessitating further architectural planning. The DAMA functional framework is discussed later in the book when we include it in an enterprise-capable approach to requirements management.

Hammergren DW Planning Matrix

As we narrow our analytical scope further, we arrive at the Hammergren DW planning matrix, which provides a straightforward means for EDW teams to systematically analyze the requirements, design, and implementation of a data management application. Tom Hammergren started his career as a data warehousing methods planner with Sybase

Environmental elements ➡ Functions requiring management ⬇	Goals & principles A	Activities B	Deliverables C	Roles & responsibilities D	Technology E	Practices & techniques F	Organization & culture G
Data governance 1							
Data architecture 2							
Data development 3							
Data operations 4							
Data security 5							
Reference & master data 6							
Data warehousing 7							
Business intelligence 8							
Documents & content 9							
Metadata 10							
Data quality 11							

FIGURE 4.7   DAMA's framework for data management functions. *Source: Adapted from DAMA DMBOK Functional FrameworkVersion 3.02.*

during the 1990s. He authored several books on data analytic system development and later published *Consensus*, an important productivity tool for EDW requirements gathering [Balanced Insight 2014]. His planning framework provides a streamlined approach to deriving well-grounded DW/BI system designs and high-level implementation plans, an approach that has been utilized by TDWI in several of its webinars.

Figure 4.8 shows the summary grid from Hammergren's overall design approach. This grid intersects six steps from the software development life cycle (the rows) with the functional layers at work within a finished data analytics project (the columns). Teams that pursue their research and design efforts in the order suggested in the diagram will arrive at a business-centric architecture for their application that not only supports the user's functional requirements but also balances them reasonably with the major nonfunctional requirements that determine how extensively end users will adopt the system. On the right of this diagram, notes identify the objectives that teams should strive for while working through the analysis for each SDLC step. The matrix from Hammergren's original representation has been transposed so that his functional layers are aligned with the data layers in DW/BI reference architecture introduced previously in this chapter. Agile EDW team leaders should keep Hammergren's matrix close by because it serves as a guide to the detailed steps that developers should execute for several of the column sets during a project that many teams place on their Kanban-style work boards, such as "analyze" and "design."

Combining all three of these frameworks provides a robust analytical approach for answering the demands arising from three different levels within the corporation: end users, IT management, and enterprise architecture. A development team can begin with Hammergren's planning matrix and quickly arrive at a workable design for the team's application as a solution to specific business users. At this point, project leads can refer to the DAMA functional framework

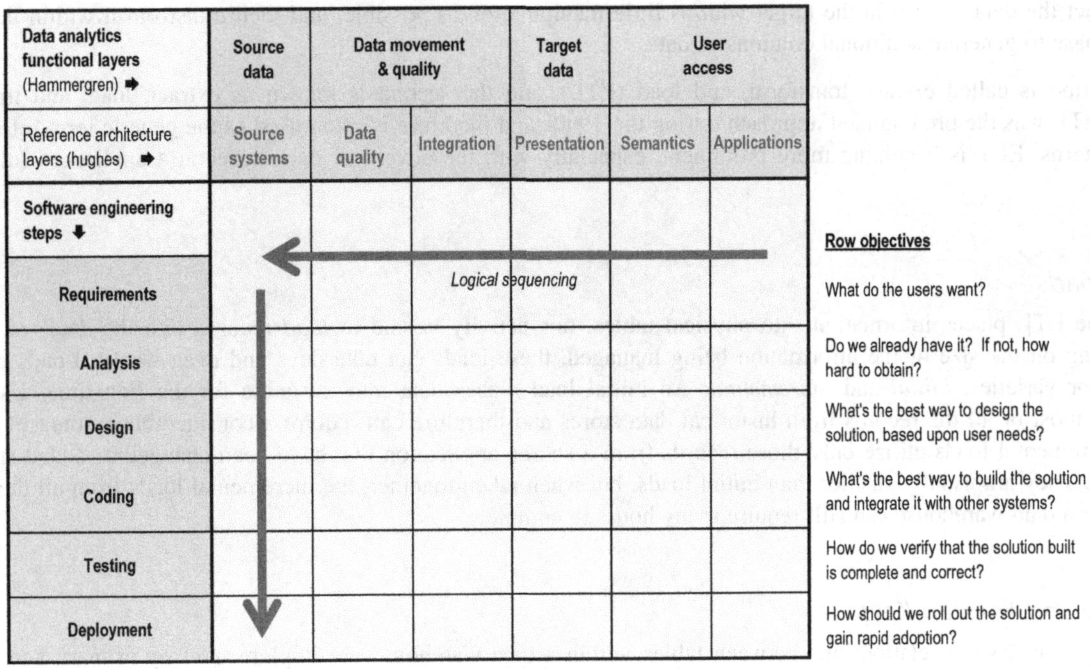

Data analytics functional layers (Hammergren) ➡	Source data	Data movement & quality		Target data	User access	
Reference architecture layers (hughes) ➡	Source systems	Data quality	Integration	Presentation	Semantics	Applications
Software engineering steps ⬇						
Requirements			*Logical sequencing*			
Analysis						
Design						
Coding						
Testing						
Deployment						

Row objectives

What do the users want?

Do we already have it? If not, how hard to obtain?

What's the best way to design the solution, based upon user needs?

What's the best way to build the solution and integrate it with other systems?

How do we verify that the solution built is complete and correct?

How should we roll out the solution and gain rapid adoption?

FIGURE 4.8 Hammergren's matrix for sequencing DW/BI development work.

to evaluate where they need to invest additional thinking in order to transform their application design into a fully conceptualized DW/BI system with low total cost of ownership. Finally, the project architect can then review the Zachman EA framework to better anticipate the company-wide requirements that the enterprise architecture group will need the new application to support.

ADDITIONAL DATA WAREHOUSING CONCEPTS

Data analytics involves a few additional terms that will cause confusion later in the book if left undefined.

Database Management System

A *database* is an organized collection of data stored in a structured way that enables rapid search and retrieval by a computer. The *database management system* (DBMS) is a multi-user, fault-tolerant application used to hold, manipulate, and answer queries upon one or more databases. Data warehouses are typically implemented using some of the world's best databases, such as Oracle, Microsoft's SQL Server, and IBM's DB2. As a core capability, all of these products support *relational databases* in which information is stored in tables each of which is dedicated to a specific information entity. These tables are organized very much like a spreadsheet, with the rows being called records. Each of these records represent a given instance of the entity that the table was modeled to support. In turn, these records contain columns, each one dedicated to a specific attribute of the focal entity. Each column has a data type and other constraints to ensure that information is properly constructed when loaded into a record. Users or applications insert, update, query, and delete the database records using the DBMS's *data manipulation language*. For the commercial DBMSs listed previously, data manipulation commands are written in an international standardized syntax known as *Structured Query Language* (SQL).

ETL/ELT

In general, information must be taken from a source and then placed into each successive layer of a data warehouse's reference architecture. There are two patterns utilized for this work:

1. Extract the data from sources, transform it as needed, and then load it into the target database belonging to the data layer being populated.

2. Extract the data, load it in the target with as little manipulation as possible, and then transform it within the target database to generate additional columns of data.

The first is called extract, transform, and load (ETL), and the second is known as extract, load, and transform (ELT). ETL was the predominant approach during the 1990s and therefore is often used as the generic term referring to both patterns. ELT is becoming more prominent, especially with the advent of data warehouse appliances (discussed later).

Data Loads

When the ETL places information into physical tables, this activity is said to *load* records into the data warehouse. Depending on the size of the information being managed, these loads can take days and even weeks. Loads come in two major varieties, *initial* and *incremental*. An initial load places data into the table for the first time. Usually it involves most or all the records from historical data stores and therefore can require a considerable amount of processing. Incremental loads utilize only those records from a source application that have been changed or added since the last load. They are usually smaller than initial loads, but when taken together, the incremental loads from all the source tables for a data warehouse can still require many hours to complete.

Primary and Foreign Keys

Typically, the desired relationships between tables within a data warehouse are implemented by primary and foreign keys. The *primary key* of a table consists of one or more columns whose values can uniquely identify a record within that table. Naturally, each value in the primary key of a table must occur only once in the table. A *foreign key* within a table is a column or set of columns whose values can be found in the primary key of another table. Foreign key values can occur many times in a given table and once for every record that should link to the primary key in another table. Therefore, a properly coordinated primary key/foreign key pair physically implements a one-to-many relationship within a database. The table with the primary key is typically referred to as the *parent* table and the table with the foreign key as the *child*.

Natural and Surrogate Keys

The tables in the source systems have primary keys for uniquely identifying their records. Data warehouses build a history of the changes to the records in a source system and can therefore acquire multiple images of any given identifier in the source data. For that reason, DW/BI teams cannot use the source system's primary keys as primary keys in the data warehouse tables. So that DW/BI applications can still uniquely identify every instance of records in a table that tracks source information history, the data warehouse often assigns its own unique serial number as it creates records in its data tables. The columns holding these new identifiers are called *surrogate primary keys* or simply "surrogate keys." The original primary key values from the source tables, such as "order number," are often of great interest to the data warehouse users, so DW/BI teams include them in the target tables alongside the surrogate keys, labeling them as the source's *natural keys*.

Indexes

DBAs typically maintain *indexes* on database tables of any appreciable size. An index is a data structure that cross references a set of values from a given domain to the places (records or rows) where each value appears, generally within a single table. Indexes must be refreshed each time a table is loaded.

Indexes facilitate the joins between database tables, especially between primary and foreign keys. Thus, indexes can greatly accelerate data retrieval for queries that follow the anticipated path that the indexes were designed to support. Often, designers anticipate that users will pull data from the database via many different retrieval paths, and they may well specify a set of indexes to support each one. If they follow this strategy to an extreme, a data warehouse can end up with so many indexes that the indexes absorb more disk space than the base data tables. When the collection of indexes approaches such a size, the time required to build or refresh a warehouse's indexes can start to rival the time needed to load the data tables.

Constraints and Referential Integrity

DBAs also configure databases with *constraints*, which are machine-applied rules governing the values that can be placed in the data tables. Some constraints, such as UNIQUE or NOT-NULL, operate on a single record. Other constraints are checks on values between tables. A common example of a multi-table constraint is a foreign key constraint, which ensures that a record will not be loaded in a table if the values in the foreign key column(s) cannot be found in the primary key column(s) of the parent table.

DBMS-enforced constraints consume processing power and therefore can slow down warehouse data loads considerably. For this reason, many DW/BI teams do not employ DBMS-enforced constraints in their databases, relying instead on the ETL to ensure that child records are not inserted without corresponding parent records. When the records in a database completely agree with the mandatory primary/foreign key constraints specified by the data modeler, the tables are said to have *referential integrity*.

Views and Data Virtualization

A pre-declared join between two or more tables is called a database *view*. End users and applications can retrieve records from a view by referencing it by name. They do not have to specify the join logic because that logic was established by the database administrator when he or she created the view.

Typically, views can be defined without special configuration by the DBAs only across the tables of a single database. However, the past few years have seen marked improvements in *data virtualization servers*, which allow developers to easily create views that bridge together separate data warehouses, multiple databases of the same vendor, and multiple databases from different vendors. They can also draw from data stores in desktop repositories, spreadsheets, and unstructured data sources including XML messages and email.

Data Schema

The *data schema* for a database defines the structure of the tables held within that database, along with some additional objects, such as indexes and views, that are needed for performance and convenience during data retrieval. Data warehouse designers use data schemas to impart a high level of organization to their databases. Often, the data layers of the reference architecture are implemented in separate data schemas so that they can be managed separately and even distributed independently across multiple hosts. Data schemas for end users can sometimes contain mostly views that pull data from tables in yet another schema, which resides deeper in the data warehouse's reference architecture.

Subject and Topic Areas

A *subject area* is a collection of related data warehouse entities or tables logically grouped for presentation and analysis together. Some subject areas are defined by the end user perspective they support, such as *marketing*, *sales*, and *finance*. Other subject areas represent a fundamental data resource within a data warehouse, such as *customer*, *product*, and *organization*.

Subject areas can be large, involving scores of tables. Often, development teams must focus their design and loading efforts on a subset of the tables composing a subject area. I call these subsets within a subject area *topic areas*. Examples are the *address* tables within a *customer* subject area, or the *product hierarchy* tables within a *product* subject area.

Data Dictionary

To make sense of the data stored in a DBMS, companies usually maintain one or more *data dictionaries*, which store business and/or technical terms and definitions for the elements within the database, including tables and views. In general, data dictionaries should document the data schemas used to organize the data warehouse and should make clear the database objects available within each. They should also provide guidance regarding the subject and topic areas of the data warehouse.

Normalized Data Model

A *normalized* data model subdivides a data schema into many single-themed tables so that the database will not be subject to undesirable deletions or duplications of information during data manipulation actions. Thorough normalization often breaks tables that represent a particular business entity into many smaller tables, resulting in a very complex data model that few business users can understand. In general, the process of normalization requires up to six steps, each one requiring a significant investment of effort and resulting in a specific "normal form." The integration layer is frequently modeled using at least "third normal form" and is therefore often labeled "3NF" on diagrams. Queries against normalized tables effectively "de-normalize" the data—that is, they logically join the normalized tables so that the output once again resembles a single table.

Dimensional Data Model

A dimensional data model organizes the information in a database so that it is highly intelligible to business users and so that the DBMS can answer queries very quickly. In general, the data is structured into *fact tables* that are dedicated to events, transactions, and other time-based metrics. These metrics are connected to *dimension tables* that hold the qualifiers needed to analyze the metrics stored in the fact tables. Users analyzing a fact table commonly start with a display of an aggregate of its metrics and then decompose those values by constraining the query to certain values of the associated dimensions—a process frequently called "slice and dice" when DW/BI professionals are speaking informally.

Data Marts

A *data mart* is a business intelligence or data analytics application that focuses on a limited subject area and uses a dimensional data model design. Typically, a data mart belongs to the departments most closely associated with its focal subject area, such as "Marketing," and acquires much of its information from the company's EDW.

Data Warehouse Appliance

Although there are many architectures for these devices, in general a data warehouse appliance is a system that contains hardware and software optimized for servicing data warehouse queries. Often, a data warehouse appliance restructures the data behind the scenes in order to reduce DW/BI query response times by one or more orders of magnitude.

Corporate Information Factory

The corporate information factory (CIF) is an enterprise data warehouse that follows a high-level data flow architecture advocated by Bill Inmon and Claudia Imhoff [Inmon & Imhoff 2001]. As popularly understood, a CIF gathers data from sources and transforms it into a repository in the integration layer of the reference architecture. From there, the information is subsetted out to departmental data marts, delivering the specific columns and rows needed by each one. In the CIF model, the data stored in the integration layer should be a "single version of the truth" within the company. Because most DW/BI designers suspect that duplicate information stored within a database inevitably allows data discrepancies to occur, most CIF integration layers are highly normalized because the normalization process leads to tables that make such redundancy impossible. The data in the integration layer is then de-normalized into a dimensionalized model and stored in an enterprise presentation layer of the warehouse. Data is later subsetted into small dimensional models as needed for specific users and is often structured to specifically support the needs of a particular class of data analysis, such as sales volumes and profitability.

Enterprise Data Bus

The enterprise data bus (EDB), as championed by Ralph Kimball, is widely considered an alternative to building a corporate information factory [Kimball & Ross 2013]. The EDB loads staged source data directly into the denormalized tables in the presentation layer of the reference architecture. For that reason, an EDB data warehouse generally does not need the normalized data tables of an integration layer. Because they avoid the effort of careful data normalization, EDB warehouses are considered by many DW/BI professionals to save time and money. However, the dimensional tables in an EDB must be "conformed"—that is, they must be defined and structured so that it can be re-used by many fact tables. An example is a conformed dimension for company store locations that can be used by the fact tables in the marketing, sales, and service subject areas. Conforming dimensions can require considerable design time and extra ETL programming, so the time and cost savings of the EDB can be less than one might expect.

TRADITIONAL PROJECT MANAGEMENT TERMS

Building an EDW involves many intersections between the disciplines of IT and project management. Given that agile greatly changes the way that teams pursue defining, executing, and validating their work, the remaining chapters frequently use the project management terms highlighted in this section. Unless otherwise noted, the following definitions quote or paraphrase terms found in the Project Management Institute's *Project Management Body of Knowledge* [Project Management Institute 2013].

Project

A *project* is a temporary endeavor undertaken to create a unique product, service, or result. Good project managers require projects to have a defined purpose, a beginning, and an end, in addition to an explicit means of determining success. In this book, projects are also assumed to have financial sponsors and a governance body that has final say over the features that will be included in the software applications that they create.

Stakeholder

A project *stakeholder* is any party involved in the endeavor that could be significantly impacted by the outcome of the work. Not all stakeholders actively participate in a project nor even realize ahead of time that they will be impacted, so good project managers actively search for and communicate with potential stakeholders. In particular, this book uses *stakeholder* to collectively refer to people on both the business and IT sides who will care about what a project achieves. On the business side, this group includes a project's sponsors, end users, and the departmental staff involved in the business process that a DW/BI application will affect, as well as the customers and vendors who will see the project change the company's performance. This group also includes the project's "close stakeholders"—that is, the business staff (other than the team's product owner) who actively work with the development team to identify requirements and validate IT's deliverables. On the IT side, stakeholders include the developers, any supporting IT groups such as DBAs, and the managers who will be held accountable if a project fails.

Programs

A *program* is a group of related projects and activities, managed in a coordinated way to obtain benefits not available from managing them individually. Commonly, executive sponsors actually fund an IT program, and a program manager distributes those funds to the component application development projects.

Companies frequently have little choice but to manage enterprise data warehousing efforts as programs, for the following chain of reasoning: Creating or changing a data warehouse impacts more than just the warehouse that the development team is working on. The operational systems supplying data will have to be altered in order to create the access points or the data extracts through which the data warehouse will receive source information. Applications depending on data transfers from the warehouse may well have to be altered, too, when the data offered to them expands, disappears, or changes definitions and formats. For each impacted system, upstream or downstream, a separate project with a dedicated team and project manager needs to be created. For the most part, executives will be uninterested in the upstream and downstream chaining of systems. Because business sponsors simply want the new analytical capability, IT will have proposed a total cost figure for the warehouse and all attendant work. These executives will award that funding, and IT will need to split it among the separate teams that will work on each impacted system, making the entire effort a program of multiple projects. As work progresses, the business sponsors will require status updates, change the requested capabilities, and alter the program funding. The program manager will combine the information from all the project activities so that it appears to the executives as a single effort.

Portfolios

A *portfolio* is a roll-up of programs and represents the collection of project work under management for an entire company, for one particular sponsor, or for a given program manager. *Project portfolio management* is the practice of taking an integrated and top-down approach to optimizing the project work and resources within the company. Companies practicing portfolio management typically profile proposed and ongoing programs in terms of cost, potential benefits, risks, and alignment with company strategic objectives. They regularly compare the profiles of the programs within the portfolio in order to more effectively decide which projects to maintain, expand, and discontinue. DW/BI departments will need to depict proposed projects in a common format so that such comparisons will be straightforward and accurate.

Program Management Office

A project management office (PMO) is a group or department within a company that defines and maintains standards for the management of projects, programs, and portfolios within the organization. For companies utilizing program management, such as described previously, this group is often called the "program management office." PMOs strive to standardize and introduce economies of repetition into the execution of projects and therefore frequently provide templates for project artifacts, guidance on practices, and definitions for metrics that measure project performance. The staff members of PMOs are typically schooled in only traditional, plan-driven project management techniques and therefore can be extremely resistant to agile approaches.

Project Charter

Traditional project management stipulates that projects should begin with a *project charter*—that is, a short document that states the key parameters defining a project, such as the sponsor, the project manager, an outline of the desired product, assumptions and constraints, the approximate funding, the time frame for delivery, and the means to measure success.

Project and Program Manager

Project and program managers are professionals charged with coordinating the resources, communications, and work steps involved in successfully completing the project charter. Agile methods offload much of the personnel management functions that many project managers normally perform during IT development projects. Even so, project managers will be required to secure resources such as facilities, equipment, and staffing. They also serve as the interface between the team and formal project governance structures within the company, shepherding requested changes in requirements or designs through a change control board. Large companies sometimes provision important projects with two project managers, one of whom represents the business and the project sponsors and the other of whom represents IT and the development team.

SUMMARY

The scope of agile enterprise data warehousing presents a challenge in terminology because the multiple IT disciplines involved, including requirements management, data modeling, quality assurance, and project management, do not share a single vocabulary. This chapter presents a set of terms standardized across these disciplines that will allow the following chapters to avoid switching lexicons each time the discussion touches upon a different software engineering discipline. This single vocabulary draws from definitions provided by professional organizations such as DAMA, TDWI, and IEEE. It covers topics such as basic business terms, data and information, information services, software engineering, data architecture, enterprise data warehousing, business intelligence, and project management. The reader should be particularly aware that the agile data warehousing method utilizes a few terms that do not represent standard definitions for the DW/BI profession, including *reference architecture*, *shadow IT*, and *topic areas*.

Chapter 5

Recap of Agile DW/BI Coding Practices

Although iterative coding is only one of several disciplines for robust software engineering, it is a foundational component of agile enterprise data warehousing (EDW) for two reasons. First, programming is the activity in which someone with his or her fingers on a keyboard actually creates new capabilities for the organization. The other disciplines, which focus on requirements, data modeling, and quality assurance, can be seen as supporting activities that simply "pave the road" so that the value-creating work of programming can roll ahead unimpeded. Second, the iterative nature of agile programming sets the tenor for the entire project. The philosophies and principles embodied within the supporting activities had better harmonize with the programming style or they will only undermine that value-creating work. Given that iterative programming is foundational, this chapter provides a summary of the agile coding techniques for data warehousing described in my previous works so that we can then craft versions of the remaining software engineering disciplines that effectively support agile's high-speed delivery approach.

ITERATIVE CODING ALONE SIGNIFICANTLY IMPROVES BI PROJECTS

Although generic agile methods leave many portions of the full software life cycle unaddressed, they can still dramatically change the economics of an EDW program or department all on their own. My colleagues and I first tried iterative delivery in 1998 while building a system for a large department of the U.S. government. We took over after a large systems integrator that had worked on the requested application for 10 years and billed more than $400 million without providing a single working version of the application. Although the term "agile" had not been coined yet, our iterative approach had all the key elements of Scrum: We co-located our developers and built the application in small increments, using eye-to-eye conversations with key users for business departments. We collected new versions of the software in an integration environment where stakeholders could continuously evaluate the evolving solution. Every couple of months or so, when the current build in the acceptance environment had acquired enough new features to justify the expense of promotion, we pushed a new version into production. Even without the benefit of the fast requirements templates, adaptable data models, and automated test engines that I describe later in this book, we were able to put the application online in 6 months, spending only $10 million including hardware. Admittedly, the particularly dysfunctional nature of the starting situation made it easy to achieve dramatic improvements in this case. Still, the iterative, results-oriented approach at the heart of Scrum cuts through the red tape and confusion of a large government program to deliver a 20-to-1 acceleration in delivery speed and 40-to-1 improvement in costs, clearly demonstrating the power of agile philosophies and principles.

Given the success of our first iterative project, my colleagues and I understandably advocated a similar approach for all our projects thereon. The agile manifesto, posted to the Internet a few years later, revealed to us a group of authors whose materials gave us a much clearer set of guidelines for further evolving our techniques. Ken Schwaber's 2004 book on Scrum gave our approach a name and some much needed structure for each coding iteration. Scrum's simplicity matched well that which had worked so well on our first iterative project, and Scrum's five-step iteration cycle offered the ceremonies, terminology, and objectives needed to make that success a repeatable process.

Yet Data Integration Remains a Challenge

Although Scrum greatly improves data warehousing/business intelligence (DW/BI) projects, new practitioners often note that front-end and back-end programmers have very different experiences with the method. Whereas BI developers on a team can usually find the means to push new features to the front-end applications every couple of weeks, the extract, transform, and load (ETL) programmers typically struggle to complete just a few pieces of their user stories,

TABLE 5.1 Areas Where Generic Scrum is Particularly Challenged by Data Integration Work

#	Challenge	Adaptation
1	Data integration stories are far too large for developers to complete in only one or two weeks	Decompose the users stories one step further into "developer stories" that each pertain to just one layer of the warehouse's reference architecture
2	The many skills the team needed were not shared widely enough for developers to swarm the issues as they appeared	1) Define some DW/BI specific roles for the team and clearly articulate the artifacts and support they will provide the remaining developers, 2) add columns to the task board for these roles, so that their work is highly visible
3	Customers demanded to know when we would deliver certain features and how much they would cost	Take a half-day during Iteration 3 or so to bracket the full backlog by the current velocity of the team, and then publish an update to this "current estimate" at the conclusion of all future iterations
4	No single business partner stayed with the project long enough to become a true product owner	Create a project architect role for one of the developers to drive requirements and design, so that the team has someone who understands the whole and stays with the project
5	Developers demanded more detailed guidance than iteration planning provided before they would start programming a module	Create a *system analyst* role for one of the developers to provide *source-to-target mappings*, but only require them to be 80% complete before coding begins
6	Even the analysis and design portion of each story could require more than one iteration	Set up a "pipeline" of work, so that the analysis and design specialties work one iteration ahead of the developers
7	Developers tended to start far too many tasks at once, making daily dependency analysis difficult	Add Kanban-style work-in-progress limits to the task board, so that the team maintains a steady flow of work through the entire development process

even with 4-week time boxes. Some of this contrast can be attributed to the different tools each type of programmer uses. Compared to the clunky ETL packages that our profession has for building the data integration modules, the BI tools seemed absolutely spry in delivering new features for end users. However, the problem runs deeper than tools, as a good look at the reference architecture introduced in the previous chapter can make clear.

The BI developers have only one or two architectural layers to worry about: semantics and dashboards. The data presented by the semantic layer is already clean, organized, and stored for the BI tools to draw upon. The ETL developers, on the other hand, must build modules within several of the most difficult layers of the entire data warehouse architecture. Their objectives are tantamount to trying to build four or five complicated applications at once. Table 5.1 lists several of the challenges that confronted the data integration specialists on project after project during the early days of agile data warehousing. The table also lists the adaptations that we eventually identified for Scrum to make it support data integration work smoothly. The reader will find summaries of many of these adaptations in the following sections. The fact that these adaptations are necessary makes an important conclusion very clear: Scrum as learned from certification classes and textbooks is simply "generic Scrum" and not yet ready for back-end data warehousing applications. When DW/BI teams add to Scrum the adaptations listed in this chapter, they begin to practice not generic iterative development but, instead, *agile data warehousing*.

NEW ROLES FOR DW/BI PROJECTS

Generic Scrum is very sparing on the roles it defines for a team. The textbook version of the method states that a team needs only a business partner to act as "product owner" in addition to another teammate to serve as "Scrum master" and facilitate the process. Everyone else is simply a "developer." When the programming begins, Scrum envisions that the team will self-organize into specific roles and define the handoffs of work that should occur between them.

Unfortunately, this self-organization process never proved easy during the early years when our DW/BI projects included much data integration work. Arriving at the correct structure for the team could sometimes take a half-dozen iterations and include a few disastrous user demos before the right organization for our developers became clear. Because the teams we coached always seemed to arrive at the same general collection of roles, my company decided to recommend that new teams start with this pattern and evolve from there if further adjustments are necessary.

The following set of roles has proven to be a good initial organization for a DW/BI team. Because these additional roles provide several dimensions of key decision making, they can be referred to collectively as the *team leads* in the project room. The role summaries presented here anticipate the involvement that these team leaders will have in the full software engineering process presented later. Detailed responsibilities for these roles can be found in my previous books. Readers considering agile for a small team should keep in mind that the following suggestions are roles and that each role does not have to be a separate individual. On small teams in particular, people must fill multiple roles. We do not experience any problems with overloading individuals in this way as long as everyone keeps in mind the role a particular person is filling at any given moment.

Project Architect

Data warehouses are incredibly expensive undertakings that can squander crucial business opportunities if they do not perform as needed when placed into production. Given this large risk, the business side of the company should demand that a single person in information technology (IT) be able to articulate, whenever needed, the reasons why the design and construction of the warehouse is correct. I call that person the *project architect* (PA), although I have worked with companies that call this role the "solution architect" or the "system engineer" instead. All three titles designate someone who possesses a whole-project view of the undertaking and who has the skills and authority to steer the design as necessary to better meet functional and performance needs.

Given this authority, the PA is in a position in which he or she must certify the DW/BI solution. When the warehouse is still just a design, the PA certifies to the sponsors that the envisioned application will solve the designated business problems. When the warehouse enters into production, the PA certifies that those business problems have been solved.

In order to be able to convincingly assert that the warehouse is a worthwhile solution, the PA will need the authority to perform three primary duties:

1. Drive requirements
2. Drive design
3. Drive quality assurance

Later, I suggest that the PA also drive recurring project estimates. The word "drive" is a deliberate choice. The PA does not need to actually perform the work implied by these bullets, but he or she needs to ensure throughout the project that someone is attending to them effectively.

Of these three duties, driving requirements is the area in which the PA typically invests the greatest measure of direct, "hands-on" time. This concentration derives from two important considerations. First, during the initiation phase (to use the Rational Unified Process terminology), someone must provide enough definition of the desired applications to get the rest of the development process funded, staffed, and moving forward. Thus, for the opening stretch, the PA will be working alone, with no other teammate to whom to delegate the work. Once the project outlines are established and a development team assembled, the PA will feel the need to continue leading the work on requirements in order to keep subsequent decisions aligned with the vision of the project that the sponsor chose to fund.

Second, the PA must certify the solution, both during construction and once delivered. Understanding in detail what the business requested is the core information that the PA will need in order to perform this certification. One can delegate authority but not responsibility. If sponsors and stakeholders decide that the application addresses the wrong business problem or is missing the features needed to allow it to succeed, only the PA will be held accountable. For that reason, PAs naturally choose to stay closer to the requirements management process than any other aspect of the project. In a later portion of this book, we examine in detail the means by which the PA can manage enterprise DW/BI requirements.

The second PA duty, *drive design*, also derives from the project architect's responsibility to certify the solution. To assure customers that the application will solve the business problem, the PA must understand what operational data the warehouse will acquire, how it will be transformed, and how it will then appear to the end users. These are the major elements of a DW/BI application's design. Given the deeper understanding of requirements that her early work on the project provides, the PA usually provides the team members with their first vision of the application's design, mapping the list of high-level features to the major requirements. From there on, the PA needs to understand the mid-level design decisions, constantly tracing them back to the application's guiding vision. When we discuss requirements management in greater detail, I suggest an agile set of design artifacts that will equip the PA to pursue this duty. The data engineering section of this book then describes the major elements that the PA should request that his team incorporate into the application's design.

Finally, the PA must *drive quality assurance* in order to certify that the application is a correct and dependable solution. Although she can ask others to run the necessary tests, she must understand enough about the team's validation efforts to assure the stakeholders that the application was tested sufficiently at all levels. The PA's role in driving this function emerges when the team realizes that it does not have the funds to test every conceivable aspect of the system. Given that she will be held accountable if the resulting application is not a dependable solution, the PA naturally must make the ultimate decision as to how to concentrate the testing that will occur. We consider later in this book what constitutes sufficient quality assurance for DW/BI projects.

Given the responsibilities listed previously, the PA is the linchpin of the development team. If a talented person has been engaged for this role and understands its duties, the rest of the team will have the leadership it needs and, given the power of the agile approach, will surely succeed to deliver a system of considerable value in a business-acceptable time frame.

Data Modeler

As discussed in the introductory chapters, DW/BI applications are complex data repositories with multiple architectural layers, each of which has a specific purpose. The team will require at least a logical and physical model for each data layer. The programmers will need a data dictionary documenting the tables, columns, and constraints within each schema, along with the database management system (DBMS) views or virtualization objects involved. Drafting these artifacts is the primary duty of the team's data modeler (DM).

The combination of layers and artifact types creates a long list of work for the DM. Harking back to the reference architecture discussed in Chapter 4, at least four data layers will require artifacts: landing, data quality, integration, and presentation. Three artifacts for four layers results in a work list with 12 major deliverables for the DM. The reference architecture for some large EDWs can have another four abstraction layers or so, making the DM's list of project deliverables even longer.

In addition to producing these artifacts, the DM will have coordination and review responsibilities. First, the DM will have to collaborate with the project's architect and analysts to ensure that the columns in the tables of each data schema are appropriate given the data available from the source systems. Second, the DW/BI project may fall within a larger ecosystem of corporate applications and thus be subject to technical requirements issued by the enterprise data architecture and data governance groups. In this event, the DM must adapt all of his project deliverables to this overarching set of requirements.

Third, the DM will need to validate the work of the other developers on the team. Following the agile principles of self-organization and deferring decisions to the last responsible moment, detailed decisions regarding data elements occur when the developers begin working with the product owner on a user story. The DM will have set some boundaries on those decisions in advance; however, he will have to participate in design sessions and later code walkthroughs in order to ensure that those boundaries were observed.

Finally, because the DM will understand the intent of each data schema better than any other teammate, he will need collaboration on validating the results of data loads once the ETL has been run. The collaborative effort will include checking the referential integrity of the loaded data, especially if the team has chosen to maintain integrity using ETL-coded business rules rather than DBMS-implemented constraints.

Systems Analyst

The systems analyst (SA) is another role that goes by many names. Calling this position a *business analyst, process architect*, or the team's *technical lead* does somewhat change the function of the role, but a core set of duties always remains. Whereas the DM supplies the design of the warehouse's data structures, the SA provides the design of the transformation processing that will populate those structures with information. This responsibility naturally imparts to the SA four subsequent duties that greatly assist developers when it comes time to code data transforms:

1. Maintain the application's upper-level data flow diagrams
2. Standardize the design patterns and technical requirements for the ETL modules
3. Author the source-to-target mappings that the ETL modules will implement (using the 80/20 specs described later)
4. Profile the source data

As with the PA role, the SA can delegate portions of the work to the other developers on the team but in the end must be able to certify the results and thus cannot escape overall responsibility for these duties.

The agile manifesto claims that the best designs arise out of self-organized teams. In practice, however, the project will move faster and achieve a more coherent result if the SA takes the lead on authoring level 0 and level 1 data flow diagrams. Similarly, for the sake of intelligibility and maintainability, all warehouse modules should follow a single set of design patterns, and DW/BI teams save time if the SA will take ownership of authoring and validating these patterns as well.

Although teams gather incredible speed and quality when ETL developers work eye-to-eye with the customer to derive source-to-target logic, this happy arrangement is unfortunately a very rare occurrence. The analysis required to plan the transforms is frequently just outside the skill set of the average ETL coder, and so most programmers are neither willing nor competent to perform this work. When the data transforms become complex and intertwined enough, most ETL developers will insist that team leaders provide at least draft specifications for them to follow while programming.

Because they are charged with drafting source-to-target maps, SAs often inherit the duty of profiling source data. One cannot draft source-to-target logics without understanding the source data, which must be explored and documented, either with a software utility or by hand. Identifying relationships and data quality problems within operational systems is also outside the interest and skills of typical ETL developers, so the SA addresses these objectives as well while profiling source data.

System Tester

Project planners can reasonably expect the developers on their warehouse teams to perform unit and component testing. However, proving that *all* the components assemble together as planned is a responsibility that is difficult for multiple people to fulfill reliably. For that reason, teams need to designate a system tester (ST), whose primary responsibilities are as follows:

1. To create a repeatable integration test that provides both full progression and full regression testing
2. To coach the developers on unit testing and later validate their results
3. To certify to the project architect and eventually the operations group that the application is worthy to be promoted into production
4. To certify to the project architect and the business stakeholders that the data in the warehouse is complete and correct

System integration testing must ensure that the application can run as a complete and coherent assembly of components. This objective requires validation of the new features (progression testing) and the previously developed features that should not have been adversely impacted by the new increments of code (regression testing). Because integration testing becomes extremely demanding as the warehouse grows, the ST must devise a way to accurately execute a plethora of test scenarios in a way that remains economical. This goal is usually achieved through automated integration testing, which is addressed in the quality assurance portion of this book.

The ST is also the best choice of role for coaching the developers on unit testing techniques. This work will position the ST to review the developers' results, allowing him to assure the PA that the team is achieving the desired level of test coverage and thoroughness. With detailed knowledge of testing activities at all levels—from unit validation through integration review—the ST is the best candidate to regularly compile and report data quality metrics to business stakeholders and the development team.

Proxy Product Owner

Lack of business involvement has from the earliest days of the IT profession been one of the most frequent complaints of both online transaction processing (OLTP) and online analytical processing development teams. EDW programs suffer from the additional challenge of having to build an application that is so large and complex that often no single business person is knowledgeable enough to guide the developers across all the subject areas they will have to address. Consequently, DW/BI projects must often contend with a new face in the product owner's chair as the focus of the project addresses each new business area. Often, these temporary product owners are not particularly enthused or qualified for the large role that they have taken on. This steady stream of less-than-perfect product owners can seriously compromise the quality of direction that the development team receives.

To stay true to Scrum's emphasis on business alignment, an agile DW/BI team must both keep the product owner as its guiding force and also backfill the position when the product owner proves to be inattentive, misguided, or underqualified for the role. To meet this challenge, many teams resort to a "proxy product owner" (PPO)—an IT person who understands the business well enough to both ensure that the current product owner is performing her role adequately and provide the missing information and decisions that the team needs to keep moving forward.

The most frequent choice for PPO is the team's project architect because, due to the fact that he is already driving requirements, he is the best informed about the needs and wants of the business. The degree to which the PA actually performs PPO duties will wax and wane over the course of a project as the competency of the product owner role fluctuates. If the project truly has the support and attention of the business, the PPO role will stay small, perhaps necessary only when business is swapping out product owners.

Whenever the PPO role is active, project risk is naturally increased because the project has become essentially driven by IT. When the team is fortunate to have a business partner who is proficient and mentally engaged, the PA should drop back into strictly project architecture work and stay ready to resume product owner activities when another lapse in input from the business becomes apparent.

Scrum Master

The duties of the new roles for Scrum listed are simply an average of what I have witnessed teams devise when working DW/BI projects that have heavy data integration requirements. The disadvantage of defining new roles is that it increases the number of interfaces between parties that a team must plan out. Thus, the Scrum master in the typical data analytics projects takes on an additional responsibility besides reminding the team of the upcoming steps in the iteration cycle. He or she must also monitor the performance of these new roles and the quality of communications between them.

Every team will arrive at a different pattern for these roles and their intercommunications, so the first step for a Scrum master may well be to simply articulate the current responsibilities for each role, displaying them on a poster on the project room wall if necessary. These responsibility outlines will need to be updated as the team's method evolves, and the Scrum master can certainly assist this process by calling attention to moments when the demands on a role seem to have changed, prompting the team to restate how it prefers to collaborate going forward.

Including the New Roles on the Team's Whale Chart

One handy way to make the roles explicit is for the Scrum master to build a diagram of effort-by-role over the life of a project. A sample of one I have used with my teams is shown in Figure 5.1. Such a diagram echoes a RUP whale chart, although the horizontal bands will represent roles rather than software engineering disciplines.

On the sample chart, one can see that the project architect gets started early, followed by the data modeler and system analyst. It also shows the proxy product owner's activity peaking as product owners trade off. Moreover, it shows the system tester activity occurring steadily throughout the project, with peaks just before demos when integration testing work runs high, and in the middle of iterations when full volume testing occurs (described later).

80/20 SPECIFICATIONS

Throughout the software engineering process, agile gains flexibility by waiting until the last responsible moment to decide on specifics. Such a practice is consistent with lean software development principles listed in Chapter 2. That practice unfortunately leaves new teams wondering exactly how detailed to make their requirements, analysis, and design specifications as they prepare for an upcoming iteration. Once we added the formal roles listed previously to generic Scrum, my colleagues and I could no longer delay providing our developers some guidance on this crucial point. After considerable experimentation, we decided the best advice is, "Start with 80/20 specs and adjust from there."

One can conceptually order the new roles listed previously in the logical sequence that they touch a user story as it works its way to a developer's workbench: product owner, project architect, data modeler, and system analyst. To prepare an 80/20 specification, each role would surmise the level of detail and amount of time that would have been invested for a given story while following a waterfall method. Under agile, then, they would plan to invest only 20% of that effort and focus on the most important 80% of the issues. The remaining 20% on any given specification will be details—details that the product owner and developers can work out if and when they start coding that particular story. Delaying detailed consideration of the last 20% works out well, in fact, because it is in this "tail block" of details that

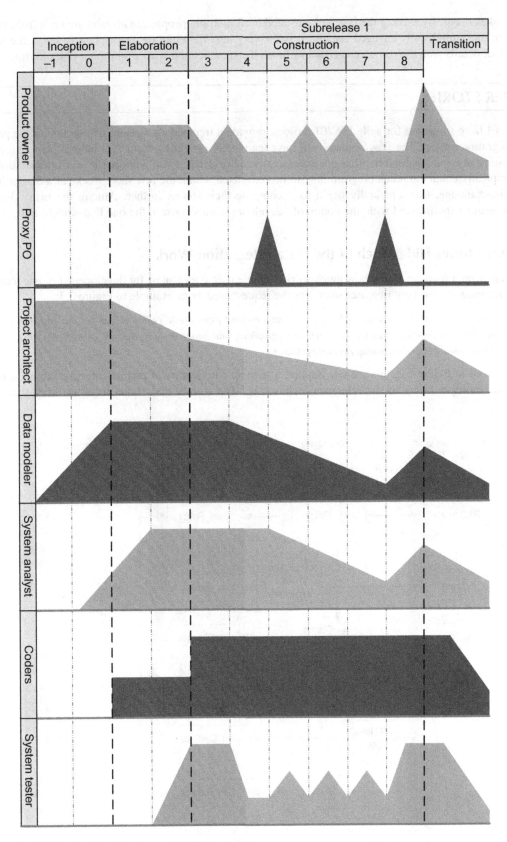

FIGURE 5.1   Typical RUP-style whale chart for an agile EDW project.

the most mistakes occur. By leaving the last 20% unstated until multiple people can collaborate on it from multiple perspectives, with their minds fully engaged because it is the very next item that the team plans to build, the team tackles this tail block of details with the resources needed to finish the specification with a minimum risk of error.

DEVELOPER STORIES

The new roles I have suggested for agile DW/BI projects provide a tremendous amount of support for the programmers on a data integration project. The programmers will have teammates providing them data models, source-to-target mappings, and testing plans at a substantial (but not excessive) level of detail. Even with that level of preparation, however, user stories typically entail too much programming to be completed within the few short weeks of a Scrum iteration. To overcome this challenge, teams naturally begin to decompose their stories further. Among the many decomposition strategies our teams experimented with, the notion of "developer stories" proved the one that worked best.

DW/BI User Stories Hide Much of the Data Integration Work

Product owners cannot imagine at first how much work a simple user story can be for developers. For one team I coached in the insurance industry, the very first user story was the request used as an example in Figure 2.7:

As a property policy rate analyst, I want to be able to compare total exposure to policy values for our top 10% of loss incidents, with drilldown by product category, customer demographics, and geography, so that we can identify clusters of customers for whom we should stop discounting property policies.

As summarized in Figure 5.2, this request implied a tremendous number of target tables for the team to build and populate in the multiple layers of the reference architecture. The team's DM stated that this story would require 6

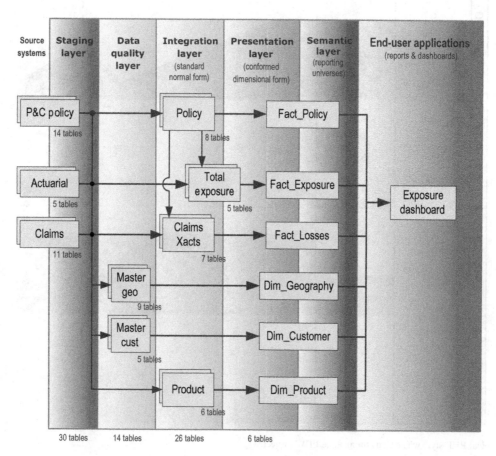

FIGURE 5.2 Agile EDW user stories result in too many developer stories for one, short Iteration.

tables in the presentation layer: three fact tables for policy, exposure, and losses, and three dimension tables for customer, products, and geographies. She then estimated that those presentation tables would have to be populated from approximately 26 tables in the integration layer and 14 tables in the data quality layer. The PA and SA examined the three separate transaction systems that would serve as a source for the integration layer and calculated that the team would have to build extracts for nearly 30 tables from the operational systems.

As depicted schematically in Figure 5.2, the decomposition of a single user story resulted in 30 landing routines and 46 data transform modules for the data integration portion of the project. The ETL coders would have to program and execute both the initial and the incremental load for these tables before the BI developer could put even the first element on a dashboard. The work was clearly far more than the team could code in a couple of months, let alone a few weeks. Such an explosion of work occurs in the first few stories of every significant data warehousing subject area. After a few months, the team will have delivered many of the landing dimensions tables so that the multiplier between user stories and the number of development modules still needing to be built diminishes somewhat.

The major lesson that new agile DW/BI teams should learn from Figure 5.2 is that the number of required tables in the depths of the reference architecture remains an unknown if they try to manage their project requirements at the user story level. It takes time for the team leaders, such as the PA, DM, and SA, to reflect and analyze the situation before estimating the number of landing, data quality, and integration tables a particular user story will require. This work cannot be accomplished with any accuracy on the fly during a story conference. If this work is not performed before each iteration begins, the multiplier between user stories and data transforms required will become a hidden landmine waiting to explode beneath the team when the team begins coding each product owner request. In my experience in rescuing dozens of new agile programs during the past couple of decades, this hidden multiplier is the primary reason that teams dabbling with agile data warehousing tend to fail miserably on their first incremental delivery project.

One solution is for the project architect to work with the product owner to further break down each user story. For our example, the product owner could translate the request into three user stories, which can be summarized as follows:

- Policies by customer, product, and geography
- Exposure by customer, product, and geography
- Losses by customer, product, and geography

However, even decomposing the original request down to just "exposure by customer for data from the actuarial system" will still require building and populating 17 tables, as can be deduced from Figure 5.2. This is still far too much work for the team to accomplish in the few short weeks allowed by a Scrum iteration.

Developer Stories Make DW/BI Work More Manageable

The solution to this challenging multiplier effect is the *developer story*. Developer stories result when a team intersects Scrum's notion of a user story with the layers of the data warehouse's reference architecture. The easiest way to identify these developer stories is to take a moment before each story conference to stretch a given user story across the data analytic application's reference architecture, as shown in Figure 5.3. At each point where the user story touches a layer of the reference architecture, the team can enumerate one or more target tables that developers will have to load before the ETL of the next layer will have the inputs it requires. With this step, a user story such as "replace the Sales Order Customer Number on our Customer Churn analyses with a company-standard customer identifier" gives rise to multiple developer stories, such as the following:

- Land customer extracts for three source systems.
- Load the landed customer data into the Party tables within the integration layer.
- Populate the Corporate Customer dimension table in the presentation layer from the Party tables.
- Add the Corporate Customer dimension to the BI tool's universe.
- Replace the Sales Order Customer Number field with Corporate Customer ID on the six Customer Churn pivot tables.

Teams decide on a case-by-case basis whether to write a developer story for each table that needs to be loaded in a given data layer, or whether they can clump a few tables together into one developer story. Clump too many tables together and the developer story becomes difficult for developers to complete in one iteration. On the other hand, writing a developer story for every little table needing ETL can make the backlog cluttered and unintelligible to the product owner. Either way, when agile DW/BI teams begin defining their backlogs with developer stories, they quickly discover how much work used to be hidden within user stories. Suddenly, everyone can see why their early attempts deliver a complete user story within a short Scrum time box were next to impossible.

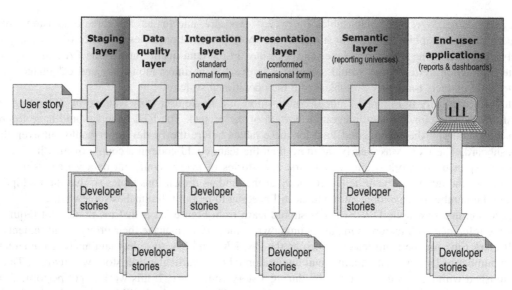

FIGURE 5.3 Deriving developer stories from user stories.

The term "developer story" is a deliberate hybrid of user story and developer task. The term is an appropriate combination given the developer story's role in bridging these two types of work items that generic Scrum defines. "Story" communicates to the team that these work items are meant to be clearly understandable to the product owner, just like user stories, so the team had better be able to articulate the business value toward which each one is driving. "Developer" acknowledges that the developers must take the lead in defining these work items because the product owner, a member of the business and not entirely fluent with the application's reference architecture, would never have been able to author them independently.

Developer Stories Require a Deeper Understanding of Value

Readers should be aware that developer stories are typically considered an anathema by most agile practitioners who do not work on data analytics projects. Generic agile purists will immediately point out that a given developer story does not deliver value to the customer. Technically, I suppose this criticism is correct. However, on an agile project, there is considerable wiggle room with regard to terms such as "value" and "customer," and a DW/BI team has to draw on these nuances to make agile work for data integration project. True, the product owner is a member of the larger community of end users, so developers will want to keep the backlog business intelligible and value driven, but the product owner is also a member of the team. By being on the team, the product owner soon learns that data must take a few intermediate forms before it can appear on a dashboard. With that fact established, value starts to come in many forms. Some forms of value can be appreciated by all business users of the application. Other forms, only the product owner can understand.

Consider, for example, the Fortune 50 aerospace company where my teams first started experimenting with developer stories. The company was halfway through a 5-year enterprise resource planning (ERP) customization effort when it realized that the ERP package would provide too little operational reporting to maintain normal company operations. The executives turned to the DW/BI department in a panic, asking if the department could replace the company's operational reporting system in the span of 2 years. DW/BI started working through the assignment incrementally, but the first iteration revealed a serious obstacle. The 1000-plus tables and their columns in this particular ERP package had all been named using German words that had been abbreviated to four characters. No one in this U.S. company could make sense of the source application's data model. The company's information seemed to be locked away so that building any reporting or analysis would be impossible.

Fortunately, the vendor of the ETL tool we were using had a bolt-on product designed for that exact ERP system with views that made the source data model intelligible to English speakers. We crafted our first few developer stories to simply land the purchase orders and vendors from the new source system. On demo day, we let our product owner test drive just three landed tables after we had joined them together using only natural keys. She stood up smiling, halfway through the test drive, and left to make a phone call to the vice president sponsoring the project. "We've been able to access the ERP data," she told him, "There's hope for this project after all." Did that quick look at nothing more than landed data have any value to the product owner and her sponsor? Certainly it did, even though finished fact and dimension tables were nowhere close to being displayed on a dashboard. Did it have any discernible value to the other stakeholders who would someday use the BI application we were planning to build? Not really, but at least it had value to a couple of key stakeholders. The same could be said of the next round of developer stories we delivered that nudged the operational data steadily closer to the dashboard.

The conclusion we drew from this early experience with developer stories has proven true in all the agile DW/BI projects that my company supported from then on: Once the product owner, sponsors, and even the near stakeholders realize how complex a DW/BI project truly is, they begin to see value each time data is advanced to another abstraction layer of the reference architecture—because these small steps steadily reduce the risk that the enormous project they have undertaken might fail.

Developer stories are a compromise between full value to the business community and an accomplishment only IT can appreciate. As such, they need to be managed carefully. As long as the product owner understands from his business perspective the incremental risk reduction that each item represents—and can brag to the sponsors about what his team has accomplished—developer stories will function in a project in the same way that user stories support generic Scrum. Developer stories allow the work of DW/BI user stories to be decomposed into iteration-sized chunks, and they trace directly back to a user story that the wider business community can appreciate, keeping IT aligned with the needs of the company.

CURRENT ESTIMATES

Developer stories allow DW/BI projects to be decomposed into small work bundles that are actionable by the programmers but still of recognizable value to the product owner. Accordingly, they become the "stories" that are assembled into backlogs, especially for the data integration aspects of an agile business intelligence project. The developer stories are estimated in story points and later decomposed into technical tasks for completion during a development iteration. The fact that developer stories can be estimated in story points also makes them the foundation for forecasting the level of effort that a particular DW/BI release or even an entire project will entail. Armed with a backlog of developer stories estimated in story points, a development team can provide stakeholders in both the business and IT with an extremely valuable approximation of the remaining work—a forecast called a "current estimate."

Many Scrum teams working on OLTP applications are strongly averse to estimating the size of a project. To make sense of this aversion, one should first understand that the stories on a project backlog are not all of equal quality. In general, the stories prioritized at the top are usually kept "crisp" by the development teams—that is, they are well articulated and intelligible to both business and IT. The team wants these stories to be atomic, estimatable, and testable because such qualities make them actionable, and being at the top of the backlog, the team will be programming them someday very soon. On the other hand, teams usually leave the stories farther down the backlog purposely vague, which makes sense following lean software development's aversion to amassing large inventories of unfinished work. If they were to keep all the stories on the backlog equally well-defined, they would pay a heavy price in wasted effort when business conditions change and the product owner decides to start dropping stories from the project backlog.

With this context, many agile teams also view estimating an entire project backlog as potentially wasteful. Moreover, they dread estimating the whole project out of fear that the customer may well treat the result as a commitment, a painful circumstance that they remember all too well from their prior waterfall projects. If they were to forecast labor for the vague stories at the middle and bottom of the backlog, they would probably underestimate them significantly due to the hidden details affecting each one.

For all these reasons, I have heard Scrum masters flatly refuse to provide a whole-project estimate, telling their product owner to settle instead for a generic agile approach: "Simply fund the team for an iteration, and if you like what we deliver, give us the money to run another iteration. We'll keep programming new features as long as you fund the team." Such an incremental planning approach may work well for transaction-capture systems in which most iterations result in changes immediately visible on an end user's interface. Unfortunately, data integration projects must populate tables buried deep in the DW/BI reference architecture so that it takes multiple iterations to deliver new results all the way from source data to the dashboard. Add the fact that everyone instinctively knows data warehousing projects are large and risky, and most DW/BI program sponsors will not accept a "take it as it comes" approach to funding their projects.

Accordingly, agile DW/BI teams must embrace whole-project estimating. Veteran Scrum masters perform release planning, in which the user stories that will go into the next release are estimated en masse in order to create a burndown chart in story points that indicates whether all the development will be done by a given calendar day. Agile data warehousing teams need to extend this technique to cover all the known developer stories on the project backlog. Not only does this allow a full project burndown chart, useful in and of itself, but also, more important, it positions the team to calculate the currently perceived, full-project cost and duration.

At approximately Iteration 3 or 4 of a new project, an agile EDW team takes a day away from programming to derive story point estimates for the remaining developer stories on the entire project backlog. The team then brackets that list using its current velocity to yield a "current estimate" of the project, as shown in Figure 5.4. In this example, the team has used its velocity of 16 story points delivered per iteration to identify that the remaining backlog will take nine more development iterations to complete. Using this technique, the team can state when particular features will be delivered, given the

- current velocity;
- current collection of stories; and

Story	Business value	Priority	Story points	Iteration	Iteration points	Subrelease
Operations analyst wants call rates so that....	1000	1	3	1		
Finance analyst wants margins so that....	948	2	8	1		
Sales analyst wants close rate so that....	895	3	1	1	15	
Marketing analyst wants lead conversions so that....	805	4	3	1		
Operations manager wants call rates so that....	779	5	5	2		1
Finance director wants close rate so that....	724	6	3	2	16	
Operations analyst wants margins so that....	687	8	8	2		
Operations analyst wants close rate so that....	699	7	13	3	16	
Marketing manager wants close rate so that....	672	9	3	3		
Sales manager wants close rate so that....	669	10	3	4		
Marketing director wants call rates so that....	659	11	8	4	16	
Operations manager wants lead conversions so that....	644	12	5	4		
Marketing manager wants margins so that....	634	13	8	5		
Marketing analyst wants close rate so that....	602	14	5	5	16	2
Sales manager wants lead conversions so that....	583	15	3	5		
Sales analyst wants margins so that....	525	16	5	6		
Marketing manager wants call rates so that....	513	18	3	6	16	
Sale director wants call rates so that....	512	19	8	6		
Marketing director wants lead conversions so that....	515	17	13	7	15	
Marketing director wants margins so that....	511	20	2	7		
Operations director wants close rate so that....	497	21	5	8		
Finance director wants margins so that....	496	22	2	8	15	3
Sales manager wants call rates so that....	492	23	5	8		
Finance analyst wants lead conversions so that....	469	24	3	8		
Operations analyst wants lead conversions so that....	461	25	8	9		
Operations manager wants margins so that....	433	26	5	9	16	
Marketing analyst wants margins so that....	412	27	3	9		

FIGURE 5.4 A "current estimate" for an agile data warehousing project.

- current story point estimates on the stories farther down the backlog (which may change when the stories are later groomed).

By counting up the total number of iterations projected and multiplying first by the length of an iteration and second by the personnel and other costs of running an iteration, the team can forecast the total duration and development expense of the project—assuming that the velocity and backlog remain the same.

Because velocities and backlogs change, agile DW/BI teams inform all stakeholders that the current estimate will be revisited at the end of each development iteration, when a new value for the team velocity will be measured. With every iteration, teams consider the current collection of developer stories, rebracket the list by the velocity just observed, and recalculate the implied duration and project cost. Unlike waterfall teams, agile DW/BI developers regularly update their project estimates, empowering their business partners to make evidence-based decisions regarding project scope and resources should the latest forecast reveal that the project will require more or less money and time to complete than previously expected.

This pattern of continually updating the whole-project estimate causes many people to state, "Agile DW/BI will never work, at least not at my company. We have to know *exactly* what a project is going to cost before we can get started." This conclusion is unfortunate because they are saying that they are willing to forego the tripling of delivery speed that agile programming offers because their stakeholders insist on one and only one estimate for a project, derived at the start of a project, when the team's ignorance of requirements, design, and source data is greatest. When they refuse the continually refreshed projections of total duration and cost that agile offers, these companies decide to manage their projects with a single target date and set themselves up for a nasty surprise when the assumptions embedded in that original estimate diverge from reality. Such a preference is like choosing a car that only has an idiot light for a fuel gauge. Instead of warning the driver that the vehicle is running low on gas, the single-estimate approach condemns everyone in the car to a long walk home when suddenly the tank is empty.

Given the importance of whole-project estimates in managing agile DW/BI programs, development teams are wise to treat seriously the matter of refreshing their current estimates. Arriving at an accurate forecast involves managing well the components that go into that calculation—the developer stories, story point estimates, and current team velocity. With the current estimate essential for matching actual results to sponsor expectations, the responsibility of managing the components and their assembly into a forecast at the end of every iteration often falls to the project architect, who is already the key leadership role on the team.

The one nuance to agile DW/BI's approach of continually refreshing current estimates is that in order to forecast total cost and duration, *new* teams must complete a couple of iterations before they will have a dependable measure of their velocity. After establishing a velocity and getting some feedback on the accuracy of the developers' story points, the project architect should be able to provide a reliable count of iterations-to-go. In contrast, established teams do not need to wait a few iterations before providing a current estimate. Assuming that their next project employs the same reference architecture and draws from a similar selection of operational systems, an experienced team can build a first current estimate by identifying and assigning story points to the new developers' stories the same way it did for the project it just completed. The team can then apply the story-point velocity measured from the last iteration on the previous project.

Guiding management to update its mindset to work with a constantly evolving estimate may take some convincing. I have found this transition challenging but not daunting. Even traditional project managers realize by the fourth or fifth iteration that an agile team's current estimate is far more accurate than the forecasts that traditional methods provide at the beginning of a project. Once convinced that the agile approach makes the project's trajectory much easier to track, project managers frequently become strong advocates for redefining project governance to allow iterative current estimates.

ADDING TECHNIQUES FROM KANBAN

My colleagues and I found that agile data warehousing teams became much easier to manage once we adapted Scrum by adding new roles, developer stories, 80/20 specifications, and current estimates. These techniques ensure that a team has the skills it needs, that right-sized requests make up the backlog, that developers have enough direction to begin coding, and that high-level stakeholders receive usable appraisal of whole-project cost and duration. Still, the work within the project room did not proceed smoothly until we also introduced "pipelined" engineering steps, which required adding a couple of techniques from Kanban. The result was a hybrid method along the lines of Scrumban, as described in Chapter 3, with a distinct data warehousing flavor.

Pipelined Delivery

Developer stories helped rightsize the work for the project backlog, but when teams further decomposed them into technical tasks to put on the task board, the sequence of work was still very difficult to complete within a single iteration. Even a developer story as simple as "load the landed customer data into the Party tables within the integration layer" generates a long list of tasks, such as the following:

- Profile the landed source data.
- Draft the source-to-target map.
- Perform the detailed design.
- Design the data tables and get them built in the database.
- Prepare the test data.
- Code the initial and incremental load logic.
- Perform unit and component testing.
- Add the module to the integration test suite.
- Draft updates for the install guide, operations manual, and user guide.
- Resolve integration testing issues.
- Script the high points for the user demo.

Such a list immediately confronts the agile DW/BI team with two challenges:

1. This list is simply too much work to finish in a few short weeks.
2. These tasks require very different skills that must be applied sequentially.

New Scrum teams will typically just place all this work on the task board and leave it for the group to self-organize a solution to these challenges. What they typically experience is that the systems analyst needs a few days to perform the analysis and produce the mapping specifications. The data modeler then needs a few days to structure and vet the tables to be loaded. Combined, these tasks that must precede the ETL programming will consume 4–8 days, which represents a major portion of a development iteration. The team must also subtract out a few days at the end of the iteration for integration testing and loading the demonstration data. Even with a 4-week sprint, which many practitioners consider too long, the programmers will have only approximately 9 days to complete all the coding required once they have made time for the necessary preparation and wrap-up activities.

The disadvantage of sprints that last 4 weeks or longer is that the team goes too long without review from the product owner, which (1) allows major mistakes to occur and (2) leaves the product owner with too little involvement to remain an integral part of the team. Even if a longer iteration were feasible, note that while the systems analyst and data modeler are busy preparing the specifications for the iteration's backlog of stories, all other members of the team have no work to do. Trying to organize a Scrum sprint with 3 days of analysis, 3 days of modeling, 9 days of coding, and then 3 days of testing is like trying to complete a waterfall inside a Scrum iteration, and it has been labeled "water-Scrum-fall" or "WaterScrum" by the agile community [Malik 2007]. As noted, WaterScrum makes it very difficult to utilize a team's resources to the fullest. Moreover, it leads to very bad interpersonal dynamics between the roles on the team. The programmers will spend the first week of the iteration harping on their analysis and design teammates, urging them to finish. Later, the system tester will be exasperated when coding runs long, leaving her only 30 minutes before the user demo to validate an entire build.

Faced with these frustrations, every DW/BI team I have ever worked with eventually decided to make the same adaptation to Scrum, one that works very well. During the retrospective for Iteration 3 or 4, the ETL developers would turn to their analysis and design teammates and ask "Can't you just work one iteration ahead of us?" Because a team's project backlog makes it fairly easy to predict which stories the programmers will work on during the next few sprints, the architect, data modeler, and analyst usually agreed with this request. Going forward, they decide to invest the extra effort needed to finish the specifications for a few stories by the time each story conference arrived so that these work items would be ready for immediate programming.

A similar realization invariably occurred to system tester role, too. "I'm so tired of getting only a half hour to perform integration testing on each build," the system tester would tell the developers. "Why don't you guys just take the whole iteration for programming—that's essentially what you're doing now. I'll run the exhaustive validation on each build one iteration behind you." By pushing analysis and design to one iteration before coding, and system testing to one iteration afterward, agile DW/BI teams self-organize their work into a three-stage pipeline, as shown in Figure 5.5.

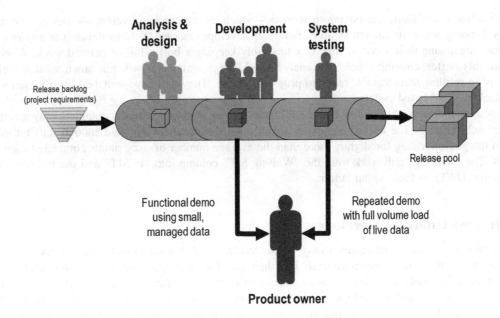

FIGURE 5.5   Agile data warehousing requires pipelined work specialties.

On first look, some people claim that this approach is essentially a return to waterfall, but that criticism misses several important points. The intent of a pipelined development approach is still to code fast and continuously deliver value to the customer. The roles that work both ends of the pipeline, such as architects, analysis, designers, and testers, still remain in the project room, ready to answer programmers' questions and collaborate with them eye-to-eye in real time. Only when the developers have what they need to move forward do the team's technical leaders then turn back to their preparation or validation work, focusing on it until the developers need further support.

Pipelining restores healthy team dynamics and leads to much better resource utilization, but it can have an inverse impact on the Scrum task board that needs to be resolved. When developers first begin to pipeline their work, they tend to create task cards for the analysis, design, and testing work, placing them on the task board and reviewing them with the entire team during the daily stand-up meetings, as if they were just another iteration task. Unfortunately, this practice makes the task board extremely difficult to understand because suddenly cards for three iterations of work have appeared, including

- tasks for stories undergoing analysis and design for the next iteration;
- tasks for stories being coded during the current iteration; and
- tasks for stories from the prior iteration now undergoing integration testing.

On large projects, the resulting clutter made the task board unintelligible to programmers to the point that they could not easily find their own work, seriously undermining the smooth functioning of the self-organized teams. Teams can solve this challenge with a technique from Kanban. As mentioned in Chapter 2, the columns of a Kanban work board represent software engineering steps rather than the status of a task card. Many teams extend their Scrum task boards with Kanban-style columns, as shown in Figure 3.7, in which columns for analysis and design work were added to the front and columns for advanced testing activities were placed at the end. This adaptation moves nonprogramming work to the edges of the board, leaving the coding task as an uncluttered collection in the middle. Note that the cards change granularity as they move from left to right. They first appear in the requirements columns as user stories, decompose into developer stories when they enter the high-level design columns, and then break down further into task cards as they enter the Scrum task board embedded in the middle of this artifact. When the programming is complete, the team may very well assemble all the tasks back into developer stories for integration testing and naturally also transfer the developer stories back into user stories for end-user acceptance testing.

Interestingly, introducing the Scrumban task board will further change the manner in which many of the nonprogramming teammates organize their work. At first, the analysis and design roles, for example, will strive to time box their specification efforts, just as they worked when the team had only a Scrum task board. Soon, however, they will perceive that the developers needed only a certain number of story points of work prepared for them each iteration.

They will realize that rather than time boxing their work—which has ceremonial overhead—they can be just as effective by simply keeping a certain amount of story points of developer stories ready to develop at any one time. They will switch from organizing their work by time box to simply keeping a buffer full of defined work. When the coders pull work from this buffer, creating a hole, the analysis and design teammates will put down whatever else they are doing and focus on refilling their team's "ready to program" buffer. They will have switched from Scrum's time-boxed approach to Kanban's pull-based system.

Similarly, system testers quickly realize that the ETL developers working upstream complete only a certain number of story points each iteration. The testers' objectives will also evolve to where they add enough staff for quality assurance to sustain integration testing for slightly more than the average number of story points completed each iteration by the developers. They will then pull work from the "Waiting SIT" column into "In SIT" and use the next column, user acceptance testing (UAT), as their output buffer.

Work-in-Progress Limits for Developers

Switching to a two-tiered task board makes it easy to incorporate another Kanban technique—work-in-progress (WIP) limits—for those teams that need it. Approximately half the teams I have coached throughout the years have had trouble staying focused on a few tasks at a time. When an iteration commenced for these teams, far too many tasks would appear in the programmers' "under development" column at once. Having that many open tasks indicated that the programmers were multitasking considerably and therefore losing velocity in switching between tasks. To slightly tamp down on this frenetic activity, we placed WIP limits on the columns, as seen in Figure 3.7. By limiting the number of stories that could enter programming and even the number of tasks that developers could start coding, team members would force themselves to finish work very soon after it was started, greatly reducing multitasking.

The WIP limits also forced some cross-training, an important long-term goal of DW/BI management. For example, when the *Under Dev* column fell empty of stories because cards were stuck in *Profile* and *Model*, an ETL developer and the system tester would volunteer to perform some of the data profiling work and help the systems analyst refill the *Programming* section of the board. By getting teammates to move between roles in order to resolve bottlenecks, the developers learned new tools and the DW/BI department began to see benefits from having developers with a widening set of skills.

Iteration −1 and 0

Pipelining the development will change the way a team prepares a project for development. From its earliest days, Scrum has advocated an "Iteration 0," which gives a team time to prepare for the development sprints that will begin with Iteration 1. Pipelined development makes it clear that a further prep step before Iteration 0 will be necessary.

By laying out the package of stores that will be developed with each iterations as shown in Figure 5.6, it can be seen that developers will program the stories in Package A during Iteration 1, then the stories in Package B during Iteration 2, and so on. With pipelining, analysis and design roles need to work on a given package one iteration before the developers start coding it. Accordingly, the figure shows that Package A must receive analysis and design work during Iteration 0 so that it will be ready for coding during Iteration 1.

The analysis and design teammates will in turn need some details regarding the business requirements and the application vision before they can draft 80/20 specs for a given package. They must get these details from the project architect. Consequently, the project architect will need to derive the vision for Package A during an Iteration −1 so that the analysis and design teammates can add their details during Iteration 0 in preparation for programming the package in Iteration 1. Combining these on the grid in Figure 5.6, it can be seen that every package of work takes a predictable, diagonal path as it moves between stations in the pipeline and across time. System testing logically occurs after coding. As can be seen in the diagram, Package A receives system testing during Iteration 2.

The plus sign marked on Package A for Iteration −1 and 0 is an important detail in Figure 5.6. Because Package A is the first set of stories that will be coded, the programming solutions utilized by these developers will set in motion the patterns to be used for the entire project. If the developers programmed the stories of Package A thinking only of the functionality needed for the first demo, they could easily establish some regrettable coding patterns and make some poor architectural decisions that would be very difficult to correct in the future. For that reason, the project architect and the analysis and design teammates should invest more in their lead-off packages in order to provide the programmers with a "whole-project context." With this extra bit of design work in their first work package, the developers will

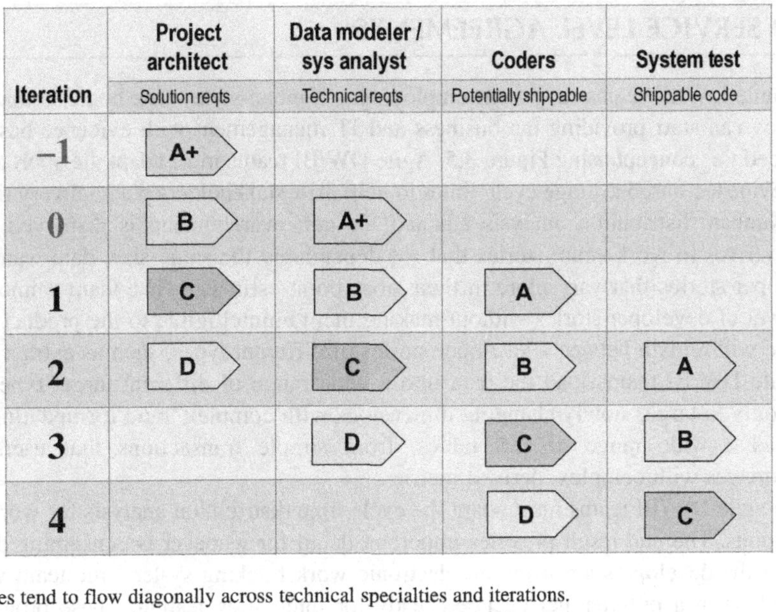

Iteration	Project architect Solution reqts	Data modeler / sys analyst Technical reqts	Coders Potentially shippable	System test Shippable code
−1	A+			
0	B	A+		
1	C	B	A	
2	D	C	B	A
3		D	C	B
4			D	C

FIGURE 5.6 Work packages tend to flow diagonally across technical specialties and iterations.

be able to keep the application modules consistent and coherent across time. Thus, Package A for both of them will have slightly more detail, so it is labeled "A + " in the diagram rather than just "A."

In acknowledging that Package A + will need to provide whole-project context, I do not mean to suggest the team should resort to the big-design-upfront work pattern that bedevils waterfall and many RUP projects. Agile DW/BI teams must keep in mind that their analysis and design teammates will provide 80/20 specifications—module descriptions that cover the most important 80% of a need component but that require only 20% as much time to author as a full waterfall spec. The project architect should aim for the same level of completeness, too, in preparing to communicate the most important aspects with his or her vision artifacts, leaving the fine details for later. For each step in the pipeline, the remaining details will emerge when the next party downstream begins working a package. The upstream party providing the specification is simply another teammate who will be close at hand to answer any questions.

Two-Pass Testing

Pipelining an agile DW/BI team's development work will also change the pattern it follows for validating its deliverables. That validation will require two reviews, which help the developers reach a higher level of thoroughness in testing than the single-pass approach envisioned before they started pipelining their activities.

As shown in Figure 5.5, the first review occurs at the end of the development step during the iteration demo. At this point, the developers allow the product owner to test drive the new features, as is normal for Scrum, but here they have to employ a rather small set of data for the iteration demo—one they can load in approximately 1 hour. Using a data set that takes longer than an hour to load simply consumes too much time during the iteration's development step, given that the programmers must frequently load, review, catch bugs, and recode their modules. A small data set may save time for coding and demonstrations, but unfortunately DW/BI professionals have learned from experience that just one or two records out of a million can break an important business rule. To be safe, each build should be validated with data that closely resembles the full load that a warehouse will receive from its source systems.

Loading near-production data requires considerable time, sometimes several days, due to the number of records. With a pipelined work approach, the system tester begins loading the near-production data set soon after the programmers have completed the iteration demo using the small, functional data set. Once the near-production data load is complete, the system tester schedules time with the product owner and repeats the previous iteration demo. Because the full-volume load may include troublesome data that the small, functional data set did not, the system tester and product owner search for features and business rules that no longer work during this second demo. Thus, with pipelined work pattern, the product owner receives two distinct demonstrations of each build, and the quality of DW/BI application improves commensurately.

EVIDENCE-BASED SERVICE LEVEL AGREEMENTS

One important benefit agile DW/BI teams reap from employing a Kanban-style work board is that after approximately a half-dozen iterations, they can start providing the business and IT management with evidence-based service level agreements (SLAs). I introduced this concept using Figure 3.5. Agile DW/BI teams must adapt the approach slightly but can still arrive at very accurate, evidence-based average cycle times to help their stakeholders plan delivery times for their projects.

An example of a Kanban distribution analysis adapted for data warehousing is displayed in Figure 5.7. Unlike generic Kanban, which strives to work small stories that are dependably the same size, data warehousing projects have a tougher mix of developer stories that vary more in their story-point estimates. The team cannot decompose the work packages beyond the level of developer stories without making them unintelligible to the product owner. Unfortunately, major differences in size will remain between developer stories of different types, such as extract scripts and integration modules. Moreover, agile DW/BI teams load the data into a wide range of different target types—from small dimensions with current data only to large, slowly changing dimensions with complex logic for updating their history records. DW/BI teams also load a wide range of fact tables, from simple transactions that users will only count to status-tracking process images with complex, derived metrics.

For these reason, the agile DW/BI teams must adapt the cycle time distribution analysis for work units that range from ½ to 13 or more story points. The end result provides important detail for whoever is consuming the team's performance metrics. Especially when the developers are using an electronic work tracking system, the team will know when a task entered development and when a programmer declared ready for integration testing. These programming times can be aggregated to provide a factual notion of what similar work requests will require in the future. For example, the information displayed in Figure 5.7 shows that 2-point stories over the past iterations of the project have taken from 10 to 40 hours from the moment they went into analysis and design to the moment they were ready for integration testing. For 2-point stories in the future, these developers can offer their stakeholders a cycle time of 25 hours or less with 27% confidence, and they can be 98% certain that they complete it in less than 35 hours. For developer stories estimated at 3 story points, the team has to make a different promise: 30 hours or less 43% of the time and less than 35 hours 90% of the time. By simply tracking its actual performance on backlog stories, the agile DW/BI team can provide its customers evidence-based SLAs instead of basing estimates on expert judgment alone and struggling to honor them.

This evidenced-based service level analysis works well with the current estimate that agile DW/BI teams were already providing its customers. Figure 5.8 shows a current estimate with the cycle time information added. The stories have been story pointed by the team using the estimating poker technique discussed in Chapter 2. In this analysis, the Scrum master has listed the cycle times for each story point estimate value used by the team. This cycle time is expressed as a mean (Column A) and a standard deviation (Column B).

The standard deviation was derived from the cycle time analysis using the assumption that a 95% confidence level represents the mean plus two standard deviations, as can be found in any college text on statistics. The forecast for all the stories for a given band of story point estimates is calculated by multiplying the mean by the number of stories at that estimate level remaining in the project backlog. The standard deviation for each band is calculated by using the square root of the sum of the squares, again as indicated by the rules of statistics. The forecast for the entire remaining project is then compiled by taking the sum of the means across the bands and the square root of the sum of squares for the standard deviations. In this manner, the cycle time analysis yields a current estimate for this example indicating that the team will require 1,436 hours to complete the remaining project backlog.

Unlike estimates under waterfall methods, the Kanban-enabled SLA provides *evidence-based* estimates. A team needs only provide stakeholders three items:

- Its remaining project backlog
- The story point estimates for the developer stories on that backlog
- The mean and standard deviations for actual hours on stories at each level of estimated story points

With this information, the stakeholders can calculate remaining project duration for themselves. They no longer need to ask the team for a completion date or wait for it to compile an estimate. The cycle time analysis indicates to stakeholders early in the project whether the team can be reasonably expected to deliver the project on time, and that insight allows them to promptly discuss change in scope and features if necessary. They can spot trouble and plan an informed solution without having to rely on developer promises to deliver by a certain date—promises that in practice can rarely be honored.

Team leads should exercise care in providing stakeholders information from cycle time analysis too soon during a transition to agile methods. One of the greatest advantages of story points is their ambiguity—business and IT management do

Frequency Counts

Actual Hours	0.5	1	2	3	5	8	13	20
(Story Points Estimated)								
Count	32	43	84	72	61	45	33	24
Mean	8.28	14.19	21.69	30.93	56.79	92.09	172.39	236.46
Std Dev	3.22	4.97	6.04	3.29	2.83	9.04	13.12	33.85
0	-	-	-	-	-	-	-	-
5	6	-	-	-	-	-	-	-
10	20	11	3	-	-	-	-	-
15	5	17	10	-	-	-	-	-
20	1	8	20	-	-	-	-	-
25	-	7	28	4	-	-	-	-
30	-	-	17	27	-	-	-	-
35	-	-	5	34	-	-	-	-
40	-	-	1	7	-	-	-	-
45	-	-	-	-	-	-	-	-
80						6	-	-
90						10	-	-
100						22	-	-
110						7	-	-
150							2	-
175							20	1
200							9	3
225							2	5
250							-	6
275							-	7
300							-	2

Cumulative Percentage by Actual Hours for Each Estimate Level

	0.5	1	2	3	5	8	13	21
	Story Points Estimated							
67% SLA:	10 hrs	20 hrs	25 hrs	35 hrs	60 hrs	100 hrs	200 hrs	275 hrs
95% SLA:	15 hrs	25 hrs	34 hrs	40 hrs	70 hrs	110 hrs	225 hrs	300 hrs
Actual Hours								
0	-	-	-	-	-	-	-	-
5	18.8%	-	-	-	-	-	-	-
10	81.3%	25.6%	3.6%	-	-	-	-	-
15	96.9%	65.1%	15.5%	-	-	-	-	-
20	100.0%	83.7%	39.3%	-	-	-	-	-
25	100.0%	100.0%	72.6%	5.6%	-	-	-	-
30	100.0%	100.0%	92.9%	43.1%	-	-	-	-
35	100.0%	100.0%	98.8%	90.3%	-	-	-	-
40	100.0%	100.0%	100.0%	100.0%	-	-	-	-
45	100.0%	100.0%	100.0%	100.0%	-	-	-	-
50	100.0%	100.0%	100.0%	100.0%	1.6%	-	-	-
60	100.0%	100.0%	100.0%	100.0%	91.8%	-	-	-
70	100.0%	100.0%	100.0%	100.0%	100.0%	-	-	-
80	100.0%	100.0%	100.0%	100.0%	100.0%	13.3%	-	-
90	100.0%	100.0%	100.0%	100.0%	100.0%	35.6%	-	-
100	100.0%	100.0%	100.0%	100.0%	100.0%	84.4%	-	-
110	100.0%	100.0%	100.0%	100.0%	100.0%	100.0%	-	
120	100.0%	100.0%	100.0%	100.0%	100.0%	100.0%	-	
130	100.0%	100.0%	100.0%	100.0%	100.0%	100.0%	-	
140	100.0%	100.0%	100.0%	100.0%	100.0%	100.0%	-	
150	100.0%	100.0%	100.0%	100.0%	100.0%	100.0%	6.1%	-
175	100.0%	100.0%	100.0%	100.0%	100.0%	100.0%	66.7%	4.2%
200	100.0%	100.0%	100.0%	100.0%	100.0%	100.0%	93.9%	16.7%
225	100.0%	100.0%	100.0%	100.0%	100.0%	100.0%	100.0%	37.5%
250	100.0%	100.0%	100.0%	100.0%	100.0%	100.0%	100.0%	62.5%
275	100.0%	100.0%	100.0%	100.0%	100.0%	100.0%	100.0%	91.7%
300	100.0%	100.0%	100.0%	100.0%	100.0%	100.0%	100.0%	100.0%
325	100.0%	100.0%	100.0%	100.0%	100.0%	100.0%	100.0%	100.0%
350	100.0%	100.0%	100.0%	100.0%	100.0%	100.0%	100.0%	100.0%
375	100.0%	100.0%	100.0%	100.0%	100.0%	100.0%	100.0%	100.0%
Total	32	43	84	72	61	45	33	24

FIGURE 5.7   Cycle time distribution analysis for an agile data warehousing project.

not understand what they represent, and that ignorance forces business and IT to accept a team's forecast regarding the number of iterations needed to complete the project. If a team provides its cycle time analysis before its managers have fully embraced agile DW/BI's notion of continually updated current estimates, these managers can unfortunately begin translating story points into hours. The easy math they will use will create the illusion that an agile development process can be

Story points (SP)	Actual hours on past projects		Planned modules by SP	Total forecasted by estimated SP	
	Mean [A]	Std [B]	[C]	Mean [D]	Std [E]
0.5	1.59	0.87	7	11.16	2.31
1	3.23	0.87	15	48.49	3.36
2	4.76	1.29	22	104.76	6.03
3	6.46	0.89	29	187.29	4.78
5	11.18	1.02	23	257.15	4.91
8	19.44	1.95	13	252.78	7.03
13	33.82	3.88	5	169.09	8.69
20	45.71	5.47	6	274.25	13.39
		Overall forecast		1,305	66
		95% Confidence		1,436 hrs	

FIGURE 5.8   A current estimate adjusted for observed delivery cycle times.

directed rather than observed. Managers who believe they know how many hours a story point should take to complete often begin criticizing the actual labor hours that a team reports its work to be consuming. Managers may start dictating that a whole collection of stories should take far fewer days than the team knows is the case.

To avoid this destructive interference, agile DW/BI Scrum masters should keep the cycle time analysis to themselves until management truly understands and accepts that a current estimate for the project will be updated with every iteration. Once that change in thinking has been achieved, the cycle time measurements can be shared with management as a validation of the current estimate that the team provides. The Scrum master will still need to provide a healthy number of provisos, such as "Only the latest current estimate is the truth, and its accuracy fades with time," followed by "The cycle time analysis is only a window that lets you see a little deeper into that truth." Fortunately, it takes many iterations to acquire enough data points at each story point level before a Scrum master can calculate a complete cycle time analysis, providing the delay needed to establish the correct perspective among a team's business partners.

PROOF THAT AGILE DW/BI WORKS

Even a quick glance at the previously discussed material suggests that switching to agile data warehousing is a serious undertaking with many details involved. DW/BI professionals will naturally want evidence that the iterative approach has been successful before they decide to abandon the waterfall approach altogether. My company has been able to collaborate with The Data Warehousing Institute on surveying the DW/BI profession to not only find those companies that are practicing incremental delivery of BI applications but also measure their success rates and even their performance on four key performance indicators (KPIs) [Hughes & Stodder 2013].

The 2013 survey provided the best response yet, with more than 400 companies providing usable answers to more than 20 questions. Figure 5.9 illustrates the overall success rates that these agile DW/BI practitioners have achieved, broken out by the number of agile projects completed. This result is extremely encouraging. Nearly 80% of agile DW/BI practitioners reported improved success rates for their development teams. The surveys of waterfall methods referenced in Chapter 1 revealed that traditionally managed projects succeed only 50% of the time at best. The Ceregenics/TDWI survey of agile data warehousing suggests that DW/BI professionals who wish to advocate an incremental delivery approach can assure stakeholders that the agile method quickly improves team performance and achieves better results than traditional project management techniques 8 times out of 10.

More pointedly, Figure 5.10 depicts the impact of agile methods on important DW/BI aspects such as programmer productivity, customer satisfaction, application quality, and project cost. These statistics reveal that companies that switch from waterfall to agile methods will see programmer effectiveness increase 8 times out of 10. Moreover, customers prefer working with agile teams three-fourths of the time.

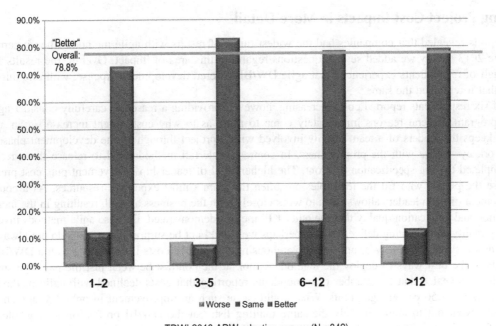

FIGURE 5.9   Success rates for agile data warehousing teams, by number of agile projects completed, compared to traditional methods.

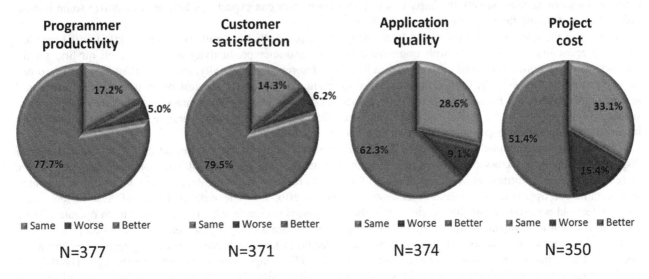

FIGURE 5.10   Agile's impact upon key performance indicators for data warehousing development projects.

Interpreting the key performance indicator (KPI) for application quality involves a bit of subtlety. Sixty percent of teams surveyed saw improved application quality, which seems low until one realizes that 30% reported that quality remained the same. Even traditional data warehousing teams experience strong pressures to focus on data quality, so it is no surprise to discover that a significant number of companies are already achieving sufficient quality with their DW/BI approach. In this light, a reasonable interpretation of the quality KPI figures might be that for companies for which the quality of DW/BI deliverables could be influenced by a new method, agile enhanced quality six times more frequently than detracting from it.

Investigating Project Cost Impacts in More Detail

Our previous polls revealed that companies had the widest range of results with agile methods when it came to project costs, so in the 2013 survey we added several questions regarding this area of impact. Overall, the results for that year showed that half of respondents experienced that agile DW/BI lowered development expense, with one-third of respondents stating that it remained the same.

One out of six respondents reported costs increasing, however, providing a reason to carefully consider agile's impact on an EDW program. Several reasons immediately come to mind as to why costs might increase on an agile project. Agile DW/BI keeps the leaders of a team heavily involved with a project throughout the development phase so that the leaders can work eye-to-eye with the programmers. In contrast, waterfall methods tend to release those resources once they have completed the big specification up front. The higher level of leadership involvement puts cost pressure on the project because the people who fill the lead roles are often the team's most expensive resources. As a counterbalance, greater involvement of team leaders allows them to work closely with the business as well, resulting in the increase in customer satisfaction and application quality that the other KPI metrics demonstrated. Because agile methods invest resources into improving quality and reducing delivery times, perhaps we should not be surprised that costs do not always go down.

The good news is that the ability of agile data warehousing to improve costs is increasing as the DW/BI profession learns more about the best ways to deploy the method. A look at the contrast between just the past two surveys, those of 2012 and 2013, revealed that the number of respondents reporting that costs declined with agile methods increased nearly 60%, from 30 to 50 percentage points. What could cause such an improvement in only 1 year? The invitations for both surveys went out to approximately the same mailing list, but the DW/BI profession as a whole had gained another year of experience with the method. Because agile DW/BI is a new approach, we should expect it to be improving quickly as practitioners work out the details. Moreover, TDWI and Ceregenics made a deliberate effort during the 2013 survey to include those companies that had either taken our agile DW/BI training classes or had been coached by Ceregenics' consultants. Not surprisingly, the improved cost figures reflect a greater inclusion of success stories and therefore measure more accurately the impact on cost that companies can expect—as long as they utilize some instruction and support during their transition to agile methods.

Analysis of these surveys also revealed a large group of companies that are truly excelling in agile DW/BI practice, achieving reductions in cost along with improvements in programmer productivity and application quality. Of the respondents that reported improved cost, more than 45% also improved productivity, and more than 35% achieved better application quality as well; thus, truly effective implementations exist for the rest of us to emulate. Ceregenics' research in the future will focus on these top performances in order to identify the common practices they follow. Their success formulas need to be shared with the companies that are struggling with iterative delivery so that the risk involved in switching development methods can be reduced even further.

The 2013 survey attempted to uncover the detailed factors that determine agile's impact on project costs. Table 5.2 displays the top four factors rated as having the greatest impact for the 39 of 403 respondents that experienced increased expenses: multitasking, waiting for other IT groups to respond or cooperate, and the complexity of the enterprise data model. Speaking as a veteran of many agile transition efforts, I believe the first three of these factors essentially reflect old waterfall habits that persist within the larger organization in which a new agile team operates. These issues may begin to dissipate as the iterative delivery projects within a company demonstrate increased productivity, quality, and customer satisfaction. IT managers may well decide to let their highest performing teams concentrate on one project at a time in order to achieve even faster deliveries. IT managers might also provide the agile DW/BI with steadily greater support vis-à-vis the other IT service groups with which they must work, an action that will mitigate the middle two challenges. Complex data models gave rise to the last item among the top four factors that increase

TABLE 5.2 Factors Having the Greatest Impact for Those Agile DW/BI Practitioners Reporting Increased Costs

Factor	Percentage Agreeing (N = 39)
Programmer multitasking	49%
Waiting for services from non-DW/BI IT service groups	49%
Time spent coordinating between IT service groups	44%
EDW data modeling	41%

TDWI 2013 ADW Adoption Survey.

	Purported weakness of agile methods	Data Pts	Agree	Disagree	Agree (bad notion is true)	Disagree (bad notion is false)
1	The developers in my organization will not support agile	293	16.7%	70.0%		
2	Management in my organization will not support agile	293	20.5%	63.5%		
3	Agile software development is undisciplined	296	26.0%	62.2%		
4	Agile teams don't plan sufficiently	293	30.0%	59.4%		
5	Agile teams don't sufficiently address analysis	293	31.7%	55.6%		
6	Agile approaches result in low quality	296	29.7%	56.8%		
7	The culture of my organization is a bad fit for agile	293	30.7%	54.3%		
8	Agile teams don't sufficiently address architecture	294	38.4%	48.3%		
9	Agile projects are difficult to govern	292	43.2%	46.9%		
10	Agile isn't appropriate for highly regulated industries	293	21.2%	42.3%		
11	We can't easily get access to our business stakeholders	292	49.7%	38.4%		
12	Agile teams don't write sufficient documentation	296	47.6%	37.2%		
13	Agile isn't appropriate to process-audited environments (e.g. CMMI)	290	23.1%	32.4%		

Note: Diagram shown omits respondents answering "no opinion."

FIGURE 5.11   Agile data warehousing surveys indicate that practitioners have overcome some challenge areas.

project cost. The agile data engineering techniques presented in Part IV of this book may soon make this challenge a thing of the past as well.

Some Myths Prove True

Since their appearance at the beginning of the 21st century, agile methods have received much criticism from the "old school" of established project managers and software engineers for being undisciplined. In the agile DW/BI adoption surveys by Ceregenics/TDWI, we included a set of questions exploring the veracity of these criticisms. A summary of our findings can be found in Figure 5.11. This summary indicates that most of these criticisms are unfounded. In the same light, there are a few areas that we need to focus on and improve.

The reader should keep in mind that the statistics in Figure 5.11 are for agile methods alone, without the comparable figures for traditional methods alongside. By omitting traditional methods from this figure, I do not mean to imply that waterfall methods perform perfectly in any of these categories. Scanning the results presented in the figure, one can spot areas in which agile data warehousing has clearly overcome areas of weakness that detractors cited in the past. For example, organizations deciding whether to switch to agile DW/BI should consider the responses for Items 2–5 and 10. The evidence shows that most practitioners have found agile compatible with disciplined software engineering, allowing teams to sufficiently analyze and plan their work, even in highly regulated industries.

On the other hand, Items 8 and 11 suggest that agile DW/BI teams frequently struggle with architecting a solution or enticing business partners to participate in the development process. Part III of this book provides a new approach to project definition—one that systematically solicits inputs from the executives of a given organization and thus addresses these concerns. Items 9 and 12 suggest that agile EDW projects have an even greater struggle with application documentation and project governance. Faults such as insufficient project documentation should be easy to address, most likely by revisiting the team's "definition of done" for task cards. Teams can best address the impression that agile DW/BI projects are difficult to govern by employing a combination of more disciplined requirements management and quality assurance, as explored throughout the remainder of this book.

SUMMARY

The agile approach to DW/BI application coding anchors the spirit and style of the larger iterative approach that this book proposes for EDW. The earliest agile warehousing projects orchestrated programming work with pure, generic Scrum, but they quickly found that they needed to add new work roles specific to DW/BI, including project architect, data modeler, systems analyst, and system tester. Other simple innovations gave rise to 80/20 specifications, developer stories, and frequent revisions to a project's "current estimate." Whereas developer stories help rightsize the work packages for the project backlog, when it comes to data integration projects, each developer story typically generates more tasks than a team can complete during a single Scrum iteration. For this reason, data integration teams commonly adopt a technique known as pipelining, meaning that the full engineering life cycle for a developer story is stretched across three iterations. Techniques from Kanban make this extended approach manageable, especially once team leaders such as analysts, designers, and testers abandon Scrum's time box and focus on moving work through input and output buffers instead.

Kanban-enhanced development pipelines involve some additional innovations, such as requiring Iterations −1 and 0, two-pass testing, and a new approach to calculating the service level agreements that a team can offer its customers. All told, this adapted agile method works well for DW/BI, as demonstrated by the results of successive surveys of companies that practice it today. Companies experience far better success rates than with waterfall methods, as well as achieving higher programmer productivity and quality of deliverables. Many companies achieve all of these and significantly lower project costs, making the agile data warehousing method an extremely valuable strategy for their business intelligence programs.

Chapter 6

Eliminating Risk Through Nested Iterations

The data warehousing profession is replete with stories of development programs that stalled for years, spent millions, and then delivered only a handful of reports that could have been acquired directly from the operational systems with far less time and money. Such experiences leave many of us yearning to find a dependable means of eliminating the risk of investing too much and receiving too little that seems inherent in data warehousing/business intelligence (DW/BI) projects. The new techniques outlined in this book for managing requirements, modeling data repositories, and validating the development team's output all address key hazards that cause enterprise data warehousing (EDW) programs to fail. However, there is another, more simple solution that sets the tone for employing those other three groups of techniques: Elevate the notion of iterative delivery as high in the program as possible. The resulting approach sets off a crucial positive feedback loop between the development team and executive business stakeholders. The agile approach mitigates risk by delivering frequently, allowing business sponsors and staff to regularly measure progress and be confident that the EDW program will provide important value without excessive cost or delay. These frequent review points thus keep the EDW customers at all levels mentally engaged with the project, which in turn leads to better requirements and quality assurance efforts that greatly improve the team's performance and further reduces risk. This overall cycle of risk reduction and improved results can be easily structured using a few concepts, which the EDW team leaders can deliberately implement with every new project and thereby make agile data warehousing a dependably safe and effective method for growing a company's enterprise business intelligence capabilities.

EDW PROGRAMS SLIP INTO "231 SWAMPS"

The first step to making EDW programs a reasonably safe investment for business sponsors is to articulate how and why DW/BI efforts become huge time and money sinks. First, EDW programs are typically enormous undertakings. It is not uncommon for EDW programs in Fortune 500 firms to have a separate multiyear project underway for each conformed dimension, such as customer, product, vendor, and location. DW/BI efforts at medium-sized companies can require two or three dozen information technology (IT) professionals for 1 or 2 years. For even small projects, the fully loaded labor costs covering wages, facilities, and equipment will total $1,000 or more per developer day so that a team of just 10 people will represent a "burn rate" approaching $2.5 million per year when the involvement of various IT teams is also taken into account.

These high burn rates raise the stakes and place business executives funding these projects in an unenviable situation. As money steadily drains out of the program budget month after month, do the executives receive any tangible work product from IT to demonstrate that the funds are being invested effectively? For an EDW program utilizing a traditional project management approach, the answer is an emphatic "no." Surveys of failure rates for traditional software development efforts point toward a picture of widespread dysfunction. The Standish Group's *Chaos Report* surveys, mentioned in Chapter 1, attest to the inability of traditional methods to dependably manage large projects. As detailed in Table 6.1, these surveys of more than 8000 application projects pursued at 365 companies revealed that the larger a software development effort became, the less likely it was to deliver on time, on budget, and with all the promised features. When projects were kept under $1 million, the failure rate was 45%—still regrettably high for most business sponsors—but each increment in project size steadily drove failure rates to 100% as budgets exceeded $14 million [Standish Group 1995]. Similar studies of business intelligence application projects in the early 2000s suggested that the average data warehouse project costs between $10 million and $15 million and failure rates were greater than 65% [Ericson 2006].

TABLE 6.1 Failure Rates for Traditionally Managed Software Development Projects

Funding Level					
	1999 Dollars	2014 Dollars*	People	Months	Failure Rate
Less than	$750 K	$1 M	6	6	**45%**
Up to	$1.5 M	$2 M	12	9	**67%**
Up to	$3 M	$4 M	25	12	**75%**
Up to	$6 M	$9 M	40	18	**85%**
Up to	$10 M	$14 M	250	24	**92%**
Over	$10 M	$14 M	500	36	**100%**

*Converted then rounded from 1999 dollars to 2014 using a CPI ratio of 1.429.
Adapted from [Standish 1999].

During the many years we have championed agile data warehousing strategies, my colleagues and I have heard many woeful stories from the companies that asked our consulting firm for a better way to pursue enterprise business intelligence:

- A major transport company once complained that "A big systems integrator spent 2 years here, charged us $10 million, and delivered only some binders."
- A Fortune 50 pharmaceutical firm lamented, "Our last DW/BI project involved 150 people for 3 years. It got so expensive it's hurt our share price. And that was our third attempt at building the system."
- A leading telecommunications company opened the meeting with us by stating, "The finance department wants to fire all 110 members of the data warehousing department because we're too slow and too expensive."
- One of the largest waste management companies in the United States described its last EDW effort by stating simply, "We spent 2 years, $3 million, and got only one report. That seemed like a really expensive report."

The last complaint in the collection was an example of a horror story so commonly encountered that we were compelled to give it a special name. Business executives everywhere seem to get lured into spending 2 years and $3 million on data warehousing just to get Report #1. I am guessing that this particular combination of time and money must be the average threshold of pain for most companies large enough to pursue enterprise data warehousing. Perhaps, sensing this threshold of pain, the large system integrators must simply orchestrate their EDW project quotes to arrive at those numbers, whether or not they plan on actually delivering anything of value once they begin development. In any case, after a year during which we spoke with at least a half-dozen companies citing this same regrettable outcome, we started calling the 2-year, $3-million report the "231 swamp." Whereas the goal of agile techniques in general can be defined as to "constantly deliver value to the customer," EDW team leaders would be right to translate this maxim as "The goal of agile enterprise data warehousing is to keep EDW programs from becoming 231 swamps."

231 Swamps Derive from a Command and Control Strategy

What is the root cause for so many EDW programs ending up mired in a 231 swamp? Although many DW/BI professionals suggest that such swamps are unavoidable because EDW is inherently complex, the fact that agile techniques can so dramatically accelerate DW/BI programs while improving quality and customer satisfaction points to a more fundamental explanation. Understanding the dynamic that gives rise to the 231 swamp illuminates what EDW team leaders must do to escape it.

Large programs begin to sink into the swamp when they choose to mitigate project risk with command and control techniques instead of with results-driven progress tracking. Out of fear of how complex a requested BI application will be, non-agile project managers adopt an approach that makes EDW development far more complicated than it has to be. To be fair, enterprise DW/BI development does present several challenges that make it difficult, messy work:

- User requirements are difficult to pin down because companies have complex business rules.
- Users cannot describe what they want from an application until they actually see it on the screen.
- Source systems provide incomplete and inaccurate data.
- Data volumes are enormous, sometimes taking days to process and load into the database.

- EDW data models are difficult to get right and require a tremendous amount of effort to adapt for mistakes or new requirements.
- Quality assurance efforts only reveal defects toward the end of the project when time and resources have grown scarce.

Whereas techniques exist to address all of these concerns, as we will explore in the remainder of this book, it is important to realize that the way our project leaders respond to such adverse events can cause as much harm to the development effort as can these challenges themselves. When complications such as those listed previously cause an adverse event for a project, managers who have worked all their lives in hierarchical organizations react to the threat by trying to further control the activities of the people working below them. Extensive, detailed control is in fact the core principle behind traditional project management methods, down to the point where individual tasks are scheduled, dispatched, and monitored by managers. In order to measure the effectiveness of the corrective actions they take in response to adverse events, traditional managers track whether *tasks* are getting started and completed. Unfortunately, tracking tasks only infers success from increased developer activity rather than from business-meaningful, working software.

As the program encounters unforeseen adverse events, the traditional project plan grows longer as the project manager defines the additional tasks needed to repair the situation. The road to success was long to start with, and when the going gets rough, the road only gets longer. Only slowly do the sponsors realize that despite all the controls that project management has put in place, the work has not delivered any tangible results that the business staff can actually use. Despite all the developer activity reported, plus the money and time invested, no improved support for better business operations has arrived. Moreover, as more adverse events occur, the project plan grows longer, turning the plan-driven, control-oriented program into a 231 swamp.

AGILE'S FUNDAMENTAL RISK MITIGATION TECHNIQUE

Agile EDW practitioners drive the risk out of EDW projects with a system of nested iterations. They eliminate hazards at the programming level using agile's basic iterative programming techniques. They then extend the iterative concepts upward to mitigate risk occurring at the higher levels of an EDW program's conceptualization. At every level, agile ADE teams rely upon increased risk detection in order to minimize impact, so we should start by looking at why that basic strategy works so well.

Agile's General Risk Mitigation Strategy

Agile general strategy can be expressed succinctly as "fail fast and fail cheap," that is increase the frequency of encountering defects in order to minimize their impact. The methods connected to the agile manifesto utilize frequent reviews of working software to detect and resolve challenges instead of relying on granular command and control of developer activities, as occurs in traditionally managed projects. To understand why this approach performs so well, EDW leaders should consider the notion of risk first from a standard project manager's point of view. One definition of "risk" is the likelihood that an uncertain event will occur. Whereas theoretically the uncertain event could have an either positive or negative impact, most project managers focus on the potential for a negative impact. They typically maintain a list of the major possible adverse events threatening their endeavors and then employ various means to quantify the risk that each represents [Borek et al 2013, Chapter 11]. The most common technique is to calculate a risk index as the product of three multiplicands:

1. The probability it will occur
2. The impact it will have should it occur
3. The possibility that it will go undetected

Multiplying these three values together quantifies the risk that each item poses. By sorting this list by these risk products, the manager can then plan responses to these potential adverse events in the order of the magnitude of threat that they pose.

Although agile practitioners would be uncritical of development teams that maintain such a detailed risk analysis, provided that they find it truly helpful, in general agile practitioners take a radically different approach to eliminating threats. They encourage development teams to steadily and quickly deliver small pieces of the application, ending each iteration of development with a review of the product. These incremental deliveries must be the actual version of components they plan to deliver, very nearly ready to add to a production instance of the application. Because delivering working, production-ready code is highly difficult, any misunderstandings concerning a module's intent, data structures, or transform algorithms will result in a nonworking module that the product owner will reject at the end of the iteration.

In choosing this difficult objective for each incremental delivery, agile methods reliably force flaws in requirements, design, and programming to the surface with every iteration, ensuring that errors and oversights are detected early and often. Thus, over the arc of a project, the iterative review of the developing collection of modules drives the risk that defects still remain in the application toward zero. By choosing to work in short iterations, the EDW leaders have in fact reorganized the project so that at any point in the effort, the team can waste at most only a few weeks of work. If an iteration turns out to be a complete failure, everyone involved will be concerned, but they will also take that opportunity to change policies and techniques so that such a disaster does not occur again. The iterative approach prevents major defects from accumulating and wasting an entire project's worth of work.

The quality standard for each iteration is "ready-to-consume" modules, which effectively forces the agile teams to keep their code unafflicted by defects. If the product review at the end of an iteration uncovers a large defect, the affected module is rejected and returns to the backlog for further work. If the defects are small, they can be placed on a "tech debt" list for quick resolution at the beginning of the next iteration. These two practices ensure that the application code remains free of flaws, thus keeping the team from losing large amounts of time in teasing apart the complex webs of cause and effect that occur when programmers layer one defect upon many others.

Reflecting upon the math involved in the traditional definition of risk, we can see how agile teams so effectively reduce the risk products on the project's list of possible adverse events:

- By coding small increments, they reduce the impact that an event can have on the project (multiplicand 2).
- By frequently reviewing the resulting application, they reduce the likelihood that an event can remain hidden (multiplicand 3).

In the chapters that follow, I illustrate how agile EDW teams can also reduce the likelihood that an adverse event will occur in the first place. However, EDW team leaders should note that even if those additional techniques did not exist, the iterative approach alone drives at least two of three factors defining project risk toward zero, thus eliminating the overall program risk, no matter how resistant the third factor might be to remediation.

Of course, the additional reviews that undergird better detection must be paid for out of the project's budget, but EDW team leaders can demonstrate that these reviews are cost-effective because they more than proportionately reduce the impact that those product flaws will have. Figure 6.1 shows a cost multiplier popularized by Dr. Barry Boehm at TRW during the 1980s. His work demonstrated that the cost of correcting a system flaw increases considerably when a team allows it to go uncorrected during the length of a project because, with time, that defect undermines progressively

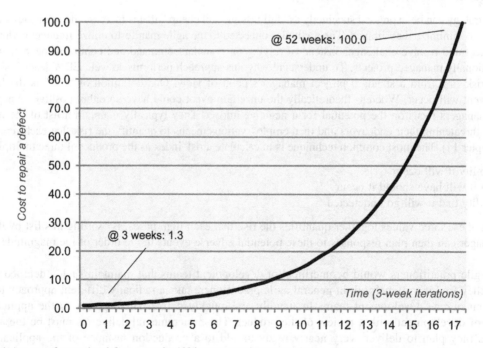

FIGURE 6.1   Relative cost of correcting defects grows by 100 between requirements and promotion into production.

more of an application's features: "Finding and fixing a software problem after delivery is 100 times more expensive than finding it and fixing it during the requirements and early design phases" [Boehm 1987]. The curve in the diagram shows the path taken by this increasing remediation cost during the course of a 1-year project. This path was drawn as an exponential curve to reflect the fact that the number of relationships between components increases geometrically as more components are added to a system.

With this context, we can approximate the costs that a method involving iterative reviews can save a project. For example, consider that the error caught during Week 1 cost only one unit to repair. During the first iteration, the product owner of a team using a 15-workday Scrum cycle will most likely discover the flaw during the product demonstration at the end of Week 3. Following the geometric growth from Figure 6.1, the impact of that defect will have increased only 30% to 1.3 units, given the short time that has elapsed. Compared to a waterfall method's pattern of holding a single business review at the end of the year-long development effort, validating the development team's work every 3 weeks represents a 17-fold increase in the number of business validations occurring within a project. This more frequent review, however, allows the team to seize a 77-fold decrease in the impact of the product flaw, making the trade-off more than worth the extra effort.

Eliminating Miscommunication with Multiplexed Engineering Phases

Considering the impact of iterative delivery through another lens, we can see that agile's frequent reviews of a growing application dramatically change the overall organization of a project in a way that greatly eliminates the risk of miscommunication between the business and IT.

The Standish Group's 1995 *Chaos Report* documented that lack of incomplete requirements, lack of user involvement, and unrealistic expectations were the major causes for project failure sited by more than 35% of respondents [Standish Group 1995]. To provide the business with frequent checkpoints for the work of the IT staff, the iterative approach effectively sandwiches together small slices of what a waterfall method would consider distinct software engineering phases, making such miscommunications a near impossibility. Figure 6.2 depicts the impact that iterative methods have on the reorganization of work. The top band of the diagram shows the timeline for a typical waterfall project. The time required to complete both the big specification up-front and the big test at the end is considerable. Unfortunately, this project duration extends beyond the time frame during which the business could have benefited

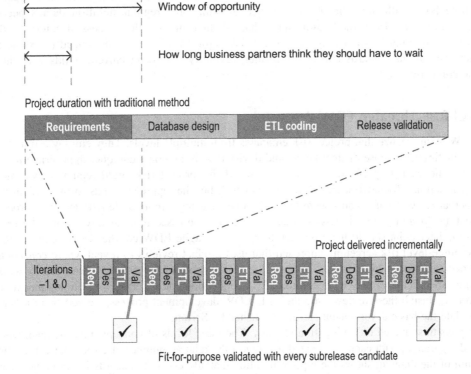

FIGURE 6.2 Incremental delivery mitigates risk by increasing the number of product check points.

from the new system, as shown by the "window of opportunity" arrow above the timeline. The situation is even more ridiculous when the traditional project plan is compared to the business staff's attention span, suggested by the next arrow down, and so the waterfall approach naturally leads to tremendous frustration among project sponsors.

Instead of fully completing each software engineering step before beginning the next, agile methods perform a little bit of requirements, followed by a little bit of design, then a little bit of coding, followed by a little bit of product validation. The bottom of Figure 6.2 depicts how, in the agile approach, these small slices from the distinct software engineering disciplines are essentially "time division multiplexed" together [Kundu 2010, p. 252]. The steady stream series of deliverables that this approach creates repeatedly puts usable product in the customers' hands, alleviating a great deal of their frustration with the slow pace of EDW development. It also provides frequent checkpoints with the business stakeholders, allowing them to keep the EDW development team aligned with the company's true needs for business intelligence services.

This last point is crucial. As much as IT staff members would like to say they understand the business, they rarely do because they do not work with the operational systems every day, as does the business staff. Without a deep understanding of the transactions applications, IT staff members can make a large number of mistakes regarding requirements and design. They need the business staff to review their work product and correct those oversights, especially in situations in which the business and/or the operational systems are changing.

The repeated validation points found in the agile approach allow the business many opportunities to evaluate how well IT understands the business requirements and how accurately IT has crafted the application's design. I have attended very few product reviews where the business has not caught at least a couple of significant mistakes on the part of IT members of the team. These frequent reviews allow the business to keep IT aligned with the true needs of the company and resolve product flaws before a large amount of code is assembled, greatly mitigating the risk of the project.

AGILE EDW'S EXTENDED RISK MITIGATION TECHNIQUES

Iterative delivery is an effective strategy for mitigating the risk of software development projects in general, but unfortunately the nature of EDW development tends to limit the effectiveness of this technique. In Chapter 5, we discussed the fact that a team's product owner is typically the only business representative attending the regular iterations' product demos because the nature of data integration work makes it difficult to demonstrate realistic data more than once per time box. With only the product owner attending, the regular iteration demos become somewhat myopic, addressing only what I call the bottom tier of hazards that threaten the success of enterprise data warehousing projects. To mitigate a much wider range of project risk, agile EDW team leaders need to extend the concept of repetitive product validations upwards two levels further, regularly reviewing current builds with the directors and executives of the company.

Three Types of Risk Threaten EDW Programs

Veteran agile EDW teams realize that project risk emanates from multiple levels. They employ a framework for identifying hazards originating from those distinct layers and devise risk mitigation techniques appropriate for each level.

Project leaders who want to perform an exhaustive search for project risk could regularly evaluate their projects using the DAMA functional framework discussed in Chapter 3, but that approach tends to overwhelm the team with a long list of perils that *might* occur. Teams seem to perform better using a more agile risk detection process that focuses on the threats that are *likely* to come to pass so that they can be addressed immediately, saving the exhaustive search techniques for some later point should there be time to spare. The agile EDW coaches in our consulting firm therefore employ a simple, three-level risk screening approach that uses product reviews to reveal where *conceptual errors* have occurred in the decisions made by the team. We use the reviews to identify where a team that is working fast from "just good-enough" specifications may have committed an application coding error, a solution concept error, or a business concept error. To install these reviews into the agile EDW development process, we add two further types of iterations that encapsulate the basic development sprint established by Scrum.

Figure 6.3 depicts this layered risk mitigation strategy. The three levels of concepts that the team wishes to scan for errors appear in the pyramid, with each layer sized to suggest the relative number of errors that can occur at each level. The center column of the diagram shows the type of iteration that addresses the hazards found in each conceptual level. On the right of the diagram is listed a couple of the major techniques that will enable a team to fail fast and fix quickly while addressing a particular level of risk. All these techniques are discussed in this book.

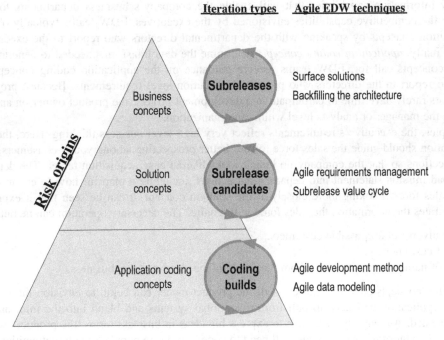

Iteration types   **Agile EDW techniques**

Business concepts — **Subreleases** — Surface solutions / Backfilling the architecture

Solution concepts — **Subrelease candidates** — Agile requirements management / Subrelease value cycle

Application coding concepts — **Coding builds** — Agile development method / Agile data modeling

Risk origins

FIGURE 6.3 The sources of EDW project risk mitigated with three types of iterations.

TABLE 6.2 Examples of Errors by Conceptual Level

Conceptual Level			
Goal	Business Partner Level	Example Directive	Validation Strategy
Business Concepts			
New Competitive Capabilities	Executive and Program Sponsors	"Use BI to create call lists for our sales force so that they can expand market share in the Gen Y age group in order to build a dependable revenue stream for the next ten years and thereby fend off an acquisition."	Directors report improved operational metrics, attributing them to organization's use of the BI application
Solution Concepts			
New Information Capabilities	Departmental Directors	"Identify likely Gen Y prospects by subtracting the households of our current customers in their 30s from the set of all households headed by individuals in that age group for each geographic region, and subset that list for the sales reps in each branch office."	Product owner demonstrates to close stakeholders new data visualizations addressing the information need, explaining source data employed and business rules applied
Application Coding Concepts			
New Data Capabilities	Managers or Senior Analysts	"Implement business rules 4 through 6 upon our policy data in order to eliminate duplicates within the current data so that the warehouse produces an accurate list of current Gen Y households.	Product owner finds correct results when reviewing data loaded from data sets with known challenges to the business rules

Examples of the Three Levels

Table 6.2 lists the three conceptual levels of an EDW project and also provides examples from the insurance industry of errors that a team can make in each. This table parallels the approach I recommend for pursuing requirements and quality assurance, as explored in later chapters. In brief, *business concepts* describe the new competitive capabilities that executives believe the company will gain with improved business intelligence applications. *Solution concepts* represent the new information capabilities that will enable the company's business departments to take the actions needed to achieve the competitive capabilities envisioned by the executives. EDW teams typically obtain the majority of a project's solution concepts by speaking with the departmental directors who report to the executives funding the DW/BI projects. Finally, *application coding concepts* determine the data transforms needed to generate the information that the solution concepts call for. EDW teams receive guidance on the application coding concepts from the staff and managers who report to the directors who provide the solution-level requirements. Because project sponsors and department directors rarely have time to participate in a development project, the product owner on an agile EDW team usually hails from the manager or analysts level within an organization.

In these examples, the executive's requirements reflect very high-level business thinking. Here, the executive stated that the BI application should guide the sales force toward better prospecting among young consumers, firming up long-term revenue projections so that the company no longer looks like an easy acquisition target. The department directors translated this broad mission statement into departmental actions, including a plan for how to create call lists that will better guide the sales force. Looking more closely at the solution concept, it can be seen that it expresses a set-based operation that generates the information the sales force will require. The necessary operation can be outlined as follows:

- Start with the universe of all possible customers.
- Subtract current customers.
- Arrive at a set of names of people with whom the company needs to develop business.

Once the solution concepts have been articulated, the product owner can begin to envision the individual data elements that the BI application will need to pull from operational systems and blend into the information sets that the directors have requested. Although he will have to express his ideas in business terms, the product owner will describe column-by-column the algorithm that the team will need to code in order to populate the target entities in the data warehouse. The example in Table 6.2 identifies the business rules the application should apply in order to create a clean list of current customers that can be subtracted later from the set of all consumers within a geographic region.

The EDW project must deliver appropriate capabilities addressing the ideas occurring in all three of these conceptual levels. Perhaps more important than assessing the quality of the programmers' extract, transform, and load (ETL) and BI modules is how the team leaders will know that the concepts they have been given to guide the project's overall development effort are correct. They can use iterations to validate all three levels of these guiding concepts. Each level calls for a different type of iteration, as outlined here, starting with the bottom layer of the risk pyramid and working upward.

Mitigating the Risk of Application Coding Concept Errors

In the foundation of the risk pyramid we find errors occurring within the application coding concepts. Application coding concepts include all the guiding information needed by the technical team members regarding how the modules within the application should be designed and programmed. These concepts represent the team's notion of how a particular module should be built and why it should be built in that way. In an agile development effort, the foundation for these notions will be the insights into source systems and required transformation rules, all expressed at a business level by the product owner working with the team. In the previous example, the product owner described the three business rules for removing duplicates from the current customer list. The rest of the team had to translate that guidance into application coding concepts involving data structures and transform algorithms.

In order to know that the application coding concepts that they employ while building a particular module are correct, the members of an agile EDW team should use the standard development iterations discussed previously. These coding cycles are the short iterations of two to four weeks that agile EDW teams use to build potentially shippable modules that will load BI data for the product owner to explore during a product demonstration. The product demonstrations at the end of each iteration will allow the product owner to interact directly with the transformed source data. During this review, the product owner will uncover flaws in the source data selected by the team, in the business rules used to transform the data, and in the integrity of the information loaded into the warehouse. If the product owner is thorough in her review, very few application coding errors will go undetected.

Mitigating the Risk of Solution Concept Errors

Solution concepts comprise the middle layer of the risk pyramid. A solution concept packages together the new data capabilities streaming out of the coding iterations. The "solution" contained in such a package is a mapping of new application features to the business problems that the team believes the application will solve. Assembling a set of new data capabilities into a solution is unfortunately a mental activity that lends itself to many possible errors, so the set of requested data capabilities needs to be checked as carefully as the code in ETL modules. The product owner must select the right business problems to solve and express them in a way that the IT members of his team can understand. Those IT teammates must then select appropriate data sources, devise transforms, and design target elements that present the company's situation in a way that enables business staff members to solve the desired business problems.

The resulting solution mapping contains statements such as "Features 1 through 3 will solve Business Problem X. Features 2, 4, and 5 will solve Business Problem Y." In the example provided in Table 6.2, the solution concept contained several features: a list of current households, a list of all possible households, a function to subtract one from the other, and the ability to filter the result by consumer age brackets. These were all mapped to a particular business problem: the need to provide better prospecting lists for the sales force.

This solution map is important to get right because it will guide the programming work of several development iterations. Regrettably, the group process that generates such mappings can go wrong in hundreds of ways. The business problem is often difficult for directors to articulate accurately. The product owner often provides only a basic outline of the features needed, overlooking those software aspects that more unusual circumstances will demand. Returning to the example, perhaps the product owner did not think of a crucial feature, namely the ability to detect as distinct consumers Gen Y individuals living in single-family dwellings owned by an older person, such as a parent.

In order to know that the current solution concept they are working from is correct, agile EDW teammates will need to validate the increments of that solution with the departmental directors who are waiting for the new information capabilities that they expect the new application to provide. Only when they see their requests translated into working solutions can the directors realize features that are missing or implemented poorly.

To obtain director-level reviews, the EDW team will need to add a validation cycle higher than the product demonstration built into the standard agile coding iteration. To drive out the risk of making a solution concept error, EDW team leaders will need to take the time to regularly hold *subrelease reviews.*

During a subrelease review, the team gathers the results of a few application coding iterations into a release candidate and presents the new information capabilities that it offers to the stakeholders that have been recently advising the team. These "close stakeholders" will probably be the directors of the departments and their lieutenants who understand the solution that the release candidate claims to provide, and who will benefit from the recently added features. The team's product owner, who has been translating the departmental input into direct guidance for the team, should present to these close stakeholders the current build of the DW/BI application, asking them to validate whether that guidance was correct.

The subrelease contains a very simple proposal to the audience of close stakeholders:

- The current build of the BI application has many new features ready to go.
- The product owner believes these features represent a "critical mass" of new capabilities that will generate significant value for the company.
- Promoting the current build into production will consume effort from both the development team and supporting IT groups.
- Such a promotion will require the team to suspend development for one iteration, so the creation of new features will temporarily stop.
- The labor from the team and the relevant IT groups will also cost money—often between $25,000 and $75,000 depending on how exacting the company's promotion procedures are.
- The close stakeholders need to review the new capabilities contained in the current build and decide whether the benefits they offer will justify the expense of the promotion effort.

If the stakeholders decide that the increment of value offered by the new build outweighs the cost of a promotion cycle, the subrelease review will have proven that the team's solution concept was essentially correct—the new features mapped well enough to the stakeholders' business problems that they want the new system in operation now. If, on the other hand, the stakeholders vote no, then the product owner and the team leaders can query them to find out why. Every gap in capability and poorly designed feature that the reviewers point out will equal a flaw in the team's solution concept. By holding these simple, subrelease candidate reviews, the team can drive solution-concept errors out of the shadows, allowing the team to improve its notion of the business problems confronting the company and the features required to solve them. Box 6.1 presents the script that my colleagues and I typically ask product owners to follow when they conduct these subrelease candidate reviews.

Figure 6.4 shows how the application coding iterations assemble into the subrelease candidate reviews that the close stakeholders should attend. Because the application coding cycles take two to four weeks each, even a few of them will

Box 6.1 A Script for Subrelease Candidate Review Sessions

Once the agile EDW team has added a reasonable number of new features to the DW/BI application, the product owner can employ the following script while presenting the system's current build to the project's close stakeholders:

1. Share with the stakeholders that the team desires them to either endorse or reject the proposal to promote the current build of the business intelligence application into production usage.
2. Share with them the estimated cost of such a promotion, which will cover the following:
   a. A "promotion iteration" by the developers during which they will prepare the build for system and user acceptance testing
   b. Time from other IT support groups needed to review and implement the build
   c. Training the end users how to operate the new version of the application
   d. Developer time for supporting those users and correcting minor defects
3. Ask the stakeholders to subjectively consider the features of the new build they are about to see and to decide whether the features, taken as a whole, merit the cost of a promotion effort.

4. State the business problem(s) that the team believes the subrelease candidate will solve.
5. Show the stakeholders how the information now available through the BI application will enable their departmental staff to better understand the fundamental nature and trajectory of the targeted business problems.
6. Show the stakeholders how the BI application will reveal whether the problem is being solved by the new actions of their staff members.
7. Explain the sources of information employed and the business rules used to transform those sources into the information being reviewed.
8. Explain how the team decided that the end users will be able to trust the information now flowing into the data warehouse.
9. Summarize why the product owner believes that the benefits offered by the new build outweigh the cost of promotion.
10. Ask the stakeholders to either endorse or reject the new build.
11. If rejected, ask the stakeholders to identify the further features and benefits necessary before they will endorse the build for promotion.

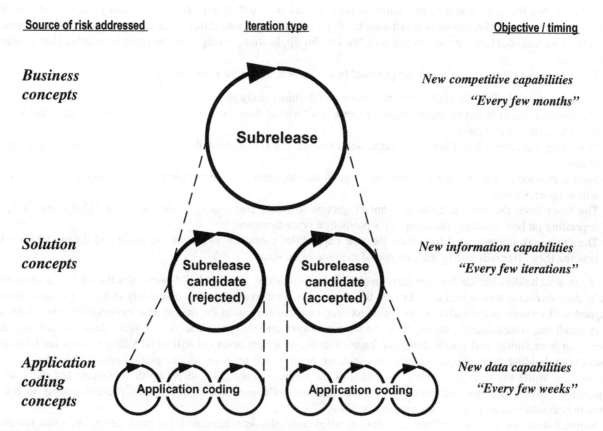

Source of risk addressed	Iteration type	Objective / timing
Business concepts	Subrelease	*New competitive capabilities* "Every few months"
Solution concepts	Subrelease candidate (rejected) Subrelease candidate (accepted)	*New information capabilities* "Every few iterations"
Application coding concepts	Application coding Application coding	*New data capabilities* "Every few weeks"

FIGURE 6.4   Relative timing for the three types of iterations that Agile EDW employs.

represent a months-long stretch during which the stakeholders will not see much new from the data warehouse team. To keep stakeholders engaged and their guidance timely, the team should present a subrelease candidate after every few development iterations. The first candidate presented may very well be rejected, so the team will need to return to the project room, invest in a couple more coding iterations, and then hold another subrelease review. Given the learning occurring with each subrelease review, it will not take long before the stakeholders accept a candidate, especially because their departmental staff members are eagerly awaiting the new business intelligence features that the EDW team is working on.

People who practice generic agile will suggest that the close stakeholders be included in the product demonstrations held at the end of every coding iteration. This suggestion touches upon one difference between agile for software development in general and agile for data warehousing. As discussed in previous chapters, data warehousing requires that information progress through the many layers of the DW/BI reference architecture. The EDW team often needs one or more iterations to build the ETL for each one of these architectural layers. Until that data arrives at the presentation layer, it will not be very interesting to the project's business stakeholders. Because the project owner has been working closely with the developers, she should eventually be able to understand the data as it lands in the preliminary layers of the reference architecture, but she may be the only business staff member who will be able to appreciate its value. Given a choice, the other business stakeholders will probably opt to wait until the data can be examined using a finished dashboard or a report.

Moreover, data volumes and ETL complexity often prevent teams from loading the target tables until the very end of a coding iteration. For this reason, iteration demos are usually the first time a product owner sees a new set of data, and it often contains some enormous defects, some of them originating from errors in the directions that the product owner provided. The product owner may very well prefer to be surprised by these product flaws without her business colleagues looking on because she may think it better to get the big defects ironed out within the privacy of the immediate development team. For these reasons, agile data warehousing teams usually choose to show the application to the project stakeholders only after they have had a chance to first look at the data themselves.

Mitigating the Risk of Business Concept Errors

At the highest level, an EDW team must be sure that the application that the team is building embodies a rational and coherent set of business concepts. The requirements for every multiproject EDW program are shaped by multiple overlapping ideas from business sponsors. These ideas motivated the executives to fund the DW/BI development in the first place because they express how the company's performance would improve if only the staff could have better information at its disposal. If these business concepts are flawed, however, the component projects or even the entire EDW program could prove to be a colossal waste of money, time, and effort.

In the examples provided in Table 6.2, the business concept asserted that identifying prospect Gen Y consumers would enable the sales force to improve the company's revenue stream. Perhaps this concept was not as well thought out as it should have been. When someone gives a prospecting list with only names and phone numbers to insurance sales agents, they will immediate ask, "How am I supposed to develop a rapport with these people when you haven't told me anything about them?" They will tell the data warehousing team to come back later with a list stating every prospect's occupation, monthly salary, hobbies, and dependents. In this case, the business executive had launched the DW/BI project with a half-baked business concept. Unfortunately, the additional capabilities that end users call for often require an entirely different collection of data sources than those for which the team has programmed, making these errors very expensive to repair. If the agile EDW team does not take steps to validate the business notions driving a project, then it risks coding fruitlessly for months, even years.

One could hope that the directors attending the subrelease reviews will catch such errors in the business concepts, but given their management positions, they may be far removed from the factors that the staff members know all too well from their daily struggles to keep the business running. To dependably detect business concept errors, the EDW leaders have to get the application they are building in front of these end users for validation in a real business setting. For that reason, the team leaders need to plan on multiple subreleases for the EDW rather than just a single, full release.

Agile data warehousing practitioners often refer to these subreleases as *minimal viable products* (MVPs), a concept borrowed from Eric Ries' 2011 book, *The Lean Startup*. As Ries explains in his book, his first two attempts at building web-based service companies failed because he and the other executives involved severely misunderstood what customers wanted from Internet products. Rather than continuing to assume they could guess at the right product, Ries and colleagues switched to a strategy of testing market demand using minimal viable products [Ries 2011]. *Minimal* meant they would keep the cost of each introduction very low so that they consumed as little of their venture capital as possible until they understood what the customers wanted. *Viable* signified that each introduction had to be reasonably usable or the customers would not have any meaningful feedback to provide. Once they switched to minimal viable products, the fate of their subsequent start-up attempts vastly improved—so much that they grew into durable firms still operating in the market today.

Given that very few people, especially project sponsors, understand business intelligence applications enough to envision in the abstract how they will look and operate once online, EDW team leaders would do well to treat their applications as new Internet services. They should market test them as Ries' companies did, using minimal viable products before overinvesting in any one business concept.

Team leaders may find it difficult to convince some product owners to support multiple subreleases due to the effort and expense involved. With generic agile, the product owner role decides when the product is ready for promotion. With data warehousing, product owners can sometimes believe that there is little value in putting an EDW into production until users can "slice and dice" all the metrics by every dimension. They believe that putting the data warehouse online with only a few metrics and a handful of dimensions will provide end users only a glimpse of the much larger truth that they need, so they will want to wait until the end users can see everything in full detail. Unfortunately, this practice will leave the EDW developers diligently programming month after month without any feedback from real users, leaving the developers vulnerable to business concept errors that the product owner, directors, and senior executives have all overlooked.

So that business concept errors can be readily uncovered, the project architects in this situation must insist on at least three or four subreleases per year. They may have to ponder the requirements and design intently to discover ways to meaningfully partition the project so that each subrelease has value to the end users. Although such planning can be complex at times, I have yet to work on a project where it could not be done. Elaborate fact tables usually have many distinct sets of metrics within them, and these metric columns often have elements replicated from source systems placed alongside the complex, derived values. Subreleases for the program can be organized to deliver each metric column set as an increment, or they can first focus on the replicated values followed by the derived columns in the subsequent subreleases. The early subreleases can also be issued with the aggregated metrics connected to only a handful of the dimensions, to be replaced with more granular fact tables connected to more dimensions later. Partitioning the project into subreleases can take imagination and effort, but the additional cost of a couple of promotions pales compared to the damage that can occur if the company has seriously miscalculated the value of the warehouse that the team is building.

Putting increments of the facts and dimensions in front of real end users to see if they laugh at the mangled and misconceived information that the data warehouse contains is the acid test that the EDW team leaders need to strive for. Part VI of this book surveys some techniques and technology that will greatly assist EDW teams in building fast and inexpensive subreleases so that they can pursue a series of minimal viable products without risking months of development effort.

SUMMARY

Enterprise data warehousing projects are full of risk. When pursued with traditional project management methods, efforts at building an EDW fail more often than they succeed. Agile EDW techniques greatly mitigate risks of failure by both using the general features of the development iteration and adding two further types of iterations to the overall project plan: one for subrelease candidates and another for actual application subreleases. The development iteration contains a product demonstration for the product owner, an event that gives him or her a regular opportunity to screen for application coding errors that may have crept into the BI system's current build. Development projects also need accurate guidance at the solution level—the realm in which application features are selected and mapped to the business problems they solve. To detect solution concept errors, the EDW team must inspire its product owner to regularly present a subrelease candidate after every few development iterations to the stakeholders most involved in guiding the team. If the close stakeholders approve the subrelease candidate, the team should promote the current build into production usage and have real business users evaluate the new subrelease. The end users will be able to test whether the business concepts shaping the data warehouse are accurate. The errors and gaps in requirements and design that these three levels of review will uncover will keep the team from investing months of programming into seriously misconceived application designs.

Application coding concepts, solution concepts, and business concepts provide a handy structure for organizing a team's risk mitigation efforts. We elaborate on and heavily rely on this same framework when we devise a requirements management approach for agile enterprise data warehousing teams—a discussion that begins in the next chapter.

Part II References

Chapter 4

Abran, A., Moore, J., Bourque, P., Dupuis, R., 2005. Guide to the Software Engineering Body of Knowledge (SWEBOK). IEEE Computer Society, Piscataway, NJ.

Angelov, S., Grefen, P., Greefhorst, D., 2012. A classification of software reference architectures. Inform. Softw. Technol. 54 (4), 417–431. <http://www.archixl.nl/files/wicsa_referencearchitecture.pdf> (accessed December 2013).

Association for Computing Machinery, 2006. Software engineering. Association for Computing Machinery (website). <http://computing-careers.acm.org/?page_id=12] > (accessed May 2014).

Balanced Insight, 2014. Accelerating information delivery. Balanced Insight (website). <http://www.balancedinsight.com> (accessed May 2014).

Brackett, M., 2005. Data resource quality. Presentation at the National Forum on Education Statistics, February 21, 2005. <http://nces.ed.gov/forum/pdf/data_res_quality_ppt.pdf> (accessed October 2013).

Brackett, M., 2011. Data Resource Simplexity. Technics, Bradley Beach, NJ.

DAMA International, 2013. About us. DAMA International (website). <http://www.dama.org> (accessed November 2013).

Department of Defense, 2010, June. Reference architecture description. Department of Defense (website). <http://dodcio.defense.gov/Portals/0/Documents/DIEA/Ref_Archi_Description_Final_v1_18Jun10.pdf> (accessed December 2013).

Earley, S., 2011. The DAMA Dictionary of Data Management, second ed. Technic, Bradley Beach, NJ.

Gartner, 2013. Gartner IT glossary. Gartner (website). <http://www.gartner.com/it-glossary> (accessed November 2013).

Giachetti, R.E., 2010. Design of enterprise systems, theory, architecture, and methods. Boca Raton, FL: CRC Press. Cited in Wikipedia entry for "enterprise."

Hughes, R., Stodder, D., 2013. Agile Data Warehousing: Putting Business Back in the Driver's Seat. Keynote Presentation at The Data Warehousing Institute's October 2013 World Conference, Boston.

Inmon, W.H., 1993. What is a data warehouse? PRISM Newsletter. vol. 1, No. 1. St. Louis, MO: Washington University, Center for the Application of Information Technology.

Inmon W.H., Imhoff, C., 2001. Corporate information factory, second ed. New York: Wiley.

Kimball, R., Ross, M., 2013. The Data Warehouse Toolkit, third ed Wiley, New York.

Malveau, R., Mowbray, T.J., 2003. Software Architect Bootcamp, second ed Prentice Hall, Upper Saddle River, NJ.

Mosley, M., Brackett, M., Earley, S., 2009. The DAMA Guide to the Data Management Body of Knowledge. Technics, Bradley Beach, NJ.

Nelson, J., 2013, April 22. The rise of Shadow IT: Should CIOs take umbrage? CXO Unplugged (website). <http://cxounplugged.com/2013/04/shadow_it>.

Project Management Institute, 2013. A Guide to the Project Management Body of Knowledge, fifth ed. Project Management Institute, Newtown Square, PA.

Sessions, R., 2007, May. A comparison of the top four enterprise-architecture methodologies. Microsoft Developer Network (website). <https://msdn.microsoft.com/en-us/library/bb466232.aspx> (accessed December 2013).

The Data Warehousing Institute, 2011, May. Data integration and data warehousing defined. What Works in Data Integration, 31, <http://tdwi.org/Issues/2011/05/What-Works-Volume-31.aspx> (accessed October 2013).

The Data Warehousing Institute, 2013. About TDWI. The Data Warehousing Institute (website). <http://www.tdwi.org> (accessed November 2013).

Zachman, J.P., 2011. "The Zachman Framework Evolution," *Zachman International* (website), <http://www.zachman.com/ea-articles-reference/54-the-zachman-framework-evolution> (accessed July 2014).

Chapter 5

Hughes, R., Stodder, D., 2013. Agile Data Warehousing: Putting Business Back in the Driver's Seat. Keynote Presentation at The Data Warehousing Institute's October 2013 World Conference, Boston.

Malik, N., 2007, June 4. WaterScrum vs. Scrummerfall. Inside Architecture (blog), Microsoft Developer Network. <http://blogs.msdn.com/b/nickmalik/archive/2007/06/04/waterscrum-vs-scrummerfall.aspx> (accessed June 2013).

Chapter 6

Boehm, D. TRW, Inc., 1987. Industrial software metrics top10 list. IEEE Software, pp. 84–85.

Borek, A., Parlikad, A.K., Webb, J., Woodall, P., 2013. Total Information Risk Management. Morgan Kaufmann, Waltham, MA.

Ericson, J. 2006, April. A simple plan. Information Management Magazine. <http://www.information-management.com/issues/2006 0401/1051182-1.html> (accessed September 2011).

Kundu, S., 2010. Analog and Digital Communications. Pearson India, Chennai.

Ries, E., 2011. The Lean Startup: How Today's Entrepreneurs Use Continuous Innovation to Create Radically Successful Businesses. Crown Business, New York.

The Standish Group International, 1995. The chaos report. <http://www.standishgroup.com> (accessed April 2006).

The Standish Group International, 1999. Chaos: A recipe for success. <http://www.standishgroup.com> (accessed April 2006).

Part III

Agile EDW Requirements Management

Chapter 7

Balancing between Two Extremes

Agile data warehousing projects teeter precariously on a knife edge when it comes to requirements. Without an accurate notion of the problems their customers face and a strong concept of the system that will solve those problems, teams can labor for months and still deliver very little of value to the business. On the other hand, defining a project's requirements in exhaustive detail can consume so much time that the team leaves itself too little opportunity and resources to build enough working modules of sufficient quality to solve any of the business problems identified. To succeed, agile practitioners need an approach to framing projects that yields requirements that are "just good enough," to quote a phrase that iterative delivery practitioners use extensively. Just-good-enough requirements in the agile context means focusing the developers on the right problems with sufficient understanding to create an effective project backlog. With an accurate backlog in hand, they can then begin programming increments of working software that meets the business needs.

An agile enterprise data warehousing (EDW) team employs a unique strategy for successfully balancing between too little and too much project definition before programming begins. It relies on a lightweight, incrementally adjustable, stereoscopic vision to enable the developers to effectively define and scope the project. *Lightweight* means this vision is based on 80/20 specifications, as discussed in the introductory chapters. *Incrementally adjustable* signifies that as the project iterations proceed, the team can selectively increase the level of detail above the 80/20 mark where needed. *Stereoscopic* indicates that a team will describe its project from two perspectives so that it can "see around the corners," spotting gaps and investing in greater detail when necessary.

Agile team leaders do not expect that defining the requirements for a project as large as an EDW will be a one-time effort. Moreover, the needs of many business departments and interacting business systems will determine the full list of features required of an enterprise data warehousing system, and these needs will not be fully apparent at the start of the project. Accordingly, team leaders should expect the business stakeholders to improve their notion of the business intelligence services they need as they learn about the insights that data warehousing can provide. Moreover, the competitive landscape for the organization may also change multiple times before the EDW team fully delivers the next release of its application. For all these reasons, agile EDW team leaders need to think in terms of "requirements management"—that is, building a good understanding of organizational needs at the start of the project but then continuing to explore and update that notion over time so that the active goals of the project remain as accurate as possible.

The mind map in Figure 7.1 shows how the five chapters of this part of the book present the elements involved in agile EDW requirements management. This chapter, in particular, begins by advocating that EDW team leaders invest at least some effort into requirements management in order to counter the notion that "agile" means programmers just start coding. This chapter concludes with an overview of the stereoscopic approach that my colleagues have successfully used for many years to identify and lightly document the full breadth of EDW project requirements. The chapters that follow provide greater details of this process by addressing the following:

- Disciplined definitions for EDW epics, themes, and user stories
- Quantifying *value* throughout the requirements management process
- The artifacts employed for a generic agile approach
- The artifacts employed for an enterprise-capable agile requirements value chain
- Intersecting those two approaches to yield a stereoscopic definition of the project
- Interfacing agile requirements management with the traditional project governance processes

By combining the generic and enterprise-capable requirements management techniques, agile EDW team leaders can compile at the beginning of a project a complete and accurate project backlog with just enough detail to properly

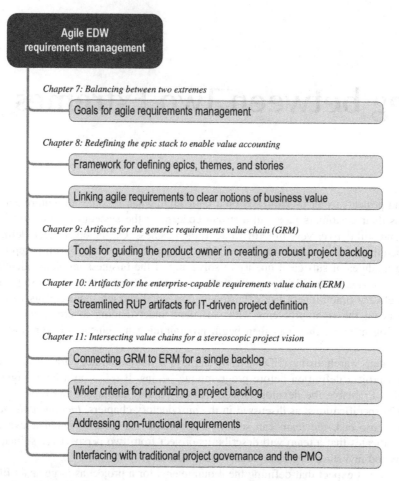

FIGURE 7.1   Mind map of topics addressed in Part III.

sequence their work items for fast, iterative delivery. Such a backlog will also enable team leaders to efficiently estimate the cost and duration of the effort and smoothly support any formal requirements management procedures that traditional project management offices might impose at a higher level.

A quick reminder regarding some of the terms that will be used frequently here and in the following chapters: Because data analytics projects include requirements for both data preparation and information visualization, I use the term *data integration* when focusing more on the back-end portion of a system, *business intelligence* when looking at it more from an end-user's point of view, and *enterprise data warehousing* when thinking of a data analytics application comprising both data integration and end-user analytical components that must combine data from many source systems and deliver it to many business departments.

BUILDING THE CASE FOR EFFECTIVE REQUIREMENTS MANAGEMENT

EDW team leaders will need to set a team's goals for requirements gathering and then motivate their developers to conscientiously perform this sometimes-tedious work. Such motivation will require a clear and compelling statement of the benefits that a team will secure by properly defining the needs and objectives that a project should address.

Speaking broadly, a project's *requirements* describe the features, functions, capabilities, and characteristics that an information-based end product or service should provide. Requirements express the conditions and capabilities needed to solve a problem or to achieve the agreed-upon objectives of a system or component [Larson & Larson 2013]. Requirements for large projects such as enterprise data warehouses are challenging to manage for multiple reasons, the foremost being the many kinds of needs that project teams should catalog and analyze before they start programming. Even a simple listing of requirements types includes functional as well as nonfunctional requirements; business, architectural, and technical requirements; and a distinction between positive and negative requirements. Moreover, requirements can be collected at a high level when the software objectives are simple, or at an excruciating level of detail when the company's business rules are complex.

One of the most important decisions that project leaders can make is the level at which requirements will be gathered and managed. Figure 7.2 provides examples of requirements expressed at three levels of detail. Level 1, although not in user story format, represents the generalized notions that one finds on most agile teams' project backlogs. The more complex Level 3 requirement demonstrates the excruciating detail that many traditional project managers insist upon. Projects that can work with Level 1 requirements will clearly begin programming far sooner than those that invest in Level 3. However, teams can doom a project to failure if they start coding with only Level 1 requirements in hand when Level 3 artifacts are truly necessary.

Level 1 (Simple):

The data mart will enable users to decompose sales-transaction metrics by the customer agent that finalized the sale on the order entry system.

Level 2 (Intermediate):

Records that cannot be loaded will be placed into a suspense table associated with each primary target table. These records will be marked with a date-time value in the INSERT_DATE column. When data on the source application changes and allows the record to be loaded, that record will be physically removed from the suspense table. At any time, business users will be able to examine the suspense tables to find a current image of all records needing correction by end users of the source system.

Level 3 (Complex):

```
/* Logic for setting the market segment for a sales order */

if the order references a contract number

then

    if contract can be found in the contract table, then dim_market.segment = dim_contract.cust_segment
    else dim_market.segment='CURRENT_CONTRACT_UNLOCATABLE'

else

    if the order has a associated retail license

    then

        if   max(order_line_item.bandwidth) > 1 GBPS
            and   (count(order_line_item)
                    where order_line_item.product_category = 'PROVIDER_MANAGED_SECURITY' )
                > 3
        then dim_market_segment = 'WHOLESALE'

        else

            if max(order_line_item.bandwidth) <= 10GBPS

            then dim_market_segment = 'SMALL_MEDIUM_BUSINESS'

            else dim_market_segment = 'LARGE_BUSINESS'

        else dim_market_segment = 'CONSUMER_MARKET'
```

FIGURE 7.2 Sample EDW requirements expressed at three levels.

Most people in the data warehousing/business intelligence (DW/BI) industry have at least one horror story about projects whose leaders invested too little in defining their requirements before starting development. Common symptoms of this mistake are as follows:

- Overlooking crucial software capabilities that the business absolutely needed in the application
- Modeling the data warehouse to support one analysis to the exclusion of other analytics that turned out to be far more important
- Overlooking a data source essential for the requested business analysis
- Misstated business rules that necessitated endless repair cycles after the application was placed into production
- Subject matter experts insisting on so many new features that the entire effort ended up costing far more than the benefits realized would merit

Agile EDW teams need a disciplined approach to requirements that lets them detect where detail is needed and allows them to use fast, high-level requirements where it is not.

Developers Often Neglect Requirements Work

Given the previously mentioned well-known risks, why do teams so frequently skimp on requirements? Truth be told, information technology (IT) people generally consider requirements gathering and analysis to be boring work, especially compared to the fun of programming new system features. Uncovering and articulating the needed application functionality can be tedious and difficult work, demanding that developers simultaneously consider business processes and system design from multiple directions. Moreover, once requirements have been documented, they need to be validated. Validating requirements involves either regenerating the requirements from separate inputs or asking a whole new group to confirm that every requested capability is in fact needed. To many systems developers, validating requirements is like spending weeks re-plowing the same field—an experience they would rather do without.

To make matters worse, all the previously mentioned effort must take place in a setting of impatience. The sponsors and end users urgently *need* the business intelligence solution they requested. Usually, the company is hemorrhaging money on an expense they cannot understand, or a crucial business opportunity is dying on the vine. Everyone from vice presidents to financial analysts wants the data integration programming to get started *now* so that new information and analytics will soon appear on their BI dashboards. EDW teams rarely feel that they have the time to derive a complete and correct list of needed capabilities. Sponsor urgency can weigh particularly heavily on agile teams, whose entire self-definition hinges on being responsive to customer needs. Moreover, agile teams have an embedded business partner who directs their efforts as product owner. This product owner often embodies the business's desire to get new capabilities programmed in a hurry.

Motivating Teams to Take Requirements Seriously

Situational pressure and dedication to speed can tempt many agile teams into severely forego even rudimentary efforts at requirements management. Thus, agile project leaders would be wise to begin every project by presenting to their teammates a convincing case for carefully planning the requirements effort and then investing the time required to achieve those objectives. After describing why requirements management will help, they then provide some recommended techniques for keeping the requirements gathering process as lightweight as possible. These techniques are discussed later, but first the case for good requirements management practices is outlined. If avoiding the horror stories mentioned previously is not enough, project leaders can employ three further notions to scare their teammates into investing the needed effort into defining requirements: the Boehm multiplier, the blivit factor, and the curse of working nights and weekends.

The Boehm Multiplier

To achieve world-class performance from their teams, project leaders need to relentlessly inspire their developers to go beyond being just programmers to become software engineers. Chapter 6 introduced Barry Boehm's research showing that teams can correct errors in requirements with one-hundredth as much effort as would be entailed in fixing errors once the system has been programmed. EDW team leaders should use Boehm's findings to inspire their agile teams to critically assess the requirements provided by the project's product owner. Every teammate—from a senior business analyst to a beginner extract, transform, and load (ETL) programmer—should be actively searching for gaps and misunderstandings each time the product owner presents items from the project backlog. Similarly, every user story should be scrutinized until the team is sure that each one is accurate and coherent with the other stories comprising the iteration, the subrelease, and the project. Agile teams discuss data transformation business rules extensively with their product owners, including sessions such as story conferences, data-modeling efforts, and daily conversations regarding desired outcomes. Certainly it is easier for teammates who are not central to the conversation to fall into a passive mode of simply following rather than contributing to the conversation, but unfortunately, Boehm's hundred-to-one penalty awaits a team that lets its members idly coast through any discussion of requirements.

Examples of such passive listening can be seen in almost any project meeting that involves three or more teammates. For example, while starting an EDW architectural review for a large bank, I was asked to sit in on a modeling session for one of the component projects. That day, the team spent more than 4 hours deciding what would be the primary keys for the major model entities. The data modeler and the product owner did the majority of the talking, while the other half-dozen teammates seemed to be there only to stay abreast of the modeling decisions. Speaking with the data modeler later, I found out that national and regional identifiers in the primary keys had not been included in the primary keys of the model, despite the fact that the project sponsors had stated many times their desire to someday implement the regional EDW at corporate headquarters. The product owner had overlooked this requirement because she viewed her constituents as only the local financial directors with whom she worked every day. The data modeler had overlooked the requirement because he was new to the project. Unfortunately, the other six developers in the room overlooked this requirement because they were listening passively to the product owner rather than mentally testing each statement against the project's big picture. How much more expensive would it have been to let that oversight persist and then correct it later by reprogramming the application once it had been implemented at headquarters? Given Boehm's multiplier, the cost would probably be 100 times larger.

The Blivit Factor

Blivit is a World War II term for cramming 10 pounds of manure into a 5-pound sack. As Kent Beck pointed out in *Extreme Programming Explained*, the entire endeavor of software development is imbued with *self-similarity*: Complexity observed at one level of consideration will be matched by an equal degree of complexity when the analysis zooms in to look at the situation more closely. Teams that only scratch the surface when discussing requirements with their product owners risk overlooking layer after layer of details, any one of which could be the origin of a crucial mistake. Teams that do not even glance at the full depth of requirements before they estimate a project's development effort will commit to far more work than they realize, condemning themselves to trying to force 10 pounds of features into a 5-pound project budget. Starving requirements management of the time needed to build a realistic view of the requested application will convert the project into the proverbial blivit, when deliveries and expenses do not match expectations, to the chagrin of everyone involved.

The Curse of Working Nights and Weekends

When a project team fails to invest sufficiently in requirements discovery and then slams into the Boehm multiplier and the blivit factor, who pays the price? First and foremost, it will be the developers on the team. Unfortunately, the unrealistic nature of their commitment will become apparent only gradually. The first few oversights and misunderstandings will be thought of as exceptions, not the start of a pattern. The team will believe that it can address them by working extra hard for a day or two to pull the project back on track. However, the unpleasant discoveries mount, the Boehm multiplier and blivit factor start to take over. The extra work required to honor the team's commitments will grow way past a day or two into a steady diet of working late nights and weekends. By skimping on requirements management, the developers are tacitly choosing to forfeit their private lives later in the project.

The combined effect of the Boehm multiplier, the blivit factor, and the curse of working through weekends should motivate all the members of the agile EDW team to participate in identifying, testing, and polishing the project requirements. Because everyone on the team has an interest in defining the delivery goals, EDW project leaders can let the work of requirements management become a team responsibility. Chapter 5 slated the project architect as the agile EDW teammate who should "drive requirements." Drive does not mean "do," but instead indicates this person's role is to ensure the team takes a methodical approach to requirements so that the results will be complete and correct. Accordingly, the business analysts on the team may perform much of the requirements work, given their training in diagramming and analyzing business processes. The systems analysts and data modelers should also be highly involved in translating business requirements into technical requirements. Everyone on the team can catch an oversight, and any particular person—no matter his or her role—may prove to be particularly good at thinking through requirements.

Given that the entire team will fail if even a few crucial requirements are overlooked, agile EDW team leaders should encourage wide participation in requirements management and support those who demonstrate initiative in this area. For this reason, I frequently refer to requirements as a team function in the following discussion, unless a particular step clearly falls within the responsibilities of a specific role.

EASY TO OVERINVEST IN REQUIREMENTS MANAGEMENT

The adverse effects of the Boehm multiplier and the blivit factor can be so alarming that they scare an agile development team back into a waterfall approach to processing project requirements. Team leaders need to guard against this overreaction and steer their developers instead toward a middle path that tempers agile's urgency to start coding with the right amount of old-school techniques for defining projects. To this end, we will now take a quick look at traditional requirements management so that the EDW team leaders will both be familiar with the disciplined techniques that it offers and understand how time-consuming it can be if employed unreservedly.

"Requirements Management" Formally Defined

On traditional projects for large organizations, requirements are usually managed by the *business analyst* (BA) role. The work of a business analyst has been well defined by the International Institute of Business Analysts (IIBA), which provides instruction and certification testing on the skills needed. The authors of the IIBA's *Business Analyst Body of Knowledge* define "requirements management" as a discipline with three major goals [Larson & Larson 2013]:

1. Planning the process for gathering, monitoring, and validating an application's requirements
2. Following that process in order to author a complete and correct set of requirements
3. Maintaining the accuracy of those requirements by properly processing requested changes

   When these steps are translated into practice, requirements management involves three activities that often overlap:

1. Requirements discovery: A divergent process during which the project leaders cast a wide net to ascertain the full extent of business needs relevant to the proposed project
2. Requirement analysis: A convergent process in which the project leaders strive to assemble those discoveries into a single, coherent and complete narrative of what the application should be when it finally arrives
3. Requirements change management: A disciplined pattern for vetting and accepting new or modified ideas that impact the nature of the application so that changing notions of intent and desired capabilities do not impede or undermine the delivery team once development is underway

Typically, the work in these phases is shared between a project architect and business analysts as they work with a wide range of business stakeholders.

The agile EDW approach to requirements attends to all three of these components. Teams *discover* requirements by taking direction from the team's product owner while also interviewing the project's stakeholders. They *analyze* those requirements by intersecting these independently derived notions of the intent and desired characteristics for the requested BI application. Finally, they *manage* requirements by first assembling a concise project backlog and then evolving it through discussion with stakeholders as the project progresses. They also negotiate a change control process with their oversight groups such as the project management office, arriving at a governance pattern that empowers the development team to independently attend to the detailed business and technical requirements of the application.

Traditional Projects Employ a Big Spec Up Front

When companies pursue applications as complex and extensive as an enterprise data warehouse, the traditional approach results in a *requirements specification document* (RSD). The RSD for an EDW project is typically a massive binder of prose and diagrams, often more than 1000 pages long. Figure 7.3 shows a summary of the steps needed to generate such a specification:

1. The company assigns a requirements team.
2. The requirements team pursues *requirements discovery*, in which the team reaches out to the project's likely stakeholders and requests input on the desired features, functions, capabilities, and characteristics for the proposed application.

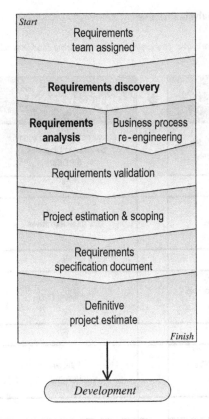

FIGURE 7.3   Waterfall-style requirements management.

3. The team invests in requirements *analysis*, during which it authors many types of requirement artifacts in order to extend, deepen, and validate its understanding of the company's needs for the new system.

4. Optionally, the team undertakes a *business process reengineering* (BPR) effort, during which the team redesigns some of the company's major work flows in order to better take advantage of the new application.

5. When the analysis and process reengineering efforts are complete, the team *validates* with stakeholders the resulting requirements, usually through some extensive presentations and feedback gathering.

6. With a validated set of requirements in hand, the team prepares a *budgeting estimate* that forecasts the level of effort needed to satisfy the requirements. Project sponsors use this estimate to set the application's *scope*, matching the project's objectives to the funding available.

7. With this subset of requirements approved for development, the team can author the project's formal *requirements specification document* (RSD). This RSD is placed under change control so that any modification to it must be first presented to and approved by the project governance committee.

8. Using the RSD, the team can update its level-of-effort estimate and provide the sponsors with a (supposedly) definitive estimate of the cost and duration of the project's development work.

These eight steps all involve considerable amounts of time and labor. Some of them, such as preparing the estimates, may take only a few weeks to complete, but most of the others, especially requirements analysis and business process engineering, can span several months for EDW projects of even moderate complexity. If these eight steps progress smoothly and average only 6 weeks each, for example, then the overall requirements management process depicted in Figure 7.3 will easily consume an entire year. Add another year or more of development on top of that delay, and many of the business opportunities that an EDW is designed to exploit will have disappeared before a project's first BI dashboard goes online. Agile methods aim to constantly deliver value to the customer and to respond quickly to changes in the business. Getting mired in a yearlong project definition process before a single module is programmed will clearly undermine this goal. To successfully streamline the requirements process, however, one must first understand the underlying complexity of requirements that drives the traditional approach to such extremes. When we craft an agile approach to requirements, it will have to somehow manage the full spectrum, from the simple to the devilishly complex.

TABLE 7.1 Traditional Requirements Analysis Process

Artifacts requiring extensive effort to author and maintain are in bold. Note process requires completing 27 artifacts before application design and development can begin. Adapted from [Larson & Larson 2013]

Abstraction Level: Disciplines	Discovery	High-Level Analysis	Detailed Analysis
Business Process Modeling	Value Chains, Context Models, Cross-Functional Models	Functional Decomp. Diagram, **Swim Lane Diagrams, SIPOCs***	**Detailed Process Maps**
Use Case Modeling	Use Case Diagrams	**Use Case Narratives**	**Activity Diagrams, Sequence Diagrams**
Data Modeling	Entity-Only Entity Relationship Diagram (ERD)	Attributed ERD	**Normalized ERD**
User Interface Modeling	High Level Write-Ups, Wire Frame Depictions	High-Level Prototype	**Detailed Prototype**
Application Definition Management	Solution Scope, Req. Mgt. Plan, Business Rules Outlines, Entity-Only Traceability Matrix	**Business Rules Narratives, High-Level Traceability Matrix**	**Requirements Specification Document, Detailed Business Rules Algorithms, Detailed Traceability Matrix**

* SIPOC: Tables of suppliers, inputs, process, outputs, and customers listings for each element on the functional decomposition diagram.

Requirements are Inherently Diverse

Before development teams can manage requirements, they must first discover and analyze them—two tasks that demand considerable effort because of the many types of requirements that exist and the extensive set of artifacts that business analysts have created to capture them. Table 7.1 summarizes the traditional requirements management approach and its artifacts and shows both discovery and two rounds of requirements analysis. To complete these three major phases adequately, the team must start at a high level and drill into considerable detail, as indicated by the rows in the diagram. Each row represents one or more BA activities that revisit the current set of requirements at a still finer level of detail.

The number of steps and artifacts involved in this traditional approach is impressive. Figure 7.4 lists more than two dozen types of artifacts that the authors of the IIBA's certification study guide believe would be a reasonable result from pursuing the process laid out in Table 7.1 [Larson & Larson 2013].

The need for such a large number and diversity of requirements artifacts is appropriate not only because of the multipass process that the traditional approach involves but also because of the wide range of requirement types implicit in any project as extensive as an EDW. Table 7.2 attempts to list all the requirements types that traditional development teams should consider documenting. This list was compiled from several international standards, such as FURPS and ISO. Also included are several requirements types listed by the Rational Unified Process (RUP), the pre-agile, iterative development method that many traditional shops still employ, at least to define their projects.

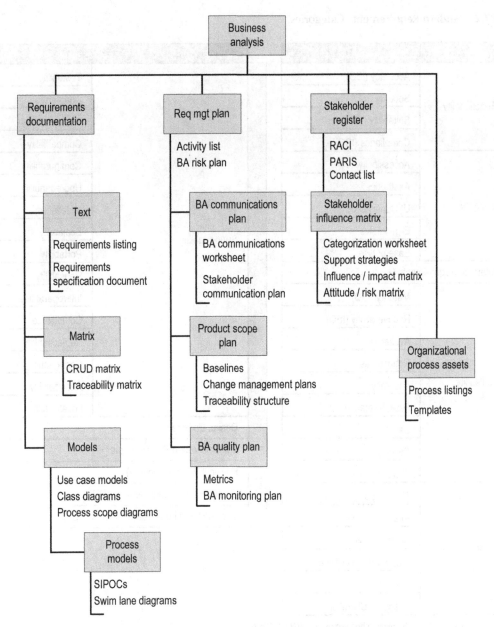

FIGURE 7.4   Typical requirements work breakdown for a traditional project. *(Adapted from Larson & Larson 2013.)*

The IIBA does encourage requirements team to selectively choose from these lists rather than aiming to produce all types of artifacts to cover all requirements types. However, traditional teams tend to invest in documenting a majority of items suggested on these lists because their project method allows them only one opportunity to capture requirements before programming begins. Because they only have one chance to define the project, team leaders often overinvest in requirements gathering so that they do not overlook anything important. Unfortunately, no matter how much effort a team invests, delivering a perfect set of requirements before programming begins is impossible for multiple reasons:

- Application requirements are extremely fractal, with each one decomposing into many others that all decompose ever further.
- Resolving conflicts between requirements becomes considerably more difficult as the level of detail increases, often requiring committee meetings and delays while stakeholders research their needs.

TABLE 7.2 Standard Requirements Categories

Functional / Non-Functional	Category	Subcategory		Category	Subcategory
Functional	Functionality	Accuracy (ISO)		Supportability	Testability
		Security (ISO)			Adaptability
		Suitability (ISO)			Maintainability
		Compliance (ISO)			Compatibility
	Usability	Accessibility			Configurability
		Aesthetics			Upgradeability
		UI Consistency			Installability
		Ergonomics			Scalability
		Ease of Use			Portability
	Interface Requirements (+)				Reusability
Non-Functional	Reliability	Maturity (ISO)			Interoperability
		Recoverability (ISO)			Compliance
		Availability			Replaceability
		Robustness			Changeability
		Accuracy			Analyzability
		Fault Tolerance			Localizability
		Safety		Design Constraints (+)	
		Security		Implementation Requirements (+)	
		Correctness		Physical Requirements (+)	
	Performance	Throughput		Documentation Requirements (RUP)	
		Response Time		Licensing and Legal Requirements (RUP)	
		Recovery Time			
		Stop/Start Cycle Time			
		Capacity			
		Resource Utilization			

All standards from FURPS unless otherwise marked [Grady 1992].

(+) Added later to FURPS, making it FURPS+

(ISO): Borrowed from [ISO 2011]

(RUP) Borrowed from Rational Unified Process. See [Zielczynski 2008] for details on elements listed.

Designations between functional and non-functional are generalizations—exceptional circumstances will occur

- Documenting complex, detailed requirements involves many lengthy artifacts that consume too much time to prepare and then later modify.

Agile methods offer a better approach—one in which teams postpone detailed requirements analysis until they begin programming each module, so that time is not wasted on documenting and accommodating requirements for portions of a system that never get built.

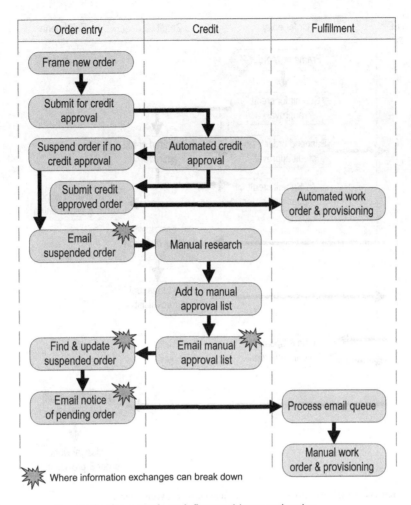

FIGURE 7.5 As-is business process diagram showing a sample work flow requiring re-engineering.

Business Process Reengineering Can Add to the Complexity

Figure 7.3 listed BPR as an optional step. This discipline can provide a valuable set of requirements, but EDW team leaders should employ this discipline judiciously because when overapplied, it can stall a project for months at a time.

Unconstrained BPR absorbs excessive team resources because it demands that the requirements team prepare both as-is and to-be diagrams of the business processes that the new application will impact. Figures 7.5 and 7.6 are simplified versions of BPR diagrams that many traditional business analysts working on enterprise data warehousing projects typically prepare. The first diagram is the dysfunctional as-is situation that the company would like to address. The second diagram shows the improved overall process that EDW will enable. The vertical swim lanes on both diagrams represent the business systems that a project will impact. The rounded boxes represent major functions within those business systems, and the arrows represent information flows. The small explosion symbols represent areas where the information flows within the organization's current business process break down, developing gaps or inaccuracies that undermine effective business performance.

These diagrams and the prose that must accompany them consume an inordinate amount of time to prepare for several reasons:

- Every flow and alternative flow in the existing business process must be considered for diagramming and modification, leading to a large number of processes to document.
- Both the current and the future business processes lie far outside IT's domain knowledge so that the business staff must spend a significant amount of time up front familiarizing IT with the basic operations of the company.
- The existing business processes are rarely documented thoroughly, leaving most of the important details existent only in the minds of the business staff.

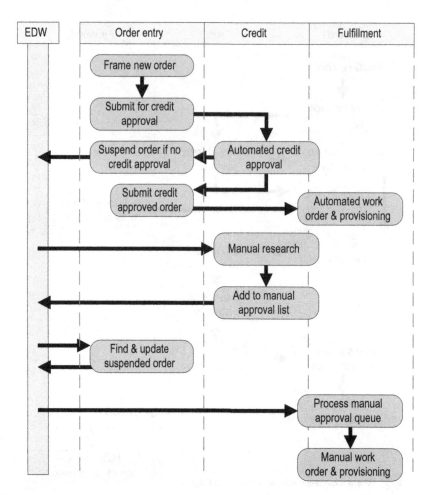

FIGURE 7.6   To-be business process re-engineered to use EDW to communicate between agents.

- The benefits of the new application are far off, so the business subject matter experts rarely have the motivation to invest the necessary time envisioning and discussing how to change the way they currently work.

More importantly, companies easily overstate how much data warehousing they will be able to achieve with a given project. When coupled with the expensive nature of BPR practices, this overstatement leads development teams into wasting far too much of their project budgets on process reengineering efforts that never get fully implemented.

In those specific functional areas where the value of a DW/BI hinges on a properly reengineered business process, BPR is an excellent choice of techniques. Agile teams should definitely retain this technique in their toolkits, but they should deploy it only when the warehouse features requiring BPR work approach the top of their project backlogs. When they do employ BPR, EDW team leaders should assiduously keep the scope of that effort well contained so that the team only spends time and money on reengineering plans that will actually be used.

BPR can also be insidious because of the mindset it encourages. During my decades on BI projects, I have noticed that business analysts who are trained in BPR seem to believe that every business process that the warehouse touches should be carefully diagrammed. If project leaders let such an assumption have too much influence, their team will spend far too much time on drawing swim lanes and vetting them with impatient business experts instead of spending that time on delivering new analytic capabilities.

REASONS NOT TO OVERINVEST IN REQUIREMENT WORK

With the background on traditional requirements management offered above, project leaders can easily understand that they must resist any temptation to complete a full requirements documentation effort before beginning programming, else they will never deliver new features in a business-reasonable time frame. Unfortunately, many parties involved in DW/BI projects—such as program and project managers—believe that an application should be defined in detail so that the programming effort can be finely controlled. The flaws in such a traditional approach are multifaceted. First, it overinvests in precision at the expense of accuracy. Statistically, it fails more than it succeeds, squandering valuable business opportunities. Moreover, business partners truly detest having to spell out exactly what they want before receiving any new capabilities, and therefore they overtly or passively refuse to support such an approach sufficiently. Because EDW team leaders may have to convince project management that these flaws exist, we will discuss each before considering the agile alternative.

Precision at the Expense of Accuracy

When people insist that a detailed requirements specification will ensure project success, they are emphasizing precision over accuracy. Unfortunately, precision prevents accuracy during protracted development efforts, and without accuracy, precision is another form of wasted effort.

We can take carpentry as a metaphor and consider accuracy and precision when it comes to cutting a board to span an opening in the frame of a house, for example. *Accuracy* is how well the carpenter identifies the necessary length of the board. Did he choose to cut the board to fit inside the vertical framing studs when a better design would have been to cut the board so that it sits on top of them? The notion of *precision* pertains to how well the carpenter marked the board once the proper length was determined so that he could put the saw blade exactly where it was needed. As shown in Figure 7.7, a dull pencil will mark a board with a wide smudge, leaving the precise point at which to cut unclear. The small bell curve suggests the variance that would occur if multiple cuts were attempted based on the same pencil mark. Note that if the carpenter had a means of adjusting the board in small ways after the cut, the accuracy of the specified length would matter far more than the precision of the cut.

In the world of EDW requirements, accuracy becomes a matter of knowing what needs to be built, whereas precision involves documenting those features in fine detail. When starting a project, or even managing work in midproject, teams receive tremendous benefit from an accurate list of features. Describing each feature with high precision will only overwhelm the team members with details to digest, leading them to lose sight of the spirit of the application and undermining the accuracy of their efforts. Perhaps because IT people work with computers, they tend to emphasize precision over accuracy in their requirements management efforts. Table 7.3 shows how typical EDW requirement questions change depending on whether an IT team emphasizes accuracy or precision. Close study of the two columns reveals that the questions emphasizing accuracy serve to set application scope—that is, boundaries around what the application will do and whom it will serve. Precision-oriented questions focus far more on the details that the developers will need when it comes time to code each module of the application. For this reason, emphasizing accuracy tends to be a breadth-first approach, one that provides a solid whole-project notion of a team's goal without diving into a detailed description of application features.

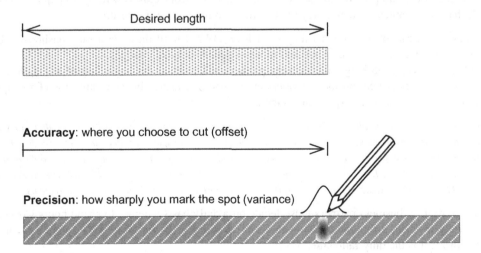

FIGURE 7.7   Accuracy vs. precision.

TABLE 7.3 Comparison of Accuracy and Precision for an Agile Enterprise Data Warehousing Project

Accuracy *Achieving the Right Objectives* *(Needed up-front to define the application)*	Precision *Achieving them in the Right Way* *(Can wait until each area of the warehouse enters programming)*
How can DWBI improve this company's competitiveness?	What drill-down path will Role "R" want to use with Fact Table "F"?
What business groups and business process need support?	What is the complete list of business rules that the application must implement?
What information do major players need to improve these processes?	What should be the Type 2 triggers for Dimension "D"?
What source systems do we need to integrate?	What is the complete list of data elements in those sources?
What are the key integration points?	What are the formats for each version of a given natural key?
How will end users know they can trust the BI information?	What are the edge cases for a particular business rule?
What features should go with each subreleases?	Where in the data model will the split between subreleases occur?

Agile teams reverse the normal tendency of an IT development team—they focus on accuracy rather than precision during requirements discovery. As they define a project, they note where precision is required and then research those details one module at a time, and only for those modules that have arrived at the top of the backlog for development. By keeping their requirements work focused on both the high and the medium level, agile teams arrive at complete and correct project definitions far more quickly than teams using traditional approaches, which tend to get mired in premature precision.

Business Partners are Adverse to Traditional Requirements Gathering Efforts

Even if the IT members of an EDW engagement could somehow make a traditional requirements effort succeed, their business partners would prove to be uncooperative participants. Veteran EDW developers have a very common set of complaints about the end-user communities with regard to requirements:

- At the start of a project, they ask for far more than they are willing to pay for.
- They will not take the time to learn the many ways that DW/BI can help the business.
- They will not make the effort to articulate how their business processes need to be improved.
- They will not take the time to explain those business processes so that IT can suggest improvements.
- The requirements that they do provide are vague and they will not work closely with IT to explore the details.
- Even when IT has deliverables for them, they are unwilling to review them carefully.

As a result, business users cannot tell IT what they want from DW/BI until they see it on a dashboard. Unfortunately, by then, the project will have run out of the time and money needed to make changes.

These age-old challenges of working with business partners still exist at the beginning of any agile EDW program. When I ask my customers about why business partners are so unenthusiastic about defining for IT the application they have requested, many of them offer an explanation such as the following:

> *Apathetic business partners were made, not born. We in the business have worked with IT for more than 30 years now. IT always wants us to spend months explaining everything we want out of a system. But, decade after decade, IT has failed to deliver even half of what we ask for. In fact, when it comes to BI projects in particular, Gartner says 70–80% of those projects fail [Kernochan 2011], and I feel like I've been on the receiving end of every one of them. My department decided long ago that working with IT is largely a waste of time, especially when the work involves big binders of requirements.*

At the start of a new project, business partners must decide on a daily basis whether to spend hours working with the IT team (which will only result in disappointment) or to focus on running the business. When they pass on collaborating wholeheartedly with IT, it is the only rational choice.

TABLE 7.4 Traditional Approaches to Requirements Performed Poorly in the Era Before Agile

| # | Factor Undermining Performance | Responses by Category of Projects | | | |
| | | Cancelled | | Challenged | |
		Rank	%	Rank	%
A	Incomplete requirements	1	13.1%	2	12.3%
B	Lack of user input	2	12.4%	1	12.8%
C	Unrealistic expectations	4	9.9%	7	5.9%
D	Changing requirements	6	8.7%	3	11.8%
E	Didn't need app any longer	8	7.5%		
F	Unrealistic time frames			9	4.3%

In order to perform noticeably better than waterfall methods, agile EDW project leaders need to offer their business partners a new approach to managing requirements—one that blends specification work with the delivery of new, exciting business intelligence capabilities. With an agile approach, every effort invested in defining an application is soon rewarded with a tangible benefit for the business. Given this reward structure, the business staff soon finds the motivation it needs to participate in the project more fully.

Traditional Requirements Management Fails More than it Succeeds

The many disadvantages to traditional requirements management listed previously result in one decisive fact that folks arguing for a complete and perfect specification up front cannot overcome: The traditional approach to requirements fails more often than it succeeds. In the seminal *Chaos* reports, published before agile methods became available, the Standish group documented that even the smallest projects, which had the best success rates, failed more than 45% of the time. As projects grew in size toward the $10 million mark, the failure rate quickly increased to 100% [Standish Group 1995, 1999]. In these studies, poor performance on requirements constituted 6 of the top 10 reasons that projects became seriously challenged or were canceled during the era of waterfall project management, as shown in Table 7.4.

Whereas this table can be read as a listing of all the ways that IT typically errs while building software, I believe it reflects all of the impediments that even the most disciplined IT developers will encounter in traditionally managed software projects. From that perspective, the factors summarized in the table become warnings to teams that believe they can amass a complete and perfect requirements specification document before development work begins:

- Incomplete requirements: Many forces will prevent you from finishing your work.
- Lack of user input: Even the end users you are serving will not give you the guidance you need.
- Unrealistic expectations: Sinking too much time into a complete spec will distract you from showing your customers how much their limited funding can really accomplish.
- Changing requirements: A perfect specification is impossible because the business will not stand still long enough to be completely described.
- Did not need the application any longer: The time window you have is far too short to consider writing out complete specifications.
- Unrealistic time frames: The feedback cycle between requirements, design, and project estimation is too long for you to keep people's expectations aligned with the true effort needed to build software.

The Greatest Failure is Losing Business Opportunity

The fact that some respondents reported that their projects were canceled because the organization no longer needed the application being built reveals a particularly pernicious disadvantage to the big, up-front requirements definition process. By delaying the flow of usable features, traditional methods force far too much opportunity cost on EDW's customers. Advocates of the complete and perfect requirements specification document believe that the big spec up-front

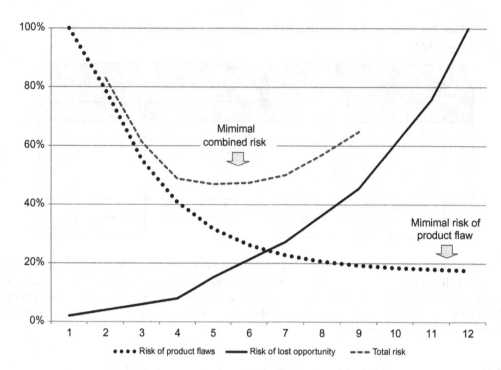

FIGURE 7.8 Standard risk analysis.

approach protects the company from risk, but they are actually amplifying risk dramatically. As depicted in Figure 7.8, which shows the probability of adverse events, the risk of product flaws and opportunity costs have opposite dynamics. IT can drive down the risk of product flaws (the dotted line descending from the upper left) using exhaustive requirements management practices, but as discussed previously, that process takes time and can only reduce the risk by so much. More importantly, as IT spends the better part of the year preparing a full requirements specification, the risk that the business opportunity driving the project will slip away increases steadily. In this example, by the end of the first year, the application is no longer needed because no competitive advantage is left for the company to capture.

The situation is even more dire when this graph is updated to show the dollar value of these two risks. I once had to convince a data modeler that our project team should use two distinct releases when updating the revenue subject area of an EDW for a telecommunications company. I wanted to start delivering new BI applications as soon as we had the requirements for only the landline portion of the business and then return later to update the subject area for the company's strategic products such as cloud backup and satellite TV services. My point was that the company, which did not offer wireless phone service, was losing 10% of its copper landline business *every quarter* as subscribers acquired cell phones and canceled their traditional phone service. The data modeler's concern was that starting work on the warehouse when we only had one portion of the requirements could force us to reengineer a large portion of our data model when we uncovered the remaining requirements. He wanted to take a full year to discover the company's complete set of requirements for the revenue analysis.

True, we had estimated that our total project would exceed $5 million, so starting development when we had only a portion of the requirements could conceivably put all of that investment at risk. However, the company executives desperately needed to determine if their new strategy of bundling landline service with new products such as high-speed Internet was slowing the defection rate of landline customers. Figure 7.9 shows that the value of the compounding loss of revenue would reach $1.8 billion within a year's time. The value of the business opportunity that sponsors wanted the EDW to help capture can be seen clearly in the diagram, whereas the $5 million potential cost of reengineering our work for the second release visually departs from zero. If we had insisted on spending a full year gathering requirements for the project before starting development, our team would have forced this enormous opportunity cost upon the company, only to avoid the comparatively tiny risk of product flaws.

In choosing how extensively to invest in defining project requirements, then, the rational approach is to consider the total of the risk confronted by the company sponsoring the warehouse. Figure 7.8 includes a third line that shows the sum of the two risks as they change over time. The lowest point on that combined curve falls somewhere near the 5-month mark, but this point is found on the graph that charts only the probability of events, not their value.

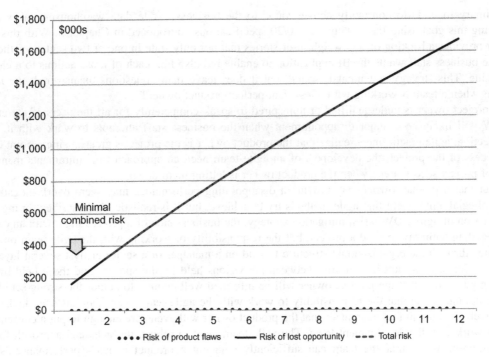

FIGURE 7.9 Standard analysis adjusted for dollar value of each type of risk.

That intersection moves completely to the left in Figure 7.9, when the dollar value of the curves is included. The EDW team clearly needs to find an approach to requirements that can accurately express the overall nature of its customer's BI needs in significantly less than half a year, and it needs to leave fussing over precise requirements until later. Agile EDW's two-perspective requirements management technique achieves exactly that goal.

AGILE'S APPROACH CENTERS ON BALANCE

The previous discussion considered the perils of investing both too little and too much into managing requirements. Fortunately, agile EDW combines traditional and iterative techniques into an effective requirements management approach that lies somewhere between those two extremes. In fact, agile EDW offers not one, but two processes for defining a project's requirements. Teams can utilize either one or both and can adapt each of them so that they achieve the blend of accuracy and precision that a given project context demands.

The first approach, which is presented in Chapter 9, is a distillation of the requirements management techniques used by generic agile development teams with some slight modifications so that it can be easily applied to the needs of data warehousing projects. The second method is a streamlined version of the requirements approach found in the Rational Unified process, the granddaddy of today's agile delivery methods. Those techniques are presented in Chapter 10. Whereas an agile EDW team can draw upon either approach, utilizing both will provide the advantage of having two separate perspectives on a given data management challenge. With two perspectives, the developers achieve "stereoscopic vision," with the combined vantage points allowing them to easily test the validity and worth of each requirement, thus enabling the team to find gaps in the overall project definition. Such validation greatly improves the accuracy of the project requirements, thus doubly assuring the program sponsors that the development team will succeed.

Agile Objectives for Requirements Management

Before diving into the details of our first requirements management approach, we should be clear on the goals we are trying to achieve. Put succinctly, agile requirements management is designed to ensure that the project's product owner performs his or her job well.

Agile's primary focus is to constantly deliver value to the business. Agile data warehousing takes a long stride toward achieving this goal using the strategy of "80/20 specifications" introduced in Chapter 5. With this strategy, the product owner provides a backlog of lightweight user stories that not only state in one or two sentences the information actions that the business staff wants the BI application to enable but also link each of those actions to a clear statement of business value. This strategy statement is sound, but it does leave many questions unanswered, the largest being, "What happens when a team is working with a less-than-perfect product owner?"

When the project owner is underqualified or uninspired to speak competently for all the users of the enterprise, the resulting EDW will likely be a major disappointment when the business staff attempts to work with it. With only a moment's reflection, agile practitioners realize that the product owner is the project's greatest single point of failure. To ensure the success of the project, the developers of an agile team need an approach to requirements management that assures them of project success even when the product owner is letting them down.

Pointing out that a product owner may provide a disappointing performance may seem overly negative given the whole-team, collegial atmosphere that agile methods try to achieve, but it is realistic. As described during the previous chapter's discussion of agile EDW's risk mitigation strategy, the business side of a project starts with an executive who has enough spending authority to fund a project, but the responsibility of working with the agile team on a daily basis quickly descends through the organizational structure to land on a manager or a senior analyst several layers below the sponsor's office. Serious disconnects can arise between the visions held by the sponsor and those held by the product owner. Nothing guarantees that the product owner will be informed well enough to author the strong set of user stories the team is expecting. Given that the responsibility to work with the agile team every day has been kicked downstairs two or three levels, nothing in fact guarantees that the product owner will even care enough to put a conscientious effort into his or her work with the development team. The agile team needs a robust, multichannel approach for identifying and vetting requirements so that the team can sufficiently augment a product owner's performance, should a gap appear.

The following qualities of a robust agile approach to requirements management were mentioned previously:

- It will heavily employ 80/20 specifications.
- It will emphasize accuracy, investing in precision only as necessary.
- It will abet an incremental delivery strategy.

To guard against or repair a serious disconnect between a program sponsor and a product owner, however, the requirements management approach will have to demonstrate several other properties as well.

Provide Enough Context to Make User Stories Easy to Author

Product owners frequently arrive without the experience or orientation needed to author user stories. In this case, the requirements management process must "prime the pump" and give the product owner the context he or she needs to begin authoring a complete and correct stream of user stories.

Engage the Close Stakeholders

The requirements management process must be engaging for not only the assigned product owner but also the subject matter experts whom the product owner will need to involve if the requirements are going to be correct. Maintaining their engagement will require keeping the process as light and enjoyable as possible so that the business partners do not start dreading their collaboration with the development team. The process should also clear the business value of the application and its likely subrelease dates, so that business users can build reasonable expectations about how the effort will soon improve their work lives.

Must Address All Types of Requirements

Data integration and business intelligence applications involve not just end-user requirements but also notions such as enterprise data quality, post-warehouse data processing, and nonfunctional requirements such as performance and security. The requirements management process needs to be rich enough to guide IT in identifying even those system aspects that the product owner cannot deeply appreciate.

Empower IT to Judge Requirements Completeness and Accuracy

Teams will never be entirely sure that the product owner has provided a reasonably complete and accurate set of requirements if they cannot independently test that collection. The requirements management process therefore needs to include a channel of insight into business needs that is independent of the product owner. Once armed with two depictions into the business's needs, the IT members of the team will be able to judge if the two visions cohere well enough to be reasonably assured that all major requirements have been detected.

Provide a Whole Project Sketch to Avoid the Big Mistakes

The requirements management process must attend to the needs of not only those who author requirements (the product owners and subject matter experts) but also those who must lead the developers during the construction of the application. Key roles such as data modeler, process architect, and systems tester need to possess enough background that they will be able to author an 80% complete outline of the project for the programmers, as well as identify the high-risk areas that need to be tackled early in the project.

Knowing when a Backlog is "Good Enough"

For an agile team, the primary result of effective requirements management is a good, actionable backlog. When a project's initial backlog reaches "good enough" status, project leaders can turn their attention to getting programming underway. Judging whether an EDW project's backlog is good enough will require some careful considerations, however, for three important reasons:

1. It will consist of a blend of different story types.
2. Readiness must be judged from several directions.
3. The clarity of stories will decrease as one travels down the list after it has been prioritized.

To address Item 1, story types, readers should keep in mind that an enterprise data warehousing project frequently involves both data integration and business intelligence features in an integrated set of back-end and front-end components. As discussed in the introductory chapters, the back-end, data integration work in particular needs to be decomposed one level farther than the front-end, business intelligence work. Thus, a typical EDW backlog will be a mix of user stories for the business intelligence components and *developer stories* for data integration, although some BI modules can involve business rules complex enough to also require developer stories.

Regarding the second element, readiness, one must apply several tests to the stories that the requirements management process generates in order to judge whether an EDW backlog can enable programming to begin. A "good" DW/BI project backlog is one that demonstrates several important qualities, namely that it

- focuses clearly on business problems that need to be solved someday soon;
- has important people in the organization that want the features it promises;
- offers outlines of the more complex business rules to anchor detail design work later;
- provides several "quick wins" to engender good will from the user community right away;
- makes discernible when in time certain features will be completed, based on the team's current delivery velocity;
- maximizes the application's value to the enterprise should development be halted early;
- offers frequent checkpoints, allowing the business to validate that the remaining items are still necessary; and
- minimizes the project's overall risk.

Item 3 highlights that project leaders must keep in mind that when a backlog becomes good enough to allow programming to start, not all of its stories will be equally "crisp." Stories that will enter development in the next iteration or two may well need a fairly extensive specification, such as physical characteristics of the data tables to be loaded, the logic of the business rules involved, and the idiosyncrasies of the source data from which ETL modules will draw. Stories that will be developed a few iterations from the present may need only enough data modeling work to spot the key integration points that they will support. Stories that will not be developed until several iterations in the future may need only enough detail that the team can estimate story points for the programming effort they will require. The rest of the details can be attended to later as those stories draw closer to actual development. In other words, the farther into the future a story's development will begin, the less precision it needs.

Enable Regular "Current Estimates"

Throughout the years, I have been able to use one criterion to determine whether a backlog is sufficiently complete and detailed—a criterion that rolls together all the considerations listed previously. That litmus test for "good enough" is to determine whether the backlog can support a *current estimate*.

For agile EDW teams, a current estimate for a project requires three elements:

1. A backlog with the stories arranged in priority order
2. Story-point estimates of the labor those stories will consume
3. The team's current delivery velocity in story points

With these elements, the team can then bracket the stories on the backlog using the team's velocity, as depicted in Figure 5.4.

Once the stories on a backlog are bracketed, the project leaders will be able to count the number of iterations needed to finish the work. Multiplying the projected number of iterations by the iteration time box yields the number of weeks of work still needed—that is, the project's remaining duration. Multiplying the number of brackets by the cost to run an iteration reveals the funding required to finish the programming—that is, the remaining development cost.

These two calculations constitute the agile team's *current estimate* of remaining project cost and duration, two numbers that are vitally important to the business sponsors of the EDW project. Naturally, providing a current estimate requires the team to have a whole-project vision of the work ahead. If the team has taken too many shortcuts in defining its backlog, many stories will be difficult or impossible to estimate with confidence. If the backlog is only half-baked, the developers will balk at using it to provide numbers for remaining cost and duration, realizing that they are slipping into a project blivit, as defined previously in this chapter. For that reason, a good agile requirements management approach is one that leads to an accurate backlog (all the stories on it are truly needed) with just enough precision that the team can calculate and provide a current estimate to management. The process of preparing a current estimate is considered in greater detail in Chapter 11.

Keeping the Requirements Management Process Agile

Beyond delivering a usable backlog that supports incremental delivery, the overall process of managing the project's requirements needs to be agile, meaning that it incorporates the values, principles, and practices from the multiple iterative delivery techniques considered in the opening chapters of this book. With their roots in the Toyota production systems and with more than a decade of refinement through usage, these principles and techniques ensure that the team will not make crucial mistakes in the requirements it gathers, nor overly invest in details that will not further the project's chances for success. Table 7.5 displays a selected list of the values and principles that I believe are most pertinent for the process of requirements gathering and analysis. How agile EDW's two-pronged requirements management style that I suggest for agile EDW fulfills these objectives will become clear as each component approach is presented, but for now the table provides the reader with the qualities to look for in the techniques described next.

TWO INTERSECTING REQUIREMENTS MANAGEMENT VALUE CHAINS

Agile enterprise data warehousing offers a system of two distinct approaches to discovering and analyzing requirements. These two approaches intersect so that they each provide a test of the other and assure an EDW development team that the resulting project backlog will be reasonably complete and correct. As depicted in Figure 7.10, the artifacts of each of the approaches can be portrayed as a value chain—that is, an ordered sequence of activities that generate a steadily better understanding and expression of a project's requirements.

The vertical chain in Figure 7.10 represents agile's generic requirements management (GRM) approach. The GRM comprises epic, theme, and user stories—notions that a majority of agile teams working on transaction-oriented projects today depend on and that were discussed extensively in my previous books. It also includes the developer story to support data integration efforts. Teams pursuing predominantly front-end work or a small data mart may find that they can manage their project definitions quite well using GRM alone.

The horizontal chain represents an enterprise-capable requirements management (ERM) approach. This value chain is a streamlined version of the requirements management artifacts available from RUP. As mentioned previously in this book, RUP is a heavy-duty development methodology used by the world's largest systems integrator to build some of the most demanding information systems of our age [Kroll & Krutchen 2003, p. 24]. Impressed by RUP's capability but wary that it would be overkill for many projects, my company has been steadily trimming RUP's collection of artifacts and templates down to the bare essentials needed to get an agile EDW project defined

TABLE 7.5 Agile Objectives for Requirements Management

Agile School
  Concept
    Compliant Agile EDW practice

Lean Principles & Tools
Eliminate waste Employ techniques such as "80/20 specifications" to keep the inventory of requirements artifacts as small (in size and number) as possible, thus minimizing cost to project when requirements change or are dropped from scope.
Set-based development Breadth-first approach defines whole project at high level first, then steadily tightens constraints via requirements and design choices made from multiple directions, minimizing the risk that important concepts will be precluded or overlooked.
Last responsible moment Leaving last 20% of requirements for development time and addressing most of those through eye-to-eye contact with the product owner allows teams to practice just-in-time details, minimizing the number of prior decisions subject to obviation.
Minimize the cost of delay Practices such as project segmentation and story prioritization combine with just-in-time details to allow incremental delivery of high-value features first, thereby maximizing benefits realization.
Agile Manifesto Philosophies & Principles
Business people and developers must work together daily throughout the project Co-location (or at least close collaboration) allows teams to a) work with a minimum of written specifications and b) catch errors as modules are developed, so a complete and perfect requirements specifications are no longer necessary.
Working software over comprehensive documentation Investing only 20% of the traditional prep time up-front allows teams to keep detail specifications to a minimum, so they can invest the remaining 80% into software module development, rather than into polishing the spec.
Simplicity—maximize the amount of work not done Eliminating the need for 80% of detailed requirements documentation for all but the complicated aspects of the system's modules allows teams to get more done far sooner than their traditional, waterfall counterparts.
Welcome changing requirements, even late in development Keeping elaborate specifications to a minimum plus Scrum's frequent planning cycles gives the business a continual opportunity to create, change, and discard requirements with minimal impact on project documentation and project plans.
XP Values & Principles
Redundancy Drawing upon both an approach from standard agile practices (GRM) and RUP (ERM) gives the team more ways to detect requirements, but also allows the requirements generated by each technique to be tested for accuracy and value.
Self-similarity Both approaches utilize a top-down stack of artifacts that increase in detail with each level of requirements decomposition, enabling teams to manage requirements at all degrees of detail with equal effectiveness.
Simplicity Not only does Agile EDW requirements management techniques utilize streamlined templates, but they also defer detail specifications until absolutely needed, maintaining a high degree of overall simplicity in project definitions.
Feedback By relying on the development process to illuminate and prove the remaining 20% of requirements, Agile EDW's requirements management technique minimizes the lag between business expression of need and IT's demonstration of a software solution.
RUP Philosophies
Address risk early in the project Agile EDW's requirements management techniques culminate in a project backlog that is prioritized by considering business value and project risk, minimizing the probability that adverse events can lie undetected in the project's future.

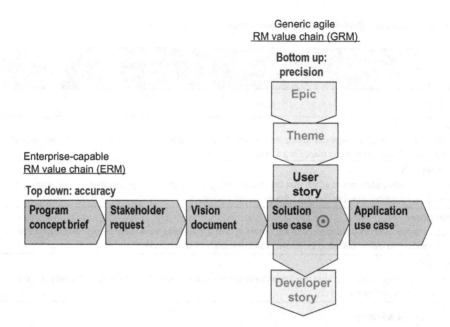

FIGURE 7.10   Agile EDW's requirements management benefits greatly from intersecting value chains.

well enough that a team can begin authoring user stories. The value chain displayed in Figure 7.10 represents the current status of that effort: five templates, with the first four requiring no more than a few pages of prose and a few diagrams each.

The GRM value chain consists of the following elements, sequenced in the order of increasing specificity:

1. Epic: Sponsor-level statements describing the needles on the gauges of the corporate cockpit that the company needs to cause to move up or down
2. Theme: Director-level statements describing the set-based operations that will provide the information needed to make the business decisions that will deflect an epic's cockpit needles in the desired direction
3. User story: Manager- or analyst-level statements describing the data validation actions that someone will need to reference while convincing a director that the information provided by a theme can be trusted
4. Developer story: A statement describing just one of the many data-transformation modules needed before an end user can perform the data validation described by a user story

Many front-end-oriented BI projects can progress well with a value chain consisting mostly of artifacts 1–3 alone. Teams pursuing any significant data integration work, however—even if that work is taking data straight from source systems to star schemas—will find themselves working with many instances of developer story artifacts as well.

The ERM value chain consists of the following five elements, again ordered for increasing specificity:

1. Sponsor's concept briefing: A half- to one-page statement derived from an interview with the project's sponsor(s) that expresses: "Here's how we're going to make money with business intelligence's help."
2. Stakeholder request: a half- to one-page statement derived from an interview with a key stakeholder group that describes: "Here's what's wrong with our current BI solution, and here's how we'd fix it if we were IT."
3. Vision document: A composite document authored by the project architect with only two lists and three diagrams, which states in essence: "Here are the business problems IT has heard from the business, and here's a sketch of the DW/BI application that will solve those operational challenges."
4. Subrelease overview: A mini vision document authored by the project architect after he or she has been able to segment the project into multiple, each expressing: "Here's a partial DW/BI system release that will solve the next, most important subset of business problems for the customer."
5. Module use case: A streamlined use case authored by the team's ETL designer that expresses in essence: "Here's a data transformation module we're going to build as a major component for the current subrelease we're assembling."

Considering the ERM value chain as a whole, we can see that it progressively moves one's thinking from the clouds (sponsor-level business requirements) down into the weeds (programmer-level technical requirements). All but the last artifact of the ERM value chain are short documents so that the team will not find itself investing too much in producing and formatting the actual pages of those documents. The last artifact, the application use case, can turn into an extensive document if necessary, so teams must choose carefully how much effort to invest each time they decide to author one.

Readers should note that I do not advocate completing all five of these artifacts, for all aspects of a system, for every project that a team undertakes. Such an approach would easily take a team back to a big-spec-up-front, waterfall mentality, and it would hardly be agile. Instead, teams should pick and choose from the ERM artifact set and utilize a subset that best addresses their needs. For projects in which the challenge is mostly with business–IT alignment and not with guiding the programmers, EDW team leaders will need only the first three documents to get a project adequately defined. On the other hand, some teams fully understand the context of their projects but have a group of programmers who demand some detail in module design specs before they will start coding. These teams would probably do well with just the last three artifacts because only the details of their projects are demanding careful management. The EDW team leaders may find, in fact, that they need to provide module use cases only for a few of the ETL components that will make up the system, namely those with complex business rules. All told, the previous list of ERM artifacts is a menu of available templates, and teams should pick and choose which of them will assist their efforts and ignore the rest.

However, most teams seem to draw upon the middle template, the vision document. In practice, that particular artifact proves to be the pivotal document that allows business-oriented thinking to transition into IT-actionable plans. For a project requiring high-level definition, the vision document serves as the goal to which the sponsor's briefing and stakeholder requests all point to. For a project employing the detail end of the ERM value chain, the vision document is the whole-project sketch to which the technical members of the agile team need to anchor all of their design decompositions. In both cases, the vision document articulates the full-scope solution concept toward which the project architect will steer the development activities of the team. It articulates the "spirit of the application" and enables the architect to certify that the application about to be developed will solve the project's central business problems.

Salient Differences between GRM and ERM

In order to enable the agile EDW team to test the indications of each value chain against the other, the generic and enterprise requirements management approaches need to be materially different. Some of the differences between them will become clear as readers start to utilize these two value chains on an actual project. To set expectations, the following list anticipates the differences that EDW team leaders will probably discover:

- GRM is far more immediate—it works directly on the project's backlog. In contrast, the ERM artifacts provide background that will later make the backlog fairly easy to author.
- GRM focuses on getting the product owner to think deeper, drawing from what he or she already knows about the company and the project. ERM is designed to elevate the knowledge of IT members of the team, giving them an independent source of information that they can use to judge whether the product owner is providing complete and accurate user stories.
- GRM has some helper artifacts (see Chapter 9) to nudge the product owner along. They are lightweight, collaborative, and generally fun for the team to work on together. ERM artifacts are streamlined versions of formal IT requirements artifacts. No one would accuse them of being fun, but most people acknowledge that they are powerful.
- The GRM approach can work top-down, bottom-up, or both simultaneously, allowing the team to meet the product owner wherever he wishes to begin his thinking. Teams can start ERM collection with any of the artifacts and backfill the rest as time allows, but the value chain does support a top-down approach more strongly.
- Teams can freely pick and choose from the helper artifacts that GRM offers, whereas with ERM, teams tend to select the first three artifacts, the last three, or all five.
- In GRM, the detail-level artifacts—either user stories or developer stories, depending on the object being programmed—are the objective, making them mandatory. In ERM, the detailed level artifact—the module use case—should be employed only where a detailed specification is needed. Accordingly, a project may well need only one or two of these use cases, and only for the ETL modules involving particularly complex business rules.

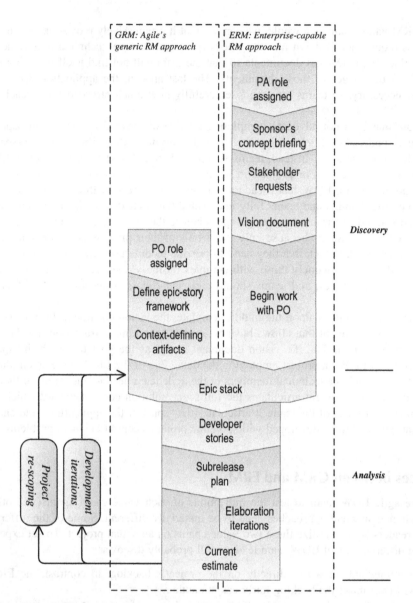

FIGURE 7.11   Overall agile EDW requirements management plan.

As can be gleaned from the previous list, GRM and ERM are clearly different approaches. Teams should selectively draw on portions of both, using the context that ERM provides to judge whether the backlog emerging from the GRM process is complete and accurate. Figure 7.11 schematically portrays a combined approach, showing how they converge. The diagram shows the logical ordering of steps, not timing, largely because the actual duration of each step is determined by the context of each project. This is especially true for teams that start the value chains at random points and backfill the missing elements later, beginning with an epic stack, for example, and then authoring a vision statement. Because GRM represents the team prompting the product owner to think more deeply, this value chain can begin when both the product owner and the project architect roles have been staffed. The first action would be for two of them to define a clear notion of what each level of the epic tree signifies. Once they have established this framework for defining epics, themes, and users stories, the team then utilizes GRM's context-defining artifacts, such as user modeling and vision boxes, until the product owner is reliably authoring good, actionable user stories, thus yielding a hierarchically organized backlog called an "epic stack."

True to agile EDW's notion of 80/20 specifications, this stack does not have to be absolutely complete. If the most important 80% of the stories have been identified, the team will be able to accurately scope the project, trusting that the remaining stories will emerge without too much disruption as development and benefits realization begins. Of course, once the project starts incremental delivery to the product owner, both business and IT will learn more about the project's requirements. This learning will uncover a few requirements that had been overlooked, but in my experience with agile teams, the real insight this learning provides is that the project's requirements were overstated, so that often the product owner ends up taking large requests out of scope. Figure 7.11 depicts this notion with arrows that show the development iterations and project rescoping contributing to new versions of the epic stack.

The ERM branch of the combined approach can begin before a product owner is assigned, as long as the project architect has been named. The project architect, and any other team leaders who wish to assist, can pursue interviews with the project sponsor and major stakeholders on his or her own, boiling down what they learn into a vision document that will scope and guide the development work. Once the product owner is assigned, the team will use the context from the first half of the ERM value chain to assist him or her in authoring a good, 80/20 collection of user stories.

The two chains merge once the product owner has authored the initial epic stack. At that point, the developers on the team can use the knowledge from their work on the ERM value chain to test the accuracy of the user stories that the product owner adds to the project backlog. For those user stories that pass muster, the IT team members can then begin decomposing them into developer stories where necessary. With a reasonable first draft of the project backlog, the project architect can group the stories together into a candidate subrelease and present the subrelease plan for the business's approval.

The backlog of developer stories can also be estimated by the team in story points leading to the project's first current estimate. This estimate can be made right away if the project draws from an established team. Projects using a new team will have to wait a couple of iterations because the developers must first discover their delivery velocity by actually working on a few stories. If the project has notable risk in its requirements or design, even an established team may want to complete a couple of "elaboration" iterations to resolve those issues before providing story points for the full backlog and issuing a first current estimate. As discussed previously, the current estimate will be updated before each development iteration, using the team's actual velocity and the backlog of remaining stories. In this way, team leaders will refresh the forecast for management regarding remaining project cost and duration. While working completely at a medium level of precision, the team following this two-prong approach will have quickly prepared for business stakeholders a palpable notion of what they will receive from the project and approximately when they will see it.

BUSINESS ANALYSTS IMPLICIT IN TWO PROJECT LEAD ROLES

Given the diversity of artifacts discussed previously, requirements gathering and analysis for most EDW projects typically involve a considerable number of people and roles. For clarity in the discussion that follows, I focus the presentation on a few central roles. Figure 7.12 depicts the formal and informal reporting relationships between these roles. Those depicted in dark text are the focal roles in the presentation made during the next four chapters.

Because not all projects staff the business analyst position, the BAs are shown in a light print, implicitly defining two approaches that a project can take. When BAs exist, they perform a large amount of requirements gathering and analysis. In fact, they tend to be the contributors who chase down all the details needed to validate the requirements gathered, so their function is crucial. They can report to either the business or IT, as shown in Figure 7.12. Business-hired BAs usually work closely with the product owner, and IT-hired BAs collaborate more with the project architect.

On the other hand, if the project has not staffed the BA position, the product owner and/or the project architect roles will have to assume these duties. To keep the presentation simple, I write as if only the product owner and the project architect exist. This simplification makes sense in that the product owner's role is to express requirements from the business perspective as user stories and place them on the project backlog. Any detail discovery and analysis work performed by BAs employed on the business side must still pass through the product owner to land on the backlog, so using the product owner term to mean "product owner and BA team" will not introduce any confusion. Subject matter experts appear in light print, too, indicating that their contributions must also flow into the project through the auspices of the product owner. It will be up to the product owner, the subject matter experts, and the business BAs to self-organize their work so that the direction they provide the developers is maximally effective.

Similarly, the role of the project architect is to translate the business requirements into a high-level design for the application that will solve the business problems identified by the product owner. The requirements and discovery work performed by IT-employed BAs must undergo project architect review before becoming part of the project's vision or specifications, so using the term "project architect" to signify a composite role involving multiple people will not detract from the discussion.

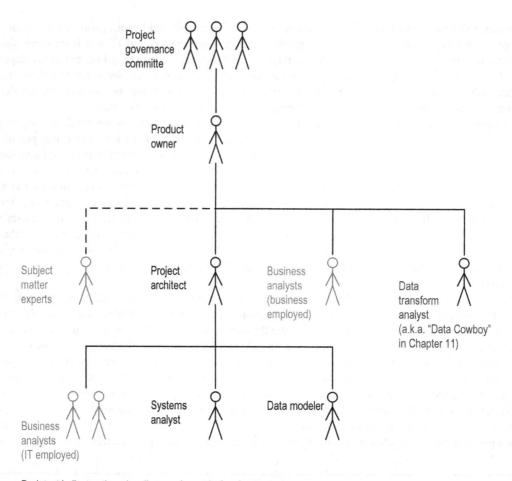

Dark text indicates the roles discussed most in the chapter text.

FIGURE 7.12 Enterprise requirements management roles.

SUMMARY

Agile EDW leaders face a dilemma when managing their project's requirements. Too little requirements management will expose them to overcommitment, missing features, and/or endless reprogramming to fix mistakes. On the other hand, investing in the extensive requirements specification document that traditionally managed teams employ will force the project sponsors to wait many months before the necessary business intelligence services appear on their end user's workstations. Both too little and too much requirements work leads to extremely unhappy customers. The agile enterprise data warehousing method addresses this dilemma using a flexible, incremental approach to requirements management. This approach involves two intersecting value chains of artifacts. The generic agile requirements management value chain strongly guides the product owner in authoring an accurate backlog for the project. The enterprise-capable requirements management value chain leads the IT members of the team to develop an independent notion of the project's requirements so that they can validate the product owner's backlog. These two perspectives on project requirements intersect at the user-story/subrelease level and thus provide the team members with a "stereoscopic vision" that allows them to spot gaps in the project concept.

Chapter 8 suggests a powerful framework for defining epics, themes, and stories, and it also offers guidance on linking each level to a quantified notion of value to the business user. Chapters 9—11 discuss the generic requirements management value chain, the enterprise-capable value chain, and how to successfully intersect them into a robust description of the application that the agile team needs to build.

Chapter 8

Redefining the Epic Stack to Enable Value Accounting

The iterations of an agile development effort revolve around the team's backlog. For a team to reach its peak effectiveness, that backlog needs to be an accurate list of needed features and ordered properly, lest the development team labor at length on modules that do not solve the business's problem or fail because the team wasted its time on the project's less important aspects. My colleagues and I have learned through hard experience that a team cannot simply trust that its embedded business partner will automatically provide an accurate backlog. Although generic Scrum stipulates that this list of stories belongs to the product owner, team leaders need to actively contribute to the quality of that list. Their involvement should focus intently on one goal: the derivation of a backlog where every story aligns with an important business purpose and clearly represents a predefined, quantified increment of value for the customer. To properly align with business purpose, the team needs to implement an effective *epic decomposition framework* for generating accurate stories that the product owner can place on the backlog. To quantify the importance of each story on the backlog, the team needs to employ *value accounting*. Without these two techniques, teams hazard coding for months without delivering enough value to convince executives that the project achieved something important or that they should continue funding it.

TOWARD A ROBUST EPIC DECOMPOSITION FRAMEWORK

Enterprise data warehousing (EDW) project leaders who gently insist that their teammates discipline their approach to defining the project backlog and then apply that discipline until the backlog is clear and coherent will enable their teams to avoid confusion and start effective programming work much sooner. Much of the needed discipline for creating and managing backlogs revolves around simple organizational concepts. Many teams fervently begin programming with only vague notions of what the epic-, theme-, and user-level stories are, only to become frustrated many iterations later when important stakeholders claim they have seen nothing of value among all the modules that the developers have delivered. To avoid such wasted effort, agile EDW leaders can apply a small amount of discipline in expressing and organizing a project's requirements. To begin with, they should

- formally define the hierarchy that the project will use to manage backlogs;
- identify the general business hierarchy for the project's stakeholders; and
- align these two hierarchies so that the team creates stories speaking to the needs of all levels within the business.

Defining the Backlog Hierarchy's Structure

Generic agile textbooks refer to the components of a project backlog in terms of epics, themes, and user stories, but they provide little guidance as to how each level is defined. Teams will need two basic terms to begin building this guidance for themselves: epic stack and epic tree.

The "epic stack" is simply the collection of terms the team will use to categorize the stories within its backlogs. For example, the terms "epic story," "theme story," and "user story" constitute the epic stack offered by most generic agile textbooks. An "epic tree" is the collection of stories at all levels that link upwards to a given epic-level story, making a project's backlog the set of all epic trees. Epic trees assist in understanding and planning a project. As a starting point, teams naturally consider delivering one epic at a time. Even when many factors eventually determine a very different order in which to develop stories, the team frequently considers the backlog one epic tree at a time, testing for accuracy and completeness.

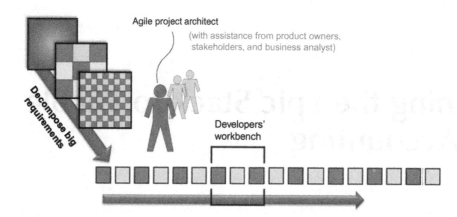

FIGURE 8.1 Big picture – decomposing epics into a backlog of stories.

In essence, an appropriately defined epic stack facilitates EDW teams in decomposing a project's requirements into accurate, intelligible, and actionable epic trees. Figure 8.1 illustrates the decomposition that agile team leaders wish to achieve. In the upper left, the product owner submits a huge, vague requirement—that is, an epic. The project architect and associated business analysts work with the product owner to steadily decompose that large need into "bite-sized" requests that can comfortably fit, three or four at a time, on the programmer's workbench. When the project's leading edge of epic requests have been decomposed to this level, the team can begin to crank through the backlog, turning these actionable requests into working software that provides business intelligence to the organization.

To make this decomposition a straightforward process, EDW team leaders need to clearly state the epic stack that the team will employ. Generic agile offers the following rudimentary epic stack:

- Huge requests are "epics."
- Themes are a little smaller, but still too large to program within an iteration.
- User stories are small enough to be actionable.

EDW team leaders should realize they are free to adapt this stack to meet the needs of their particular project. In previous chapters, I introduced one major modification that many agile data warehousing/business intelligence (DW/BI) teams make to the epic stack: Add developer stories to further break down user stories into modules that link to the layers within the company's DW/BI reference architecture. Some projects require even further adaptations, the most common being dividing theme-level stories into "subthemes." For example, an EDW team delivering enterprise dashboards that each contain many graphical modules such as pivot tables and line graphs may decide that a given dashboard is a *theme-level* story and its graphical modules will be *subthemes* within it.

With a clear epic stack defined, agile EDW leaders can guide their teammates in authoring stories so that each one can be clearly categorized with a level from the epic stack and then linked into the proper place within an epic tree. Chapter 6 urged teams to plan their deliveries in subreleases in order to greatly lower overall project risk. The simple use of epic stacks and epic trees advocated here will greatly help teams ensure that every story they work on has a clear lineage to its parents and children, making it much easier for the team to deliver coherent portions of the backlog with each subrelease candidate they propose. Establishing a clear epic stack and epic trees early in the project will keep the project highly intelligible to both the product owner and the developers, facilitating their communication and allowing them to begin effective programming much sooner.

Aligning the Epic Stack to the Company's Hierarchy

As hinted at previously, lackluster product owner performance occurs frequently. Should this occur, agile EDW project leaders need to be ready to "manage upwards" and ensure that the team somehow receives the quality backlog it needs for smooth and effective development. Aside from defining the epic stack the project will use, the next step they can take toward this end is to align that stack with the company's business hierarchy.

The team needs the person filling the role of product owner to perform a complex, multipart duty:

- Envision all the different stakeholders for the EDW that exist within the company
- Envision what each of them needs from business intelligence in order to be more effective

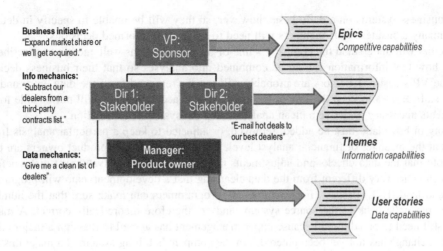

Business initiative:
"Expand market share or we'll get acquired."

Info mechanics:
"Subtract our dealers from a third-party contracts list."

Data mechanics:
"Give me a clean list of dealers"

VP: Sponsor

Dir 1: Stakeholder   Dir 2: Stakeholder

"E-mail hot deals to our best dealers"

Manager: Product owner

Epics
Competitive capabilities

Themes
Information capabilities

User stories
Data capabilities

FIGURE 8.2   Immediate business stakeholder formalizing all levels of stories by linking them to the hierarchy among business stakeholders.

- Articulate all those needs in bite-size pieces that the agile development team can program quickly
- Organize those pieces in the order they should be delivered

Many factors can prevent product owners from authoring an actionable set of epic trees. Product owners can be

- underqualified for a leadership position;
- too inexperienced in the industry or with the company;
- loaded with too much work from their regular duties in their assigned business department;
- too new to DW/BI to envision how it can improve a business process;
- harboring serious doubt about EDW in general given the size and complexity of the applications; or
- quietly hostile toward information technology (IT) given a bad experience in his or her past.

Any of these factors will result in a toxically poor backlog for the team to work from and, consequently, project failure.

Team leaders cannot simply resign themselves to failure if the product owner is underperforming in his or her role. Instead, they must jump in and assist in polishing the stories so that they form an accurate, coherent, and actionable backlog. They will be far more effective in this effort if they have a framework that imbues each story with clarity and categorizes it within the appropriate level of the project's epic trees. One handy framework for categorizing and shaping stories from the product owner is to link the levels of the epic stack to levels within the organization.

Figure 8.2 provides a simplified notion of a company's business hierarchy that makes this linkage easy to perceive and manage. This framework defines epic stories so that they link to project sponsors, theme stories so they connect to department directors, and user stories so that they speak to the experience of managers or analysts. Other frameworks are possible, so I do not suggest that this particular approach will work for every team without modification. However, all teams will arrive at far better backlogs if they employ a framework such as the one illustrated here, so readers can consider the approach depicted in Figure 8.2 as a starting notion for their own requirements management system.

To link the epic stack to the organization hierarchy, a team must first have a working model of the stakeholders in the company and how they connect to the EDW project. Starting from the top of the organization, executives from the vice president (VP) level or higher usually sponsor EDW projects because these projects are very expensive. The agile EDW team must realize that although the VP is funding the application development, he or she will not be the team's embedded business partner. The responsibilities of a VP will not allow her to spend every day working with the developers, so she will delegate that responsibility to one of the directors who report to her. Unfortunately, directors usually have demanding high-level responsibilities, too. They will quickly push the burden of working with the agile EDW team down yet another level onto a manager or senior analyst working for them.

All this delegation of responsibility creates a communication challenge that the agile team leaders must manage. Although the VP and director both delegated the chore of product owner downward, they still have requirements for the project that are very dear to them and that the agile team must discover and include in the application's design. As shown in the Figure 8.2, VP sponsors understand the strategic goals of the company that the DW/BI project needs to support. They can describe the well-informed decisions they want their staff to someday make, and it is hoped that they accurately understand how those decisions will bring the company competitive success. VPs do not work with the company's line of business systems on a daily basis, however, so they will be unable to specify in detail what pools of information the company's business staff members will need to make well-informed decisions.

In contrast, directors will understand the company's line-of-business systems well enough to describe the information available there and how that information should be combined into analyses so that their business decisions become as well informed as the VP's desire. Directors are probably still too far removed from the data entry and error correction processes that their staff utilizes to keep the line-of-business systems accurate. They will not be able to specify the data checks and adjustments necessary to derive a clean analysis from the system's information.

The understanding of how data must be added, removed, or adjusted to keep a particular analysis from misleading a decision maker lies at the manager or financial analyst level, the level from which product owners are typically drafted. It is important to note that the data checks and adjustments that managers and analysts must make before providing an analysis to their directors are very different from the data cleansing that a development team will program into the EDWs extract, transform, and load (ETL) process. For example, the programmers can make sure that the numbers reported for accounts receivables reconcile back to the source systems and are therefore theoretically correct. A manager can know that those numbers still need to be adjusted because upper management has agreed to reassign a major contract to another business unit, but that change has not yet been entered into the company's billing system. To make this distinction clear, I speak of "programmable data validations" that the developers can embed into the code of an EDW's data transformation, in contrast with "business-level data validations" that only a human steeped in the day-to-day operations of the company can perform.

Clearly Defining Each Level within the Epic Stack

At this point, EDW team leaders have a solid definition of their epic stack and a multilevel model of their project's stakeholders. To bring clarity to the project's backlog and to ensure that requirements at all levels are addressed, the leaders need only to link the levels of the epic stack to the levels of the business organization.

The starter epic decomposition framework that my consulting firm uses links each class of agile requirements story to a distinct level in the company hierarchy so that our teams will systematically discover and address the full set of requirements that an application must satisfy. In this framework, we say that VP sponsors provide epic stories—that is, stories describing the corporate-level business initiatives that the application must support. We say that directors of the business departments provide theme stories. Each theme describes an analysis that a director will need before he will know what his department staff should do in order to achieve the business initiatives set forth by the VP sponsors. We say that managers and analysts in those departments provide user stories. Each user story focuses on a business-level data validation that must be performed before the organization knows that the analyses about to be provided to the departmental directors are not misleading.

Table 8.1 shows how my colleagues and I connect an organizational model to the levels of an epic stack to create a handy framework for defining the stories within each epic tree. Starting at the highest level, the project's sponsor, who will be signing the checks that pay for the project, names the gauges on the corporate cockpit he or she wants to affect and then states approximately where those needles should move to. Each request from the VP sponsors for greater competitive capability is a natural candidate for epics-level stories. The team needs only to ensure that these requests are atomic. Sometimes sponsors express multilayered goals for the company, such as "improve market share by providing the lowest-cost product in its class." That particular statement contains two objectives, one for sales volume and another for product pricing. EDW team leaders will need to process this request until they have unpacked it down to the individual or "atomic" components, at which point they will have positioned themselves to develop them independently, as befits agile's incremental delivery strategy.

Looking within each epic from the sponsor, the framework guides the team leaders to seek how one or more business departments need to change their behavior in order to move the VP's selected needles in the corporate cockpit in the right direction. The team will need statements from the directors of those departments regarding which analyses it needs in order to achieve the desired corporate performance. These statements will represent director-level theme stories. For an insurance company, for example, a director could decide, "The fastest way to expand market share as our VP has requested will be to cross-sell additional coverage to existing customers who currently hold a policy from only one of the product lines we offer." To pursue such a strategy, this director's staff will need an analysis showing

- financially sound customers holding only one product; and
- products that would interest each customer, given the customer's demographics and other personal attributes.

TABLE 8.1 Example of How to Codify an Epic Stack for Agile EDW Teams

Requirements level	Purpose: To define...	Expressed casually	Sample statements (medical equipment financing company)
Epics	Atomic **competitive** capabilities	Identify the needles on gauges in the corporate cockpit that have to move and approximately where they have to get to	VP project sponsor: "Expand our market share through better prospecting"
Themes	Atomic **information** capabilities	Describe the set-based operations on company information needed for an analysis that will let business users act	Director of Direct Sales: "Financially sound customers minus customers holding all three types of products equals cross-sell prospects"
User stories	Atomic **business data validation** capabilities	Name the context checking needed before users will trust the parent theme's analysis	Manager of sales reporting: "Here's how will check that the list of current customers is free of any hidden duplicates..."
Developer stories (for data integration work)	Atomic **transform** capabilities	Names a load module needed to provide the data required by a user story	EDW systems analyst: "Here's how to load the next set of customer records from Source #3 into the integration layer of the warehouse"

With such an analysis in hand, the director can instruct his or her sales force to "call the people listed in this report and offer them indicated products for the reasons listed on each line." Each of the analyses the director requests will make good candidates for theme-level stories.

Again, the first expression of each theme may have many ideas folded together, so the project architect will need to work with the directors to tease apart the individual notions until they are atomic and thus more manageable within an agile development process. One way to translate such director-level requests into atomic EDW-appropriate theme stories is to consider each deliverable as a set-based operation upon the company's information. To continue with our example, the EDW team could work with the director to clarify the previous request to where he or she expresses it as follows:

- Get me a clean list of customers' households.
- Subtract out all those that hold three or more policies.
- Split that list by the last broker who had contact with the customer.
- Assign any customers missing a broker by intersecting the likely cross-sell product with our agents' area of specialty.

Each of these set-based operations resulting in actionable information is a perfect candidate for theme-level stores for a DW/BI application.

Finally, the analyses on which the business staff will act cannot be misleading. Double-checking an analysis for missing business context is typically left to the managers and analysts who report to the department directors. Here, the agile team leaders can turn to the product owner and ask for the business-level data validation steps that the staff will have to perform before the implications of the theme-level analysis can be trusted. The product owner might say,

We will need to take a second look every time we have two phone numbers listed for the same address. That might be a middle-aged couple with an adult child living in a carriage house in the back. That household should only get one phone call, else we'll annoy that prospect so much that they'll never buy another product from us.

Each necessary data check that the product owner identifies will make a perfect user story because it will be a stand-alone, extremely focused query against the information in the data warehouse. Often such user stories will suggest further data transform programming that will be possible in the future once the business-level validation steps are better understood by the product owner. With some polishing, human data-check steps will become atomic business-level data validation capabilities required by the user community.

The graphics for this section provide a few more examples of stories defined using this framework. The last column in Table 8.1 provides an abbreviated sample for each class of story, distilled from the backlog for one of my company's projects in the automobile financing industry. Table 8.2 provides a more fully expressed example of an epic tree for a revenue assurance project in the subscriber-based telecommunications industry. This table expresses these stories in the full, three-part format that agile textbooks recommend with clauses for *who*, *what*, and *why*. Some teams also add a fourth element, "How will this be validated?" that can assist the developers in the test-led development technique described in Chapter 16. The particular instance of the backlog shown in the table is in mid-creation, so the product owner has not yet provided user stories for all of the epics and themes. In both examples, the strongly typed nature of each story class should be apparent: Epic stories are new competitive capabilities, theme stories are new analyses for action, and user stories represent all the necessary business-level data validation steps.

Strongly typed stories empower the developers on the agile team to evaluate more astutely the quality of the backlog provided by the product owner. They can check that the data validation represented by every user story traces back to an information analysis linked to a director and then verify that theme's analysis links appropriately to a competitive capability requested by the sponsors. Now enabled to validate the backlog, the team leaders will be able to quickly detect whether the product owner has skimped on his or her backlog-definition duties. If, for example, the product owner offers a story about compiling customer survey data when all the epic trees address improving product margins, the team can respectively suggest that something is awry with the project's requirements. Either a particular epic tree has not been stated yet or this user story belongs in another project.

The remaining element of the agile EDW epic stack is the developer story. As discussed in my previous books, developer stories become straightforward to author once the team arrives at a solid set of epics, themes, and user stories. The team needs to simply take each user story and "stretch" it across the EDW's reference architecture, as shown in Figure 8.3. At each intersection, the project architect and other team leads will be able to quickly name the data transformations needed to load the data that the given user story will require. This effort will identify the atomic transform modules that the application requires, with each of those modules being a perfect focus for a developer story.

TESTING WHETHER STORIES ARE GOOD ENOUGH

The epic decomposition framework described previously helps teams author stories at the right level for each class of requirements they must manage, but it does not guarantee the quality of each story they create. Teams will need a means to judge whether the stories on that backlog are good enough.

Generic Scrum practitioners employ an "INVEST" test to determine whether a given user story is sufficiently polished. Because they work with *developer* stories, especially for the data integration portion of their projects, agile data warehousing practitioners have had to extend and rename components of the INVEST test elements, transforming them into "DILBERT'S" test. EDW teams employ this test many times throughout a project, such as during Sprint 0, story conferences, mid-iteration backlog grooming, and even user demos when the quality of a story appears to be the root cause of a rejected feature. Figure 8.4 shows the components of each test and how the elements of agile's generic INVEST test for user stories have transformed into the components of the DILBERT'S test for DW/BI developer stories. We need to consider only the DILBERT'S elements because each INVEST test element has been carried forward.

Demonstrable

Demonstrable indicates that the deliverables for each developer story should result in something that can be demonstrated to the product owner during a user demo. Because developer stories can define data loads for schemas far removed from an end-user dashboard, teams often have to demonstrate their progress using temporary BI modules connected to the ordinarily hidden architectural layers of the warehouse. With a little imagination, teams can usually demonstrate business value to the product owner even if the data for the demo comes from an intermediate data layer such as the landing area or the integration layer. Seeing the data drawing closer step-by-step to the end-user dashboard is usually enough to convince the product owner that the team has made significant, tangible progress. As long as the product

TABLE 8.2 Sample Epic Tree from the Revenue Assurance Example

Background Statement from Chief Operating Officer		
Our share prices have under performed in the past two years, making our company an attractive takeover target. The board of directors has set net margin improvement goals of plus 5% for this year and the next, in order to mitigate this risk. As Chief Operating Officer, I believe operations can attain these goals through three primary efforts: a) bundle our products to include high-margin basic services with the high-volume new products b) decrease our fulfillment cycle times to shorten the lag between order and first dollar of revenue c) find and correct the cause of "broken orders" that get neither filled nor billed after the customer purchases services		
Epic	1	As the Central Region's vice president of operations, I want my directors to be able to find and show trends for areas of overly long cycle times so that we can assess the effectiveness of our process redesign efforts.
Theme	1.1	As director of business services provisioning, I need to identify the problem work orders by subtracting out the 80% with the fastest cycle times and then breakout the remainder by personnel involved so that we will know who to manage more closely.
Epic	2	As the vice president of business services, I want my accounting directors to be able to quantify and assess root cause for sales orders that do not get fulfilled so that we can reclaim at least a quarter of the $50M per year of earned revenue that manual audits show we're not collecting.
Theme	2.1	As director of Tri-States district accounting, I need sales orders that do not acquire a matching work order within three working days so that we can label and analyze them as "broken sales orders."
User Story		2.1.1 As manager of business services accounting, I need to see the work orders marked with their originating sales orders by number of days between order dates so that I know those with a lag of less than four days have been removed from the director's "broken sales orders" analysis.
User Story		2.1.2 As manager of business services accounting, I need to see the work orders marked with sales orders superseded by revised sales orders so that I know those have been removed from the director's "broken sales order" analysis.
User Story		2.1.3 As manager of business services accounting, I need to see unrevised and revision sales orders with late work orders where product codings on the revisions don't match the product codings on the original sales orders so that I know those have been removed from the director's "broken sales order" analysis. (We will have to solve the product coding issues, but that's a different problem.)
User Story		2.1.4 As manager of business services accounting, I need to see unrevised and revision sales orders with late work orders where the dates on credit approval or previous account hold flag is more than 3 days after the active sales order's creation date so that I know those have been removed from the director's "broken sales order" analysis. (We'll have to address late reversals on credit rejections and previous account holds, but that's a different problem also.)
Theme	2.2	As director of Tri-States district accounting, I need work order line items that do not acquire matching billing records service items within three working days so that we can label and analyze them as "orphaned work items."
Epic	3	As the vice president of business services, I want my accounting directors to be able to quantify and assess root cause for provisioned services that do not get billed so that we can reclaim another quarter of the $50M per year of earned revenue that manual audits show we're not collecting.

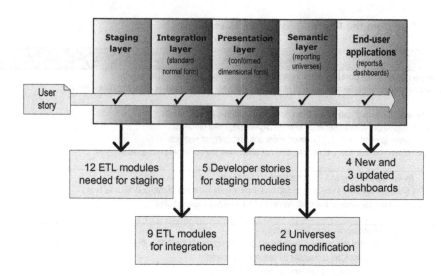

FIGURE 8.3   Primary technique for decomposing user stories into developers stories. Note the 25-to-1 multiplier for this project's user story.

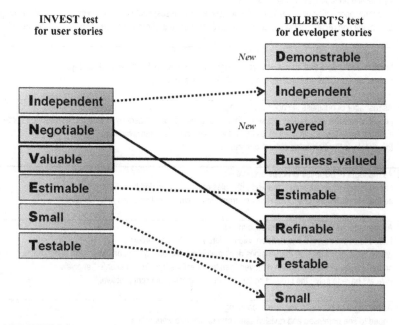

FIGURE 8.4   INVEST and DILBERT'S test.

owner can drive the BI module himself and begin to answer the business question represented by the parent user story, he should be able to see how the work done so far has reduced the risk of the project and will contribute to a usable feature for business users, someday soon.

Independent

Developer stories are said to be *independent* if they are defined so that, given where they occur in the project backlog, the team will be able to develop them without having to resolve other dependencies first. This definition of independence takes into account the ordering of the backlog, so when teammates re-sequence the stories, they often feel the need to scan the list again to determine whether the new order has created any unintended dependencies.

Layered

The *layered* criterion indicates that the team has defined the developer story so that it addresses only one layer of the DW/BI reference data architecture. Focusing on one layer at a time will also help considerably to make each story *independent*, especially if all its inputs and outputs connect to data objects located outside the layer in question.

Business-valued

Closely associated with the notion of demonstrable, the business-valued consideration reminds the team that it must define and communicate every developer story so that the product owner can appreciate it as a significant step toward delivering the parent user story and the overall application. Drawing from the epic decomposition framework discussed previously, business-valued also suggests that developer stories need to be clearly traceable to the hierarchy within a particular epic tree. Moreover, each parent story for a given backlog item should be clearly expressed as an atomic capability of the proper requirement class, as listed in Table 8.1. Only when the team can clearly state the competitive, information, and business data validation capabilities that a given developer story will help bring to life can the team be sure that its developer story represents undeniable value to the business.

Estimateable

Developer stories in a backlog should be expressed so that the team can forecast the level of effort that the module will require, in both story points and labor hours. If the team cannot forecast the work that a developer story will take, quite likely the parent user story is still too big or vague, indicating that the product owner should invest more time in decomposing it further.

Refinable

Refinable for developer stories is the equivalent of the INVEST test's "negotiable" for user stories, which is often phrased as "not too specific" by agile practitioners. For generic agile projects, "negotiable" reminds teams to keep the user story to a single sentence or two. Agile teams do not want the product owner to write pages of details because that practice would take the team back toward the waterfall approach of detailed requirements specification, and it would risk wasting large amounts of effort when business conditions change.

Agile data warehousing practitioners use "refinable" to remind themselves also to rely on 80/20 specifications. The developer story and its parent user story need only to capture the essence of what services the new features must enable. The remaining details should be covered during development time when programmers can gather true, detailed requirements while working eye-to-eye with the product owner.

Testable

We borrowed the *testable* criterion directly from the INVEST test, which states that a story should describe a unit of functionality that is small and distinct enough to be validated in a straightforward manner. For agile DW/BI projects, developer stories should be fairly close to the programmed units that will make up the application, so if the programmers cannot envision how to unit test a developer story, that story or its parent user story is still too large to enter the iterative development process.

Small

Generic agile practitioners state that user stories should be *small* enough that each one will consume only a fraction of the team's capability during a single iteration. Whether "small enough" means that the developers can deliver, for example, five stories in an iteration rather than just four will be something that the team members will have to establish for themselves during the first few sprints of their project. Fortunately, if the team properly applies the earlier criteria of *independent*, *layered*, *estimateable*, and *testable*, "small" usually results. Occasionally, a developer story describing an ETL module still proves to be too large to develop within one iteration. At that point, teams employ additional decomposition techniques, such as defining separate stories for each natural subset of target-table columns or rows, so that not all of the business rules for a given module have to be programmed in a single effort.

CLARIFYING EVERYTHING WITH VALUE ACCOUNTING

Teams that adopt a clear framework for creating focused, compelling epic trees greatly increase their effectiveness. A strong epic tree communicates clearly to the developers what they must do during an iteration and even across sprints. Developers can begin fast development of DW/BI components once a backlog reaches this level of organization. The missing piece, however, will still be an appreciation of their work by end users and project sponsors. A heap of new modules by themselves means very little to the business departments funding the EDW programming effort. Somehow the many components created by the programming team must be assembled into deliverables that the business can appreciate. That appreciation will emerge when the EDW team leaders can demonstrate that they have had

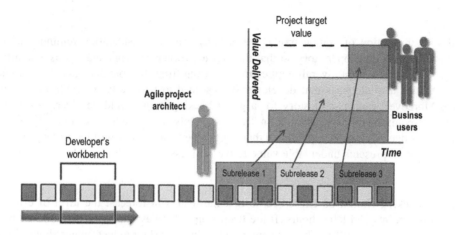

FIGURE 8.5   Big picture – recompling modules for perceived value.

a positive impact on the organization. Teams can use a technique called "value accounting" to make such a claim. Value accounting requires some effort, but it pays great dividends by lowering the risk of a project and bolstering team morale, both of which translate into increasing delivery speeds.

Figure 8.5 portrays the tail end of the process started in Figure 8.1, which depicted the process by which the team decomposed the originally large and vague business requests down to a backlog of bite-sized work bundles for programming on a developer's workbench. In the second half of the process shown in Figure 8.5, the project architect orchestrates the assembly of the many modules that the developers have programmed into a package which end users can operate and derive value. Given that data must move across several layers of a data warehouse's reference architecture, every set of new, business-appreciable capabilities in an EDW project will take two or three iterations to emerge from the development process. Moreover, for the reasons stated previously, teams cannot assume that a product owner will adequately advertise the team's accomplishments among the business stakeholders. These dynamics may create a public relations gap for the EDW project as sponsors and end users impatiently wait for the new features to appear, and leaders should address this gap in order to ensure the continued funding of their team. Value accounting provides EDW team leaders with an objective means for communicating accomplishments to all levels of stakeholders throughout the life of a project.

The Basics of Value Accounting

Value accounting is the practice of placing a numeric measure of worth on every item on the backlog and actively claiming credit for that contribution with each delivery, even intermediate ones. The end result of value accounting is shown in the upper right of Figure 8.5 as a *buildup chart* depicting the value of the deliverables that the team has delivered into production usage. Other versions of this chart show the deliveries of modules to the intermediate environments such as system testing and user acceptance testing as well. Traditional data warehousing projects typically accumulate a reputation for being expensive and near useless as the company waits many months before seeing something of value emerge from the extensive programming effort. Agile EDW teams that use value accounting can prevent this bad impression from taking root by regularly advertising their achievements through value buildup charts. With every deliverable that the developers make, the team adds the worth of that delivery to the buildup chart and gets credit for making another contribution to the success of the enterprise. Should a stakeholder inquire as to what value a particular uptick on the buildup chart represents, the team can either have the product owner explain what he or she said during the last user demo or can read the value statements from the user story cards that the team members were programming during the last iteration. Not only does this small bit of public relations insulate the agile team from criticism, it also builds enthusiasm for the project among the business staff members and elicits greater participation from them for guiding the next round of deliverables.

The most difficult aspect of value accounting is defining a unit of measure by which the value of epics, themes, and user stories can be expressed. The numbers displayed on the buildup charts will have to represent something real to the casual business observer. The project architect will need to research and select an overall measure of value for the project, such as the return on investment that project sponsors had in mind when they approved the project for development. If teams are using the backlog definition framework described previously in this chapter, these statements of value can be associated with the epic stories that the project's VP sponsors provided.

As discussed later, once the value of the epics has been articulated, the remaining distribution of value becomes fairly straightforward. The executives allocate the value of each epic down to the theme stories that it contains. The development team then distributes the value of each theme to its component user stories. When the team places a theme into production usage, the team increases the buildup chart by the value that had been apportioned to that theme. If the theme gets split across subreleases, then the team claims credit for the value of only the user stories that the team has put into production.

Because value accounting requires some thought and effort, the advantages it provides for a team are discussed first, before the details of apportioning epic value to themes and user stories are presented. The advantages manifest in two general areas: team effectiveness and risk mitigation.

Value Accounting Makes Developers More Effective

Once value has been assigned to the project's epics, themes, and user stories, prioritizing the backlog becomes far easier because the team acquires a second and very clear measure of importance for backlog items. This second measure of importance augments the product owner's personal notion, which can sometimes be unfounded and change erratically between iterations. In fact, the process of allocating the epic- and theme-level values identified by executives to the user stories on a backlog is often the pivotal experience that inspires half-hearted product owners to take their role seriously. When the team leaders begin driving toward full value accounting, the context for the product owner changes from "Please tell us which of these stories is more important to you" to "Here's how much the company has said these epics and themes mean to everyone." With that change, the product owner realizes that the company expects him or her to lead the delivery of benefits that the company is eagerly waiting for. That realization is often all the pressure needed to snap many product owners out of their apathy.

Value accounting causes the product owner to think more deeply about the project, which often generates more and better user stories. When confronted with two themes that seem to have the same worth to the product owner but that the organization has labeled with widely different values of, for example, $100,000 and $5 million, the product owner can ask himself, "Why is the second so much more important than the first?" The question will lead him to trace through the thinking of the executives from whom the values were derived, connecting him thoroughly with the goals of the company, and in the end, acquiring greater business acumen with which to lead the development team.

Value accounting is also powerful because it can rescue teams that are drifting. Without quantifying the worth of backlog items, the team is at the mercy of the product owner's whims regarding what features to build next. Value accounting provides an external reference regarding which project components are most important. This external input positions the team leaders to reason with the product owner regarding the ordering of backlog. They can keep him or her better focused on the most worthy system elements, and they can ward off any impulse to chase something new before finishing the work that has already been started. By reducing any such "requirements churn" from the product owner, the team gets more appreciable work done in a shorter time and thus becomes far more effective.

Once the team has derived value ratings for the entire backlog, organizing a project into subreleases becomes far easier. The process transforms from "Sort this big box of rocks, where they all look the same" to one of "Let's get the diamonds moved to the front of the line, ahead of these lumps of coal." Once the team has used value to sort the big sections of the backlog, issues such as inter-story dependencies and resource availability become much easier to reason through and resolve.

Value accounting brings clarity to the project because the value ratings on the backlog are numbers that everyone on the team can see and understand. This positions all team members to have an opinion regarding what should be worked on next, greatly amplifying the motivation that leads to self-organization. By catalyzing spirited self-organization, value accounting improves the agile project's delivery speed.

Value accounting also provides a strong, positive feedback loop rewarding the team for organizing and delivering software modules. With every user demo, the project leaders can quantify team accomplishments with statements such as, "Fabulous. We just delivered another $750K of value to the company." Couple that feedback with knowledge of the team's labor cost per iterations, and everyone involved can derive an objective notion of the team's "profit margin." If the project costs $150,000 per iteration, then that hypothetical sprint just made the company $600,000 better off. Naturally, teams that are returning four times what they cost feel good about their contribution. They have something tangible to be proud of and a clear reason to believe that the company should appreciate their work and continue funding it. I have seen this perception alone transform a lackluster team with sloppy software engineering habits into a spirited collective, dead serious about what it was building and intent on constructing it correctly. Such improvement in the esprit de corps directly increases the speed and thoroughness of teams' everyday decision making, resulting in a higher team velocity and fewer defects in the modules delivered.

Value Accounting Mitigates Project Risk

Beyond increasing team effectiveness, agile DW project leaders should realize that value accounting greatly reduces actual and perceived project risk. EDW project leaders face some daunting hazards to their projects and their careers. Enterprise data integration work takes so long to build correctly that when project leaders finally deliver the application, they can discover heartbreakers such as the following:

- The business has changed and no longer needs the product.
- The stakeholders asked for features that do not solve the business problem.
- The design omitted one or more crucial information sources.

Teams that put off proving the value of their work until the end of the project risk these undesirable outcomes. Teams following a generic agile process such as Scrum deliver coded modules in increments, but they can still leave the proof of value to the end of the project when all the EDW pieces are in place.

Even the subrelease strategy advocated previously in this book will help little if the team does not actively claim and advertise the value of the intermediate application versions that it puts into production. To mitigate project risk, teams need to combine a subrelease strategy with value accounting. When EDW team leaders claim to have delivered a serious increment of value, they will spur the business stakeholders, from managers all the way up to the sponsoring executives, to look more carefully at the latest subrelease in order to see whether those claims are overblown. When the stakeholders look more closely at the application, they will more likely find that some requirements have been overlooked or misunderstood, allowing the team to correct its backlog and soon improve the software. This interplay between the team's claims of value and the feedback that it generates will greatly reduce the chance that the project team is working on the wrong goals and failing to build DW/BI features that matter.

Value accounting provides teams a compelling way to visualize team progress so that stakeholders also see a steady reduction in the remaining project risk. Returning to Figure 8.5, the horizontal line along the top of the value buildup graph represents the total value that the executives have asked the EDW team to help them realize. At any point in the project, the gap between the value delivered and validated by the business and the target value line is the harm that could occur if the project were to fail at that point. With each increment in the buildup graph, the EDW leaders should not only advertise the additional value realized but also express it as another large portion of project risk removed. On a purely practical level, EDW teams that appear to be steadily delivering valued software and eliminating risk are the teams that executives prefer to keep together and continue funding.

Executives who understand the value buildup chart often turn into powerful allies for agile EDW team leaders, especially when the team begins to have conflicts with the project management office. Traditional project managers often push agile teams back toward a big specification up front so that all work is defined before coding begins, giving them a greater sense of control during the programming work. This conflict between incremental and traditional management preferences can turn into a heated standoff, at which point the agile team will need to appeal to the project sponsors. I have been in program governance meetings in which the project managers have insisted that the developers abandon their incremental approach, only to have the sponsor intervene by saying, "These teams have already delivered several good results over the past few months. My directors and managers understand completely what they're delivering and like how the gap between what we have and what need keeps shrinking on the buildup chart. They seem to know what they're doing. Why not let them keep going as they are?"

When the annual budget cycle comes around, the agile team will also benefit from having clear, well-organized epic trees that have been used to communicate the value delivered and the risks eliminated. When the company needs to reduce DW/BI funding, which of the following development efforts is more likely to get the ax?

- The project in which leaders can draw a results chart with not only a well-understood goal line but also steadily increasing bars that represent proven, delivered value
- The project in which the requirements are difficult to understand and the leaders cannot articulate what they contributed to the company lately

Most steering committees will prefer to support the first project. Project leaders who forego value accounting leave the outcome of these budgeting decisions to fate. Project leaders who invest in organizing their epic trees and honest value accounting take their future into their own hands.

ALLOCATING VALUE THROUGHOUT AN EPIC TREE

Given the many advantages that value accounting can bring to the team, the effort needed to quantify the worth of the backlog stories will seem modest. Quantifying value for the items on a backlog begins with the value of the project itself so that later the team can distribute that value to the component epics, themes, and user stories.

Identifying the Value of a Project

What is the value of a project? Finding a hard number to which to anchor the value of a project can take a good deal of thoughtful discussion and imagination. In commercial business settings, my company's consultants usually pursue the matter with the following sequence of questions:

- What was the business case for this project when it was proposed and approved for development?
- What was the return on investment (ROI) cited in that business case?
- If no ROI was stated, do any of the project approvers have in mind a hard measure of financial benefits?

One would think that every company embarking on a multimillion-dollar EDW project would have a solid business case prepared, but to my continuing surprise, the vast majority of ongoing projects we encounter do not. When no business case exists for a project, the sponsor is usually one or two very high-placed individuals who feel confident that the application is needed and that they know what it should do. Such projects are typically discussed and chartered in terms of features and costs, and the overall benefit of the project is rarely quantified with any rigor.

For situations in which the executives have not articulated a single ROI figure for the project, the EDW team leaders will have to quantify value one level down, measuring benefits for each epic story instead. Here, a clear definition of an epic will serve the project architect well during this research, as he or she asks questions such as the following:

- Which needle on the corporate cockpit gauges will this epic move?
- What fundamental business notion does that needle represent: customers, revenue, margin, velocity of assets, or regulatory compliance?
- What is each increment of movement in that needle worth to the company?

Not every epic has a value that can be expressed in dollars, so the project architect must be prepared to switch to other units of measure. For example, when a company needs an EDW to maintain operational reporting once the company switches to a new accounting system, how does one place a dollar amount on the value that each report delivers? The company needs just about all of the original reports to maintain the business, making it difficult to value each report separately.

During the approximately 25 years we have been providing agile EDW leadership, the consultants in my company have had to resort to many different units of measure in order to quantify value such as:

- Hours saved in the work of very important staff members
- Reduction in staff members needed to maintain a major business process
- Number of embarrassing reporting discrepancies caught before they reach partners and customers
- Days shaved off important business processes' cycle times
- The additional decisions that key staff people can make in a day
- Counting the non-warehouse information sources that decision makers have to consult per transaction

Arriving at a usable unit of measure for benefits realization can take time and creativity. Whenever possible, project leaders should invest enough effort to find a single unit of measure that they can use for all the epic stories in a project so that their latter assertions of value delivery will not be challenged simply for "mixing apples and oranges."

It can be particularly difficult to measure value for noncommercial enterprises because the mission of the organization may not focus on transactions that generate currency-denominated revenue. If none of the alternative measures mentioned previously provide a solution, then project leaders can resort to the size of the budget of the organization or department that the EDW application will support. Although this type of measure does not link to something as clear-cut and compelling as company revenue, it still has a respectable rationale. Throughout the years, an organization will allocate more operating budget to the departments and business processes with the greatest perceived worth to the company. Following this reasoning, EDW project leaders working for noncommercial organizations can claim to have delivered objectively measured value with assertions such as "With the last release, we put online dashboards supporting another $13 million of operations. With the coming release, the data warehouse front-ends will meet the needs of another $7 million of business processes."

In driving toward value quantification, project leaders should remember that they do not need to employ the perfect unit of measure, and nor do their claims of value contribution require an inordinate degree of precision. The goal is to provide a reliable measurement of the importance of the team's incremental deliveries, around which both business and IT can align. The fact that an agile team can reasonably quantify the value delivered with each subrelease signals that its leaders probably understand the project requirements well enough to keep the development effort on track and driving toward success. The exercise of value accounting brings that clarity to the team. Any measurement means that is objective and quantifiable, with a small enough grain to be able to show the team's steady delivery iteration by iteration, will suffice.

Allocating Value to Epics

Once the project architect has identified the value of the project, the team can begin allocating that value down to epics, themes, and user stories. The mechanism for allocating value varies with each of these levels. Given a value for an entire project, the project architect should then ask the project governance committee or at least the project sponsors to divide that single number between the epics that make up the project. Sometimes the steering group can perform this division easily, either verbally or via a poll orchestrated through the company's survey engine. The project architect needs only to check that the individual amounts assigned add up to value stipulated for the project as a whole.

In other circumstances, the relative values will be unclear to the executives, and they will struggle to agree on a single allocation of value across epics. Here, the project architect can resort to a game to derive the official values of each epic. First, he or she creates a poster for each epic, listing its definition and perhaps the major themes associated with it. The poster for a given epic will have a space designated for each governance council member. The project architect places those posters around the governance council's meeting room with plenty of space to walk around each one. He also provides each governance member with a stack of poker chips that totals $1,000, for example. At that point, he invites the governance members to spend the next 15 minutes walking around the room, with each member placing chips in any given epics poster. The governance members can leave as many poker chips on a given poster as they want, as long as that amount represents the value they subjectively place on the epic described by the poster. In practice, this process can take far longer than 15 minutes because the governance members will congregate around a few of the epics and discuss them at length before deciding how many chips to give them. These discussions may well reveal some additional executive-level requirements to the project architects.

After the chips have been placed on the posters, the project architect calculates the tallies for each epic and asks whether the totals truly represent the value of the epics. This part of the process may take a few iterations because the first round may yield some surprising tallies, such as an epic with negligible value, which may generate new insights and group discussion. The project architect welcomes the council members to redistribute their chips, if desired, until the tallies reflect the council's collective opinion of the epics' relative worth. Once he has secured agreement from the governance committee on the overall allocation of chips, the project architect will have a solid basis for allocating the overall value of the project to the epics, whether in dollars or some other unit of measure. For a backlog of epics with values expressed in different units of measure, this poker chip voting process can provide the conversion ratios for translating between those units. Consider, for example, a project in which one epic is valued as "20 full-time equivalent (FTE) positions saved" and receives 2000 poker chips, and another epic that is valued at "1000 process errors avoided" ends up with only 1000 chips. Here, the project architect can rationally propose to the governance committee that with regard to reporting value that the project team will deliver, every 100 process errors avoided will bump up the value accounting graph by the same degree as 1 FTE saved.

Allocating Value to Themes and User Stories

Once the governance council has allocated project value to epics, distributing value to the remainder of the epic tree is comparatively easy. The value of the themes comprising a given epic should add up to the value of that epic. For major themes, the project architect can ask the governance committee to distribute an epic's value using either analysis and discussion or the poker chip voting game described previously. However, the governance council will often defer to the directors who are most familiar with the business area of each epic to allocate the value to the themes.

In working with the directors who will be impacted by a given epic, the project architect can present his or her request for value allocations in a manner similar to the following:

- Epics represent new competitive capabilities for the company.
- This particular epic will enable the company to do X.
- The project sponsors and executive stakeholders stated that this capability is worth $Y million per year.
- Themes reflect analyses that merge, intersect, and subtract one set of information from another, giving directors such as yourself the insight needed to make sound business decisions.
- The epic we're considering now involves analyses A, B, and C.
- If these analyses taken together will allow the company to achieve $Y million, what contribution to that amount is reasonable to attribute to each analysis separately?
- Your answer can be as subjective as you like, and it does not have to be precise as long as it is something you can agree with over the next year or so while we build out the data warehouse.

At this point, the project architect turns the conversation over to the directors, who will then allocate the epic's value to the component themes.

Using the framework outlined previously usually empowers directors to assess the value of themes. The value of the user stories that make up a theme, however, becomes much more difficult for business people to assess. In the epic decomposition framework considered here, user stories represent business-level data checks that support staff need to perform to assure themselves that a particular theme-level analysis will not mislead the decision support system's end users. If asked to subjectively proportion the value of a given theme down to the user stories that support it, the business staff may answer, "What's the value of checking that all the suspended transactions were included versus knowing that no customers have been double-counted? It's impossible to say." The business staff cannot honestly identify the value of individual data checks because one must perform them all before the information from the warehouse will be useful. For that reason, EDW project leaders usually recommend that the business staff allocate the value of each theme to the underlying user stories using the story point estimate of each. The reasoning here is simply as follows:

If you need all 24 story points of data checks before you can use an analysis valued at $12 million, then when we deliver 8 story points in one iteration, we have gotten you one-third of the way closer to performing the analysis, and therefore that story is more or less worth one-third of the $12 million.

Readers should keep in mind that the team will be measuring value delivered by user stories only as a provisional tracking mechanism. The real objective is to deliver a full, usable analysis in a subrelease candidate. This level of accomplishment is represented by theme-level stories, which can be ascribed value individually. When teams award themselves value credit for delivering a few user stories, the team members are only communicating within the confines of the project room and only among themselves and with the product owner. Tracking value at the granular, user-story level helps the developers stay focused, but no one will try to equate those micro-accomplishments with themes delivered in a subrelease.

VALUE BUILDUPS BY ENVIRONMENT PROVIDE MOTIVATION AND CLARITY

The process of actually claiming credit for value delivered involves some subtlety that agile EDW project leaders will need to manage carefully. To make the process meaningful to both teammates and business stakeholders, the project leaders need to distinguish between the environments to which they have delivered finished modules.

Figure 8.6 shows the value delivered by two distinct teams. The top band on both these graphs shows the value of modules delivered to the system integration test (SIT) environment, a platform in which the team confirms that all the modules assemble properly together. Two other bands show the value promoted to user acceptance testing (UAT) and production environments. Although both teams have delivered approximately the same amount to SIT, clearly Team 1 is doing far better than Team 2 in truly creating value for the organization. Team 2 went 9 months before placing anything in UAT for end users to consider, and then another 9 months after that before offering them a second version of the application to review. Even worse, this team went 22 months before putting any services into production usage, and then it was only a small fraction of the warehouse's already programmed capability. As revealed by this graph, the customers of this project are paying dearly for new business capabilities that have been programmed but still denied to them. If the developers of Team 2 had claimed in Month 8 or even Month 20 to have delivered important value to the company, many staff members of the organization would have rightly scoffed at this assertion. That team's contribution

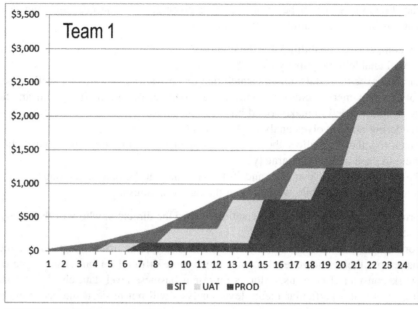

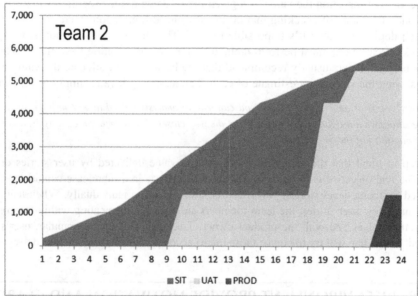

FIGURE 8.6 Value build-up charts distingishing between delivery environments.

is clearly locked up in the SIT or UAT environment, where it may be pretty to look at but is still providing no business benefits to end users who can only profit from features that are in production.

In contrast, the value buildup chart for Team 1 shows that it not only maintains a steady flow of value to the SIT environment but also makes frequent pushes of new application versions to UAT and nearly as frequent promotions of them into production. In essence, the first two bands are important leading indicators of team performance, but the bottom band is the only value deliveries that count. The top two bands on the value buildup charts are still worth drawing because they show stakeholders what is in the project's pipeline. They can also reveal project issues such as too many modules suffering large defects in SIT or too few features meeting with business approval in UAT and therefore being kept from production. When these graphs plateau, many different reasons could lie behind the bottleneck revealed. Seeing the problem highlighted by the value buildup in any of the three environments allows team leads, project governance committee members, and the project management office to realize that there are issues to investigate.

SUMMARY

EDW team leaders can take two actions that will quickly make their project backlogs clear and well aligned with business needs. First, they can adopt an epic decomposition framework that strongly types the stories in the backlog, giving a memorable and distinct purpose to epics, themes, and user stories. In one commonly used framework, epics come from sponsors and vice presidents, themes come from department directors, and user stories originate from the manager or analyst who serves as the product owner. Teams can utilize such a framework to define and refine items on the project backlog until they pass DILBERT'S test, indicating that they are good enough to enable programming to begin.

Second, EDW team leaders can ensure business alignment and requirements traceability with value accounting. Value accounting starts with the overall benefit expected from the EDW project, allocating it downward to the epics, themes, and user stories. The thinking required to distribute value smoothly down the levels of an epic tree ensures that the backlog is intelligible and coherent. Moreover, value accounting enables team leaders to state that they have made a quantifiable contribution to the company with every subrelease, in a way that will stand up to business stakeholder scrutiny. These claims of value delivery easily constitute a modest public relations effort that will build excitement and participation for the project among the business departments and that might someday save the EDW project from the yearly "budget ax."

Chapter 9

Artifacts for the Generic Requirements Value Chain

The goal of agile enterprise data warehousing (EDW) requirements management is to provide the team with a project backlog of stories accurate enough that the developers can begin transforming the business needs listed there into data warehousing/business intelligence (DW/BI) modules that provide valuable business insights to end users. Hopefully the team is working with a product owner who is sharp and motivated enough to author such a backlog. Yet even a capable product owner may have some trouble starting the process or staying focused over the long term. As a means of supporting a product owner who is struggling with her role, generic agile practitioners have identified several "context-defining artifacts" that can help considerably. My colleagues and I employ them so often while working with product owners on epics, themes, and stories that we consider them simply part of agile's generic requirements management (GRM) value chain. These helper artifacts assist the product owner in envisioning the situation at a deeper level so that she can effectively author user stories. They enable the information technology (IT) members of the team to assist in polishing the stories, making the backlog complete, and keeping the requested features within the proper scope. By providing a bit of structure to the story-writing process, helper artifacts also greatly reduce the requirements churn that can undermine the developers' agility when the team has made no provisions to keep the backlog pointed toward a single goal. Agile EDW team leaders should be familiar with this collection of context-defining artifacts so that they have tools to use in those moments when their product owner struggles to create a backlog or begins to author stories that seem inappropriate for the given project.

This chapter presents the most common context-defining techniques that support well the generic agile requirements management value chain introduced in Chapter 7. These techniques are listed in Table 9.1. The artifacts involved in this value chain demand some deep thinking but are very easy to draw, so they enable teams to avoid both underinvesting in discovery work and overinvesting in extensive requirements documentation. Team leaders should not feel that they need to employ any or all of them from the very start of their project, but instead should pick and choose from this collection as the situation merits. To better illustrate the usage of artifacts, this chapter provides an example for each one that ties conceptually to the revenue assurance project introduced earlier in Table 8.2.

BEWARE OF REQUIREMENTS CHURN

"Requirements churn" occurs when the product owner provides erratic direction for the team from one iteration to the next, to the point where no meaningful progress toward a goal can be made. This antipattern can waste so much time and effort that it will cause an agile team to fail.

Business customers who believe that agile methods are intended primarily to make the development team responsive to the business often indulge in the highest levels of churn. I once worked on a project in which the developers received the following requests from the product owner during the course of the first six iterations:

1. "I need features that show me what's happening with revenues."
2. "You know, it's actually cost reduction where we're having the greatest challenges."
3. "I've got to be able to combine revenue and costs to reveal where profitability is suffering."
4. "I think it's vendor performance that's hurting profits—show me metrics on deliveries."
5. "The company is taking too long to ship after receipt of order—show me fulfillment cycle times."
6. "The VP of sales just complained about customer retention—I need metrics on buyer satisfaction."

TABLE 9.1 Generic Agile RM Techniques

Technique	Purpose
Epics, themes, user stories*	Hierarchy to assist managing large number of stories
INVEST & DILBERT'S tests*	Check list for high-level evaluation of story quality
User modeling / personas	Profiles for placing stakeholder needs in sharp focus
User's hierarchy of needs	Service categories for keeping solutions as simple as possible
Mind maps & fishbone diagrams	Visual aids for decomposing complex problems
Vision boxes	Tangible artifacts for expressing the spirit of an application
Vision statements	Short, high-powered for forging agreements and advertising goals
Product roadmaps	Deliveries located in time to assist prioritization and buy-in

* Presented in earlier chapters.

Within 2 months, this product owner had the team switching erratically between data found in billing, manufacturing, fulfillment, and customer care systems. We were barely able to get a few tables landed from a given source system before we were suddenly chasing a whole new universe of operational data. Three months into the project, when the sponsor demanded to know why she had not yet seen any analyses on revenue, the IT members of the team could only say that the product owner had kept us scrambling and unfocused. It felt like a very thin reason for allowing such deep customer disappointment to occur.

EDW team leaders need to watch for the product owner-driven requirements churn and call attention to it when it begins to undermine team effectiveness. At that point, they will need to clarify that the intent of agile methods is to constantly deliver value to the business, not to program in endless circles. When churn reaches a pernicious level, these leaders must be ready to deploy some of the GRM artifacts in order to put gentle constraints on their product owner's thinking and thus yield a stable goal for the project. When a product owner's direction proves to be erratic, using a few of the GRM context-defining artifacts listed in this chapter will guide the team's business partners toward a more stable project definition and give the team a realistic goal toward which to steer.

USER MODELING/PERSONAS

Product owners are only human, and it is easy for them to focus too much on the needs of only the department to which they belong, given that those are the business challenges that will be foremost in their minds. Even the most conscientious product owners will need help envisioning the situation of business stakeholders in departments with which they are not as familiar. *User modeling* is a popular technique for heightening the product owner's understanding of a project's full range of stakeholders. It also helps with positioning the rest of the team to judge whether the backlog is complete and correct.

User modeling involves creating *personas* to make tangible the complete spectrum of users that an application must support. Personas were defined by the "father of Visual Basic," Alan Cooper, a thought leader in the software user experience movement. A "persona" is an imaginary representation of a particular user role, so vivid that everyone on the team feels like they know the person and can easily imagine his need for better software services [Cohn 2004].

During user modeling, the team members collaboratively create a set of archetypical users, at least one for every business department that the EDW is going to support. When creating these hypothetical individuals, the team gives each one a name, a face, and enough relevant details to make them seem real to the project members. The best persona names link to the role for each, such as "Sandy in Shipping" or "Frank in Finance." It is easy to find a likely portrait photo for each of them on the Internet, and teams print those portraits for display on their project board. Teammates then create a biography for each persona, describing the role that each persona currently has in the corporation and what his or her work experience must be like.

Biographies for user personas need to be detailed enough to capture the goals and priorities that each hypothetical person will have when he or she turns to the envisioned application, seeking business intelligence. Teams commonly include biographical components such as the following:

- The persona's job title, his boss, and direct reports
- His official and unofficial roles in the organization

Franny in Finance

Title:	Director of Accounting, Commercial Marketing Business Unit
Manager:	Tri-States District Controller
Direct Reports:	Revenue Analyst, Fulfillment Ledger Analyst, Sales Sub Ledger Analyst
Official role:	Certify monthly financials for the business unit selling to businesses
Cross-Organizational Committees:	Product Catalog Consolidation, Data Quality Stewards Center of Excellence
Annual Review Criteria:	Financial close by 5th day of account period, no more than 300 general ledger corrections
Upstream Business Partners	District controllers, regional provisioning directors
Downstream Business Partners:	Corporate strategy, public reporting analysts, operational directors (budgeting)
Works late because:	Reconciliation of district sub ledgers requires too many judgement calls to delegate it to her department's analysts
Biggest data challenges:	Joining district and regional sub ledgers extremely difficult due to conflicting master data elements, especially geography and product catalogs

FIGURE 9.1   User modeling example.

- Cross-organizational committees to which he belongs
- The criteria that will be used in his annual review
- How his work affects the company's customers
- His upstream and downstream business partners
- What forces him to stay late or work weekends
- His biggest challenges with information timeliness and accuracy

Figure 9.1 shows one of the personas created by the team that built the revenue assurance application used as an example in this chapter. By investing a moment in creating such profiles, even for only the primary users of an application, the team members empower themselves to extensively desk check their product owner's user stories. When given stories that do not ring true for at least one person in the user model, the developers can challenge the backlog's accuracy. When backlogs do not contain several user stories for each persona in the user model, the team can legitimately ask the product owner whether the backlog is complete.

END USERS' HIERARCHY OF NEEDS

Defining a complete and coherent set of stories for a project backlog is difficult work. Part of the challenge is the complexity of an EDW. End users from multiple departments have asked for business intelligence, but the precise application needed is strongly determined by the mix of requirements. Does the intended user community need mostly front-end dashboarding, back-end data integrations, or a complex combination of the two? The EDW team leaders will arrive at a better understanding of the users' requirements mix if they employ a systematic approach that guides their thinking.

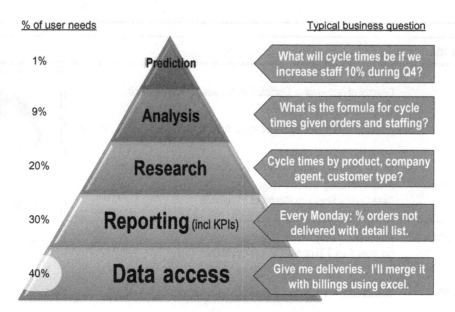

% of user needs   Typical business question

1%   Prediction   What will cycle times be if we increase staff 10% during Q4?

9%   Analysis   What is the formula for cycle times given orders and staffing?

20%   Research   Cycle times by product, company agent, customer type?

30%   Reporting (incl KPIs)   Every Monday: % orders not delivered with detail list.

40%   Data access   Give me deliveries. I'll merge it with billings using excel.

FIGURE 9.2   Business intelligence user's hierarchy of needs for the example project.

Throughout the years, I have relied on a very simple tool to help product owners better envision the requirements of a project business stakeholder: the *business intelligence hierarchy of needs*. In psychology, Maslow's "hierarchy of human needs" posits that people must progress through a sequence of distinct physical and emotional needs in a particular order that begins with food, water, and safety and then moves on to higher callings, such as friendship, companionship, achievement, and, finally, morality [Maslow 1943]. Use of a similar hierarchy of needs when modeling the customers of an EDW project can make the agile team more perceptive and faster to deliver appropriate solutions for the business they work for.

Figure 9.2 provides the BI hierarchy of end-user needs that my colleagues and I use at the start of our projects. It organizes five major delivery modalities for DW/BI services as a pyramid. With this pyramid, the agile team places at the bottom the services that it believes are more basic, foundational, and the easiest to deliver. Those services addressing more specialized needs and involving more technology, deeper designs, and rarified technical skills end up toward the pyramid's top.

Data Access

At the bottom of the pyramid is the most basic value that an EDW team can provide stakeholder departments: plain old data access. The presence of this layer asks the team to consider what percentage of the end users' BI needs could be satisfied by simply giving them access to the raw data staged from the source systems.

Many DW/BI professionals do not believe that simple data access is a solution modality that they should consider—until an EDW project takes too long to deliver anything of value. At that point, the sponsors and directors overseeing the project grow exasperated with IT and insist, "Just give my end users the dang data! I'll have them knit together some answers using spreadsheets because we need some visibility *now* on what is happening with our business." In fact, departmental power users, data miners, and shadow IT can all derive great value for the business department using nothing but raw data, and such an approach is far faster for developers to deliver than all other service modalities.

One challenge to this solution mode is the fact that business departments are often tempted to stop funding system development once they have access to raw operational data. DW/BI managers naturally fear that with every department taking a similar path, the organization will be flooded with many incoherent copies of source information, with hundreds of incomparable derived values based on them. Team leaders need to be clear that the point of including data access in the hierarchy of needs is not to eliminate the EDW in favor of data anarchy but instead to engender a deeper understanding of the concept of "solution" as they plan a business intelligence system. Perhaps the realities within the company will require straight access to landed data to be either a very temporary solution or ruled out altogether. In either case, the agile EDW leaders should not silently exclude simple data access from consideration without discussion.

They need to explicitly articulate the business case for their recommended use of straight data access because (1) there may be small ways in which this technique can save time and avoid enormous opportunity costs, and (2) explaining an alternative approach to the customers and the team will cause everyone to explore and balance the needs of the company thoroughly, leading to far better requirements. Accordingly, this simple solution to business problems should not be discarded off-handedly by EDW teams that are hoping to be agile.

Reporting

The next layer up is reporting—regular and predictable representations of aggregates, including key performance indicators (KPIs) for the company. Reporting often requires some data preparation and appealing visualizations, so this layer involves more work than simple data access. Reporting is valuable to end users who must answer the same question day after day, but many BI professionals these days do their best to avoid asking end users how their business problems can be solved with this approach. They prefer to discuss "self-service BI," suggesting that it will have greater value for the end users in the long term. Some of these BI professionals will admit that they prefer to discuss self-service BI in hopes of keeping IT out of the "report writing business" because in the past that solution modality left developers in an endless swamp of coding and fixing outputs. Many of them also shun reporting solutions because it involves some of our profession's oldest and most boring technology. However, IT can often write a few reports in one-tenth of the time it takes to build the star schemas that support self-service BI. Given that an agile team's goal is to constantly deliver value to the customer, the fact that reporting is an order of magnitude faster than IT's preferred EDW delivery mode means it still deserves careful consideration.

Research

The middle layer of the hierarchy provides *research* capabilities—that is, BI applications that allow end users to see the numbers behind the elements on a report. Users need to perform such investigations when reporting reveals an unexpected value or a KPI moves into the red. Such analyses can take many forms. For decision-support applications, empowering end users to see the numbers behind the KPIs would involve the dimensional analysis at which star schemas excel. End users can start with aggregate measures and drill to detail as the business context dictates. For BI applications involving more advanced analytics, seeing the numbers behind the KPIs may involve any one of a dozen favorite algorithms employed today by data miners [Chauhan 2012]. Whatever the style of analysis required, providing this capability in the research layer will necessitate a careful work on requirements, design, development, and validation, making the services of this layer in the hierarchy of needs far more expensive to build than those from the first two layers. Given the additional time and expense of applications in this layer, agile teams need to include them in their solution designs only when simpler approaches will not suffice.

Analysis

The last two layers of BI users' needs represent more special-purpose solutions. *Analysis* involves building statistical models that can explain what has happened in the company. For example, data miners may want to identify a set of independent variables that account for the movement of dependent variables with a high degree of precision. Once the model is perfected, it can be regularly executed by an application scheduler, so that trends in the dependent variables will be continually tracked and understandable.

Prediction

Prediction is similar to analysis, but it focuses on what will happen rather than on what has happened. Although analysis and prediction are growing in importance these days with the advent of technologies such as big data and purchasable social networking data, most EDW programs still consider data access, reporting, and research as more foundational and therefore place repeatable analysis and prediction at the top of the pyramid.

Benefits Offered by the BI Hierarchy of Needs

Business users' hierarchy of needs provides many benefits to those teams that take the time to identify an appropriate pyramid of requirement types for their end users.

First, the hierarchy provides a good agenda for requirements discovery sessions between the product owner and other subject matter experts from the business departments who will provide the team with requirements. Not only will stepping through the layers cause business stakeholders to think of the needs they have, but the practice will also lead the project architect to systematically test each requirement offered. By simply identifying the layer where the discussion seems to have concentrated, he or she can ask the stakeholders to try recasting each decision to fit the levels above and below that layer. If no one can think of a reason to address a requested capability from a different layer, then the group has probably envisioned the nature of that requirement correctly.

When stakeholders often get stuck disagreeing on how to express a requirement, team leaders can use the hierarchy to prompt them to think around the problem. By considering alternative layers, they will often imagine a new solution, one that involves a temporary service that yields instant value that can be followed by a more complete solution later in the project.

From the IT perspective, the hierarchy of needs helps keep the technical members of the agile EDW team from becoming "one-trick ponies." BI developers often become fixated on one technology, such as dimensional modeling or big data, and then pursue projects as if every need must be solved with their preferred solution. Star schemas, for example, are powerful constructs, but they require considerable time to design well and are expensive to populate with data, especially when they track the history of major business entities. Unfortunately, star schemas are difficult to defend when projects run too long and go grievously over budget.

By simply checking the BI hierarchy of needs on a regular basis, the team can kick itself out of its preoccupation with a single technical approach when a simpler solution might provide just as much value to the company. The lower layers of the pyramid will prompt the team to discuss easier, faster solutions with the product owner—solutions such as a simple spreadsheet connected to landing data or a simple report distributed to hundreds of business people that will let them coordinate efforts on a daily basis. By coming up with simpler solutions to the more banal services that an EDW must provide, teams can often save their resources to better deliver the complex features that the business also desperately needs.

Conversely, the higher layers will guide team leaders to ask more penetrating questions in situations in which the product owner instructs them to "simply put all the company data in a pivot table." By considering analysis models and predictive analytics, the team can ask, "What crucial causes and effects do you think our operational data could reveal?" and, "If we were to set up a model linking major operational drivers with business outcomes, what kind of if–then questions would you be able to answer?"

Figure 9.2 includes examples of requirements that emerged at all five levels of our hierarchy of needs during the revenue assurance project. The percentages listed for each level reflects the proportion of requirements that discussions with business stakeholders revealed could be met with services from each layer. These percentages proved very instructive to the development team. We could ask ourselves questions such as "Why are we spending all our time on designing a star schema for every aspect of this project when 50% of the requirements can be addressed with spreadsheets and scheduled reports linked to the staging layer?" Sometimes we found good reasons to press on with a star schema solution, but we also found places where we could remove fairly expensive components from the design, ultimately allowing our team to deliver more benefits while consuming less time and energy.

Many DW/BI designers and managers become alarmed when they see that a team's hierarchy of needs includes reporting, and especially simple data access. Readers should take care to realize that just because the hierarchy of needs includes these notions does not dictate that those types of solutions will be used. Instead, the hierarchy only forces the team members to ask themselves two important questions that should never be ignored by an agile team intent on delivering value quickly: (1) "Are we overengineering any aspect of the system we propose to build?" and (2) "Are their some temporary solutions available in the simpler layers of the hierarchy that will allow us to address an urgent business need and give us the chance to gather better requirements by observing how the users employ a nonpermanent capability?"

By nudging the product owner and developers to stretch their thinking throughout the requirements management process, the BI hierarchy of needs leads agile teams to far more focused and perceptive application requirements, thus giving them a higher probability of success.

MIND MAPS AND FISHBONE DIAGRAMS

Product owners sometimes have trouble decomposing requirements for an EDW in a disciplined, hierarchical manner, and this frustration can prevent them from drafting a solid set of user stories. Mind maps provide an easy, visual means for decomposing complicated business problems into multiple layers of components. Once the layers become clear, stories at all levels seem to be much easier to write.

Figure 9.3 shows a portion of the mind map we used for our revenue assurance project. The central problem statement came from the sponsor, making it a perfect place to start articulating an epic story. The sponsor suggested a couple of the first level of bubbles, but it was the director overseeing the project who gave us the definitive list, making it probable that each of these items would properly anchor a theme story. The director also gave us the factors making

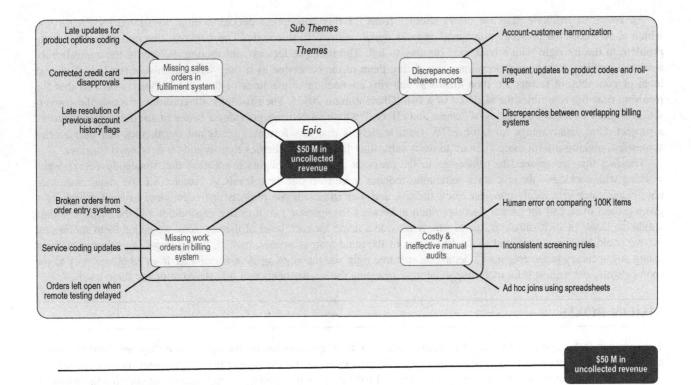

FIGURE 9.3   Mind map & fish bone diagrams.

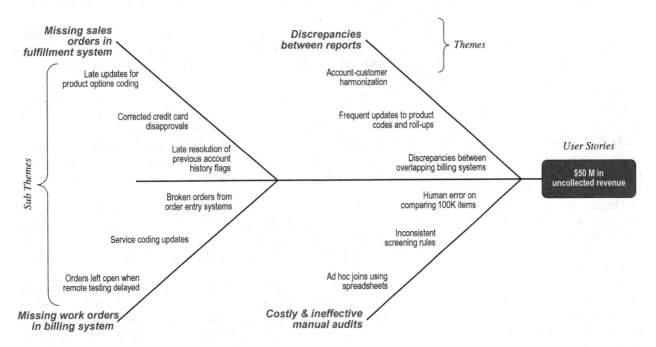

FIGURE 9.4   Previous mind map re-drawn as a fishbone diagram.

up the third-level items; looking at them, our team believed they were still information capabilities rather than business-level data validation steps. Thus, we categorized the third rung as subthemes rather than user stories. Even this simple diagram was enough to give our product owner the bearings needed to envision all the business validation activities he would have to perform before forwarding a particular EDW-based analysis to his director. That vision was enough to get him started dictating a long list of user stories for our team.

An *Ishikawa fishbone diagram* offers another form for this conceptual decomposition, illustrated by Figure 9.4, which shows how the previous mind map appears when redrawn in this style. The fishbone diagram puts the central problem to the far right with a backbone running to left. The multiple factors contributing directly to the central problem are then drawn with secondary lines connecting them to the backbone as if they were the ribs of the fish. The next level of contributing factors are then drawn as sub-ribs connecting to the lines of the next higher concept so that the resulting drawing resembles the skeleton of a fish [Charantimath 2011]. Such fishbone diagramming recasts the conversation slightly to focus on a series of "cause and effects," which sometimes provides a better fit for the requirements of a project. One disadvantage for agile EDW team leaders is that this format spreads out the themes and user stories somewhat, making it a bit more difficult to draw subsetting lines around themes that should be developed together.

The fact that we resorted to subthemes in the previous example highlights a situation that frequently occurs when working with backlogs—the epic stack sometimes requires more than just three levels. A business's EDW requirements do not always categorize nicely into just epics, themes, and user stories. Some projects and even some isolated aspects of a given project often call for greater decomposition in between the sponsor's competitive capabilities and the manager's data validation steps. In such situations, teams simply provide a name for each level of theme. Here, we called them *subthemes*, but we could have easily referred to the leaf nodes of the mind map as *themes*, making their parents *superthemes*, without losing any accuracy in the epic stack. Getting an epic tree right and maintaining clear traceability from each user story to the sponsor's original request is far more important than arranging the requirements in a tidy structure of just three levels.

VISION BOXES

Teams move faster and avoid wasteful tangents when they have a consensus on the application they are building. Many agile teams start their projects by collaborating on building a *vision box* for the project in order to foster such a consensus.

In building a vision box, the product owner leads the developers in creating an appealing container for the software they are about to build together. To draw a good vision box, teammates must imagine that they will offer their application for sale on a store shelf, as if it were a package of cereal or a shrink-wrapped software product for someone's home computer [Highsmith 2009]. Teams gain a solid, shared understanding of a project when they collaboratively author the content for the front and back of such a box.

As can be seen in Figure 9.5, the front of the vision box should show an interesting graphic and the major benefits that would compel the project sponsors to buy the product. The end-user hierarchy of needs, discussed previously, provides a good tool for making sure that the benefits cited on the box front represent the most important qualities that the stakeholders expect the BI application to provide.

The back of the box should provide some of the most important features and provide greater detail on benefits. I have found that teams can easily identify features and benefits at the right level for a vision box back by looking at high-level data models, even straw man dimensional models, for the data marts that they believe the EDW should support.

At the bottom of the box back, the team should also list the major "operating requirements" that the software will involve. These items should reflect the project's major assumptions and constraints, in addition to any important parallel investments that the project sponsors should plan on making (e.g., end-user training or better visualization software) in order to make the project a success.

Usually, a team only needs half a day or less to generate such a box. For newly formed teams, vision box sessions are a great way to break the ice between the business partners and the IT staff that will be collaborating on the software system. Inviting some of the major stakeholders who the product owner should represent during the project to the vision box session can greatly improve communications on the business side of the project and thus the accuracy of the project backlog that will emerge from that collaboration.

The end result is a tangible artifact that the team can keep on its project room table. When the product owner gets stuck authoring user stories, the team can toss him or her the vision box and ask, "What more do we need to build to deliver on this promise?" Alternatively, when the product owner suggests a user story that is wildly inappropriate, the team can turn to the vision box and say, "We don't see where that story fits on this vision box. Do we need to update the box or change the story?" In this way, the vision box can often provide just enough dampening on the product owner's erratic direction that the team achieves a linear direction toward its overall goals, preventing a large amount of wasted effort.

VISION STATEMENTS

Vision boxes work well to build a team consensus, but they are awkward to carry around the company. *Vision statements* provide a far more portable means of expressing the spirit of an application, and that portability can pay handsome dividends.

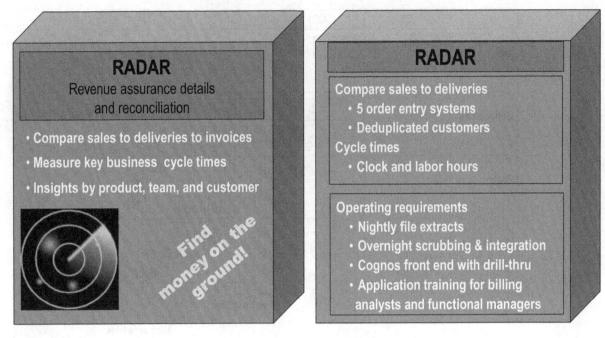

FIGURE 9.5   Front and back of a project vision box.

> For the billing analyst
>
> who needs to ensure that all products ordered are delivered, and all product delivered are billed for
>
> the Revenue Assurance Data Mart is a reconciliation tracking and analysis tool
>
> that integrates sales orders, work orders, and billing events across multiple business units and line-of-business systems,
>
>   allowing automated detection and detailed analysis of revenue generation fallout.
>
> Unlike the current, manual process of comparing monthly aggregate totals between LOB applications,
>
> our product identifies fallout daily, requires one twentieth as much labor, and has an order of magnitude greater accuracy.

FIGURE 9.6   Example of a project vision statement.

Figure 9.6 shows the vision statement for the example application used in this chapter. As one can see, a vision statement should include a phrase addressing each of the following points [Cobb 2011]:

- For (target customer)
- Who (statement of the need or opportunity)
- The (product name) is a (product category)
- That will (key benefit or compelling reason to sponsor the project)
- Unlike (primary competitive alternative)
- Our product will (statement of primary differentiation)

Although simple in form, vision statements can be amazingly difficult to author. They sometimes require half a day to get right, but the discussions leading up to the final phrasing will cement a single notion of the project's goals into the minds of every team member.

Like the vision box, the vision statement can dampen any requirements churn in which the product owner might be tempted to indulge. Its laser-sharp focus also greatly minimizes design churn and unproductive tangents by the IT members of the team, eliminating another major cause of wasted effort on many projects.

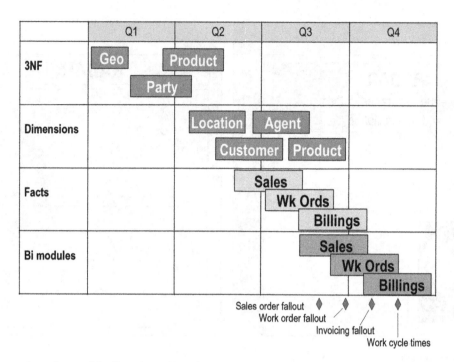

FIGURE 9.7 Product road map formatted for discussions with product owner.

I advocate asking every teammate to memorize the vision statement once the product owner believes it is worded correctly, not only to achieve clarity within the development iterations but also to build support for the programming effort outside the project room. When the developers memorize the vision statement, the project acquires a dozen or more ambassadors, all armed with a compelling value statement that describes the project's goals. The vision statement becomes the project's "elevator pitch" because it is short and makes an impression on those who hear it.

Whenever one of the developers finds herself riding up the elevator with the CEO or some other highly placed individual, she can share in one breath the exciting project on which she is working. As the developers circulate around the company during the next several months, many important people will eventually hear about the EDW project from them. When the next budget cycle occurs and the executives need some projects to cut, many of them will have heard the EDW's elevator pitch and therefore know of a compelling reason to continue funding it. That small dollop of good will may be all that deflects the budget ax away from the EDW and toward some other project that did not do as good of a job at advertising its value.

PRODUCT ROADMAPS

Agile focuses on constantly delivering value to the business. The *product roadmap* is the last of the context-defining artifacts for the GRM value chain, and it focuses on visualizing the delivery of value across time.

As shown in Figures 9.7 and 9.8, the agile EDW teams can prepare a product roadmap in two different formats. The examples shown here are for the same revenue assurance project used to illustrate the other artifacts discussed previously. The first format will speak more to the team's product owner than to other business stakeholders. It shows the time spans during which the team will be working on each major component that makes up the warehouse. Milestones toward the bottom indicate the point when users will receive the information capabilities of the major themes listed on the backlog. When the project architect creates this type of roadmap, he or she considers the total story points for the developer stories of the objects displayed. The story points for an object divided by the team's current delivery velocity translates directly into the number of weeks it will take to deliver the information capability, giving the project architect the durations to depict with each block.

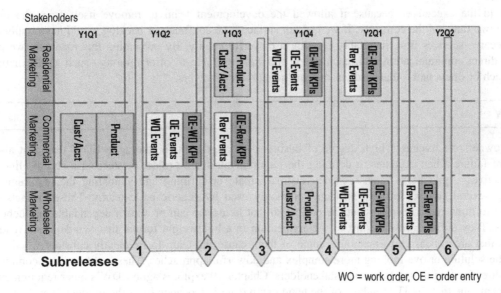

FIGURE 9.8 Product road map formatted for presentation to conflicting stakeholders.

The blocks representing major capabilities are placed in swim lanes named after the layers of the EDW's reference architecture, making it easy for both the team and the product owner to see when the project will achieve its major technical milestones. For example, Figure 9.7 shows that the stories comprising the conformed dimensions for party, product, and geography will take the team most of two quarters to construct in the integration (3NF) layer of the warehouse, although the move of that data into the dimensional layer will be finished soon after the third quarter begins. This roadmap also shows that the team will then focus on the fact tables and dashboard of the sales subject area, followed by those for work orders, and complete them before starting on the analytics for billing information.

These durations are based on two pieces of information that the team knows very well: the team's story point estimates and their current velocity. Because the team measures and confirms both of these quantities every iteration, the product roadmap is an *evidence-based* delivery forecast rather than a set of dates pulled out of the air, as happens with waterfall projects. With the roadmap shown in Figure 9.7 in hand, the product owner gets feedback on what his backlog looks like when projected onto the calendar, given the stories he has provided and the priority order he has given them. If he is disappointed with the delivery dates for particular themes, the product roadmap puts him in a good position to reason with his technical teammates about rearranging stories on the backlog until the desired services arrive in a business-reasonable time frame.

Such discussion can become very innovative and indeed agile. Consider, for example, that the product owner is frustrated that sales analytics will not be online until the fourth quarter. The roadmap shown in Figure 9.7 suggests that if he can live with a sales fact table without party information, the team could put the dashboard into production within 6 months. Of course, some rework would be required to later fold the party information into the star schema, but the roadmap gave the product owner the opportunity to think of splitting the implementation of the sales fact table. He was able to assert to both sponsors and teammates that the necessary rework would be more than balanced by the business value of a preliminary deliverable.

The second format, as shown in Figure 9.8, communicates better with stakeholders beyond the product owner. It removes the swim lanes for architectural layer, replacing them with bands that reflect major end user groups. Optionally, it also indicates when the team will place the application's subreleases into production. The example in the figure shows that the product owner's backlog dictates that the Commercial Marketing business unit will receive its three dashboards long before Residential Marketing users will see theirs.

When my colleagues and I presented this roadmap to the project steering committee, of course the vice presidents for Residential Marketing objected: "We represent 75% of this company's revenue, so our dashboards should be delivered first." "You may currently generate the bulk of revenue," answered the vice president for Commercial Marketing, "but my business unit is growing by 35% per year, and yours is shrinking by 10% per quarter. We represent the future of this company, so our analytics have got to be at the top of the list." IT benefited greatly from presenting this roadmap to the executives because it allowed the development team to remove itself from the disagreement between these two titans of the company. If we had not surfaced the conflict, our backlog would have implicitly decided who would receive services first, inevitably creating a powerful enemy. By presenting this roadmap, we put the vice presidents in direct communication with each other, and we were able to offer options—such as alternating between features for each business unit—that made us appear to be problem solvers.

SUMMARY

The product owner role assures a high degree of business—IT alignment for the agile EDW team but also creates a single point of failure when it comes to defining the requirements for a project or steering a straight line toward the project's objectives. Agile EDW teams can actively participate in defining and validating the requirements of their projects using several context-defining artifacts commonly used by generic agile teams. These artifacts prompt the product owner to think more deeply about the project so that he or she can provide a dependable and coherent stream of user stories. They define well the spirit of the application in a lightweight format that avoids overinvesting in large specifications that are expensive to maintain. Some of them cause the team to frequently consider whether it is over-engineering the solution or overlooking more complex and powerful approaches. These artifacts also communicate well the project's direction and timing to outside stakeholders. Chapter 10 explores agile EDW's other requirements management value chain, one that the IT members of the team can pursue independently of the product owner. Once these two value chains are combined, the requirements for an EDW project will be expressed from two separate viewpoints that can be used to validate each other and ensure that the team has not overlooked any crucial business needs.

Chapter 10

Artifacts for the Enterprise Requirements Value Chain

As useful as the generic agile approach to defining a project and reducing requirements churn might be, agile enterprise data warehousing (EDW) teams typically invest in a second requirements value chain to provide themselves with an independent viewpoint of the solution they should build. This second value chain represents an adaptation of techniques borrowed from the Rational Unified Process (RUP)—a pre-agile, iterative method that large systems integrators still employ to build large and complex software systems. Agile data warehousing teams strip the original value chain down to its bare essentials, borrowing only five of RUP's dozens of templates. The resulting requirements value chain can be completed quickly yet still provides a comprehensive project definition that takes into account a company-wide notion of system requirements. Moreover, the information technology (IT) members on an EDW team can pursue this second value chain without the product owner's participation, thus acquiring an independent perspective on their project that can be used to test the backlog provided by the product owner.

In reviewing the five templates we have chosen, some practitioners have suggested that the enterprise-capable value chain is too heavy-weight for an agile team. I typically respond to such comments by pointing out that all the adapted templates but the last are fairly brief, allowing them to be authored and updated quickly as business conditions change. Furthermore, teams are free to utilize these templates as supplements to the generic requirements management process that the product owner will be driving, rather than as the central requirements management process. Thus, EDW team leaders can safely employ the artifacts from RUP-based value chain selectively, in only those areas where the templates will resolve confusion or foster a stronger team consensus on the nature of the project.

THE GENERIC VALUE CHAIN CAN OVERLOOK CRUCIAL REQUIREMENTS

Although having a business partner embedded in the team to author a backlog for the EDW project results in high business—IT alignment, many veteran developers will notice that the resulting requirements lack a considerable amount of rigor compared to those generated by an IT-driven waterfall process. Developers familiar with traditional requirements gathering can instantly spot three important gaps in the generic agile approach outlined in Chapter 9. First, it leaves out many techniques that constitute disciplined software engineering as taught in university computer science programs. For EDW, it omits many of the interrogatories suggested by the time-tested frameworks used by TDWI and DAMA. These frameworks provide a systematic approach to deriving requirements, and veteran analysts rely on them so that they remember to consider all major types of requirements, not just functional needs. Fail to follow these frameworks, they warn, and a team can easily overlook crucial requirements that will become obvious only when the EDW needs to add an additional source or support a different aspect of the business than one planned for.

The second aspect of generic agile requirements management that concerns formally trained analysts is its reliance on the product owner. Scrum's collaboration model makes the product owner the keeper of the backlog. The remaining members of the team must trust that he or she has included everything essential in the backlog, such as the following:

- Sufficient requirements for all business departments, not just the one that the product owner works for
- Both large and small requirements for the end users in each department
- The larger analytical needs of the directors
- The strategic initiatives belonging to the executives
- The longer term trajectory of the company and its products
- The upcoming changes that one or more departments have planned for their business processes

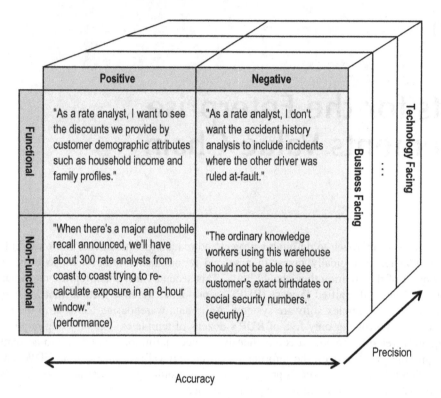

FIGURE 10.1   Three important dimensions to application requirements.

I have yet to work on a project in which the product owner's first backlog met even three or four of these criteria for a complete requirements set.

Third, veteran analysts warn that the product owner will be far too focused on functional requirements—that is, focused on what the application should do once it is online. Two other major categories of requirements must be incorporated in an application design before it will be a lasting asset for the corporation: nonfunctional and negative requirements. Figure 10.1 shows these major dimensions organized into a matrix. The two-by-two face of this matrix offers an example of requirements that the product owner should provide for each intersection of functionality and polarity. EDW team leaders can use this matrix to screen a backlog for major gaps in the requirements that it expresses.

The horizontal bands in Figure 10.1 reflect the distinction between functional and nonfunctional. The columns focus on positive versus negative requirements, described later. The depth dimension on this diagram refers to whether the analysts' current expression of a requirement is for the end user's consumption (business requirements) or more for providing direction to the developers (technical requirements).

The matter of functional versus nonfunctional requirements represents an area with which product owners often struggle. Functional requirements express how the applications should behave, that is, how they should look to the end users, respond to their actions, and the information they should manage or provide. Nonfunctional requirements pertain to all other aspects that make a system fit for its purpose, including crucial matters such as performance, security, and manageability. Hailing from the end-user community, product owners naturally focus on what the requested BI application should do, so that often a backlog omits most of the nonfunctional requirements that the system must meet.

The distinction between positive and negative requirements typically reveals another important gap for EDW team leaders to search for in a product owner's backlog. Positive requirements are relatively easy for business partners to author once they imagine using the data warehouse information to solve business problems. Negative requirements articulate undesirable outcomes that the company does *not* want to happen when the data or operating conditions for the system fall outside the expected boundaries. Unfortunately, the boundaries of a system prove difficult for business staff to understand, especially with a system that does not yet exist, and so product owners invariably neglect to author negative requirements, as important as they are to the detailed design of the application.

As for the third dimension on the diagram, business-facing versus technology-facing requirements, the product owner's backlog will naturally include mostly the former unless he or she has worked with data warehousing teams in the past. The derivation of developer stories from users stories speaks to this dimension, but developer stories are still single sentences describing components to build. The product owner will have to help developers with many further questions that straddle the border between a pure business requirement and a design decision.

TABLE 10.1 Contrast between Generic and Enterprise Requirements Management Value Chains

Agile's Generic Requirements Management (GRM)	Agile Enterprise-Capable Requirements Management (ERM)
Designed to elicit requirements from the product owner	Driven by the project architect—in fact, he or she can complete much of it before a product owner is assigned to the project
Largely limited to the product owner's vision, intent, and business knowledge	Seeks out needs and constraints from all relevant parties within the enterprise
Focuses on business requirements	Designed to pivot from business requirements into technical requirements
Focuses on positive and functional requirements	Deliberately prompts IT to consider negative requirements and nonfunctional aspects of the system
Generally requires team to utilize each level of artifacts, from epic to user stories	Either end of the value chain is optional, depending on context and development team

In my experience, good product owners provide a solid collection of positive, functional, business-facing requirements that leave the negative, nonfunctional, and technology-facing needs of the organization unaddressed. EDW team leaders need an additional tool that allows them to take the lead on closing these gaps, lest the company end up with another development project that churns on for years, never delivering true business value and squandering crucial business opportunities. Accordingly, team leaders should help the product owner complete their backlog using the generic requirements management (GRM) value chain outlined in Chapter 9 and should simultaneously have the product owner help them with the enterprise-capable requirements management (ERM) process described next. The ERM work will allow developers to test the results of the product owner's GRM process and thus ensure that the project has a complete and accurate collection of requirements. Table 10.1 highlights the major differences between these two approaches.

ERM AS A FLEXIBLE RM APPROACH

When we were first searching for an incremental approach to building EDW systems, my colleagues and I tried RUP on a few projects but found it to be far too ponderous for teams that need to start delivering services to the customer quickly. RUP's numerous and detailed templates led teams back into a big-specification-up-front approach reminiscent of waterfall project management. Ironically, analysts would get lost in all the detail that RUP generated so that crucial requirements still got overlooked despite all the effort to identify them completely. To make the RUP approach to product definition workable, we streamlined its requirements management process. From the dozens of artifacts it stipulates, we boiled the process down to just five documents, arriving at the ERM value chain described here. For each of the artifacts we kept in our process, we distilled the template from dozens of pages to a few bullet points each.

The resulting enterprise requirements management approach still attains RUP's comprehensive orientation, but it defers all the detail that can wait, true to agile EDW's preference for 80/20 specifications. The result is a technique that is fast to complete and will take a team's product definition effort all the way from the clouds down into the weeds, when and where such detail is warranted. Table 10.2 provides a quick summary of the RUP-based requirements management artifacts presented in this chapter, including a capsule summary of the intent of each document. Note that the value chain begins with very short artifacts authored by important business stakeholders and then transitions to still brief items authored by the project architect. In practice, the EDW team leaders take the effort to interview key business stakeholders, with or without the product owner, and then write up the first two artifacts for them. This work provides the team leaders with the information needed to begin authoring the remaining ERM artifacts where they are needed.

When we lead agile EDW projects, my colleagues and I benefit greatly from this second value chain for project definition because it provides an independent perspective on what an application should be, giving us "stereoscopic vision" on the endeavor and largely ensuring that important requirements are not overlooked. As indicated in Figure 7.10, the ERM value chain intersects with the GRM approach at the user story level. When teams find that the requirements generated by these two systems do not intersect, they have uncovered a fatal risk to the project—the product owner has a very different application in mind than the rest of the organization, which IT has just finished interviewing. Agile EDW's two-prong requirements management approach gives the team the opportunity it needs to resolve such fatal miscommunications before coding begins.

TABLE 10.2 Summary of the Artifacts Comprising the Enterprise Value Chain

Artifact	Pages	Author	Intent
Sponsor's concept briefing	1–2	Project sponsor/VP (interviewed by the project architect)	"Here's how we're going to make money with DW/BI's help …"
Stakeholder requests	1–2 each	Department director (interviewed by the project architect)	"Here's what is weak about our current DW/BI support and how we would fix it if we were IT …"
Vision document	3–5 with three diagrams	Project architect	"Here's the BI solution for all of the business problems in scope …"
Subrelease overview	3–5	Project architect	"Here's the outline for a particular subset of solutions we should build soon …"
Module use case	5–10	Systems analyst	"Here's the outline of a major module needed in the next subrelease …"

The previously mentioned artifacts alarm many agile purists who claim that such a multistep process will push projects back into waterfall's big spec up front. Two considerations should assuage this concern. First, all of the ERM artifacts are optional. Agile EDW teams should use each artifact when and where it will mitigate risk. The rest of the ERM artifacts should be omitted from the project definition effort because the GRM approach of epics, themes, and users stories will do well to get the project started. The only exception to this notion might be the vision document. We have yet to work an agile project that succeeded without the clear picture of the team's destination, a picture that this artifact provides very well.

Second, all of these artifacts except for the last one, the module use case, are very short. They range from only one page of content to five pages plus three diagrams, as noted in Figure 10.1, so agile teams can still get a project defined in a short time and move on to coding their first subrelease without great delay. True to agile artifacts in general, the ERM artifacts are all very quick to author once a team has gotten the deep thinking done, making them very fast to update when requirements change. Sometimes, the module use case can become a longer document, but mostly because it includes source-to-target mappings, first mentioned in Chapter 5. Many data integration programmers insist on source-to-target maps, no matter what method the team employs, so the ERM approach does not add any appreciable documentation burden beyond what a team has already had to plan on.

FOCUSING ON ENTERPRISE ASPECTS OF PROJECT REQUIREMENTS

The three dimensions of requirements depicted in Figure 10.1 play a major role in planning a full requirements management approach, so they deserve more detail. Astute readers will see all three of these dimensions at work in the remaining sections of this chapter, in which we examine the artifacts making up the ERM value chain.

Functionality Dimension

Requirements tend to divide into functional and nonfunctional sets of system capabilities. Functional requirements focus on the behavior that the application should manifest for the immediate user or other system with which it exchanges information. They express what the application should "do" for the person utilizing its user interface and the behaviors that the user's inputs should unleash. The example provided in the upper left quadrant of Figure 10.1 speaks to what the user should be able to see in the BI dashboard after having drilled into a subject area.

Nonfunctional requirements are application aspects viewed outside of this immediate human–machine interface. As illustrated in Table 7.2, they focus on qualities of the application as a system, including many qualities that determine the application's total cost of ownership. When these requirements are not met, the costs of maintenance and re-engineering over the lifetime of the application typically grow dramatically. The example in the lower left quadrant of Figure 10.1 pertains to performance, an important nonfunctional requirement. Teams that understand an application's performance requirements before finishing construction will not have to re-engineer the system when user demand peaks, saving considerable development expense and thus keeping the cost of system ownership from climbing after implementation.

Nonfunctional requirements divide further into two groups: application-specific and externally set architectural groups. The technical members of the agile EDW team will be well positioned to identify some nonfunctional requirements, such as manageability and recovery times, as they start thinking about the system's design. However, many nonfunctional criteria will be established by other enterprise planning teams, and the project leaders may have to put some effort into gathering this input from these groups. For example, the company's enterprise architecture group may have declared that all major systems should be able to communicate with other systems using the company's standard for service-oriented architecture. Moreover, the company's data governance council may have stipulated that all data management teams will support a shared repository of customer information rather than building a separate repository for each project. The agile EDW team will need to incorporate these standards in its system design. If they do not manage these nonfunctional requirements, the external architectural groups will undoubtedly try to stop the team's development efforts until the discrepancy is addressed.

Product owners and business stakeholders naturally focus on the services they desire from the application, so they contribute mostly functional requirements. The templates of the ERM value chain deliberately include several key questions prompting the agile team to consider the application's nonfunctional requirements so that team leaders can appropriately judge whether their design has sufficiently controlled the system's likely cost of ownership.

Polarity Dimension

The second dimension that EDW teams need to keep in mind is the distinction between positive and negative requirements. Positive requirements express responses that the team desires the application to make when given inputs and triggers fall within an expected domain. Negative requirements state responses that the team hopes will not occur, including situations in which inputs and triggers fall outside of the anticipated range. The functional example in the upper right quadrant of Figure 10.1 involves sets of records that the users want excluded from the analysis in response to an expected query. The nonfunctional example below it describes records that should not be visible when the user requesting data lacks the necessary access credentials.

Every positive requirement that users can imagine involves a combination of expected inputs and triggers. Because there are typically several possible violations of the boundaries that define those inputs and triggers, multiple negative requirements exist for every positive requirement, making the negative requirements more numerous and often exhausting to fully identify. For that reason, users tend to focus on only the positive requirements, thus making the GRM value chain susceptible to large oversights in the negative realm. By providing a disciplined approach for the project architect to pursue, the ERM value chain gives the development team the forum it needs to ensure that the application's negative requirements can be adequately addressed as well.

Orientation Dimension

The third aspect of a project's requirements that agile teams wish to actively manage during discovery and analysis is its orientation. Some requirements statements are clearly business facing—that is, they articulate the need in a way that business users can recognize and validate as an important need of theirs. At the other extreme of this dimension are technical requirements—that is, statements that speak to the technical members of the team and express system features and capability in a manner that enables system design and programming. The classic example of a DW/BI technical requirement is the source-to-target map, which details which source attributes combine into one or more derived values in the target tables, as well as the transformation logic necessary to create those values. Typically, product owners will not spontaneously begin to spell out this detailed level of need until after they author each user story. Instead, the EDW team leaders must make the time to query for this level of guidance.

Because the team's greatest responsibility is to provide software that users can employ to further the company's objectives, requirements typically start out business oriented, phrased mostly as positive, functional needs. As the bulk of the discovery process is completed, the developers on the team begin to think about what the business requirements imply about the coded modules they must build. Thus, business requirements steadily become more technology facing as the team works with them. As the start of construction draws near, the developers find that the product owner believes that he or she has finally articulated the business needs well so that the team can focus mostly on translating them to a more technical level. This progression from business to technical requirements does not occur in a single step, but it should instead evolve along a repeatable pattern so that important factors are not overlooked and the resulting GRM and ERM value chains intersect well, as we need them to do.

Teams typically define their own waypoints for this continuum, such as the following:

- High-level business requirements
- Detailed business requirements
- High-level technical requirements
- Detailed technical requirements

The key step for project leaders is to realize that they will need to manage this progression, so they should prepare in the early stages of the project by explicitly defining the waypoints they want to use and any special artifacts to associate with each.

Streamlined ERM Templates

The enterprise-capable requirements management approach that my colleagues and I adapted from RUP achieves the objectives laid out previously. It allows requirements discussions to focus at first on positive, functional, business requirements. However, once the team reaches the third artifact—the vision document—the templates ask the team to focus progressively more deeply on negative, nonfunctional, technical requirements. As can be seen in the listings that follow, we reduced the templates for the ERM artifacts so that they remain lightweight. Each template has six or fewer components, so they have been calibrated to still provide 80/20-level requirements or design specifications. If we had kept any more than the core elements for each template, we would have sunk agile EDW teams back into the protracted project definitions efforts that make RUP so onerous to use.

Because some EDW projects might be able to benefit from the lengthier version of these templates with their full complement of questions, agile data warehousing teams should know that the original templates can be retrieved from the website for OpenUP, the public domain version of RUP [Eclipse Foundation 2012]. I suggest that EDW team leaders familiarize themselves with the full outlines of the artifacts because every project has a unique challenge that one or two questions from the original template can sometimes solve handily.

UNCOVERING PROJECT GOALS WITH SPONSOR'S CONCEPT BRIEFING

Every EDW project *should be* founded on a clear notion of how data warehousing will enable the company to achieve the business goals selected by project sponsors. Unfortunately, those goals are often left unspoken, or at least hidden from the developers who might then spend years of their lives programming toward a purpose they do not understand. In my experience, leaving the mission of a project unexpressed only sets up the development team for confusion, oversights, and mistakes that easily lead to a devastating waste of time and money. To mitigate that risk, EDW team leaders should invest a short time drafting the first artifact in the ERM value chain, the sponsor's concept briefing (SCB).

The SCB is a single page of text that states how the executives funding the project believe that the company will achieve new competitive capabilities using DW/BI technology. The input needed to create this artifact is best gathered through an interview of the executive who is requesting *and willing to pay for* the application envisioned by the project. An executive who wants to contribute requirements but no funding should be approached to provide a stakeholder request, which we discuss next. Usually, IT staff members will only be able to get 15−20 minutes of a sponsoring executive's time, so the template guiding their questions will have to be short.

Figure 10.2 provides the streamlined template for an SCB that we use in my consulting company. This template should result in no more than a page of prose, and the ideas it captures should contain clear statements of project intent and value to which all other artifacts can be traced. With a concise statement of the entire project's overall value proposition, this document will anchor all subsequent requirements artifacts, as well as decisions regarding scope and application design, to a core set of notions that the sponsors consider important.

As mentioned in Chapter 8, sponsors should be asked for the new competitive capabilities that they hope to obtain for company. The sponsor's concept template focuses precisely on new capabilities, and thus the elements mentioned in this artifact should directly generate epics for the project backlog.

Figure 10.2 lists the minimal subset of topics needed to get a project underway, in my experience. Readers who are trained in the Project Management Institute's (PMI) approach to defining projects will note some overlap with PMI's notion of a *project charter*, another short artifact. The project charter differs in that it focuses on (1) the nature of the application once delivered and (2) the authority of the project manager, whereas this template is a *requirements* document that expresses only business needs and the value that the requested application should bring to the company. Teams that have extra energy may profit from drafting a project charter also, although this document may have been already completed by the project manager associated with the EDW engagement, in which case team leaders should check that the two documents do not contradict one another.

EDW Sponsor's concept briefing (Template)

Justification

How have the sponsors justified the need for this project?

- e.g., revenue generation, cost savings, government mandate, maintain the business

Customer experience

What will be the impact upon our customer's experience with the company by business unit and functional group?

- e.g., marketing, ordering, provisioning, repair, support, billing, self-service

Internal impacts

What will be the internal impacts upon those functional groups?

- e.g., marketing, ordering, provisioning, repair, support, billing, self-service

Value of the project

{Insert a description of the driving value that the sponsors plan to capture with the proposed application, quantified in units such as dollars revenue, hours saved, audit discrepancies eliminated.}

Program metrics and benefits

- How will the sponsors measure the success of this project especially before the value of the project has fully materialized, that is, what "leading indicators" will they be watching?
- What measures will be employed and who will be collecting them?
- What are the target levels those measures should achieve and by when?

FIGURE 10.2 Streamlined template for a streamlined *Sponsor's Concept Briefing* (SCB).

Justification Type

This section of the sponsor's concept template asks the sponsor to classify the overall motivation for the large amount of money that the company is about to invest in DW/BI. Such motivations can be expressed in many ways, so the reader will have to take a moment and customize the template here for the needs of his or her particular organization. In the SCB template, I listed the most common categories for justification on the template: revenue generation, cost savings, government mandate, and maintaining the business. I have seen justification decomposed in other ways, such as the following:

- Integrating business systems
- Deepening business partnerships
- Expanding market share of strategic products
- Achieving operational efficiency
- Balancing investment and returns

Still a third set of justification categories that I prefer to use originates from Ram Charan's short and powerful primer for corporate staff members, *What Your CEO Wants You to Know* [Charan 2001]. In his presentation, Charan states that every company contains a "money-making machine," and project leaders can contribute much by creating applications that enhance that machine. According to Charan, a company's money-making machine has five goals:

- Attracting and retaining customers
- Generating revenue
- Expanding the margin between revenue and costs
- Accelerating the velocity of assets (e.g., increasing inventory "turns")
- Achieving regulatory compliance

Given considerations such as these, any other objectives that stakeholders and product owners might later obsess over will pale in comparison. Thus, the sponsor's concept briefing gives the team leaders a powerful tool for keeping the project correctly aligned.

When I get the rare chance to ask an application's sponsor for the justification of the project, I ask him or her to name only one from the list I am using. Sponsors naturally want all they can get for their money, so they will be tempted to list three or four of these enormous goals, but in my experience that is a setup that will lead the EDW to grief. If a sponsor cannot identify a single, overriding justification for the project, his uncertainty suggests that he is actually attempting to get two or more projects developed with a single budget. For me to lead a team into a commitment that is so drastically underfunded from the start is grossly unfair to my teammates. Gently insisting on a single justification at this very early stage of the project is the single most effective way I have found to protect my team from such overcommitment. Even if I lose in this effort, the executive usually sees some wisdom in not trying to "boil the ocean" with a single project and is able to narrow down the mission considerably, making it all that more achievable for the development team.

Customer Experience Impacts

A project as expensive as an EDW will need to change the organization is some crucial way. The most valuable of projects will manifest improvements that the company's customers can see and appreciate. This section of the template prompts the sponsor to articulate the impact on customers and other external partners by considering how operational changes across the company's major business divisions will appear to these outside parties. The template outline provides a starter set of business groups, namely marketing, ordering, provisioning, repair, support, billing, and self-service. Team leaders will have to adapt these rubrics to match the actual organization of their company. They should keep in mind that some important categories, such as "self-service," will not appear on a formal organization chart for the enterprise. However, these hidden categories may be inferable from the current set of business initiatives being promoted by the company's executive team. For that reason, project leaders might wish to review recent directives from the executive suite while customizing this list of business areas to consider.

Functional Area Impacts Assessments

EDW projects should not only improve the company's attractiveness to customers but also make life better for the business staff. Such improvements may manifest as cost savings, but it is hoped that the EDW's impact will amount to something even more valuable, such as getting more done in a given amount of time or even making better decisions with less stress. This portion of the template prompts the sponsor to articulate those improvements across the company in a first level of detail by breaking them down into the same functional areas used for customer experience impacts. Together, these two sections suggest that there is a single reality to the company—the functional divisions—and the goals of a project must be understood via that structure when viewed both from within (the staff's perspective) and from without (the customer's perspective).

Value of the Program

In my experience, if the sponsor cannot state the value of the project with clarity, then the development team will struggle incessantly to achieve success. Accordingly, the sponsor's concept template anchors the project's value accounting effort by prompting the sponsor to quantify the value that she hopes to achieve with the BI investment she is proposing to make. Perhaps the sponsor will require some time to derive a reasonable answer to this request. Perhaps she will need some help gathering and crunching the numbers to calculate the project's value. The project architect should volunteer to perform as much of this work as necessary to get a sponsor-sanctioned statement of value for the project. Getting a solid number on which to base the rest of the project is worth nearly any effort because when the project is complete, the project leaders will be able to claim a compelling contribution to the company, in a form such as "We have now ..."

- brought visibility and manageability to $15 million of new annual revenue;
- enabled a $10 million reduction of annual materials consumption;
- provided the reporting necessary to run 15% of this $50 billion company; or
- saved each sales rep in Global Accounts 15 hours monthly, which is worth $200 million in annual revenue when multiplied by the business the sales reps generate.

When linked to an unambiguous quantity quoted straight from the project's executive sponsor, such claims of contribution of value will ring true. Without such an anchor, others in the business will view such claims as only grandstanding.

Program Success Metrics

This section of the template essentially asks the sponsor to provide some definitional and logistical details to the statement of value derived previously. Success can be a more detailed notion than the project's overall value. Often, the value of a project, such as expanding market share, will be realized over years, in which case the success of the project needs to be measured on a far shorter time frame. This measurement might need to focus on the "leading indicators" that the executive sponsor will employ to decide whether the long-term value is being realized on a monthly or quarterly basis. Those measures of success will need to be quantified, and those quantities gathered, calculated, and compared to a target level. This section of the template, by stating all of these considerations—even at a high level— essentially outlines the contract between sponsor and IT for the construction of the warehouse.

Chapter 9 provided an example for authoring themes and stories for an epic for an insurance company that focused on "expanding market share by providing call lists to sales agents for cross selling to existing customers." When the sponsor of that project was asked for leading indicators that would tell him week by week if market share was bound to expand soon, he suggested the EDW team show him evidence that

- the monthly number of calls by sales reps to customers with only one or two products has increased;
- the number of quotes to these customers for new products has grown;
- closure rates on such quotes have improved; and
- total dollars for first payment on these quotes have increased $25 million per quarter.

Often, discussion of leading indicators reveals additional metrics that the warehouse will need to provide to the business. Such a realization is a positive event because those needs were requirements that existed but were hidden, coming to light only because the EDW project leaders were disciplined enough to ask how to measure their success.

IDENTIFYING PROJECT OBJECTIVES WITH STAKEHOLDER'S REQUESTS

The SCB will explicitly mention the major parties impacted by the EDW project. EDW team leaders should then interview each of these parties because they are clearly major business stakeholders in the project. These stakeholders will be easily identified in the two sponsor concept sections that asked how the experience of customer and internal staff in each major company function would improve. The team's project architect and business analysts should interview the directors of each of these divisions or departments in order to obtain the next level of detail regarding the requirements of the EDW application. As suggested in Chapter 9, directors typically provide theme-level stories for a project; thus, each stakeholder request should map directly to a small collection of themes on the project backlog. Because these directors often provide only fleeting opportunities for an interview, the project leads need to enter these discussions prepared, with an effective outline of essential questions to have answered. The core of a stakeholder's request is listed in the template provided by Figure 10.3. Descriptions for these essential elements follow.

Business System Challenges

Given the degree of computerization in today's companies, business departments typically think of their processes in terms of a series of applications. Members of the typical finance department, for example, usually describe their operations by listing how transactions and aggregations move between the subledger systems, the general ledger application, and utilities such as fixed assets and standard costing, to name a few. Accordingly, the opening section of the stakeholder request template asks them to reflect upon those business applications with which they are struggling. Often, this will be expressed in terms of information flows between systems, such as "We cannot get the sales order system to reliably transfer new orders to the provisioning system, so the sales force will take an order but fail to roll a truck to the customer's home for product installation." In asking where each department is challenged, the EDW leaders should try to limit the discussion to fit within the context of the sponsor's concept for the project; otherwise, a department might dump an unmanageable collection of ongoing frustrations upon the development team.

Current Manual Solution

Long before the EDW team interviews them, the business departments will have addressed their systems frustrations with clever, manual workarounds. Accordingly, this section of the template prompts stakeholders to describe at a high to medium level the steps that they currently take to fill the gaps that their current business applications leave

EDW Stakeholder's request (Template)

Business systems challenges

Which business processes problems lack good solutions?

- Within the scope of the reigning sponsor's concept briefing, of course.

Current manual solution

How do you solve these problems now?

Desired business solution

How would you like to solve these problems given the company's information?

Data volumes

Describe the number of transactions the systems mentioned above manage in a given unit of time.

Scope of the user community

Who are the users?

How many in each business unit and department?

Scope of dependent systems

Which other applications do you need to interface with both as source and targets of information?

FIGURE 10.3 Streamlined template for a streamlined *Stakeholder Request* (SHR).

unaddressed. The development team needs to understand these because they often represent a process amazingly close to the solution that the warehouse will need to automate.

Desired Business Solution

Each department's current workarounds will consist of a mix of manual work and computer-assisted work. As clever as these provisional solutions might be, they are undoubtedly not as capable, reliable, or repeatable as the business would want. This section of the template prompts the stakeholders to describe what a complete solution would look like to them. If the developers listen carefully, they will hear a rough description of the algorithm they need to implement in the warehouse, usually via business rules programmed into the extract, transform, and load (ETL) modules for the data integration layer of the reference architecture.

Volume Requirements and End-User Census

The project leaders will need some notion of the data volumes that a department wrestles with and the end-user community that the BI application will need to support. In this section, the template prompts the team leaders to inquire about both so that they can surmise the approximate size of the application they are going to build. A requirement based on 50,000 transactions and 10 users results is a very different system design from designs involving billions of transactions and thousands of users.

Dependent Systems

Data warehouses may have been only targets for information during approximately the first 20 years of our profession, but today they are an increasing part of an overall information ecosystem. They often gather and transform data in bulk, only to pass subsets on to one or more operational systems that need summary or forecasted figures. They also provide data extracts for a wide variety of analysts in departments other than those sponsoring the EDW. This section of the template prompts the project leaders to ask about such downstream systems so that the project's "nonhuman stakeholders" can be identified and supported as well.

SKETCHING THE SOLUTION WITH A VISION DOCUMENT

The vision document is the pivotal artifact in the ERM's value chain of five templates. It connects upstream requirements discovery efforts to downstream requirements analysis work. When shown to the project's business partners, it communicates the functional intent of the project so that they can assess and confirm that the application, as conceived, will solve the organization's pressing business problems. When shown to the project's technical teammates, it communicates the spirit of the proposed application so that each specialty can begin digging into the aspects of requirements analysis that lie within its skill domain.

For all its power, the vision document is an amazingly short document with only two written lists and three diagrams, as depicted in the template provided by Figure 10.4. Because of its brevity, it can be easily authored and updated by the team's project architect, making it a reliable polar star for the team and the project's stakeholders to steer by. Because the entire artifact rarely exceeds 10 pages, a project architect really has no excuse not to take a half day to pull together a vision document, especially because this single artifact so readily ensures that IT understands the business's desires and constraints, thus dramatically reducing project risk.

Solutions Statements

The first list in the vision document is a small collection of *solutions statements*. Solutions statements take a standard structure so that they can be readily understood:

- The business problem of {A} affects groups and major operational systems {B} and {C}.
- So, the company needs to do {D} in order to increase/decrease hard measures {F} and {G}.

Figure 10.5 provides sample solutions statements for the revenue assurance project that is being used as an example.

Readers who consult the original templates will see that RUP calls this component of the vision document *problem statements*, but I believe the word "problem" is far too negative, especially because the second part of problem statements clearly provides a solution to the business pain identified. Note that the second half of the statement states the business value that solving the problem should yield. This portion of the statement should trace back to the benefits listed in the sponsors' concept briefing, positioning the development team to begin the practice of value accounting.

Practitioners may need to exercise care when stating the hard measures for the second half of each statement, depending on the culture of the company within which they are working. For example, if the solution statement called for a 30% reduction in reconciliation errors, and the application only achieves a 29% improvement, critics in some organizations would actually fault the team for falling short of the target rather than praise it for making an important contribution.

Features and Benefits List

This section of the template prompts teams to list the major solution capabilities that they promise to deliver. The stakeholders and project managers can use this collection as a punch list at any point in the project to quickly assess what has been delivered and to discuss timing for the remainder. Figure 10.6 provides a sample list of features for the example revenue assurance application.

In practice, agile teams do well to employ their project backlog to discuss features that have been delivered and those that are soon due, especially once that backlog acquires story-point estimates that allow evidence-based positioning of deliverables in time. Keep in mind, however, that the vision document is often prepared many weeks before a backlog is started so that while the company is striving to define the project, this list will be the only census of desired features that the team will have to work with.

Note that this section calls for features *and benefits*. Just prompting the business to explain the benefit expected from each listed capability will provide a valuable reference when the team must prompt its product owner to provide rationales in the "so that" portion of the users stories.

For all its simplicity, the features and benefits list actually represents a crucial milestone in the life cycle of the project because it is the definition of the application as a solution to the overall business problem. Consider Figure 10.7, in which the individual business problems have been placed to the left and the proposed features of the application to the

---
EDW Vision document (Template)

Solution statements

The following solution statements distill the business problems identified by the project sponsors and major stakeholder groups while discussing the desired outcome of this project.

- The problem of...
- Impacts groups of... (either customers or internal functional departments)
- So, our company should... (business description of the proposed solution)
- In order to impact the following hard measures:
    o Measure 1: (description, target measurement level, time frame)
    o Measure 2: ....

Major features and their benefits

The following major features will provide the benefits listed.

- Feature 1
    o Benefit 1 (description, target measurement level, time frame)
    o Benefit 2 ....
- Feature 2....

Context diagram (Level 0 data flow diagram)

This diagram depicts three crucial elements of the proposed application, all shown upstream or downstream from the EDW solution, as appropriate:

- Sources of data
- Supported end user groups
- Supported downstream business systems

{insert context diagram here)

Target Business Model

This diagram depicts how the company's information will appear to business users once available via the proposed application. This information is shown by major category, not necessarily at the entity level. The attributes for these information categories will be established later, as each component of the proposed application approaches the time of its development. Darker elements are dimensions, lighter elements represent measures (a.k.a. facts or metrics).

{insert target business model here)

High-Level Architecture Diagram (Level 1 Data Flow Diagram)

This diagram depicts how the proposed application will acquire major categories of data and then cleanse, integrate, and present it for end-user analytics. The vertical bands represent separate layers within the enterprise data warehouse. Darker elements are existing components.

{insert high-level architecture diagram here)

Non-Functional Requirements

This list identifies qualities of the data services the application must provide besides the actual data offered for end-user analysis or downstream application support.

- Non-Functional Requirement 1:
    o Category:
    o Short description:
    o Quantified goal:
- Non-Functional Requirement 2:
    o ....

FIGURE 10.4 Template for a streamlined *Vision Document* (VDoc).

EDW / RADAR Subject area: Solutions statement #3

The fact that Customer Care's order entry system does not successfully transfer all sales order to the fulfillment scheduling system is causing a) 1,300 customer orders worth $150M per year to go unfilled, and b) staff in both Customer Care and Fulfillment to waste 1,500 hours annually (costing $180,000 fully loaded) searching for transaction fallout.

So we need business analytics systems that allows analysts to identify, understand, and correct sales-order to work-order fallout, with the goal of preventing or quickly rectifying at least 80 percent of the dropped orders each year.

FIGURE 10.5   Sample vision document solution statements.

EDW / RADAR Subject area: Major features & benefits

The Revenue Assurance Detection And Remediation (RADAR) will provide business departments the following major features and benefits:

Feature	Benefits
Integrated direct sales order information	Single, all-company picture of sales orders created by all three regions of the customer care organization.
Integrated work order information	Single, all-company picture of work orders created by any of the four fulfillment applications.
Integrated billing order information	Single, all-company picture of billing records and invoicing activity created in both regional billing systems.
Integrated account and customer dimensions	Eliminate need to interpret accounts and customers by which system they were created upon. Far less staff time spent in reconciling input data sets for analyses.
Integrated product dimensions	Eliminate need for product management to hand-join and reconcile 11 separate product catalogs in order to analyze and present company transactions and inter-system fallout by the equipment and services ordered.
Staff and source system dimensions	Allow analysts and managers to trace errors in transactions to the individual and source system contributing to the problem.
Sales-order to work-order traceability	Ensures staff to start analysis with a list of sales orders that did not become work orders, so that they can immediately address the concerns of (potentially) unhappy customers without first having to compile a problem list.
Work-order to billing-event traceability	Enables staff to start with a list of unbilled equipment and services, so that they can allocate far more time to correcting inter-system fallout and thereby correct the majority of $50M of annual unbilled earned revenue.

FIGURE 10.6   Sample vision document solution statements.

---

right. The benefits that the application will provide are expressed here, in detail, by the lines connecting features to the problems they will solve. Taken together, the lines that comprise these mappings represent the application *as a solution*.

As business and technical stakeholders work through the many iterations of an agile project, they will refer to "the solution" many times during their discussions, as they mention concepts such as "solution use cases," "solution scope," and "solution architecture." As central as the term *solution* can be in these conversations, many people can leave the exact definition of this word unarticulated, which only causes miscommunication and increases project risk. Actually drawing a diagram such as Figure 10.7 for a project as large as an EDW would be unwieldy and very expensive to keep updated. However, EDW project leaders should realize that such a mapping of features to benefits is possible, and if drawn it would be *the solution* that so many stakeholders reference in their statements.

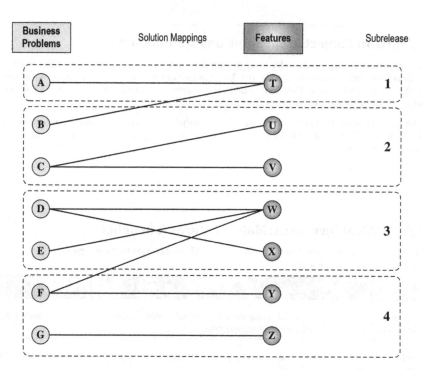

FIGURE 10.7   Defining a business solution.

Team leaders should also realize that such a mapping is dynamic and that it exists simultaneously in different versions in the minds of the many people involved in the project. EDW team leaders will better position themselves to manage project requirements if they keep in mind that (1) the solution is a mapping, (2) that mapping has not been diagramed, and (3) the details of the mapping are changing and inconsistently understood among stakeholders. With this understanding, teams can spot and deal with miscommunications as they occur. When two stakeholders seem to be talking past one another during a requirements meeting, it may be that they are working from conflicting notions of *the solution*. To bring them to where they can agree or at least clarify their disagreement, the EDW project leaders can often ask, "What is the mapping of features and benefits that each of you believes this particular version of the solution entails?" Drawing just a subset of the lines connecting two columns such as shown in Figure 10.7 is often all that is needed to identify where the parties disagree.

For the vision document, the project architect drafts the list of features and benefits at a very high level, so this artifact can only be a sketch of the true solution. However, given that the primary function of the project architect is to certify that the application that the EDW team is building will be a solution to the business problem, the mapping between features and benefits documented in this section of the vision document becomes all-important to his or her success as a team leader.

Note that the mapping shown in Figure 10.7 makes defining subreleases diagrammatically easier to understand. The boundary for Subrelease 1, for example, is modest and will only solve a single business problem, although it lays a good portion of the groundwork that will be required to solve the next business problem with the second subrelease. Whether to actually draw the mapping lines of the solution or leave it inferred by the features and benefits list is a decision the project architect will have to make. The full solution mapping for a large EDW project can be complicated and difficult to read. Still, knowing that a subrelease plan could be depicted if the mapping lines were drawn clarifies what partitioning a project into subreleases truly means.

Context Diagram

The *context diagram* of a vision document is a simple diagram that shows the source systems contributing data to a DW/BI system, as well as the major user constituents and downstream information systems that is supports. This simple diagram only takes a few minutes to draw once the project architect has completed all the research and the hard thinking that it represents. This diagram's simplicity makes it perfect for agile requirements management. With such a specific purpose and simple grammar, existing versions of this artifact prove to be very easy to update as business

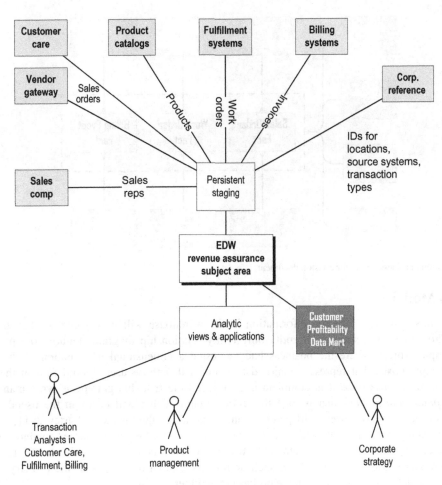

FIGURE 10.8   Sample context diagram for a vision document.

conditions evolve and as design insights occur during the life of the project. Figure 10.8 shows the context diagram that one might find in our sample revenue assurance project's vision document.

Context diagrams are often called "Level 0" data flow diagrams because if one were to put arrows on the connections between sources and targets, the diagram could serve as the cover sheet of a data flow diagram packet that many analysts prepare for traditionally managed projects. The agile context diagram can display only one box for the EDW in the middle or a few, as shown in the example, depending on whether breaking out the major layers of the DW/BI facility adds any clarity for the business stakeholder and the technical teammates.

Often the most difficult aspect of getting this diagram correct is simply picking the sources to depict. I have worked in organizations in which IT had 250 major lines of business systems under management. Deciding which sources for just the customer data to place on the context diagram for a modest EDW enhancement required 2 months of meetings and analysis.

Context diagrams greatly reduce project risk because they are easy for a team's business partners to understand. I have often had subject matter experts catch high-level design mistakes while reviewing this artifact. "Don't pull sales rep data from the HR system," I remember a director of finance telling me on one project. "Our sales reps couldn't care less if we've processed their income tax forms, but they really care whether we're ready to pay them their commission checks. So, grab the data out of the compensation system—it's the most accurate list we have of active sales reps."

By depicting the applications downstream user groups and systems, context diagrams also make it clear which user groups the development team considers to be its customers. The project sponsors often have strong opinions as to whom in the corporation they are willing to spend money to help. Several of my projects have been delayed for weeks while department heads argued about whether or not one of them was going to get a crucial data extract even though he was not going to help fund the development effort. I was thankful that the context diagram forced these conflicts to occur early during requirements analysis. If such an issue had come to light after the coding iterations started, months of invested teamwork could have been easily wasted when the executives changed their minds about whom the EDW was going to serve.

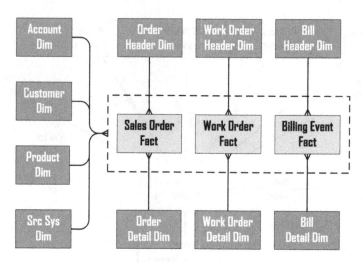

FIGURE 10.9 Sample target business model for a vision document.

Target Business Model

The target business model depicts how the information in the warehouse will be organized when the end users can finally access it. This model is a simplified, entity-only entity relationship diagram. Figure 10.9 provides the target model for the example project, where the business had requested a dimensional presentation of the final data. This diagram has only simple boxes that represent major data features that those users would find in the presentation or semantic layer of the warehouse once it is complete and online. Note that this graphic is what many data architects would call a *conceptual data model*—that is, one that reflects entities that will occur in the users' world, drawn as closely as possible to the way those users will perceive and think about the business [Earley 2011, p. 80]. The target business model is certainly not a logical data model because it does not depict the target database as other applications—notably the ETL engine—will see the data. The attributes of each entity are notably absent. The diagram is also not a physical data model because it does not list such notions as column data types or the primary and foreign keys that will be found in the database tables once the team has created them.

For all that it lacks, however, this picture of the target business model is worth a thousand words. By pointing at the highly abstract boxes on this model, the project architect can tell many important stories about how the end users will be able to derive crucial business value from the warehouse once it is online.

Examples of the stories that the project architect can tell using this simple model for our sample project include the following.

- The value of the sales orders for any given time period will be found here, in the Sales Orders Fact table.
- This fact table will have dedicated dimensions for data elements from both the order headers and the line items, so you will be able to slice and dice the value of sales orders by transaction aspects such as order type and backorder status at the time the customer purchased an item.
- The warehouse will also have fact tables for work orders and billing records.
- All these fact tables will share these four dimensions—customer, account, product, and source system—so you will be able to slice and dice the metrics from any one of the fact tables in the same way.
- In fact, you can move across these fact tables using those shared dimensions, so you will be able to connect notions such as the completed sales, fulfillment, and billing events for any given customer, and then any given product.

Because the target business model's format makes it easy for business users to comprehend, this diagram greatly reduces project risk. I have had subject matter experts, department directors, and project sponsors all catch solution concept mistakes by examining the proposed target business model. Considering our sample target model, for instance, a billing analyst might say, "You need to add a dimension for the agent owning each transaction so that we can learn which members of our customer service and fulfillment teams are causing the most errors." Catching such an oversight at an early point in the project when a vision document is compiled can easily save weeks of rework that would have been necessary if such an error had been discovered after coding had begun.

Moreover, the vision document's context diagram and target business model interact to reduce project risk even further. The first diagram identifies the sources of the information, and the second graphic shows the tables into which information will be loaded. Knowing both source and target, even at a high level, places a major constraint on the requirements churn that can occur during the project. Consider, for example, that the product owner for the project represented by Figures 10.8 and 10.9 creates a user story that includes the term "net income." The fact that a data set called "standard costing" does not appear on either of these diagrams, which represent the sources and targets to be included in the application, strongly implies that the requested story is completely out of scope. Should the product owner add an epic regarding net income during the middle of the project, the source and target models in the vision document allow EDW team leaders to gently push back, saying, "We don't see data elements supporting net income on the diagrams of the vision document. Do we need to defer these stories until another project or do we need to go back to the sponsor and stakeholders to get the vision document changed?" These simple diagrams, then, provide just enough dampening on requirements churn to keep an agile team pointed toward the true and steady goal over the entire arch of the project. Given this stabilizing effect provided by a few quick-to-draw diagrams, projects that incorporate these artifacts of the ERM value chain for requirements management tend to be far more linear and therefore successful than agile projects that rely on the generic agile requirements value chain alone.

High-Level Architectural Diagram

The next component of the vision document is a *high-level architectural diagram*, which summarizes the data transforms that the team proposes to apply to the source data. Figure 10.10 provides a sample of this artifact, one that many business analysts will recognize as a "Level 1" data flow diagram because it is simply the first decomposition of the Level 0 diagram provided by the vision document's context diagram, now drawn with data flows. Like the context diagram, the high-level architectural diagram still depicts sources and target data elements without a great amount of detail. The diagram's goal is to communicate the big picture regarding how the ETL modules will transform, merge, and store these "gloms" of data as they move across the EDW's reference architecture.

With the high-level architectural diagram, the vision document begins to bridge business requirements and technical requirements by providing a diagram that each side of the project can utilize in its own way. Business stakeholders will recognize elements on this data flow diagram from the context diagram and the target business model, and they can check that this initial design is complete and correct given their knowledge of the business systems that serve as information sources. From the other point of view, the technical members of the team will see on this diagram the major transformations required, and they can begin imagining the ETL modules that will be needed in each layer of the reference architecture. The high-level architectural diagram can thus be validated from these two perspectives, providing a stereoscopic vision of the proposed application that further ensures business–IT alignment concerning the nature of application.

Considering just the sales data in Figure 10.10, for example, the reviewer can see that the application will derive both customer and location information from the sales order systems. Once cleansed, the customer information will be transformed to become "party" records, a change that will enhance its reusability for later business intelligence projects. The reviewer can also see that the EDW will take sales transaction information directly into a sales fact table. The business stakeholders may adore this decision because it will save them the expense of placing the data first in integration tables, but the company's enterprise architect may well insist that all information in the EDW should first land in the integration layer, where data is stored in tables complying with a third-normal form data model. At this point, the EDW project leaders may wish to counter with notions of economy, agility, or temporary measures, but at least the high-level data flow diagram sparked this architectural discussion before the programming began, possibly saving months of rework.

By placing this diagram alongside the four other sections described previously, the vision document makes it as easy as possible for stakeholders to judge whether the application's design—at its highest level—is consistent with the promises being made to the business users. The systems analyst, for example, can easily check whether a general transformation plan exists for every source identified in the context diagram by simply considering the first column of the high-level data flow diagram. Similarly, the business analyst can check whether the EDW team has planned to provide all the information components necessary for the desired front-end applications by examining the last column of the same diagram.

Nonfunctional Requirements

In this last section of the vision document, the project architect can list a summary of the special characteristics that the finished application must someday possess, beyond the data analysis actions that it will offer end users. Because the vision document represents the highest possible depiction of the application's nature, it needs only to identify, not detail, the nonfunctional requirements that the project architect can anticipate at this time. The next two templates will

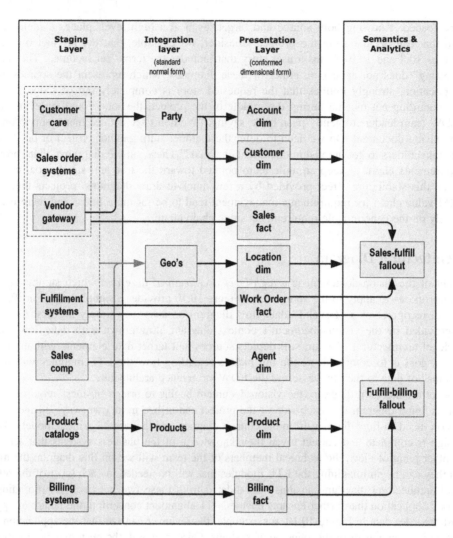

FIGURE 10.10 Sample high level architecture diagram for a vision document.

contain sections for more detailed nonfunctional requirements, allowing the team to describe these needs more carefully before programming begins.

The project architect can identify plenty of nonfunctional requirements for the system by considering, even briefly, the items listed in two independently published references: (1) sections for nonfunctional requirements in published IT standards for requirements management, as summarized in Table 7.2, and (2) the DAMA data management functional framework, as illustrated in Figure 4.6. While scanning Table 7.2, "security" might suggest itself to the project architect, causing him to note in the vision document something as simple as, "The application will need to control access to table columns by user group so that the personal protected information (PPI) of customers is visible only to a particular category of managers." While examining the DAMA framework, the intersection of "Data Quality Management" and "Technology" may cause him to add another single sentence such as, "The application should rely on the Parts Data Management system for standardized identifiers for all products manufactured in-house." Chapter 11 further discusses the analyzing nonfunctional requirements.

SEGMENTING THE PROJECT WITH SUBRELEASE OVERVIEW

By preparing a vision document, the project architect was able to communicate to a wide group of both business and technical stakeholders, securing buy-in on both sides at a very high level. With the next artifact in the ERM value chain, the *subrelease overview*, the project architect will communicate mid-level, increasingly technical requirements to

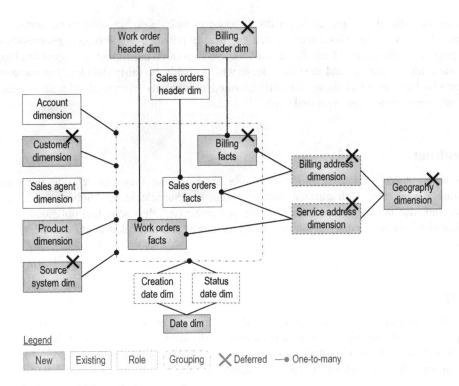

FIGURE 10.11 Target business model for a subrelease overview.

the members of the development team. As a member of the team who is learning quickly about data warehousing through her involvement with the project, the product owner should at some point be able to understand the subrelease overview as well.

The subrelease overview is a mid-level description of an incremental version of the DW/BI system that the project architect believes will make a good subrelease candidate at a particular point in the project. A good way to communicate the restricted scope of a given subrelease is to update a copy of the target business model included in the vision document, striking out all but what will be included in the next version of the application that the end users will see. Figure 10.11 provides an example of how such a revised business target model would appear. Some aspects of the subrelease overview template are geared to systems that provide a rather mainstream set of business analyses that use facts and dimensions. Teams working with data mining or specialized analytics platforms will want to adapt these sections with the typical elements with which they work. If EDW program frequently involved time series analysis, for example, then the project leaders might want to update the Technical Description section of the template to include the various smoothing algorithms the company prefers and the high-level parameters controlling those algorithms [Milhøj 2013].

The purpose of a subrelease overview is twofold:

1. Enable the project architect and product owner to reason about partitioning the project into multiple subreleases so that the team can pursue the risk management approach suggested in Part II of this book.
2. Communicate to the technical members of the team just enough information about what they will be building during the next few development iterations that they can all start pursuing their work in a self-organized manner.

The project architect may draft all the subrelease overviews for a project at one time, before any programming begins, in order to depict a complete, multistep release plan, or he may draft these overviews as they are needed, focusing instead on only the next version of the application that the team should place into production.

The template for the subrelease overview calls for more sections than any of the previous templates in the ERM value chain. Because many of them are diagrams, they are quicker to author than prose, but they will still require appreciable time to prepare and validate. In my experience with this artifact, only a few of the diagrams listed are actually required for any given project, although the actual set needed varies from project to project. Thus, keeping with the theme of "just enough requirements," the project architect should choose carefully from the many sections of the subrelease overview template and only include in any particular overview those diagrams needed to achieve the two objectives mentioned previously.

Moreover, the sections that the project architect does choose to include do not have to be perfectly complete with his or her first draft of the overview. Those sections can be steadily polished as the project progresses and more questions concerning project partitioning get answered. Just as the stories at the top of a project backlog are the most polished, the overview for the current and next subrelease will probably be fairly detailed, but those describing more distant subreleases will have many elements left still unstated or partially expressed. The short descriptions of the sections of the subrelease overview are presented here.

Subrelease Identifier

The team and its stakeholders need a name for each subrelease so that they can refer to them individually. My preference is to simply label them with cardinal numbers—that is, "Subrelease 1," "Subrelease 2," etc. When teams name them for their intended delivery dates, such as "August Subrelease," they soon feel obligated to meet the implicit deadline and quickly slip back into a date-driven project management mentality that worked so poorly in the traditional waterfall methods.

Subrelease Scope

The scope of a subrelease can be expressed in any combination of three ways: the data services that the proposed version of the application will provide, the logical data entities the data repository should contain, or a subset of the facts and dimension attributes that it will offer end users (for star schema-based solutions). The project architect should decide which combination of these formats the current situation requires.

Expressed as Data Services

To express scoping by data services, the project architect can create a "dimensions of value" diagram that I discussed extensively in my previous two books. Figure 10.12 provides an example of this diagram type for the back end of a DW/BI application. Dimensions of value diagrams first identify the major aspects of a project that deliver benefits for the customers in terms of data services. Because DW/BI solutions are so diverse, each EDW project may have its own particular set of dimensions for these diagrams. In the example, the aspects determining the value that an intermediate subrelease can provide are largely as follows:

- The layer of the reference architecture in which the data is located (the closer to the semantic layer, the better)
- The types of transformation that have been added so far (the more derived columns, the more informative the data will be)
- How advanced the loads have become (incremental loads can handle more data than "kill and fill")
- How frequently the data gets refreshed (daily is better than monthly, although it takes more scripting)

Next, these diagrams indicate the "waypoints" along those dimensions and order them by increasing value to the customer. In the example, the waypoints of the architectural layer suggest that customers may be able to derive some small value out of the data warehouse's landing data alone, but they obtain more value when IT can provide integration of current data, and even more when IT can deliver all the data into a dimensional data mart.

To express the proposed scope for a particular subrelease overview document, then, the project architect needs only to draw a boundary that connects the intended waypoints from each of the dimensions of value. Such a boundary line clearly depicts the data services that will be achieved when the team places the proposed subrelease into production usage. Upon viewing Figure 10.12, in particular, the product owner can view the boundary line and understand instantly that the proposed subrelease will provide only current data from an integration layer, loading everything but the harder derived columns via weekly, incremental loads with no error trapping.

Figure 10.13 depicts sample dimensions of value for the front end of a DW/BI system. It repeats the dimensions for transformation type and refresh frequency from Figure 10.12, but the other two dimensions have been replaced with one for the user friendliness of the dashboard and another representing the scope of the users groups that will have access to a particular version of the application. Instead of depicting just one subrelease, however, this version of the diagram shows three boundary lines drawn, indicating the increasing level of service that users will receive from the sequential subreleases.

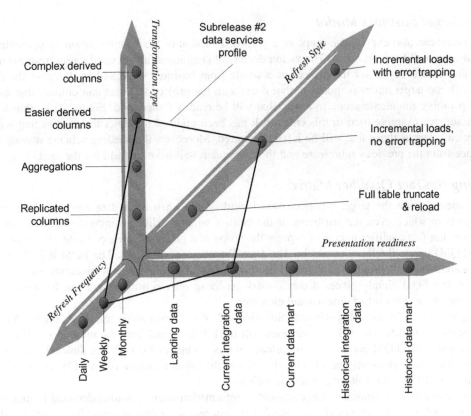

FIGURE 10.12 Subrelease scope drawn on a dimensions of value diagram.

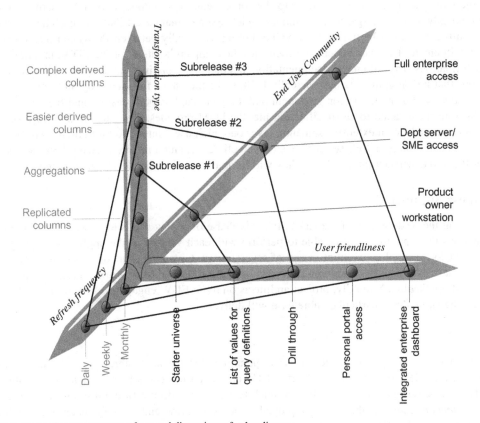

FIGURE 10.13 Subrelease plan summary on a front-end dimensions of value diagram.

Expressed as a Target Business Model

A subrelease overview can also express the scope of a proposed version of the BI application by communicating which data elements end users will have access to. The vision document contains a fully scoped target business model in order to communicate and secure buy-in for the project as a whole from business stakeholders. Because the product owner will be familiar with the target business model in that document, the project architect can employ that model to depict the limits of an upcoming subrelease scope in a way that will be readily understood. Figure 10.11 shows such a model for the revenue assurance example used in this chapter. It has been updated to depict the entities that will be in scope for the next subrelease versus those that will be left undelivered. Moreover, the shading scheme reveals which entities are already in place from the previous subrelease and those the team will have to build for the next.

Expressed Using the Fact Qualifier Matrix

Describing a subrelease using the target business model works well when each data entity will be delivered in its entirety. For projects in which even the attributes of the entities will be delivered incrementally, the project architect may want to employ the fact qualifier matrix to express the scope of a given subrelease. Table 10.3 shows a typical fact qualifier matrix (FQM) much like those taught by The Data Warehousing Institute. The FQM lists the metrics that the fact tables of a warehouse will provide as columns in this matrix. The dimensional elements are listed as rows. In its simplest notion, the FQM simply places a check mark on those intersections where the BI users will be able to decompose a measure by a given set of dimensional elements.

Table 10.3 depicts the FQM for a hypothetical Subrelease 2 of the revenue assurance example. Aside from some helpful enhancements to indicate where the dimensions will track history and how the measures will be packaged into fact tables, the version of the FQM contains a "Subrelease Status" indicator for both the dimensions and the measures. This indicator identifies those elements that (1) already exist in the current version online, (2) will be added during the next subrelease, or (3) will have to wait for a future subrelease.

Fact-qualifier matrices do communicate a large amount of information in an easy-to-understand format, but agile EDW projects tend not to employ them as regularly as waterfall project teams for two reasons. First, they are detail-oriented, making them slow and expensive to not only create but also later maintain. For those fact or dimension tables that will be delivered as whole tables, teams need only to refer to the components of a subrelease by table name. They can manage table names more quickly using the target business model, which assumes that the attributes of each table "travel together."

Second, FQM artifacts tend to be transitory in value, falling temporally between the vision document and the ETL modules the team will create. The vision document identifies the company's intent for the EDW, in terms of both sources and desired transformations. The automated documentation that most ETL engines can provide will identify the details of the transformations that the programmers have actually built. Once they have finished programming a module, the team can understand it quite well using the vision document and the generated as-built design, and the team will obtain little additional insight from the detailed to-be specification that the FQM provides. The exceptions I have seen to this trend are EDW programs that include an extensive semantic layer on which users intend to build their own dashboards. In this case, the users have been promised "self-service" business intelligence, and a matrix showing how facts and dimensions intersect enables them to understand in detail how they will be able to work with each element in the data marts.

Business Process Supported

In addition to scoping the next version of the EDW, the subrelease overview needs to make clear to the product owner the business functions that end users will be able to perform with each version of the application. The project architect can express this envisioned set of capabilities in any of several ways. Given the four formats suggested here, the project architect should include in any given subrelease overview only those needed to describe a particular planned version of the project's DW/BI application. Naturally, project architects on *agile* EDW engagements will prefer those formats that best communicate the *value* that a particular subrelease will deliver.

Use Case Model

Perhaps the simplest means of describing the business operations that the next subrelease will enable is the summary diagram of a use case model. As mentioned in Part I, RUP employed use cases to document the capabilities of a proposed system. The uses cases themselves involve so much text that they do not fit comfortably into an agile approach, but the *use case summary diagram* that RUP employed is quick to draw and communicates well with a company's business staff members. Agile EDW teams often employ the summary diagram and forego writing out the use cases.

TABLE 10.3 Fact-Qualifier Matrix for a Subrelease Description

Enterprise data warehouse / **revenue assurance subject area\
Fact-qualifier matrix for subrelease 2**

Dimension / Attribute	Track history	Subrelease Status	Sales order facts				Work order facts				Billing facts		
			Ordered qty	Current qty	Ordered value	Current value	Ordered qty	Current qty	Ordered value	Current value	Tariff value	Discount value	Billed value
		Status →	Exists	Deferred	Exists	Deferred	Add	Deferred	Add	Deferred	Deferred	Deferred	Deferred
Account dimension		↓											
Account number		Exists											
Subscriber name		Exists			✓			✓				✓	
Account value rating	Y	Add											
Credit denial		Add											
Credit denial waiver record ID		Add											
Customer dimension													
Standardized customer number		Deferred											
Customer name	Y	Deferred			✓			✓				✓	
Customer value rating	Y	Deferred											
Bad history flag		Deferred											
Bad history waiver record ID		Deferred											
Sales agent													
Agent personnel ID		Exists											
Name	Y	Exists			✓			✓				✓	
Original start date	Y	Exists											
Line manager	Y	Deferred											
Product dimension													
Native product code		Exists											
Native product description	Y	Exists											
Standardized product code		Add											
Standardized product description	Y	Add			✓			✓				✓	
Std product coding date		Add											
Product line	Y	Deferred											
Product class	Y	Deferred											
Product group	Y	Add											
Sales order header dimension													
Sales order number		Exists		✓									
Status	Y	Exists											
Work order header dimension													
WO Number		Add						✓					
Status	Y	Add											
Billing header dimension													
Invoice number		Deferred										✓	
Billing cycle		Deferred											
Source system dimension													
Source system code		Deferred		✓				✓				✓	
Source system description		Deferred											
Date dimension													
Date		Exists											
Day of week		Exists		✓				✓				✓	
Holiday		Deferred											

Figure 10.15 shows a summary use case diagram for a particular subrelease of the sample revenue assurance project described in this chapter. The stick figures depict the EDW's major user constituencies who will receive new services with the next version of the data warehouse. The bubbles provide short descriptions of what those services will be. The target business model in Figure 10.14 stated that our sample application's next version would add work order facts to the already existing sales order facts. This use case summary diagram states that with both those collections of facts in place, the billing analyst and customer care manager will be able to quantify the number of sales orders that did not get transmitted to the fulfillment system, and the fulfillment manager will be able to decompose that fallout by the products involved.

Analysis Venn Diagram

A Venn diagram is a simple illustration that uses ovals to picture the universe of data that an analysis begins with and the subsetting, unions, and intersections that one can make within that data. In the epic stack presented in Chapter 8,

---

EDW Subrelease overview (Template)

Subrelease identifier

Provide an identifier devoid of any suggested implementation time frame, since many factors outside of the control of the team can determine the actual delivery date.

Subrelease scope

Employ as many of the following three artifacts as necessary to define the scope of the subrelease.

Data services diagram subset

{insert data service scoping (a.k.a. a "dimensions of value") diagram here}

Target business model subset

{insert diagram here}

Fact qualifier matrix

{insert diagram here}

Business description

Employ as many of the following artifacts as needed to provide the business stakeholders with a clear understanding of the capabilities the proposed subrelease will provide.

Use case model

{insert diagram here}

Venn diagrams for supported analyses

{insert diagram here}

Data validation steps

Analysis 1:

- o   Step 1:
- o   Step 2: ....

Analysis 2:

- o   Step 1:
- o   Step 2: ....

Sample business queries

During project inception, elaboration, and construction, business stakeholders and project analysts have mentioned interest in conducting the following queries against the EDW once available. These queries are important to track, but are not "large" enough to manage as separate user stories.

- Query 1: (presentation-layer entities required, goal of the query, joins expressed in natural keys)
- Query 2: ....

FIGURE 10.14   Template for a streamlined *Subrelease Overview* (SRO)

themes represented atomic information capabilities that support a specific analysis requested by high-ranking members of the business staff. Most of those information capabilities can be expressed as set-based operations—that is, as unions, intersections, and subtractions of large assemblies of records that yield a final set of records that mean something to the business. If themes represent set-based operations, then a Venn diagram is a perfect way to document the themes that a subrelease will support.

Figure 10.16 illustrates the fallout analysis depicted in the use case summary diagram just considered. The diagram states that, with the next EDW version, users will be able to distinguish sales orders that have been open for 3 days or more and then subtract out those associated with work orders, reversed credit denials, and late product codlings.

Technical description

This section provides high-level technical requirements that the project architect needs to communicate to the design and development team.

Target measures details

{a.k.a. "facts," list relevant details here}

Reusable target dimensions details

{list relevant details here}

Non-reusable target dimensions details

{list relevant details here}

Data sourcing details

{list relevant details here}

Non-functional requirements

This list identifies qualities of the data services the application must provide besides the actual data offered for end-user analysis or downstream application support.

- Non-functional requirement 1:
  - o Category:
  - o Short description:
  - o Quantified goal:
- Non-functional requirement 2:
  - o ....

FIGURE 10.14   (*Continued*)

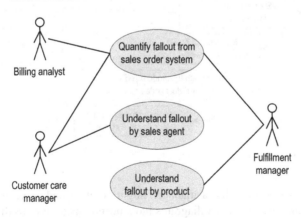

Scope of subrelease #2

Billing analyst

Quantify fallout from sales order system

Understand fallout by sales agent

Customer care manager

Understand fallout by product

Fulfillment manager

FIGURE 10.15   Use case model for a subrelease description.

The diagram also states that with regard to seeing the impact of late bad history waivers, the end users will have to wait until the next subrelease.

Business-Level Data Validation Steps

The epic decomposition framework I have suggested for agile EDW projects encourages teams to consider user stories as the business-level data validation steps that a manager would want to take before forwarding an analysis to his or her director, knowing that the director will proceed to take perhaps irreversible actions based on the insights that this analysis provides. The *data validation steps* section of the subrelease overview simply lists those data validation actions that the next version of the application will support.

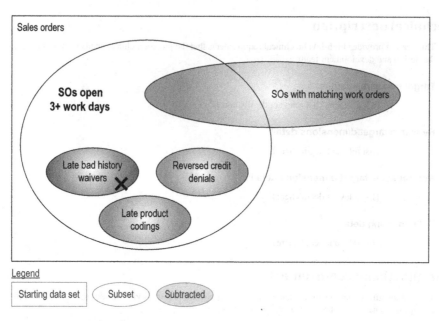

FIGURE 10.16 Venn diagram for a subrelease description.

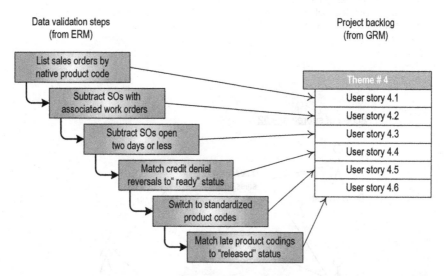

FIGURE 10.17 Data validation steps for a subrelease description.

Figure 10.17 shows the data validations that a manager might want to undertake for the fallout analysis that the previously discussed use case summary and Venn diagrams have been considering. In this case, the product owner has imagined holding a report showing the sales orders that did not transfer to the fulfillment system. He understands that when he provides this analysis to the director of the customer care department, the director will speak—perhaps harshly—to the sales agents and fulfillment managers involved with those transactions that were not properly handled. If the sales agents and fulfillment managers refute the analysis from the EDW by showing that the orders were suspended for an obvious and legitimate business reason, the director will be returning to speak—probably harshly—to the billing analyst who provided the faulty analysis. Because of this risk, most managers will want several means of vetting the information presented by the EDW for any given analysis.

The list of data validations section is therefore a crucial portion of the subrelease overview to plan out carefully. Each of these data validation steps represents a small operation that end users will want to perform with the EDW front-end application. Not only are these actions small but also each has a very specific objective, such as ensuring that a certain set of transactions were excluded or that an intermediate result still reconciles to an independent tally of problem cases. Given that they are small and focused, these data validation steps map well to user stories. Therefore, this section of the subrelease overview provides the area where the product owner and the entire team can validate that the ERM value chain is intersecting properly with the user stories in the project backlog derived from the GRM approach described in Chapter 9. This mapping is indicated on the right portion of Figure 10.17.

Sample Business Queries

This last component of the business description for a subrelease provides the project architect with an area to record the small investigations into warehouse data that the product owner has mentioned he will want to perform once the warehouse has been loaded. Product owners typically mention dozens of small actions they look forward to taking once they can get their hands on the company's operational data. These passing comments are too minor to merit converting them into bona fide user stories that must go on the backlog and be processed and estimated during story conferences. However, the team cannot afford to discard these desires of the product owner, no matter how small. If the project architect simply gathers them as a list in this section of the subrelease overview, the team members can draw from them in the future when they validate an upcoming subrelease.

This list of intended queries can greatly help technical teammates who are working with a product owner who is being too casual with his or her validation duties. I have often observed iteration demos in which the product owner only glances at a dashboard full of new information and then gets up to leave, saying off-handedly, "Looks OK to me." In such cases, the team leaders can draw from this section of the subrelease overview, saying, "Please wait. Here's the list of 40 things you said you wanted to try with the warehouse once we had data loaded. Why not see if you can accomplish a few of them with this demo version you're looking at now?" The resulting user demo session will be a far more productive review, perhaps uncovering several defects and even some new requirements.

Technical Description

The content of the scoping and business description sections contains information that the technical members of the development team certainly appreciate receiving. The developers will need still further information, however, before the subrelease overview will contain enough mid-level details that they will consider it an 80/20 specification that provides enough guidance to support early design work. In particular, my colleagues and I have found this section of the overview to be a convenient place to record the many special-purpose design solutions that Ralph Kimball has popularized throughout the years for star schemas.

Target Fact Tables Details

This section of the overview gives the project architect a place to record a clearer description of the fact table(s) to be included in the subrelease than the vision document allowed space for. Here, the project architect would spell out notions such as the following:

- Factors determining the grain of each fact table, especially if they are changing from the last EDW version
- Whether each fact table involved tracks single-moment events, an evolving process, or recurring transactions
- Metrics that are semi-additive, such as percentages
- Allocated facts [Kimball & Ross 2013]
- Degenerate dimensions [Kimball & Ross 2013]
- Factless fact tables [Kimball & Ross 2013]
- Removing records that have exceeded the customer's desired retention period
- Special coding for references to nonexistent dimensional records
- Special handling for records that are unloadable because they are incomplete

Reusable Target Dimensions Details

This section of the subrelease overview should include mid-level technical requirements for dimension tables shared by multiple fact tables.

The Kimball Group discusses extensively the practice of *conforming* the dimensions of a BI application whenever possible. When a modeler conforms a dimension table, he or she generalizes it so that it can be linked to many fact tables within an EDW. By making dimensions reusable, the data modeler allows the business to analyze a large collection of metrics using the same representations of major business entities such as customer, product, sales force, and geographies.

Conforming dimensions is a major challenge for the EDW developers for several reasons. First, they require standardized definitions, often at the enterprise level. Such standardization can involve data governance committees, meaning many people outside the project must weigh in before the EDW team can design a particular dimension table. Second, several sources contain data for these shared entities, so conformed dimensions typically require extensive data integration coding. Third, users frequently want to understand the history of the standardized representations, making these conformed tables some of the EDW's more complicated slowly changing dimensions. Fourth, these dimensions can involve complicated business rules for "late arriving dimensions"—that is, situations in which a fact table must be loaded before all the information needed to properly set the attributes for a dimension is available.

Given this complexity, the developers will need the project architect to describe his or her intent for reusable dimensions in this section of the subrelease overview so that technical teammates such as the data modeler and systems analysts can get started on the extensive analysis and design work that such situations require.

Non-Reusable Target Dimensions Details

Aside from the EDW's conformed dimensions, any particular fact table may have qualifiers that only it will employ, such as the Sales Order Header dimension in the example used in this chapter. Both these dedicated dimensions and conformed dimensions involve many technical requirements, such as the following:

- Hierarchies contained
- Strategy for slowly changing data—that is, whether the dimension is Type 1, 2, 3, 4, or 6 [Kimball 2011]
- Seeding records for unknown references in the transaction data
- Business rules for removing records once they exceed the desired retention period

This section of the template gives the product owner a place to summarize any such thoughts on these single-use dimensions.

Data Sourcing Details

This section of the subrelease overview is where the developers will find the project architect's recommendations for how to acquire the necessary data to load into the data warehouse. Especially in large companies, multiple sources of information often exist for a given element of the target business model, especially for reusable dimensions such as customer, product, and locations. The developers will validate the project architect's choice, but to get started they will need to understand the criteria that the architect employed to make his or her original recommendation. This section provides an area for the project architect to communicate not only that selection rationale but also a high-level description of the following:

- Major business rules for cleansing and transforming the major data flows from each source
- The mechanism that the team can use to pull only the new information from each source—that is, the "change data capture" logic to employ
- Processing the less-than-perfect records acquired from each source, whether to load them with flags, reroute them to a suspense table, and/or notify users of the source system that corrections need to be made

Nonfunctional Requirements

This section of the subrelease overview provides the project architect with a place to communicate to his or her technical teammates any relevant notions concerning the application's nonfunctional requirements for the envisioned version of the application. Material for this section will often be rooted in a list of nonfunctional requirements such as was provided by Table 7.2 or the DAMA data management framework, summarized in Figure 4.6. For example, if the project architect refers to the nonfunctional requirements list while preparing an outline of the second subrelease of the EDW, the "capacity" heading might cause him to note in the subrelease overview that "The physical storage will need to be 1 TB or larger because the additional sources in this subrelease will add 350 GB to the 450 GB consumed by the first subrelease." Similarly, the intersection of "Reference and Master Data Management" and "Roles and Responsibilities" in the data management functional framework might inspire him to add another single sentence, such as "The Product

Management group within finance will need to provide three data stewards to review and make updates to part records given the new data quality reports that this version of the application will provide."

PROVIDING DEVELOPER GUIDANCE WITH MODULE USE CASES

If and when the project backlog contains a particular module that requires more careful planning, the EDW team leaders can organize the necessary details using a module use case. Sometimes a particular module involves enough complexity or risk that the programmers will want lower-level guidance before they start coding, and the module use case provides the system analyst a structured artifact for recording those details. Note the change in authorship that occurs at this point in the ERM value chain. The business's sponsor and department directors provided the content of the concept briefing and stakeholder requests. The team's project architect supplied the material for the vision document and the multiple subrelease overviews. With the module use case, the team's system analyst and perhaps technical lead become active to document any remaining technical requirements that the programmers will require before they can begin collaborative development with the product owner and other subject matter experts. Typically, these team leaders do not bother to draft a module use case for those modules that are readily understood through higher-level documents and direct conversation with their teammates. Only when a module involves details that could be forgotten if not written down do they start placing that information in a module use case. Moreover, they use the sections of the module case selectively, completing those that speak to the points of uncertainty for a given module and leaving the rest of the topics to be addressed while speaking eye-to-eye with the programmers when they start coding the module.

Given its structure, the module use case is aptly named because it focuses on a single ETL or BI module and closely follows the use case template available from RUP. As revealed by the template in Figure 10.18, the core of this artifact describes the flow of events that should occur within a particular system module or component (here used as synonymous terms). For ETL systems, a module may be one mapping or several that run together in a single workflow. For a BI front end, a module may be a simple graphical device such as a pie chart, an entire display complete with menu bars, or a managed portal that has been distributed enterprise-wide. The systems analyst authoring the use case will have to decide the correct scope for this artifact.

As with all the other documents within the ERM value chain, the author of a module use case should aim for an 80/20 spec—investing only one-fifth as much time as a waterfall specification would require but capturing the most important 80% of the concepts that the component should embody. The remaining details can be decided when the team begins developing the module described. The sections of this module use case are as follows.

Goal

Stating the goal at the onset of a use case provides context that makes the remaining material much easier to understand. RUP defined use cases to document a flow of events that generates value for an actor, whether that actor might be a human or another automated system. For module use cases, the actor is usually the application to which the component will belong, so benefit will be for the EDW system rather than an EDW user. If the module is part of the ETL system, for example, the actor receiving the benefit is often the EDW data repository, so the goal of the module use case will be typically some version of "further enrichment of the information stored within table set X of the data warehouse."

For the sample project discussed in this chapter, the focal component for a module use case could be "Load Customer Data from Central Region Work Order Data," in which case the goal would be "Cleanse and conform staged customer records from system X and place them into the EDW's integration layer." Note that this sounds very much like the developer stories from the generic value chain that were examined in Chapter 9. In fact, if the goal of a component use case did not match a developer story found in the project backlog, it would signal that the GRM and ERM value chains have arrived at different notions regarding the application. In that case, the gap between the two value chains will have revealed a major risk to the project. To resolve this disconnect, the project architect will need to invest time on artifacts upstream from the module use case, realigning the conclusions of the two requirements management efforts.

Standard Flow of Events

In RUP, a flow of events is an ordered list of actions that the software should take. For use cases that rely on prose, documenting a flow of events can take up the bulk of a use case write-up, sometimes as long as several dozen pages for complex processing components. Writing, validating, and maintaining such prose is expensive, and it also represents

---

EDW module use case (Template)

Module goal

Single sentence description if module's reason for existence, in terms of:

- Category of data accessed and its EDW reference architectural layer
- Category of target data to create and its EDW reference architectural layer
- Major value added during the data's transformation

Standard flow of events

This level 2 data flow diagram depicts at a high level the steps required to access, transform, and load the data into the necessary target tables, including any master data elements, external processes, and look-up tables required.
{insert diagram here}

Alternative flow of events

These level 2 data flow diagrams depict the variation on the standard flow of events required during the initial load of the target tables or for the proper handling of unloadable records.
{insert diagram here}

Special requirements

This list enumerates the logical programming elements that will be needed to properly manage the data and meta data affected by this transform module.

- How to handle failed lookups:
- How to handle incompletely loaded data from a prior module run:
- Parties to notify upon modules success:
- Parties to notify upon module failure:
- ....

Supplemental specification: source-to-target mapping

{attach source-to-target map here or indicate location in project document repository}

Non-functional requirements as supplemental specifications

This list identifies qualities of the data services the application must provide besides the actual data offered for end-user analysis or downstream application support.

- Non-Functional Requirement 1:
  - o Category:
  - o Short description:
  - o Quantified goal:
- Non-Functional Requirement 2:

  - o ....

FIGURE 10.18   Template for a streamlined *Module Use Case* (MUC).

the last 20% of the details that an 80/20 spec would leave unaddressed until development time. For that reason, my colleagues and I prefer to express flow of events as simply a Level 2 data flow diagram, as shown in Figure 10.19. Where a particular bubble on the Level 2 diagram requires greater detail, the designers can document a link to a data flow diagram drawn at an even deeper level of abstraction or resort to prose, whichever would be more effective.

To make a process such as the one shown in Figure 10.19 describe a *standard* flow of events, the team usually constructs it to depict the nominal or "happy path" processing pattern that records should follow within a system's ETL. Here, *nominal* means "everything progressing according to plan," signifying standard, everyday data that the team expects to load with exceptions.

Alternative Flow of Events

Not all data will comply with expectations of the nominal case, however, and for those records that do not comply, the designers will need to spell out an alternative flow of events. The most common alternative flow documented in an ETL module use is the initial load of data. Initial loads often come from a different source than those that provide daily data increments to the warehouse. Initial load records are often pulled from archive tapes or an old data mart that the company

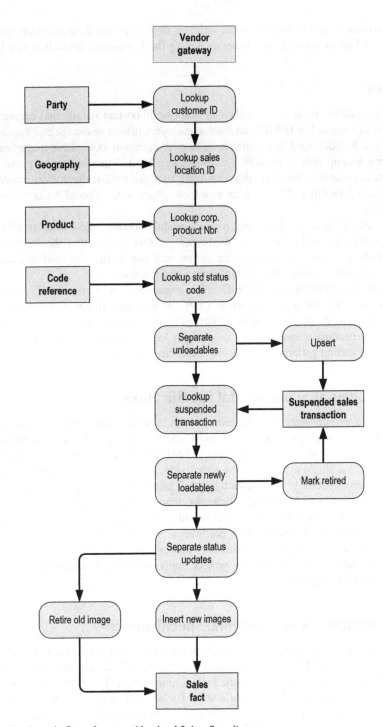

FIGURE 10.19   Communicating the main flow of events with a level 2 data flow diagram.

hopes to retire. The business rules for initial load records invariably have some differences from the processing needed for incremental data. The special handling they require should be spelled out in a variant of the Level 2 data flows documented for the nominal case.

A second common alternative flow found in EDW component use cases is error management logic. Sometimes EDW modules halt an entire batch run when a record proves to be unloadable, but more mature applications place the record in a suspense table. Modules that utilize suspense tables frequently have logic that watches for a corrected version of each suspended record. When a corrected version is encountered, the ETL module not only loads it into the warehouse but also removes the faulty record from the suspense table.

When such logic is too complicated to include in the standard flow of events diagram, designers will need to be move these details to an alternative flow document, sometimes switching the format to a flow chart or a UML activity diagram.

Special Requirements

This section of the use case allows the systems analyst to describe important details that cannot be recorded easily on the diagrams used for flow of events. For DW/BI modules, developers often use the special requirements section to document design topics that can be addressed in a sentence or two. A common example is the action that a fact-table load module should take when a lookup fails to provide a surrogate key for a dimension table record. Typically, EDW load modules place a surrogate key value in the fact table that links to a pre-seeded dimension record indicating "unknown value." The need for a seeded record and its role as a default return value should be noted in a module use case's special requirements section.

Another common example is the restart logic that a given module should follow after an ETL run ends abnormally. The systems analyst preparing the module use case might note in this section that the records loaded by the earlier, failed ETL process should be removed at the beginning of the next run so that the load module can simply restart its work at the top of the landing table without fear of duplicating target records.

A third special requirement frequently found in ETL module use cases is the desire of certain roles in the organization to be notified when the ETL for a given portion of EDW data has finished processing. Frequently, different managers monitor different areas of the warehouse. Order entry management cares most about conformed customer dimension, for example, and product managers care only about loading the conformed product tables. A module use case would spell out this notification pattern in the special requirements section.

Source-to-Target Mappings as Supplemental Specifications

The RUP templates include a *supplemental specification* section in which a designer can express early design details specifying notions about how the application should be built. EDW teams use this section in particular for a standard data warehousing artifact called the *source-to-target map* (STM). STMs specify how one or more columns in source data tables will be merged into a single column on the target side. Some agile data warehousing teams do not employ STMs because their programmers prefer to work directly with a product owner who can explain the necessary business rules as they are coding a module. Just as frequently, however, teams include programmers who want only to code ETL and are not comfortable filling an analyst role. The teams would rather program from a specification rather than hashing out business rules with a subject matter expert. This preference is particularly common for teams involving subcontractors for module coding, or when a language barrier may prevent the subject matter experts and programmers from readily understanding each other. In such cases, the project leads can fill out a spreadsheet detailing transformation rules, such as the excerpt shown in Figure 10.20.

Nonfunctional Requirements as Supplemental Specifications

Finally, the EDW designers can add a supplemental specification section to the module use case to record the nonfunctional requirements for a given module. Again, the team leaders should consult the table of standard nonfunctional requirements shown in Table 7.2 and the DAMA functional framework in Figure 4.6. For example, a *manageability* requirement might prescribe that the given ETL module should send XML messages upon startup to a particular queue so that particular data transform can be monitored and restarted when necessary by the administrators of the company's supply chain system. While reviewing the DAMA framework, the systems analyst might encounter the intersection between "Reference and Master Data Management" and "Activities" and realize that the data steward in the Vendor Maintenance Office should send the EDW a spreadsheet of authorized vendors weekly so that the warehouse can report on purchasing compliance.

Many nonfunctional requirements are inherited from IT or DW/BI departmental standards, but each EDW module can have several items deserving a nonstandard specification. For example, a module performing predictive analytics may have a particularly difficult performance challenge and cannot meet the standard response time that the enterprise architecture group specified for data warehouses in general. Such discrepancies should be spelled out in the supplemental specification section so that they can be discussed and tracked when the module enters into programming and deployment.

Target table type:	Single event fact table
Main Source:	View of sales transactions in the EDW integration layer, INTG_VW_SALES_LOAD, where UPDATE_DTM > ETL_PARM.AS_OF_DATE

Target Logic:	Prepare record, check for defects
	   if defects, note defects in LOAD_REJECT_CD and insert into SALES_FACT_SUSPENSE
	    else insert into target

Source Table	Source Column	Target Table	Target Column	Transform Logic
---	---	Sales_Fact	Sales_Fact_SID	GET_SQNC("SALES_FACT")
---	---	Sales_Fact	Insert_Process_ID	ETL_PARM.ETL_PROCESS_ID
INTG_VW_SALES_LOAD	SO_Nbr	Sales_Fact	Sales_Order_Nbr	replicate
INTG_VW_SALES_LOAD	Src_Sys_Msg_ID	Sales_Fact	OES_Tracer	replicate
INTG_VW_SALES_LOAD	Product_Class	Sales_Fact	Selling_Business_Unit	replicate
INTG_VW_SALES_LOAD	Src_Sys	Sales_Fact	Source_System	replicate
INTG_VW_SALES_LOAD	SOLI_Nbr	Sales_Fact	Line_Item_Nbr	replicate
INTG_VW_SALES_LOAD	SOLI_Qty	Sales_Fact	Line_Item_Qty	replicate
INTG_VW_SALES_LOAD	SOLI_Price_List	Sales_Fact	Line_Item_List_Price	replicate
INTG_VW_SALES_LOAD	SOLI_Price_Quoted	Sales_Fact	Line_Item_Sale_Price	replicate
---	---	Sales_Fact	Line_Item_Ext	Line_Item_List_Price * Line_Item_Ext
INTG_VW_SALES_LOAD	SO_Open_DTM	Sales_Fact	Process_Begin_Dtm	replicate
INTG_VW_SALES_LOAD	SO_Close_DTM	Sales_Fact	Process_Complete_Dtm	replicate
---	---	Sales_Fact	Sales_Cycle_Time	Process_Complete_Dtm - Process_Begin_Dtm
INTG_VW_SALES_LOAD	Line_Item_Prdct_Nbr	Sales_Fact	Dim_Product_SID	Call LOOKUP_DIM_PRODUCT(Line_Item_Prdct_Nbr, ETL_PARM.AS_OF_DATE)
INTG_VW_SALES_LOAD	SO_Header_Zip	Sales_Fact	Dim_Sales_Location	Call LOOKUP_DIM_GEOGRAPHY("ZIPCODE", SO_HEADER_ZIP, ETL_PARM.AS_OF_DATE)
INTG_VW_SALES_LOAD	SO_Header_Status	Sales_Fact	Dim_Sales_Status	Call LOOKUP_DIM_MISCCODE("SALES_STATUS", SO_HEADER_STATUS, ETL_PARM.AS_OF_DATE)
INTG_VW_SALES_LOAD	SO_Customer_Nbr	Sales_Fact	Dim_Sales_Customer	Call LOOKUP_DIM_PARTY("CUSTOMER", SRC_SYS, ETL_PARM.AS_OF_DATE)
---	---	Sales_Fact	Load_Reject_Cd	if any DIM_*_SID <= 0 then Load_Reject_Cd || 'BAD_DIM^'
---	---	Sales_Fact	Load_Reject_Cd	if any Sales_Cycle_Time <= 0, then Load_Reject_Cd || 'BAD_CYCLE_TIME^'
---	---	Sales_Fact	Insert_Dtm	ETL_PARM.ETL_AS_OF_DATE

FIGURE 10.20   Example of a source-to-target map.

SUMMARY

The generic agile approach to managing requirements involves a useful hierarchy of epics, themes, and user stories, but it relies exclusively on the input of the product owner. Because there are many reasons why the product owner might perform poorly in authoring users stories, the technical members of an agile EDW team may well want to invest in a parallel requirements discovery and analysis process. Moreover, product owners naturally focus on positive, functional business requirements, leaving important notions such as negative, nonfunctional, and technical requirements largely unaddressed. Agile EDW practitioners utilize an ERM process to prevent such gaps in their project definitions.

The ERM value chain consists of five streamlined artifacts borrowed from RUP. They have been streamlined so that they represent 80/20 specifications and fit well within an agile development context. The team leaders of an agile EDW engagement should selectively employ the ERM artifacts as needed to provide a second perspective on the product owner's project backlog. The *sponsor's concept briefing* outlines how the executives believe the company will make money with DW/BI's help. *Stakeholder requests* allows business departments to briefly describe what they find lacking in their BI systems and how they would fix it if they were IT. The *vision document* allows the project architect to sketch a high-level design for the application in order to garner buy-in from both business and the development team. A series of *subrelease overviews* permits the project architect to record the mid-level details for a particular incremental version of the application that the team is building. Finally, the *module use case* provides the system analyst a document in which to record many technical requirements that programmers sometimes insist upon before they will start coding, especially when there are complex system data transformation components involved.

With both the generic and the enterprise-capable requirements management approaches now defined, Chapter 11 discusses how to constructively intersect them and prioritize the user stories that result so that the agile EDW team will have a solid project backlog to feed into its rapid, incremental development process.

Chapter 11

Intersecting Value Chains for a Stereoscopic Project Definition

The two approaches to requirements discovery and analysis discussed in the previous chapters involve different drivers and artifacts. The product owner drives the generic requirements management (GRM) value chain by authoring the standard set of agile artifacts: epics, themes, and user stories. Information technology's (IT's) project architect drives the enterprise-capable requirements management (ERM) value chain through a set of artifacts that begins with a high-level sponsor's concept briefing and concludes with a subrelease overview, in addition to a few module use cases in those areas in which the programmers need greater detail. These two sets of requirements will add up to more than the sum of their parts. Combined, they should give the team a "stereoscopic vision" of the project, allowing the team to detect significant gaps in the definition of the application when considered from the business perspective versus what it looks like to IT.

The process of considering a project from two directions does not occur spontaneously, however. The team must make an effort to look through both eyes and deliberately scan the requirements for aspects that do not appear the same. In order to make this scanning effort a dependable and repeatable process, agile enterprise data warehousing (EDW) teams follow a particular train of thought and set of steps. Not only do these steps result in a crisp, prioritized project backlog but also they prepare the leading edge of the backlog for immediate programming, double-check the list of nonfunctional requirements, and provide materials for working with the project's governance team.

INTERSECTING THE TWO VALUE CHAINS

With just a bit of effort from the agile EDW team leaders, the two agile requirements management value chains described in the previous chapters will intersect well to generate a highly actionable project backlog of developer stories. "Highly actionable" in this context signifies that

- the team believes the most important 80% of the project is captured by the existing stories;
- all of the stories on the backlog are clearly desired by the business stakeholders, not just the product owner;
- those stories occur in a reasonable order that takes into account value, risk, and dependencies; and
- the top of the backlog has just enough specifications to be ready for immediate agile programming.

Once the team has completed a good portion of both value chains, the project leaders should begin checking for consistency and traceability between the two sets of artifacts.

Agile EDW's Version of Requirements Traceability

Intersecting the two requirements value chains results in requirements traceability, an important technique for reducing project risk. In general, "requirements traceability" is the ability to identify and document the lineage of each requirement, including its derivation and its allocation, and its relationship to other requirements [Brennan 2009]. In other words, traceability allows project planners to confirm that every requested feature ended up in the application's design and that every designed feature started with a real business request.

Figure 11.1 portrays agile EDW's version of requirements traceability. This graphic begins with the two value chains introduced in Figure 7.10, in which the generic value chain runs vertically from top to bottom, and the enterprise value chain runs horizontally from left to right. The epic decomposition framework offered to readers in Chapter 8 suggested that epic stories should represent sponsor-level requirements, whereas themes should link to director needs, and user stories

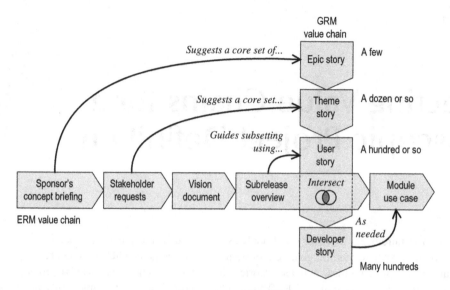

FIGURE 11.1   Tracing requirements between value chains.

should link to the business-level data validation objectives of managers and analysts. Following that framework, then, the team should be able to trace between ERM and GRM in the pattern suggested by the arrows added to Figure 11.1. For the top two levels of the generic value chain, confirming traceability means that the team can conceptually link

- every epic story on the product owner's backlog to one of the competitive capabilities requested by the project sponsors, as listed in the project architects' sponsor's concept briefing; and
- every theme in the backlog to a director-requested analysis listed in a stakeholder request.

To complete the traceability analysis, the team leaders attempt to run those links in reverse to verify that

- each of the new vice president-requested competitive capabilities is fully supported by the proposed set of backlog epics; and
- each director-requested analysis is fully supported by the proposed set of themes.

This process of intersecting the results from two requirements management value chains should greatly assist the product owner in refining the project backlog. When considering epic stories, should the team discover a "needle on a gauge in the corporate cockpit" that is not addressed by an epic, the project architect can ask the product owner to investigate how the project, with its current backlog, will address this requirement expressed by the sponsor. The opposite type of discrepancy can occur, where the product owner has added to the backlog epics that do not connect to the gauge needles in the corporate cockpit, as identified by IT's ERM process. The project architect can state that either the team needs to ask the sponsor to expand the project scope and update the sponsor's concept briefing or the product owner needs to drop that epic story. Either way, it is the logic of the situation, not IT, that guides the product owner to improve the accuracy of the backlog, allowing the technical project leaders to avoid a conflict of opinions with their embedded business partner.

The dialog concerning gaps in backlog themes will be similar. The project architect can use the stakeholder requests (SHRs) to guide the product owner in validating and polishing the theme stories on the project backlog. Themes should represent new informational capabilities that achieve a set-based operation that sparks and tracks business actions by the company's staff. If the directors' SHRs include an analysis not found on the backlog, the logic of the situation will nudge the product owner to add themes to cover the discrepancy or provide the context for asking the directors to expand the scope of their requests.

The team leaders need to change tactics slightly when it comes to confirming traceability for user stories. The ERM value chain does not provide an independent list of business-level data validations that managers have requested. Instead, the project architect has provided a subrelease overview, which, as discussed in Chapter 10, contains several graphs depicting how the end users will be able to work with and benefit from the next release of the EDW. With these graphics, confirming traceability is a matter of the project architect and product owner confirming that

- every user story can be linked to an end-user action or benefit depicted in one of the subrelease overview's graphics; and
- the user stories that will be developed and delivered with the next subrelease will fully realize those illustrated actions and benefits.

The final step in this traceability process is to confirm the last level of the generic value chain, the developer story. To achieve this, the team leaders need to simply scan the backlog of developer stories that will compose the next subrelease and identify those that are complicated enough to merit a more detailed to-be description than the single-sentence developer story provides. They can then confirm that the systems analyst has provided a module use case for each of those developer stories. They might also confirm that each module use can be associated with a developer story slated for in the next subrelease because if this is not the case, the systems analyst is building up an inventory of to-be specifications that could easily go to waste if the direction of the project were to change.

Readers may have noticed that ERM's vision document was omitted from the traceability check described previously. Vision documents will support much of the traceability described previously, but it is a high-level summary of information from the sponsor concept briefing and stakeholder requests, so if the team has already confirmed links from the backlog's epics and themes back to those artifacts, including the vision document in a deliberate traceability validation step will be redundant. Similarly, subrelease overviews derive from the vision document so that validating support for all user stories against a proposed subrelease makes checking them against the vision document unnecessary. If the project architect has chosen not to provide subrelease overviews, however, then checking traceability of users stories against the vision document is a good substitute.

Confirming traceability in the manner described previously may sound complex at first, but we need to remember that in truth it means little more than checking the items on a list (the project backlog) against a few short documents that contain a modest number of diagrams (the ERM artifacts). Taking the small amount of effort required to perform this check will ensure that no major requirements have been overlooked and that an identifiable person in the organization is eagerly waiting for every item that the team is about to program. Knowing that no gaps exist and that every feature to be built will be used greatly reduces the risk that the team will spend weeks or months developing a system that does not generate value for the company.

ADDRESSING NONFUNCTIONAL REQUIREMENTS

The previous discussion of traceability focused on predominantly *functional* needs of the users. In order to deliver EDW applications with reasonable total cost to ownership, the project leaders will need to also incorporate nonfunctional requirements into their planning activities. The last three templates for the ERM value chain contain prompts for the project architect and systems analyst to capture the salient nonfunctional requirements as they consider the project at increasingly finer levels of abstraction. However, those few short sections represent nonfunctional requirements discovery more than careful requirements analysis. Agile EDW teams will have to invest some effort in analyzing nonfunctional requirements if they are to avoid overlooking crucial considerations that will seriously undermine the performance, overall value, and long-term viability of the application they are building.

The agile EDW project life cycle addresses nonfunctional requirements at many points and at many levels, making it difficult to describe in a few short paragraphs. Instead, I touch upon this topic steadily during the remaining sections of this chapter while describing other requirements management topics, such as embedding agile EDW development into a larger application release cycle, prioritizing project backlogs, managing incremental precision, orchestrating effort levels between team roles, and interfacing with project governance. Before beginning that extended treatment, however, we need to first scope the discussion of nonfunctional requirements because it is easy to overload an EDW development team with far more infrastructure work than it will have bandwidth to manage.

The Proper Problem Domain for Agile EDW

Addressing nonfunctional requirements for enterprise data warehousing projects is a tricky subject because the "enterprise" and "data" components of these projects border on a whole further class of corporate-level architectural requirements that the organization needs to manage assiduously. Topics such as enterprise information management, data governance, enterprise architecture, and data architecture can easily smother an EDW development team with some thorny, abstract challenges that often take months or years to resolve. The key to keeping agile EDW development teams from losing their velocity to these enterprise-level topics is to understand how to properly allocate these additional responsibilities between project teams and other IT planning groups.

Figure 11.2 shows one way that companies approach these areas of planning and implementation. *Enterprise information management* (EIM) serves as an umbrella term incorporating all the work required to successfully manage a company's information as a strategic asset, including definitions, planning, staffing, managing repositories, and tracking the results of that effort. EIM is only one aspect of *enterprise architecture* (EA), which, as mentioned previously,

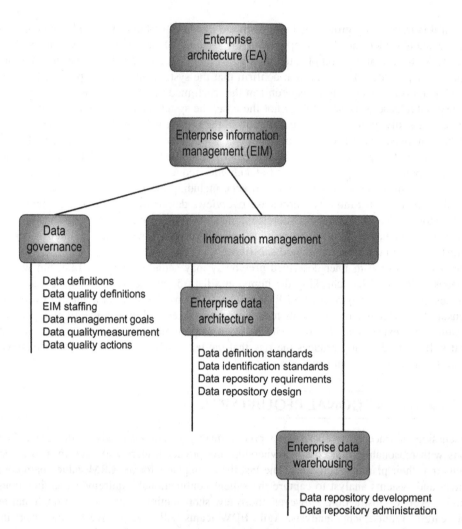

FIGURE 11.2 Corporate-level planning functions that generate architectural requirements.

comprises strategic plans for standardizing, integrating, and optimizing the company's overall business processes for delivering goods and services to customers. As a component of EA, EIM divides into two major areas of concentrated effort: data governance (DG) and information management (IM) [Ladley 2012]. *Data governance*, broadly speaking, focuses on EIM work that the business staff needs to pursue, especially the definition of shared information elements, aligning them with corporate strategy, and the dispatching of staff from the business departments to monitor and maintain data quality. Conversely, *information management* lies on the IT side of EIM and focuses on the design and delivery of systems that enable the business staff to achieve the goals and objectives set forth by data governance work. Information management necessarily involves some complex data management topics, including enterprise data architecture, master data management, and corporate data quality applications. Note that in this approach, enterprise data warehousing has an explicit and rather restricted role: It facilitates information management, but it is not responsible for defining the standards that have been allocated to the process of enterprise data architecture.

During the past 15 years of writing and presenting agile enterprise data warehousing at conferences, I have encountered many data professionals who believe the agile EDW method to be somehow incomplete or insufficient because it does not instruct the developers on the creation of data governance programs and enterprise data architectures. These people are absolutely correct that these organizational and architectural requirements need to be addressed. My question to them is whether we will be going far beyond the true purpose of enterprise data warehousing if we include techniques for authoring all activities that fall under EIM in Figure 11.2. It seems that agile EDW should be responsible for no more than the objectives that non-agile EDW is expected to fulfill, which is only the activities shown single bubble in the lower right of the diagram. Data governance and enterprise data architecture are broader challenges than EDW of any type should be responsible for.

When people suggest that an agile EDW method should provide guidance on data governance and data architecture in addition to data warehousing, they remind me of a gentleman who interrupted one of my Agile Data Warehousing 101 classes many years ago. "The problem we have with whole-team development in our company," he said, "is that management has equipped the project rooms with these really old laptop computers that overheat in a couple of hours, crash, and lose all our work." He stared at me for a moment and then demanded, "What's agile going to do about that?"

Of course he was right to be frustrated with his company's programming workstations, but I believe he was mistaking agile development techniques with some kind of silver bullet to be used against all forms of organizational insanity. Silver bullets do not exist. Every discipline has its proper area of application, and project leaders must carefully apply each technique to its appropriate domain of problems. EA, EIM, and IM are all challenges that must be addressed, but to demand that agile data warehousing teams provide solutions for all of these disciplines is taking both data warehousing/business intelligence (DW/BI) techniques and agile methods out of their proper problem domains. The responsibility of enterprise data warehousing is to provide data repositories that support the organizational activities that data governance and information management have identified as necessary. Agile EDW is no more than a very effective way to pursue enterprise data warehousing. The fact that it is "agile" does not expand its focal problem domain beyond that of EDW. It is true that agile EDW has a role to play in solving the challenges in the other problem domains, but it will lead to disaster to consider it a full solution for all the larger challenges that surround an EDW project.

Agile EDW Supports Broader Architectural Activities

Table 11.1 depicts what I believe to be the proper positioning of agile EDW with regard to the question of identifying and fulfilling the architectural requirements involved in enterprise data warehousing. The table lists a corporate hierarchy, all the way from the directors in the boardroom at the top down to the EDW project leaders working in the project rooms with the developers. Each rung in the corporate ladder has responsibilities it must attend to directly. It also supports the functions of the levels above and below it. Much of this support can be characterized by whether a given level is a creator or a consumer of a particular objective, whether it be a corporate strategy or an information architecture.

The company's board of directors and the CEO, for example, create corporate strategy, whereas the CxOs consume that strategy and strive to achieve the goals that it lays out. Similarly, companies should have dedicated teams to formulate enterprise architecture, set enterprise information management goals, and author architectures for enterprise data and enterprise data warehouses. The proper role of the EDW project governance and EDW project leaders should not be to develop enterprise data warehousing architectures. Instead, EDW teams should focus on delivering applications that solve specific business problems while honoring the objectives provided by the architectural bodies above them, including the company's enterprise data warehouse architecture team. To ask the development team members to provide these architectures as part of their work in delivering applications would not only distract them from their core responsibility of solving specific business problems but also confuse their proper role as a consumer of an architecture with that of being its author. It would be like asking the chief operation officer to decide whether her company's primary objective for the next 5 years was to expand into new product lines overseas or simply find a buyer, given all the debt that the corporation has acquired. That decision is properly left to the board of directors and is out of scope for a CxO. Of course, the company could dump such a decision on its team of CxOs, but the risk of arriving at the wrong decision via this route is too high to make that choice advisable.

Parties can still be involved with the work outside their scope of responsibilities, however. The CxOs do not silently consume the corporate strategy and pursue it whether it is right or wrong. They provide feedback on its feasibility because only they can test whether the goals are practical given the realities at work within their business units. Similarly, EDW development teams are consumers of the architectural requirements authored by the EA, EIM, EDA, and EDW architectural groups. In fact, some EDW project leads may well sit on those groups, but sharing personnel does not make authoring enterprise architectures a responsibility of the development teams. Instead, the development teams' responsibility can only be to (1) implement the direction provided by the architectural groups, (2) provide feedback on whether those strategies are practical, and (3) make suggestions as to how to fill the gaps found between the architecture and the real-world constraints encountered during system design and coding.

From this perspective, then, expecting the agile development team to author a host of enterprise architectural specifications *before* focusing on the needs of their immediate business customers is ludicrous. To expect them to author these architectural goals *during* development—when they are struggling to manage functional requirements, application-specific nonfunctional requirements, incremental design, database construction, and programming in a time-boxed environment—is insane. Companies who lack the discipline to establish separate EA, EIM, DG, and EDA groups can try to make those high-level specifications the responsibility of the agile EDW team, but in most cases the results will be

TABLE 11.1 Hierarchy of Enterprise Data Warehouse Planning

Feedback ←

Direction →

Role	Party / Function	Responsibility
Creators of Corporate Strategy	**Board of Directors**	Protect and further the interest of the corporation's shareholders through setting the mission of the organization, acquiring financial resources, and selecting and directing the company's chief executives.
	CEO	Achieve the mission of the organization by setting strategy at the highest level, driving change within the organization, and presiding over the entirety of company's operations.
Consumers of Corporate Strategy	**CxO**	Implement the corporate strategy within major functional divisions of the company and maintain the effectiveness of day-to-day activities by setting high-level policies, measures, and control mechanisms.
	CIO	Enable the company's day-to-day operations through the acquisition, development, and management of a sound, secure, and cost-effective information infrastructure.
	Enterprise Architecture	Author and maintain strategic plans for standardizing, integrating, optimizing the company's overall processes for delivering goods and services to customers.
	Enterprise Information Management	Author and maintain corporate policies, technologies, staff, and processes that maximize the benefits from the company's investment in data and content [adapted from Ladley 2012, p 8].
Creators of DW/BI Architecture	**Enterprise Data Architecture**	Provide the desired model of the enterprise information management environment, its components, and their interactions, interrelating the people, processes, technologies, and policies needed to manage and effectively use enterprise information assets [adapted from Ladley 2012, p 10].
	EDW Director	Hire and direct resources in the acquisition, development, and administration of a data management platform capable of achieving the EA, EIM, and data architecture objectives of the company.
	EDW Architect	High level specification of the data warehousing components and their interactions with an emphasis on achieving EA, EIM, and enterprise data architectural objectives plus corporate non-functional requirements such as performance, security, scalability, manageability, and extensibility.
Consumers of DW/BI Architecture	**EDW Project Governance**	Setting and adapting the high-level goals and constraints for an EDW project, balancing specific functional objectives with the directives from EA and EIM, plus directing and monitoring project timelines, inter-project milestones, and the use of resources and funds
	EDW Project Leaders	Discovery and proper articulation of a project's requirements, crafting a design that delivers upon those requirements and honors the constraints set by project governance, and the economical creation and implementation of software systems fulfilling that design.

[Ladley 2012] John Ladley, *Data Governance*, 2012, Morgan Kaufman.
My thanks to my colleague, Mark Mays, for providing an early version of this table.

disastrous. If the teams listed above the EDW project leaders in Table 11.1 do not exist, IT management needs to advocate that these groups be formed. Perhaps some of the agile EDW team members can serve on these groups, but the EDW team itself must be considered only a consumer and reviewer of the direction statements these groups should provide. To ask agile EDW to also provide enterprise architectures in addition to reducing system delivery time, increasing application quality, and solving the end user's specific business problems is to overload the method. It is taking a solution out of context and placing it in an inappropriate problem domain.

SUPPORTING THE ORGANIZATION'S SOFTWARE RELEASE CYCLE

With agile EDW properly conceptualized as a consumer and reviewer of enterprise information architectures, teams will need some guidance as to how their work patterns should support the larger planning efforts provided by the higher-level architectural teams. This guidance will require first a clear model of the company's release cycle for EDW projects and then a notion of effort curves so that the project leaders can find the time to fulfill their responsibilities to appraise higher-level architectures and suggest corrections. Properly aligning agile EDW efforts with the company release cycle will also provide team leaders with the opportunity to invest in clarifying their application's nonfunctional requirements.

Phases Borrowed from Rational Unified Process

Large projects, such as constructing a major enhancement to an EDW, proceed in phases. These phases are designed to address the organization's need for risk management and the hand-offs of major deliverables. Although the names and numbers of these phases vary slightly from company to company, every large organization with a corporate IT function will have a "release cycle" that defines them. The agile EDW project leaders will have to support the release cycle that their company follows.

The inner circle shown in Figure 11.3 portrays a typical release cycle. This depiction is a simplified version of the cycle offered by the iterative method Rational Unified Process (RUP). Although RUP is an iterative method, its release cycle has proven general enough that many companies that are thoroughly committed to the waterfall approach use its terminology to describe their release cycles. For that reason, Given that flexibility, I will use the RUP release cycle as an iconic approach to systems development whether or not a company employs an iterative method.

In the waterfall version of this release cycle, a project begins with the *inception phase*, typically driven by a project architect with perhaps some business analysts to assist him or her. Their objective is to define the system and application requirements just enough to provide an initial scoping of application features and a cost estimate, so that sponsors can decide whether to pursue the project. Should the project get funded, the team staffs up for the *elaboration phase* by adding the other leading roles, such as a data modeler, system analyst, and system tester. Management also provides a few coders. The objective of elaboration is to address the key risks of the project and to prove out the application's architecture. Once the architecture is proven and the major risks are mitigated, the team moves into the *construction phase*. Management staffs the team with its full complement of coders, and the team delivers all the remaining project features. Finally, the team arrives at the *transition phase*, during which it collaborates with (1) business customers to complete a user-acceptance test and (2) operations to plan the application's deployment to production usage and an initial period of operational support. At this point, the team can begin another release cycle for the application should additional features be required.

Iterations −1 and 0 Fit into the Inception Phase

Agile EDW teams can begin adapting to a standard release cycle, such as the one described previously, by utilizing a notion of "Iteration −1 and 0" to fulfill the role of an inception phase. As discussed in Chapter 5, Iteration 0 is a standard technique for agile teams to begin projects in general, and Iteration −1 is an adaptation that agile DW/BI teams make to better support data integration work. As illustrated in Figure 5.6, Iteration −1 represents the time that a project architect needs to prepare guidance for his or her team's data modeler and system analyst. Iteration 0 creates time for those two roles in turn to author 80/20 specs for the programmers concerning the modules they will build during Iteration 1.

In theory, the specifications resulting from these two preparatory iterations should also include just enough whole-project information to allow the team to incorporate good architecture and nonfunctional requirements into the design

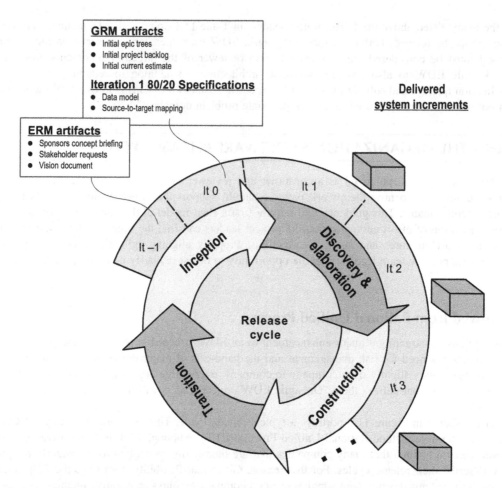

GRM artifacts
- Initial epic trees
- Initial project backlog
- Initial current estimate

Iteration 1 80/20 Specifications
- Data model
- Source-to-target mapping

ERM artifacts
- Sponsors concept briefing
- Stakeholder requests
- Vision document

Delivered
system increments

It 0   It 1

It −1

Inception

Discovery & elaboration

It 2

Release cycle

Transition

Construction

It 3

FIGURE 11.3   Typical project release cycle used by large companies.

of the modules that programmers will code during Iteration 1 and beyond. Calling these two predevelopment periods "iterations" is a bit of a misnomer, however. On many projects, the team leaders need significantly more than a standard iteration time box to envision the application as a whole and complete the needed guidance, even at an 80/20 level.

Given the two requirements management value chains described in this part of the book, we can paint a more detailed picture of the work that occurs during these predevelopment iterations. Figure 11.4 depicts the ERM and GRM artifacts to Iteration −1 and 0. The project architect's goal for Iteration −1 is to articulate a whole-project vision. That work is accomplished with the first four artifacts of the ERM value chain. The sponsor concept briefing and stakeholder requests provide the discovery work needed, and the vision document and the first couple of subrelease overviews represent the project architect's requirements analysis work.

Iteration 0 provides the opportunity to connect the project architect's guidance to the first set of specifications for the programmers. Programmers need a crisp, reasonably complete backlog down to the developer story level in order to understand the work ahead. They will also need physical models for the relevant portions of the target database, source-to-target maps (STMs), and module use cases for whatever components involve complex business rules. The project architect, data modeler, and systems analyst can collectively provide these artifacts as a reasonable set of objectives for Iteration 0. Combined, Iterations −1 and 0 fulfill the goals of the release cycle's inception phase because they position the team to begin at least the elaboration work, during which the team will address the project's greatest risks.

Figure 11.3 also lists a first project estimate as an output from the inception phase. The team leaders can actually derive two estimates from the requirements management artifacts listed previously. The vision document positions the project architect to draft a *rough order of magnitude estimate* or "T-shirt estimate" (−25 to +50% [Project Management Institute 2013]). Later, the team can employ an early version of the project backlog to assign story points to developer stories and then calculate a first current estimate, which will serve as the basis for a *budgeting estimate* (−25 to +10% for that specific collection of stories).

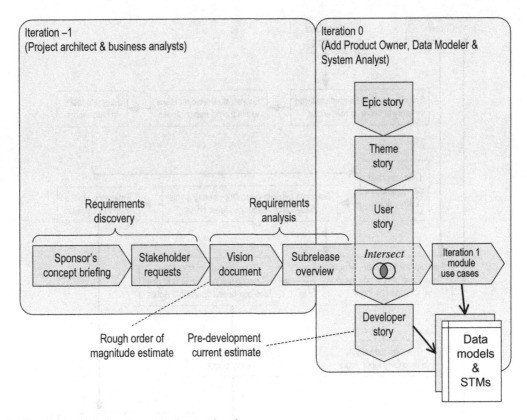

FIGURE 11.4   Fitting RM artifacts into the pre-development iterations.

Arriving at a Predevelopment Project Estimate

Figure 11.4 qualified the budgeting estimate at the end of an inception phase as a "predevelopment current estimate" because the team leaders will compile it before programming gets underway with Iteration 1. Once development begins, they will prepare many more current estimates, one at the conclusion of each programming iteration. The predevelopment labor forecast will pose a unique challenge, however, because the team will be lacking two crucial pieces of information needed for an accurate current estimate: story points on the stories of the backlog and a team velocity. Agile EDW practitioners call this the "green team estimating problem," which vexes every new agile data warehousing program. Fortunately, agile teams have created a means for overcoming this problem. The practice entails some risk if the estimate provided is taken too seriously, but it does allow project leaders to offer business stakeholders a whole-project forecast of cost and duration that all managers naturally desire at the start of a project.

As was illustrated with Figure 5.4, teams generate current estimates at the end of each iteration. These current estimates are easy to calculate at the end of an iteration because the team needs only to divide total story points for stories still awaiting development by the team's current "velocity," the number of story points the team just delivered during the past iteration. The result indicates how many additional iterations will be needed to complete the programming. If the developers are progressing at rate of, for example, 20 story points per iteration, and they have 200 points of developer stories ahead, one can easily project that they will need 10 more iterations to finish the programming. This forecasted project duration can then be converted into estimated programming cost by multiplying the projected number of iterations by the labor cost incurred during a sprint. Estimating project duration before development iterations have started is difficult, however, because the developers have not yet programmed a single story, so they have no velocity measurement to use. Moreover, the team does not have even story points assigned to the items on the backlog yet.

As covered in my previous books, ongoing agile teams can estimate the story points of a requested module by envisioning the work it will require and comparing that effort to the work they have already invested in two or three other modules that they have recently delivered. These "reference modules" allow them to estimate by comparison the level of effort needed for any item on the project backlog ahead. For example, if in the last iteration, the account dimension module was 3 story points of work and the customer dimension was 13, then the team could well estimate that the effort required to deliver the geographies dimension, which feels like it falls between the two reference modules in terms of difficulty, will be 8 story points.

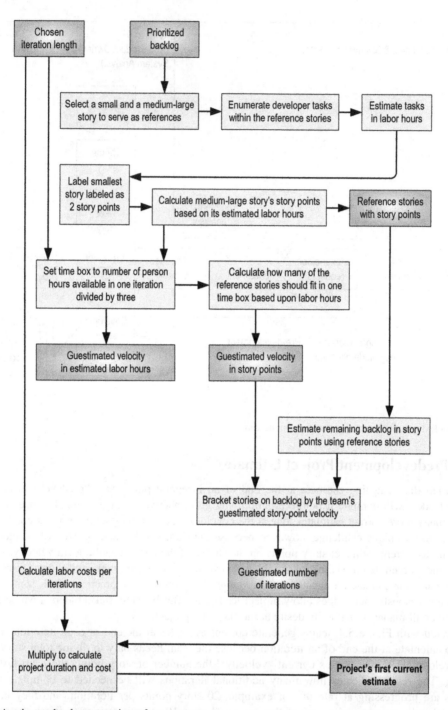

FIGURE 11.5   Preparing the pre-development estimate for a new team.

At the end of the inception phase, the team will have an initial backlog of stories that need programming; however, the team members will be "green"—that is, lacking any programming experience that would give them the reference modules needed to perform story point estimation. To provide an initial estimate of labor required for the project, then, the team will need to create reference modules and a team velocity from thin air. Throughout the years, agile EDW teams have devised a way for green teams to "back into" story point estimates for reference modules and a velocity. Of course, this technique provides only a rough estimate, so team leaders should carefully manage the expectation that stakeholders form when they receive this first labor forecast for the project.

Figure 11.5 shows the steps that the leaders of a green agile EDW team typically follow in preparing a project's first current estimate. In essence, the developers must surmise a reasonable number of story points for a pair of stories they plan to build, and then use the story points on those hypothetical reference stories to not only story point the rest of the backlog but also guess what the team's velocity will be once it starts programming. The first step in this process is to find on the backlog a couple of developer stories for each layer of the reference architecture that would be good benchmarks for estimates if only they had been already developed. A good pair of benchmarks for a given layer of the reference architecture would include a story that seems smaller than the rest and another that seems medium to large.

To calculate story points for each of these hypothetical benchmarks, developers will need to identify the development tasks implicit in each story and then estimate that work in labor hours, yielding a total labor hours for each story. Arranging the benchmark stories from smallest to largest based on these estimated labor hours, the team awards the smallest story an arbitrary "size" of two story points, for example. The developers then use the ratio of the labor hours of each remaining benchmark story to that of the smallest story and thereby derive story points for the remainder of the reference stories.

Agile teams allow themselves to use only a few numbers in estimating story points, typically the Fibonacci series (0, 1, 2, 3, 5, 8, 13, 21, 34, ...). Using a sparse collection of possible numbers prevents developers from splitting hairs during estimating—that is, wasting time arguing whether a particular story is a "5" or a "6." Teams may have to revisit the story points they have derived for their hypothetical reference stories so that they will align with the sparse number scale that the teams wish to use. Once they have story pointed a set of reference stories using their sparse number scale, the developers can then employ these reference stories to estimate the rest of the project's backlog using estimating poker [Rubin 2012].

The story points on these hypothetical reference stories will also allow the developers to guestimate a reasonable velocity for the team. First, they calculate how many work hours will exist for a standard iteration, usually by multiplying the length of the workday by both the number of developers and the number of workdays in the development time box they have chosen. They then adjust this number by a "get real" factor, typically dividing it by three, to arrive at the number of estimated programming hours that the team will probably be able to complete during one iteration. This number represents a reasonable velocity in labor hours for the team to shoot for during its first iteration.

The project leaders then take stories from the backlog, identify the development tasks for each, and estimate those tasks in labor hours. They continue to add stories to the iteration backlog until the total estimated labor hours matches the reasonable labor-hour velocity that they calculated previously. They had already assigned story points to these stories, so once they add up the story points for the stories in the iteration backlog, they will have a reasonable velocity for Iteration 1 measured in story points. At this point, the team needs only to apply that guestimated velocity in story points against its project backlog to forecast how many development iterations it will need to complete the project.

Some people might think it is too severe to divide the work hours available during a development time box by three in order to calculate a likely velocity for the team in labor hours. Teams that skip this reduction step unfortunately assume that the developers on the team will be able to program during every hour of the workdays available within an iteration. In practice, however, developers lose considerable programming time to emails, phone calls, and informal communications between teammates. Moreover, programmers can never anticipate all the work that programming a given module will require. As they start work on each one, they uncover new development tasks, especially during early iterations in which the team will be challenged by issues involving unfamiliar tools and unconfigured platforms. Finally, teams should be careful with their first current estimate because corporate managers may well use that number against them for the remainder of the project. Given that the organization will tend to remember their initial estimate, developers are wise to understate what they think they might be able to accomplish. All these reasons combine to make "divide by three" a reasonable adjustment when guessing a team's likely velocity during Iteration 0.

Managing the Predevelopment Estimate

Rather than a single deliverable, the agile EDW team leaders should realize that providing the predevelopment project estimate to project governance is just the beginning of an information flow that they will have to maintain. If not soon supplied with yet further current estimates at the conclusion of Iteration 1, and 2, and so on, project governance will adopt the predevelopment forecast of labor and duration as *the* estimate for the project. Undoubtedly, business stakeholders will interpret the only current estimate they have received as the EDW team leader's promise to deliver X scope of features by Y date, turning the entire endeavor into yet another waterfall project with a high risk of failure.

The team needs to actively submit current estimates at the conclusion of each iteration and emphasize that each is the most recent—and therefore the only accurate—appraisal of the time and development labor needed to finish the project. Business and IT managers who are new to agile will be unreceptive to updated estimates at first and may even criticize the agile EDW team for its inconsistency. In the projects I have led, two arguments have helped me move project governance past this counterproductive mindset. First, the predevelopment estimate was compiled when the team and its business partners were at the peak of their ignorance regarding the level of effort the project will require. Clinging to an estimate made by uninformed people is foolhardy when better forecasts exist.

Second, to refuse to factor the new current estimates is to remain deliberately blind to the latest information. That practice is tantamount to buying a new car with only an idiot light for a fuel gauge. The light will remain dark as one drives relentlessly into the desert and then suddenly come on when the gas is gone and the driver is hundreds of miles from any help. Just as drivers will make better decisions if they rely on incremental fuel gauges in their cars, project governance teams will be able to better keep their project scoped and funded if they will accept an honest reappraisal of remaining effort and duration at the end of each iteration.

Completing the Release Cycle

With the conclusion of the inception phase, agile EDW team leaders need to turn to their attention to moving their developers expeditiously through the elaboration phase of their company's application release cycle. As depicted by the outer ring in Figure 11.3, Iterations −1 and 0 make up the inception phase as expected. The elaboration phase spans the first few development sprints, starting with iteration 1. The RUP method advocates an elaboration phase in order to give the team an opportunity to (1) draft a technical architecture for the application, (2) demonstrate its appropriateness for the project, and (3) mitigate the project's greatest development risks [Rational Software 1998].

Naturally, it is impossible to say *a priori* how many iterations will be required to prove an architecture and mitigate serious risk. Agile EDW teams usually believe they have achieved "just enough" risk mitigation within one to three iterations, depending especially on the length of the development time box they are using. The developers will need to estimate the actual number required once they have had a chance to consider the project vision provided by the project architect as part of the inception phase. The outer band in Figure 11.3 depicts a project for which the team decided that two iterations would suffice, and those two sprints are shown fitting into the elaboration phase accordingly.

The remaining development iterations make up the project's construction phase. These sprints are followed by the work of promoting a subrelease into production during an iteration that constitutes the transition phase. This promotion iteration typically involves user validation, system testing, and promotion activities, which will be discussed in the next part of this book when we take up quality assurance.

TECHNIQUES FOR THE ELABORATION PHASE

After the opening inception phase, the RUP release cycle begins an elaboration phase in which the goal is to both identify a viable architecture for an application and mitigate the major risks of a project. Agile EDW practitioners can draw from two techniques to accomplish this phase of work quickly and effectively.

Choosing Developer Stories for the Elaboration Phase

RUP and traditional project management methods actively assess a project's work breakdown structure for risk [Aked 2003]. Agile EDW project leaders should emulate this practice and appraise their project backlogs accordingly in order to identify those stories to include in the elaboration phase of a project. Table 11.2 depicts a simple framework for calculating the risk represented by a collection of developer stories. The risk of a developer story is simply the product of the points awarded to it based on three considerations: how likely the risk is to occur (its probability), the damage it will cause if it does occur (its impact), and the difficulty the team will have in judging whether it has occurred (its undetectability). Developer stories with the lowest probability, impact, and undetectability receive points that multiply out to 1. Stories with the highest degrees of these considerations multiply out to 27. Some teams do not employ the undetectability consideration, in which case the risks scores will range from 1 to 9.

Before scanning the backlog for risk, the team leaders decide what score indicates a hazard that deserves assiduous risk mitigation. Usually, the threshold is 9 or greater (when using all three considerations), which means that the project leaders will leave to the normal development process risks with medium or lesser levels of probability, impact, and undetectability.

Using this risk assessment framework, the project leaders start the elaboration phase by working through the backlog, calculating the degree of risk that each developer story represents. The team might evaluate user stories and entire themes in a similar manner to determine if any of them stand out as particularly risky. Stories with risk points exceeding the preestablished threshold will be moved upward in the backlog so that they will undergo development during the

TABLE 11.2 Risk Calculation Framework and Example

Epic / Theme / User Story / Developer Story	Probability	Impact	Undetectability	Risk Level	Action	Risk Description / Mitigation Plan
Reduce number of loss events						
Loss events by location						
Harmonized locations	3	2	2	12	Y	Different geocoding between bus units Translation table
Harmonized events						
Stage transaction files	3	3	2	18	Y	XML data without XSD schemas Change request to vendor
Integrate transaction / source 1	2	1	3	6		
Increase cross selling						
Call lists for customer with only 1 product	1	3	2	6		
Lower customer churn						
List of customers at-risk						
At-risk profiles	1	2	2	4	N	
Calculate at risk scores	3	1	3	9	Y	Move call to external procedure into the steel thread subrelease

elaboration phase. Given the dependencies between stories on the backlog, some work items with under-threshold risk will also travel upwards on the backlog as companions to the high-risk stories. Later, we discuss the process of prioritizing a full backlog for multiple considerations, including risk.

Proving Out Architectures Using a "Steel Thread"

RUP practitioners advocate a further technique that agile EDW teams will find very helpful during the elaboration phase of their projects. Given a typical EDW project's complex mix of functional, architectural, and nonfunctional requirements, how can a team know that the programming architecture, tool set, and platforms chosen for the project represent a workable combination? Agile EDW teams can answer this by constructing a "steel thread"—that is, by programming a single small line of information services all the way from the landing area to a front-end dashboard.

As explained to me by RUP practitioners, the name of this technique derives from the construction of suspension bridges, such as the Golden Gate Bridge in San Francisco. The roadbed of these bridges hangs from massive cables that stretch between piers set in bedrock, often miles apart. Those massive cables were not delivered ready-made and then lifted to the appropriate height but, instead, had to be assembled, in place, one strand of steel at a time. Once the first small thread of steel was situated along the correct arc, the construction crews used a special winding device that would travel along the partially completed cable, back and forth between the piers, laying down one wire after another until the full cable was complete.

This anecdote immediately brings one question to mind: Where did the original steel thread that the winding machine began following come from? Someone had to start at the top of the first pier, attach the starter strand, and then climb down, travel by boat to the next pier, and climb the second tower to put the first steel thread in place. Once the first steel thread was situated, the rest of the work of building the full cables could proceed at pace.

To prove out the project's architecture, then, the agile EDW developers need to identify a small slice of functionality that will travel from source extract to business intelligence dashboard. They need to think through their design and pick the path of this steel thread carefully so that it touches on as many of the doubtable components in the architecture as possible without involving too large a set of developer stories. If possible, the team should strive to select developer stories that not only prove viability of the project architecture but also add up to a valuable business service so that the product owner can appreciate from a business perspective the deliverables of the elaboration phase when reviewing them during the project's first few user demos.

For some projects, the steel thread will involve a majority of technical issues so that the team may need the product owner to allow it an "architectural sprint" that everyone understands will provide very little for an end user to appreciate. Such architectural sprints should be kept to a minimum, however, because they violate the central agile tenet of constantly delivering value to the customer. By definition, a steel thread for EDW projects brings at least a few data elements to the end-user dashboard, so with a little imagination, project leaders should be able to include in this work multiple end-user features.

Viewing the previously discussed notions through the lens of requirements management, then, team leaders can anticipate that the steel thread will somewhat impact their project's starting backlog. The risk mitigation analysis elevated the riskiest stories in the backlog. The steel thread analysis then rearranges the backlog further to ensure that the opening iterations not only address the technical concerns over risk but also add up to something of appreciable value for end users.

PRIORITIZING PROJECT BACKLOGS

Agile development teams aspire to be responsive to the changing business conditions faced by their business customers. For that reason, they often collaborate with their product owners to re-sequence the stories in the project backlog at the end of each iteration so that, as much as possible, the stories that are most important at that moment enter development during the next sprint. In addition to business value, the risk inherent in a developer story will also affect the point at which it will be developed during the project, as discussed in the previous section.

Throughout the years of practicing agile EDW, my colleagues and I have found several other criteria for properly sequencing the stories on project backlogs. Some involve business considerations, whereas others are more technical in nature. So that the reprioritization process works for both the business and the technical aspects of the project, agile EDW project leaders should negotiate up front with their product owner and project governance council the criteria to be employed while sequencing a backlog and their relative importance. To provide a starting point for such a conversation, the following list names the criteria from which my colleagues and I draw upon for the project teams we lead, in the order that we typically apply them.

Many of the following steps assume that project leaders are considering their backlog in *current estimate* format, illustrated in Figure 5.4. That format shows the sequence of developer stories for the project, the story points for each story, and brackets grouping the stories into the iterations during which they will be developed. Those brackets are sized to match the current velocity of the team, as measured by the number of story points delivered by the last iteration completed.

Priority 1: Business Value

True to our agile mission to constantly deliver value to the customer, the business value of a particular story is the first criteria we use to sequence the items on the project backlog. It is hoped that the value is expressed in terms of value points resulting from the value accounting process that I recommended in Chapter 8, but at a minimum, the product owner can simply sort the backlog by the importance that he or she places on each one.

Priority 2: Predecessor/Successor Dependencies

After business value, the most important consideration in a data warehousing project has to be the technical dependencies that exist between stories. Dimensions must exist before fact tables are loaded, for example, otherwise, the product owner and other users will not be able to perform analytics on the measures provided by the data warehouse. During this step, the technical members of the project leadership team need to push the dependent stories lower in the backlog while doing their best to honor the business priorities previously established by the product owner. This step provides a valuable opportunity, by the way, for the project architect to validate his or her subrelease plan with the developers on the team. For example, if a few fact tables are slated for delivery before all the dimension tables have been created, does the delayed arrival of the various dimensions create more rework than is justified by the benefits of providing certain facts earlier in the project? The project architect can also discuss with the developers shortcuts for delivering value to the customer, such as backfilling the architecture, a technique that is discussed in the next part of this book.

Priority 3: Architectural Uncertainties

The previously mentioned priorities will yield a technically rational backlog that reflects what the business requires of the data warehouse. At this point, the technical team leaders should employ the risk assessment technique discussed previously to identify the developer stories that may seriously impact the project if they cannot be delivered as planned. At the start of the project, the riskier stories should be elevated so that they fall into the first few iterations that will make up the elaboration phase of the release cycle. These stories will need to be moved as a block with the other stories on which they depend, so sequencing for risk must occur after predecessor/successor dependencies between stories have been identified. After the team completes the elaboration phase, high-risk stories should be far fewer in number. Conditions may still change, so re-sequencing by risk will be necessary to a small degree throughout the project.

Priority 4: Meeting Interproject Milestones

Once the backlog addresses the major issues of value, dependencies, and risk, team leaders can consider rearranging large blocks of stories to better meet the requirements of other projects that wish to exchange data or services with the enterprise data warehouse. The current estimate clearly shows the iterations in which certain features will be programmed, making it easy to deduce whether the requested capability will be developed and online by a given date. If a large block of stories must be pushed upwards—that is, earlier in time to meet an external milestone—the team leaders will have to revisit the first three steps to ensure that business, risk, and architectural priorities are still being intelligently addressed by the resulting development schedule.

Priority 5: Smoothing Out Iterations

As a team brackets its developer stories for upcoming iterations, some items at the bottom of each bracket may be a few story points too big to fit perfectly into that iteration. Rather than splitting the story between iterations, teams can more simply swap that story with a more appropriately sized story further down in the backlog. The product owner must agree with this recommendation or propose another substitution that he or she would like better.

Priority 6: "Funding Waypoints"

Agile EDW projects often span fiscal years and thus might lose funding when the budgets are prepared for the next year. Team leaders should locate on the current estimate the iteration where the fiscal year will end, and they should ask the product owner if any story below that cutoff is one that end users will absolutely need to have. Often, the product owner will find a few stories toward the bottom of the list that, although low in overall importance, are still essential for the system, such as the module for expunging transactions that have exceeded the warehouse's data retention period. In order to play it safe, the product owner may well wish to elevate these stories above the fiscal year cutoff and then push a corresponding number of story points for other stories below that boundary line.

Priority 7: Resource Scheduling

Finally, the order of stories on the backlog must be adjusted to reflect resource availability. If the BI developers will not be available for 4 months, for example, it makes no sense to have front-end stories occur before their arrival. Project leaders should place stories with missing resources lower on the list in order to accommodate the given constraints.

MANAGING INCREMENTAL PRECISION

Once the agile EDW project leaders have properly intersected the GRM and ERM value chains for requirements and have completed the backlog prioritization process described previously, they will possess a solid backlog for their project. They will be able to story point the entire backlog and generate a current estimate by which they and other project stakeholders can understand the arc of the coming months of labor and track the team's steady progress. However, the fact that a backlog is well organized does not imply that the project's stories will be equally actionable. Any story more than a few iterations away may eventually be dropped from the backlog as business conditions change or when one of the project leaders discovers an easier way to achieve the same business goal. To minimize the risk of wasted effort, then, the team should have the leading edge of stories ready for development but should leave more vague those that will not be programmed until much later.

The variable level of precision occurring within the requirements expressed in the project backlog has to be deliberately controlled. A distant story may be vague now, but in a few months, when it enters development, the programmers will demand clear instructions if they are to code it accurately. Although the details required for coding a module will depend on the particular programmers assigned to a team, the list of possible specification artifacts is quite extensive, as one can see by considering the templates for the subrelease overview and module use case presented in Chapter 10. These specifications cannot be provided spontaneously, and therefore project leaders need to plan to steadily enrich the documentation available for a given story as it approaches the top of the backlog. At the start of a project, team leaders should agree upon a repeatable pattern for progressively elaborating the guidance accompanying a story. Besides facilitating effective programming, the team's incremental specification approach should also create the opportunity for project leaders to address the nonfunctional requirements relevant to the upcoming modules.

A Framework for Visualizing Progressive Requirements

The fact that agile EDW teams allow distant stories on the backlog to be vague until they are truly needed harks back to the notion of accuracy versus precision introduced in Chapter 7. When the product owner authors a user story, the developers want that story to both possess business value and comply with the stated purpose of the application. But until the planning day in which the associated developer stories will be coded, the programmers could not care less if their technical leaders understand the technical details of a given user story. In short, the developers will insist on accuracy in the backlog's stories, but they can wait for precision.

For the team leaders such as the data modeler and the systems analyst, precision is not a quality they can provide overnight. The business rules and data structures involved in a single developer story can take days to articulate. Often, they will need time to research the impact of many nonfunctional requirements as well. For these reasons, the project leaders should employ a clear process for progressively elaborating the requirements of user and developer stories as they draw nearer to their day of programming.

Table 11.3 shows one approach to managing progressive requirement elaboration within an agile EDW project. This frameworks knits together the many notions regarding requirements discussed in the past three chapters and locates all the artifacts we have examined within a repeatable process. Focusing on the artifacts, we can see that most of the ERM value chain—from sponsor's concept briefing to subrelease overview—occurs in the first two rows. The requirements process then switches over to the GRM work of authoring an initial set of epics, themes, and user stories on row 3. The remaining ERM artifact, the module use case, can be found at the end of requirements analysis on row 5. The artifacts from both these value chains are highlighted in heavy script to make them easier to find.

The structure of the framework corresponds to many of the dimensions of requirements management that have been examined in this part of the book. The artifacts occur in the shaded portion in columns 4–9 in Table 11.3. The rows of this area reflect the deepening precision in the requirements, whereas the columns reflect temporal sequencing. A label is provided for each level of precision in column 3, although readers are invited to rename these should they think of terms that better describe the degrees of elaboration achieved. In general, the process of progressive elaboration is reflected by a diagonal movement from the upper left to the lower right, as indicated by the arrow.

Starting with the row labels in column 1, this framework distinguishes between requirements discovery, requirements analysis, and design, showing that requirements discovery transitions into analysis as the epic stack becomes steadily more complete in row 3. It can also be seen where business requirements progresses into technical requirements as the progressive elaboration moves into row 4.

In row 7, the framework lists the software engineering phase that the artifacts achieve. Immediately below that row is listed the role on the team that typically takes the lead with each set of artifacts. Taken altogether, this framework provides a handy reference to the crucial questions of who, what, and when within the domain of agile EDW requirements management.

The Freezer, Fridge, Counter Metaphor

The last row in the agile EDW requirements management framework describes "storage" and reflects a simple metaphor that many teams with which I have worked like to use in order to more easily communicate the progressive elaboration pattern to which they have agreed. The metaphor describes the journey of a package of frozen food as it makes its way from the freezer onto your kitchen cooktop [Rawsthorne and Shimp 2011]. This journey begins for an agile EDW requirement when a product owner first articulates a user story and the project architect can vet that it fits within the spirit of the application, as expressed in the project's vision document. The project architect also analyzes how the

TABLE 11.3 Progressive Requirements Elaboration Pattern

Col ⇒	1	2	3	4	5	6	7	8	9	Abbreviation Meanings
Row	**Activity**	**Orientation**	**Precision**				Artifacts			
1	Requirements Discovery		Notional	SCB / SHR						Sponsor's Concept Briefing / Stakeholder's Request
2		Business Facing (Business Requirements)	Scoped		VDoc		SRO s (Subrelease Plan)			Vision Document / Stub Release Overview
3			Queued		User & Developer Stories within an Epic Stack	70% Complete	80% Complete	95% Complete		
4	Requirements Analysis	Technology Facing (Technical Requirements)	High Level			LDM @ Key Integration Points (integration & presentation layers)	80/20 LDM			Logical Data Model / Business Rules / Data Warehouse / Non-Functional Requirements
5			Actionable				BR Sketches / DW Architecture / NFRs	Data profiles / 80/20 PDM / MUC s (STMs)	Remaining PDM / Whiteboard DFD / Pseudo code / Test script / Coded Modules	Physical Data Model / Module Use Case / Source-to-Target Mapping
6	Design & Development (pursued simultaneously during development iterations)									Physical Data Model / Dataflow Diagram
7	SWE Phase >			Requirements Gathering			Requirements Analysis	High Level Design	Detailed Design	
8	Who >			Project Architect & Business Analysts		Product Owner & Project Architect	Project Architect, Business Analyst, & Data Modeler	Data Modeler & System Analyst	System Analyst & Developers	
9	"Storage" >					Freezer	Fridge	Countertop	Cooktop	

Progressive elaboration

user story will intersect with the EDW's reference architecture and generates a starter set of developer stories. The data modeler then considers the impact that this set of developer stories will have on his or her logical data model (LDM), especially the key integration points that will connect its data to the subject areas already populated in the warehouse. If this user story is placed at the bottom of the backlog, development will not occur soon, and the story needs no further requirements elaboration. We say that the team has placed this story in the *freezer* for long-term storage.

As the time for coding approaches, the project architect realizes that the story needs to acquire greater clarity regarding logical data modeling, business rules, and the impact of nonfunctional requirements. Thus, the architect places the story into the team's pipeline for the data modeler and business analyst to begin working on. The data modeler will draft the attributes for the relevant entities of the logical data model that will support the user story while leaving the least important 20 percent of the attributes unspecified. The data modeler will also invest effort to comply with the non-functional architectural requirements received from external bodies, such as enterprise information management, enterprise architecture, and the enterprise data warehouse architect. At this point, the team has completed high-level, technical requirements analysis, and we say that the story has moved from the freezer into the *fridge*.

One or two iterations before the programmers will start coding the developer stories for this product owner request, the system analyst will begin data profiling the source data and the data modeler will draft an increment to the physical data model for the most important 80 percent of the attributes. Once the data modeling is complete, the systems analyst will document the transformation logic, at least the derived columns implied by the story, placing these specifications in an STM for the programmers to follow. At this point, we say that the story has moved from the fridge onto the kitchen *countertop*, ready for the developers to throw it in a pot and place it on their cooktops for final transformation into a meal.

EFFORT LEVELS BY TEAM ROLES

Table 11.3 focuses on the progressive elaboration of a single requirement. It lists the objectives that requirements work should achieve, but it does not convey the overall effort required from project leaders during requirements management. These demands will peak and ebb at different times for the various roles on a team as the work of defining a project, and later a given iteration, progresses through the software engineering disciplines such as requirements and design. Teams can visualize the expected demands on each teammate using *effort curves*. These charts allow project leaders to better plan resource acquisition, communicate expectations, and, just as important, budget time for each role to address the project's nonfunctional requirements.

Visualizing Requirements Management Demands with Effort Curves

Figures 11.6 and 11.7 portray the labor time that the typical agile EDW project requires from each role. These curves are analogous to the RUP whale charts mentioned in Chapter 3 and represent the level of effort required from a given role at a given time in the project. Figure 11.6 focuses on the roles of the project architect and the product owner. The second drawing shows the pattern of involvement expected from the remaining roles on the team. The columns of the graph identify the iterations during which the work should occur, starting with −1 and 0. In both figures, a lighter block suggests the portion of time that the role will invest in quality assurance (QA), which is discussed in detail in Part V. The darker block depicts the non-QA effort that a role must invest, which for most roles is dedicated to functional requirements.

The particular project depicted in Figures 11.6 and 11.7 utilized the combined requirements management approach, investing in both ERM and GRM in order to gain stereoscopic vision on the needs of the company. The requirements management demand on the project architect is heavy at first but then tapers off once he or she has completed the vision document. Only as the team approaches each subrelease does the requirements management effort spike again because the project architect must (1) check on many details in order to certify that each version of the application going online is a solution to the proper subset of business problems and (2) invest some additional effort to communicate to the team the intent of the next subrelease as its development gets started.

The product owner's involvement is zero during Iteration −1 because that is the period in which the project architect is gathering content for the vision document from sponsors and major business stakeholders. As usually occurs in large companies, the project sponsors and governance council require a vision and a budgeting estimate from IT before they will assign someone from the business staff to work every day with a development team as a product owner.

Once project governance has named a product owner, the time demands on this person peak in Iteration 0, during which he or she collaborates with the project architect on a first collection of user stories that will make up the project's

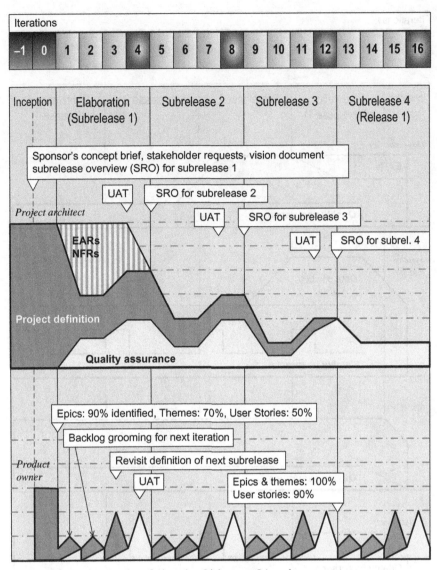

Iterations

| -1 | 0 | 1 | 2 | 3 | 4 | 5 | 6 | 7 | 8 | 9 | 10 | 11 | 12 | 13 | 14 | 15 | 16 |

| Inception | Elaboration (Subrelease 1) | Subrelease 2 | Subrelease 3 | Subrelease 4 (Release 1) |

Sponsor's concept brief, stakeholder requests, vision document subrelease overview (SRO) for subrelease 1

Project architect

UAT   SRO for subrelease 2

UAT   SRO for subrelease 3

UAT   SRO for subrel. 4

EARs
NFRs

Project definition

Quality assurance

Epics: 90% identified, Themes: 70%, User Stories: 50%

Backlog grooming for next iteration

Revisit definition of next subrelease

Product owner

UAT

Epics & themes: 100%
User stories: 90%

Dark areas: Development (non-QA) work   Light areas: QA work
Abbreviations used: UAT = user acceptance testing
EAR = enterprise architecture requirements   NFR = non-functional requirements

FIGURE 11.6   Requirements management effort curves and timing of artifacts over length of a project (part I).

backlog. After that, the project's IT leaders strive to keep the time demand on the product owner low overall so that the engagement only consumes a small fraction of his or her average workday. Small spikes in the effort needed for requirements occur midway through each sprint when the product owner and the team leaders invest some time in grooming the leading edge of the backlog for the next iteration. An even larger spike in requirements management work occurs during the iteration before a subrelease, representing the effort necessary to review the requirements to be addressed during the coming user acceptance test.

Figure 11.7 depicts the requirements management work needed from the remaining roles of a typical agile EDW project. Except where noted, these effort curves here represent requirements analysis yielding technical requirements rather than work on nonfunctional requirements. The data modeler's loading peaks at the start of the project, as soon as the project architect has authored a project vision document for him or her to work from. The modeler's involvement tapers off once the project data model gels and the programmers gain a fuller understanding of the data repository they are building.

Of all the roles, the systems analyst has the highest loading throughout the project because he or she is busy profiling the next set of source data, writing STMs, or validating that the programmers have correctly implemented the

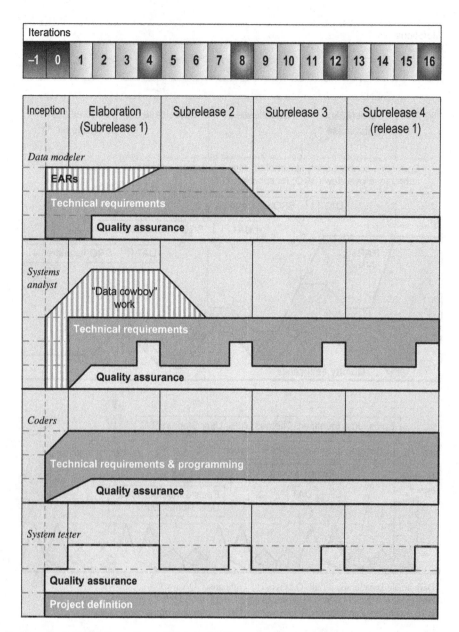

FIGURE 11.7   Requirements management effort curves and timing of artifacts over length of a project (part II).

business rules expressed in the STM. The coders only hit their peak loading when elaboration gets underway. Their involvement should stay maximized throughout the remainder of the project, which only makes sense if the agile team wants to deliver the greatest possible value to the organization. Finally, the system tester role contributes somewhat to project definition, reflecting the fact that test-led development can be practiced to some degree at the level of the project and not just that of the module, as will be discussed in the chapters on quality assurance.

Allocating Time for Nonfunctional Requirements

The effort curves in the preceding diagrams provide the team with a means to plan for addressing the nonfunctional requirements of a project. As discussed previously, there are two types of nonfunctional requirements that EDW project leaders need to address. First, there are application-level "abilities," as listed in Table 7.2, that make up the standard notion of "nonfunctional" requirements for any computer application. Second, there are higher-order, enterprise requirements provided by architectural groups such as the enterprise information management, enterprise architecture, and enterprise data warehouse architecture groups. As discussed previously, an agile EDW team is a consumer of these requirements and is responsible for both supporting them during the construction of individual projects and providing feedback and ideas where those high-level specifications prove infeasible.

Addressing both of these classes of requirements consumes effort, so processing time for them needs to be budgeted by the project leaders. Looking at the effort curve for the project architect, the time demand on this role lessens soon after he provides a functional definition of the project via the vision document and subrelease plan. Eventually, DW/BI management will ask the project architect to begin definition work on another project because the project depicted in the graph no longer needs him full-time. Before he begins on that second project, however, he will have the bandwidth starting with the first iteration of elaboration to consider both enterprise architecture requirements (EARs) and classic nonfunctional requirements (NFRs). This effort is indicated by the cross-hatched area marked "EARs, NFRs" in Figure 11.6, occurring during Iterations 1–3. As a result of this effort, he may need to revise slightly the project's vision document and subrelease plan. Such refinements should not disrupt his teammates much because the refinements will come to light during elaboration, before the team has locked in a desired application architecture.

For the data modeler, this role could probably complete the bulk of her schema designs in the first few iterations, if all she were focusing on were functional requirements. We want her to incorporate the company's enterprise architectural requirements, however, so her effort curve will probably extend well into the development time of the second subrelease. Although the exact mix of functional and nonfunctional work effort cannot be depicted precisely for the data modeler, at least a graph such as Figure 11.7 will illustrate that both are involved. Team leaders can use the total of both types of effort during conversations with DW/BI management to illustrate why the data modeler will need a longer involvement with the agile EDW project than the functional requirements alone might suggest.

CONQUERING COMPLEX BUSINESS RULES WITH AN EMBEDDED METHOD

Carefully planning the progressive elaboration of application requirements will greatly help the project leaders generate a smooth supply of design guidance for their programmers, but one serious challenge will remain. Projects receiving poor data quality from sources systems and/or involving complex business rules easily fall prey to "analysis paralysis." When the analysis and design roles cannot make immediate sense of the source systems and subject matter experts fail to adequately explain how the source data should be integrated and transformed into metrics, the project leaders will be unable to continue creating 80/20 specifications for their coders. Without guidance, the programmers will run out of work, they will fall idle, and the entire agile delivery process will grind to a halt.

This situation requires the team to readjust its process quickly lest it begin to squander valuable development resources and forfeit crucial business opportunities. The challenges posed by sources and transform logic are large unknowns at the beginning of a project. In my experience, these massive unknowns must be met with a surge of analysis as soon as the vision document has been approved. The best solution is for the project to engage a short-term "data cowboy" to wrangle the more unruly areas within the source data and to illustrate the full intricacies of the project's most complex business rules. Naturally, this cowboy will need a special blend of skills and tools to master this situation, but just as important, he will be most effective if he employs a special method of his own.

Add the Data Cowboy Role

A more formal name for this role might be *data transform specification analyst* because that is the mission this person takes on: Dive into the source data; make sense of it as quickly as possible; decide how the extract, transform, and load (ETL) process should transform it in order to create the desired information in the EDW repository; and document those rules for programmers to follow during coding. I prefer the *data cowboy* label for this person, for just as the cattle wranglers of the past had to be willing to leap off a horse and wrestle errant cattle to the ground, this analyst must be ready to try anything to pummel a heap of poorly documented sources and business rules into yielding their secrets. Our company has one associate specializing in this role who actually prefers to be called the "data spanker," a fitting moniker even if it is slightly difficult to use when introducing the team members to a new customer.

When it comes to source data, individuals filling this cowboy role will need true bravado because the data quality problems can be a horrid mix of nightmares, such as the following:

- Inconsistent element definitions
- Nonexistent data models
- Unreliable join patterns between tables

- Missing or incomplete lookup tables
- Overloaded columns in a transaction system that each data entry operator used for a different purpose
- Columns with binary encoding instead of text

Source data quality problems seem to be particularly common in the records originating from mainframe and personal computer applications because the transaction systems created for these platforms often impose few checks on the information submitted by the users. Atop this frustration, the project must contend with subject matter experts who cannot clearly articulate the business rules defining the target data elements because they involve scores of if—then—else statements that no one in the company has ever documented. Compound these challenges with tight time frames imposed by project sponsors anxious to start using business intelligence *now*, and the data cowboy will need to be a miracle worker indeed.

Special Skills and Tools for the Data Cowboy

The perfect person for this role will possess an extensive experience in profiling, cleansing, and migrating poorly behaved source data. Often, individuals who have spent some time serving as shadow IT make excellent candidates because such experience will have made them practiced at knitting together corporate and noncorporate data sources, usually with minimal help from the corporate systems owners. Such work will have taught them how to rapidly iterate through an invent-and-try cycle until they find a means to match candidate keys, accomplishing a difficult join between tables from different source systems. They will have also had to dispose of any self-imposed notions of "doing things the right way" and focus instead on just getting the job done quickly. Such an attitude would be dangerous to instill in ETL or BI programmers because it could undermine the culture of disciplined software development that the team leaders would like to establish in the project room, but the attitude is perfect for a specialist whose mission is to discover and record hidden patterns in source data.

This specialist will be comfortable building up complex transform algorithms during interactive sessions with the data and then repeatedly transferring the algorithms that work to a script that embodies the overall sequence required to groom and join the source information into the desired output. Many of the rules that the specialist identifies can also be directed to the data governance group because they describe editing and harmonization rules needed to create a reliable set of master data that applications upstream from the data warehouse should employ.

To work at this demanding level, the data cowboy will need several data-taming weapons in his arsenal. He will need fluency in SQL, the lingua franca of databases, and a scripting language such as Python or Perl. Some aplomb with programming languages such as C and Java will allow him to manage binary data representations. He should certainly be comfortable with one or more data profiling tools, which can provide some basic intelligence regarding a new data source fairly quickly. The other skills he will need will depend on the sources involved, such as mainframe applications demanding COBOL or web-based applications requiring Java and XML.

The data cowboy will undoubtedly need strong capabilities in one or two tools for data visualization. The data spanker who works with my company prefers to use a self-service BI tool that employs an enormous memory-resident data repository so that he can toss, churn, and display a tremendous number of source records in real time until he forces them to make sense.

Agile DWBI project leaders should not be concerned that the data cowboy wishes to employ a tool outside the technology selected for the project. This maverick works only in the discovery and elaboration portion of the software engineering life cycle. His mission is to jump into a heap of lousy source records and half-baked business rules in order to discover their secrets, then convey the necessary transform logic to the team. His deliverables can be as simple as a page of ETL pseudo-code for every target column that the team's regular systems analysts could not profile or understand. Speed and insights are the goals of the data cowboys, not maintainable or compliant code. They should use whatever tools allow them to get this job completed quickly because the longer they take, the more likely the ETL programmers will run out of coding specifications and fall idle.

Modified Data Mining Method Can Help

Although the data cowboy's choice of tools is largely immaterial to project success, the process he employs should still be lightly managed in order to avoid adverse impacts on the other developers. Adding such a free spirit to a project team, even for a short while, represents risk. If not properly channeled, the data cowboy can create a large distraction with his nonstandard tools and work habits. Moreover, if the cowboy is allowed to work any way he desires, project leaders cannot be sure that his efforts will result in complete and correct specifications. To mitigate this risk on our

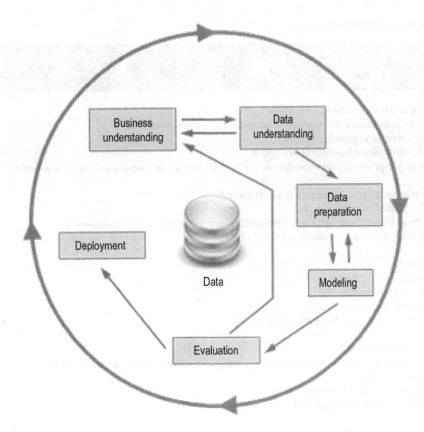

FIGURE 11.8 The CRISP-DM process for data mining.

projects, my company's project architects often request that the data cowboy follow a simple iterative process adapted from CRISP-DM, an international method for disciplined data mining.

The Cross-Industry Standard Process for Data Mining (CRISP-DM) originated in the late 1990s as part of the European Union's ongoing initiatives to coordinate research, development, and knowledge transfer in the realm of information technology. Recent surveys have identified CRISP-DM as the "de facto standard for developing data mining and knowledge discovery projects" [Marbán and Segovia 2009]. Figure 11.8 portrays CRISP-DM's six major steps and shows how they are arranged into a repeatable process.

Table 11.4 provides greater detail for steps composing the CRISP-DM cycle. I have adapted these steps to better meet the needs of a DW/BI project, but readers can find a reference to the official formulation of this process at the bottom of the table so that they can compare my version to the wording of the original. I have also added the two *involvement* columns, which emphasizes that the business rule discovery is a collaboration between the data cowboy and the project's product owner or other subject matter experts. These two roles will trade off the lead frequently as they progress through the CRISP-DM process.

The discovery of business rules hidden within source data or target transforms begins with understanding the business context. The process then gives the data cowboy a chance to acquire a sizable collection of source records to explore. At this point, the product owner and data cowboy focus on modeling the business rules and validating each guess against real records. When they believe they have modeled the transform for a given target column in the EDW, they demo that understanding to other subject matter experts who work with the source data but did not share in the modeling. When these subject matter experts accept the proposed business rules, the agile team's leaders can be reasonably assured that the data cowboy and product owner have accurately divined how to work with the source data system. Finally, this pair compiles its validated knowledge into a pseudo-code narrative of the necessary transform steps, or even an STM that the EDW team can later elaborate upon and follow when coding ETL modules.

By placing just a small amount of structure on the work of the data cowboy, EDW team leaders will make business rule discovery a transparent practice that the team can understand, track, and steer. Giving the data cowboy his own process allows the team to optimize that discovery effort without having to alter the way all the other developers on the agile team pursue their work. The result is a small process running in parallel during the early days of an agile EDW

TABLE 11.4 Steps of the CRISP-DM Process

CRISP-DM Step Tasks (Adapted for EDW Business Rules Discovery)	Involvement Data Transform Specialist	Product Owner
Business understanding		
Clearly articulate the business rules needing documentation	Assist	**Lead**
Assess how much data exploration the current resources, assumptions, and constraints will allow	**Lead**	Assist
Translate each business rule to a input/output model	Assist	**Lead**
Sketch the current understanding of how inputs become outputs	Assist	**Lead**
List the exploration work steps needed to confirm each business rule, articulating them as a series of questions to be answered	**Lead**	Assist
Data understanding		
Gather initial data collection, integrate as necessary to support intended exploration	**Lead**	Assist
Document "gross" or "surface" properties of the data	**Lead**	Assist
Begin the exploration work steps, answering the associated questions using queries, reports, and visualization.	**Lead**	Assist
Assess whether acquired data is complete, correct, and of sufficient scope	**Lead**	Assist
Data preparation		
Acquire secondary sources	**Lead**	Assist
Clean secondary data	**Lead**	Assist
Construct derived attributes as needed	**Lead**	Assist
Integrate secondary data with primary	**Lead**	Assist
Format data with syntactic modifications that do not change meaning	**Lead**	Assist
Modeling		
Select business rule modeling techniques	**Lead**	Assist
Generate test scenario(s) for assessing validity of the model, e.g., specific transactions to run through the business rule	Assist	**Lead**
Create expected results for each test	Assist	**Lead**
Create models using modeling tool on the prepared dataset	**Lead**	Assist
Assess whether models generated the expected and/or correct results	Assist	**Lead**
Evaluation		
Present to SMEs the models' current ability to match expected results and remaining gaps	Assist	**Lead**
Document changes in logic and business requirements suggested by SMEs	**Lead**	Assist
Document the complete understanding of how inputs become outputs	**Lead**	Assist
Decide whether to send current models to development team	Assist	**Lead**
Deployment		
Communicate validated business rules to systems analyst for documentation in source-to-target maps	**Lead**	Assist
Review new business rules capabilities during iteration demos	Assist	**Lead**
Present new business rule capabilities to stakeholders during UAT	Assist	**Lead**

engagement that provides the team's regular developers with reliable data transform specifications while keeping them undistracted from the careful coding that their ETL modules require.

Placing Business Rules Discovery and Analysis into the Effort Curves

In my experience, the data cowboy role is a relatively short-lived assignment. The individual filling that role may well stay on with the team, given his valuable problem-solving skills, but at some point the need for wild, rapid data discovery disappears. That transition frequently begins with the end of the elaboration phase of the project and concludes a few iterations thereafter. Winding down the rapid business rules discovery process at this time coincides well with the rest of the developers' transition to the steady work of programming the applications ETL modules in the context of a proven, stable architecture.

To illustrate this transition, I placed a supplemental effort curve on the tasking for the system analyst role in Figure 11.7. The work of business rules discovery can begin as soon as the project architect secures approval of the vision document. Working from the sources listed on the vision document's context diagram, the data cowboy can jump into data extracts from the transaction systems and start making sense of the records they contain. The work of data cowboys complements that of the systems analyst in that it provides the insights that the latter needs to prepare decent STMs for the coders. In this collaboration, the data cowboy reconnoiters the unknown territory ahead, and the systems analyst serves as cartographer, documenting the landscape in a way that connects the cowboy's discoveries with landmarks already known, creating an intelligible map that developers can readily follow.

Adding a data cowboy to the development team for a few months at the start of the project allows the team to get out ahead of the large learning curve that each new source system represents and avoid analysis paralysis during the construction phase of the project.

INTERFACING WITH PROJECT GOVERNANCE

The definition of requirements management cited in Chapter 7 included three key elements: planning the work, gathering and validating the requirements, and maintaining the accuracy of those requirements. The previous discussions have focused largely on the first two of the elements, leaving management of the requirements unaddressed until now. Agile EDW teams frequently butt heads with project governance structures in many corporations, largely due to the style in which the latter wants to manage requirements. The solution to this conflict usually requires a "negotiated settlement." A quick outline of such a settlement will provide agile EDW project leaders with a good notion of the type of solution to insist upon. Having a solution in mind will help them quickly propose a workable pattern and avoid losing months of agile development to excessive interference from a project oversight group.

Project governance can be a multilayered structure in large corporations. It often includes a steering committee of executives funding the project and then, informally, all of their direct reports charged with tracking the development of the EDW in detail. It also invariably involves agents from the project management office (PMO) and often includes project managers on both the technical and business sides of a program.

For those organizations that have not yet developed an incremental project management mindset, an agile data warehousing effort will appear very alien and threatening to many of the parties in project governance. The traditional mindset requires that all work be defined before programming begins so that the parties overseeing the project can check off work packages from a defined list as they are completed. Traditional project management also demands that the level of effort be estimated with precision before work begins so that managers can keep the project's expenses within the budget that the sponsors have approved. Traditional managers frequently disapprove of the development methods of agile EDW teams for multiple reasons. First, EDW teams work with 80/20 specifications—the final details will be unavailable until coding is underway. Second, agile EDW backlogs also operate at an 80/20 level—a good number of user stories and even some themes will be identified mid-project as the business learns progressively more about its BI requirements. Third, agile EDW teams can provide only a current estimate for the project and not a single, definitive estimate, as all traditionally trained project managers will demand.

To take some of the friction out of this relationship, I recommend agile EDW teams start the stream of current estimates right away, as previously discussed. It is true that most agile EDW teams will struggle at first to convince project governance to accept a regularly updated estimate of the remaining work, but in my experience, rational people soon see the value of working with up-to-date forecasts rather than sticking to an increasingly outdated original estimate.

Convincing traditionally minded managers to accept the fact that a project's backlog and the requirements that it contains are never fully complete, however, is a much tougher sell. Countless project managers have told me, "I want every piece of work defined before you start coding, so I can control what's happening in the project room." In my experience, the notion of a nontechnical person truly controlling the details of a protracted programming effort is an illusion, but that illusion is seductive to both project managers and the executives to whom they report. Because requirements so strongly determine the objectives and labor costs of a project, the PMO typically demands total control over changes to requirements. In their world, the requirements and funding approved by the sponsors represent a contract with IT to deliver an exact list of features for something very close to the agreed-upon price. Every desired modification to the collection of requirements must therefore be submitted as a *change request* to the project governance board along with a careful estimate of the impact that the request will have on the project's development costs.

Unfortunately, agile EDW teams need to be, well, *agile*. To deliver real value to the customers in the shortest amount of time and effort, the agile team needs to be responsive to its product owner when she informs the team of changing business conditions. The developers also need to adapt the details of the system when the product owner changes her mind regarding features, in response to what she is learning about business analytics, the source data, and the problem domain of the project. Preparing the description and cost impact for a formal change request takes time, sometimes days. The project governance council then frequently takes even more time to consider and approve it, sometime multiple weeks. Submitting every little decision that needs to be made to project governance will paralyze the agile EDW team's decision making and force its programmers to fall idle, squandering valuable resources and, more important, business opportunities.

I have found that the trick to finding a workable compromise with the traditional project governance's command-and-control mindset is to set clear limits as to how far into the team's decision-making process the PMO's change

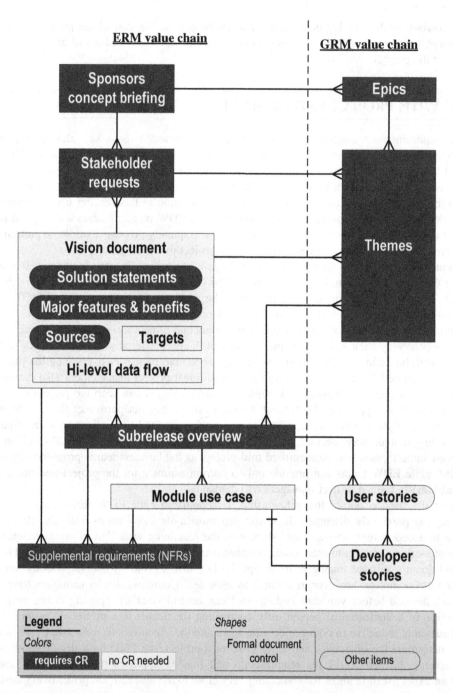

FIGURE 11.9   Interfacing agile EDW RM with project governance.

control process extends. The agile EDW team will need to cede some territory to the traditional management approach but then jealously guard the rest of the landscape against invasion. To effectively negotiate the boundaries to external control, the agile team will need a map of the territory and a clear definition of the objects on that map.

Figure 11.9 depicts the settlement that my colleagues and I can usually reach with the traditional project management office of a typical large corporation. This diagram lists the requirements management artifacts presented in the past few chapters and even the components of some of those documents. They are divided into those artifacts originating from the generic agile requirements value chain and those emerging from the enterprise-capable approach, with lines and cardinalities showing the relationship between them. The darker objects represent items that the agile team cannot change without first securing an approved change request. The team can change all of the remaining objects at will in order to keep the project focused, moving ahead, and responsive to changing conditions.

The fact that the EDW development team follows the direction of a business-based product owner should alleviate some of the traditional project manager's concerns over unmanaged development because business approval for all changes is built into the very work method that the developers are following. Negotiating a boundary over external control often involves agreeing upon the extent to which this built-in business oversight can effectively keep the project aligned with the business's interests. Generally, PMOs seem able to accept a division of controls stating that the team will seek approval of any new epics or themes, but beyond that, the product owner is free to create new user stories as he or she sees fit. Using the epic stack definition offered in previous chapters, this agreement will amount to giving the PMO a say on the EDW project targets' new competitive capabilities or business analyses. The business-level data validations, however, will be up to the team to define.

Figure 11.9 also identifies the artifacts that must reside in a formal document repository, another project management aspect that needs boundaries and that should be negotiated ahead of time with project managers. Many agile EDW projects are subject to process audits, especially in companies striving to maintain formal quality or maturity certifications. In those companies, development teams are required to register all project artifacts and their revisions into a document repository. The simple version control that a document repository provides for project documents benefits the developers by letting them recover previous versions of their artifacts.

Formal document control, however, is different and indeed challenging. Formal document control requires that artifacts be reviewed and approved before changes are committed to the repository, greatly lengthening the cycle time for updating a requirement or design element. Formal document control also requires extensive metadata concerning changes. Keeping that metadata updated well enough to provide an auditable history for each document requires even more effort, as does resolving the inevitable discrepancies between official versions of the artifacts in the repository. Developers caught in formal document control regimes often grumble that for most of the documents they work with, they only need them to be correct. Being able to state the reason for a small change six months earlier has absolutely zero value in terms of the programming decisions they need to make today. However, such overhead is valuable for the major artifacts of a project, such as stakeholder requests, but it becomes a paralytic time sink when applied to the more numerous, detailed artifacts that experience high rates of change, such as user and developer stories.

Because formal document control can paralyze a team when applied to the smaller documents it employs, the suggested settlement diagram shown in Figure 11.9 also denotes the document management style for the artifacts. Documents that the team should be maintained in the project's formal document repository have sharp corners, and those that the team can manage informally possess a rounded shape. The settlement portrayed in the diagram stipulates that the agile EDW team will practice change control and a formal repository for the high-level artifacts of the project. On the ERM side of the diagram, the controlled artifacts include the sponsor's concept briefing, stakeholder requests, and the business-oriented portions of the vision document. The vision document's high-level architecture, subrelease overviews, and module diagrams lie outside of formal document control because this particular team convinced external management that the project would proceed faster and better with easily changed designs as long as the major requirements driving those designs were carefully managed.

On the GRM side, epics and themes are controlled, but user and developer stories are not. The effectiveness of this arrangement is strongly rooted in the agreed-upon definitions of each type of backlog story. For teams using the epic decomposition framework presented in Chapter 8, epics are the new competitive capabilities that the sponsors believe data warehousing can provide the company. Themes are the analyses that directors will use to take action in order to achieve the epic's desired competitive results. Revisions and churn at this level could devastate a team by redirecting development in so many different directions that the team finds it impossible to make any meaningful progress. Accordingly, a bit of control actually helps the team to be more effective, so once the epics and themes are expressed correctly, the project governance council should insist that their wording remain unchanged without formal review. User stories, on the other hand, are business-level data validation steps that managers will need to make before they forward an analysis to a director. Change at this level of stories can only help the project because it represents the product owner steadily getting clearer on exactly how the numbers on each analysis should be checked. Similarly, change among developer stories represents that the team is both learning how to best deliver those data validations and keeping up with the new ideas from the product owner. Formal document control at either of these levels would only impede the developers' ability to match their development decisions to the business needs expressed, greatly undermining their effectiveness.

Figure 11.9 is only an example of the settlement for one agile EDW project. Every team will need to adapt the shading and the corners of the artifacts shown to meet their particular context. However, starting with an example of such an agreement can greatly empower the team leaders to negotiate a better arrangement at the beginning of the project and allow them to forestall destructive micromanagement from project governance councils and the PMO.

NOT RETURNING TO A WATERFALL APPROACH

The approach to requirements management described in the past few chapters has many components. It includes approximately a dozen artifacts, a process for authoring them, and an approach to changing some of them quite carefully. These aspects often inspire folks who profess to be agile purists to dismiss this approach, thinking it takes the agile EDW method back to a waterfall mindset. I believe this conclusion misinterprets the intent and style of our approach for two reasons.

First, the agile EDW requirements management approach presented here is a "pick and choose" proposition. All the artifacts and techniques described in these chapters represent only a menu of elements that can be employed. The combination of companies, industries, and project objectives involved in enterprise data warehousing creates a wide range of development circumstances and risk levels with which to contend. For that reason, any team will find that some of the requirements management components described here apply to their project and the rest are superfluous. My colleagues and I in fact arrived at the relatively small collection of artifacts discussed previously by steadily whittling away at the recommended documents from several other agile methods, and we expect readers to continue that reduction process diligently. Project leaders should make an effort to learn about the agile EDW artifacts available, discuss requirements management with their stakeholders, and then adopt only those artifacts that are needed by their particular engagement.

In many situations, a sufficiently stereoscopic vision will emerge if only a couple of the artifacts or techniques from each value chain are utilized. For many subject areas of an enterprise warehouse, a backlog with crisp epics, themes, and user stories complemented by only a vision document and a couple of subrelease overviews will be all that the team needs to quickly deliver an excellent business solution without any false starts. In other words, the requirements management approach advocated here still allows team leaders to "maximize the work not done" by skipping the artifacts they do not need, thus remaining true to the agile manifesto.

Second, my colleagues and I feel assured that the approach described in the preceding sections is definitely agile because we can trace so many of its aspects back to the values and principles espoused by agile methods such as XP, Scrum, Kanban, and the lean school of software development. Those linkages are listed in Table 11.5. They indicate that although we have worked hard to codify agile requirements management into a disciplined, repeatable process that will scale up to the needs of an enterprise data warehousing program involving multiple projects, we have in no way abandoned our agile roots. We welcome the innovations that another generation of agile practitioners can bring to the approach we have documented here. Such a contribution can only make the resulting method all the more robust and efficient.

SUMMARY

EDW team leaders can use the IT-driven, enterprise-capable approach to requirements management presented in Chapter 10 to validate the results of their product owner's more informal process for authoring a project's epic stack. The intersection between these two requirements value chains should yield a highly accurate backlog that developers can use to prioritize the work of the team in ways that meet multiple criteria. In particular, team leaders should elevate areas of high risk to fall within the elaboration phase of the company's release cycle. Project success can be further enhanced by selecting stories for early development that represent a "steel thread" that delivers a handful of valuable services for end users while simultaneously proving that the application's architecture is sound.

Team leaders should establish a pattern of progressive elaboration with their backlog rather than striving to make all stories equally precise from the start. They can use the freeze–fridge–countertop metaphor to steadily hone the precision of technical requirements as stories approach the day their development begins. Progressive elaboration will cause the workload for each team role to wax and wane differently. The overall pattern of team member workloads can be visualized with effort curves that will enable better resource planning and the creation of realistic expectations by team members, including the product owner. These effort curves will also provide a means for budgeting time for the project leaders to address nonfunctional and architectural requirements. The systems analyst in particular will have an excessive amount of work at the start of a project, given that he or she must provide 80/20 specs for the programmers, no matter how difficult the source data may be to understand. Teams can flatten out the effort curve for the systems analyst by engaging a "data cowboy" during the elaboration phase. The data cowboy combines advanced data skills, nonstandard analytic tools, and a method called CRISP-DM to rapidly discover and sufficiently document solutions to the most difficult challenges that lie hidden in the source data.

TABLE 11.5 Assessment of Agile EDW Requirements Management Approach for Agility

Thoughts on how agile enterprise data warehousing's approach to requirements management addresses the 72 values and principles promoted by four agile schools, showing only those items that apply.

ID	Agile School*	Value Principle	Agile EDW RM Manifestation
1	AM	**Individuals and interactions over processes and tools**	Product owner and SMEs provide detailed requirements directly at development time
2	AM	**Working software over comprehensive documentation**	Subrelease cycle validates requirements through usage by actual end users
3	AM	**Customer collaboration over contract negotiation**	See 2
4	AM	**Responding to change over following a plan**	Product owner free to reshape project backlog as necessary
7	AM	Welcome changing requirements and deliver working software frequently	See 2 and 4
9	AM	Ensure business people and developers work together daily	See 1
12	AM	Trust that the best architectures, requirements, and designs will emerge from self-organized teams	Though additional leadership roles augment team, developers still expected to adapt process themselves as needed
13	AM	Find and support the team's sustainable pace of work	Current estimate approach utilizes team's velocity to determine number of iterations needed
14	AM	Pay continuous attention to technical excellence	Freezer-fridge approach represents progressive requirements grooming
15	AM	Strive for simplicity and maximize the work not done	User stories still the fundamental requirements management vehicle
16	AM	Consider and improve team effectiveness at regular intervals	Teams expected to discuss quality of user and technical requirements during iteration retrospectives
17	XP	**Communication**	Stereoscopic approach ensures that product owner, stakeholders, and developers develop a consensus on the project's requirements
18	XP	**Simplicity**	Teams utilize only as much of the two RM value chains as they need to get the job done
19	XP	**Feedback**	See 16
20	XP	**Courage**	Proceeding with 80/20 specs requires trusting that remaining details will emerge during module construction
23	XP	Economics	Current estimates keep business apprised of likely project cost, allowing them to make scoping decisions early
25	XP	Self-Similarity	Both RM value chains abet progressive elaboration, acknowledging that requirements must be managed at all levels
29	XP	Flow	Freezer-fridge approach minimizes premature investment in detail specifications, alllowing development work to begin as soon as possible for individual modules
32	XP	Failure	Early iterations (during elaboration) will reveal whether level of requirements detail will suffice
36	Lean	**Eliminate Waste**	80/20 specs and selective utilization of ERM value chain artifacts keeps inventory of requirements to a minimum
43	Lean	Tool 6: Set-Based Development	Freezer-fridge approach emphasizes breadth-first and accuracy over precision, avoiding premature specificity
46	Lean	Tool 8: The Last Responsible Moment	See 43
47	Lean	Tool 9: Making Decisions	ERM value chain provides breadth-first approach, avoids excessive details, and steadily draws upon team leader's intuition
49	Lean	Tool 10: Pull Systems	Freezer-fridge and pipelined delivery approaches position team to pull requirements into development when new work is needed
51	Lean	Tool 12: Cost Of Delay	Product owner's participation, lead-off ERM artifacts, and project segmentation allow business value to shape the subrelease plan
55	Lean	Tool 15: Leadership	Product owner and project architect ensure team has support of a product champion and a master developer
67	RUP	Develop iteratively, with risk as the primary iteration driver	Elaboration phase and subrelease plan specifically designed to drive risk out of the project
68	RUP	Manage requirements	Two value chains leading to clear current estimates ensures team works on requirements throughout the project and iterations
70	RUP	Model software visually	Vision documents ensures that every project begins with a high-level visualization that can be later elaborated as needed
72	RUP	Control changes	Change control planning artifacts links both RM value chains to project governance and document auditing needs

*AM = Agile Manifesto school of iterative delivery methods.

Overarching all of the team's discovery and analysis work is the need to manage requirements in a way that satisfies the demands for predictability and control often voiced by project governance and the project management office. A simple graphic will allow the agile EDW team to envision a workable compromise between agility and compliance so that team leaders can negotiate up front a sufficient degree of freedom from the micromanagement that would otherwise eliminate their agility.

We have now concluded the discussion of agile requirements management, a collection of techniques that allows team leaders to quickly define and prep an EDW project for incremental development. Veteran data warehousing professionals will still doubt whether agile data warehousing is truly possible. "It doesn't matter if you can quickly define an EDW component," they might say, "If you make a mistake in the design of a warehouse table you will have billions of records loaded that will take forever to restructure and reload. You'd be better off designing the whole system first, like we do when following waterfall methods." To address that challenge, EDW teams will need to employ agile data engineering techniques that allow the schema of a loaded production data warehouse to be updated in place without expensive conversion scripting. That practice is the subject of the next several chapters.

Part III References

Chapter 7

Grady, R., 1992. Practical Software Metrics for Project Management and Process Improvement. Prentice Hall.

ISO, 2011 International Standards Organization, *ISO/IEC 25010:2011* (Systems and Software Quality Requirements and Evaluation), iso.org, 2011.

Kernochan, W., 2011, May 2. Why most business intelligence projects fail. Enterprise Apps Today. <http://www.enterpriseappstoday.com/business-intelligence/why-most-business-intelligence-projects-fail-1.html> (accessed January 2015).

Kroll, P., Kruchten, P., 2003. The Rational Unified Process Made Easy: A Practitioner's Guide to the RUP. Addison-Wesley, Boston.

Larson, E., Larson, R., 2013. Requiremetns Managments. Watermark Learning, Minneapolis, MN.

The Standish Group International. 1995. The chaos report. <http://www.standishgroup.com> (accessed April 2006).

The Standish Group International. 1999. Chaos: A recipe for success. <http://www.standishgroup.com> (accessed April 2006).

Zielczynski, P., 2008. Requirements Management Using IBM Rational RequisitePro. IBM Press, Indianapolis, IN.

Chapter 9

Charantimath, P.M., 2011. Total Quality Management. second ed. Pearson India, Chennai.

Chauhan, A., 2012, May 4. Top most algorithms used in data mining. Big Data Analytics, Data Visualization and Infographics (website). <https://cloudcelebrity.wordpress.com/2012/05/04/top-most-algorithms-used-in-data-mining>.

Cobb, C.G., 2011. Making Sense of Agile Project Management: Balancing Control and Agility. Wiley, New York.

Cohn, M., 2004. User Stories Applied: For Agile Software Development. Addison-Wesley, Boston.

Highsmith, J., 2009. Agile Project Management: Creating Innovative Products, second ed. Addison-Wesley, Boston.

Maslow, A.H., 1943. A theory of human motivation. Psychol. Rev. 50 (4), 370–396, <http://psychclassics.yorku.ca/Maslow/motivation.htm> (accessed October 2014).

Chapter 10

Charan, R., 2001. What the CEO Wants You to Know. Crown, New York.

Earley, S., 2011. The DAMA Dictionary of Data Management. second ed. Technic, Bradley Beach, NJ.

Eclipse Foundation, 2012. Intro to OpenUP, OpenUP (website). <http://epf.eclipse.org/wikis/openup> (accessed February 2014).

Kimball, R., Ross, M., 2013. The Data Warehouse Toolkit: The Definitive Guide to Dimensional Modeling, third ed. Wiley, New York.

Milhøj, A., 2013. Practical Time Series Analysis Using SAS. SAS Institute, Cary, NC.

Chapter 11

Aked, M., 2003, November 25. Risk reduction with the RUP phase plan. IBM Developer Works (website). <http://www.ibm.com/developer-works/rational/library/1826.html> (accessed April 2014).

Brennan, K. (Ed.), 2009. A Guide to the Business Analysis Body of Knowledge (BABOK guide). International Institute of Business Analysis, Whitby, Ontario, Canada.

Ladley, J., 2012. Data Governance: How to Design, Deploy and Sustain an Effective Data Governance Program. Morgan Kaufmann, Waltham, MA.

Marbán, G.M., Segovia, J., 2009. A data mining and knowledge discovery process model. In: Ponce, J., Karahoca, A. (Eds.), Data Mining and Knowledge Discovery in Real Life Applications. I-Tech, Vienna, Austria, pp. 438–453.

Project Management Institute, 2013. A Guide to the Project Management Body of Knowledge (PMBOK guide), fifth ed. Project Management Institute, Newton Square, PA.

Rational Software, 1998. Rational Unified Process: Best practices for software development teams. <www.ibm.com/developerworks/rational/library/content/03July/1000/1251/1251_bestpractices_TP026B.pdf> (accessed August 2013).

Rawsthorne, D., Shimp, D., 2011. Exploring Scrum: The Fundamentals. second ed. CreateSpace Independent Publishing.

Rubin, K.S., 2012. Essential Scrum: A Practical Guide to the Most Popular Agile Process. Addison-Wesley, Upper Saddle River, NJ.

Part IV

Agile EDW Data Engineering

Chapter 12

Traditional Data Modeling Paradigms and Their Discontents

The agile approach to requirements management presented in the past several chapters allows enterprise data warehouse (EDW) project leaders to adroitly discover and express the goals and objectives that stakeholders have in mind for the requested data warehousing/business intelligence (DW/BI) application. As powerful as those techniques are, they only bring the team to the doorstep of the design process. From that point on, the team leaders will have to choose functional and nonfunctional attributes for the system that will actually fulfill both the requirements identified to date and those that will later emerge during the iterative development process. For enterprise data warehousing projects, the design element of primary concern is the data model. A poorly crafted data model can impede or entirely prevent end users from performing the analyses identified by the requirements artifacts. Moreover, a poorly designed data model can be inordinately expensive to alter once the schema it describes has been loaded with many millions of records. Such impacts can leave customers sorely disappointed and plunge the developers into a protracted period of emergency programming in order to retrofit an application's data schemas and transform modules to support the unmet business needs.

An agile approach to DW/BI design would let a team build and populate the EDW in small increments so that both information technology (IT) and the business partners can explore possible designs throughout the project and adjust their direction without major consequences. Most traditional data modelers would say such an objective is impossible, given the limits of the database technology DW/BI teams currently have at their disposal. Fortunately, adaptive data modeling techniques now exist, along with tools that support them, so that today we can deliver an EDW one small portion at a time, fluidly adapting the design and the already loaded data in response to end-user feedback.

Part IV of this book focuses on such techniques and tools that allow EDW teams to fail fast and cheaply and then fix quickly. Presenting these new tools and techniques requires several segments. First, this chapter outlines the traditional approach to BI data design, summarizes its weaknesses that leave EDW teams searching for an alternative, and introduces the notion of agile data engineering. Chapter 13 presents the notion of "surface solutions," which involves three easy improvements that EDW team leaders can make to their solution strategy that will accelerate deliveries before they radically change their data modeling techniques. Chapter 14 outlines *hyper normalized* data models and discusses how they can accelerate construction and adaptation of the integration layer of the DW/BI reference architecture. Finally, Chapter 15 describes *hyper generalized* data models, which can bring agility to a far wider portion of the reference architecture than hyper normalized data modeling can address, namely the application's integration, presentation, and semantic layers.

EDW AT A CROSSROADS

Reviewing the Reference Architecture

EDW are odd beasts in that their data repositories typically blend multiple sets of physical tables that follow wildly different structural designs. The reference architecture of a traditional EDW can be seen in Figure 12.1, which is a slight update of a diagram employed in a previous chapter. As the reader might recall from Chapter 4, a reference architecture depicts the data design of an EDW application at a very high level, delineating distinct layers across which a company's information must move during its journey from source system to end-user BI applications. Every company defines its own particular reference architecture, so Figure 12.1 portrays a quite generic version designed to illustrate the principles of data engineering and the four data modeling paradigms we need to discuss.

Landing layer	Integration layer	Presentation layer	Semantic layer	End-user apps
Raw data extracts	*Standard normal form*	*Conformed dimensions*	*BI tool "Universe"*	*Dashboards & reports*

Metadata

Definitions
- -
Genealogy
- -
Processing

FIGURE 12.1   Basic EDW reference architecture with data paradigms listed. *This particular reference architecture supports the "standard approach" to data warehousing and does not list data modeling paradigms for the metadata layer.*

The layers in this plain-vanilla EDW reference architecture have the following general purposes:

Landing: Provides temporary storage for raw data replicated or captured from source systems.
Integration: Allows persistent storage of integrated enterprise data, modeled for accurate representation of the company's informational entities and business events. It represents the organization's "single version of the truth." Many people refer to this layer as simply "the warehouse," although that practice tends to generate confusion.
Presentation: Supplies ready-to-consume data for end-user reporting, modeled for business intelligibility and query performance. Department-specific, derived values are often stored here. Many people refer to this layer as "the data marts," although again this practice can be misleading.
Semantic: Offers logical objects that control the appearance and access to presentation-layer data stores.
End-user applications: Employs the semantic layer to provide access to presentation-layer data and is typically the only layer DW/BI allows end users to actually see. It includes dashboards, reports, and displays sent to users' workstations and mobile devices.

I have also added a layer for metadata to the diagram, important components for team leaders to keep in mind as they use agile data engineering techniques to steadily evolve their EDW data repositories.

The reference architecture presents the EDW team with a challenge: They must choose a data modeling style for each of its layers. Most teams find that no single data modeling approach will meet the purposes they have for all the layers. The spectrum of choices available today for a data warehouse designer breaks into two groups with two data modeling paradigms in each, as illustrated in Figure 12.2. The traditional group contains, of course, the two paradigms that the DW/BI community has been teaching for more than 20 years. The first is *standard normal forms* (SNF), which for many EDW projects is third normal form, the data modeling paradigm most often used for the integration layer. The second is *conformed dimensional form* (CDF), which data mart designers often call simply "conformed dimensions," a style of data models that is commonly employed for the presentation layer. Together, these familiar modeling paradigms are referred to here as "traditionally modeled forms" (TMF).

The new modeling approaches constitute a group that enables iterative and incremental delivery, making them "agile" paradigms. This group includes the following:

- Hyper normalized form (HNF), so named because it results in more physical tables in the data repository than a standard normal form requires
- Hyper generalized form (HGF), so named because it takes the common data modeling technique of generalization and applies it to an extreme

These latter two paradigms both involve a notion of "hyper," so collectively I refer to them as "hyper modeled forms" (HMF). Both HMF approaches provide data modeling guidance for the integration layer in particular. The

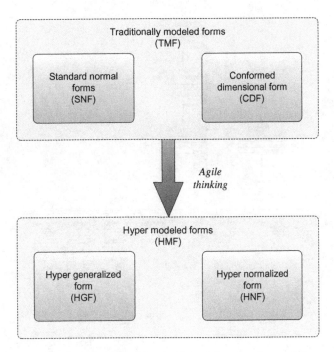

FIGURE 12.2   Given the advent of hyper-modeled forms, EDW project leaders now have four data modeling paradigms to choose from.

presentation layer (when it is still needed), is modeled in conformed dimensional form. The HNF paradigm allows EDW teams to employ programming automation for the modules of the integration layer, whereas HGF extends this automation to cover aspects of all but the end-user application layer.

Although ways exist for getting traditional and hyper modeled data tables to coexist within a single EDW, teams find it easier to pursue a project using one primary paradigm per layer rather than blending together a little bit of each. Because each of the four paradigms has strengths and weakness, the choice between them requires careful consideration. Given that switching between them in mid project can deeply disrupt the development effort, this choice of data modeling paradigms needs to be made early in the engagement, thus placing every new DW/BI project at a crucial crossroad at the beginning of each project that the team leaders must navigate carefully.

Standard Normal Forms Lead to Complex Integration Layers

In the traditional approach, teams structure the database of the integration layer using a standard normal form, somewhere between third and fifth normal form. One need only glance at the data model of a typical EDW integration layer to appreciate the effort required to build and maintain such a data repository.

Figure 12.3 shows an SNF integration layer from simple to complex, starting with a rudimentary depiction of a sales order transaction in the top panel. The square boxes represent tables maintained by the database management system (DBMS). The short lines of text visible in each table box represent attributes of the entity, which will translate into columns in a table when this model is implemented in the database. The lines depict the relationships that exist between the tables, with the round dot on the end representing the "many" side of a one-to-many relationship.

Panel 2 in Figure 12.3 shows the data model for a relatively small EDW, with the background shading distinguishing between subject areas such as Customer, Marketing, and Finance. Most data modelers try to arrange models such that they are intelligible to others on their development teams. In my experience, however, any project involving scores of business entities probably has already crossed a threshold of complexity where only one or two teammates effectively understand the data model in its entirety.

A mature EDW for a company of any appreciable size will be so complex that a detailed model will no longer fit into a single diagram, even when drawn on plotter paper. Teams frequently resort to summary depictions for these data models, such as shown in Panel 3 in Figure 12.3. Here, the tables and the relationships between them have grown

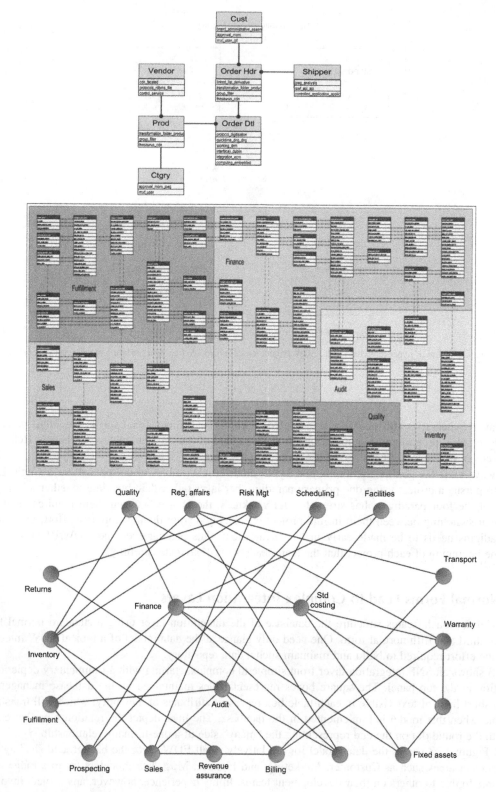

FIGURE 12.3   Examples of standard normal form data models of increasing complexity.

so extensive that there is too little space to depict tables individually, let alone their attribution. Each dot represents instead a group of entities.

Team leaders embarking on an EDW development effort involving a spider's web data model such as this last panel should be filled with trepidation. Every point on that diagram will require multiple extract, transform, and load (ETL) modules that must be "engineered"—that is, teammates will have to gather requirements for it and then proceed with the module's design, coding, validation, and promotion into production usage. Given the large number of items depicted in the web of objects, the team members will have many doubts about whether they are up to the challenge ahead, including the following:

- Can we really master the detailed requirements and design for such a complex application?
- Will we be able to properly construct so many components in a reasonable amount of time?
- Do we have sufficient time and resources to test that much code adequately?
- As we build out this behemoth, will we reach a point where we will be unable to predict the impact of a change in one area on the functionality of the rest of the application—especially for objects in the middle of the diagram that seem to connect to everything else in the application?

This last point is crucial. I have encountered many companies with data models so complicated that they can no longer discern in a reasonable amount of time the effect maintenance programming will have on their EDW. Having passed this threshold, the DW/BI staff members become very resistant to accommodating new or changing requirements because, without the ability to accurately gauge the impact of changes, they fear breaking the EDW should they touch it. When new business needs appear, these DW/BI departments take the defensive strategy of building new tables on the side of the existing warehouse in order to leave the core of the EDW alone. Unfortunately, this practice leaves them with an EDW in name alone, for without an integrated and coherent set of data tables, the warehouse is even more difficult to understand in its entirety, and the company no longer has a single point of truth.

Some DW/BI pundits might challenge companies with a growing data warehouse to simply keep tighter control over their designers so that they will not need to resort to this strategy of peripheral tables. I believe it is more useful instead to confront the inconvenient truth that large data repositories in standard normal form are unsustainable over the long term. As a profession, DW/BI needs to find instead a more practical data modeling paradigm.

Conformed Dimensions Lead to Complex Presentation Layers

Traditionally, EDW professionals prescribes a conformed dimensional model for the presentation layer. Panel 1 of Figure 12.4 portrays a simple dimensional data model, which is certainly very easy to understand. Like the standard normal form diagram, this model contains entities and relationships, but here the fact table at the center holds the metrics that the BI applications will display in their dashboards and reports. The surrounding dimension tables provide the qualifiers by which the metrics in the central fact table will be analyzed ("sliced and diced"). Because of the inherent clarity provided by this arrangement of fact and dimension tables, some portion of the DW/BI community advocates storing all of a data warehouse's information in dimensionally modeled tables. This strategy seems reasonable when the warehouse is small, but it suffers the same fate as standard normal form models when the EDW starts to grow.

Panel 2 in Figure 12.4 demonstrates that the dimensional model for a full enterprise data warehouse becomes as difficult to visually comprehend as the standard normal form model. This diagram depicts a presentation layer in which the fact tables are joined together by shared ("conformed") dimensions so that end-user analyses can employ the same definition and value domains for their qualifiers. However, at this point in the EDW's growth, the team will have trouble readily discerning from the layout which tables are facts and which are dimensions.

Panel 3 in Figure 12.4 suggests that dimensional depictions of enterprise data warehouses eventually suffer the same fate as standard normal form models as the DW/BI system grows in size. The development team can depict the complete warehouse in summary form only, with groupings representing the subject areas. Again, individual entities and attributes have disappeared. The developers can only comprehend the model one area at a time, and with so many interdependencies, fast impact analysis has become nearly impossible. Especially when a new requirement suggests changing the structure of one of the major, shared dimensions such as customer, product, or location, adapting the warehouse to meet new business needs becomes a risky solution that DW/BI management will sanction only when the situation becomes extreme.

The fate of both traditional model forms is the same: The interconnected nature of the tables increases as the data warehouse grows until the risk of making structural changes becomes impossible to assess or bear. This outcome is extremely important for advocates of agile data warehousing to confront honestly. The agile techniques for

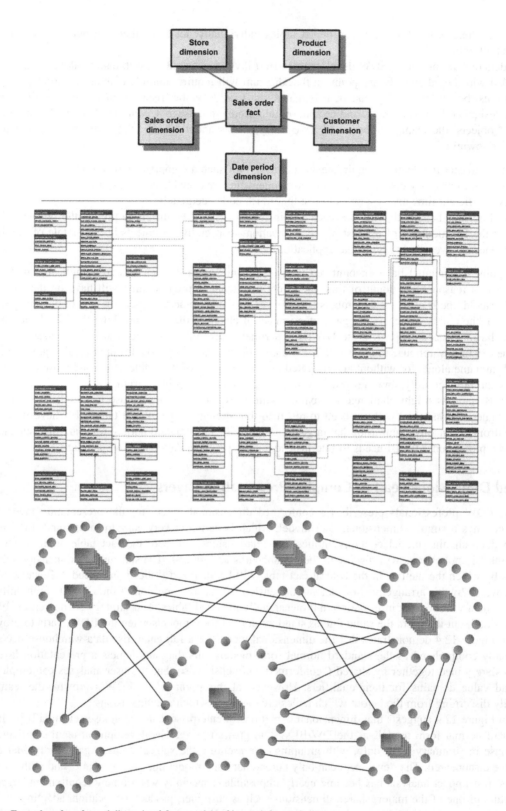

FIGURE 12.4   Examples of conformed dimensional form models of increasing complexity.

requirements gathering and coding may well allow a team to create a new data warehouse quickly, but to what end? An incremental development method alone offers no solutions to the paralysis that develops as an EDW's data model increases in size. Over the long term, agile teams that employ a traditional data modeling technique only offer their customers a faster trip into the swamp of unmaintainable data repositories. The fact that the traditional BI data modeling paradigms are thoroughly documented, well promoted, and the basis of many existing data warehouses does not mean they are the best approach nor even a good strategy for the entire life span of the typical EDW.

Faced with this situation, the major advantage that agile EDW team leaders have is their incremental mindset because it will lead them to a solution. Agile methods are all about constantly delivering value to the customer, even when the warehouse has grown large. With that mission in mind, agile teams will refuse to accept the inevitable paralysis that comes with traditional design paradigms. They will be the first to search for alternatives, and fortunately they now have more than one to choose from.

A Peek at the Agile Alternatives

Figure 12.2 shows the full choice that all EDW teams should consider as they start on an enterprise data warehousing application or even undertake adding a new subject area within an existing system. Standard normal and conformed dimensional forms are shown there, but so are the hyper modeled forms. In addition to enabling new data warehouses to be developed faster, the hyper modeled paradigms have the benefit of producing EDWs that can be far more easily maintained over the long term. In fact, they enable production data warehouses, fully loaded with data, to be incrementally re-engineered in place, without requiring the team to pursue ruinously expensive data conversion programming for existing table records. They empower the agile team to not only deliver the first release of an EDW quickly but also economically evolve the warehouse to meet new business requirements that emerge when their customers learn more about the BI problem space or when the fundamentals of the business change.

Figure 12.5 provides a good look at the hyper normalized model. It has only three types of entities. Tables of business keys, prefixed with "BK_," are isolated into small, dedicated tables. Simple many-to-many linking tables join the business keys, whether the relationship between them is one-to-many or many-to-many. The attributes of both business key and linking tables are split out into their own separate tables, prefixed with "A_."

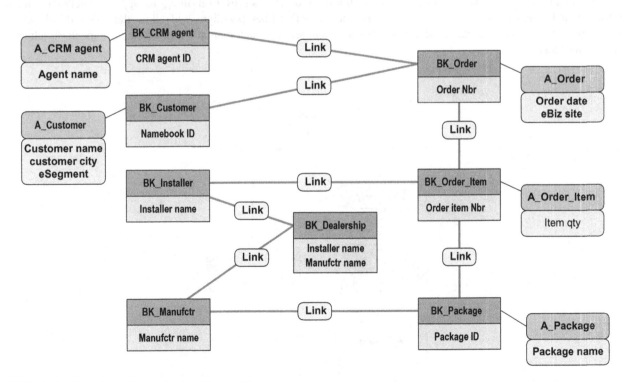

FIGURE 12.5   Example of a hyper normalized data model.

As detailed in a later chapter, a hyper normalized data repository has many advantages, but perhaps most important among them is the fact that only one parameter-driven ETL module is required to load all the data stores of a given table type. Because an HNF data warehouse consists of only three table types, the EDW development team needs to build only three reusable ETL modules, and the data loading programming for the integration layer is largely complete. The risk of model change is significantly reduced because new requirements can be addressed by (1) utilizing these reusable ETL modules to populate a new business key or linking table and then (2) dropping the other tables that no longer reflect the business conditions of the enterprise.

Figure 12.6 provides a good look at the hyper generalized approach. This data model depicts the core of the integration layer for any and all enterprise data warehouses built using the hyper generalized data modeling paradigm. The company's dimensional data can be stored in only six logical tables. Transaction data is stored in one simple "fact" table per group of metrics sent to the data warehouse. The advantages of the hyper generalized paradigm are manyfold, including the fact that an EDW automation tool can now understand both the company's data model and the data that it contains. By making both the model and the data machine intelligible, development teams need only to describe the required data warehouse in terms of business-level concepts. The warehouse automation tool can then read the business-level depiction and generate from it nearly all the ETL programs needed for loading the layers of the DW/BI application. It can also frequently convert the existing EDW data already to fit a new model necessitated by changing business conditions. For data conversions that the automation tool cannot manage on its own, the development team can program them at a business model level, saving a tremendous amount of labor over the physical-level design and coding required by the traditional modeled forms.

In both the HNF and HGF paradigms, the information in the data warehouse appears to end users the same as it did using a standard DW/BI approach. The hyper modeled forms focus primarily on the structure and agility of the integration layer. In both of these new paradigms, data is projected from the integration layer into the dimensional model of the presentation layer. Changes in the integration layer can be selectively expressed to the presentation layer, so impact on downstream BI applications is minimal, often nonexistent except for making additional data items available through the semantic layer.

Teams can interface hyper modeled solutions to traditionally modeled forms of their legacy data warehouses, making it possible for EDW projects that were started using a traditional approach to embrace these new data modeling paradigms. When choosing between the two new data modeling paradigms, team leaders must decide whether they want (1) HNF's solution, which involves three reusable ETL modules loading a large number of tables, or (2) HGF's approach composed of a data warehouse administration tool that stores everything in approximately six highly abstracted tables and projects consumable data sets as needed. Either paradigm will allow the EDW developers to evolve the data warehouse in place, using reusable ETL modules or an automation tool that manages much of data conversions for them.

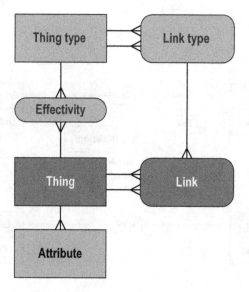

FIGURE 12.6   The main portion of a hyper generalized data model.

These new data modeling paradigms usher in the era of the adaptive data warehouse. Because they eliminate much of the cost of re-engineering a warehouse for changing requirements, they greatly reduce the harm that can occur if a team gets the EDW data model wrong at first. By reducing the impact of modeling mistakes, they free EDW teams to focus more intently on delivering the next subrelease without having to get the entire EDW model perfect before they start coding. EDW teams no longer risk falling into the swamp of a brittle data repository once the data is loaded, so they can take business requirements as they come, build the best solution for the moment, and then bend both the ETL and information stores in the warehouse to the next best solution when further requirements arrive. This process of building a warehouse that meets current needs and then adapting as new requirements emerge is what I call *agile data engineering*. EDW team leaders need to seriously considered the hyper modeling techniques because agile data engineering allows developers to keep the EDW aligned with business needs with very low total cost of ownership. Agile data engineering eliminates the temptation to solve new requirements with siloed data marts alongside the main warehouse simply because the effort and risk of adapting the warehouse has gotten out of hand.

MODELS, ARCHITECTURES, AND PARADIGMS

In the previous overview, I employed some terms without providing or adhering to stringent definitions. Seasoned DW/BI professionals will have noted that the discussion at times mixed notions of *architecture* with *models*. The discussion also failed to distinguish carefully between *logical* with *physical* models. Going forward, the presentation must be more exacting with its language in order to clearly express the concepts involved. I take a moment here to define and explain some key terms we will need and their usage.

Data Architecture

Figure 12.7 shows the key terms needed to discuss data modeling paradigms and how they establish progressive constraints on each other. This stack begins with the notion of data architecture. Speaking roughly, a **data architecture** provides the overall design pattern for the information storage of an application. It enumerates the major data components of that application and the interrelationships between them. More formally, a data architecture specifies the set of models, policies, rules, and standards that govern which data elements will be collected, described, arranged, integrated, stored, and employed in a particular application.

A data architecture can be deliberately scoped to a specific application, such as the company's enterprise data warehouse, or it can be specified to apply to all applications within a category. The staff working in a company's enterprise data architecture group may provide, for example, a more general architecture that all data marts within the organization should follow so that these data marts will integrate constructively together and thus form an enterprise data warehouse.

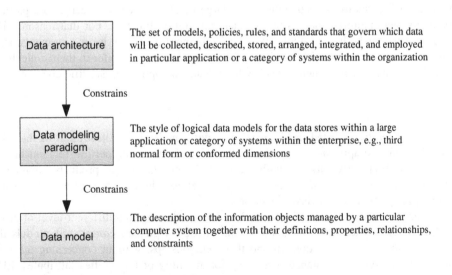

FIGURE 12.7   Data architectures, paradigms, and models.

The practice of providing a general architecture for all DW/BI applications naturally gives rise to the notion of a reference architecture that is employed widely throughout this book. In Chapter 4, I cited the Department of Defense's definition of a reference architecture as a generic, high-level design pattern for a class of information systems that can be used as a foundation for designing specific solutions within that class and that can be readily used for comparison and alignment purposes between projects.

In practice, I find that the data architectures that development teams create for specific applications tend to govern both high-level and a small set of low-level concerns. The high-level concerns generally focus on meeting nonfunctional requirements such as security, maintainability, and recoverability. DW/BI departments strive for standardization on these high-level concerns in order to achieve a degree of predictability in the designs and capabilities across system, although these standards usually evolve considerably for a given company as the years go by.

The select set of low-level concerns addressed by an application's data architecture usually pertain to a few major challenges that the new system will have to overcome. For example, data architectures for telecommunications application often have a specific architectural solution specified for call detail records because these records have very wide record structures and are very numerous, threatening the performance of applications that are not carefully designed to manage this difficult data element from the start. Accordingly, the enterprise architecture teams at many telecommunications firms have invested in a standardized approach to managing call detail records that they can suggest to any team preparing to build a data management system involving a new collection of this type of records.

The data integration function that EDW applications must achieve is heavily dependent on the quality of their data architectures because integration involves interactions between data systems that can be optimized only by aligning certain aspects of their high-level designs. For example, EDW teams often struggle to integrate the customer information between two systems if both identify customers with smart keys. Smart keys bury important business object attributes into the structure and value of the record identifiers themselves, making the history of each record very difficult to follow should the values of these qualifiers change. Such integration challenges can be prevented if the company adopts a data architecture for transaction systems stipulating that all records will be identified using a unique, meaningless, and dimensionless serial number for each record created.

Data architectures are typically drafted by data architects rather than data modelers. The **data architect** authors the target architecture of an application or category of systems and often works to align the actual designs of multiple projects. When data architects specify the data architecture of a specific application, they typically identify the major types and sources of data necessary to support desired, enterprise-wide capabilities, such as a coherent identification of products across all the divisions within a conglomerate. They may well specify a subset of the attributes that shared business entities must all have in order to facilitate data integration. Soon, however, design aspects start to pertain to only a specific application, at which point the data architects typically choose to delegate further specifications to the project's data modeler. A **data modeler** is responsible for actually creating the various data models of the application, ensuring that they comply with the guidance and constraints set forth by the reigning data architecture. Often, the data architects hold architectural review sessions with the project data modelers in order to ensure that the specific application designs have honored the dictates of the shared specifications.

Data warehouses can be enormous projects with both a large number of details specific to a particular subject area and also numerous intersystem requirements given their data integration function. For that reason, EDW projects tend to involve considerable work for both data architects, who focus more on enterprise requirements, and data modelers, who attend more to subject-area needs. For brevity in the following discussion, I refer to them collectively as data architects, being sure to specify data modeler when necessary to indicate an application-specific concern.

Data Model

Occurring at the bottom of the terms listed in Figure 12.7, a **data model** is an illustration of the information objects managed by a particular software application, together with their definitions, properties, relationships, and constraints. The objects within a model frequently correlate with "real-world" objects such as products, suppliers, customers, and orders, although data modelers place a good number of "system" entities in the model of an EDW that serve to support information acquisition, integration, and retrieval functions.

Data modelers prepare three major types of data models, each pertaining to a different level of abstraction, as illustrated by Figure 12.8. At the highest level abstraction, data modelers prepare **conceptual models** that focus on the major business entities within a modeling domain and their relationships, without concerning the reader with details such as fully enumerating the types of instances occurring for an entity or the entities' attributes. EDW team leaders often employ conceptual models to discuss with the business people the overriding requirements for a computer system.

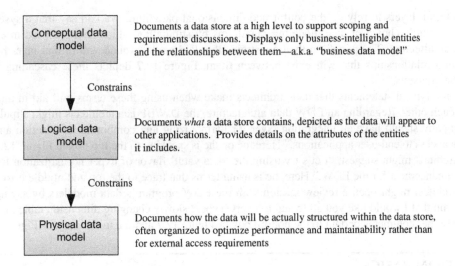

FIGURE 12.8   Business, logical, and physical data models.

For this reason, conceptual models are often called "business conceptual models" or just "business models," but this labeling must be used with care because the business staff often has other documents referencing "business models" that describe commerical partnerships and profit formulas and which have nothing to do with DW/BI projects. The target business model that the enterprise-capable requirements management (ERM) value chain includes in its vision document is a good example of a conceptual model, as was illustrated with Figure 10.9.

At a more detailed level of abstraction, data modelers create **logical data models** that depict the data of a computer system as it should appear to people or computer applications that must use it. Such a model must identify all the entities the system will manage and also specify details concerning their semantics, relationships, attributes, and constraints [Earley 2011]. Given this additional detail, business users usually struggle to understand logical data models, leaving them to technical staff members who employ them for many purposes, such as the following:

- Understanding the data contained within sources systems
- Planning integration of data between systems
- Matching the capabilities of a DW/BI data repository to the requirements it must support

At the lowest level of abstraction, data modelers utilize **physical data models** to illustrate how data specified by a logical model will actually be stored within the disk-based and solid-state storage devices of an application. In a physical model, the logical data model's entities and attributes become tables and columns. Physical models can vary significantly from the corresponding logical data models as entities are combined or subdivided into physical tables in order to better achieve nonfunctional requirements such as security and performance. Preparing a good physical model requires solid knowledge of the specific data storage system a project will employ, because each DBMS offers a different set of performance and security features. For this reason, data modelers often collaborate closely with database administrators in the preparation of physical models.

Given the purpose of each level of abstraction, data modelers employ business models to constrain a logical model—that is, to define its scope and set its objectives. This pattern of constraints is depicted by arrows in Figure 12.8. Similarly, logical models constrain a system's physical data model. When a complete EDW design honors these cascading constraints, developers will be able to trace all features of the physical model to a stipulation within the logical model and, similarly, all features of the logical model to requirements established by the business conceptual model.

Data Modeling Paradigm

With the notions of data architecture and data models defined, we can return to the remaining concept found in Figure 12.7. A **data modeling paradigm** is a term I have adopted to specify the style of logical data models to be employed within a particular realm of an enterprise data warehouse. These realms are frequently defined by the reference architecture stipulated by the DW/BI architects for all the warehouses within the organization. For example, the traditional DW/BI approach calls for integration layers to employ the standard normal form data modeling paradigm and for the presentation layers to rely on the conformed dimensional paradigm. We can say that a system's data architecture constrains a team's choice of data modeling paradigms by stipulating which shall be used in each layer of the EDW's reference architecture. The paradigm then constrains the data models found within that layer by specifying the types of entities and relationships that will exist between them. Figure 12.7 depicts these cascading constraints with arrows between the concepts.

Considering some typical statements that data architects make when using these terms will aid in understanding how they stack within each other. Regarding an EDW data architecture, the DW/BI data architects might stipulate, "Data warehouses in this company should have an integration layer for harmonizing and combining information and a presentation layer that provides access to end-user applications." Here, he or she is speaking to the top box in Figure 12.7. For data paradigms, a project architect might suggest, "Let's try using the 'data vault' flavor of hyper normalization for the integration layer of this next enhancement for the EDW." Here, he is using terms that trace to the top and middle boxes of Figure 12.7. The team's data architect might open a review session with the EDW program's data modelers by saying, "I've added a new metadata column that I would like you all to add to every Type 2 slowly changing dimension table in your logical data models." In this case, her comments pertain to the bottom box of Figure 12.7 and the middle box of Figure 12.8.

NORMALIZATION BASICS

Before I can present how *hyper* modeling can allow agile EDW teams to fluidly adapt their production warehouses to new and changing requirements, we first need to discuss the basic data modeling techniques of normalization and generalization that underlie nearly all DW/BI data design work today. **Normalization** prepares the data model so that it can hold the business information of the enterprise without distortion as it captures the events and relationships occurring within the organization. **Generalization** typically starts with a normalized, logical data model and combines highly similar objects in a way that some or all of their attributes can be managed through a shared entity so that the team ends up with fewer entities and ETL modules to build and support. A quick introduction to normalization is provided next, and a similar overview of generalization is provided in the following section.

Designing Databases to Eliminate Update Anomalies

Database normalization is the process of organizing the columns and tables of a relational database in order to minimize the data distortions that can occur when a system makes inserts, deletes, or modification data records. Normalization achieves this goal through a multistep process that steadily eliminates the redundancies and dependencies between the objects in a relational data store. By following a specific set of design modifications in the proper sequence, a data modeler normalizes a data model by progressively dividing large tables into smaller, "single-themed" tables and redefining the relationships between them [Wyllys 2003].

Normalization drives redundant storage out of a data model so that each piece of information is stored only once. The properly designed relationships within the database guarantee that any given datum can be connected to all other records that need to be associated with it. Thus, changes to a single value in the database will "flow" through all the relationships created between the tables and properly appear in the results of all relevant data retrieval queries.

Each of the formal normalization steps theoretically makes the data model better reflect the truth about objects and relationships within the business. If the data modeler is diligent enough, he or she can supposedly create a model that needs little or even no restructuring later because all the business objects and relationships comprising the business will have been anticipated and supported by the model.

The first versions of this technique were defined in the early 1970s by the an IBM researcher, E. F. "Ted" Codd, who called it "normalization" to echo the normalization of relationships occurring between the United States and the Soviet Union at the time [Date 2012, p. 36]. Codd was searching for a means to dependably design the tables of a database so that an information system would be free from the distortions cause by "update anomalies." As illustrated in Figure 12.9, update anomalies can occur in poorly designed tables from three causes, namely operations to delete, insert, or modify the data records of the table. In the discussion that follows, I will take advantage of the fact that modification actions can be viewed as a delete followed by an insert event, and provide at times only examples for a modification or a insert-plus-delete actions.

We expect the information in a company's databases to accurately reflect the reality of the businesses. Insert anomalies occur when an inconsistent view of reality arises after a record is added to the database, but others holding redundant data are not modified in a coordinated way. Delete anomalies occur when removing an entire record in order to

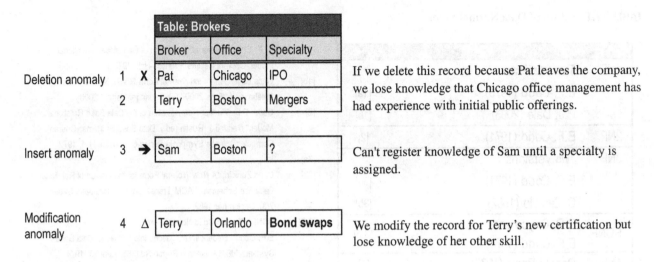

Deletion anomaly   1   X   If we delete this record because Pat leaves the company, we lose knowledge that Chicago office management has had experience with initial public offerings.

Insert anomaly   3   →   Can't register knowledge of Sam until a specialty is assigned.

Modification anomaly   4   Δ   We modify the record for Terry's new certification but lose knowledge of her other skill.

FIGURE 12.9   The update anomalies data normalization is designed to prevent.

eliminate one field causes too much information to be destroyed because all the other, still valuable fields on that record are discarded as well.

Figure 12.9, for example, shows a table that combines broker, office, and broker specialty for a wealth management company. The delete anomaly occurs when broker Pat leaves the company, causing the database administrator to delete her record. Unfortunately, Pat's departure eliminates the database's knowledge that the company has a Chicago office because, at that time, Pat was the only agent working in that city. Somehow, the elements of this database are too tightly coupled.

Figure 12.9 also shows that this overcoupling between data elements can prevent the company from keeping its data as up-to-date as possible. Sam has joined the Boston office, but his specialty has not yet been identified. If we were to add a record for Sam, the information in the database would imply that we can have brokers without a specialty, which in truth is against the company's business rules. The organization can choose to simply not record Sam's existence in order to avoid such an insert anomaly, but this leads to a distortion in the other direction because an accurate company roster cannot be retrieved from the database.

The third example in Figure 12.9 illustrates the distorted picture of the truth that a database can acquire through update anomalies. The company's IPO expert, Terry, moved to the company's new office in Orlando as soon as she became certified to perform bond swaps. If the database drops her old record for Boston and inserts her new record for Orlando, marking her specialty as bond swaps causes the company to lose all knowledge of her skills in mergers.

Table 12.1 presents the seven steps currently defined for correcting a database design to eliminate update anomalies. This table also names the database theorists that have most actively worked to define each step, starting with Ted Codd in 1970. Three considerations should strike the reader immediately. First, data normalization is a nontrivial practice involving multiple steps. Searching for "data normalization" on the website for any mainstream bookseller yields 2000–3000 references from which to choose. Second, the practice still entails some controversy, given that two versions exist for the first, third, and sixth normal forms. Third, the overall process is still in a state of change, with Chris Date still suggesting new approaches as recently as 2003.

The complexity of the subject and its ongoing refinement give rise to one of the greatest weaknesses with the practice of normalization. EDW projects would be far more manageable if data normalization were a repeatable process with a reliable outcome, but that is not the case today. Data normalization is a slow and labor-intensive practice, especially when teams aim for the higher fourth and fifth normal forms. Two equally skilled data modelers normalizing the same starting data structure will typically come up with two different yet equally valid designs. Even a single data modeler normalizing the same starting database twice will produce a different specification. Given that normalization does not provide repeatable results, how can DW/BI managers and programming teams have confidence that a team's current data model represents a sound basis for months, even years of ETL development? The variability in the results of normalization makes this area of database design an enormous threat to the success of a project. So that they can reliably drive enterprise data warehouse projects to a successful completion, EDW project leaders need to understand not only normalization and its weaknesses but

TABLE 12.1 History of Data Normalization

Form	Definition events	Reference
1NF	Two versions: E.F. Codd (1970) C.J. Date (2003)	 [1a] [1b]
2NF	E.F. Codd (1971)	[2]
3NF	Two versions: E.F. Codd (1971) C. Zaniolo (1982)	 [3a] [3b]
BCNF	R.R. Boyce and E.F. Codd (1974)	[3.5]
4NF	Ronald Fagin (1977)	[4]
5NF	Ronald Fagin (1979)	[5]
6NF	Two versions: Ronald Fagin (1981) C.J. Date, et al (2002)	 [6a] [6b]

Notes:

[1a] E. F. Codd, Further normalization of the database relational model, Courant Institute: Prentice-Hall, 1972

[1b] Chris Date, "What First Normal Form Really Means", Date on Database: Writings 2000-2006, Springer-Verlag, 2006

[2]   Codd, E.F. "Further Normalization of the Data Base Relational Model," Randall J. Rustin (ed.), Data Base Systems: Courant Computer Science Symposia Series 6. Prentice-Hall, 1972

[3a] Ibid.

[3b] Carlo Zaniolo, "A New Normal Form for the Design of Relational Database Schemata." ACM Transactions on Database Systems 7(3), September 1982

[3.5] BCNFL "Boyce-Codd Normal Form"
      E.F. Codd, "Recent Investigations into Relational Data Base Systems," IBM Research Report RJ1385, April 23, 1974

[4]   Ronald Fagin, "Multivalued Dependencies and a New Normal Form for Relational Databases," ACM Transactions on Database Systems, Vol. 2, No. 3, September 1977

[5]   Ronald Fagin, "Normal Forms and Relational Database Operators", ACM SIGMOD International Conference on Management of Data, May 31-June 1, 1979, Boston, Mass.

[6a] Ronald Fagin, "A Normal Form for Relational Databases That Is Based on Domains and Keys,"
      ACM Transactions on Database Systems, Vol. 6, No. 3,

[6b] Chris Date, Hugh Darwen, and Nikos Lorentzos, Temporal Data and the Relational Model, Elsevier LTD, January 2003.

also the costs and benefits of each level of normalization so that they can choose the right style of normalization to pursue.

Example: One Table from First to Fifth Normal Form

To provide an example that illustrates the previously discussed concepts, I now take one table from a state of total "denormalization" to fifth normal form. This section serves only as a quick introduction to normalization, and it assumes that the reader has some basic vocabulary regarding relational databases, such as tables, columns, and keys. Moreover, to keep the presentation streamlined, this example excludes Boyce–Codd and sixth normal form because Boyce–Codd is a variation on third normal form and sixth normal form is still controversial. An example showing only levels one through five will be complete enough to familiarize readers with the practice of normalization and the hazards involved. A more complete presentation of these terms and data normalization can be found in reference books such as that by Date [Date 2012].

Figure 12.10 shows the context model for the hypothetical data warehouse we will be normalizing. This DW/BI application belongs to a telecommunications company that sells services such as cell phones, video on demand, and high-speed Internet. This company advertises its products via ads on other companies' websites. Customers who click on those ads are taken to the telcom company's consumer ordering website, where they can pick one or more packages of services and select a third-party company that will deliver and install the equipment. One can think of the company's marketing program as comprising three major components:

1. The sales management team initiates reseller advertising agreements with major ad managers such as Google and Yahoo!, which will display ads across the Internet.
2. The fulfillment management team recruits a cadre of installers throughout the nation who are qualified to implement the equipment and services that consumers purchase.
3. The sales website team maintains the company's consumer ordering website so that consumers can find the products advertising and purchase them.

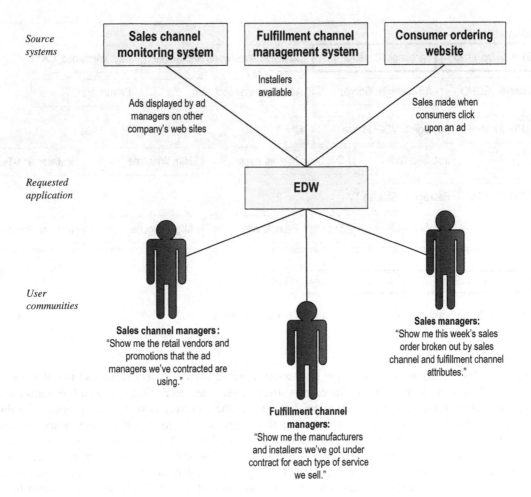

FIGURE 12.10 Context diagram for the normalization example.

As shown Figure 12.10, the Sales Channel Monitoring System provides the EDW with information regarding the advertising that the ad managers such as Google and Yahoo! provide for the company's products. Downstream, the sales channel managers want to query this data to learn how faithfully ad managers are displaying the company's promotions to the people surfing the web. The Fulfillment Channel Management System provides information regarding the installers contracted to service the consumers. The fulfillment channel management team will want to ask questions about who is ready to support which types of equipment that the telecommunications company provides. The Consumer Ordering Website provides information about the sales that occur, and the sales managers will want to analyze which retailers and promotions have proven to be the most effective at enticing the public to buy the company's products.

Figure 12.11 presents a starting data model in which a single data record called "Sales Order" contains all the information provided by these three source systems on a single data record. The particular data record shown in the figure represents a sale of two packages of equipment and services to a city recreational center in California. The designers of this starting database chose the consumer's Facebook ID and the order's date-time as the business attributes that will uniquely identify each sales record. They have designated this combination as the table's primary key, as indicated by the bold borders in the diagram. For the transaction depicted, the customer actually purchased two packages after clicking on an advertisement she saw while viewing the website for OnlineDepot.com. That particular ad was displayed to her by the Google ad management service, and it offered her half-off on her installation charges.

With all the attributes of a sale placed in one table, Figure 12.11 depicts a database in "zeroth normal form" or 0NF. This example shows how a design team takes a 0NF database and progressively normalizes its structure from 1NF to 5NF.

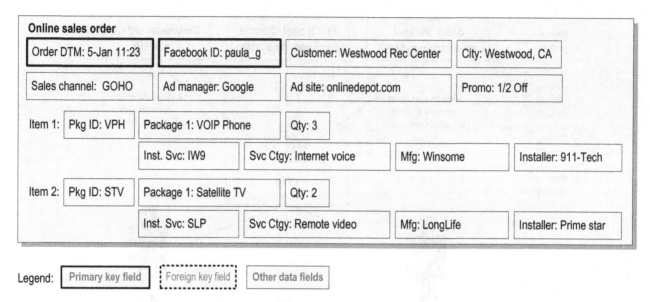

FIGURE 12.11   Sample case's data in its starting arrangement, i.e., zeroth nomal form.

1NF Correction

According to the rules of data normalization, the first design flaw we should correct is the fact that this database has a repeating set of columns for the items sold. The current structure provides storage for only two line items for each sale, which makes the database vulnerable to insert anomalies. Should the company next receive an order with three items, the warehouse would either be blocked from recording this event or have to duplicate sales header information on another, new record that would be necessary only to record the third item. The first choice prevents the organization from knowing that it had demand for the third item. The second choice will cause misinformation when the company tries to determine how many orders it has received by counting order headers. Similarly, if this record were dropped, a delete anomaly would occur because it might hold the only instance of the VOIP phone manufactured by Winsome, causing the company to lose knowledge that such product exists for sale.

First normal form dictates that no elements within a record can represent sets of values. Every attribute of an entity should contain only one atomic value from a particular domain. In the 0NF configuration, Package ID is actually an array containing two values, VPH and STV.

The first panel in Figure 12.12 shows the corrected database record, in which the problem of repeating columns has been eliminated. The second panel in this figure depicts the change in the data model when viewed as a high-level entity relationship diagram. The items sold have been moved to their own "Line Item" table, which contains one record per item sold. The designers established a many-to-one relationship between the tables through a foreign key (designated with bold dashed borders) on the Line Item table, composed of Order DTM and Facebook ID. The values in these fields link each Package record to a single parent record in Sales Order Header, whose primary key fields are Order DTM and Facebook ID. The primary key of the Line Item table is this foreign key plus the item number.

2NF Correction

At this point, the designers consider the fields remaining in Sales Order Header table and notice that the non-key customer attributes have nothing to do with the order date-time. Second normal form requires that a database be in first normal form and that the values of all non-key columns be determined by all of the table's primary key, not just part of it. With the record's current design, a delete anomaly could occur if this order were cancelled and its record removed, because this record might be the company's only indication that the Westwood Rec Center exists as an interested customer. Conversely, an insert anomaly might occur if a sales transaction arrived to the company's server that was missing the customer's city and the city had been designated as a required value. Because it was missing a required customer field, the warehouse would be prevented from recording a sales transaction, causing the sales counts provided by the database to be in error.

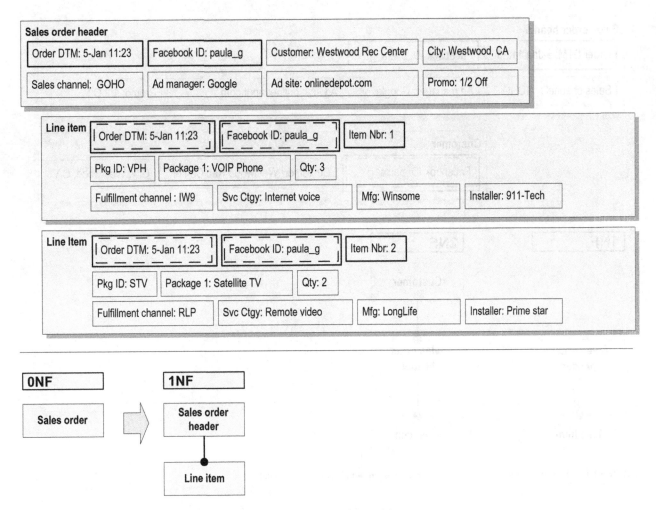

FIGURE 12.12 Impact of a first normal form correction upon sample case's data model.

Figure 12.13 shows the database after it has been redesigned to meet second normal form. The fields identifying the purchaser have been moved to their own dedicated table called Customer. The Facebook ID field links each record in the Sales Order Header table to the single appropriate customer record in Customer.

3NF Correction

Continuing on with the normalization process, the designers now search their new structures for violations of third normal form, which rules out "transitive dependencies." Transitive dependencies occur when a non-key element determines the value for another non-key element. We can see three such dependencies in the second normal form version of this database. First, in the Sales Order Header table, the sales channel code is not part of the records' primary key, but it does determine the values for the ad manager, ad site, and promotion that make up the buyer's path to the purchasing site. Second, in the Line Item table, Package ID is not part of the primary key, but it determines the Package Name. This connection is another transitive relationship that violates third normal form. Finally, the Fulfillment Channel code is not part of the Line Item records' primary key either, but it dictates the values for Service Category, Manufacturer, and Installer. Considering the update anomalies for just the first of these dependencies, we can see that if this record were to be deleted, the company could lose all knowledge that the Google ad manager has displayed half-off advertisements or any ads on OnlineDepot.com at all. Similarly, if the business rules made advertising sites or promotional styles mandatory values for the record, a transaction missing either of them would get blocked during an insert action, making incomplete the data warehouse's information regarding ads that have been displayed.

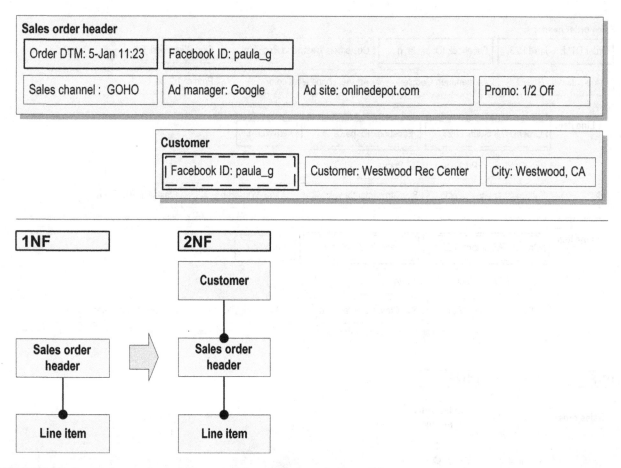

FIGURE 12.13   Impact of a second normal form correction upon sample case's data model.

To correct these weaknesses, the designers diligently eliminate each transitive dependency so that each set of items that were not determined directly by a data record's primary key receive their own single-themed table. In this case, the data modelers updated the design as follows, all of which are illustrated in Figure 12.14:

- Sales channel fields receive a dedicated table with columns for Ad Manager, Ad Site, and Promo. Sales order headers will link to this table using the field for the Sales Channel code.
- Package Description is split out to a separate table also. Line item records will link to this table via the Package ID.
- The fulfillment channel fields land in a table of their own that will have columns for Service Category, Manufacturer, and Installer. Line item records will link to this table using the Fulfillment Channel code.

Note that this type of correction was used for the Package ID and Package Name fields, which represent a code and its meaning. Data modelers learn early on to look for code-decode pairs within the same table, since they are usually third normal form violations. As a general practice, EDW teams will create many reference tables for data warehouses that hold code meanings in order to avoid the update anomalies that third normal form violations engender.

4NF Correction

Some designers believe that moving a database to third normal form is sufficiently free of update anomalies and stop their design work there. Modelers on more advanced projects, however, believe it is necessary to insulate their database designs against another class of anomalies, namely *multivalued dependencies*, and this belief causes them to search their third normal form schemas for fourth and fifth normal form violations.

A multivalued dependency exists if the keys of a table determine not just one occurrence of the remaining values in a table but instead multiple values. Consequently, if a multivalued dependency exists in a table, we need to create more than one record to store the information associated with a given key value [Singh 2011, Chapter 10]. One disadvantage

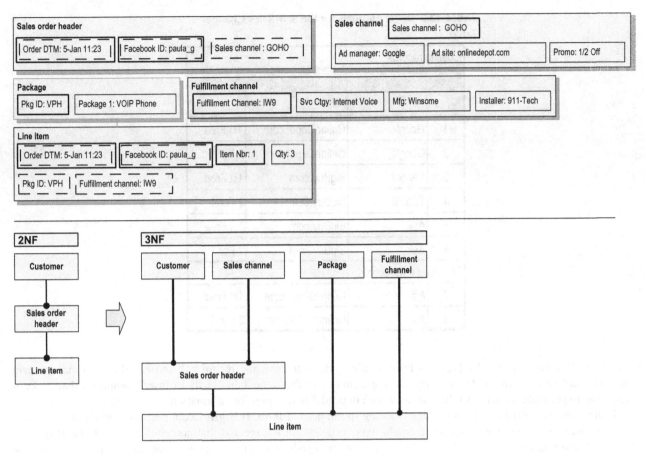

FIGURE 12.14 Impact of a third normal form correction upon sample case's data model.

of allowing this condition to exist in a data warehouse is that additional, inter-record logic must be designed and programmed into the ETL so that all the necessary records are created each time a new set of key values is added. Such multirecord logic is difficult to specify and program correctly, and so it is a common source of vexing quality errors within a data warehouse.

Multivalue dependencies can be more difficult to spot than the first three normal-form violations because one must consider the values that can occur across several records in a table, not just the values stored on a single record. To take our model beyond third normal form, we must search it for two types of multivalued dependencies. Two or more independently varying, non-key fields lead to a fourth normal form violation. Two or more fields whose values can be determined by an exogenous reference domain, such as a control list, violate the requirements for firth normal form.

To understand the fourth normal form violation, consider Table 12.2, which shows the full domain for the Sales Channel table in the third normal form data model. Looking at this listing, the designers discovered that there is more than one way to interpret the records that it holds. With multiple interpretations possible, the sales management team may draw the wrong conclusions when it uses these records to review the company's advertising campaigns that are running on the Internet. The ambiguity emerged when the designers asked themselves what updates to this table should the ETL make when the Ask ad manager started displaying the company's advertisements via the OnlineDepot.com website. The company is currently running two types of promotion: "1st Free" and "2 for 1." If the data warehouse created records for both of these promotions, as shown at the bottom of Figure 12.14, it would imply that Ask displays both types of ads on OnlineDepot.com, but perhaps that would be a false picture of reality. Ask's ad servers may have a problem with the images used for the 2-for-1 promotions, so populating this reference table with both records will imply a counterfactual notion that Ask is fulfilling its contract obligations. Conversely, if the warehouse created a record for only 2-for-1 promotions because that is the only ad found in the sales channel monitoring system, the end users might infer that Ask has deliberately chosen not to run 1st-Free ads for the company. Perhaps it is only

TABLE 12.2 Insert Anomaly for the 3NF Sales Channel
Table

Existing records			
Sales channel table			
ID	Ad Manager	Ad Site	Promo
1	Google	OnlineDepot.com	1st Free
2	Google	OnlineDepot.com	2 For 1
3	Yahoo!	BigBuy.com	1st Free
4	Yahoo!	BigBuy.com	2 For 1
5	Ask	BigBuy.com	1st Free
6	Ask	BigBuy.com	2 For 1
Proposed new records			
7	Ask	OnlineDepot.com	1st Free
8	Ask	OnlineDepot.com	2 For 1

coincidence that has kept the 1st-Free ads from running yet, so the missing record will mislead the sales management team. The inclusion of two independently varying columns in the same table leads to insert anomalies that make it impossible to populate the table so that end users can dependably interpret its information.

Delete anomalies exist as well for tables violating fourth normal form. If BigBuy.com decides to block Ask as an ad server for its website, the data warehouse would have to delete all the records that contain "Ask" and "BigBuy.com" (Records 5 and 6 in Figure 12.14). Record 4 would be the only indication in the data warehouse that 2-for-1 ads are running on the BigBuy.com website. If Record 4 did not exist, then deleting Records 5 and 6 would have eliminated all knowledge of this particular combination of ads and ad sites, leading to incorrect information for the sales team. In real-life data warehouses, the number of columns and records involved with fourth normal form violations will be many times higher than the two small records here; thus, the rules for avoiding and correcting the possible update anomalies can be very difficult to specify. Multivalued dependencies also require complex ETL routines that act on more than one record per event, programming, so most veteran EDW data modelers work hard to remove them from their designs.

Correcting for a fourth normal form violation follows a similar strategy that data modelers used for the first through third normal forms: The columns involved in multivalue dependencies should be relocated into their own special-themed tables. As illustrated in Figure 12.15, a fourth normal form design will split the columns in the last model's Sales Channel table into three separate entities: Ad Manager, Ad Site, and Promotion. Furthermore, the designers will need to add two associative tables in order to express the relationships between the records in the three entities—one for tracking relationships between ad managers and ad sites and another for links between ad manager and promotions. Table 12.3 illustrates how the rows of the original Sales Channel table would be distributed across the five new tables. With this design, only one record is needed in the first associative table to document that Ask will be running the company's advertisements on the OnlineDepot.com website. Whether that contract supports 1st-Free or 2-for-1 promotions will be documented independently in the second associative table. The existence of an advertising contract is now decoupled from the promotion it covers so that end users will not be misled by the update anomalies that could occur in the previous design. Updates to the Ad Manager—Promotions table incur no requirement to affect the records in the Ad Manager—Ad Site table, so the programming for maintaining an accurate database becomes much simpler. Business users still create the full set of records making up the previous Sales Channel table by joining these five tables together, only now the business situations that those results imply will be clear.

This correction for a relatively simple fourth normal form violation should serve as a cautionary tale for EDW team leaders. Our example identified several columns in an apparently functional table that turned out to be varying independently. When the EDW team realized that some of the attributes no longer represented a simple set of values qualifying the primary key of a table but had instead taken on independent lives of their own, the design fix required turned out to be very involved. The correction required five new tables, each needing an ETL module of its own, in addition to data

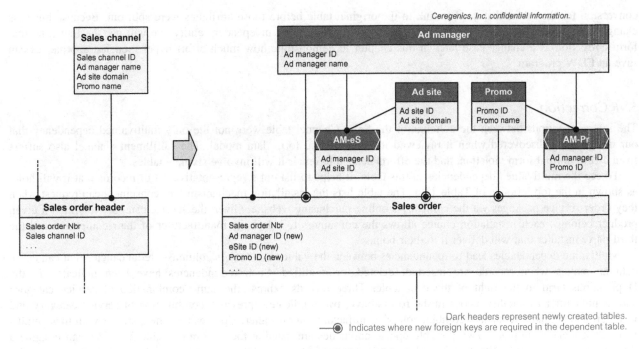

FIGURE 12.15   Impact of a fourth normal form correction upon sample case's data model.

TABLE 12.3 Sample Case's Tables After 4NF Correction Applied

Entity tables	Associative tables*

Ad Manager Table

Ad Manager ID	Ad Manager name
101	Google
102	Yahoo!
103	Ask

Ad Site Table

Ad Site ID	Ad Site Name
201	OnlineDepot.com
202	BigBuy.com

Promo Table

Promo ID	Promo name
301	1st Free
302	2 For 1

Ad Manager-Ad Site Table

Ad Manager		Ad Site	
101	(Google)	201	(OnlineDepot.com)
101	(Google)	202	(BigBuy.com)
102	(Yahoo!)	201	(OnlineDepot.com)
103	(Ask)	201	(OnlineDepot.com)
103	(Ask)	202	(BigBuy.com)

Ad Manager-Promo Table

Ad Manager		Promo	
101	(Google)	301	(1st Free)
101	(Google)	302	(2 for 1)
102	(Yahoo!)	301	(1st Free)
103	(Ask)	301	(1st Free)
103	(Ask)	302	(2 for 1)

* Associative records populated with IDs of the entity table records that they relate.
 Names for each ID shown in parentheses for clarity.

conversion for the tables that used to link to the original table before those attributes were split out. Because business changes can frequently transform simple attributes in a table into an independent entity, we will use the fourth normal form correction as a change case later in this chapter to demonstrate how much effort hyper modeled approaches can save an EDW program.

5NF Correction

The interconnections between the columns of the Sales Channel table were not the only multivalued dependency that our design team discovered when it reviewed its third normal form data model. The fulfillment channel also suffers from a fifth normal form violation, and the efforts needed to repair it will involve six new tables.

To see the multivalued dependencies in this table, it helps to list out a representative set of records that it will hold, as shown in the top left side of Table 12.4. The table lists the installation mechanism that consumers can request when they order service packages via the company's online purchasing website. Given the service category to which a given product belongs, each installation choice allows the consumers to select the manufacturer of their equipment and the third-party installer that will deliver it to their homes.

Multivalue dependencies lead to redundancies between the values in a table's columns—redundancies that can cause data anomalies when records are inserted, deleted, or modified. Such redundancies have been indicated in the Duplications Grid to the right of the data table. Three records express the same combination of service category and manufacturer as another record in the rows above, two duplicate a previous combination of service category and installer, and six list a redundant combination of manufacturer and installer. Updates become complex with these multi-value dependencies in place. Two possible update anomalies are listed at the bottom of Table 2.14. We can imagine a third type of complex update that would occur if a manufacturer decided to stop doing business with a particular

TABLE 12.4 Records Demonstrating a Fifth-Normal Form Violation

Fulfillment channel table				Duplications grid		
ID	Svc. Category	Manufacturer	Installer	Svc Ctgry-Manufactr	Svc Ctgry-Installer	Manufactr-Installer
1	Cloud Storage	TwoProng	GeekSquad			
2	Demand Video	Winsome	GeekSquad			
3	Hi Speed Copper	LongLife	Prime Star			
4	Internet Voice	LongLife	Prime Star			Y
5	Internet Voice	Winsome	911-Tech			
6	Internet Voice	Winsome	GeekSquad	Y		Y
7	Mobile Hotspot	LongLife	GeekSquad			
8	Remote Video	LongLife	Prime Star			Y
9	Internet Voice	LongLife	GeekSquad	Y	Y	Y
10	On-Premises Wifi	LongLife	Prime Star			Y
11	On-Premises Wifi	Winsome	911-Tech			Y
12	On-Premises Wifi	Winsome	Prime Star	Y	Y	

"Y" indicates a record contains the same values for the given pair of columns as a record above it

Problem cases			
Delete anomaly			
1	Cloud Storage	TwoProng	GeekSquad

If deleted, database loses all knowledge that there is a "cloud storage" product type.

Insert Anomaly			
13	Remote Video	LongLife	911-Tech

If added, ETL will also need to add two further records for the 911-Tech and LongLife combination to cover the other two service categories that 911-Tech already works in.

installer. If LongLife suddenly refused to support Prime Star, for example, it would not be enough to delete Record 3. Records 4, 5, 10, and 12 would have to be removed as well. Ensuring that the ETL performs multiple, coordinated deletes can require a nontrivial effort, especially when the business rules determining the affected rows involve many columns.

The consideration that makes this design a fifth normal form violation is the fact that the company's s subject matter experts have provided insight that will help the DW/BI team correct this table's multivalued dependencies. They have assured the team that there is no need to track all the known combinations of manufacturers and installers for each service category because if a particular installer is authorized to install a manufacturer's equipment for one service category, it is qualified to perform installations for that manufacturer in all the other service categories that the installer can handle. In fact, the company possesses a list of dealerships—that is, a control list of installers authorized for each manufacturer. With that information available, the Fulfillment Channel table can be decomposed into three core entities with three associative tables linking them, as shown in Table 12.5. The data modelers isolate service categories, manufacturers, and installers into their own special-themed tables. Then they create associative tables to link the valid combinations between any two of these core entities.

Once the original Fulfillment Channel data has been distributed to the new design, the relationships between service categories and manufacturers can be maintained separately from relationships between service categories and installers and also separately from the links between manufacturers and installers. To re-create the Fulfillment Channel table of the original design, the end users can join the six new tables as shown in the high-level entity diagram of Figure 12.16. Records can be inserted in or deleted from the appropriate table to express new truths about the theme of that table without altering the truths held about the other, unaffected entities in this corner of the data model. Consider the insert anomaly identified in Table 12.4, for example. In the third normal form design, the ETL would have had to add three records when 911-Tech started installing equipment made by LongLife, one for each of the service categories in which 911-Tech works. Perhaps the ETL would perform that insert correctly, or perhaps coding errors would cause one or two of the records to be omitted. Once the design is compliant with fifth normal form, however, only one record has to be inserted in the Dealership table, namely, one linking 911-Tech with LongLife. Programming the ETL to add a single record is far easier than coding modules to execute three coordinated inserts.

GENERALIZATION BASICS

The other fundamental EDW data modeling technique besides normalization is *generalization*. Generalization is a modeling technique that transforms data structures that are specific to a particular entity to a form that can support a wider range of entity types.

The classic use of generalization is the party model. Without generalization, a data model could specify a separate table for each of a company's customers, employee, and vendor entities. However, the modelers could note that instances of all three of these entities are either companies or individuals. With some thought, they could consolidate the three specific tables into a single generalized set of tables that can store instances of a *party*, whether it be a person or a company. Such an adaptation makes it far easier to update the data warehouse's design when the company creates a new way to work with other companies, such as marketing partnerships, because it can simply declare a new type of party and begin storing that flavor of data in the existing party tables. When one generalizes a denormalized table such as a flat file extract from a source system, the resulting model tends to have a generalized parent table (a supertype) that holds the common fields shared by the entities plus a set of related child tables (subtypes) that will hold the attributes specific to entity types. We will see this pattern play out when we step through a generalization example later.

Advantages and Disadvantages of Generalization

As an overall advantage, generalization consolidates data transform logic within a DW/BI application, thus eliminating redundant blocks of programming within the ETL modules. With fewer redundant blocks of code, developers have fewer locations to consider while performing impact analysis and maintenance programming so that they can update the EDW's functionality faster and with fewer mistakes. For example, if customer, employee, manufacturer, and installer all share some basic attributes and the data modelers locate these attributes together in a shared entity, the EDW developers can program the transformation logic for these attributes in a single, reusable module, leaving themselves only one block of code to update when the business rules affecting these entities change in the future.

TABLE 12.5 Table Records After 5NF Correction Applied

Entity tables   _Associative tables*_

Service category table	
ID	Name
101	Cloud Storage
102	Demand Video
103	Hi Speed Copper
104	Internet Voice
105	Mobile Hotspot
106	Remote Video
107	On-Premises Wifi

Service category-manufacturer table			
Svc. Category		Manufacturer	
101	(Cloud Storage)	301	(TwoProng)
102	(Demand Video)	303	(Winsome)
103	(Hi Speed Copper)	302	(LongLife)
104	(Internet Voice)	302	(LongLife)
104	(Internet Voice)	303	(Winsome)
105	(Mobile Hotspot)	302	(LongLife)
106	(Remote Video)	302	(LongLife)
107	(On-Premises Wifi)	302	(LongLife)
107	(On-Premises Wifi)	303	(Winsome)

Manufacturer table	
ID	Name
301	TwoProng
302	LongLife
303	Winsome

Service category-installer table			
Svc. Category		Installer	
101	(Cloud Storage)	201	(GeekSquad)
102	(Demand Video)	201	(GeekSquad)
103	(Hi Speed Copper)	202	(Prime Star)
104	(Internet Voice)	202	(Prime Star)
104	(Internet Voice)	203	(911-Tech)
104	(Internet Voice)	201	(GeekSquad)
105	(Mobile Hotspot)	201	(GeekSquad)
106	(Remote Video)	202	(Prime Star)
106	(Remote Video)	201	(GeekSquad)
107	(On-Premises Wifi)	202	(Prime Star)
107	(On-Premises Wifi)	203	(911-Tech)

Installer table	
ID	Name
201	GeekSquad
202	Prime Star
203	911-Tech

Dealership Table*			
Mfctr		Installer	
301	(TwoProng)	201	(GeekSquad)
302	(LongLife)	202	(Prime Star)
302	(LongLife)	201	(GeekSquad)
303	(Winsome)	201	(GeekSquad)
303	(Winsome)	203	(911-Tech)
303	(Winsome)	202	(Prime Star)

* Associative records populated with IDs of the entity table records that they relate.
  Names for each ID shown in parentheses for clarity.
** Also known as the "Manufacturer-Installer Associative Table."

Generalization is not guaranteed to always reduce complexity, however. If the data modelers must take extraordinary steps while abstracting data field names, domains, or data types, for example, generalization can lead to designs that are more opaque and ETL programs that are more internally complex, overshadowing the advantage of locating the logic in one module.

Generalization is different than abstraction, another concept in data modeling. Whereas abstraction is a loss of unnecessary detail as one takes a progressively higher viewpoint upon a system, generalized data structures can still manage all the required detail—they just utilize tables that can store more than one type of entity [Silverston and Agnew 2008].

Unlike data normalization, the practice of generalization does not yet have a single set of modeling techniques that a data modeler can follow across all types of entities. In general, data modelers can take two or three steps in

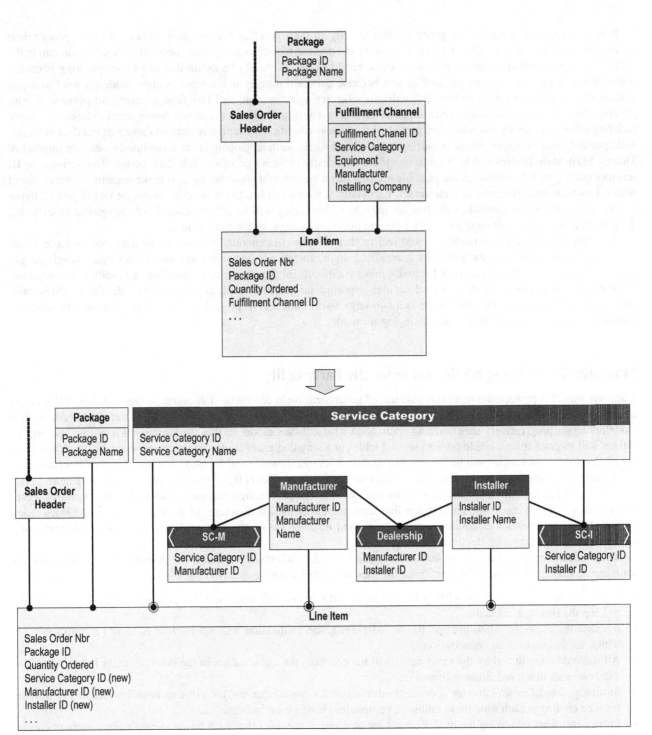

Dark headers represent newly created tables.
──● Indicates where new foreign keys are required in the dependent table.

FIGURE 12.16 Impact of a fifth normal form correction upon sample case's data model.

generalizing a starting flat-table design, but for some common topics, such as status codes and methods of contact, a fourth step is possible. Not only does the number of possible steps vary between topics but also the goal of each generalization step can be different. Generalization is therefore more of an art than normalization. With each step, the data modelers must carefully weigh the gains in simplifying the ETL code against the obfuscation caused by having a single structure that can serve two or more purposes.

Many data modelers emphasize generalization heavily in their practice because they believe it *future proofs* their application's data structures against possible changes in business requirements. Some forms of generalization can make data models more robust against new requirements, but EDW teams should be aware that full future proofing is costly. Because the future can only be guessed at and because generalization is not a science, data modelers tend to argue extensively over some of the smallest design details when trying to insulate an EDW design against all possible contingencies. Consequently, ambitious generalization efforts can seriously distract a development team. Moreover, future proofing efforts frequently fail when confronted with business conditions completely outside those that the data modelers anticipated. Given the rapid change occurring today due to forces such as globalization, e-commerce, and the Internet of Things, EDW team leaders will be wise to invest only modestly in future proofing their data models. Delivering new BI services quickly will far outweigh the possible updates that a team might someday have to make because it moved ahead with a less-than-fully generalized data model. Especially if teams employ the agile data modeling techniques of hyper normalization and hyper generalization that are introduced later, they will be able to adapt EDW designs so quickly that there will be very little advantage gained by trying to guess and design for the murky future.

As a final note of caution, readers should realize that mistakes in generalization can make data models more brittle rather than more flexible. If the modelers generalized an organization's customers and employees into a single *people* entity, for example, that decision could actually make it difficult for the company to someday start selling to companies because there would be nowhere to record company-appropriate qualifiers such as employer tax identifiers, Duns numbers, or resellers licenses. Generalization is a two-edge sword, and EDW project leaders should manage the situation carefully when their data modelers start swinging it broadly.

Example: Generalizing a Sales Table for the Party Entity

The party model is perhaps the most common use of generalization in enterprise data warehousing and thus will serve as a good illustration of the steps involved in this data modeling technique. Figures 12.17–12.21 demonstrate how data modelers might progressively generalize an application's logical data model so that the attributes for people and organizations will migrate from a single table to several tables in a way that enables greater reuse and adaptability. When completed, a single set of entities will be able to play several roles in a database and support widescale reuse of information.

As with the normalization example, these diagrams begin with a "Level 0" representation, as shown in Figure 12.17. In the Level 0 configuration, the data model has been normalized just enough that each sales order header record serves as a parent for one to many line items. Each line item references the manufacturer of the equipment on the sales order. Note that the attributes for customer, contract agent, and installer are on the sales order header, and similar attributes have been placed on the manufacturer's table.

The modelers may well choose to leave the database in a Level 0 configuration if the project's context does not call for reusable entities. However, this configuration does have the following disadvantages:

- If a particular customer changes his or her last name, all sales records involving that person must be updated in order to keep the database accurate.
- Because the customer fields are specific to individuals, the application will not be able to record a transaction for which the customer is an organization.
- All the orders facilitated by the same agent will have to hold the same values in the contract agent fields, filling the database with much redundant information.
- Similarly, the database will store redundant information for manufacturers that serve as installers, leading to a maintenance challenge each time these multirole companies change their information.
- Project members reviewing the model cannot see at a glance the roles that each business entity plays without considering the details of the table's attributes.
- The model cannot support the rollups that occur when hierarchies exist between customers (as in a household) or between installers (as exists when the company contracts out to the members of a services conglomerate).
- By collocating so many columns, the designers have created a very wide table that may incur poor performance when the database server must process huge blocks of data even if the query requires values from only a few fields.

Several of these disadvantages represent the update anomalies considered previously during the discussion on data normalization, and many would be corrected by normalizing this logical model. Rather than employing normalization, the following three steps will correct these disadvantages through the related practice of generalization—that is, remodeling tables to achieve greater applicability rather that redistributing keys and breaking up multivalued dependencies.

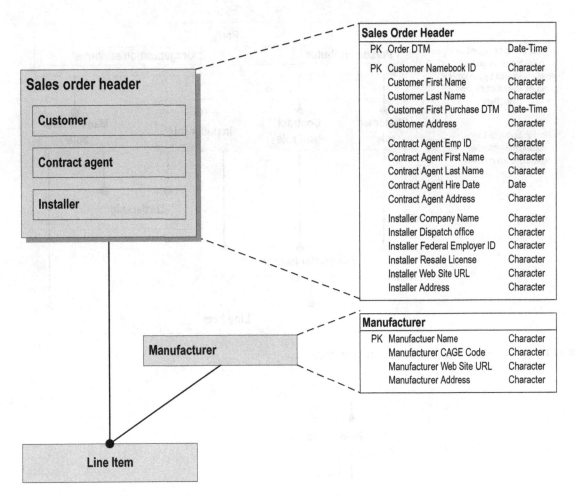

FIGURE 12.17   Level zero data generalization.

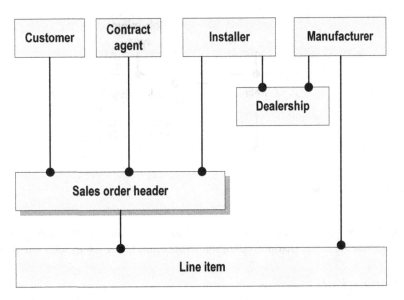

FIGURE 12.18   Level one data generalization for the party model.

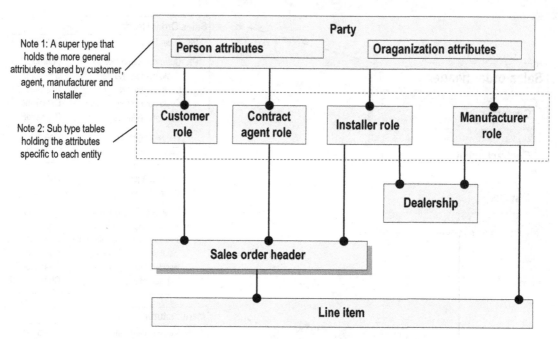

FIGURE 12.19 Level two data generalization for the party model.

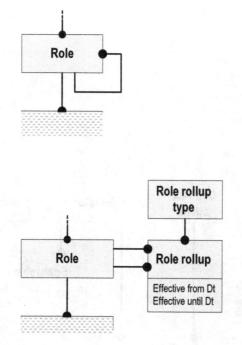

FIGURE 12.20 Data generalization roll-up patterns.

As will be shown, normalization generally aligns with Level 1 generalization, but the later generalization steps tend to consolidate the many single-theme tables that normalization creates into fewer tables with reusable attributes.

Level 1 Generalization for Party

Figure 12.18 shows the results of Level 1 generalization, which begins our design's journey toward a standard party model. This step moves each set of attributes representing a person or an organizations to a separate table, leaving the

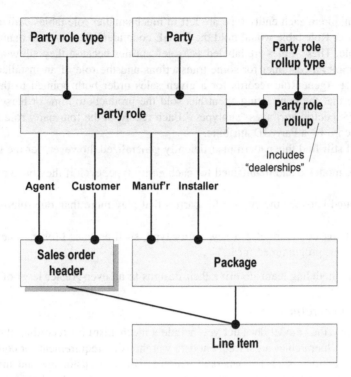

FIGURE 12.21 Level three data generalization for the party model.

design with distinct entities for customer, contract agent, manufacturer, and installer. The model also shows the impact of some additional normalization where a Dealership table has been created to manage the relationship between installers and manufacturers, as discussed in the previous section. The dealership entity is used in later generalization steps to demonstrate how rollups are managed.

This new version of the model addresses much of the disadvantages noted previously regarding redundancy. Now orders created by the same contract agent, for example, can all refer to a single Contract Agent record. With fewer attributes, the Sales Order record is "skinnier," suggesting performance will probably improve for queries that link sales orders to only one of these four entities.

This new arrangement still suffers from some important challenges, however. If a contract agent becomes a customer, then a redundant record must be created and maintained. This is also the case for manufacturers who can serve as installers. Manufacturers and installers cannot become customers because customer is still modeled as if it were a person. Moreover, consider the work that will be required should the EDW team decide to manage the address fields with greater sophistication—for example, dividing out elements such as street names and cities and ensuring that all such elements have been cleansed and standardized. That rather complex logic will have to be replicated to the ETL modules dedicated to each entity, leading to a maintenance challenge over the long term. This redundant programming will be required everywhere people and organizations share similar attributes. In the minds of many data modelers, such a situation calls out for further model generalization so that the necessary ETL logic can be consolidated.

Level 2 Generalization

Figure 12.19 shows how this database will be structured after Level 2 generalization for people and organizations. All such business entities are now treated as just another instance of a notion called Party. This entity contains a set of attributes for people and another for organizations so that it can receive the information of any party to a transaction, whether it be an individual or a company. The person attributes would hold an individual's first and last names, for example. The organization attributes would provide fields for company name and federal employer identifiers. By collecting these common attributes into the party table, the EDW developers consolidate the logic that maintains these various fields into the single ETL module that populates the Party entity, making defect analysis and logic updates far easier to manage.

The attributes that are unique to each entity type are left in much smaller role tables dedicated to specific role types. Perhaps only the Manufacturer Role table would hold the CAGE code identifier given to manufacturers by the U.S. federal government, for example. These tables are labeled as "role" entities because they allow a single instance of a party to play the role of, for example, a customer for some transactions and the role of an installer for others. In fact, if the Customer Role and Contract Agent Role records for a given sales order both pointed to the same Party record, that arrangement would indicate that the contracting agent has sold the products to him- or herself. Data modelers call the smaller tables holding entity-specific attributes "subtypes." Each record in the four party role subtype tables is linked to a parent, supertype Party record by a Party ID attribute.

Some data modelers will still find this pattern insufficiently generalized, however, for the following reasons:

- Separate entities must be modeled and maintained for each entity type, even if they have essentially the same collections of attributes.
- Records must be duplicated between the entities for parties that play more than one role in the database's collection of transaction.
- Each time the business transactions involve a new entity type, such as sales broker, a new subtype table has to be added to the model and ETL programmed for it.

Such concerns lead many modeling teams to drive their designs to an ever-greater level of generalization.

Two Patterns for Role Hierarchies

As a further limitation, the previous model does not yet include a mechanism for recording the hierarchies that can exist between parties. Rollups along hierarchies are a frequent data warehousing requirement for companies that want to better manage nested structures of entities, such as ownership patterns between customers and multilevel product catalogs. Common examples of hierarchies between parties are customers who are people who share a single household, customers that are companies embedded within a conglomerate's ownership structure, and employees who have managers and directors within their departments. Supporting information about hierarchical relationships can greatly increase the value of an enterprise data warehouse. Tracking the relationships between individual customers alone can easily support better marketing, discounting, and customer care decisions. When working with the party model, hierarchies are typically applied to the roles a party plays rather than the party itself. This practice allows for a given party to participate in one hierarchy scheme when active as a customer, for example, and another when viewed as a vendor.

While generalizing the logical data models, data designers implement rollups in two ways, as shown in Figure 12.20. The top half of the figure shows a simple mechanism that supports only a single recursive rollup scheme. Here, the data modelers have given a party role table a Parent ID attribute in which the ETL will place a value identifying the next higher party role record in the hierarchy. This approach works but has two limitations, the first being that it restricts each role to participating in only one type of hierarchy. Second, it supports only one rollup *instance* between any two role records so that when the database updates the relationship between two party roles, all knowledge of a previous relationship disappears.

The bottom half of the figure shows a more flexible rollup scheme. A separate associative table called Party Role Rollup will support multiple many-to-many links between any two parties roles. Attributes on the rollup record hold values for an Effective-From date and an Effective-Until date that allow these records to be marked as retired but left in the database when the relationships they reflect end, so that the data warehouse can track the full history of the hierarchies between parties roles. In order to support many rollups patterns involving a given party role, each rollup instance links to a record in a Party Role Rollup Type reference table.

Level 3 Generalization

Figure 12.21 shows a Level 3 generalization of our starter model that addresses the remaining challenges cited in the Level 2 model and employs the more flexible style of rollups between parties. This model still contains the party entity, but now the multiple role tables of the previous model have been consolidated into a single Party Role table. The Party table holds a rich collection of information about each participant in the company's transactions, whether they be a person or an organization. Each party record can play many different types of roles in the transactions, even multiple roles within a single transaction. This flexibility arises from the fact that each Sales Order now references a Party Role record for each type of participation in a given transaction, such as customer or installer. By reusing the Party Role instances, this design eliminates the redundant information storage seen in lower levels of generalization and allows an EDW team to place all the transformation logic for parties and party roles in one module for each table.

The database can apply different rules to match various kinds of roles because each Party Role instance has a parent Party Role Type reference record describing the class of role to which it belongs. New roles can now be easily implemented by simply adding a new role type record and updating the ETL for the Party Role module to follow a new set of business rules for records referencing that role type.

With the new Party Rollup Type entity, this design can also track more than one rollup scheme between parties roles. For example, it can support the ownership relationships between parties serving as manufacturers and also their membership in industry organizations. For consumers who are people, the same rollup tables can track how customers share the same households.

Further Generalization Concepts

The previous discussion of generalization steps will serve to familiarize readers with this data modeling concept well enough to understand the new agile approaches to EDW data modeling. This presentation only scratched the surface of the technique, however. Techniques for generalizing topics such as products, locations, contact mechanisms, and transaction statuses all follow their own patterns, which are very different from the one employed for people and organizations. Moreover, an entire second layer of tables for roles and role types is typically needed to manage the difference between declarative and contextual relationships, where *declarative* entities manage the roles an organization allows for a given party, and *contextual* tracks the relationships that actually manifest as the company pursues its business.

I invite all EDW project leaders to thoroughly familiarize themselves with the rich and extremely powerful discipline of data model generalization by reading the books by my colleague at The Data Warehousing Institute, Len Silverston. The *Data Model Resource Book* series that he has published during the past 15 years provides an invaluable reference for reusable patterns that can provide extensive guidance for EDW project leaders, saving them the effort of reinventing models and helping them avoid the frustration of deploying improperly structured repositories for business analytic systems.

THE STANDARD APPROACH AND ITS DATA MODELING PARADIGMS

The notions of data normalization and generalization sketched previously position us to now discuss what I refer to as the traditional or standard approach to enterprise data warehousing. The standard approach is robust and very well documented, but it is hardly agile, in no small part due to the type of data modeling that traditional EDW teams employ. The notions of normalization and generalization allow me to present in the following chapters alternatives to the traditional approach that are far faster to deliver and more flexible in the face of changing business requirements.

The concept of enterprise data warehousing took root in the 1990s and 2000s through the writings of Bill Inmon, Claudia Imhoff, Gartner Analytics, and many others. (See [Inmon et al. 2001] for a definitive guide to what I call the standard approach.) To provide readers with a simplified version of the consensus emerging from this community of thought leaders, Figure 12.22 depicts the data topology of the standard approach, and Figure 12.1, which was considered previously, portrays the layered data architecture one typically finds in traditional EDWs.

Figure 12.22 expresses the notion that the EDW should gather and harmonize all of the company's key decision support information and then distribute subsets of the resulting integrated information to special-purpose data marts. The

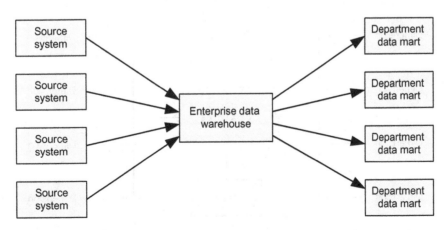

FIGURE 12.22   The hub & spoke conception of an enterprise data warehouse.

intent of the data warehouse is to provide a "single version of the truth" for the organization. The data in the EDW has been cleansed, transformed, and validated so that it supposedly provides measures and qualifiers that all departments within the company can trust to be standardized and correct. The DW/BI team subsets this information out to departmental data marts so that end users need only sift through a small portion of corporate data to receive fast answers to their business questions. DW/BI is free to choose whether these data marts operate on separate data servers or are simply logical subdivisions of the information available on the data warehouse host.

Stepping down one layer of abstraction to look more closely at the data architecture found in a standard approach, we can see that the warehouse and data marts typically employ different data modeling techniques to meet the distinct purposes. As noted in Figure 12.1, the Landing layer holds source system extracts. Traditionally, these extracts are held only long enough to load into the warehouse and are then discarded. EDW teams typically structure Landing layer tables to closely match the source database, with the addition of a few metadata attributes such as extract date, so that the source systems are the biggest determinant of the structure that Landing tables take. Frequently, Landing-layer objects are loaded with only the subsets of the records found on the source systems, namely those records that have not yet been captured by the warehouse. Because these subsets represent the difference between what the current operational systems and the data warehouse have last loaded, DW/BI developers often say that the Landing layer holds "delta" record sets.

In contrast, the design of the Integration layer is largely determined by the EDW team. Because its purpose to hold a single integrated collection of enterprise data, data modelers commonly place this layer in one of the standard normal forms, either third, fourth, or fifth, depending on how much they wish to guard against the update anomalies discussed previously in this chapter. Given that data normalization divides starting data models into many single themed tables, a standard normal form EDW Integration layer can contain hundreds of tables, becoming a time-consuming challenge for the EDW team to design, populate with data, and then maintain.

In the standard approach, the Presentation layer reverses the data normalization of the Integration layer. Whereas the measure and qualifier attributes are typically spread across scores of tables in the Integration layer, the Presentation layer thematically reduces the information down to a few dozen fact and dimension tables. As shown in Figure 12.23, the Presentation layer surrounds each fact table with consolidated dimension tables, making it easy for end users to "slice and dice" metrics by the business attributes that qualify them. Each fact table represents a coherent set of measures for the enterprise, such as sales, revenue, or shipment numbers. Each fact record is stamped with foreign keys that link it to records in the dimensional tables that provide context for each value provided. The dimension tables typically contain textual qualifiers that allow the facts in a table to be divided into steadily smaller subsets, allowing the end users to "drill drown" to groups or specific instances of business notions such as a given product, department, or sales agent.

EDW teams choose to transform and store Integration-layer data into the simplified structures of the Presentation layer for multiple reasons. The first reason is performance. The denormalized nature of the data means that the information has been essentially "pre-joined" for the end-user departments. Because most of the joins were executed when the data was transformed and stored in the Presentation layer, the response time to end-user queries is far faster. In fact, EDW teams strive to achieve "train of thought" performance for end-user queries, meaning that answers arrive before the user's attention wanders off the business question he or she is trying to answer. When end users construct queries against the hundreds of tables found in the Integration layer, they frequently author poorly designed queries that can sometimes take days to return an answer. If a star schema of prejoined, atomic data does not return answers quickly

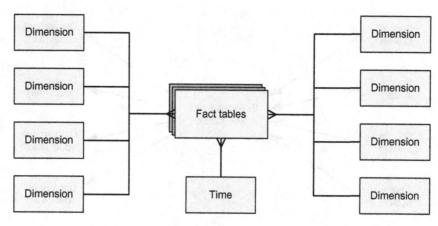

FIGURE 12.23   A schematic representation of a simple subject area in an EDW presentation layer.

enough, the DW/BI team can choose to aggregate the Integration-layer data before placing it in the Presentation-layer tables. Should the end users of aggregated star schemas eventually need the atomic detail behind these aggregates, the EDW designers can enable the front-end applications to "drill through" to the individual records stored in the Integration layer.

Second, prejoining Integration data into Presentation-layer tables allows the EDW team to ensure that the corporate information arriving to the end-user dashboards and reports has been properly assembled. Allowing the general end user to construct his own retrievals from the hundreds of tables in the Integration layer only invites him to make mistakes, sometimes double or triple counting transactions, for example. Should the business users base an important decision on a faulty analysis that the end user insists was retrieved from the data warehouse, the EDW teammates may well find themselves looking for a new job. The fact that it was the end users who put the corporate information together wrong will offer little protection. After the large amount of time and money consumed by the data warehouse development effort, executives rightly expect everything retrieved will be correct.

The last layer of the reference architecture is the Semantic layer. In essence, it provides a set of views draped over the EDW Presentation layer, and thus it typically reflects the dimensional design implemented in the Presentation layer. However, these views can impose more user-friendly names to the objects than found in the Presentation layer. It can also provide the EDW team with another level of control over how the queries pulling data from the Presentation layer will be constructed.

THE TRADITIONAL INTEGRATION LAYER AS A CHALLENGED CONCEPT

We now have all the vocabulary and concepts needed to fully discuss the data modeling paradigms from which EDW team leaders have to choose. The choice of data modeling paradigm for each layer is perhaps the greatest architectural decision that these leaders can make. More than any other decision, it will determine *by an order of magnitude* how well EDW development teams will perform, including the following:

- The speed by which the business will receive new decisions support
- The cost of establishing those capabilities
- The ease with which the warehouse can adapt to mistakes in design and new business conditions
- The long-term costs of maintaining the warehouse

Whereas EDW teams can theoretically choose to combine data modeling paradigms within each layer of the reference architecture, in practice most fast-delivery teams want to keep their architecture as simple as possible and therefore desire a single paradigm per layer. The choice of paradigm thereby takes on an "all-encompassing" importance and needs to be made carefully. To fully inform EDW project leaders so that they can make this choice well, I first present the weaknesses frequently found in the standard approach and then present two alternative data modeling paradigms. I conclude the chapter with four data-modeling "change cases" by which we can measure the advantages these alternative approaches can provide.

Involves an Expensive Hidden Layer

The standard approach is very solid in theory. In practice, however, its careful step-by-step approach leads to EDW project plans that take too long to deliver and cost far too much for even large corporations to be comfortable with. The best example of this lamentable situation during my career was when I joined an EDW project at a Fortune 50 pharmaceuticals company to help construct the "lights-out" automation of its ETL job stream. The project leaders were following the standard approach as closely as they could. Overall, this development effort had consumed 150 programmers over 3 years and required three project managers to keep it on track. In the end, the effort grew so expensive that it began to negatively affect the company's share price, and it was therefore dramatically scaled down by the board of directors. Unfortunately, this particular effort was the company's third attempt at the project, with each attempt being led by one of the major systems integrators in the field.

The previous example is only the most extreme case of many standard EDW projects I witnessed during the late 1990s and early 2000s that exploded in cost and duration beyond all reasonable bounds while delivering very little. Such evidence clearly indicates that something is wrong with the standard approach and demands that we reconsider the fundamentals of EDW projects. Many factors point to the complexity and expense of the integration layer as a major root cause for EDW project failure. Many years ago, I began asking DW/BI directors for the back-of-the-envelope cost-estimating parameters they use when considering whether to build a new EDW subject area. A director of a major telecom provided the clearest guidelines, which fall in the middle of what I have heard from many others. To build a new EDW subject area following the standard approach, he suggested allocating the program's development budget as follows:

- 30 percent for constructing the data extract routines that load the Landing layer
- 50 percent for building the Integration layer
- 20 percent for developing the Presentation and Semantic layers

Although these figures are rough planning guidelines that must be adapted for the specifics of any given project, one aspect of them should cause DW/BI professionals to seriously question our standard approach: The Integration layer consumes approximately half of an EDW project.

Data architects are fond of saying that the internal design of a warehouse is a technical decision. That frame of mind frequently leads EDW professionals into a blindness of hubris that can seriously affect their careers. Consider the reference architecture from the perspective of the project's business sponsor: "You mean adding an 'Integration layer' to my data warehouse is going to *double* the cost of this project? Then forget it. Find another way to build the warehouse." The situation is equivalent to a patient having to make a choice over a major surgery. He does not have the medical training of the surgeon, so he should not have to evaluate competing surgical techniques on his own. On the other hand, it is *his body and his life* under discussion, so his input truly counts. Just as surgeons have a responsibility to seek out all the best options for their patients and explain them clearly, EDW project leaders need to be familiar with the full spectrum of DW/BI architectural choices and present the advantages and disadvantages to their business sponsors so their customers can make an informed decision regarding their budgets and outcomes.

Results are Difficult to Understand

DW/BI data architects often claim that the standard approach is optimal because carefully designed Integration layers fully document the realities of the organization sponsoring the data warehouse. Unfortunately, the value of this documentation rarely lives up to these high expectations.

The standard approach calls for an extensively normalized and generalized data model before the programmers can begin coding the ETL modules. Creating such a detailed specification requires the developers to ask a myriad of questions, leading data architects to believe that the modeling process ferrets out the hidden entities and relationships at work within the business. With this in-depth research invested, they believe that the data model and the data that is eventually stored in the specified structures will essentially represent *the truth* of the business.

Data architects cite many advantages to possessing such a complete and well-documented notion of a company's truth. Supposedly, business and technical staff members can refer to it to accurately understand the company's information requirements. Its clarity will allow developers to better validate their designs with business experts before coding begins, allowing them to build more accurate information systems. With well-validated models, all the business's fundamental data items will be included in the data warehouse, and the team will have prevented situations in which they need to restructure a warehouse due to a requirements oversight or a design error. Because normalization has removed the model's redundancy and because generalization has endowed it with adaptable entities, the EDW team will be able to support future requirements by simply adding new classes of transactions that simply reference those fundamentals. If only documenting the truth was equivalent to making it understandable to everyone.

During my 20 years of observing and working with the standard approach, the data model for an EDW never lives up to these promises. First, the fully normalized and generalized data models are simply too big to understand. Many of them exceed what can fit on plotter-sized paper. Second, despite the care that data architects use to build these models, the results are still too detailed and technical for business people to comprehend. Even the technical members of an EDW team will struggle to understand a typical Integration-layer data model. They can usually follow narrow portions of it after careful study, but in practice only the few developers who spend months working with the model are able to appraise the impact of the design changes a new business requirement demands. In practice, these models do not provide the clarity data architects expect. Without clarity, the organization cannot validate the model, allowing oversights and errors to creep into the EDW design. The developers must make their best guess when they build the ETL and discover the modeling mistakes many months later when the end users object to the nature of the data displayed on their dashboards.

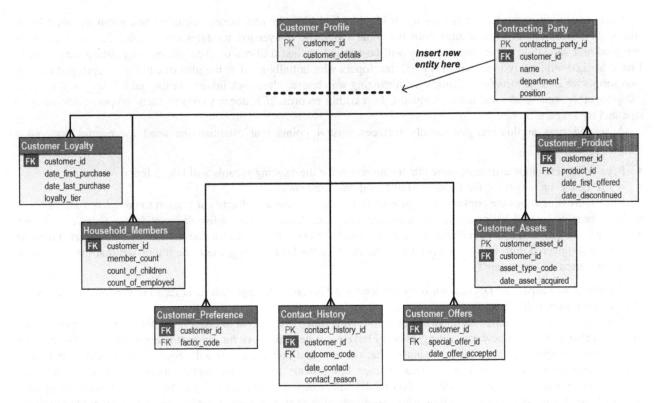

FIGURE 12.24   Standard normal form models are brittle in the face of changing requirements.

These observations do not suggest that EDW teams should forego modeling their projects before programming the ETL. However, with regard to evaluating alternative architectural approaches, I do not believe we can honestly insist that traditionally designed Integration layers that make up the standard approach are *intelligible*.

Entails High Maintenance Conversion Costs

Another factor that undermines the effectiveness of the standard approach is the fact that traditional integration layers never provide the insulation against future adaption costs that architects promise. Highly normalized and generalized data models require a tremendous amount of thought to be invested in every corner of the model. One might think that such an investment would future proof a model, but it in fact only makes it more brittle to requirements changes and design oversights. Figure 12.24 illustrates the type of brittleness implicit in highly engineered Integration layers that employ data models in standard normal form. The tables shown represent only a small corner of an EDW logical data model, namely the customer subject area, and in fact only the portion that ties to a Customer Profile table. Consider that a business decides it must support a facilitated purchasing model for some of its major customers, making it crucial to track *who* put each deal together rather than just which company made the purchase. In this case, the impact is easy to express, as shown in the figure: The EDW team must insert a Contracting Party entity between Customer Profile and all the entities that link to it.

Unfortunately, this easily stated change in business requirements will require the development team to undertake new development and re-engineering work for eight physical tables (assuming that the physical model follows the logical model rather closely). Granted, a table and corresponding ETL must be designed, built, validated, and deployed for the new entity, Contracting Party. However, the bulk of the work involved will occur when the team turns to adapting the remaining seven tables shown in Figure 12.24 for the new join pattern this change will require. Each of those tables must be reconstructed to join via foreign key to Contracting Party rather than Customer Profile. All the data already loaded in the existing tables must then be converted so that the foreign key values will link to the correct record in the new parent table. Achieving this two-step goal unfortunately requires double development: one to update existing tables and their ETL modules and another to build a conversion script for the data already loaded into the data warehouse.

Data conversion programming is very much like building ETL for new tables, requiring just about as much labor. Although often they are programmed with the same tools, the conversion modules can require far more carefully designed and validation efforts because they will be applied against millions or even billions of existing data records. I have worked with many journeyman DW/BI developers who initially scoff at the idea of carefully developed conversion scripts for making structural changes to an existing warehouse. "Just back up the existing table," they will suggest. "Slap together some code, and throw it against the existing records. If it doesn't convert them properly, restore from tape and try it again."

A second pass at this analysis usually surfaces several points that establish the need for careful conversion programming:

- Back-of-the-envelope estimates show that a conversion for the existing records will take a few days to run.
- It will take even longer for the business staff to validate the results.
- How many times does the conversion team want to sit and wait for a multiday conversion to complete running?
- How many times will business users put aside what they are doing to spend a few days validating a conversion run?
- What if the business and IT make only a half-hearted business rules validation and defects in the converted data set are not discovered until many months later? Who in IT or the business is going to be impressed that the data has to be converted all over again?

If there is any aspect of DW/BI that does not lend itself to an agile approach, it is data conversions during model changes for traditionally structured integration layers.

The previous analysis raises an important question: How much does it cost to convert a table with the proper amount of care? Table 12.6 shows how my colleagues and I have estimated this work for our customers in the past. The calculation has been simplified somewhat by assuming that the new and updated tables will require 2 days of data transform programming *on average* (see line 7). This average has proven accurate for highly engineered Integration layers because data normalization tends to fill the data model with many smaller tables. We assumed only 6 hours of productive work per day to account for the usual office overhead, such as status meetings, email, and supporting other projects. The estimate is organized as a RASCI chart (responsible, accountable, supporting, consulting, and informed) to reflect the fact that most roles generally need to interact with others on the team during this type of work. The estimate takes into account tasks that must be completed just once per update effort, no matter how many separate tables are involved—that is, "shared" tasks. The remaining work items are tasks that must be completed once for each table affected by the database design change. These tables must have their structure updated and their existing data converted and loaded into the new or modified schema.

Note that careful data conversion efforts must invest time in analysis, design, test planning, and test data preparation in addition to coding, just like one would undertake for a regular, reusable ETL module. Moreover, conversion scripts must be promoted, executed, and validated at least twice—once to move them into system integration testing ("SIT") and again to move them into production usage ("PROD"). The sheer number of steps involved is one aspect that leads this estimate to a surprisingly large cost projection per table affected. Another aspect increasing the estimate is the support time required from the others in this RASCI analysis—time that might be hidden in the clutter of the average workday but that must be paid for nonetheless.

According to this estimate, converting an EDW for a design change that impacts existing tables loaded with data will involve labor for both overhead activities and tasks required on a per-table basis. The once-per-batch overhead will be approximately 7 calendar days for the developers in addition to 20 calendar days for the business staff to review the outcomes first in SIT and then in production. The per-table labor will be approximately 180 labor hours per table. EDW team leaders who multiply these hour estimates by a reasonable compensation rate for developer labor will see that the cost to re-engineer just one production warehouse table breaks into the five figures.

These numbers may come as a shock to many readers, who are invited to re-do these estimates with parameters that reflect their experience. When substituting in their own parameters, they should keep in mind that a realistic estimates must (1) reflect the time required for all the roles on the team, not just the primary actor (2) reflect careful software engineering practices for data conversion because the existing records contain valuable decision-support data that for the most part cannot be replaced; and (3) DW/BI work almost always takes far more labor than anyone anticipates. The previous sample labor forecast employs some very conservative estimates for each task. For example, the labor for creating coding specs and test data was set below the programming time, which proves true only approximately half the time in my experience. Even with these conservative numbers, the situation is clear: Re-engineering standard integration layers is an expensive and time-consuming proposition.

TABLE 12.6 Realistic Level-of-Effort Per Table for Non-Trivial EDW Re-Engineering Assignments

For tables requiring two programming days of data transform programming[2]

Presented as a RASCI chart with the following codes in the effort-by-role columns:
R: Responsible, the role for which labor hours are estimated
C: Consults (considerable involvement), participation calculated as   50 percent of responsible party's time
S: Supports (occasional involvement), participation calculated as   15 percent of responsible party's time

			RASCI & Effort in charged labor hours							Total Effort Hours	Duration	
Ln #	Tasks	Performed Once Per...	Project Architect	Business Analyst	IT Analyst	Data Modeler	Coder	Admin	Tester		IT Team[3]	Business SMEs[4]
1	Analyze and select sources	Model Change	S 1	R 6	C 3					10 hrs	1.00	
2	Create new business data model	Model Change	S 1	C 3	S 1	R 6				11 hrs	1.00	
3	Create new logical data model	Model Change	S 1	S 1	C 3	R 5				10 hrs	0.83	
4	Create new physical data model	Model Change				R 4				4 hrs	0.67	
5	Analyze existing target data	Model Change	S 3	C 10	R 20					33 hrs	3.33	
6	Author STMs[1]	Affected Table	S 2	C 6	R 12	S 2				22 hrs	2.00	
7	Data Transform Programming[2]	Affected Table			S 2	S 2	R 16		S 2	22 hrs	2.67	
8	Author test cases	Affected Table	S 1	C 3	C 3	C 3	C 3		R 6	19 hrs	1.00	
9	Write test scripts	Affected Table			S 1	S 1	R 4		S 1	7 hrs	0.67	
10	Create test data	Affected Table		C 3	C 3	C 3	R 6		C 3	18 hrs	1.00	
11	Validate test scripts in DEV	Affected Table		S 1	C 3	C 3	C 3		R 6	16 hrs	1.00	
12	Promote to SIT	Affected Table			S 0	S 0	C 1	R 2		3 hrs	0.33	
13	Execute scripts	Affected Table					S 0	R 2		2 hrs	0.33	
14	Drive IT's conversion validation	Affected Table	S 1	S 1	C 2	S 1	S 1		R 4	10 hrs	0.67	
15	Support business' validation	Affected Table		R 6						6 hrs	1.00	10 days
16	Document errors	Affected Table		C 3	R 6	C 3	C 3			15 hrs	1.00	
17	Promote scripts to PROD	Affected Table			S 0	S 0	C 1	R 2		3 hrs	0.33	
18	Execute scripts	Affected Table					S 0	R 2		2 hrs	0.33	
19	Drive IT's conversion validation	Affected Table	S 1	S 1	C 3	S 1	S 1		R 6	13 hrs	1.00	
20	Support business' validation	Affected Table		R 8						8 hrs	1.33	10 days
21	Document errors	Affected Table		C 3	R 6	C 3	C 3			15 hrs	1.00	
	Per-model-change task totals (Lines 1-5)		6 hrs	20 hrs	27 hrs	15 hrs	0 hrs	0 hrs	0 hrs	**68 hrs**	7 days	20 days
	Per-affected-table time totals (Lines 6-21)		5 hrs	35 hrs	41 hrs	22 hrs	42 hrs	8 hrs	28 hrs	**181 hrs**	16 days	

[1] Source-to-Target Maps
[2] The average programming effort on a past project of the author's for an EDW with many hundred tables, large and small. Represents ETL programming for new tables, conversion scripting for existing tables.
[3] Reflects how many days the longest task will take, assuming that team members work on that task   6   hours per day.
[4] Task duration for business Subject Matter Experts to validate IT work, shared across all table involved.

Given these costs, it can be seen why companies that depend on the standard approach become extremely reluctant to change the design of an existing data warehouse in the face of changing business requirements. This reluctance in turn leads organizations to believe they must model the EDW integration layer perfectly and make it completely future proof before ETL coding begins. If the model has to be perfect before programming starts, DW/BI management will naturally emphasize a big data model up front—the antithesis of agile development. Clearly, agile EDW leaders need to find an alternative to standard normal form Integration layers if they wish to incrementally deliver data warehouses that can economically adapt to changing business needs.

"STRAIGHT-TO-STAR" AS A CONTROVERSIAL ALTERNATIVE

Many people who have considered the weaknesses of the standard approach have suggested instead that data be taken straight from the Landing area into the star schema of the Presentation layer. In the standard approach, the Integration layer is summarized and then projected into the Presentation layer's dimensional model. An option promoted by the Kimball group is to instead use the star schema to store the atomic data in dimensional form [Kimball and Ross 2013]. In this approach, the data is pulled directly from the Landing area and dimensionalized as loaded, after which the Landing data is discarded. The Kimball group urges EDW designers to consider "conforming" the dimensions and facts. At the atomic level, a conformed warehouse in this approach contains only one version of each dimension which should be linked to all fact tables that can make use of it. The fact tables within the multiple subject areas should be defined so that they can link to these reusable dimensional tables (also known as "qualifiers").

To be fair, the thought leaders in the Kimball group do state that some normalized helper tables might make data transformation easier where the business rules governing conformed objects get complex [Becker 2007]. However, they generally believe that the effort needed to build a large Integration layer, with its standard normal form data models, is an unnecessary expense. They find it pointless to place the company information in a data repository that few can understand and query. Although disk space is declining in price, they also point out that it is not inexpensive. They ask why an EDW program should have to pay for the storage required to hold a preliminary copy of the data that provides no immediate decision support directly to the BI user.

Standard approach advocates have some powerful rebuttals to the Kimball group's position, so neither approach is clearly superior in all situations. First, a dimensional model—with its fact tables linked to the dimensions—tends to support specific patterns of analysis. The star schema's design in effect presupposes the questions the business will be able to ask of the warehouse. The value of a specific pattern of analysis lasts only as long as the business confronts the same challenges day after day. The minute business requirements change for a new product, a new competitor, or a new regulation, a different analysis will be required, making some or all of the current star schemas obsolete.

Second, when a team must update the design of a star schema, it will have to convert the existing information so that it can be loaded into the new tables. Transforming the data from one star schema to another requires breaking the information into small, independent pieces and reassembling them to match the new patterns of analysis. That decomposition process will in fact require a third to fifth normal form model, so why not permanently keep the data in such a format from the start so that the EDW team can meet new requirements by simply reprojecting Integration-layer information into new star schemas as they become necessary?

Third, consider the star schema model in the middle panel of Figure 12.4, which we examined previously. By definition, "conformed dimensions" implies that a Kimball-style warehouse will contain tables to which many other tables connect. Change the design of one of these shared tables, and the EDW team will be knee-deep again into an expensive data conversion effort for all of the related tables, just as we estimated previously. No major advantage has been secured by skipping the Integration layer.

This analysis is essentially the infamous Inmon–Kimball debate that has been simmering for decades without much advantage gained by either side. What this debate overlooks is that both design approaches suffer from the same weakness—one cannot truly future proof a data model against all the unanticipated changes that a business will experience in the years ahead. There is no way to design against Donald Rumsfeld's "unknown unknowns" [U.S. Department of Defense 2002]. EDW teams following either the standard approach or the conformed dimensional strategy will find themselves paying heavily for data conversion work when the supported business operations must evolve. The data warehousing industry does not need an answer to the Inmon–Kimball debate. It needs a totally new approach to data modeling that can cut through the Gorgon's knot of data conversion.

FOUR CHANGE CASES FOR APPRAISING A DATA MODELING PARADIGM

Converting the information contained in an enterprise data warehouse is arduous and expensive if the EDW's design employs either form of the traditional data modeling paradigms. The solution to this unfortunate situation is to utilize a different data modeling technique—an adaptable one that allows data warehouses to evolve as fast as business conditions change.

Fortunately, agile data engineering provides two alternatives to the traditional data modeling paradigms—alternatives that allow teams to economically adapt EDW data repositories in the face of unfolding business requirements, even after those repositories are full of many years of transaction records. So that readers can appreciate that these alternative data repositories are far less expensive to evolve and therefore enable truly agile enterprise data warehousing, I examine and quantify in the discussions ahead the cost of updating an EDW using four common "change cases." These change cases reflect some of the surprise requirements that DW/BI programs must contend with the most. The effort required to accommodate these change cases is analyzed using the cost estimates for new and updated tables presented in Table 12.6. Table 12.7 shows the likely labor time and re-engineering costs incurred by these four change cases under the traditional modeling approaches.

Change Case 1: Correcting Fourth Normal Form Errors

The first change case will be the fourth normal form correction that was used to illustrate data normalization previously in this chapter (see Figure 12.15). Enterprise data warehouses frequently confront the situation in which a simple business notion such as Ad Site or Promotions becomes more important or complex over time. As the developers must steadily add more attributes to an existing table to support new versions of such an item, they can realize that the notion clearly has a life of its own, independent of the theme of the table in which it is located. This situation can easily become a multivalue dependency with two or more independently varying, embedded entities, such as we saw when we considered a fourth normal form violation. At this point, the attributes for each component of the multivalued dependency should be removed from the original table and relocated to a separate entity.

In our normalization example, the Ad Manager, Ad Site, and Promotions all had to be broken out into separate entities, requiring five new tables to support three new entities and the two associations between them. (See Table 12.3.) In addition, the Sales Order Header table needed its foreign key for Sales Channel converted into three different foreign keys for the new entity tables. Although in this example, the items migrating to new tables were only one attribute apiece, in real EDWs most entity split outs can involve dozens of attributes. If we focus instead on situations in which the entities to be split out involve tables complex enough to require on average two ETL programming days each, we can use the estimating parameters established previously to forecast the expense and elapsed time for accomplishing this design change.

Table 12.7 employs the per-table and once-per-effort labor forecasts from Table 12.6 to estimate the investment a company will need to make for each of the four change cases, resulting in a quantitative contrast of the traditional and agile data modeling paradigms. Using those parameters, correcting the fourth normal form violation described previously will require creating five new tables and the re-engineering of a third, which will exceed 1100 total team hours and $140,000 (2015 dollars). Moreover, as detailed in the last column of Table 12.6, this work will also entail two reviews by the business stakeholders taking 10 days of elapsed time each—if IT is fortunate to be working with a business department that is reasonably responsive.

An important downstream impact of the contemplated design change is missing from both this estimate and the one for Change Case 2. The Integration layer represents a source system for the Presentation layer so that when EDW teams alter the design of their Integration layers, they typically must update the ETL to the Presentation layer's star schemas as well. The estimates for the standard-normal-form change cases omit this work item because an EDW's particular design will determine how much Presentation-layer work will be required. In cases in which the Integration layer is projected to the Presentation layer via database views, the team may be able to mask out most of the impact of the new design on the star schemas using simple updates to those views. If ETL modules with complex business rules load the Presentation layer, then updating these data transforms may be as expensive to accomplish as the Integration-layer changes. The change cases assume the former case, in which Integration-layer changes can be hidden behind easy modifications to database views. Even with this simplification in place, these estimates for Change Case 1 should make one fact very clear: Making even simple changes to an existing data warehouse based on the standard approach is neither fast nor cheap.

Change Case 2: Generalizing to the Party Model

The second, more extensive change case comes from our generalization study, namely the effort required to consolidate four business entities into the party model. The starting point for this change case is the situation depicted in Figure 12.18, which, after conversion, arrives at the model depicted in Figure 12.21. EDW teams frequently face situations such as this, especially when they realize they have drastically underestimated how many different people and organizations play a role in their organization's business processes. In the case considered here, the EDW had believed that there were only two parties involved in the demand channel and two in the supply channel. New regulations or

TABLE 12.7 Summary of Re-Engineering Labor for Four Change Cases when Using a Traditionally Modeled Modeling Paradigm

Implied re-engineering costs for four common DW/BI change case

Per table estimates		
Blended hourly rate across roles for expenses:	$125	

IT Activities	Effort	Expense
Per conversion	68 hrs	$8,500
Per affected table	181 hrs	$22,625

Standard normal form

	#1: 4NF Correction			#2: Party model		
IT Activities	Tables	Effort	Expense	Tables	Effort	Expense
Per conversion		68 hrs	$8,500		68 hrs	$8,500
Per affected table	6	1,086 hrs	$135,750	8	1,448 hrs	$181,000
Total		1,154 hrs	$144,250		1,516 hrs	$189,500

Conformed dimensional form: Minimal case[1]

	#3: New SCD trigger			#4: Change of grain		
	Tables	Effort	Expense	Tables	Effort	Expense
Per conversion		68 hrs	$8,500		68 hrs	$8,500
Per affected table	2	362 hrs	$45,250	4	724 hrs	$90,500
Total		430 hrs	$53,750		792 hrs	$99,000

Conformed dimensional form: Typical case[2]

	#3: New SCD trigger			#4: Change of grain		
IT Activities	Tables	Effort	Expense	Tables	Effort	Expense
Per conversion		68 hrs	$8,500		68 hrs	$8,500
Per affected table	11	1,991 hrs	$248,875	13	2,353 hrs	$294,125
Total		2,059 hrs	$257,375		2,421 hrs	$302,625

[1] Assumes affected fact tables as shown in Figure 12.25

[2] Assumes ten fact tables affected by the change in dimension tables

business conditions such as social networking or software-as-a-service can quickly introduce additional players into a company's business model. Sensing this, the EDW team decided it was time to invest in generalization so that future roles can be accommodated with less programming. As can be discovered from studying the diagrams used previously, such a change will require the following:

- Creating five new tables: party, party role, party role type, party role rollup, and party role rollup type
- Converting four tables in order to subsume their data into the new party tables: customer, contract agent, installer, and manufacturer
- Converting two further tables so that their foreign keys now link to the party tables: sales order and line item

Even for an EDW data model as simple as the one used here (one transaction table involved), the company should expect to invest more than 1500 development hours and more than \$175,000. Our example assumes that only the sales subject area will be affected. In most EDWs, however, the entities being moved into the party model here would link to many other subject areas, so the amounts forecasted here vastly underestimate the cost of this design change. It can be seen from the parameters employed for Table 12.7 that each additional table referencing the party roles will require approximately 180 labor hours and cost \$22,000 to complete.

Party is not the only central entity found in the typical enterprise data warehouse. Products, geographies, and processes are other notions that DW/BI teams frequently realize must be generalized in the data model. Given these cost estimates for making such conversions after the first version of the EDW is built and loaded, one can understand why (1) data modelers using traditional data modeling paradigms want their designs to be perfect before ETL programming begins and (2) so many companies choose to just patch their existing EDWs with single-purpose "outrigger" tables rather than re-engineering them correctly when requirements change. Because both practices are the antithesis of agility for enterprise business intelligence programs, EDW team leaders need to find an alternative to the standard approach if they want their companies to remain competitive.

Change Case 3: New Trigger Attribute for a Slowly Changing Dimension

The third change case involves a common update required for teams that have chosen a Kimball-style conformed dimensional approach that takes operational data straight from a landing area into a star schema. When first designing a Kimball-style warehouse, the EDW team must choose the columns of each slowly changing dimension table that will trigger the creation of a new history record for a given business key. When the ETL application detects a new value in a "trigger attribute," it marks the existing record in the repository as "retired" and inserts a new record with updated values for all attributes. Most designers avoid making every column a change trigger so that the ETL is not constantly creating updates, eating up processing horsepower and storage space just to track the history on the attributes of lesser interest. Such discretion entails risk, however, because often business stakeholders will approach the EDW after the data warehouse is in production to ask that history be tracked on an attribute that they had originally claimed was unimportant. Moreover, they will not be satisfied with accumulating history records going forward but, rather, will want this change to be implemented with as much prior history loaded as possible. Because more history means a proliferation of records in the dimension table, many existing links between the fact table and the outdated dimension records will have to be updated in order to honor this request.

Figure 12.25 provides the starting dimensional model for the two change cases we will consider for data warehouses that follow the conformed dimensional approach. Change Case 3 focuses on the work required to expand the set of attributes in the Vendor table that cause a Type 2 slowly changing dimension update. In this scenario, the business did not originally believe the company needed to track changes in the CAGE code that the federal government assigns to manufacturers. However, the executives decided recently that CAGE codes provide a tracking mechanism that can sometimes allow the company to offer better discounts than would be warranted by transaction histories assembled by other company identifiers such as name or location. In order to understand a company by its CAGE code, the sales team will now need the warehouse to provide the full history of this newly important attribute.

Examining the logical model in Figure 12.25 reveals that answering this change request will require updating two tables: Vendor and Expense event. Vendor will have to be converted when the EDW team draws upon any archived landing data still on backup media in order to backfill as much history as possible. The net result will be a noticeable increase in the number of Vendor records. Records in the Expense Events table will have to be re-keyed in order to link to the new set of surrogate keys that the conversion of the Vendor table will create.

For both conformed dimensional form change cases, Table 12.7 summarizes the cost of performing this change case under two scenarios. The first is the minimal case in which we assume that the impact of the new design can only affect tables shown in Figure 12.25. Although the minimal case is possible, it is not realistic because both the

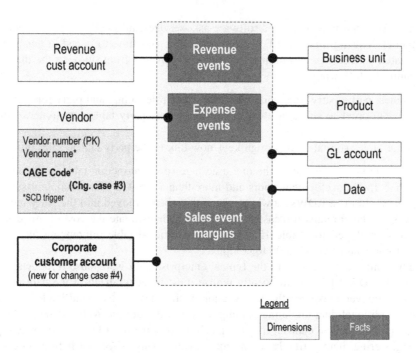

FIGURE 12.25   Change Cases #3 and #4 for conformed dimensional form model.

design changes contemplated here affect dimensions tables with widespread presence in enterprise data warehouse employing conformed dimensions. To make the estimates more typical, the second scenario assumes that changes to the Vendor and Corporate Customer Account dimensions will affect 10 fact tables, and it increases the labor projections accordingly.

As totaled in Table 12.7, converting two tables in order to meet this simple change request and retrofitting multiple fact tables for the change will involve more than 2000 developer hours and cost $250,000. Given the fact that the conformed dimensional form strives to reuse dimension tables as much as possible, re-engineering even a modestly important dimension can easily impact dozens of tables. Of course, the cost of this design change depends heavily on how many fact tables will have to be updated given the new design of the conformed dimension. EDW team leaders should take to heart that altering a conformed dimension has a large ripple effect within a data warehouse following the conformed dimensional approach. The large number estimated previously underscores what I have observed many times during my years of consulting: The savings that Kimball school adherents claim will be garnered by following the conformed dimensional approach largely disappear when one considers the cost of *maintaining* rather than simply *building* an EDW.

This change case began when the customer requested an additional history trigger for the conformed dimension. Although the EDW team would like to know all the history triggers the business will require over the life of the data warehouse, such insight is unlikely, so their choices over the long term will be limited to the following:

- Make every column a trigger (which will lead to far more programming of the original ETL modules)
- Get used to making these expensive changes as new triggers are needed
- Refuse to make such model changes due to the high expense and allow the warehouse to become increasingly unaligned with business needs

Because none of these choices are attractive, EDW team leaders will want to find a more agile data modeling paradigm than the conformed dimensional approach.

Change Case 4: Changing a Fact Table's Grain

Change Case 4 represents another common update scenario required of data warehouses based on conformed dimensions without an integration layer. Changing business conditions often require that the EDW create a new shared dimension. This additional dimension can provide a new means of slicing and dicing existing fact tables. Should this new avenue of decomposition provide a more detailed or a completely unrelated level of analysis, the additional dimension will require a change of grain for all existing fact tables to which it links.

Figure 12.25 also depicts the situation in which a company was interested in product-oriented analyses. Accordingly, the data warehouse's first design linked the fact tables to the account numbers found in the operational systems of each business unit. Later, the business realized that it would not be able to reduce customer churn until it started understanding the consumer. The EDW sponsor requested that DW/BI add a corporate-level Customer dimension that consolidates consumer information across the conglomerate, uniting the multiple account numbers a given customer might have. Such consolidated information will allow corporate analysts to retrieve a "360-degree" view of the customer, allowing the company to offer better discounts and, it is hoped, to reveal what makes some large customer leave.

As Figure 12.25 indicates, such a change will require that a new dimension table be added for Customer, and the foreign keys of all three fact tables be updated, so one new table and three table conversions will be necessary. Fortunately, the EDW in this hypothetical case has kept 3 months of landing data on active backup tapes, so the developers will be able to generate some prior history for each customer. This work will require updating the existing Customer records in order to capture as many acquisition and merger events among those parties as possible. As summarized in Table 12.7, fully analyzing, coding, validating, and deploying these changes against even this small, Kimball-style data warehouse once it is in production will require approximately 2400 developer hours and cost more than $300,000.

Again, this estimate was compiled assuming 10 impacted fact tables. A team may actually need to update fewer fact tables than assumed, but the shared dimensions most vulnerable to changes as business conditions evolve are precisely those that most fact tables employ, such as customer, vendors, product, and geographies. Large dimensional enterprise warehouses can hold hundreds of tables, with the core dimensions linking to nearly every fact table in the data model. Moreover, dimension tables can require more than one version in order to accommodate the business nuances frequently found in heavily used business entities such as customer, product, and geography. Telecommunications companies, for example, are frequently vexed by the fact that the early versions of their decision support systems failed to distinguish between *billing address* and *service address* but that marketing and network engineering analysts eventually insist that the distinction is crucial. Performance considerations can also require multiple versions of both dimensions and facts because analyses that employ less detail run far faster if they pull data from preaggregated fact tables joined to preaggregated versions of each major dimension.

All told, a simple change in grain as illustrated previously can easily impact 50–60 fact tables in an established enterprise warehouse with conformed dimensions, making a more reasonable estimate for updating the BI applications many times larger than the figure I have calculated for this change case. Advocates of Kimball-style EDWs often claim that their approach leads to agile data warehouses, but given the estimates provided by the previous analysis, there is little reason to believe that this claim can be proven. With such high maintenance costs for even simple feature requests, sponsors and DW/BI management may well refuse to update even a Kimball-style data warehouse when changing business conditions demand it, leading to an EDW with a design increasingly at odds with business needs. For this reason, EDW team leaders need to find an agile alternative to the conformed dimensional approach. As we will see in the coming chapters, hyper-modeled paradigms provide precisely the alternative approaches that agile EDW teams desire.

SUMMARY

Every EDW team starting upon a new warehouse or major subject area is at a crossroads where they must choose to follow either traditional data modeling techniques or one of the new agile approaches. To understand the advantages of the agile techniques that are demonstrated in the following chapters, EDW team leaders must first understand the weaknesses of the two traditional approaches: standard normal forms and conformed dimensional forms.

The standard normal form implies a very traditionally structured data warehouse, one with an Integration layer and a Presentation layer. Designers will model a traditional Integration layer with tables in third, fourth, or fifth normal form. ETL will load this normalized Integration layer first before transforming it again to populate the star schemas of the Presentation layer, which better support user-friendly BI applications. The conformed dimensional data warehouse skips building much or all of the Integration layer in order to load the company's operational data directly into star schemas.

Both of these modeling approaches lead to data warehouses that are very expensive to modify once data is loaded into their data repositories, making them brittle in the face of changing business requirements. In order to provide a data warehouse that can evolve as fast as the business context can change, EDW team leaders will need to draw upon an agile approach to DW/BI design. The alternative delivery and data modeling techniques that will make such "agile data engineering" possible are presented later, but in the next chapter we first consider some provisional agile solutions that can be achieved even without adopting a new data modeling technique.

Chapter 13

Surface Solutions Using Data Virtualization and Big Data

A primary challenge to agile delivery of business intelligence applications is the complexity of the data warehousing/ business intelligence (DW/BI) architecture. As we explored in Chapter 12, delivering clean, integrated, and standardized data for the enterprise requires several distinct data layers, all requiring their own type of data schema and extract, transform, and load (ETL) transformations. These requirements give rise to the typical DW/BI reference architecture that contains separate layers for landing, integration, presentation, semantics, and end-user applications. However, the fact that the reference architecture contains multiple layers does not mean that every strand of data must land in each data layer as it progresses from the source applications to the end user's dashboard. Insisting that enterprise data warehousing (EDW) applications persist data in each of these layers without exception from the very beginning of a project will easily undermine agile's goal of early and repeated delivery of value to the customer.

Even without resorting to new data modeling techniques, EDW team leaders can greatly improve their speed of delivery and end-user satisfaction by employing a strategy that I call "surface solutions with architectural backfilling." With this strategy, the EDW team delivers a provisional application that, considered from the surface, looks like a business solution or an important piece of one. In reality, this provisional application utilizes just one or two layers of the reference architecture and skips the rest. Of course, the developers need to eventually provide a fully governed and reliable corporate information asset, so this surface solution approach simply buys them some time to define and construct a more robust version of the application. Although the surface solution may soon be replaced with a more complete application, the end users see at least a quick, partial answer to their pressing business needs, and then a steady stream of improved capabilities that address whatever information gaps the users may have found in the first few deliveries. This surface solution with subsequent backfilling of the architecture looks *agile* to the business consumer, allowing the EDW team to both learn quickly and achieve high levels of customer satisfaction.

Agile EDW teams can pursue surface solutions in three ways, listed here in the order of increasing completeness:

- Leveraging a business department's shadow information technology (IT)
- Data virtualization servers
- Big data technologies

These three strategies couple well with the hyper modeled data design techniques that are discussed in detail in the next two chapters. Hyper modeling enables teams to build a full data warehouse more quickly than traditional methods, but the process still takes significant time. In contrast, surface solutions allow super-fast delivery of applications, but those deliveries must address a smaller scope of requirements. Frequently, EDW teams employ surface solutions to provide an immediate answer to a few key business problems and then use that provisional application to learn about the project's full spectrum of requirements in greater depth. With more complete requirements in hand, they then employ hyper modeling techniques to construct a complete solution that addresses not only a fuller range of the business's functional needs but also the system's nonfunctional requirements.

EDW teams will benefit from adding surface solutions to their bag of tricks because even in areas where this approach provides only a temporary fix, it blazes the trail that the fully engineered solutions should follow. Moreover, there are some situations in which the surface solution works well enough for specific business problems that they can be converted into production systems, answering customer needs inexpensively and thus freeing up EDW resources for work on features for which more labor-intensive approaches are absolutely necessary.

LEVERAGING SHADOW IT

The first and simplest approach to surface solutions and architectural backfilling involves no new technology whatsoever. This technique requires only that the DW/BI developers join forces with the appropriate shadow IT resources in order to quickly solve crucial business problems. This approach is a dynamic strategy involving several subreleases, each of which buys the EDW team more time to build a better solution, simultaneously identifying for the developers improved business and technical requirements. In essence, this approach is a collaborative discovery process that provides usable solutions with every step in the learning cycle.

The company for which I first suggested this approach was an online game publisher that owned many of the most popular electronic game titles at the time. This company's medium- and long-term revenue depended on its customers feeling challenged just enough at each point in a game's design. Places in the game where characters repeatedly died had to be detected and designed out of the play path lest customers decide it was impossible to win and abandon the product for another company's game. High-challenge locations could also be addressed by placing a bottle of magic potion or an all-powerful sword within the game player's view. The players needed only to pay for the instant solution to surpass the obstacles and adversaries confronting them. These pay-as-you-go shortcuts represented a significant revenue stream, but they could also backfire if not designed and monitored carefully because too many of them could make the customer feel fleeced rather than entertained.

Like most online games, the actual events took place upon centralized servers, leaving the player's workstations to serve as display consoles linked to the company's servers via the Internet. This architecture gave the company great flexibility in that it could bring in a dozen or so programmers and completely re-engineer the game over the span of 10 days or so, deploying the new version back to "the cloud." Naturally, after investing in several weeks of round-the-clock programming, the design and finance groups wanted to know immediately whether the changes were improving customer satisfaction and company revenue.

Unfortunately, the speed with which the company could change its products created a particularly stiff challenge for the DW/BI department. When the product managers re-engineered a game, they essentially restructured most of DW/BI's data sources, usually breaking a large portion of the company's ETL modules. To reprogram the majority of the warehouse's ETL was a multimonth proposition, but DW/BI's corporate customers were willing to wait only a week or two for their answers.

Example of a Five-Step Collaborative Effort

Figure 13.1 sketches an approach based on surface solutions and architectural backfilling that resolved this impasse. This diagram shows that the full solution was delivered in five subreleases, the first four of which relied heavily on the interim solutions provided by "shadow IT"—that is, computer-empowered data analysts and front-end tool programmers employed by the end-user business departments rather than corporate IT. Readers who are familiar with the requirements management strategies presented in Part III of this book will see in Figure 13.1 a steady progression through the BI end-user's hierarchy of needs.

The surface solution begins when the EDW team, confronted with a large programming assignment and impatient end users, simply lands the new source data onto the warehouse servers with Subrelease 1. EDW team leaders have equipped the department data miners with an associative query engine (similar to the type of tool that was recommended for "data cowboys" in Chapter 11) along with selective access to this raw source data. With this tool and access, the end-user departments can at least see and process for themselves the new click stream data that the updated game servers have started to provide.

Upon providing this access to the shadow IT staff, the EDW project leaders warned the departmental analysts not to overinvest in their front-end applications because very soon that temporary solution would be replaced with another offering more data and greater capabilities. The EDW team leaders also only provided access to 1% of the game events so that no one can claim to have possession yet of the whole truth. However, even that small percentage of the source was enough to let the data miners begin asking some fundamental questions and provide company executives with a notion on whether the new game design was achieving its goals.

With the small dose of new data provided with Subrelease 1, the shadow IT analysts spent several happy weeks writing new analyses and reports, taking the pressure off of EDW to deliver a full solution immediately. The EDW team leaders used this time to observe the applications that the shadow IT staff created, gathering for their data warehousing teammates some very accurate solution requirements. The EDW team also used this time to build the next surface solution.

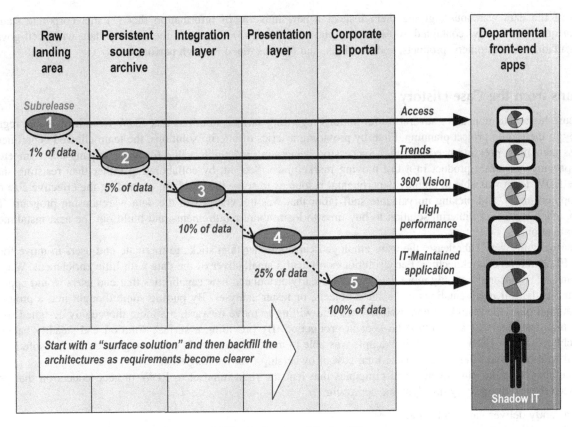

FIGURE 13.1 A surface solution with architectural backfilling that leverages "Shadow IT".

For Subrelease 2, the EDW team leaders updated their persistent source archive for the sources data sitting in the Raw Landing layer. The team leaders communicated to the shadow IT analysts that access to the landing area was going to disappear so they should start "rolling their front applications forward" to utilize the new data that would be available in the next layer of the reference architecture. So that the shadow IT would not rebel against this change, the EDW team leaders offered two new features: a fivefold increase in the amount of data available (to 5% of the click stream) and the historical capabilities that the Persistent Source Archive provided. The history capabilities of this layer would allow shadow IT to analyze and report on *trends* in player behavior rather than just summarizing current activity.

These new capabilities again kept the shadow IT analysts happily engaged with creating new data visualizations for weeks, during which the EDW team again observed the new development for solutions requirements and used the time to build out the next surface solution. With Subrelease 3, EDW instructed shadow IT analysts to once again roll their front-end applications forward to the Integration layer, where they would now be able to construct 360° views of customers and products while receiving doubling in the amount of data available. As the departmental analysts expanded and created applications to employ this larger universe of information, the EDW team leaders gathered further solution requirements by watching usage patterns. They also used the time to bring the new data into the star schemas of their data warehouse's Presentation layer.

When the Presentation layer was finally re-engineered, the EDW team leads initiated Subrelease 4, where end users would find the data in a dimensional model. Once this next solution was ready, they asked shadow IT to connect their front-end applications to the Presentation layer, where analysts would find more than twice the information as before, as well as the ability to slice and dice game events using the multidimensional features of their visualization tools.

By again noting new usages and adding them to all the observations made during the three earlier subreleases, the EDW team was able at this time to compile a comprehensive list of requirements. The team used the full requirements list to construct a new version of the company's official BI portal. Because this well-guided BI update had finally back-filled all of the architectural layers, it was no longer a surface solution but instead a full and robust application for the enterprise. This version was therefore promoted not as a subrelease but, rather, as the next full release of the corporate analytics application. With this last step, EDW team leaders announced they would be removing access to intermediate layers of the data warehouse, giving them instead a new universe of information that (1) met corporate standards of data quality; (2) now contained 100% of the player activity; (3) integrated the activity data with well-governed representations of customers, products, and locations; and (4) was tuned for high performance.

Lessons from the Case History

This case history demonstrates several useful notions regarding surface solutions that EDW team leaders can regularly employ in their agile project planning. First, by providing a series of interim solutions, the team allowed departments to address their most pressing needs in quick succession, generating incredible value for any company that competes via an improving consumer product in a fast-moving marketplace. Second, by collaborating rather than resisting shadow IT, the EDW team was able to employ departmental resources to solve the problem, expanding the effective size of the development team, and picking up valuable staff labor that was not charged to the data warehousing program. Third, the approach used every interim solution to buy time to learn about requirements and build out the next installment in the application.

Finally, with every subrelease, the team employed carrots rather than sticks to motivate end users to move forward in the EDW reference architecture. Early solutions only had a small sliver of the data with little enrichment. With later solutions, EDW offered not only more data but also clearly articulated new capabilities that end users would appreciate such as trends, full representations of business objects, or faster analyses. By putting some thought into a progressive motivational plan, the team kept end users excited and willing to move forward to a more thoroughly designed solution rather than insisting that a prototype be kept in production. By providing a surface solution and steadily backfilling the architecture, the EDW team in this example was able to meet its customer's conflicting needs for fast solutions that are still well built and offering reasonable total cost of ownership over the long term.

Note also the agile philosophies and principles that lent the right mindset to EDW project leaders on that project that made them willing to try this dynamic approach:

- Constantly deliver value to the customer.
- Seek specifications and designs that are "just good enough."
- Collaborate rather than contract with customers.
- Work in small iterations and learn as you go.

Striving for a perfect solution on the first release would have ruled out the collaborative and highly successful incremental solution described previously. The EDW team would have taken months to derive a 100% perfect vision of the new BI system needed and then, even with agile development techniques, many more months to build out the ETL with a front end that supported the new data warehouse design. The business would have waited the better part of a year to learn whether its end-product enhancement effort, which took only a few weeks to implement, had generated any positive results for the business. If the game redesign had offended and driven away customers, the company would have been entirely blind to the reasons why this occurred, able to vaguely detect the changing tide only months later through falling corporate revenues. Although the agile approach involved some extra expense to pay for multiple subreleases and some re-engineering here and there, it provided decision support in a business-reasonable time frame.

FASTER VALUE DELIVERY WITH DATA VIRTUALIZATION

The second approach to surface solutions and backfilling the data warehouse architecture involves a technology that many companies already have and that the rest should consider acquiring—data virtualization servers. The case study presented previously simply combined departmental shadow IT and a good front-end tool to provide a type of "self-service BI." As much as it pleased end users with fast answers to crucial questions, this departmentally powered solution will alarm many veteran data managers because at any point the company management might declare one of the subreleases as "good enough" and insist that DW/BI leave it in permanent production. These "production prototypes" are usually a dangerous decision because they leave unanswered many important questions, such as the following:

- What guarantees that shadow IT groups have correctly represented the company's information with their hastily assembled front ends?
- What assures the company that these new BI applications will have low ongoing maintenance requirements and can be economically enhanced for new business requirements in the future?

- Are the important analytics they provide well documented so that IT can support them when they break months later, after the folks who created them have moved on to other opportunities?

By allowing DW/BI to participate more fully in the creation of the prototypes, a data virtualization server (DVS) allows EDW teams to provide surface solutions without incurring that type of major risk. DVS can quickly deliver low-cost BI services that are reliable corporate assets, with many of them so robust that they can be safely treated as permanent analytic solutions.

Defining Data Virtualization

The major database management systems in the marketplace today all provide a handy construct called "views." A view is a logical representation of one or more tables within the database that is predefined and ready for execution whenever that particular representation is needed, making them in essence a stored query. Often, they join numerous tables together and return only a select set of columns, many of them renamed for the particular usage the designers intended to support. Creating a view is a very efficient approach to tailoring what the surface of a large database looks like to end users because they simply need to be declared. No additional data is created when a view executes. Instead, the particular combination of data that a view defines is simply assembled by the database management system (DBMS) when end users draw upon the view and is later automatically released when no longer needed. Where a run-time query can solve a business problem, views are an economical approach because they do not incur additional disk storage and thus require very little management effort.

Unfortunately for DW/BI, views are bounded to the database within which they execute. Designers can extend them somewhat by including tables linked from other databases into the FROM clause of the view's SQL declaration, but database links require additional setup and at best are limited to tables residing in databases from the same vendor. This severely limits the value of traditional views for data warehousing because they cannot be easily used to perform real-time integration services across the wide variety of source systems that typically feed into an EDW.

Data virtualization servers break down this last barrier, allowing an EDW team to create views that span many brands of databases. In fact, DVS views can span many classes of data—relational, semistructured, and unstructured. Modern database servers rely on an "optimizer" component that translates every SQL statement into a highly efficient execution plan for retrieving and assembling the data with a database. Data virtualization servers represent a "superoptimizer" that builds highly efficient execution plans that can tap information from source systems from competing vendors and widely varying data formats.

This superoptimizer provides several features that allow EDW teams to rapidly build robust, useable, and maintainable solutions for DW/BI applications and end users. First, a DVS uses SQL, allowing EDW teams to build surface solutions using this lingua franca of the database world, no matter how many different types and sources of data a given view actually draws upon. We say that the DVS *encapsulates* the organization's data, allowing it to be retrieved without any concern for where it resides, what the technical interface is, how it has been implemented, which platform it uses, and how much of it is available [van der Lans 2012, Chapter 1.3]. Encapsulation masks away all those technical details, allowing DW/BI applications and end users to work with a single simplified interface based on a language that many developers and consumers already know.

Second, DVSs provide *abstraction* for companies' enormous collection of data. As controlled by the specific definition of a given DVS view, the consumers see only the elements and rows of the data that fits their needs. The information may be presented on a detailed level or on an aggregated level, concatenated or transformed, as best suits the needs of the consuming applications and end users [van der Lans 2012, Chapter 1.6].

Third, DVS tools provide metadata management support, so that EDW can more easily review the genealogy of queries that accumulate and so that end users can understand the information they have retrieved. All told, DVSs enable EDW teams to offer data consumers a unified, simplified, and intelligible collection of integrated data through easily created data objects. Moreover, the fact that these virtual data resources are declared rather than materialized dramatically improves the economics of providing BI solutions, as will be shown later.

The Basic Use Case

Figures 13.2 and 13.3 show the before and after pictures of the basic data integration use case that employs a DVS. The context for this case is a pair of applications that must draw upon four data sources as diverse as an ERP system, an existing EDW, an independent departmental data mart, and an assembly-line process controller. Although the two

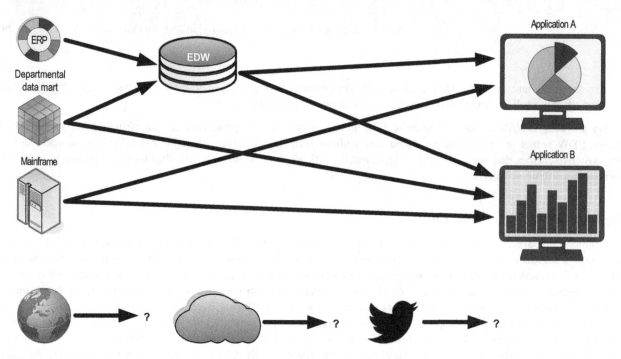

FIGURE 13.2 Basic data integration use case, delivered without data virtualization.

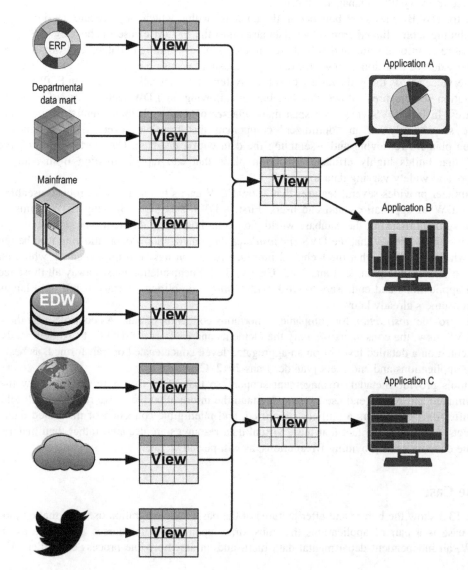

FIGURE 13.3 Basic data integration use case, delivered using a data virtualization server.

end-user applications shown deliver much of the same information, they were built independently, thus the company's information takes two separate paths to the data consumer. No structural guarantees exist that the data consumed by these two groups of end users have been extracted, transformed, or stored in a compatible manner. Nor does the company have any guarantee that the definitions for similarly named elements are equivalent, because the metadata for the informational elements also takes two independent paths to the applications. Such a situation leaves the company vulnerable to situations in which end users will retrieve very different values for what they think is the same data element. Decisions based on such conflicting information can easily interfere with each other, allowing the data disparities to become operational paralysis. Moreover, the information provided in the "before" situation is severely limited. Because the company's traditional DBMS tool set is missing an easy means for including data from sources such as the Internet, cloud applications, and social networking sites, the decisions made using the two end-user applications will be imperfectly informed and therefore easily flawed.

The second diagram in this pair shows a much improved state. A DVS has been placed in between sources and end users so that the EDW team can declare a single set of highly managed views, integrating data from all the necessary sources. The DVS will also deliver a single pool of metadata, allowing the company to understand how the EDW information is defined and derived. Now the end users of the two applications know that they both receive equivalently defined data elements, empowering them to pursue comparable analyses and complementary decisions. Moreover, EDW can now support new applications that include the wider variety of information available via Internet sources today.

Notably, the EDW team provides these benefits without programming ETL modules or materializing new data objects. All these services are provided by virtual data resources created via declarations, a much faster process than designing data tables for information storage and programming ETL to load them. This reliance on declarations makes DVS solutions faster not only to create but also to update. Should a particular view prove to be imperfectly defined, the EDW team can simply modify and republish the SQL that defined it. By working with a high-level language such as SQL, this republishing is faster than coding. Because the results are pulled in real time from the sources, previous versions of the solution did not create persisted data stores that have to be located, analyzed, and converted or expunged. The faster try-and-fix cycle that DVS allows greatly amplifies the agility by which the EDW team can address end users' needs and adapt to changing requirements.

Data virtualization provides EDW teams with many new opportunities for providing the surface solutions and architectural backfill discussed previously. This incredibly agile approach is subject to two important limitations, however. Although these limitations are manageable, they need to be considered when incorporating DVS into an EDW architecture. First, a DVS can only deliver data that exists in the source systems. For views built solely on the transaction systems, the result will be current information only without any derived history that trending analyses would need to display. Second, because it knits together existing sources using the network, the speed of the network and the volume of records returned will largely impact the speed with which results arrive to end users. Even with these limitations, a large number of business problems can be addressed using a reasonable amount of current information, and for those problems, DVS offers an inexpensive solution, rapidly delivered.

DVS Performance Features

The limitation that a data communications network might impose on a DVS is only one aspect of a broader topic of "performance," a concern that DVS vendors have made serious efforts to address. When most DW/BI practitioners first hear that DVSs provide real-time data integration using views against heterogeneous sources, they rightly worry that query response times will exceed end users' willingness to wait for answers. They ponder how quickly intermediate results from the multiple data sources can be channeled across the network to a single delivery point and then integrated and transformed by the lone data virtualization server.

Not surprisingly, when the DVS does attempt to perform all the processing on its own, end users can experience such excessive data latency that they will consider the service largely unusable. Fortunately, the DVS products available today have a decade or more of design and programming behind them and thus include many high-performance features that eliminate a good portion of the performance issues. As superoptimizers, they employ analogs of the strategies that relational database management system (RDBMS) servers utilize in their execution plans, except the DVSs no longer limit these strategies to a single database, single brand of databases, or a single type of source data. The following are the primary performance technologies that data virtualization packages employ so that a wide variety of queries can complete in a business-reasonable time frame:

Pushdown processing: The DVS does not have to perform all of an execution plan on its own computer host. Instead, the DVS inquires and learns about the capabilities of each data source from which it must draw information.

It then pushes as much of the integration, filtering, and sorting work as possible down onto the database servers of these sources, thereby distributing the process load and executing the resource-intensive aspects of each view on hosts with superior resources.

Query substitution: There is no reason why a DVS must execute the queries precisely as written by the EDW team. With query substitution, the DVS translates the overall request into a collection of subqueries so that each portion can be pushed down to the underlying database servers, allowing data requests to be fulfilled as effectively as possible.

Query injection: While rewriting the queries, the DVS moves up constraints in an execution plan so that they can be pushed down to the underlying database servers earlier in the overall process. "Injecting" these constraints into the early query segments running on source resources reduces the rows returned and thereby minimizes the join work the DVS needs to do when assembling the final presentation of the data.

Ship joins: The DVS can go as far as sending data from one data store to another so that the database server that runs the fastest can process both sides of a join.

Sort-merge joins: The DVS can also push down only the ORDER BY clauses implied by a join so that the original data sources sort their records before sending them downstream, leaving the DVS to perform only the merge portion of an operation.

Statistical data: The DVS continually gathers information from the source data stores regarding the objects they possess, such as the number of rows in a table, the average width of the rows, the columns that have been indexed, and the number of different values and nulls in each column. Such statistics allow the DVS to optimally rewrite execution plans using a wide variety of shortcuts.

Hints: The EDW developers can review the DVS execution plans, and sometimes they will spot an optimization trick the server has not thought of. In this situation, they can instruct the DVS to use their preferred technique by providing a small piece of execution guidance within the SQL defining the view.

SQL override: Sometimes the EDW developers will want to affect the query far beyond a small hint. The DVS will allow them to provide a fully formed SQL statement that will override the DVS execution plan, allowing the developers to completely control which query segments pushed down to the source DBMSs.

Data caches: When the previous techniques do not achieve sufficient performance, the DVS can build a data cache by materializing intermediate or final results of queries run against the source data stores so that later queries calling for the same information will draw data from physical tables. These caches are managed and refreshed by the DVS so that they do not become programmed objects that the EDW team must spend time maintaining.

The Economics of Virtual Solutions

With all the advanced features listed previously, DVSs can deliver amazingly complex queries with impressive speed, but in many cases the latency will still be greater than if the end users were receiving results from a single set of tables with data already preprocessed for analytics. Whether the latency for a given result is small enough to be business-reasonable requires a fairly subtle calculation. The first element to that calculation should be the raw economics of virtual versus fully engineered solutions.

Although the savings offered by a given DVS-based solution will depend on the particulars of the application, one can make a strong case that in general the DVS approach should cost a small fraction of the effort that an ETL-based solution will require. Figure 13.4 depicts the alternatives for quickly delivering three new analytic applications via ad hoc ETL (shown on the left) versus DVS (shown on the right). For the ETL-based approach, a separate data access channel must be created between every source and the application that uses it. The total number of channels needed here by three applications drawing upon six sources is 18 ETL modules that must be analyzed, designed, coded, validated, and promoted. Of course, it would make more sense to gather all these data sources into a single EDW and then send the integrated information to the applications. However, this organization, like many others, has decided that the new modules for the EDW (already one of the sources in the diagram) take far too long to adapt, hence the resulting mess of three separate, stove-piped solutions.

How should the EDW team proceed using a DVS if the team's primary objective was fast delivery of a solution? The right side of Figure 13.4 depicts a design for providing the same analytic services using a DVS. Using a DVS, EDW team leaders can deliver new services by declaring views, allowing them to provide a shared data transform service in a matter of hours or days rather than months. They first declare six views to acquire information from the source systems. They then declare three views based on the first six that each finishes shaping the data needed by one of the end-user applications. All told, they need only declare 9 objects instead of the 18 needed using ETL, leading to a 50% reduction in the number of new components required.

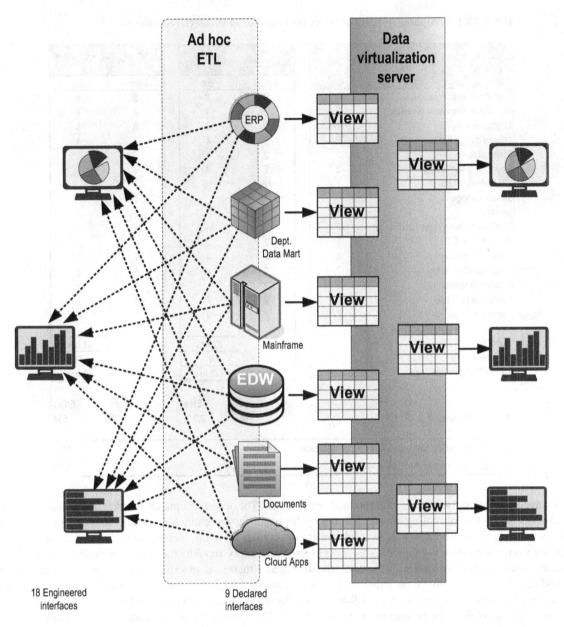

FIGURE 13.4 Data virtualization reduces the number of interfaces required for a given set of solutions.

The fact that the DVS objects are declared rather than engineered leads to even greater savings. Table 13.1 provides an analysis of the level of effort required to build an ETL module—which must be designed, coded, and validated—versus the labor required to simply declare a DVS component. Some of the creation steps on this list, such as identifying transformation rules and logical design, are required in both approaches and require approximately the same amount of time. Other steps appear only in one approach or the other. ETL programming is needed only for the engineered approach, for example, and only the DVS requires a "write view logic" step. The labor requirement between these two activities is notable. The DVS object is declared and therefore delivers the service in 1 hour versus the 2 days of work required to program an ETL module that would materialize the required data. Granted, another person might estimate the steps shown in this table differently than me, but the speed with which that object can be declared versus programmed should cause our two results to agree in approximate magnitude. This difference arises from the fact that ETL tools are procedural, forcing developers to specify every action the module must take. The SQL statements employed in a DVS query are declarative, relying on descriptions of the set-based results desired and leaving the enumeration of logical processing steps to the optimizer to perform.

Table 13.1 also lists a set of steps that appear in both approaches but require less time in a declarative approach. For example, logical design review and unit testing absorb less time in the DVS approach because of the lower level of

TABLE 13.1 Comparative Level of Effort for Engineered vs. Declared Objects

Action	# of People	Engineered (Programmed ETL)			Declared (Data virtualization views)	
		Hours	Ext		Hours	Ext
Transform mapping and rules	1	8	8	=	8	8
Functional requirements review	2	2	4	>	2	4
Logical design	1	8	8	=	8	8
Logical design review	2	2	4	=	2	4
Physical design	2	2	4			
Physical design review	2	2	4			
ETL programming	1	16	16			
Write view logic					1	4
Unit test	1	4	4	>	2	2
Unit test review & code walkthrough	2	2	4	>	1	2
Promotion to SIT	1	2	2			
Integration testing	1	4	4	>	1	1
Integration test review	2	2	4	>	1	2
Readiness review	3	2	6	>	1	3
Promotion to PROD	1	2	2	>	1	1
Validation	2	4	8	>	1	2
Subtotal			**82 hrs**			**41 hrs**
Rework @ 50%			41			21
Total Effort per Interface			**123 hrs**			**62 hrs**
		Count	Effort		Count	Effort
Interfaces Required (Fig. DVRO)		**18**	**2,214**		**9**	**554**
Savings offered by data virtualization per interface						**50%**
Total Savings Across the EDW (Fig. DVRO)						**75%**

detail involved in declarative versus programmed approaches. The lower estimates for the DVS tasks also reflect a lower level of risk. Because creating—testing—fixing cycles occur far more quickly when a team is declaring a solution, developers can rely more on validation to catch errors rather than laboring over specifications up front and verifying programming once a module is built. Because developers can simply republish a view that proves insufficient for its purpose, the consequences of making a mistake are lower, and therefore specifications, reviews, and unit testing for DVS modules do not need to be as exhaustive. For this reason, many of the steps listed for both approaches in Table 13.1 are estimated far lower for the DVS-based solution than for the programmed ETL.

As shown in the totals at the bottom of the main table, the DVS approach allows teams to create modules in approximately half the time that fully engineering ETL modules would require. For the hypothetical case of six sources and three targets depicted in Figure 13.4, this 50% reduction in module development effort along with the 50% reduction in the number of objects necessary combine to give the DVS approach a 4-to-1 advantage over ad hoc ETL solutions, as summarized at the bottom of the table.

Because the previous analysis focused on an ad hoc ETL solution, we should ask whether a DVS would have the same advantage over the standard approach to enterprise data warehousing, where a carefully designed ETL-based system consolidates the data before delivering it to applications. The standard approach can provide high-quality information to the enterprise, but it cannot match DVS in terms of fast delivery of solutions. EDW teams that pursue a traditional hub-and-spoke delivery strategy take even more time than developers pursuing an ad hoc ETL approach because they must plan data transforms for harmonizing disparate data sources and design the appropriate data stores. Replicating the DVS "shared bus" approach shown on the right side of Figure 13.4 using ETL would be considerably more involved, creating an even greater economic advantage for DVS than that demonstrated in the previous case.

DVS Surface Solutions and Progressive Deployment

Reconsidering the case history presented at the beginning of this chapter, DVSs can provide an even better means for providing surface solutions than leveraging shadow IT. Figure 13.5 provides a four-step approach that an EDW team might

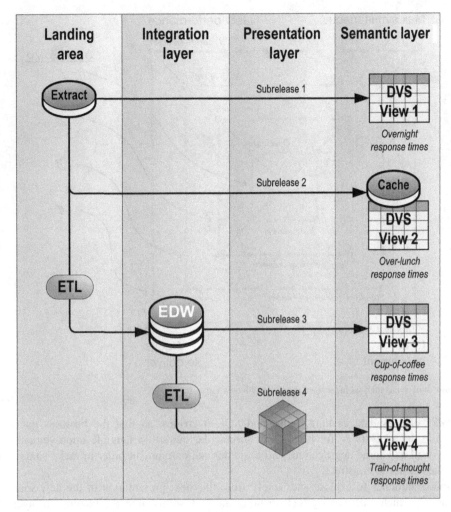

FIGURE 13.5 General surface-solutions delivery pattern with data virtualization.

take to iteratively deliver analytical information from a new or significantly updated data source. The line marked Subrelease 1 represents the first deliverable the team might plan on. Although DVS would allow creating multisource views that pull data directly from the transaction systems, usually companies do not want to burden their line-of-business systems with BI reporting requests. Accordingly, Subrelease 1 depicts a surface solution based on a simple extract from the source systems that the EDW team has placed in the landing area of its reference architecture. The team can then create a DVS view that reformats this replicated new source data for the end users, exposing it through the semantic layer of the company's BI application. Assuming a daily refresh for the extracted tables, this first subrelease is a quick solution that offers current data from the new updated source systems. The team has not yet taken the time to cleanse, harmonize, or aggregate the data, however. Nor has it created any value-added fields, largely because the source is unfamiliar to the company and the business users cannot yet say how they want it transformed or enriched.

If the raw data is large and requires many joins or special processing to surface it as an intelligible, relational table, then queries against this new data may well perform poorly, despite the fact that it has been extracted from source systems and placed on EDW servers. Some of the key queries may need to run overnight to finish, so the only sure value of this first step is providing the business with a partial design of a solution with some real data with which to evaluate it. Still, the cost was low because the EDW probably only needed a day or two to create and validate this view. Moreover, the team may well have been able to link the new data to information already in the EDW, so the business may have been able to review the results in a rich corporate context. At a minimum, this first subrelease will allow departmental analysts to begin exploring the new source data and answer some basic business questions.

While the end users work with this first deliverable as best they can, the EDW team begins developing a next version, shown as Subrelease 2 in Figure 13.5. With this version, the EDW team draws upon the performance-enhancing

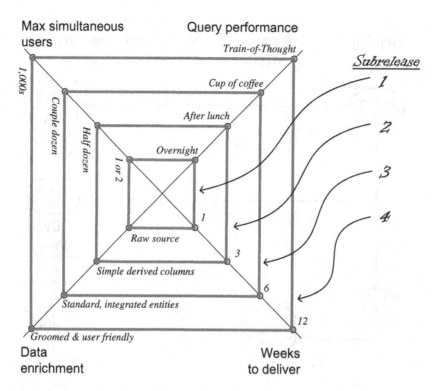

FIGURE 13.6 Dimensions-of-value analysis for surface solutions with data virtualization.

features of the DVS, such as data caching, hints, and SQL overrides, so that the business queries complete more quickly, perhaps while the analysts go for lunch—not spectacular but still a tangible improvement over Subrelease 1. The developers may well add some aggregations and basic derived columns in order to make some analytical reporting on the new source data easier to construct.

While the business continues to explore and benefit from this next presentation of the new source, the EDW team invests in Subrelease 3, which will employ ETL to bring the new source into the integration layer of the data warehouse. This subrelease may actually be several mini-subreleases. Each one would look the same to the end users, but in the background the EDW team will be steadily moving the join and transformation logic from the DVS views to the ETL engine in order to improve the solution's overall performance. These hidden iterations should steadily improve the completion times of end-user queries to the point where business questions are answered in the time it takes the analysts to fetch a cup of coffee. Moreover, users will be able to ask a wider collection of more illuminating questions given the cleansing and derived columns that the EDW team has had the time to add to the information.

Finally, based on the usage observed during all three of the prior subreleases, the EDW team has been able to not only cleanse and integrate the data from the new source but also add a star-schema base presentation layer in Subrelease 4 so that business questions are now answered fast enough for end users to maintain a steady train of thought during their analyses.

Figure 13.5 showed how each subrelease differs architecturally from the next, but agile EDW team leaders will also need to articulate the additional business value of each application version, lest management prematurely decide to make one of the prototypes the production version. Figure 13.6 employs a *dimensions of value analysis*, introduced in Part III, to illustrate the incremental value offered by each step in the chain of subreleases described previously. As the team delivers the quick surface solution and then steadily backfills the architecture using the DVS, the ring of realized data capabilities on this dimensions of value analysis expands outward.

Comparing DVS Surface Solutions to the Previous Example

The dynamic delivery approach using a DVS is far better in both capabilities and value accounting than the shadow IT-based approach sketched previously. Because agile EDW team leaders will need to regularly improvize subrelease plans involving surface solutions and backfilling, taking a moment to compare the previous two examples will highlight some of the major issues they should be prepared to consider. In the first example, the EDW team employed a quick burst of

TABLE 13.2 Contrast between Surface Solutions Using Shadow IT Versus Data Virtualization Servers

Surface Solutions via Early Data Access for Shadow IT	Surface Solutions via Data Virtualization Servers
End users work with data models in many different reference architecture layers, some of which are not structured for intelligibility.	End users always work with a semantic layer of views that EDW controls and can make user-friendly.
Each subrelease requires physical deployment, which demands greater care and effort.	EDW simply publishes a new view for each subrelease, which requires less effort and far less time.
Metadata probably incomplete and overly technical.	Solution utilizes DVS's facility for easy-to-use metadata that adapts as developers steadily increment the views.
Departmental developers must constantly re-engineer their applications for the new sources EDW provides.	Source may steadily offer new entities and additional attributes, but the source itself stays in the same logical location, making end-user applications easier to update.
	Moreover, because views are less labor-intensive to deploy and manage, EDW can maintain old and new versions, allowing end users to update their applications on their own time schedule.
End users determine all the logic of the data retrieval queries.	By defining the access views, EDW retains considerable influence on the retrieval query logic.
End users may write queries that run inefficiently or distort the information retrieved with flaws such as double counting due to missing join conditions.	EDW team members can ensure proper query construction, and by monitoring run times via the DVS administration front end, they can correct inefficient queries.
Poorly written departmental queries may impose heavy loads on normally hidden EDW layers, perhaps requiring EDW to tune those layers for end-user access.	DVS optimizer and data caching give EDW better tools for reducing the burden on the EDW servers.
Every intermediate subrelease is undoubtedly not an application EDW would want to leave in production.	As long as performance is good enough, any acceptable view can be safely left in production because the DVS guarantees it is well-defined, intelligible, monitored, and manageable.

ETL development and allowed data-savvy departmental analysts to access the results in whatever layer the data next landed. Whether the business staff received analyses employing standardized data definitions, code translations, or transformation business rules was completely up to the departmental analysts who built the provisional reports and dashboards.

In the DVS example, EDW surfaced everything through the semantic layer, leaving only the final data visualization for the end users to build. Both approaches allowed for fast cycles of discovery and incremental solution improvement and thus enabled the agile EDW team to constantly deliver value to the customer. Yet there are several points of contrast between the two solution paths, as enumerated in Table 13.2. Overall, the DVS-based approach can offer higher value and therefore merits the greater up-front cost required to put a DVS platform in place.

Data Virtualization's Value Proposition

Do the benefits provided by a DVS justify the cost and effort to acquire and deploy such a tool? Teams can utilize the value buildup chart discussed in Part III of this book to make this case. Figure 13.7 shows three such buildup graphs, representing the three agile approaches discussed so far:

- Engineered ETL modules programmed by the EDW team
- Surface solutions with EDW providing data to shadow IT groups
- Surface solutions using a DVS

These graphs have been overlaid so that the effectiveness of the various approaches can be compared.

The all-EDW approach requires the DW/BI team to program ETL for all four layers of the reference architecture for each subrelease but focusing on only a theme or two with each delivery. Even with agile techniques, this approach requires multiple months before end users receive each installment of usable applications, so the value buildup graph for this approach grows the slowest, as shown by line 1's location to the far right. Importantly, because this work

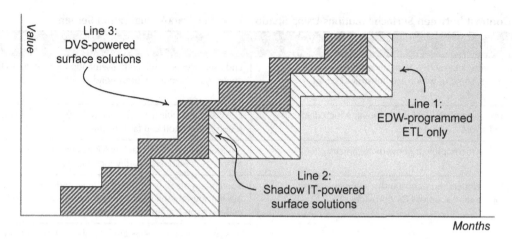

FIGURE 13.7 Data virtualization's value proposition for agile EDW teams.

pattern delivers the fewest installments, the learning experienced by DW/BI and the business staff with this approach is the lowest of all three strategies.

Line 2 represents a surface-solution strategy leveraging shadow IT groups. EDW progressively programs ETL for one layer of the reference architecture and makes the results available to the end-user department. The business receives usable data far earlier than with the previous strategy, and DW/BI start learning about the project problem space and source data sooner. Faster learning shortens the overall delivery time of the entire project, as indicated by line 2's location to the left of the all-EDW programmed approach. However, there is only so much the departmental analysts can do with their front-end tools, so the end users still find themselves repeatedly waiting for EDW to provide the next installment of ETL.

Such waiting disappears with the DVS-powered approach, in which the EDW team can begin creating views as soon as source data is available and validating them with the business staff. There are still some capabilities that EDW cannot deliver until the data is fully persisted in the Integration layer or reformatted for business consumption in the Presentation layer, but because DVS allows faster build–review cycles with the business, more features undoubtedly appeared in each subrelease than in the ETL-dependent approach. Moreover, because this strategy allows for the most frequent deliveries, learning occurs fastest with this approach, leading to a further shortening of the overall project delivery time, as indicated by line 3's placement to the far left.

With these value buildup charts, the area under each curve represents the benefits to the business delivered by each strategy. Because the DVS-powered approach creates the largest value under the curve, it is a strategy that all agile EDW team leaders should consider.

EDW's Reference Architecture Becomes Dynamic

Because data virtualization allows EDW teams to quickly deliver a wide variety of new data capabilities, this technology should be fundamentally incorporated into the reference architecture of a data warehouse. EDW leaders need only establish the following maxim for their teammates to follow:

> *Because DVS views allow us to quickly extend the value of available information and mask out problems within the source data, such views should be placed around every DW/BI object so that we can insulate consumers of EDW data from confusion and needless change.*

Figure 13.8 shows the multiple impacts that this guidance will have on the EDW reference architecture—impacts that will make the EDW considerably more agile in the face of new and changing business requirements. First, every layer in the EDW is "wrapped" within a set of DVS views so that each layer can no longer draw data directly from its upstream source. The Landing area acquires data from DVS views of the source systems, the Integration layer obtains data from DVS views of the Landing layer, and so on. If one layer requires no special adaptations to the data in its upstream source, then these views are just pass-through constructs based on simple "select * from {source}" statements. Following this pattern, views will be in place and incorporated into all EDW data access statements, ready to intercept challenges when the situation changes unexpectedly. When challenges occur, the EDW team will be able to solve many

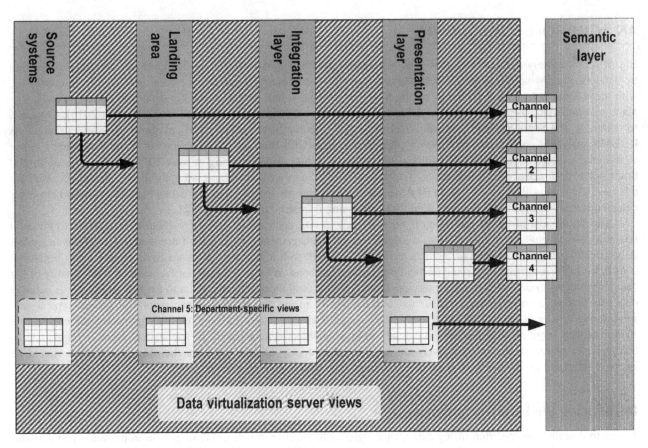

FIGURE 13.8 Surface solutions "channels" enabled by data virtualization.

of them by changing the wrapper view surrounding the objects in the affected reference architecture layer. Because these views are fast to re-declare, this strategy allows the EDW team to respond far more quickly to surprises than if it had to redesign and reprogram a large collection of ETL modules. With wrapper views, the general response pattern becomes (1) change the wrapper view first, then (2) substantiate the new design by refactoring the ETL, and (3) reset the wrapper view to pass-through mode.

The second major impact that a wrapper-view strategy will have on an agile EDW program is that it creates several channels for surface solutions from which the EDW team leaders can choose. Figure 13.8 depicts these choices as "Channels 1 through 5," which reflects the order in which they should occur in a surface solution approach. Channel 1 represents making source data available to end-user departments for self-service discovery and BI solutions whenever the line-of-business systems can tolerate the additional burden of a few reporting queries. Channel 2 corresponds with the first two surface solutions shown in Figure 13.5, in which an EDW-administered view delivered Landing layer data directly to the end users, with and without data caching. Channel 3 represents the progressive backfilling that Subreleases 3 in that diagram provided. Channel 4 is equivalent to the fully implemented standard approach in which data moves one step at a time through the layers of the EDW, but in this case it passes through DVS wrapper views, which are left in place in case they can enable a fast adaptation in the future.

End users will also greatly benefit from a third impact that data virtualization servers will have on an agile EDW program. Because DVS allows developers to inexpensively create views, EDW may well be willing to provide department-specific access to objects throughout the reference architecture. Examples of such utility views are the reconciliation reports that Finance needs to run only a few times each year. Instead of investing the time and expense to create this capability using ETL programming and persisted data stores, the EDW project leaders can solve the business needs with one or more custom views, as shown by the department-specific views labeled "Channel 5" at the bottom of Figure 13.8.

All told, data virtualization allows EDW team leaders to answer business needs in a fast and well-managed manner using steadily improving surface solutions that generate high value for the business in dramatically shorter time frames than ETL programming and persisted data stores can achieve. Because of these advantages, EDW team leaders will benefit greatly by adding data virtualization to their agile toolkits.

AN AGILE ROLE FOR BIG DATA

Big data is a loosely defined cohort of new and rapidly evolving data management technologies currently generating tremendous interest within IT and DW/BI departments. The technology is perhaps a bit too popular for its own good, with many thought leaders and vendors asking how much longer it will be before the big data products completely supplant relational database technologies in the realm of business analytics [Henschen 2013] and [Kumar 2013]. Consider, for example, the Sears Roebuck company decision in 2010 to scrap its mainframe BI platform in order to replace its RDBMS analytical applications with new applications written with Hadoop: "Eliminating all of the mainframes in use would enable Sears to save 'tens of millions' of dollars ... while also delivering at least 20, sometimes 50, up to 100 times better performance on batch times" [Henschen 2012]. Sears in fact became so enthralled with the potential for this new technology that it spun off its BI department to become an independent big data consulting firm to help other companies make the same overhaul on their data processing infrastructures [King 2012].

Although the rest of the BI profession is not yet ready to take such a leap of faith, we can at least begin to factor in this new class of products in the solutions we devise to data management problems both new and old. EDW team leaders in particular should be cognizant of big data technology, even though it is at an early stage in its development, because it does indeed offer another handy route for building surface solutions. We can leverage the "schema on read" quality of big data technologies to deliver partial data services quickly to our customers, allowing them to explore and discover value in data sets that were formerly too large or too unstructured to make use of. Even when employed against typical data sources, big data products will allow us to assemble simple end-user access early on and then gradually add engineering rigor until the overall solution has just enough heft to be a reliable and manageable BI application. Because big data technologies can power an iterative discovery-and-engineering process, all agile data warehousing practitioners should be aware of them and understand how to fit them into their agile data engineering toolkits.

Introducing Big Data Technologies

Trying to describe the spectrum of big data technologies is like trying to nail a slab of gelatin to the wall. The constant innovation currently occurring with these products makes them wriggle and morph so that a single static definition will fail to capture the subject's totality or remain accurate for long. The description offered here, then, is intended to be just good enough to present some notions on how to fit big data products into an iterative BI delivery program.

Big data technology emerged when engineers at large web companies created programming frameworks to take advantage of inexpensive "commodity" computers and disk drives. These inexpensive components allowed companies to economically assemble enormous clusters of data servers that could not only store a tremendous amount of data but also read and transform the information using massively parallel processing (MPP). Such large capacity was sorely needed as they struggled to tame the flood of new information pouring in from the new, Internet-based economy, much of it in unfamiliar and poorly constrained formats. Web logs, social networking sites, cell phones, RFIDS, and instrumentation on nearly every device from thermostats to jet engines were generating a sudden surge in the volume and variety of data available, all pouring in at high velocity, as fast as these devices could transmit it over the internal networks and the Internet [Finley 2014]. Observers noted that these "three V's"—volume, velocity, and variety—of data in the web age far exceeded the ability of traditional RDBMSs to management it and thus demanded a new class of tools [Laney 2001].

Companies soon realized that although any given sample of this relentless stream was worth very little, putting it all together could generate some important insights into the behavior of commercial processes and actors in the economy. Thus was born new or dramatically improved services such as preference engines, fraud detection, preventive maintenance alerts, and one-to-one marketing. Several of the Internet companies that created the first versions of the big data programming frameworks placed them in the public domain as open source software (OSS) projects, making it easy and economical for teams in other companies to experiment with these ideas and improve upon the early products. New versions of big data technology began to rapidly appear. When some particularly innovative companies began generating huge revenue streams from this convergence of high data volumes, inexpensive platforms, and readily available software, the big data gold rush of the 2010s was set into motion.

Whether big data products soon replace traditional data management tools or just take their place alongside them, this technology will be increasingly important to DW/BI because the quantity of information in the world is growing exponentially. In a 2014 survey, more than 500 big data professionals revealed that they expect the data volumes they must manage to grow by 45% during the next 2 years [QuinStreet 2014]. Another forecast suggests that by 2020, the world will generate information at 50 times today's frantic pace [Maguire, 2014]. If these trends continue, soon all the data generated in the world between the beginning of time through the first decade of this century will be generated every minute [Marr 2014].

Much of this growth will be powered by the emerging *Internet of Things*, where even ordinary devices such as automobiles and HVAC systems will transmit a steady stream of information to enable better monitoring and control. The aviation industry, for example, expects that the Boeing 787 will generate a half terabyte with every flight it makes. For the airlines, the ability to quickly warehouse and analyze events and status for everything from planes to cargo devices and personnel will soon become a competitive weapon as each company tries to outperform the other in adapting schedules and other delivery logistics [Finnegan 2013].

The Need for Big Data Technology

The flood of information generated by all these new sources far exceeds the capabilities of the traditional relational database technologies and techniques that the data warehousing industry has employed until now. As the marketplace scrambles to provide solutions for these rapidly growing data sets, data managers have adopted the term *big data* to refer to a new generation of the software tools that can capture, curate, manage, and process this new quantity of information within a business-reasonable time frame.

Entrepreneurs and venture capitalists have flocked into this market space, which is currently growing six times faster than the overall IT market [Press 2013]. Today, the number and diversity of companies offering big data solutions are overwhelming. A survey of the vendors offering products in this general category includes more than 250 companies [Turck 2014]. These products fall into more than 30 different categories, each varying in either the aspect of the big data challenge that they address or the technical strategy with which they attempt to solve it. An introduction to one of the most popular solutions, the Hadoop distributed file system (HDFS) and MapReduce as offered through an OSS package called Hadoop, is provided later. But to be even vaguely conversant in this field today, one would have to be able to appraise the relative strengths and weaknesses of a much wider range of products, such as NoSQL databases, data warehouse appliances, and the big data extensions that vendors are adding to the traditional relational database packages.

The discussion of Hadoop offered later focuses on providing faster surface solutions in an enterprise data warehousing context, but this use case only scratches the surface of big data products. This technology can support many other technical strategies besides enterprise data warehousing, including the following:

- Real-time analytics of high-volume data streams
- Complex event processing
- Predictive analytics
- Data mining software
- Text analytics software
- Web log analysis

Today, companies employ big data to solve an astonishingly diverse range of problems, such as the following:

- Risk modeling
- Customer churn analysis
- Ad targeting
- Trade surveillance
- Threat analysis
- Predicting network failures

Big data technology has already proven its ability to yield great value, and it will continue to expand its range for many years to come.

Where these applications can be deployed quickly and iteratively, big data will be an excellent addition to the agile toolkit. However, readers new to this field should be alert to big data's dark side. Because it relies on OSS and commodity hardware, too many people hastily concluded that it will solve data management challenges with next to zero cost and in next to zero time. Such enthusiasm has led them to pursue big data application development with too little discipline. Perhaps the most serious and common manifestation of this dangerous approach can be paraphrased as "just grab all our company's data and throw it in the 'data lake.' We'll figure out what to do with it later."

Perhaps such a reckless orientation has taken root because the economy's exploding data volume has created a sense of panic among corporate executives. *Forbes* translated big data's three V's to the three I's of big data [Feinleib, 2012]:

- Ill-defined: Everyone is still asking "What is it?"
- Immediate: Everyone feels they had better do something about it now.
- Intimidating: Everyone fears what will happen if they do not.

One executive expressed the mental malaise gripping executives by quipping, "We used to ask whether we could afford to store information. Today we ask whether we can afford to throw it away" [Henschen 2013]. IT has been plagued by successive waves of anxiety from the top ever since the invention of the computer. We invented structured requirements management precisely to counterbalance the WISCY pressure ("Why isn't somebody coding yet??") typically supplied by business partners once they decide to sponsor an application development project. In many ways, the low cost and power of *some* big data solutions has led to a further push from executives, namely WIHSODA—"Why isn't Hadoop storing our data already?" We can see the impact of this panic in a HelpIT and Teradata survey of nearly 200 companies of $1 billion annual revenue or more, which revealed that more than half of the big data projects today are being pursued without a business case [Du Preez 2014]. The same executives who pay for these unguided missiles would never think of hiring a half-dozen clerical staff members without carefully outlining the roles and responsibilities that these people would assume when they join their departments. Why they would spin up a big data project that could easily exceed that level of spending without first carefully articulating goals, objectives, and business impacts is a true mystery.

To guard against wasting big time and big money on big data technology, I encourage readers to utilize at least the first two or three of the lightweight, enterprise-capable requirements management artifacts discussed in Part III to properly frame every big data project they take on. Before any funds are invested, every IT project deserves a few sentences describing the sponsor's concept, the stakeholder's complaints with current capabilities, and an IT vision of what the new business solution will look like. Moreover, I believe that all IT projects, including big data implementations, would also greatly benefit from at least a single draft of a subrelease plan that expresses in just a few sentences the value that business stakeholders will receive over the span of the next three or four versions of the requested application.

The Promise of Schema-On-Read

The caveats expressed above notwithstanding, big data technology offers agile EDW teams a fabulous path to quick value if for no other reason than it enables "schema on read." The traditional approach to presenting corporate information on a dashboard involves landing data into relational tables that closely match a source system's data structure and then integrating it into a data warehouse. The data warehouse tables are structured not to reflect the source systems but instead the combined realities and needs of the enterprise. In the late 1990s, most of the source data systems were built with either COBOL or relational databases, so acquiring data from them was simply a matter of discerning the source tables' inherent structure. Today, BI sources increasing include spreadsheets, email, web services, machine logs, document images, and social networking streams. The location and format of the data elements in these sources commonly vary over time and often from document to document, making it impossible to ascribe a structure to many information streams at the time when a data capture application for them is designed. Instead, the structure must be discerned when the data is utilized—that is, when it's read into the analytical program.

The growing proportion of such unstructured or semistructured information in the enterprise poses a major challenge to the DW/BI team equipped with traditional tools. Relational databases management systems do allow designers to place information in columns typed for binary or character-based "large objects" (BLOBs and CLOBs). EDW teams can place largely undefined data items in these columns, but the overall data still has to be interpreted as records with keys so that it can be placed in a table structure. Moreover, writing these records will involve all the overheads of relational tables and rows, making acquisition too slow for billions of records and the resulting repository large and expensive to maintain.

Big data technologies allow a far more agile approach to managing poorly structured data. An application can store the raw extracts or source events directly in simple disk files, in whatever form in which they arrive, rather than trying to interpret them as records or impose any structure on them before saving them away. In this approach, the end consumers of the data can decide what structure to impose on the information if and when they decide to use these files. They can impose a schema on the data using the program that reads the data so that the application's ability to make sense of the source can be changed and improved as easily as one can change a line of code in the access program. With this schema-on-read approach, data can be grabbed and salted away as it is generated without incurring any delay in trying to make sense of it.

This strategy is perfectly in line with an agile philosophy of eliminating waste in the software development process. If one insisted on imposing structure on every item stored, that effort would have been wasted on whatever portion of the company's information that is never used after it has been gathered. It is far more effective to pursue the expensive process of discovering and imposing structure on only the minority of items that actually get utilized for decision making. As we will see in the following discussion of Hadoop with its HDFS storage technology and MapReduce processing, big data products embody this schema-on-read approach extensively, making it natural to include them in an agile data warehousing program.

Of all the big data technologies listed previously, the Hadoop software suite is the cohort of big data products that companies most often employ today to accomplish exactly this "grab now, parse later" strategy. To illustrate how EDW team leads can harness this technology for agility, we need a basic outline of Hadoop. Readers should keep in mind that (1) Hadoop is only one style of managing big data and (2) all the flexibility that it provides comes at a cost, a point I return to later.

An Introduction to Hadoop

Hadoop is an ecosystem of solutions based on HDFS and MapReduce (MR). Written in Java, HDFS can automatically distribute large files over many computers so that high-volume reads can execute in parallel. MR is a particular technique for spreading queries involving large data sets across many computers so that they, too, can be executed in parallel.

Hadoop will serve as a good introduction to big data technologies for multiple reasons. First, it is by far the most popular big data technology. Now that big data fever has taken hold of the world economy, more than half of the Fortune 50 companies are using or experimenting with Hadoop [Altior 2012]. Its mindshare has grown such that today many people use the terms "big data" and "Hadoop" synonymously, despite the fact that there are many other, equally effective and completely different approaches available in the marketplace. The popularity of Hadoop is probably due to the fact that it was one of the first big data solutions widely available as OSS, so it spread far and wide very quickly. Second, Hadoop represents the cohort of big data products that are evolving most rapidly, again probably due to its OSS availability, so that many of big data's "rough edges" get addressed and solved in the Hadoop ecosystem first.

Third, the path that the market is taking with big data will in many ways make it soon "just another data source" for standard DW/BI products, so understanding just one big data product will enable EDW team leaders to envision surface solutions using this new technology family. For example, many of the Hadoop products have been weak in interactive speeds and good programming interfaces, as can be expected with open-source initiatives [Turck 2014]. Accordingly, commercial vendors offer an increasing number of user-friendly and high-performance versions of these components, interfacing them with the older, more polished data management products with which most DW/BI teams already work. With this support, EDW teams can expect to eventually work with big data repositories while staying within the administration system of their preferred RDBMS.

Hadoop originated in the early 2000s when academics and Silicon Valley engineers chose to scale up web crawler utilities to manage the extremely large ("web-scale") data sources proliferating on the Internet. Contributors participating in Internet cornerstone ventures such as Yahoo!, Google, Facebook, and Wikipedia chose to create an Apache Foundation project as an umbrella for Hadoop's further development, which allows for usage and contributions from a global community of independent programmers and commercial software companies.

Figure 13.9 provides a basic presentation of the components making up the core of Hadoop distributions available today. The assembly shown is simply the baseline collection of products that most people have in mind when they speak of big data and/or Hadoop in general. By design, these components are loosely coupled to one another so that data management teams can use them selectively and swap out many of them to arrive at a technology stack adapted to a specific purpose.

The open source community has also steadily built economic scaling into the foundations of the Hadoop project, notably assuming that all modules will run on "commodity servers" employing inexpensive disk resources. With this backdrop, the community has designed these software components to widely distribute their functions and controls so that a Hadoop data facility can respond elegantly when a disk, server, or an entire rack of servers fails.

The economies of open source combined with distributed, fault-tolerant designs have allowed companies to build massive data centers based on Hadoop. The Hadoop cluster for the web search application at Yahoo!, which contributed much of the early source code to the Apache project, exceeded 10,000 Linux cores by 2010 [Babcock 2012]. In the same time frame, Facebook claimed that its Hadoop cluster had surpassed 21 PB of storage [Borthakur 2010]. This cluster then expanded to 100 PB 2 years later, and it continues to grow by roughly half a PB per day [Ryan 2012 and Facebook 2012]. To better understand how Hadoop enables scalability and schema-on-read, we need to briefly examine its two core products, HDFS and MapReduce.

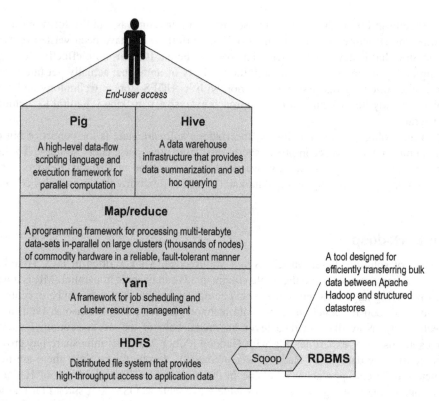

FIGURE 13.9   Notable Apache Hadoop software components. *Definitions adapted slightly from Apache Software Foundation, www.apache.org.*

Hadoop Distributed File System

Although big data implementations can operate with many different file systems, HDFS is by far the most popular choice for storing the data in a Hadoop cluster. Written in Java, HDFS can be deployed on a wide range of machines. It was designed from the start to support read-mostly data access and to redundantly distribute large files across many disks. When given a file, HDFS partitions it into the massive blocks and spreads these blocks across the disks of a given Hadoop cluster so that read actions can draw upon them in parallel. This partition-and-distribute strategy allows a file to be larger than any single disk in the network. It uses huge block sizes (typically 1000 times larger than normal file system blocks) in order to reduce the seek times and increase data transfer for applications to be nearly the read speed of the underlying hardware [White 2012].

HDFS also maintains many copies of each block, locating them on separate disks and racks, so that read operations will be able to circumvent any particular device failure. When blocks become corrupted or failed devices are replaced, HDFS will automatically restore the desired redundancy and distribution of the cluster's data by referencing the reliable copies of the blocks it has maintained elsewhere.

The design decisions that give HDFS scalability and fault tolerance come at the cost of some other capabilities. First, being optimized for large block size in order to achieve high throughput, HDFS data stores can experience high data latencies. Applications that require responsive data access—for example, in the range of tens of milliseconds—will not work well with HDFS. In such cases, switching to HBase, Hadoop's low-latency file systems, should be considered. Second, applications involving many separate files will be constrained by the HDFS name node, which maintains the metadata of each file, because it must fit within the memory space of a single machine in the cluster. Storing millions of files is feasible, but storing billions is beyond the capability of current hardware [White 2012]. Third, writes are always made at the end of an HDFS file by a single write process, making HDFS inappropriate for applications needing fast data capture and random updates.

Hadoop MapReduce

MapReduce is a programming model for data processing large datasets designed to scale a data request to process over multiple computing nodes. In Hadoop, developers can write MR programs written in various languages, such as Java,

Ruby, Python, and C++. Although one can chain together utilities to simulate an interactive session, in a plain-vanilla Hadoop implementation, the input is stored in HDFS files and MR jobs send their output to a file stored in either HDFS or on a traditional disk directory, whichever the programmer chooses. MR programs inherently employ parallel execution, thus putting very large-scale data analytics into the hands of teams with mid-level programming skills and enough computer hardware. The original developers of Hadoop designed MR and HDFS concurrently so that despite the fact that one can write MR programs against a variety of file systems, MR's capabilities and execution modes fit perfectly on top of an HDFS cluster.

The key to understanding MR technology is to consider the map and reduce portions of the programming model as separate and sequenced components. In an MR program, the developer provides a core piece of logic for the Map portion and another for the Reduce. In essence, the mapper should filter and transform the input files into a stream of records that the reducer can readily aggregate [Lohr 2013]. Wrappers provided by the Hadoop implementation take care of the execution and scaling of the two pieces, automatically invoking them in sequence. Because the logic that the developer places in either component determines what the MR programs actually do, these modules can perform a wide range of data analysis tasks, such as text analytics for customer sentiments profiling or recommendations for one web user based on past surfing pattern records for both him and thousands of people like him. Hadoop, by providing both the HDFS and the MR framework, enables these analyses to reach high levels of parallel processing and accelerates run times against truly enormous collections of data many orders of magnitude faster than traditional relational databases can achieve against the same data volumes.

Figure 13.10 gives readers new to big data an overview of how MR would process a simple join between two tables. For our example, consider the following five-line SQL statement:

```
select    CUST._ID,    CUST._NAME,    CUST._CITY,
          SO.ID,       SO.CUST_ID,    SO.DATE,    SO.AMOUNT
from CUSTOMERS CUST, SALES_ORDERS SO
where CUST.ID = SO.CUST_ID
order by CUST.ID, SO.ID;
```

In MR, one would have to write a program similar to the 70 lines of Java code listed in Figure 13.11 and then place them in a proper MR wrapper for execution.

In Figure 13.10, File One is the CUSTOMERS, and File Two is SALES_ORDERS. The right side of the diagram provides a stylized data flow between the components of the MR program and shows the actual output from each step so that the reader can see the transformations achieved with each action. The comments on the left call out the essence of each step in the program. As is typical in MR programming, this join module's strategy will be to progressively interpret the data entering each step as one kind of key-value pair, re-parse it to establish a different key-value pairing, and then sort or combine the new key-value pairs in preparation for the next step. In this example, the programmer provided a mapper component with enough smarts to process both of the input files correctly, despite the different layouts of the data elements they contain. For customer, the first key-value parsing was Customer ID as k1, and all other columns as v1. For Sales Orders, order number was k1, and all other columns were treated as v1. The core logic the developer provided simply puts distinct tags on each record to mark it as either a Customer or Sales Order and then re-parses either type of record so that the Customer ID becomes the new group key, k2.

When this mapper component executes, scaling is accomplished automatically from two directions. First, HDFS had already distributed storage of the two input files across as many data nodes as the cluster could offer so that many disks can collaborate in providing many parallel input streams. Second, Hadoop's MR framework automatically partitions the k1 keys and spreads the processing of the resulting partitions across as many processers as available.

After the many instances of the mapper component conclude their work, Hadoop automatically performs a shuffle and sort with those output segments ("shards"), deciding how to partition and distribute the full domain of new k2 values across processors. When these partitions are sent to a reducer component, each reduce instance will work with an appropriately sized range of contiguous k2 values.

Note that because MR treats the data as key-value pairs, only the key portions of the input data have to be compatibly defined and formatted. The non-key portion of the original Customer and Sales Order record now occurs in the value portion of the mapper output, with each record appropriately tagged so that the reducer can later process them correctly.

Once shuffled and sorted into ready-to-process shards, Hadoop sends them to multiple reducers where the developer's logic will have Sales Order predicates concatenated to the end of Customer predicates for each occurrence of the group key (Customer ID). Hadoop will automatically take the output from each of these reducer instances and insert them into the output file in group key order.

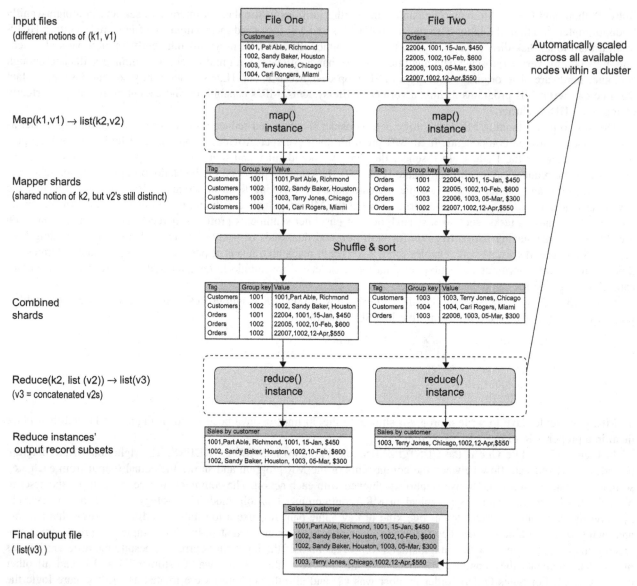

FIGURE 13.10 Processing pattern for a simple Map/Reduce join operation.

Notable Contrasts between SQL and MapReduce

A simple two-table join example should suffice to highlight for the reader several differences between big data products and traditional data management tools. Given the high level of enthusiasm Hadoop currently inspires in DW/BI decision makers, EDW team leaders need to be able to accurately contrast the two approaches and provide balanced guidance regarding the areas where each technology will perform the best.

To counterbalance the hype one hears about big data, consider the warning that two of the open source database luminaries have offered regarding the Hadoop's core technology [DeWitt and Stonebraker 2008]:

MapReduce may be a good idea for writing certain types of general-purpose computations, but to the database community, it is:

- *A giant step backward in the programming paradigm for large-scale data intensive applications*
- *A suboptimal implementation, in that it uses brute force instead of indexing*

```
Mapper for First Table

public class JoinStationMapper
    extends Mapper<LongWritable, Text, TextPair, Text> {
  private NcdcStationMetadataParser parser = new NcdcStationMetadataParser();
  @Override
  protected void map(LongWritable key, Text value, Context context)
    throws IOException, InterruptedException {
  if (parser.parse(value)) {
    context.write(new TextPair(parser.getStationId(), "0"),
      new Text(parser.getStationName()));
  } } }

Mapper for Second Table

public class JoinRecordMapper
    extends Mapper<LongWritable, Text, TextPair, Text> {
  private NcdcRecordParser parser = new NcdcRecordParser();
  @Override
  protected void map(LongWritable key, Text value, Context context)
    throws IOException, InterruptedException {
  parser.parse(value);
  context.write(new TextPair(parser.getStationId(), "1"), value);
  } } }

Reducer

public class JoinReducer extends Reducer<TextPair, Text, Text, Text> {
  @Override
  protected void reduce(TextPair key, Iterable<Text> values, Context context)
    throws IOException, InterruptedException {
  Iterator<Text> iter = values.iterator();
  Text stationName = new Text(iter.next());
  while (iter.hasNext()) {
    Text record = iter.next();
    Text outValue = new Text(stationName.toString() + "\t" + record.toString());
      context.write(key.getFirst(), outValue);
    } } }
```

FIGURE 13.11 Sample Map/Reduce code for a simple two-table join. *Taken from [White 2012, Examples 8−12 through 8−15], used by permission.*

- *Not novel at all—It represents a specific implementation of well-known techniques developed nearly 25 years ago*
- *Missing most of the features that are routinely included in current DBMS*
- *Incompatible with all of the tools DBMS users have come to depend on*

We can put a finer point on this sentiment by contrasting the two approaches we just considered, as shown in Table 13.3. Keep in mind that this comparison is based on a simple two-table join. The advantages for the higher-level SQL language will only increase in situations in which the number of tables grows and the set-based logic begins to require complex logic such as outer joins and correlated subqueries. The advantages for the MR approach

Driver Script to Call the Above Components

```
public class JoinRecordWithStationName extends Configured implements Tool {
    public static class KeyPartitioner extends Partitioner<TextPair, Text> {
    @Override
    public int getPartition(TextPair key, Text value, int numPartitions) {
      return (key.getFirst().hashCode() & Integer.MAX_VALUE) % numPartitions;
    } }


    @Override
    public int run(String[] args) throws Exception {
    if (args.length != 3) {
      JobBuilder.printUsage(this, "<ncdc input> <station input> <output>");
      return -1;
    }

    Job job = new Job(getConf(), "Join weather records with station names");
    job.setJarByClass(getClass());
    Path ncdcInputPath = new Path(args[0]);
    Path stationInputPath = new Path(args[1]);
    Path outputPath = new Path(args[2]);

    MultipleInputs.addInputPath(job, ncdcInputPath,
        TextInputFormat.class, JoinRecordMapper.class);
    MultipleInputs.addInputPath(job, stationInputPath,
        TextInputFormat.class, JoinStationMapper.class);
    FileOutputFormat.setOutputPath(job, outputPath);

    job.setPartitionerClass(KeyPartitioner.class);
    job.setGroupingComparatorClass(TextPair.FirstComparator.class);
    job.setMapOutputKeyClass(TextPair.class);
    job.setReducerClass(JoinReducer.class);
    job.setOutputKeyClass(Text.class);

    return job.waitForCompletion(true) ? 0 : 1;
    }

    public static void main(String[] args) throws Exception {
    int exitCode = ToolRunner.run(new JoinRecordWithStationName(), args);
    System.exit(exitCode);
    } }
```

FIGURE 13.11   (*Continued*)

TABLE 13.3 Contrasting the SQL and MapReduce Queries Used for the Two-Table Join Example

SQL	MapReduce
Requires one statement, comprising five lines of code when formatted for fast comprehension	Requires six times as many statements spread over 75 lines of code in four separately developed modules
Expressed in near-English text, making it easier for journeyman developers to understand and maintain	Expressed in Java, with some complex statements such as overrides required and many nested braces to keep aligned
Declares the set-based operation desired, letting the optimizer perform the actual programming	Requires the coder to engineer the exact processing steps needed to achieve the desired goal; the Hadoop framework attends only to distributing that logic over multiple processing nodes once it works
Requires the data to be loaded into well-structured tables with data-typed columns before a command will execute	Developers decide how to parse each input file when programming a mapper, allowing the module to extract a completely different set of elements each time an input file is used
Scaling requires careful planning and distribution of keys across disk-based partitions	Scaling largely handled by the Hadoop framework, with partitioning determined by the program, so that it can be determined late and changed as fast as one can update the MapReduce code

will emerge when data volumes reach very high levels or the exotic format of source data requires one or more complex parsing algorithms.

Given the strengths and weaknesses of each technology cited previously, one can see that Hadoop is not going to be a solution to every challenge encountered in a DW/BI program and, at the same time, SQL will struggle to scale as easily as Hadoop. EDW team leaders who desire more details on factors favoring one of the technologies over the other can consult Table 13.4.

Making MapReduce Look Like SQL with Hive

Table 13.4 paints the contrast between SQL and HDFS/MR quite starkly in order to help inoculate readers new to Hadoop against the extreme big-data enthusiasm gripping the market today. It is important to see past the "silver bullet" hype and realize that all major tools have areas in which they work well and others in which they do not. It was slightly unfair, however, to compare SQL against HDFS/MR because SQL is a high-level command set with many decades of development behind it. Using a polished high-level tool will naturally make programmers far more productive than a tool for which all capabilities have to be created by hand in a low-level language such as Java. The Hadoop community understands this point, of course, and has introduced a SQL-like add-on for MR called *Hive*.

Hive started as a subproject of Hadoop, but as it gained popularity, the Apache Software Foundation promoted it to a top-level, open source project of its own. The Apache community states that Hive is

> data warehouse software [that] *facilitates querying and managing large data sets residing in distributed storage. Hive provides a mechanism to project structure onto this data and query the data using a SQL-like language called HiveQL. At the same time this language also allows traditional map/reduce programmers to plug in their custom mappers and reducers when it is inconvenient or inefficient to express this logic in HiveQL [Apache 2014].*

To understand the potential for Hive to enable surface solutions in an agile data warehousing context, one only has to consider the wide range of data analytics that a company such as Facebook was quickly able to achieve using this language. Facebook has been a major contributor of programming to the Hive open source project. In early 2008, the members of the Facebook data team confronted the need to produce a plethora of analyses based on the astronomical amount of data their servers were generating through web logs and user activities on the site. The volume of data in just 32 source files had already exceeded 2 TB, with 200 GB flowing in each day [Shao 2008].

To answer this challenge using traditional data warehousing tools, Facebook would have had to carefully engineer target tables and then many ETL modules to preprocess the data for end-user analytics. This traditional engineering would have required months of analysis and design so that the resulting tables would support all the analyses the end

TABLE 13.4 Relative Strengths of Data Management Paradigms

| | Conditions Favoring One Approach Over the Other | | |
Factor	Traditional BI with Relational Database	HDFS-Based Data Management System	Notes
Structure within the source data	A single, explicitly designed structure exists	Little, changing, or many overlapping structures exist	Traditional DBMS need to impose a schema when data stored, each MR program imposes its own notion of structure when data is read
Clarity of source structure	Discernible through documentation or a bit of research	Discernible only after extensive research	Expensive to re-engineer traditional tables and ETL for change in structure; MR programming can be easily tweaked until it works
Nature of the queries consumers will submit	Numerous, but variations on a pattern	Relatively few and each largely unique	Traditional EDW allows users to request different values for multiple dimensions that have been pre-linked to transaction data
Consumers' level of comfort with programming and statistical languages	Little	Considerable	Traditional DW/BI pre-defines dimensions, so that it does not have to write custom queries for every slight variation in business question; big data users willing to program their own queries
Data volumes	Small to large	Huge	Traditional DW/BI relies on expensive disk and pre-processing for dimension-based queries, so will struggle to keep pace with increasing variety and volumes of data
Connectors to data sources	Parameter Driven	Custom Coded	Traditional DW/BI applications focus upon a finite number of source types, switching between them with changes in connect strings; MR connectors handle variety of types because some custom connect programming assumed
Longest users will wait for a query results	Train-of-thought to a minute or two	Cup-of-coffee to after lunch	BI teams may well tackle queries running a day or more in either technology with a more specialized database technology such as columnar or graph databases
Longest the business can wait for a redesign	Weeks and months OK	Hours or days	EDWs require coordinated modifications to many architectural layers, whereas HDFS apps need only change one or two program files
Nature of the complex derivations	Step-by-step applications of relatively simply transforms (business rules)	Statistical inferences or advanced mathematical transforms	Traditional ETL good at applying long chains of logic, especially with merging data streams; MR programs can easily link in far more advanced code libraries
Required degree of organization consensus upon key data definitions	Widely accepted	Siloed	EDW drives organizations toward shared business objects, whereas MR applications allow the programmer to apply his own rules as needed
Number of people directly influenced by the derived information	Large number	Fewer in number	EDWs need well-governed data elements because many people will take their cues from the values provided; HDFS applications need definitions that make sense to the individual or department asking a particular question

users hoped to perform. In addition, the size of the source data would have forced them to choose an aggregation strategy to reduce the data to at least a hundredth of its original size in order to gain reasonable query performance using their BI tools. Unfortunately, aggregation would have eliminated much of the detail the end users hoped to drill down to, thus greatly reducing the value of the data in crucial ways.

The members of the Facebook analytics team did have MR, but instead of writing extensive Java programs such as the join logic shown in the previous example, they used Hive to achieve the same results via high-level statements that were very much like SQL. Although Hive does not provide the full set of primitives found in a true SQL implementation, it allows end users to request output using JOIN and ORDER BY commands. Behind the scenes, Hive translates the SQL-like commands into MR jobs that run against the appropriate files stored in HDFS.

Figure 13.12 provides a summary of the solution architecture they used [Shao 2008]. In general, they planned to let business departments use "SQL-on-HDFS" to batch process the data into structured output files that a wide range of end users could query. They chose Hive because their users already knew SQL, making MR programming an unnecessary stretch.

To create the table in Hive, they used commands such as

```
CREATE TABLE employees (
name STRING,
salary FLOAT,
subordinates ARRAY<STRING>,
deductions MAP<STRING, FLOAT>,
address STRUCT<street:STRING, city:STRING, state:STRING, zip:INT>
) PARTITIONED BY (country STRING, state STRING);
```

To load the data, they used commands such as

```
LOAD DATA LOCAL INPATH '${env:HOME}/california-employees'
OVERWRITE INTO TABLE employees
PARTITION (country = 'US', state = 'CA');
```

This command pulls data from an HDFS source file (still in native format from the source applications) into a structured, Hive-managed table located elsewhere in the HDFS file system. Now analysts throughout the company could submit queries to this data in order to answer decision support questions.

For example, consider that the content management team wanted to profile the age of the users by page viewed so that they could ensure that sites designated as "mature" are being accessed only by subscribers older than the age of 18 years. With data tables created and loaded using commands such as the ones shown previously, these end users could submit queries such as

```
SELECT pv.pageid, u.age, count(1)
FROM page_view pv JOIN user u ON (pv.userid = u.userid)
GROUP BY pageid, age;
```

With HDFS as the foundation, the data team was able to load a wide variety of files with data types that ranged from binary to sequential text files that end users could query using only Hive SQL statements. The Hadoop framework also allowed the team to embed scripts in the processing path to extend Hive's capability, in order to provide nonstandard analyses. The output can be viewed using Hive's command-line interface, inserted into another Hive table for further SQL-style processing, or dumped to a normal file directory as comma-delimited output for importation into the end user's preferred spreadsheet or data visualization tools.

Despite the enormous size and exotic formats of the source data, Facebook's Hive-based data warehouse allowed end users to use SQL-like commands to write a wide variety of summarizations and ad hoc analyses to support operational decision making such as the following:

- Period aggregations of ad impressions served and browser click-throughs
- Counts of website users by geographies
- Ad placement optimization
- Complex measures of website users and their activities by biographic attributes
- Spam and intrusions detection via anomalies in the site's user-generated content and API usage

Notably, the combination of HDFS and Hive allowed the DW/BI team and the power users to build BI applications following a fairly agile approach of "load some new data, define a schema, try a query, repeat" until they determined the value contained in a new source and got their SQL statements correct. This fast try-and-fix cycle provided the company with far shorter "time to value" for the first version of the data warehouse plus much greater adaptability later in the face of changing requirements.

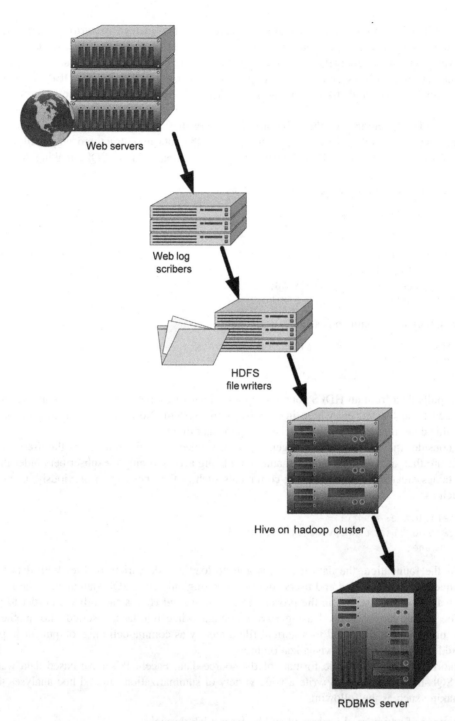

FIGURE 13.12 Solution architecture for the Facebook Hive data warehousing example.

A Tempered View of Hive

The analytics team in the previous case study was indeed able to deliver an impressive amount of BI functionality using OSS running on commodity servers. The fact that end users wrote their own queries to secure answers as fast as they could articulate questions certainly seems to be the epitome of an agile decision-support system. Given successes such as this, many observers naturally ask why everyone should not imitate Sears' decision to scrap its traditional analytics platform and "do it all with HiveQL." Unfortunately, such an impulse is too extreme and could easily land the agile EDW team in an open-source swamp. A quick overview of this use case will reveal some other trade-offs.

Apache Hive is only a data warehouse *infrastructure* built on top of Hadoop. To claim companies should build their EDWs entirely with Hive is equivalent to saying 10 years ago that everyone should have built their data warehouses with procedural SQL (e.g., Oracle's P/SQL). Such a statement implies that DW/BI departments never really needed tools such as visual ETL interfaces, change data capture utilities, and data virtualization. During the 1990s, I encountered folks who advocated building EDWs using only P/SQL in order to save the time and money needed to implement visual ETL tools. These folks found themselves in a small minority once the other DW/BI architects and managers grasped that such a reductionist approach would

- generate a huge number of long, hand-coded procedures;
- create a nightmare in trying to organize and manage so many text-based source files over the long term;
- require heavy and consistent supervision to get programmers to annotate their code;
- require "reinventing many wheels in SQL" for components such as change data capture agents; and
- limit analytics to what one relational database server could access.

In the end, the project leaders realized they did not have energy to ensure that challenges such as those just mentioned were properly remedied. Many of those challenges would require closely monitoring their developers over the arc of a long project. For applications as big as EDWs, management usually decides it will need to rely on tools to uniformly constrain bad behaviors and encourage constructive practices from the large number of developers that will be involved.

We face the same predicament today with Hadoop, and agile EDW team leaders need to see beyond the hype of a "silver bullet" data warehousing language. They need to carefully identify the limits of each product in the marketplace and then assemble the best of them into an agile value cycle that can quickly deliver data integration modules with lasting worth through a series of subreleases that allow both business and IT to drive the risk out of the requirements, design, and programming processes.

Careful study of the Facebook case history reveals several limitations that are common to "do it all with HiveQL" solutions:

1. The data management team only placed data in Hive tables, a format that many applications throughout a company will find unintelligible. A company could use another Hadoop component called Sqoop to export information to relational tables, but that would be tantamount to creating a spider's web of stovepiped data transfers.
2. The end users were responsible for writing the SQL to make sense out of the information, whether at the command line or by loading it into a data visualization product. This approach only worked because those end users were comfortable with SQL. Perhaps widespread SQL skills exist in Silicon Valley companies, but not in the rest of the economy. Most companies must support the needs of hundreds and thousands of business analysts without skills in any computer language. Most of them will not be able to load more than a single simple output file into the data visualization tool. Yet much of their analyses will draw information from multiple source tables that need to be cleansed before they can be joined.
3. Hive translates into MR programs, which have to perform the equivalent to full-table scans against each partition. As a consequence, HQL queries do not typically deliver train-of-thought-level performance but instead experience go-get-a-cup-of-coffee-or-even-grab-lunch latencies. Long data latencies can be acceptable for one-off queries where one or two end users are working to discover something for the first time. They are not acceptable for thousands of users who will be running the same basic query with simple variations in parameters, which is the dimensional analysis that star schemas, implemented with more traditional data management tools, support very well.
4. Hive does have indexing available to address these performance problems. In fact, one can load all the necessary data in yet another high-performance Hadoop database called HBase. However, now the EDW developers will be relying on multiple tools again, requiring them to combine these tools carefully. Moreover, they are back to a schema-on-design approach. They have essentially landed back into a traditional DW/BI approach, only now they are using open source tools that have been recently invented, leaving them vulnerable to all the bugs and missing features these new-born products entail.

This last point concerning response times deserves further emphasis.

DW/BI incorporates many types of analytics, from one-off questions that data scientists focus on to queries that a large community of analysts run every day or even hundreds of times within the span of a single hour. No single solution covers this full range, and it would be almost impossible for an agile EDW team to try to solve their employer's diverse business needs with a single tool, whether it be SQL, data virtualization, Hive, or HBase. To understand the

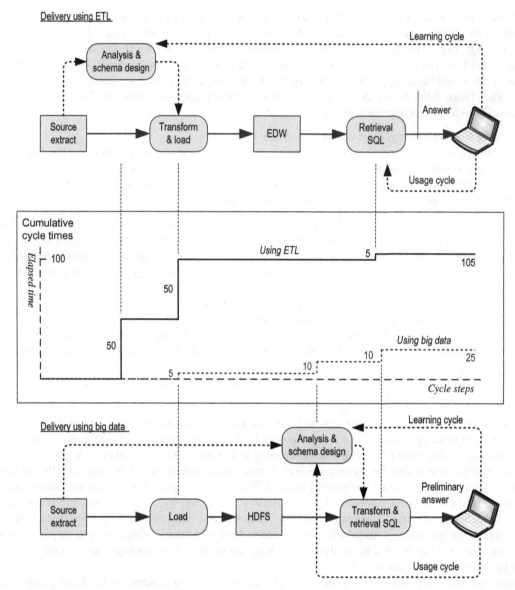

FIGURE 13.13 Cycle-time analysis for building the components of traditional and big-data DW/BI solutions.

larger reality, we need to compare the cycle times of traditional BI applications to Hive-based solutions from the end user's point of view and then see how those cycle times add up as we multiply them out by the various usage patterns a company expects an EDW to support.

Figure 13.13 provides the foundation for this analysis by showing the process needed to build the components of a solution using traditional ETL tools versus Hive. Both processes involve a source extract, transform, data load, and retrieval SQL. The difference is in the ordering and the portions of the process that get repeated during subsequent queries. Note two very important differences between these two approaches:

- The analysis and schema design is deferred in the Hive process. That accelerates providing end users basic data access. If data access is the key to a particular use case, then this is the better approach.
- The work of data transformation has also been delayed in the Hive process. It is in fact pushed upon the end users, who must invest the necessary analysis and design effort before they can write the SQL that their analyses require.

The graph placed between these two data flows shows the cumulative cycle time curve for building each solution. The ETL process's cycle time is shown in a solid line, with that of Hive depicted as a dotted line. The steps for each process are laid out at arbitrary distances from each other along the horizontal axis. The vertical axis shows the cumulative time that each cycle has consumed by the time it completes each step. The amount of time depicted for each cycle step is admittedly subjective, and readers familiar with both technologies would probably choose different amounts, but it is the relative difference between these two graphs that is important.

The cycle time for building the ETL-based approach naturally takes a big jump during the analysis and schema design step and then again during the transform and load. These big jumps reflect the work required to analyze *all* the data being placed into the warehouse and pretransform *all* the derived values, whether or not the end-user queries will draw upon them. In my experience, adding a new subject area to an existing data warehouse typically requires three or four senior developers to complete the business and data analysis and schema design, and then it requires four or five less expensive programmers to build the ETL and BI components. Because the product of hours worked and billing rates for these two subteams is approximately the same, the jumps for these two steps were both set to 50 "points" each. The effort to build the retrieval query was set to a nominal 5 points, reflecting how little work is needed to pull information from a traditional warehouse once it has been thoroughly preprocessed for dimensional analysis.

In drawing the cycle time curve for the Hive-based approach, the key distinction is that teams using Hadoop first load the data without considering its structure or worth. The organization performs analysis and schema design only on the portion that will be used, and only when an end user needs it. Because it does not have to be understood first, loading the source data into HDFS is fairly trivial, say 5 points of work. The analysis and schema design step is set at one-fifth what is necessary in the ETL-based cycle because with Hive's schema-on-read approach, the EDW team needs to consider only the portion of the new data that will be used immediately rather than having to analyze everything in the source before it is stored and used. For the retrieval step, the effort required will certainly be greater using Hive because any transform work has to be accomplished then. Accordingly, the effort for this step amounts to 10 points, or twice what is required to create another dimensional query using the ETL-based approach. All told, the level-of-effort needed to deliver the very first query for a new subject area is 105 points when using standard ETL tools, approximately four times the 25 points required to achieve the same result with a Hive-based solution.

The differences between data warehousing with the ETL versus big data tools can now be seen in Figure 13.13 by considering the difference in Learning Cycles and Usage Cycles shown on the diagram. Teams follow the Learning Cycle when they must accomplish something new with the data warehouse, such as adding a new source or implementing a new subject area. Companies follow the Usage Cycle when their business staff take a developed solution and distribute it for widescale execution across the many business units and departments in the organization. When building a new solution, a team will want a fast Learning Cycle, as shown for the big data approach illustrated in Figure 13.13, and will not concern itself much with the length of the Usage Cycle. On the other hand, companies with users who constantly use an existing solution will want a short Usage Cycle, as seen for the ETL-based process.

Using the cumulative times diagramed for each cycle in Figure 13.13, we can quantify the relative strengths of these two technologies for enterprise data warehousing. Figure 13.14 depicts the cumulative learning time for the two technologies and reveals that the total effort required to deliver a Hive solution (dotted line) grows far more slowly than the traditional approach (solid line) as the number of subreleases (repeated Learning Cycles) increases. When the number of subreleases is the driver, Hive will be the better choice.

Figure 13.15 focuses instead on cumulative usage time and speaks to the situation faced by companies interested in EDW solutions that will experience high repeated use. It shows the cumulative time the business staff spends in the Usage Cycle as it utilizes a given set of queries at increasing frequencies. Looking back on Figure 13.13, we can see that although Hive's Learning Cycle time is approximately one-fourth of that shown for the ETL-based approach (25 vs. 105 points), its Usage Cycle time is five times greater (25 vs. 5 points). This relative difference has a major impact for queries that will be used enterprise-wide tens of thousands of times. In Figure 13.15, the cumulative Usage Cycle time for the ETL-based approach grows far more slowly than that for the Hive technology, revealing that when the driver is number of executions, Hive's schema-on-read paradigm makes it the less desirable technology. For this reason, EDW teams building solutions for intensive use or a large number of users cannot throw away their ETL tools and switch all their company's business intelligence to Hadoop.

This example illustrates that the advantage of big data technologies for agile data warehousing project is specific, not universal. The advantage considered previously was based on re-usage patterns only. When one adds in other factors, such as performance, single sign-on, metadata support, and data security, the traditional EDW approach will seem preferable for an even greater number of use cases. The advantage for the traditional toolkit will increase further for analytics requiring layer after layer of ordinary business rules because that type of programming is far easier to accomplish and manage using a graphical ETL tool than in the rudimentary SQL that Hive provides. Big data technologies will regain the advantage when advanced analytics are necessary, but only approximately 5% of the total queries within

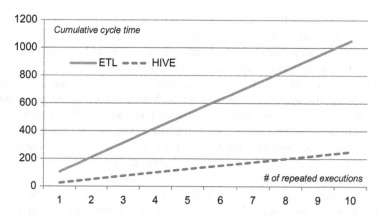

FIGURE 13.14 Cycle-time analysis – cumulative time in learning cycles. Showing how time invested accumulates as learning cycles are repeated.

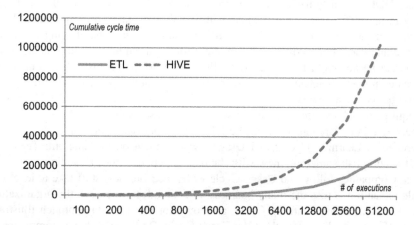

FIGURE 13.15 Cycle-time analysis – cumulative time in usage cycles. Showing how time invested grows as application is adapted by thousands of end users answering everyday business questions. Rapidly growing cost of HDFS in this scenario should give pause to those considering routing all of an organizations information into a "data lake."

the typical enterprise require that level of mathematical sophistication. Far from representing a "silver bullet" that will slay all the dragons plaguing BI, big data is a nice copper bullet. Rather than discarding all other bullets in favor of a Hadoop-only strategy, agile EDW teams should keep a variety of ordnance in their magazines.

Big Data Is Not Just Hive

Readers who are familiar with the Hadoop products and other big data technologies may believe that the previous analysis has been unfair to the world of big data products in several ways. First, a quick glance at the Apache Hive project's roadmap reveals that its community of developers plans to continue refining Hive's SQL capabilities. Moreover, the Hadoop project continues to provide new components that can greatly assist an EDW team in building a high-performance multi-user BI application—products such as HBase, Spark, Yarn, and Sqoop. Whereas Hadoop might be only a copper bullet today, plenty of people argue that it will soon be turning silver. Fortunately, despite the rapid evolution of big data products, EDW team leaders need not scrap the technologies they already know. They can still devise an effective incremental delivery strategy without making a wholesale switch in their toolkits because in the medium-to long-term the impact of big data products will be moot.

First, consider the fact that "little data" will not be going away. Well-defined and assiduously curated information will continue to be absolutely necessary in the enterprise data warehouse of the future. Organizations will still care about master data for such key business entities as customers, vendors, products, employees, and geographies. For example, a big data application might be able to show management that four or more phone calls to product warranty

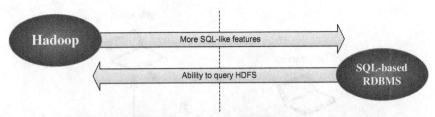

What is the best strategy for the agile EDW teams once these
two worlds overlap, allowing them to employ both big data and
"little data" technologies in a single value architecture?

FIGURE 13.16   Big data and traditional RDBMSs are converging.

are highly associated with incipient customer churn. But what has it accomplished if it cannot provide a call center manager a personalized depiction of the specific customer who is on the line, frustrated with the company's service right now? To intervene effectively, that manager must be able to see details about a given customer, such as whether he owns a product that is impossible to support or whether he is behind in his payments and therefore not worth keeping in the first place. If little data will still be vital going forward, then so will be the RDBMS packages that make little data manageable and the traditional ETL tools that allow EDW teams to cleanse, integrate, and dimensionalize those components of the company's operational information.

Moreover, the vendors providing these databases and transform tools are not sitting idle while open source Hadoop products scoop up their market share. They are quickly adding Hadoop capabilities to the mainstream data warehousing products we already know, so that many of them can now present HDFS disk farms as just another data source. As a result, we have the situation depicted by Figure 13.16, in which Hadoop will soon have added so many SQL-like features that it will have drawn closer in capabilities to SQL-based RDBMSs, but the RDBMS will have traveled just as fast in the opposite direction to tap HDFS file stores. In fact, because today's RDBMSs are mature products with decades of programming behind them, they may well become far better at incorporating big data sources than big data products will be at replicating what current database tools can do.

EDW team leaders can best devise an agile DW/BI platform by searching for the *convergence* of big and little data. Teams on a budget will want to work with the open source products, whereas those in the larger programs will appreciate the maturity of traditional tools. Neither group will be at a disadvantage. Confronted with new, unfamiliar data, both of them will be able to quickly build a surface solution by throwing the data into HDFS and exploring it with a version of SQL that can support a schema-on-read strategy. Where the data volumes are manageable, they will then both be able to *modulate* the warehouse's management of that information, addressing requirements needing fast response time into preprocessed tables using a schema-on-design approach. Given that both groups will be able to steer their information between big and little data strategies as needed, the question then becomes, "Which of the many value chains that our EDW team can follow will generate the highest value given the particular set of information we need to add to the data warehouse?"

Using Big Data to Enhance EDW Agility

Figure 13.17 provides one picture of an answer to that question. It shows the data for business intelligence information flowing toward the end user via any one of four paths. Dataflow 0 is the starting point: The organization has a data warehouse that contains master data for business entities such as customer and product. Data is loaded into the EDW using traditional ETL applications. A wide community of end users can draw upon it using easily adjusted constraints on highly reusable queries.

When a new and possibly quite large data source appears, the EDW team will need to employ Dataflow 1. Here, the new source files are simply loaded into an HDFS cluster. A small community of IT and business power users can then invent schemas on the fly and query the new resource. They will use Hive if their company has implemented Hadoop. They will use HDFS-enabled SQL if they are using a new version of a traditional RDBMS.

Once these first users have discovered an effective way to parse and output the new data that reliably yields business value, the EDW team will have a choice. If MR delivers reasonable performance times, the team can make the big data queries available to the wider EDW user community through Dataflow 2, which requires that the team simply publish that access through the company's DVS. The DVS can even join the results of a Hive query with the master data found

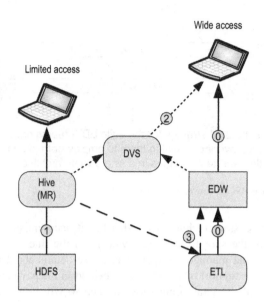

FIGURE 13.17   A succession of surface solutions leveraging big data.

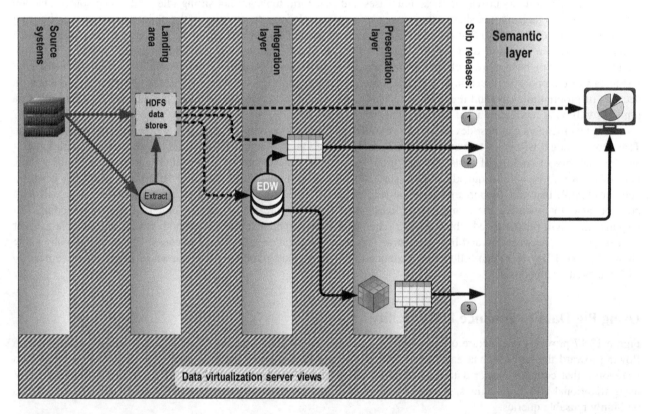

FIGURE 13.18   EDW reference architecture with surface solutions employing big data technology.

in the EDW in order to provide information with standardized references so that it can be used without confusion by departments throughout the enterprise. If, on the other hand, the end users require preprocessing for faster performance, then Dataflow 3 simply utilizes the Hive output as just another source for the ETL. The ETL modules will load relevant aggregations and subsets of atomic records into the company's "little data repository," otherwise known as the enterprise data warehouse.

We can view this iterative and incremental development of the application's high-level design as another flavor of surface solutions with backfilling, which can be depicted in terms of the EDW reference architecture. As shown in Figure 13.18, the first subrelease allows end users to pursue data discovery by accessing the results of Hive directly. This provisional solution can serve a small user community, and it will allow both business and IT to become familiar with the new data, define accurate requirements, and reduce project risk.

With the second subrelease, the Hive output is routed to the Integration layer, enriched with the EDW's existing "little data," and made accessible to end users via a data virtualization server view. By the time they construct the third subrelease, the EDW team and end users understand enough of the big data stream that they can combine it completely into the dimensional analyses that the Presentation layer of the EDW supports. In this case, EDW team delivered something cheap and easy at first, then steadily backfilled the architecture with increasing capable and robust solutions. The end users saw a quick solution and then a steady improvement in the data services provided, all amounting to a constant delivery of value, true to the goals of agile development.

SUMMARY

Incremental delivery, requirements discover, and project risk mitigation can all be achieved using a strategy called "surface solutions and architectural backfilling." Following this strategy, agile EDW teams focus first on a simple solution—perhaps based on raw data from the source—in order to allow their customers to begin solving business problems. The EDW team then steadily backfills the reference architecture to provide a series of more complete and robust solutions, eventually arriving at a full DW/BI application after several subreleases.

Agile EDW teams have three basic approaches they can take when pursuing a surface solution strategy: leveraging shadow IT, data virtualization, and big data. When leveraging shadow IT, the EDW team delivers progressively richer data sets to departmental staff, who build their own temporary BI solutions using that information. The EDW team spends the time between each subrelease observing how end users employ the data and using that information to design the next, more capable solution.

The data virtualization strategy relies on a "superoptimizer" that can create views across databases and data types, even including semistructured data as needed. With data virtualization, EDW retains more control so that data governance and performance can be better managed. The data virtualization technology has some limitations in terms of performance and the scope of data it can offer, but its solutions are declared rather than engineered, so they offer much shorter time-to-value for the business customer.

The big data strategy employs a new category of products, such as Hadoop's HDFS, MapReduce, and Hive, to provide access to new data, whether it be very large, poorly structured, and/or just unfamiliar to IT and the business users. Given that big data and traditional DBMSs are converging, EDW team leaders can plan on a new architecture that allows them to selectively modulate BI solutions from HDFS to RDBM in order to fulfill a wide variety of use cases.

All these surface solution strategies provide live-data prototypes that offer the business learning opportunities and temporary services, but for many business intelligence requirements, these lightweight solutions will not be enough. There are still many situations in which the EDW team will need to build out a fully architected data warehouse that provides reliable and well-governed information with high performance. Moreover, EDW team leaders will want to have an agile approach to delivering this highly engineered data warehouse, one that allows them to build it incrementally and evolve it easily as business requirements change. As discussed in Chapter 12, the traditional data modeling paradigms actually work counter to this goal. Starting with Chapter 14, we consider the hyper modeling paradigms that allow EDW teams to achieve truly agile enterprise data warehousing.

Chapter 14

Agile Integration Layers with Hyper Normalization

The previous chapters presented many techniques for creating fast enterprise data warehousing (EDW) solutions for business customers by leveraging data virtualization servers, big data technologies, and shadow information technology (IT) resources. As powerful as these techniques might be, EDW team leaders will still encounter many data warehousing/ business intelligence (DW/BI) requirements that can only be supported by a large repository of well-defined and assiduously prepared and persisted data elements—the kind of data repositories that enterprise data warehouses offer. When requirements tip over into this category, it is of course the outcome that everyone dreads because building or extending an enterprise data warehouse typically demands many months of engineering, involving large expense and high risk. As explored in Chapter 12, much of the expense and risk of building large DW/BI applications arise from the rigidity and brittleness of the traditional data modeling paradigms that EDW teams typically employ. Data repositories built using standard normal or conformed dimensional forms simply require far too much re-engineering and data conversion whenever business requirements change to support a truly agile data warehousing program.

Fortunately, two hyper modeling alternatives exist that can eliminate a good deal of the work and mitigate much of the risk imposed by traditionally modeled data warehouses. This chapter introduces readers to the hyper *normalized* data modeling paradigm, which lends considerable agility to the EDW's integration layer in particular. Chapter 15 presents the hyper *generalized* data modeling approach, which extends those benefits to the presentation and semantic layers of the EDW reference architecture. Because space limitations allow for only a brief presentation, these chapters aim to simply introduce the hyper modeling techniques to EDW team leaders and demonstrate why they hold such promise for making enterprise data warehousing truly agile. The citations to multiple reference works will provide DW/BI professionals wanting to explore these topics further with a place to start.

At the time of this writing, hyper normalization has a strong toehold in northern Europe and, to a lesser extent, Australia and Canada, where it has dramatically improved the economics and success rates of enterprise data warehousing teams—to the point where DW/BI professionals participating in these efforts agree that they will never voluntarily build a data warehouse using a traditional data modeling technique again. As we will see using the four change cases established previously, hyper modeling can eliminate 30−90 percent of the labor required to construct an enterprise data warehouse. The data warehousing community only began using these techniques slightly more than 10 years ago, but given their power to accelerate deliveries and reduce project risk, I predict that in another 10 years hyper modeling paradigms will be the mainstream approach for most new enterprise data warehousing initiatives. Thus, EDW team leaders need to become familiar with them now if they wish to be part of the coming sea change in DW/BI design practices.

HYPER NORMALIZATION HINGES ON "ENSEMBLE MODELING"

I use the term *hyper normalization* to refer to a family of data modeling techniques that all employ *ensemble data modeling*. As depicted in Figure 14.1, ensemble modeling is a strategy for representing data within a data warehouse that decouples the three categories of elements found in traditionally modeled data tables. Entities are captured from the source systems and broken into the following components:

- The core identifier for the entity—that is, its *business key*
- The relationships between entities—that is, the *links*
- All the other elements that provide context for these business keys and links—that is, their *attributes*

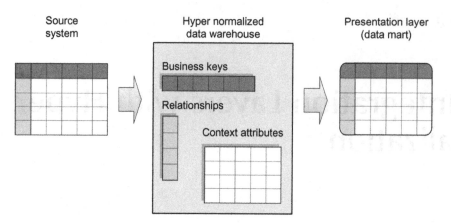

FIGURE 14.1 Ensemble data modeling.

Ensemble modeling does not destroy any information. By joining the business keys and attributes together using the links, organizations can not only reassemble the original data but also project the data into a myriad of other presentations that better support specific end-user analytics.

Delivery speeds for the first version of an EDW improve by decoupling these fundamental data components into atomic business keys, links, and attributes because then the delivery team can manage the operational data using highly pattern-based data structures that lend themselves to population by reusable data transform modules. More important, these decoupled components dramatically enhance a team's ability to maintain and extend an existing EDW, even once production data is loaded, because they insulate each component from changes occurring in related entities. Such insulation makes it far easier to respond to new requirements with only a small amount of data schema re-engineering, with the data often quickly and easily converted using the same reusable extract, transform, and load (ETL) modules. As discussed later, this pattern-based approach allows EDW developers to rapidly collect all the organization's operational data into an integrated and persistent data store using only three parameter-driven data transformation routines. Although programming these parameter-driven load modules requires some thought and effort, overall the time saved by reusing the three modules allows teams to deliver key portions of the enterprise data warehouse in an order of magnitude less time. By empowering flexible projections, fast data capture, and speedy re-engineering for end-user analytics, ensemble modeling allows DW/BI departments to be incredibly responsive to new business requirements in ways traditional EDW teams cannot match.

Several Varieties of Hyper Normalization Exist

Many styles of ensemble modeling exist today. Figure 14.2 shows a family tree of the more codified styles I have encountered during the past 10 years. The American style is called *data vaulting*, which was started by a series of white papers published by Dan Linstedt [Linstedt 2003]. Several of the developers on the first few data vaulting projects compiled their practices into a *Data Vault 1.0* standard and published these guidelines so that others could also experiment with this new data modeling paradigm [Linstedt and Graziano 2011]. This original standard was eagerly adopted by a large contingent of DW/BI consultants in The Netherlands who implemented well over 600 separate data vault warehouses within the next 10 years. The Dutch developers began sharing the challenges and solutions they encountered on these early implementations, creating a vibrant community of data vault practitioners with an enormous collection of best practices that informally defines a "Dutch" standard to hyper modeling [Hultgren 2013].

As the Dutch school of data vaulting took off, Linstedt and his colleagues were busy extending their approach. They have recently introduced a *Data Vault 2.0* standard, which adds a few technical innovations such as hashed surrogate keys and some new practice elements that incorporate Scrum, big data, and data virtualization into one's project planning [Linstedt 2014a].

Within these three schools of data vaulting standards, there are three styles for how the resulting data objects should function within the layers of the EDW reference architecture [Damhof 2011a]. As an example, which is discussed in more detail later, the *classic style* advocates applying only a minimum of business rules while integrating operational data, whereas practitioners of the *enhanced style* will readily add derived values to the tables of the Integration layer. Such a diversity in approaches is a testament to adaptability of the ensemble modeling concept and the great success that data vault practitioners have encountered in the field. Fortunately, these standards and styles are not mutually exclusive so that agile DW/BI teams can derive a hybrid approach that best matches the unique context confronting a particular DW/BI department [Linstedt 2014b].

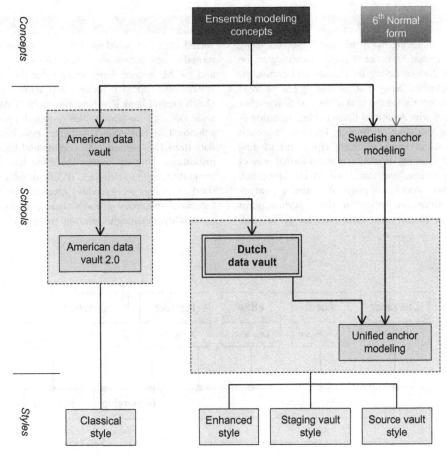

Note: Schools and styles renamed and simplified somewhat for presentation clarity

FIGURE 14.2   Family tree of hyper normalized modeling approaches.

Because the Dutch standard for data vaulting seems to have the largest user community of any hyper normalization approach, I employ their guidelines for the remainder of this chapter. Unless stated otherwise, I also follow the "enhanced style" of design. Both of these points will be far easier to understand after we have discussed the basics of hyper normalization data modeling.

Running in parallel to the rapid innovation occurring among the data vaulting communities is a Swedish version of ensemble modeling called *anchor modeling*. Invented by Olle Regardt, Lars Rönnbäck, and several other computer science academics at the University of Sweden in Stockholm, anchor modeling extends the notion of ensemble modeling with concepts from Chris Date's sixth normal form. The creators of anchor modeling honed their approach while building data warehouses for some of the largest insurance and retail companies in Sweden. They formally introduced the technique to the world in 2009 at the International Conference on Conceptual Modeling in Gramado, Brazil [Regardt et al. 2009]. Anchor modeling represents a second data design approach that results in more tables than data vaulting. Because both anchor modeling and data vaulting result in models with more tables than third through fifth normal form would create, I refer to them collectively as "hyper normalization" techniques. Interestingly, the Dutch school of data vaulting has begun to merge with data vaulting (see the sidebar), so EDW team leaders should be at least aware of how anchor modeling differs from data vault so they can choose wisely from all the hyper normalized options available for their DW/BI projects. The salient differences between anchor modeling and the data vaulting approaches are outlined later.

HYPER NORMALIZED DATA MODELING CONCEPTS

Hyper normalization data modeling is a set of techniques for designing the integration layer of a data warehouse. More pointedly, an EDW team typically uses hyper normalization to design a lightly integrated, persistent staging area for data from a company's operational systems. As detailed later in Figure 14.25, the data in this persistent staging area

Interestingly, after achieving many successful projects using data vaulting, the Dutch have not stopped innovating in the area of advanced data modeling techniques and computer-generated EDW solutions. Several of the leading practitioners there have recently combined the best of the Swedish anchor modeling technique with American data vaulting, resulting in a "Unified Anchor Modeling" technique. This new approach offers more options in terms of entity types and loading patterns than data vaulting, as well as a more formal way of modeling the transformations that need to be supported. The Unified Anchor Model is a physical modeling strategy that is derived from an enhanced third normal form (Boyce–Codd) and requires the data modeler to be well versed with fact-based modeling, a type of modeling that is rooted in new data analysis standards such as FCO-IM, ORM, and NIAM. Recent demonstrations of this hybrid and more streamlined approach include a program completed for the Dutch central bank (De Nederlandsche Bank) whose nation-wide oversight responsibilities required a fast, model-driven solution that can collect, validate, enrich, and disseminate data from The Netherlands' commercial banks and financial institutions. Unified Anchor Modeling has allowed the data integration team to deliver EDW increments in time boxes as short as a few weeks while meeting the strictest of non-functional requirements for accuracy, reliability, consistency, availability, meaningfulness, and traceability.

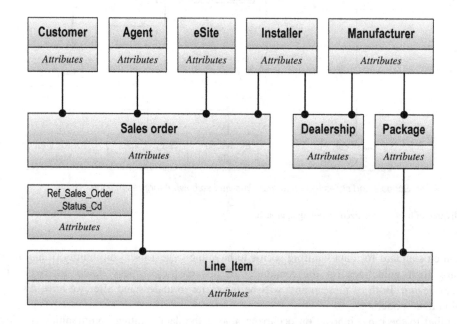

FIGURE 14.3 Hyper normalizing a 3NF data model – starting point.

can be enriched by linking it to additional hyper normalized data tables that store the results of applied business rules. Data from both the persistent staging area and the enriched tables can then be projected at will into a conformed dimensional presentation layer.

In practice, EDW teams pursue hyper normalized data modeling in very much the same way they conduct standard normalization techniques. They identify core business entities, the relationships between them, and the attributes that provide context information about both entities and relationships. Understanding the difference between standard normalization and hyper normalization is easiest if we apply hyper normalization techniques against a data model already in third normal form.

The starting point of this exercise is shown in Figure 14.3, which replicates the third normal form integration layer for the simple sales transactions data warehouse we considered in Chapter 12. The square boxes are data tables, with a

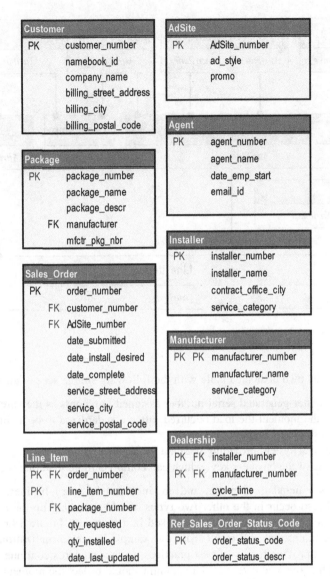

FIGURE 14.4 Structures for the starting model (in 3rd normal form).

horizontal line separating a table's business key fields from its context attributes below. This model also includes a reference table for Order Status that we will need to demonstrate how one would hyper normalize code lookups using anchor modeling. The table structures for all the objects in this starting model can be found in Figure 14.4.

Business Key Entities

The first step in hyper normalizing a starting data model is to simply identify the pivotal business keys underlying the organization and its transactions that we want the data warehouse to support. As shown in Figure 14.5, the modelers here decided the entities shown with dark headers are the major business elements the warehouse will need to track. Not all of the starting tables were deemed to be major business keys. The sales orders themselves were included because "Order Number" is an identifier that many business people know and use extensively in their everyday business processes. Line Item was not designated a major business entity not only because "Line Item Number" is rarely a stand-alone business concept but also because it can be considered simply a relationship that joins Order with Package on an item-by-item basis.

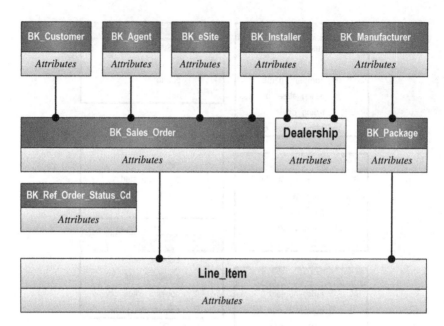

FIGURE 14.5   Hyper normalization Step 1 — declare business keys.

Each business key is given its own dedicated table with the following simple set of data columns:

- Surrogate ID (SID)—a computer-generated serial number assigned to records as they are inserted into a table
- Load date time—identifies the moment the load occurred, often standardized to be a single value across the records added to all tables during a single ETL run
- Source system—the operational system providing the data for a given record
- The human-recognized value of the business key, which can comprise more than one source column

The first three columns are metadata elements and are included in every business key table defined by data vaulting. These columns will also occur in the other two types of tables making up the data vault standard (with the exception of a surrogate key for the attribute tables, discussed in a moment). Figure 14.6 illustrates the structures of the business key and attribute tables that will result from this sample hyper normalization exercise.

Data vaulting is a steadily improving family of best practices, so the standards continue to change. For example, the standards originally specified that the load date metadata column should reflect the moment a record was inserted into a data warehouse table, but many practitioners now prefer to set it to the moment the source record was captured in the EDW's landing area so that it can remain static and traceable throughout all the layers of the reference architecture. As another example, the V2.0 data vaulting standards now recommend using MD5 hash values of the business keys rather than sequences as the primary keys on data warehouse tables. This enables ETL modules to calculate primary key values from the source data, avoiding many resource-intensive lookup actions against business key tables while loading links and attributes. Moreover, by calculating the primary keys independently, the link and attribute loads no longer have to run after the ETL for the business keys, allowing the data warehouse to load far more tables in parallel, increasing EDW performance. Nuances such as these are the primary differentiator between the various flavors of data vaulting techniques available today.

Linking Entities

In the second step of hyper normalization, the joins of the original model are all converted to many-to-many (M–M) relationships. As shown in Figure 14.7, this step requires declaring "linking" tables between all business keys that have a relationship. In the diagram, these associative tables have been labeled with "link." Figure 14.8 provides the structures for the linking tables of our example. As can be seen there, they are very simple tables, holding only the surrogate keys to the business key records that relate and also the standard metadata columns.

FIGURE 14.6   Structures for the hyper normalized model — business keys and their attributes.

Because they have such simple and predictable structures, in future diagrams they are abbreviated to diamonds marked only with the letter "L."

Note that although these linking tables are built for M—M joins, they can support both one-to-many (1—M) and M—1 relationships. This modeling technique eliminates the risk that we will have to re-engineer our model and convert our data when joins that we thought were 1—M later become M—M or even reverse into 1—M. The small price to pay is that the data model no longer structurally communicates the cardinality between business key tables so that information has to be documented elsewhere, perhaps as comments on the integration layer model.

Attribute Entities

With the third hyper normalization step, the modelers move the remaining attributes of the original tables to their own "attribute tables," as shown in Figure 14.9. Attribute tables can provide context for either business key tables or link

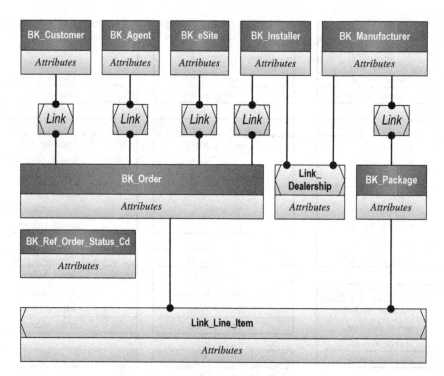

FIGURE 14.7 Hyper normalization Step 2 — install many-to-many links between business keys.

tables. Aside from one column per attribute to be stored, the data vault standard requires these "Attrib_" tables to also have the following metadata elements:

- The SID for the Parent BK or link table (PK)
- Load time stamp (PK)
- Record source

The structures for the tables of this final model can be found in Figures 14.6 and 14.8.

Note that instead of a surrogate key of its own, an attribute table employs the SID of its parent table, whether that be a business key or a linking entity. This fact speaks to the purpose of a record in an attribute table: to provide the context for a given parent record as of the moment it last changed in the source system. Accordingly, a given business key or linking record can have many attribute records associated with it, namely one for each time any of the source fields captured by the attribute tables experiences a change of value. A dedicated surrogate key for each attribute record proves unnecessary because combining the parent SID and the load timestamp is enough to uniquely identify the attribute record holding the new context values for a particular parent record and at a particular moment in time.

Note also that a business key or link table can also have multiple attribute tables associated with it, depending on how the data modeler wants to group the context fields found in the source system. If the parent business key or relationship has only a few descriptive elements, he or she will typically keep them all in a single attribute table. In these situations, my figures will depict the attribute tables in an abbreviated form as a simple object marked with an "A," as shown in Figure 14.10. Each of these attribute "stubs" in this diagram implies that all the required context elements have been collected into satellite tables and linked through key values to its parent table.

Data modelers do not always place all the context columns for a business key or link into a single table. When context columns are very numerous, they will divide them by topical area or by their rate of change in the source systems. A customer business key, for example, could have an attribute table for identifying qualifiers, another for address elements, and a third for credit worthiness. In a hospital EDW, a patient business key might have one attribute table for values observed at the time of admission, another for measures taken during daily physician rounds, and a third for holding vitals gathered by the minute during surgeries.

Attributes may also contain columns recording effective dates, such as the Effective_From_Date and Effective_Until_Date as seen in Attrib_Link_Dealership in Figure 14.8. These columns hold the business dates for

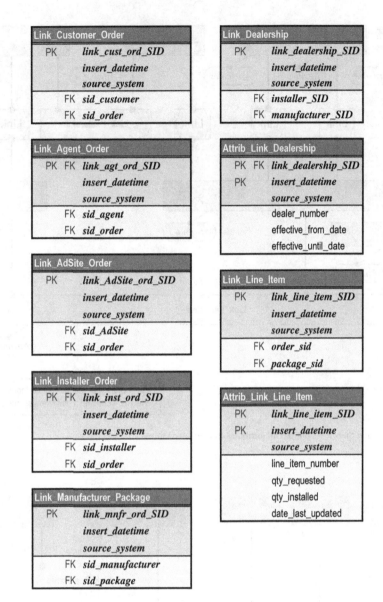

FIGURE 14.8 Structures for the hyper normalized model — links and their attributes.

which the values in the given attribute table apply to the associated record in the parent business key or link table. Effective dates are a business concept, so the values they store are conceptually independent from the load_datetime metadata column found in each table, per the data vault standard. Some modelers do not provide a column for end effectivity because the start date of the next record for a given business key implicitly defines the end of the time span the first record describes. When an end date column is included, it requires the ETL to perform an update to existing records, which runs counter to the data vault's "insert only" orientation, which is discussed later.

Lightly Integrated, Persistent Staging Area

Now that we have identified the three components for a hyper normalized data store, we can reflect upon how this form supports the desired function for an integration layer. Especially in the classic style of data vaulting, the intent of hyper normalization is to provide a persistent recording of business entities and operations in a way that we can later project the company's operational data into dimensional presentation layers for responsive business analytics. This goal implies several objectives for the hyper normalized data store; namely, it must allow

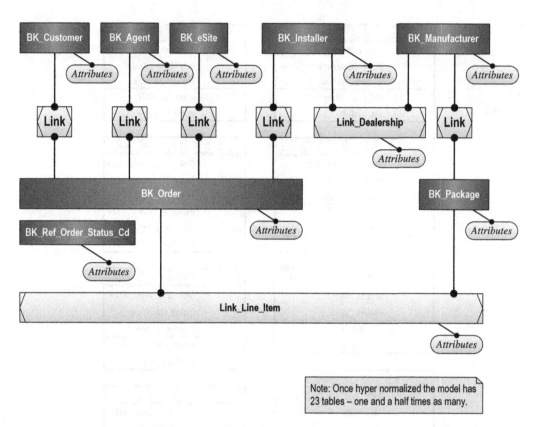

FIGURE 14.9 Hyper normalization Step 3 — split out all attributes to their own tables.

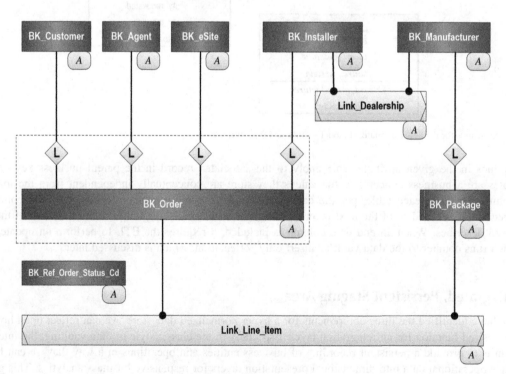

FIGURE 14.10 Hyper normalized model with abbreviated depiction of link and attribute entities.
Note that one can always restore the data to a third normal form by re-joining the components, as the dotted line indicates for the Order entity.

- the structure of the warehouse to be quickly updated so that EDW developers can rapidly respond to new data sources;
- the data of the warehouse to be economically adaptable so that existing data can be massaged to fit into the newly updated table structures; and
- light integration so that the data collected from source systems contributes to a single view of the enterprise rather than forming multiple, unrelated "data heaps" that are each specific to the operational system from which it was sourced.

The term "light integration" indicates only that all the source records pertaining to a core business entity such as customer or product end up in the same target structure whenever they clearly represent the same concept. Many EDWs perform further processing beyond this straightforward collocation of business entities. For example, they take a second look at customers, vendors, and other business partners to determine if they are indeed the same entity masquerading under different names, such as trade names belonging to the same corporation. As another example, they might use complex analytics to assign a "partner value score" so the organization can know which partners are most important to the business.

The creation of company-wide master data elements and the application of business rules go beyond "light integration." Hyper normalized data stores can support these postcapture, value-added activities, but they typically store them in a distinct sublayer of the reference architecture. This two-sublayer approach is the hallmark of the "enhanced style" of data vaulting. In that style, a data vault with a fairly simple design rapidly captures data arriving from source systems, processing that data just enough to store it appropriately in a shared set of business key and linking tables. A subsequent ETL session then applies business rules to generate derived values, harmonize information across business units, and support master data elements. This second ETL session deposits newly created information in additional hyper normalized tables that reside in a second area of the reference architecture called the "business vault." This secondary sublayer will be examined in greater depth later when we discuss Figure 14.25.

Ensemble Modeling Components Allow Light Integration and Agility

Now that we have defined the three structural components stipulated by ensemble modeling, we can consider how each abets the goal of a light, persistent staging area for operational data.

Business Key Tables Abet Agility

First, the notion of dedicated entities for each type of business key enables fast capture of shared information. Many business applications have a notion of a *customer*, for example. Each time the business requests that the EDW team add a new data source to the data warehouse, the data modelers simply look through that applications data model for how it represents customers and other common business concepts. Once they have discerned the fields that the new system uses to uniquely identify these common objects, they create an ETL to add those values to the data vault's business key tables, such as BK_CUSTOMER. If two or more systems are using overlapping sequences of integers, the modelers will simply need to make the natural key for the target business key tables the source system plus customer number in order to resolve those collisions. In either case, the EDW team can quickly employ the pattern-based modeling rules to define a shareable table for these two sets of business keys and then utilize a reusable ETL module to capture the source data. Moreover, because these business key entities reflect the real, core business concepts underlying the enterprise and its operations, a data vault's collection of business keys stabilizes very soon and then rarely needs to be expanded or redesigned. Although source systems may be subject to change, only occasionally do those changes change the types of entities that make up the structure and processes of the organization.

Linking Tables Abet Agility

A second advantage to hyper normalized designs derives from the dedicated linking tables. They too are simple in structure so that they are fast to define and can be loaded with a parameter-driven, reusable ETL module. Moreover, their minimal contents dramatically reduces the impact that many changes in the source systems might impose.

Linking tables contain just the keys of the objects they relate to and also some metadata columns. Because of this construction, they are designed for many-to-many joins. Most relationships in an enterprise data model are one-to-many, but occasionally new requirements require us to suddenly record a many-to-many association. For example, a product owner believes that brokers own their sales opportunities, so the company needs only one broker record per prospective contract. However, in the data, the development team found instances in which brokers were sharing sales

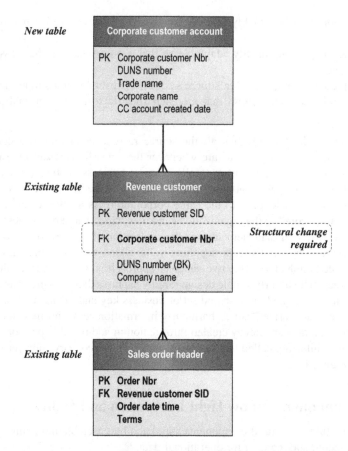

FIGURE 14.11 Third normal form data warehouses are heavily impacted by new entities.

prospects. Because linking tables are designed for many-to-many joins, the links the team believed would be one-to-many can be simply populated with additional records to manifest the bidirectional join. The structure of the warehouse does not need to be updated, nor does any existing data have to be converted.

Moreover, these single-minded association tables insulate the data warehouse from major impacts when new entities appear. The excerpt of a EDW module included in Figure 14.11 shows the impact a new entity can have on traditionally modeled data warehouses. The company has recently implemented a master data repository for customers, so the EDW must add a Corporate_Customer_Account table, and because it will serve as a parent to the customer table coming from the revenue system, this latter table will need to be restructured to add a new foreign key, and its data will need to be converted. Hyper normalization eliminates this restructuring and data conversion, as can be seen in Figure 14.12. There, the EDW team needs to add only three tables to support the new corporate customer account entity—a business key, its attributes, and a many-to-many linking table that will be used to join the BK_Corporate_Customer to BK_Revenue_Customer using records implementing a one-to-many relationship. This design achieves the same functionality but leaves the structure and data of the original entity unaffected, allowing teams to make these changes far faster than when they utilize a standard normal form model [Boyina and Breur 2013].

Attribute Tables Abet Agility

Finally, attribute tables also support the data vault's purpose of agile data integration. For data vaults designed to simply record operational data as it occurs without adding additional value, data modelers frequently structure the attribute columns to closely reflect the source elements they are designed to capture, even naming them to match the identifiers used in the source system. Given that the data vault typically integrates the information from multiple sources, some situations may entail conflicts between the names chosen for the same concept by the different upstream systems—for example, "CUST_NME" versus "CUSTOMER_NAME." To resolve this type of conflict, many data vault modelers choose to create a separate attribute table for each source, as shown on the left side of Figure 14.13. Here, data from the company's prospecting system, sales management application, and warranty registration utility land in a separate attribute

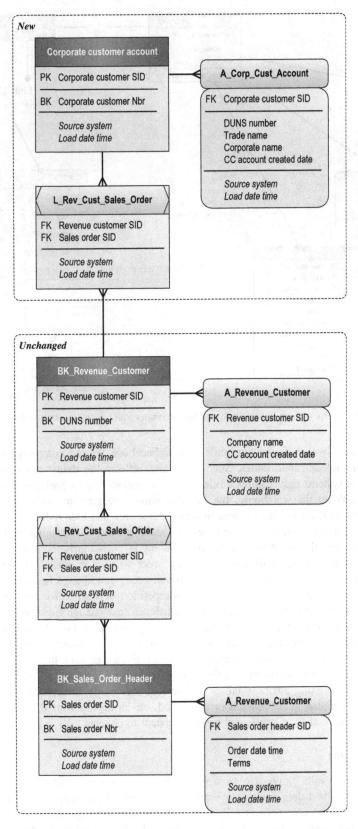

FIGURE 14.12   Linking tables in a hyper normalized data warehouse insulate existing tables against disruption when new entities are added.

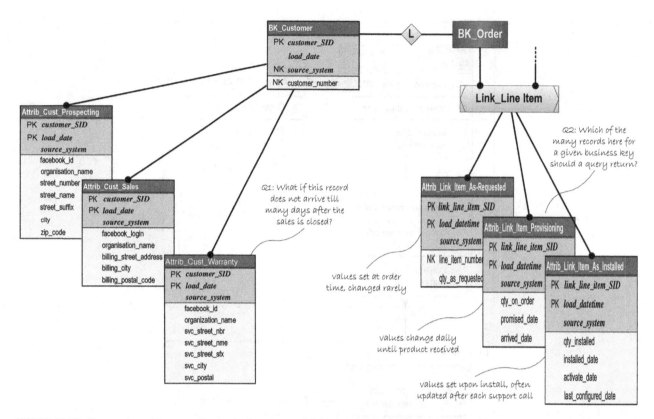

FIGURE 14.13 Data vault model excerpt showing business keys and linking entities with multiple attribute tables.

table dedicated to each source. Notice similar attributes such as Facebook ID and company name have slightly different spellings between the data vault attribute tables. Such a practice reflects the data vault's intent to provide a quickly deployable archive of source systems that requires a minimum of reengineering as business requirements change. When a new source becomes available to the warehouse, the modeler simply declares an additional table to receive the new collection of attributes it provides, giving them names to match the source and thus reducing the decisions that need to be made while simultaneously enhancing the integration layer's traceability back to the source systems.

Utilizing multiple tables for the attributes of a given parent is particularly common when different groups of qualifiers change at different tempos. Qualifiers describing an order when it is placed, for example, are relatively permanent, whereas the values describing current status during provisioning can change frequently. Splitting apart these two groups of qualifiers based on change cadence saves needless repetition of storage for the more static attributes. Often, modelers provide a different attribute table for each set of attributes that change together—for example, one table for attributes that change daily and another for those that change monthly, as depicted on the right side of Figure 14.13.

With the flexible approach to capturing business context that data vault attribute tables provide, new sources can come and go, they can change structure, and the elements within them can vary the frequency of their updates. The EDW team adapts to these new conditions by simply adding new attribute tables to reflect the new situation in the upstream system. Records in existing attribute tables still reflect the reality that prevailed when those records were captured, and therefore do not need to be adapted or converted, obviating much of the maintenance work that makes data warehouses in standard normal form brittle and highly resistant to change.

An Insert-Only Paradigm

Readers should note that data vaults emphasize an "insert-only" paradigm by design. We can visualize this notion at work by considering an established data vault in operation. When any of the supported source systems creates a new instance of a business entity, such as a customer or an order, a new business key value will appear in the extracts fed to the data vault. When this new business key value appears, the ETL simply inserts it into the appropriate business key table. The load process simply ignores the other business key values found in the extract that are already in the integration layer's business key table. Business keys are never deleted because once they are seen, the fact that they once existed remains true forever. Their status in the source system may change to deleted, but that situation is recorded in the status column of an associated attribute table, not in the business key records themselves.

The same treatment occurs when the ETL scans the input data stream for links. If the operational data contains a previously unseen combination of business keys, the ETL inserts a new link record into the appropriate table, translating the business key's natural values into surrogate keys by looking them up in the appropriate BK tables or calculating a hash value. The fact that these two business keys once had an association will be true from that moment forward, so this link record will never need to be deleted. The effective date, status, and other qualifiers for a given relationship between business key values are recorded in the records of an attribute table associated with the link table, not in the link table itself [Data Vault Discussion Group 2014].

Two aspects of the data vault paradigm make business keys and linking records impervious to later events and free them from deletes or updates: (1) They record facts that were once true rather than concerning themselves with whether those facts are still true, and (2) they have been isolated from the attribute records, which in fact can contain effective dates. These considerations make business keys and linking tables *insert-only* entities. We will see later that this fact greatly simplifies the ETL needed to support these table types.

The design of attribute tables should emphasize insert-only also, but the situation here is slightly more nuanced. The data vault creates a corresponding attribute record when the parent business key or linking record is first captured. When the context elements for this parent change in the source system, a new attribute record is created, reflecting the new truth. The old attribute record still accurately reflects the previous truth, so we should not delete it. If the source provides a begin effectivity date column, then the value in this column should be replicated to the warehouse to indicate when in time the operational system believes the record's information begins to apply. If no begin effectivity column is available in the source, the load_datetime value or the landing layer capture date time of the attribute record can provide a substitute [Vos 2014a]. In either case, the begin effectivity time of the new record implicitly defines the end effectivity of the previous attribute record for that business key, so no end effectivity columns need to be created or maintained. Following this pattern, even attributes are insert-only, again making the necessary ETL far simpler.

If the modelers place end effectivity columns on the warehouse tables, the ETL would have to search for the existing record that has become obsolete and update its end effectivity value before a new record could be inserted, making the ETL more difficult to program and slower to execute. It must be remembered that the integration layer is a repository to hold information to be projected into the star schemas of the Presentation layer. During that projection, end effectivity values can be added to the target objects where end users can find and benefit from them.

Swedish Variation: Anchor Modeling

With the three entity types involved in ensemble data modeling identified, we can now point out the major difference between the data vaulting standards and the Swedish anchor modeling technique. Readers desiring a more detailed comparison that the major points offered here can consult [Ronnback et al. 2013].

Figure 14.14 shows the sales orders data model of Figure 14.10 converted into an anchor model. This model was built using the online modeling tool provided by anchor modeling's creators and that can be found at http://www.anchormodeling.com. This site also provides online tutorials and a "generate" function that creates key data warehousing components such as target data definition language (DDL), views with triggers that facilitate table loading, and basic retrieval views that simplify data access. This level of online support makes anchor modeling an easy type of hyper normalization for DW/BI professionals to get started with.

Perhaps the most noticeable difference between the data vault and anchor modeling standards is nomenclature, as shown in Table 14.1. A second difference between the two approaches is the different treatment they give reference tables. Reference tables typically hold the codes that are used throughout a data warehouse, such as the Order Status qualifier found in the sample model I have been using. In data vaults, reference tables are typically modeled as a hub with a satellite, as shown in Figure 14.9. Each coded value is a unique record in the business key table. The decode for each code is stored in an attribute table record that, with its load date time column, enables the warehouse to track the changes a company makes in the meanings associated with its code values. In contrast, anchor models explicitly depict reference tables as a connected part of the model, using a fourth element type called "knots." One can see a knot called Order Status attached to the Order anchor in the figure.

A final difference to mention is probably the most important. Anchor models provide a separate entity for every attribute column the data warehouse contains. This approach can be seen in Figure 14.14 for the Agent anchor, which has separate attributes modeled for agent number, agent name, agent email id, and data started. If the modeler chooses to "historize" an attribute, then the online tool will give that attribute table a *ChangedAt* date time column to record

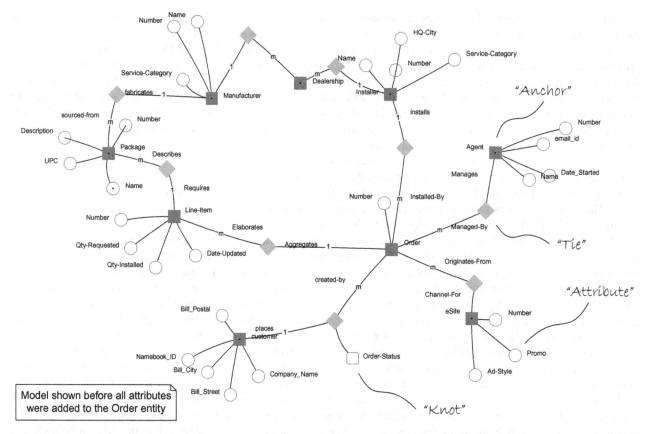

FIGURE 14.14 Anchor modeled equivalent of the HNF order model.

TABLE 14.1 Nomenclature Differences between Data Vault and Anchor Modeling Standards

Generic Concept	Data Vault Name	Anchor Modeling Name
Business key tables	Hubs	Anchors
Linking tables	Links	Ties
Attribute tables	Satellites	Attributes

when its values have changed. By splitting out every attribute to its own separate table and tracking the history of the values in each (when that option is selected), anchor modeling achieves many of the design objectives spelled out for a completely temporal database in the sixth normal form, as described by Chris Date [Date et al. 2002].

Data vaults, in contrast, assemble many qualifier columns together in the attributes tables, either one or a few, depending on their business themes and their rate of change. With many attributes sharing the table, data vaults require far fewer physical objects to actually store the information arriving from the source applications.

REUSABLE ETL MODULES ACCELERATE NEW DEVELOPMENT

The flexibility of the resulting EDW data models is an important feature of hyper normalized designs. DW/BI teams receive even greater advantage from the fact that hyper normalization frequently allows them to capture all the data of their source systems using only three parameter-driven ETL modules. In other words, when asked to create a new enterprise data warehouse, the team needs only to program three modules and the integration layer is done. That last sentence overstates the situation somewhat. It says nothing about a data warehouse's derived columns, and it overlooks the fact that many teams need a utility for writing retrieval queries against the hyper normalized data warehouse once it is loaded with information. But if we refine the statement to "build three parameter-driven ETL modules and the *data capture* portion of your warehouse's integration layer is complete," we will be getting very close to the truth.

One ETL Pattern Needed Per Hyper Normalized Table Type

Some readers may have viewed the transition of the third normal form in Figure 14.3 to the hyper normalized structure in Figure 14.9 with alarm. The model started with 9 tables and ended with 23. EDW teams following a traditional processing architecture typically develop one ETL module per target table being loaded. Would not hyper normalization then more than double a development team's programming work?

The pattern-based nature of the hyper normalized tables plays a crucial role in keeping the higher number of tables from translating into considerably more development labor. Consider the structure of the business key tables in Figure 14.6. Every business key table has the same structure: three metadata columns and a natural key value, which might be a single column or a concatenation of two or more. Many EDW developers are well versed in the technique of dynamic SQL—an approach in which the computer writes and then executes its own SQL statement, with the details of the instruction the machine creates for itself determined by the input conditions. EDW teams can take this approach to develop a reusable, parameter-driven ETL module for business keys.

Consider the BK_Customer table, for example. Why not write an ETL module so that a developer invokes in two different ways for two different sources? The first invocation of this module might amount to "Scan the Prospecting System's CUST table for new values in PROSPECT_NUMBER, and every time you find a previously unseen value, insert a record into BK_CUSTOMER." The second call might be "Now scan the Sales System's CUSTOMER table for new values in CUST_ID, and insert any new values into BK_CUSTOMER." In both cases, the ETL will create a surrogate key value for the CUSTOMER_SID column and put an appropriate value in the LOAD_DATETIME column. SOURCE_SYSTEM will be set to the name of the application that provided the data to be scanned. If designed properly, this shared LOAD_BK_TABLE module should need only the following parameters to be able to determine for itself the actual processing it should do:

Parameter Name	Value for 1st Call	Value for 2nd Call
Source System	PROSPECTOR	ONLINE_SALES
Target Table	BK_CUSTOMER	BK_CUSTOMER
Source Table	CUST	CUSTOMER
Source Business Key Field	PROSPECT_NUMBER	CUST_ID

Similarly, all linking tables have the same structure: three metadata columns and then the surrogate keys of the business key records being related. For the table linking BK_Customer and BK_Order in Figure 14.10, for example, the call for the first source system would be as follows:

1. Scan the Prospecting System's INQUIRY table for quotes new marked "CLOSED."
2. Look up new combinations of PROSPECT_NUMBER and QUOTE_NUMBER in BK_CUSTOMER and BK_ORDER, respectively.
3. Create a new LINK_CUSTOMER_ORDER record using the surrogate keys retrieved.

The call for the second source system would then be:

1. Scan the Sales System's SALES_ORDER table for new combinations of CUST_ID and ORDER_NBR.
2. Repeat steps 2 and 3 given previously.

Again, the ETL module can derive values for surrogate keys, load timestamps, and source systems on its own from either the parameters provided or the conditions prevailing when it creates each output record.

Attribute tables are slightly more complex, but they still yield to a pattern-based treatment. All attribute tables have the same three metadata columns: a parent surrogate key, load date time, and source system. Each attribute table will have a different set of columns for receiving the context columns from the source tables. Some EDW teams structure attribute table columns to match a source system's column names and data types so that the ETL can infer the column identifiers of the target schema from the structure of the landing table it is processing.

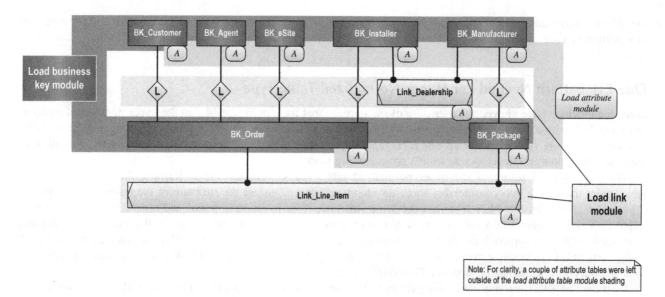

Note: For clarity, a couple of attribute tables were left outside of the *load attribute table module* shading

FIGURE 14.15   Only a few, parm-driven ETL modules are needed to load the bulk of the data warehouse.

In this case, the invocation of the ETL for the attribute table of our example is quite simple. The first call would be as follows:

1. Scan the Prospecting System's CUST table for a new set of values in the following columns....
2. Look up the combination of SOURCE_SYSTEM = "PROSPECT_SYSTEM" and CUSTOMER_NUMBER = PROSPECT_NUMBER in BK_CUSTOMER.
3. Use that surrogate key to create a new record in ATTRIB_CUSTOMER and transfer the values found in the columns listed in Step 1.

Alternatively, the LOAD_ATTRIB_ETL module could be programmed with an INCL-EXCL parameter in which "INCLUDE" would cause all the context columns listed to be transferred to the warehouse, and "EXCLUDE" would cause all the columns *except* those listed to be captured.

The development team might find it too restrictive to have to structure and name all of the target columns so that they match a source system's elements. In that case, the previous logic would still apply except that the developers would have to provide a mapping table that indicates a target column for each source attribute. Many EDW teams intend their data vaults to enable fast capture of source system information and plan on restructuring it later when they move it to the presentation layer for analytics. These teams find it easy to structure the target schemas to match source elements, and for ease of exposition, it is assumed that this is the case for the remainder of this discussion.

Parameter-Driven ETL Module Prototypes

The previously discussed concepts provide clear guidance for EDW teams wanting to craft a set of parameter-driven ETL modules. Figure 14.15 depicts the goal for this work—to build three reusable ETL procedures that can load the entirety of a data warehouse's sources into the tables of a "source" data vault. (The distinction between source and business data vaults will be discussed in a moment.) Procedure LOAD_BK (business key) populates all the business key tables following the pattern just described. LOAD_LINK and LOAD_ATRRIB perform the same service for link tables and attribute tables, respectively. Figure 14.16 lists the parameters my colleagues and I typically employ when creating these three ETL modules for our projects. We usually implement these modules using a scripting language such as Python or Perl for portability between projects, but we have built them using the procedural language of the target system's database management system (DBMS) as well.

LOAD_BK needs only seven parameters to give it the guidance needed to populate a business key table. The "source natural key columns set" parameter is usually a comma-delimited list of the column(s) that the target table should use as a natural key in order to determine the unique occurrence of records within the source entity. The ETL will scan those columns to spot entities not yet in the data warehouse. Working in terms of *column sets* rather than

```
Modules Prototypes

Load_BK ( source table, target table,
    {source natural key column set}, {target column set},
    ETL start DTM, [last delta datetime], [distinct option] )

Load_Link ( source table, target table,
    source column 1, reference table 1, {source natural key column set 1}, target column 1,
    . . .
    source column N, reference table N, {source natural key column set N}, target column N,
    ETL start DTM, [last delta datetime], [distinct option] )

Load_BK_Attrib ( source table, target table,
    parent_table, {parent natural key column set}, {source natural key column set},
    incl/excl flag, {source attribute column set},
    ETL start DTM, [last delta datetime], [distinct option] )

Load_Link_Attrib ( source table, target table, parent_table,
    lookup_table 1, {lookup 1 natural key column set}, {source natural key 1 column set}, target column 1,
    lookup_table 2, {lookup 2 natural key column set}, {source natural key 2 column set}, target column 2,
    incl/excl flag, {source attribute column set},
    ETL start DTM, [last delta datetime], [distinct option] )


Parameter Details

{sets of values}
[optional parameters]
target: name of object into which the module will insert records
source: name of object from which input records will be retrieved
ETL start DTM: shared date-time value with which all records created within one load will be stamped
incl/excl flag: indicates whether the following list of columns should be included or excluded from the attributes to be loaded
distinct option: TRUE causes the DISTINCT reserve word to be added to the SQL command that pulls records from source
```

FIGURE 14.16   Prototypes for reusable hyper normalized load modules.

expressions allows the ETL to manage the concatenation and delimiters between values, lending consistency and avoiding programming errors, but some teams use a column expression for the column set parameters instead.

The timestamp value in *ETL_start_DTM* will be placed in the LOAD_DATETIME column of every record captured to the warehouse. If the same value is employed for all calls to these reusable ETL modules in a given batch, then an entire cohort of new records within the data vault can be easily identified by this shared load date time. In order to facilitate effective tagging of record cohorts, some teams utilize a "load process ID" value in the place of the load date time field, with a LOAD_PROCESS reference table maintained separately that holds a rich set of event data for each load process the warehouse undertakes. The *last_delta_datetime* parameter allows the ETL module to process a much smaller subset of source records, namely those with create or update timestamps that occur after this value.

The *distinct_option* will cause the database to utilize a DISTINCT clause on the source records (when landed in a DBMS table or at least accessed as external table). Letting the database provide a stream of distinct input values often results in shorter overall execution times than occurs when an ETL script must work its way through a large number of redundant records.

For link tables that relate only two tables, *LOAD_LINK* requires 13 parameters. When it relates more than two tables, it requires an additional 4 parameters per additional table. Unlike *LOAD_BK*, this ETL module must name some reference entities already in the data warehouse so that the programming will know where and how to find the surrogate keys already assigned to the business key value the new link will refer to.

LOAD_ATTRIB requires a reference table to be named as well, but here the reference is its parent table, and the parameters provided instruct the module how to identify the parent record for a given set of context elements it wants to capture. This module also utilizes an include/exclude flag so the ETL module will know whether the following list of columns are those to be captured or ignored. The use of this last column list allows the developers to selectively capture the source context columns, thus separating the attributes by business theme or change cadence, as discussed previously.

```
Using Modules That Each Read Through The Source Data Set
    Procedure calls follow prototypes listed in Figure 14.16 except sources assumed to be flat file extracts.
    (Shaded lines will be found adapted in the second approach below)


/* Begin script
declare LOAD_DTM = now( )
declare EXTRACT_DIR = "/usr/edw/extract/western_region"
declare NULL_STR = ""


/* Fundamental tables with dedicated extracts */
Load_BK ( "$EXTRACT_DIR/sales_customer_extract.txt", "BK_CUSTOMER", "customer_nbr", "bk_customer_sid", $LOAD_DTM )
Load_BK ( "$EXTRACT_DIR/hr_extract.txt, BK_AGENT", "agent_number", "bk_agent_sid", $LOAD_DTM )
Load_BK ( "$EXTRACT_DIR/product_catalog_extract.txt", "BK_PACKAGE", "package_number", "bk_package_sid", $LOAD_DTM )
Load_BK ( "$EXTRACT_DIR/online_mktg_extract.txt", "BK_AD_SITE", "ad_site_domain" "bk_ad_site_sid", $LOAD_DTM )
Load_BK ( "$EXTRACT_DIR/daily_sales_transactions.txt", "BK_SALES_ORDER", "sales_order_number", "bk_sales_order_sid", $LOAD_DTM )


/* Fundamental tables sourced from the service channel extract */
Load_BK ( "$EXTRACT_DIR/service_channel_extract.txt", "BK_INSTALLER", "installer_number", "bk_installer_sid", $LOAD_DTM )
Load_BK ( "$EXTRACT_DIR/service_channel_extract.txt", "BK_MANUFACTURER, "manufacturer_number", "bk_manufacturer_sid", $LOAD_DTM )


/* Link tables sourced from the service channel extract */
Load_Link( "$EXTRACT_DIR/service_channel_extract.txt", "LINK_MANUFACTURER_PACKAGE",
    "manufacturer_number", "BK_MANUFACTURER", "manufacturer_number", "manufacturer_sid",
    "package_number", "BK_PACKAGE", "package_number", "package_sid", $LOAD_DTM )
Load_Link ( "$EXTRACT_DIR/service_channel_extract.txt", "LINK_DEALERSHIP",
    "manufacturer_number", "BK_MANUFACTURER", "manufacturer_number", "manufacturer_sid",
    "installer_number", "BK_INSTALLER", "installer_number", "installer_sid", $LOAD_DTM )


/* Links source from the sales transaction system */
Load_Link ( "$EXTRACT_DIR/daily_sales_transactions.txt", "LINK_CUSTOMER_SALES_ORDER",
    "customer_number, "BK_CUSTOMER", customer_number, customer_sid,
    "sales_order_number", BK_SALES_ORDER, "sales_order_number", "sales_order_sid", $LOAD_DTM )
Load_Link ( "$EXTRACT_DIR/daily_sales_transactions.txt", "LINK_AGENT_SALES_ORDER",
    "agent_number", "BK_AGENT", "agent_number", "agent_sid",
    "sales_order_number", BK_SALES_ORDER, "sales_order_number", "sales_order_sid", $LOAD_DTM )
Load_Link ( "$EXTRACT_DIR/daily_sales_transactions.txt", "LINK_AD_SITE_SALES_ORDER",
    "ad_site_number", "BK_AD_SITE", "ad_site_domain", "ad_site_sid",
    "sales_order_number", BK_SALES_ORDER, "sales_order_number", "sales_order_sid", $LOAD_DTM )
Load_Link ( "$EXTRACT_DIR/daily_sales_transactions.txt", "LINK_INSTALLER_SALES_ORDER",
    "installer_number", "BK_INSTALLER", "installer_number", "installer_sid",
    "sales_order_number", BK_SALES_ORDER, "sales_order_number", "sales_order_sid", $LOAD_DTM )
Load_Link ( "$EXTRACT_DIR/daily_sales_transactions.txt"", "LINK_LINE_ITEM",
    "package_number", "BK_PACKAGE", "package_number", "package_sid",
    "sales_order_number", BK_SALES_ORDER, "sales_order_number", "sales_order_sid", $LOAD_DTM )
```

FIGURE 14.17 Driver script employing reusable load modules.

These examples assume that the targets have been modeled to closely match the source system so that the names of target columns are predictable. If this constraint is too demanding, these procedure prototypes can be easily adapted by adding parameters to name mapping files that will allow the ETL modules to understand how source column names flow into distinctly named target columns.

Calling the Reusable ETL Modules

Once a team has created the three ETL modules needed to populate the source data vault tables, those modules have to be invoked in the proper sequence. Figure 14.17 shows a driver script utilizing the reusable ETL modules for our example data vault model from Figure 14.10.

```
/* Attributes for fundamental tables */
Load_BK_Attrib ( "$EXTRACT_DIR/sales_customer_extract.txt", "ATTRIB_CUSTOMER",
    "BK_CUSTOMER","customer_number", "customer_number",
    "EXCL", "$NULL_STR", $LOAD_DTM )
Load_BK_Attrib ( "$EXTRACT_DIR/hr_extract.txt", "ATTRIB_AGENT",
    "BK_AGENT","agent_number", "agent_number",
    "EXCL", "$NULL_STR", $LOAD_DTM )
Load_BK_Attrib ( "$EXTRACT_DIR/online_mktg_extract.txt", "ATTRIB_AD_SITE",
    "BK_AD_SITE","ad_site_domain", "ad_site_domain",
    "EXCL", "$NULL_STR", $LOAD_DTM )
Load_BK_Attrib ( "$EXTRACT_DIR/product_catalog_extract.txt", "ATTRIB_PACKAGE",
    "BK_PACKAGE","package_number", "package_number",
    "EXCL", "$NULL_STR", $LOAD_DTM )

/* Attributes from the service channel extract */
Load_BK_Attrib ( "$EXTRACT_DIR/service_channel_extract.txt", "ATTRIB_INSTALLER",
    BK_INSTALLER, "installer_number", "installer_number,
    "INCL", "installer_name, contract_office_city, service_category", $LOAD_DTM )
Load_BK_Attrib ( "$EXTRACT_DIR/service_channel_extract.txt", "ATTRIB_MANUFACTUER",
    BK_MANUFACTURER, "manufacturer_number", "manufacturer_number",
    "INCL", "manufacturer_name, service_category", $LOAD_DTM )

Load_Link_Attrib ( "$EXTRACT_DIR/service_channel_extract.txt", "ATTRIB_LINK_DEALERSHIP", "LINK_DEALERSHIP",
    BK_INSTALLER, "installer_number", "installer_number", "installer_sid",
    BK_MANUFACTURER, "manufacturer_number", "manufacturer_number", "manufacturer_sid",
    "INCL", "cycle_time", $LOAD_DTM )

/* Attributes from the transaction extract */
Load_BK_Attrib ( "$EXTRACT_DIR/daily_sales_transactions.txt", "ATTRIB_SALES_ORDER",
    "BK_SALES_ORDER, "sales_order_number", "sales_order_number",
    "INCL", "date_submitted, date_install_desired, date_complete, service_street_address, service_city, service_postal_code", $LOAD_DTM )
Load_Link_Attrib ( "$EXTRACT_DIR/daily_sales_transactions.txt", "attrib_link_line_item", "LINK_LINE_ITEM",
    "BK_SALES_ORDER", "sales_order_number", "sales_order_number", "sales_order_sid",
    "BK_PACKAGE, "package_number", "package_number", "package_sid",
    "INCL", "line_item_number, qty_requested, qty_installed, date_last_updated", $LOAD_DTM )
```

FIGURE 14.17   (*Continued*)

This script first sets a single load date time value for all the modules to share so that each cohort of records can be identified easily later, although many teams would employ a LOAD_ID value here instead. The invocation of the parameter-driven load modules then begins and follows the logical order implied by the data model. All the business keys are loaded first, which is possible because these tables are fully independent given that all foreign keys have been relegated to linking tables. Varying source tables are used to load these business keys. Agent and product, for example, are populated using extracts from the human resource and product catalog applications, given that they hold master records that the sales application will later utilize as reference tables. The invocations against the same source data object, such as *service_channel_extract*, have been grouped together to provide a small bit of predictability within the driver script. Next in the driver script come the calls for loading the linking tables, which have also been grouped by the source data object utilized. Finally, the driver script calls the *LOAD_ATTRIB* modules, progressing by shared source data object, until all the context needed for the business keys and links loaded previously has been captured.

Astute readers may have noted that the approach taken in Figure 14.17 requires a given source data object to be read multiple times if more than one load module draws records from it. Given that the primary tables of a hyper normalized data warehouse operate in an insert-only mode and do not update target records, one can expect high enough performance with each call. For data warehouses employing small- to medium-sized data sources, the performance will be high enough that the repeated read operations implied by Figure 14.17 will still complete within a reasonably short time window.

When data sources become very large, however, the load times for this approach may grow beyond what can be tolerated. In that event, the reusable ETL modules should be designed as subscripts to be called in sequence as each record

```
Excerpt from a Script Calling Multiple Modules On Each Record As It Is Read From A Single Source Data Set
    (illustrating processing of the service channel extract only)


procudure load_from_service_channel_extract (
    declare CURRENT_RECORD = $parameter_1

    /* Fundamental tables sourced from the service channel extract */
    Load_BK ("$CURRENT_RECORD", "BK_INSTALLER", "installer_number", "bk_installer_sid", $LOAD_DTM )
    Load_BK ("$CURRENT_RECORD", "BK_MANUFACTURER, "manufacturer_number", "bk_manufacturer_sid", $LOAD_DTM )

    /* Link tables sourced from the service channel extract */
    Load_Link( "$CURRENT_RECORD", "LINK_MANUFACTURER_PACKAGE",
        "manufacturer_number", "BK_MANUFACTURER", "manufacturer_number", "manufacturer_sid",
        "package_number", "BK_PACKAGE", "package_number", "package_sid", $LOAD_DTM )
    Load_Link ("$CURRENT_RECORD", "LINK_DEALERSHIP",
        "manufacturer_number", "BK_MANUFACTURER", "manufacturer_number", "manufacturer_sid",
        "installer_number", "BK_INSTALLER", "installer_number", "installer_sid", $LOAD_DTM )

    /* Attributes from the service channel extract */
    Load_BK_Attrib ( "$CURRENT_RECORD", "ATTRIB_INSTALLER",
        BK_INSTALLER, "installer_number", "installer_number,
        "INCL", "installer_name, contract_office_city, service_category", $LOAD_DTM )
    Load_BK_Attrib ( "$CURRENT_RECORD", "ATTRIB_MANUFACTUER",
        BK_MANUFACTURER, "manufacturer_number", "manufacturer_number",
        "INCL", "manufacturer_name, service_category", $LOAD_DTM )
    Load_Link_Attrib ( "$CURRENT_RECORD", "ATTRIB_LINK_DEALERSHIP", "LINK_DEALERSHIP",
        BK_INSTALLER, "installer_number", "installer_number", "installer_sid",
        BK_MANUFACTURER, "manufacturer_number", "manufacturer_number", "manufacturer_sid",
        "INCL", "cycle_time", $LOAD_DTM )
)
```

FIGURE 14.18   Driver script employing reusable load modules

of a large data source is read so that all the loads stemming from the same extract can be completed via only a single read through the source data. Figure 14.18 lists a pseudo code excerpt for such a "high-performance" approach, showing how the calls made in Figure 14.17 against the *service channel extract* (shaded in gray) can be all called in sequence for each record of a source data set.

Teams facing very high load volumes often add *source_partition* parameters to their reusable ETL modules. These parameters cause an instance of a load module to operate only upon a certain value range of natural keys or other driving attributes found in the source data of the business entity that the module is loading. With such parameters, the EDW developers can distribute the data capture processing for their hyper normalized loading operations across many ETL servers. These parameters can be easily updated in driver scripts, making a high degree of parallel processing very manageable. Moreover, the insert-only paradigm underlying hyper normalized data stores keeps the load processing very lightweight and allows EDW teams to implement their data capture routines on very inexpensive servers. Combine that with the easy management afforded by the natural key partitioning just described, and EDW teams find that hyper normalized integration layers scale very well indeed.

Self-Validating Reusable ETL Modules

The standard structures of a hyper normalized data store allow an EDW team to write reusable, pattern-based ETL modules to load the data. Many teams also leverage the pattern-driven structure of source data vault tables to create reusable, parameter-driven validation routines as well. By combining these two concepts, DW/BI departments can quickly program and adapt the components of an EDW Integration layer that both captures and quality assures the company's operational data with a single driver script.

```
Reusable Test Widget Prototypes (Examples)

/* Validate that both extract and target table records just loaded have the same set of unique values */
procedure confirm_domain ( HNF_table, HNF_column,
     source_extract_file, source_field, HNF_Load_Date )


/* Validate that both extract and target table records just loaded have the same median values
(works for both numeric, text, and date columns) */
procedure confirm_median ( HNF_table, HNF_column,
     source_extract_file, source_field, HNF_Load_Date )


/* Validate that both extract and target table records just loaded have the same number of null values */
procedure count_nulls ( HNF_table, HNF_column,
     source_extract_file, source_field, HNF_Load_Date )


Sub driver procedure to validate all columns of a given target table


procedure validate_hnf_table_load
     declare HNF_TABLE = parameter_1
     declare HNF_COLUMN = parameter_2
     declare SOURCE_EXTRACT = parameter_3
     declare SOURCE_FIELD = parameter_4
     declare HNF_LOAD_DATE = parameter_5


     for all columns
         if upper(right(column_name,4)) <> "_SID"
         and upper(column_name) not in ( "INSERT_DATE", "SOURCE_SYSTEM" )

             confirm_domain ( $HNF_TABLE, $HNF_COLUMN,
                 $SOURCE_EXTRACT, $SOURCE_FIELD, $HNF_LOAD_DATE )
             confirm_median ( $HNF_TABLE, $HNF_COLUMN,
                 $SOURCE_EXTRACT, $SOURCE_FIELD, $HNF_LOAD_DATE )

             if upper(left(column_name,7) <> "ATTRIB_" )
                 confirm_nulls  ( $HNF_TABLE, $HNF_COLUMN,
                     $SOURCE_EXTRACT, $SOURCE_FIELD, $HNF_LOAD_DATE )
             endif


         endif
     endfor
endproc
```

FIGURE 14.19   Prototypes of reusable test widgets and a driver script calling them.

Figure 14.19 anticipates some of the material we will consider in the quality assurance portion of this book by first providing three examples of some parameter-based testing widgets: *confirm_domain*, *confirm_median*, and *count_nulls*. These widgets are examples of a class of simple widgets that agile EDW teams often create to automate the bulk of their ETL unit testing. Any one of these widgets does not accomplish very much on its own, but teams can employ many of them against all the target columns, every time they load the warehouse. By "swarming" the target tables with many simple tests, they in fact catch the bulk of the programming errors introduced into ETL code during design changes and other application maintenance activities.

Confirm_domain, for example, ensures that a given column found in both an extract and the target table records just loaded from it have the same set of unique values. *Confirm_median* checks that a particular column in a source extract delta and the new target records created from it have the same median value. The median statistic works better than average because it can be applied against many data types, including numeric, string, and dates. *Count_nulls* can be used for non-key columns of an attribute table to ensure that the new records in a context column have the same number of null values as the source delta from which it was replicated. EDW developers typically write a dedicated test driver script that applies these widgets as appropriate against all the columns in the primary vault tables of the integration layer, calling it after each load session. These simple widgets do not require a tremendous amount of horsepower, so often the full validation script can fit comfortably within the EDW's nightly load window. When the validation routine for a given module represents such little overhead, some teams actually incorporate these test widgets into the load process. Where the ETL performance and load window allow such an approach to be employed, this strategy will guarantee that at least the leading edge of the data vault contains a clean, accurate, and therefore *trustworthy* portrayal of all the operational data sent to it.

Whether EDW team leaders decide to incorporate data validation steps directly into their load processes or run them as a separate script, the overall advantage of the hyper normalized approach is clear. By allowing a highly patterned approach to both data transformation and quality assurance, hyper normalization permits programming and validation to be achieved far more easily than traditional DW/BI design paradigms allow. Both traditional and hyper normalized approaches start with a conceptual model of the target entities and relationships the team believes the data warehouse will need. In practice, it takes only a small effort to find the business entities and links prescribed by the target conceptual model in each source system, and it takes even less effort to add calls to LOAD_BK and LOAD_LINK to the EDW's ETL driver script. Specifying the appropriate calls to LOAD_ATTRIB takes only slightly more effort, and suddenly the EDW will be poised to begin archiving data for a new source system or subject area. With a small amount of additional time to add calls to a set of reusable test widgets, the team will have implemented the bulk of necessary unit-level quality assurance, and the foundational components of the enterprise data warehouse will be ready to run.

Estimate of Comparative Development Efforts

Given that loading and testing the leading edge of the data warehouse can now be configured using modular components, we should revisit Chapter 12's estimate for implementing new EDW objects. Table 14.2 both summarizes the estimate last seen in Table 12.6 and adjusts it for the far lower level of effort required by a hyper normalized data repository.

The first two items in the estimate cover the source and requirements analysis necessary to arrive at a conceptual data model and the understanding needed to specify a source-to-target map. Because this work in unaffected by the choice of data modeling paradigm, its estimated labor is the same for both the standard approach and hyper normalization. The remaining elements will take far less labor when working with hyper normalized designs, however. The developers will be able to accomplish many tasks, such as analyzing existing target objects, programming data transforms, and validating newly programmed units, far more quickly with the hyper normalized approach because (1) the work is now highly pattern based and (2) it focuses only on implementing the lightly integrated, persistent repository. Applied business rules will be tackled later after the operational data has been safely stored away.

My observation is that EDW teams working with data vaults tend to complete approximately 90 percent of the tasks listed previously with approximately 10 percent of the effort, and the remaining 10 percent proceeds only twice as fast. These factors combine so that many of the tasks pursued with hyper normalized data models require less than one-third of the effort they would take when working with a traditional data model in standard normal form. The remaining tasks, such as creating a new logical model and supporting business validation efforts, are noticeably faster under hyper normalization but require work involving several people so that they still take approximately half the effort of a traditional approach. These adjustment factors are noted in Column H of Table 14.2.

The combined impact of these different accelerations can be seen in the totals at the bottom right of Table 14.2. For creating or updating the primary vault tables for an EDW, working with a hyper normalized data model can save an EDW team approximately three-fourths of the labor per table. In terms of billable time, the hyper normalized approach saves the EDW team and its sponsors approximately 60 hours per table—a sizable amount that should inspire all enterprise data warehousing teams to at least consider this innovative data modeling approach.

COMMON DATA RETRIEVAL CHALLENGES AND THEIR SOLUTIONS

The old saying, "There is no free lunch," certainly applies to hyper normalized data warehousing. Now that we have examined the basic components and outlined the benefits the technique offers, it is time to consider the price we pay for these advantages. A balanced appraisal will allow EDW team leaders to make a fully informed choice regarding a data modeling paradigm when they start their next major project.

TABLE 14.2 Comparable Conversion Costs Per Table when Employing the Hyper Normalized Data Modeling Paradigm

For tables requiring two programming days of data transform programming[1]

Ln #	Tasks	Performed Once Per...	Standard Approach[2] Total Effort Hours	Duration Days	Hyper Normalized HNF Adjustment	Total Effort Hours	
1	Analyze sources	Model Change	10 hrs	2.70	100 percent	10 hrs	
2	Create new business data model	Model Change	11 hrs	0.70	100 percent	11 hrs	
3	Create new logical data model	Model Change	10 hrs	1.30	50 percent	5 hrs	
4	Create new physical data model	Model Change	4 hrs	0.70	28 percent	1.1 hrs	
5	Analyze existing target data	Model Change	33 hrs	0.70	28 percent	9.2 hrs	
6	Author STMs[1]	Affected Table	22 hrs	1.30	28 percent	6.2 hrs	
7	Data Transform Programming[2]	Affected Table	22 hrs	2.00	28 percent	6.2 hrs	
8	Author test cases	Affected Table	19 hrs	0.70	28 percent	5.3 hrs	
9	Write test scripts	Affected Table	7 hrs	0.70	28 percent	2.0 hrs	
10	Create test data	Affected Table	18 hrs	0.70	28 percent	5.0 hrs	
11	Validate test scripts in DEV	Affected Table	16 hrs	0.70	28 percent	4.5 hrs	
12	Promote to SIT	Affected Table	3 hrs	0.20	28 percent	0.8 hrs	
13	Execute scripts	Affected Table	2 hrs	0.20	28 percent	0.6 hrs	
14	Drive IT's conversion validation	Affected Table	10 hrs	0.30	50 percent	5.0 hrs	
15	Support business' validation	Affected Table	6 hrs	0.30	50 percent	3.0 hrs	
16	Document errors	Affected Table	15 hrs	0.30	50 percent	7.5 hrs	
17	Promote scripts to PROD	Affected Table	3 hrs	0.20	28 percent	0.8 hrs	
18	Execute scripts	Affected Table	2 hrs	0.20	28 percent	0.6 hrs	
19	Drive IT's conversion validation	Affected Table	13 hrs	0.50	50 percent	6.5 hrs	HNF-Generated Savings
20	Support business' validation	Affected Table	8 hrs	0.50	50 percent	4.0 hrs	
21	Document errors	Affected Table	15 hrs	0.20	50 percent	7.5 hrs	Hours
	Per-Model-Change Task Totals (Lines 1-5)		**68 hrs**	5 days		**27 hrs**	60 percent
	Per-Affected-Table Time Totals (Lines 6-21)		**181 hrs**	13 days		**65 hrs**	64 percent

[1] The average programming effort for an established EDW including ETL programming for new tables, conversion scripting for existing tables.

[2] Numbers for standard approach duplicated from Table 12.6.

HNF Aids the Leading Edge of the Integration Layer Only

For all the ways that hyper normalization makes data warehouses easier to design and ETL easier to program, there are several limitations and difficulties that must be kept in mind. First, hyper normalization only addresses the integration layer of the EDW reference architecture. EDW teams must still generate the presentation layer of business analytics solutions using the same labor-intensive techniques they have followed for decades. Of course, a data virtualization server (DVS) may well make that task far easier, as described in Chapter 13, as long as the data volumes do not exceed the DVS's bandwidth and begin taking overnight to answer queries.

Second, the work represented in the labor savings previously estimated covers only light integration. One could be forgiven for saying that this leading edge of the data warehouse is only a fancy staging layer. The data there has been lightly integrated, but no business rules or master data elements have been added, so very little value has been added to the data. Data vaults in this portion of the warehouse contain table structures and data that closely resemble the operational data. Because teams can always reconcile the contents of these source-oriented structures back to the source systems, especially given the insert_datetime and source_system metadata columns, I refer to this portion of the reference architecture as an "audit layer." The audit layer's goal is to simply capture the source system data in a permanent time-oriented repository so that later the company can base trustworthy analytics on it.

With the shared business key entities, however, the audit vault does provide a further service that makes it significantly more valuable than just a persistent staging layer. By collocating the business key instances, the audit vault offers the company access to well-defined data with a first level of integration applied. One can draw upon the audit vault for 360-degree views of the enterprise, as long as those views pivot on core business entities—such as customer, product, and location—that can be found in the source systems. Because the pattern of business keys and links reflect business reality, they will not change any more than the business conditions they reflect, so the audit vault is a solid foundation on which departmental analysts can build temporary reports and analyses. Advanced users can certainly begin data mining this stable repository of operational data as soon as the EDW team begins loading it.

Reflecting on the end-user's hierarchy of needs that we considered during our look at agile requirements management, we can say that the audit sublayer of the hyper normalized data warehouse does address both the "data access" stratum and perhaps 50 percent of the value sought in the remaining layers. Not bad for a data pool that can be modeled quickly and populated with reusable, parameter-driven ETL. To be fair, however, the business will soon need derived columns and master data elements. Because those needs eventually appear, hyper normalization, with all its speed-to-market, is not a complete solution, and EDW team leaders should be sure not to oversell this approach to their customers.

Retrieving Data from an HNF Repository Doubly Difficult

Another important caveat for EDW team leaders to keep in mind is that everyone—business and even SQL wonks—finds it very difficult to retrieve data from hyper normalized data repositories. Consider the question marked "Q1" in the model excerpt we reviewed in Figure 14.13. BK_CUSTOMER has three attribute tables, one for each source system providing operational transactions to the data warehouse. A sale can easily close weeks before the customer sends in his or her warranty registration card. Say analysts in the sales department used a desktop SQL tool to query for the current status of all customers purchasing products during the past month, and that they built that query using equijoins to link together these four tables. Such a query would generate the wrong answer. All customers who had not yet appeared in the warranty system would be missing from the result because records for them would not exist in ATTRIB_CUST_WARRANT. To properly retrieve data from a hyper normalized data warehouse, then, query writers must make sure to use outer joins for those portions of clauses that pull data from attribute tables.

The question marked "Q2" in Figure 14.13 represents an even more daunting challenge. Any given record in the LINK_LINE_ITEM table can have multiple associated attribute records in ATTRIB_LINK_ITEM_PROVISIONING, each one reflecting a different state of a line item's provisioning status. Say the sales analysts wanted to report on the average promised date for the company's undelivered line items. The typical query statement one would construct with a desktop SQL tool would again use straight equijoins to all the tables involved in the request. These joins would bring back all the statuses from ATTRIB_LINK_ITEM_PROVISIONING, not just the latest record, which would again give the sales department an inaccurate answer to its business question.

Without additional preparation, one has to employ not only outer joins but also *correlated subqueries* on all the attribute tables to properly retrieve data from a hyper normalized data warehouse. Figure 14.20 provides an example of a retrieval query for selecting data from only the very small splinter of the hyper normalized data model shown on the left side of Figure 14.13. This example retrieves data from one business key table and three attribute tables. The syntax answers the challenge posed by question Q1 in the figure, namely how to prevent a missing record in an attribute table from causing no records to be returned for a given record of the business key table driving the query. It also addresses the challenge posed by Q2—that is, retrieving just one child record per attribute table for each parent record even though more than one set of attributes have been recorded for a business key value over time. Note how complex the query retrieving data from just these three tables has become with the combined effect of correlated subqueries and outer joins. Given that hyper normalization greatly increases the number of objects in a data model, the EDW teams will need to author far more complicated SQL than this statement when the queries start to include 10, 20, or more tables. Each one will require significant labor to write.

```
select      CUST.CUSTOMER_NUMBER

,           PRSPC.CITY

,           SALES.BILLING_CITY

,           WRNTY.SVC_CITY

from        BK_CUST                     CUST

left outer join   ATTRIB_CUST_PROSPECTING   PRSPC

on          CUST.CUSTOMER_SID =   PRSPC.CUSTOMER_SID

and         CUST.LOAD_DATE >=

                    ( select max( Z.LOAD_DATE )

                      from   ATTRIB_CUST_PROSPECTING Z

                      where  CUST.CUSTOMER_SID = Z.CUSTOMER_SID

                    )

left outer join   ATTRIB_CUST_SALES         SALES

on          CUST.CUSTOMER_SID =   SALES.CUSTOMER_SID

and         CUST.LOAD_DATE >=

                    ( select max( Z.LOAD_DATE )

                      from   ATTRIB_CUST_SALES Z

                      where  CUST.CUSTOMER_SID = Z.CUSTOMER_SID

                    )

left outer join   ATTRIB_CUST_WARRANT       WRNTY

on          CUST.CUSTOMER_SID =   WRNTY.CUSTOMER_SID

and         CUST.LOAD_DATE >=

                    ( select max( Z.LOAD_DATE )

                      from   ATTRIB_CUST_WRNTY Z

                      where  CUST.CUSTOMER_SID = Z.CUSTOMER_SID

                    )

and         CUST.LOAD_DATE = TO_DATE('01-JAN-15','dd-mon-yy')

;
```

FIGURE 14.20 SQL query demonstrating the correlated subqueries needed to retrieve information from hyper normalized data warehouses.

With the retrieval queries becoming so labor-intensive to write, one could justifiably suggest that hyper normalization has only relocated, not reduced, the complexity of creating an EDW. The EDW team has only deferred the complicated data transforms found in the integration-layer loading routines of the standard approach and will have to confront those challenges when it comes time to build the presentation layer objects. Moreover, both outer joins and correlated subqueries consume considerable memory and processing horsepower in the typical SQL engine, so perfectly reasonable business questions may involve a long wait or may never get answered at all.

The previous caveats require one to seriously consider both data capture and data retrieval before committing whole-heartedly to a hyper normalization strategy. Fortunately, there are several partial solutions to these challenges that keep hyper normalization as a viable strategy. EDW team leaders need to understand these solutions so that they can make an informed choice regarding data modeling paradigms and prepare a sufficient platform for their applications should they decide to pursue this flavor of hyper modeling during their next project.

Solution 0: Focus on Presentation Layer Objects

The first solution is not really a technique but, rather, simply a reminder of original intent. Hyper normalized data stores provide a persistent data staging area that provides light integration, holding operational information for further transformation into the star schemas that will be found in the EDW's presentation layer. Many of the frustrations that EDW teams experience when they begin writing queries against hyper normalized data stores arise because they are trying to create fully denormalized reporting data sets that skip the presentation layer and report directly out of the integration layer. Many EDW teams can report directly off their data vaults for *some* reports, but their leaders also realize that they will need to create a dimensional repository to support the more complex reporting and analytical requirements. When populating a presentation layer from hyper normalized integration tables, the data retrieval queries will focus on loading one dimension or fact table at a time. These queries involve far fewer objects each and are thus much easier to write. Once the data has been projected into a dimensional model, users can turn to business intelligence tools to answer questions such as an order's status on a given date or year-on-year comparisons. By deferring these advance analytical operations until the data is in a form suitable for presentation, these EDW teams avoid trying to make a hyper normalized data repository achieve too much.

Solution 1: Dummy Attribute Records

Teams can remove the need for outer joins by ensuring that at least one record exists in all the attribute tables for every record in their parent business key or linking entity. They can achieve this by providing an additional parameter for their reusable ETL modules for business key tables and links that causes the routine to seed a null record in every attribute table identified by the parameter. Regarding the situation for the LINK_LINE_ITEM table depicted in Figure 14.13, this additional parameter would name the three attribute tables for items as requested, being provisioned, and installed. After creating a given parent record, these ETL modules would place a record in each named attribute table that had NULL or default values for all columns except the primary key and record source [Linstedt 2010b]. If the query writers know for a fact that all attributes will contain at least one record for each parent business key, they can omit the outer join clauses from their SQL logic, making the queries much easier to author and maintain.

Solution 2: Current Record Indicators

Because so many end-user queries focus on the current status of business affairs, some EDW teams opt to add *current record indicators* to their attribute tables in order to reduce how many correlated subqueries they must include in their retrieval queries. On the records of every attribute table, a current record indicator has a value of TRUE if that record is the last one added to the table. All other records will have an indicator value of FALSE. For end-user queries focusing on the current state of affairs, a simple condition of CURRENT_IND = TRUE will eliminate the need for correlated subqueries because only the latest record from each attribute table will be retrieved [Vos 2014b].

A minor disadvantage to this strategy is the small amount of additional load processing it requires and the violation of the insert-only paradigm that it represents. With each run, the reusable ETL modules will need to somehow detect previously current records that have now been superseded by a more recent addition and then modify their current indicators to FALSE. Such processing usually involves a second pass and an update of the indicator's value. For EDW that must answer many queries regarding the company's current status, this slight aberration from the single-pass, insert-only model described previously is a small price to pay in exchange for being able to drop correlated subqueries from many data retrieval steps.

Solution 3: Point-in-Time Tables

A more elegant workaround that eliminates the need for both correlated subqueries and outer joins is the point-in-time table. Figure 14.21 shows the situation we need to solve using the customer topic area we considered in Figure 14.13. To retrieve information regarding a customer, BK_CUSTOMER is joined to three attribute tables that correspond to three different time points in the sales cycle: prospecting, sales, and warranty registrations. Simply constructed queries

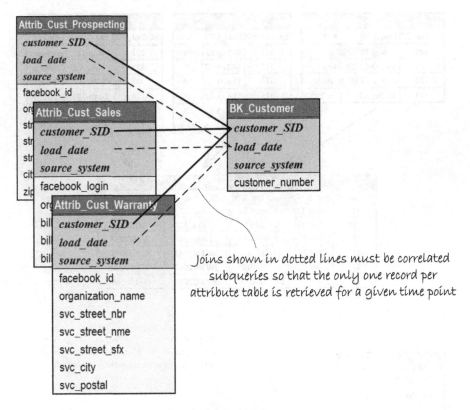

FIGURE 14.21   Hyper normalized designs can require many correlated subqueries.

intended to join these three tables into a comprehensive view will need to use outer joins for all of them so that customers missing a record, such as warranty, are not dropped from the query results. They will also have to use correlated subqueries so that each customer business key is returned only once, even if it has more than one time point recorded for it in one or more of the associated attribute tables.

EDW teams that want to make such a query easier to write or that have data volumes high enough to create performance problems can create a *point-in-time* (PIT) table, as shown in Figure 14.22. A point-in-time table contains a foreign key for each attribute table that corresponds with a select set of time points addressed by the data. The example in the figure supports beginning-of-month time points, but the team could decide instead to create records for every load date time present in the attribute tables. The retrieval query is then rewritten by (1) inserting the PIT table in between the attribute and business key entities, as shown in the bottom of the figure; (2) adding join logic that matches up the load date time values; and (3) converting the outer joins to inner joins. With this adaptation, each BK_CUSTOMER record can be easily joined to the appropriate attribute record because the PIT table contains foreign keys for both the BK_CUSTOMER_SID column and the appropriate load date time. For any given time point, the appropriate record from each attribute table will appear in the result set, whether it was created on the date recorded on the business key recorded or loaded sometime earlier. Because the correct record for each point in time has been identified by this preprocessing, correlated subqueries are no longer needed to retrieve the most current records or the records for any other moment in history.

EDW team leaders should not worry that their developers will be populating a large number of point-in-time tables because in practice hyper normalized data performs well enough that such preprocessing is necessary only occasionally. Keep in mind that hyper normalization is employed for the integration layer. Data is typically transformed into a star schema in the presentation layer to provide end users with high performance for their dashboards. Given that, point-in-time tables are only necessary for those portions of the integration-to-presentation ETL that run so slow that the overall presentation-layer load exceeds the load window allowed. Although people often worry that hyper normalization will cause EDW performance problems, the overhead of the extra tables and more technical join logic rarely impacts the speed of presentation-layer loads noticeably, especially with today's fast disk subsystems and high-memory server configurations.

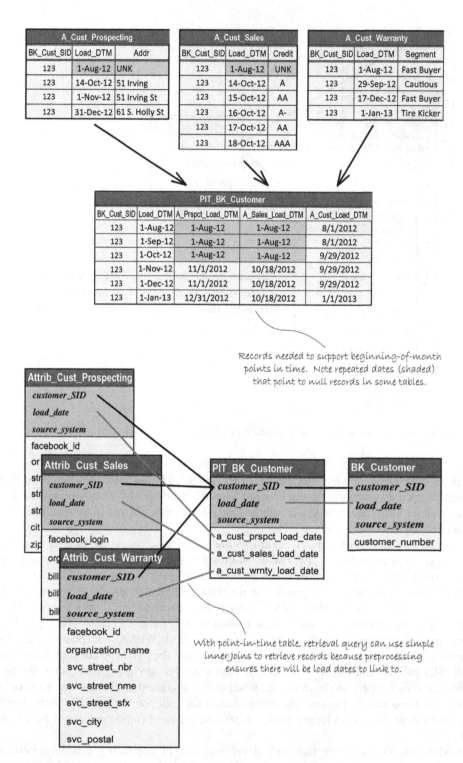

FIGURE 14.22 By using point-in-time tables where needed, we can simplify retrieval queries.

Solution 4: Table Pruning

Another tactical solution called *table pruning* frequently prevents the performance problems that many people expect hyper normalized data stores to encounter. To see table pruning in action, consider Figure 14.23. This figure shows how the data model of 4.10 would be employed to answer a query that stretches across the model and involves many tables, namely, "How many products made by a specific manufacturer and sold by a given agent have been installed in a given geography?"

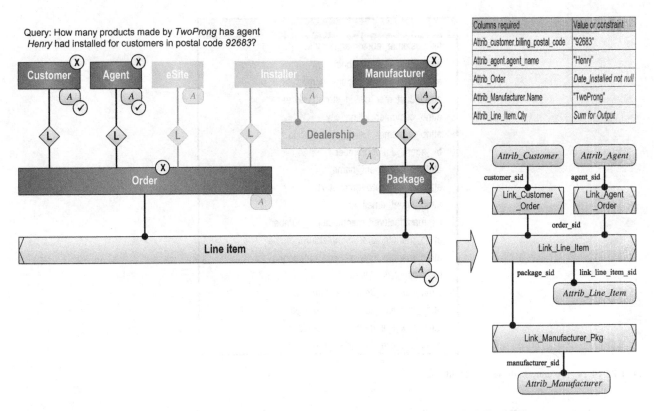

Query: How many products made by *TwoProng* has agent *Henry* had installed for customers in postal code *92683*?

Columns required	Value or constraint
Attrib_customer.billing_postal_code	"92683"
Attrib_agent.agent_name	"Henry"
Attrib_Order	Date_Installed not null
Attrib_Manufacturer.Name	"TwoProng"
Attrib_Line_Item.Qty	Sum for Output

FIGURE 14.23 Data retrieval queries can be (a) simplified through table pruning and (b) generated from DBMS constraints.

In Figure 14.23, check marks are placed on the tables that have columns needed in the result set for this query, and a few tables that neither provide data values or participate in the join logic have been faded out. However, even more entities can be eliminated from the logic of this query through table pruning. The practice of table pruning examines the contribution of each table to determine if the information in another table can fill that role, allowing the first table to be eliminated from the query. Take customers, for example. The query needs only the postal code of people placing orders, not their customer numbers. Accordingly, only the customer attribute table is needed, not the business key. Because the attribute table contains the surrogate key for the customer, it can be joined directly to the LINK_CUSTOMER_ORDER table, which already refers to the customer using that surrogate value. The BK_CUSTOMER table can be eliminated from the query language. Similarly, the query focuses on a sales agent's name rather than the agent number that is stored in BK_AGENT, so that table can be pruned from the query as well.

By connecting data mostly through the surrogate keys found in linking tables, many business key tables can be pruned from every query. Figure 14.23 uses X's to show that, upon analysis, this example had no need for the five business key tables originally included in the query. Moreover, only the attribute tables contributing values to the end result need to be included. A schematic representation of the resulting join is shown on the right. The set of 14 tables first identified on the left has been reduced to 8—a 42% reduction.

Although hyper normalization significantly increases the number of tables in a data model, table pruning reduces much of that impact upon retrieval query complexity. The previous example presented table pruning as a design-time process that developers must invest in while writing a retrieval query. In practice, most DBMSs today will natively apply table elimination to drop superfluous joins, reducing the labor required to retrieve information from the hyper normalized data warehouse. For the remaining tables, it should be kept in mind that business key and linking tables have very "skinny" records that is, they contain very few columns, making a large number of them pass through the database server's I/O buffers quickly. With table pruning and the reliance on skinny tables, most queries against hyper normalized data stores perform just fine.

Solution 5: Bridging Tables

Table pruning and point-in-time preprocessing aside, the increased number of tables comprising a hyper normalized data repository can sometimes cause performance problems for queries involving many tables. To correct this

Bridge_Customer_To_Manufacturer
bk_customer_customer_number
attrib_customer_facebook_id
attrib_customer_company_name
attrib_customer_billing_street_address
attrib_customer_billing_city
attrib_customer_billing_postal_code
bk_agent_agent_number
attrib_agent_agent_name
attrib_agent_date_emp_start
attrib_agent_email_id
bk_manufacturer_manufacturer_number
attrib_manufacturer_manufacturer_name
attrib_manufacturer_service_category
bk_order_order_number
attrib_link_line_item_line_item_number
attrib_link_line_item_qty_requested
attrib_link_line_item_qty_installed
attrib_link_line_item_date_last_updated

FIGURE 14.24   Columns in the resulting bridge table.

occasional challenge, EDW teams extend the preprocessing strategy employed for point-in-time tables to where they preload results of specific queries into *bridging tables*. A bridging table is like a materialized view—it stores the results of a frequently run query so questions against a particular join pattern can be answered from a preprocessed data store rather than requiring the base tables to be rejoined again.

Say the example considered in Figure 14.23 started consuming too much of the EDW's overnight load window. The team could prejoin the eight tables of the pruned retrieval query and place records for the combined column set in a new table, as shown in the table structure found in Figure 14.24. Each column in this figure has been prefixed with the name of the base table from which it was derived. To keep this example realistic, the collection of elements shown in the figure includes the business keys from the associated BK_ tables because downstream usages frequently need such identifiers. The resulting table can serve as a *bridge* between the hyper normalized base tables and the queries that need particularly fast performance. Subsequent queries needing this particular combination of tables will be able to pull a subset of columns as needed directly from this bridging table.

Solution 6: Retrieval Query Writers

Even with all the previous tactics, the team will still need to write many queries that cannot employ bridging or point-in-time tables. These queries will involve a good number of outer joins and correlated subqueries and thus be difficult to write and maintain. Fortunately, EDW developers do not have to resign themselves to manually writing such complex joins every time they need a new query. They can either acquire a query writer from the hyper normalization community or build one of their own.

Before such query writers can begin to assist, the EDW developers will need to declare the primary and foreign key constraints when creating the tables of the hyper normalized integration layer. Many teams do not plan to use such constraints to ensure referential integrity because they slow down data loads. However, a team can declare these constraints and leave them "unenforced" so that they still document how tables in the data warehouse should be linked together but do not incur data checks when records are inserted into the database. With primary and foreign key constraints declared, query-writing programs can use them to discover the relationships between tables and intelligently construct a query's WHERE clause.

Consider again the pruned model shown in the lower right of Figure 14.23. The most dependent table is ATTRIB_MANUFACTURER, from which we need values that are stored in the Manufacturer_Name column. With primary and foreign key constraints declared in the database, a program introspecting the DBMS's system catalog regarding

ATTRIB_MANUFACTURER will see that it has a foreign key that resolves to the column Manufacturer_SID in the LINK_MANUFACTURER_PACKAGE. The program could then introspect this table in turn, discovering that it similarly shares a key of Package_SID with LINK_LINE_ITEM. The program could progress in this manner until it has discovered all the tables required to traverse from ATTRIB_MANUFACTURER at the bottom to both ATTRIB_CUSTOMER and ATTRIB_AGENT at the top. It could then generate a query that includes joins between the business keys and linking tables, employing outer joins and correlated subqueries as needed to retrieve records from the hyper normalized data store.

EDW team leaders who wish to employ one of the data vault standards can find several online communities that are sharing already programmed query writers. Typically, such borrowed utilities are close to what a given team will need, but they will require some polishing. Thus, EDW leaders opting for hyper normalization should include some time for tuning query writers into their project plans. Once a tuned query-writing utility is in place, the EDW team will be able to upload to it the data definition language of the team's hyper normalized warehouse, which will include the primary and foreign key constraints declared in the team's database. After the utility has parsed the tables and constraints, the developers may have to declare "roles" for tables that participate in more than one join path. At this point, they will be able to select desired elements from a list of columns in the database, push a button, and receive the text of a data query that will provide the requested fields.

Clearing an Architectural Review

Despite the advantages of hyper normalized designs presented previously, many EDW teams still worry that they will never get their company's IT architectural review board to approve this data modeling approach. Careful positioning of the concept may make the difference in the outcome such a review might produce.

First, EDW team leaders can cite the distinction between logical and physical data modeling. As we saw in the example provided via Figures 14.5–14.9, a standard normal form (SNF) data model always exists as a foundation for a design in hyper normalized form (HNF). Because the HNF design concepts are very easy to apply, many teams of course skip creating an SNF design and author the HNF model immediately. When the design must pass a review, however, investing the time needed to prepare a SNF representation of the HNF design may help. The EDW team leaders can then present to the reviewers the SNF logical model first and then mention that they intend to decouple business keys, links, and attributes in the physical model—for all the benefits discussed in this chapter. Some review boards focus on logical models because their priority is how data will appear to end users and other systems, so leading with the SNF logical model answers their concerns and avoids giving them design points they will object to.

Second, EDW team leaders can demonstrate that data in HNF can always be projected into SNF. The business keys, links, and attributes of a business entity can be reassembled by a query that joins those components back together. In practice, it is not difficult to spot the tables needed to re-create any desired entity, as the dotted line in Figure 14.10 demonstrates for the ORDERS object we started with in the original SNF model shown in Figure 14.3.

The previous considerations are often enough to turn the conversation with the architectural review board completely around. If a logical SNF model lies at the heart of an HNF design, and one can always physically reassemble SNF objects when needed, why should the EDW *not* utilize a hyper normalized physical model for the data warehouse? The team can bolster this rhetorical question by pointing out that an HNF physical model will allow the EDW team to

- create an entire integrating data capture facility after programming only three modules;
- load faster than a third normal form physical model given that it involves many fewer database constraints;
- start delivering sooner in small pieces, following a path that greatly reduces project risk; and
- adapt the warehouse once online for new business requirements without ruinously expensive re-engineering and data conversion scripting.

As a final argument in favor of hyper normalization of one flavor or the other, EDW team leaders can share that Bill Inmon, the creator of the data warehousing concept, has endorsed the data vault style in particular for his Data Warehouse 2.0 specification (quoted in [Linstedt 2015]). Positioning the hyper normalized approach in this manner usually leaves data modeling traditionalists with few arguments powerful enough to convince business sponsors they should fund the slow, more expensive, and riskier standard approach to enterprise data warehousing.

RE-ARCHITECTING THE EDW FOR HYPER NORMALIZATION

Until now, I have said very little about supporting derived EDW components such as advanced metrics and master data elements within a hyper normalized integration layer. To manage derived elements, we need to divide the integration layer

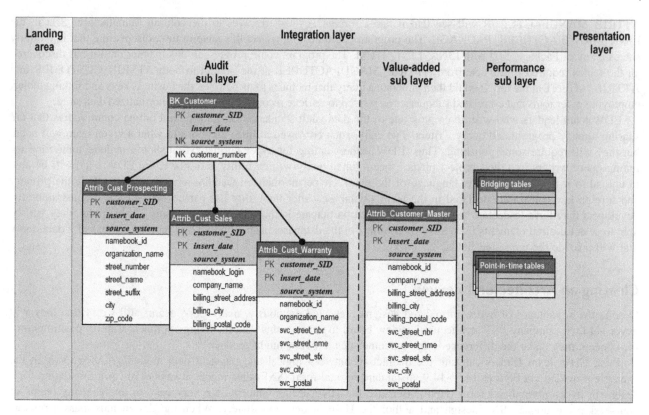

FIGURE 14.25   EDW reference architecture adapted for a hyper normalized integration layer.

into sublayers, as shown in Figure 14.25. Each EDW team has to decide whether to implement these sublayers as separate physical schemas within a database or instead through a naming convention for identifying tables within a shared schema.

The audit layer in Figure 14.25 supports the purpose of quick data capture and light integration discussed extensively above. Every record in this sublayer can be tied back to a record in a source system. The value-added sublayer that this diagram adds to the integration portion of the reference architecture will store derived elements that secondary ETL operations create based on the data in the audit layer. The business rules applied in creating this new layer add value to the information, for example, by populating derived metrics, or they consolidate multiple audit records down to one. Because these results cannot always be tied directly back to source system records, the elements in this sublayer must be validated through solid quality assurance practices. The diagram also shows a third, performance sublayer, in which helper objects such as bridging and point-in-time tables are placed.

With the audit and value-added layers defined, the EDW team faces some interesting choices on how to spread the processing across the sublayers of the data warehouse. The data vault community in particular provides several styles on how to be best accomplish this secondary processing, although the same patterns would apply to anchor-model data repositories as well. These styles are largely architectural patterns that offer solution components that can be mixed and matched in many ways. The few styles discussed here are thus just archetypes that EDW team leaders need to understand in order to arrive at a design that matches their project's particular needs. In outlining these styles, I have borrowed from one of the thought leaders of the Dutch school of practitioners, although I have relabeled their ideas slightly for greater clarity here [Damhof 2011b].

The Simple Vault Style

The architectural pattern promoted by the classical school of data vaulting is closest to what the original creator of data vaulting described in his earliest works [Linstedt and Graziano 2011]. As portrayed in Figure 14.26, data is extracted from the source systems and placed into a data vault in the warehouse's audit layer. In this style, the target data vault employs business keys that can be found in the operational data, and the ETL creates no new information aside from generating the surrogate keys and adding metadata columns for auditing purposes. The remaining columns in the integration layer contain only data replicated from the source systems.

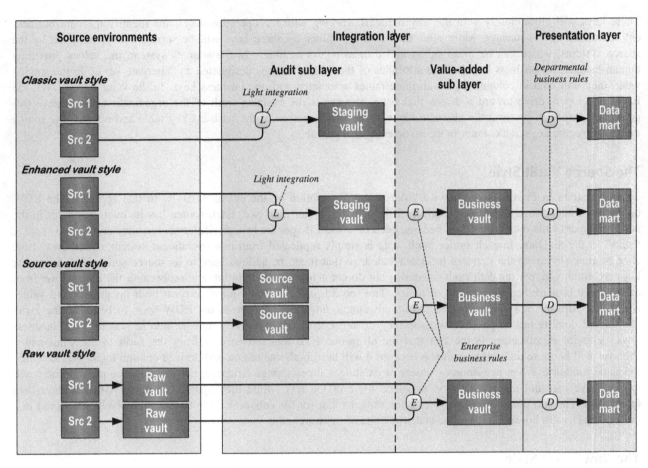

FIGURE 14.26   Four styles for distributing hyper normalized repositories across the EDW reference architecture.

This flavor of vault does perform "light integration," but only as much as can be achieved with the natural key values replicated from source. Any value-added column derivations, cleansing, or second-level integration is performed when the data is projected into a star schema structure and delivered to a data mart. Such value-added activities are marked as "departmental business rules" in the diagram, although in practice they may be applied by the EDW team when it creates the data mart on the department's behalf. Because these data vaults serve to stage the data for transformation into star schema, they are labeled "staging vaults" in Figure 14.26.

The Enhanced Vault Style

The EDW team does create value-added ETL for the integration layer in the next style of data vaulting, which builds on the classic style by adding another vault-structured repository to hold the results of any second-pass processing. As shown in Figure 14.26, this enhanced style applies enterprise-level business rules to the data found in a staging vault and then places the results in a repository kept separate from the primary vault by either a physical schema or a naming convention for the target tables.

The first stage of ETL does nothing more than (1) place another time slice of captured operational data in the EDW's persistent staging area and (2) lightly integrate that data by collocating business keys based on source-based values for common business notions such as customer and product. The second stage of the ETL, however, does some "heavy lifting" by cleansing, reformatting, and harmonizing the data. It performs further integration and consolidation of the operational data, often generating master data records and creating some derived values as well, all of which will be stored in the tables of a value-added "business vault" sublayer, as shown in Figure 14.25.

The business keys may change considerably for data moving from the audit to the value-added sublayers. The audit layer's staging vault typically builds business key records based on the identifier found in the source data with little or no modification, even if they are dimensionless values without any independent meaning, such as "order number."

These keys will align closely with the way the staff working with the operational systems identify the core business entities their systems manage. More often than not, the values for these keys will be surrogate keys assigned by the source systems, which can be meaningless and dimensionless numbers. In the sources system, the values providing human-meaningful business keys will be attributes of the tables, perhaps designated as "alternate keys." In the staging vault, they will land in columns of the attribute tables associated with the business keys. In the value-added layer, the EDW developers drive toward a design that better represents the business truth of the organization. To achieve this goal, they may well promote the alternate key values to the columns of the business key table and relegate the source system surrogate keys to a column in the associated attribute tables.

The Source Vault Style

The third strata in Figure 14.26 shows a "source vault" variation on the enhanced style. In this approach, the EDW defers any integraton and then accomplishes it in one step rather than two. Each source has its own data vault in the audit sublayer of the data warehouse. Because each data vault is specific to a particular source, they are labeled "source vaults" in the diagram. In each source vault, data is simply replicated from one operational system, stored away time slice by time slice with the standard metadata added, so that it can be audited back to its source application. Surrogate keys are employed, per the data vault standards, but do not achieve even light integration because the information from each source is placed in its own set of tables. The second-pass ETL then must perform both integration and value-added activities all in a single process. As an advantage, this approach allows the EDW team to begin saving away operational data as fast as possible because they do not even have to identify and harmonize staging layer business keys. A major disadvantage is the fact that the all-in-one ETL that moves data from the audit to the value-added sublayer will be more difficult to maintain because it will have both integration and derived column logic located within the same modules. When new sources appear or existing sources change structure, the maintenance programmers will have to take care not to impact the value-added logic of the ETL while they update the portions that achieve data integration. The end point, however, will be the same as that for the enhanced style because the results get stored in a business data vault housed in the value-added schema of the warehouse.

The Raw Vault Style

The last archetypical style of data vaulting requires a change in ownership rather than simply a change in schema. In the fourth strata of Figure 14.26, data is replicated from source into a "raw data vault." These vaults are in fact identical in structure and content to the source vaults discussed previously. The only difference is that they reside in the source layer of the reference architecture, meaning they are created and maintained by the teams that own the source applications.

Such a change in ownership is not as far-fetched as it might first appear, and this style offers some important advantages to the company's EDW program. The rules for designing and populating a data vault are so pattern-based that "nearly anyone can do it." I have met project managers, stuck on projects without an EDW team yet assigned, who have commandeered programmers and successfully instructed them on building out the first incarnation of the data warehouse using the data vaulting standards. By separating the functional components of the traditional data warehouse into business keys, links, and attributes, ensemble data modeling has positioned us where we no longer need data modeling geniuses to build repositories for every business analytics application.

Given the decoupling that hyper normalization makes possible, pushing responsibility for the persistent staging layer to the owners of the source systems is a perfectly rational policy decision. In the organizations in which I have seen this done, the statement from the executives to the source application owners has been simply, "If you're going to run a major business application such as customer relationship management, fulfillment, or billing, you need to make that data available for tracking and analysis by the rest of the company." In other words, it is not fair for one department to own such a valuable information resource and lock away its data from others in the business who need it.

In practice, wrapping source systems with raw data vaults has led to much better organizational dynamics. Before, parties wanting a new data feed from the major line-of-business systems had to beg the system owners for an extract. These extracts were always specific to a particular purpose so that the next party needing a different extract—including the EDW team—would have to go through the same groveling to get the desired data feed created. Once the raw vaults were in place, getting data from these source systems for any reason became a self-service function, removing not only a large delay in the creation of new data flows within the company but also the source of frequent and heated confrontations with source system owners.

Although these raw data vaults do not perform any integration, because their data derives from a single source, they do provide persistence of the operational information, which solves a common frustration for companies that undertake an enterprise data warehousing program belatedly. Without raw data vaults, many companies find that the past data in the operational systems has evaporated by the time they finally decide to build an EDW. Companies that adopt a policy of wrapping source systems with raw data vaults, however, find that they have a readily intelligible pool of historical data to load into the enterprise data warehouse once it is built and ready to operate. All told, raw data vaults offer an easy-to-build, self-service data source for the entire organization, and they provide EDW with a reliable source of history, making them a smart policy choice for large organizations, even before they begin data warehousing.

Blending Styles to Achieve Agility

Considering the four styles of data vaulting shown in Figure 14.26, the enhanced style offers the greatest support for an agile enterprise data warehousing, but if the organization will not support this choice, the raw vault style will still allow for a fairly nimble EDW program.

In the enhanced style, the EDW team can quickly pull together the primary vaulting tables. All they must do is identify the semantically equivalent business keys spread among the disparate sources they have been asked to warehouse and then configure their driver scripts to begin storing away the operational data. By wrapping some data-virtualization or semantic-layer views around this primary vault, they will be able to provide a very useful surface solution for the business in very little time. This first subrelease will have light integration on simple business keys that everyone in the company will admit do exist. Even if the definitions of the business keys are not as all-encompassing as the stakeholders would like, at least some enterprise reporting can begin. Moreover, this primary vault will be able to provide counts of business entities and events that end users will be able to slice and dice by all the attributes available in the source systems. Such qualifiers may not be harmonized across source applications yet, but departmental BI programming resources can bridge the gap by crafting their own cross-reference tables. The data necessary to build such Band-Aids will exist in the warehouse.

Some companies do not allow the EDW team the time or resources to build a staging vault, but if the organization has at least implemented a raw vault policy, the path to enterprise data warehousing will be considerably shorter. With raw vaults in place, the EDW team will find not only that source extracts exist but also that the contents of the business applications have already been categorized into business keys, links, and attributes by the subject matter experts who know those systems well. Given that start, the developers can skip the staging vault found in the other styles and begin immediately building an enterprise-oriented business vault in the value-added sublayer. Moreover, because their developers will be populating data vault structures in this secondary area of the integration layer, they can build out the EDW "one slice at a time," knowing that if they make a design mistake, it can be corrected by re-engineering only a small portion of the model. If they really mess up an increment of their business vault, the EDW team will be able to start over using the original data from the persistent raw vaults. With such a low-risk profile for their intended approach, the EDW team can rapidly deliver EDW increments in a "fail fast and cheap, then fix quickly" mode, much to the delight of their business sponsors who will easily forgive a couple of small mistakes as long as the overall warehouse takes shape with speed.

The hyper normalization styles described previously are just archetypes. With only a moment's study of Figure 14.26, one can spot ways to mix and match these separate notions into a wide range of additional solutions. For example, a hyper normalized EDW could build a business vault from four sources—one captured with a raw vault, another stored in a source vault, and the other two already integrated in a staging vault. Speaking from the agile perspective, the key to overall project success will be identifying the pattern that provides the business customers the greatest area under the value buildup chart we considered in Figure 13.7. Perhaps the team's first surface solutions will be a virtual star wrapped around a staging vault to be replaced later by a full business vault and a traditional presentation layer once the subject matter experts can fully discern the end users' requirements.

With so many combinations of styles possible, and because all choices involve integration structures that can be adapted easily, hyper normalization has shifted the work of building enterprise data warehousing from what we used to face with traditional data modeling approaches. In the past, EDW teams had to wade through mountains of technical details to arrive at a perfect solution, which they then had to deliver in a single development effort. Now, the more effective teams sprint through a few subreleases, hoping that the users object substantially to the first one or two so that the uncertainty regarding business needs is resolved. With end-user requirements clarified, the early version of the warehouse can be quickly adjusted to serve the business correctly.

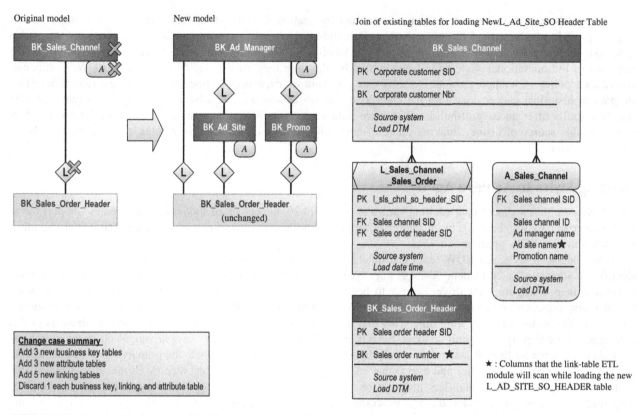

Original model   New model   Join of existing tables for loading NewL_Ad_Site_SO Header Table

Change case summary
Add 3 new business key tables
Add 3 new attribute tables
Add 5 new linking tables
Discard 1 each business key, linking, and attribute table

★ : Columns that the link-table ETL
module will scan while loading the new
L_AD_SITE_SO_HEADER table

FIGURE 14.27   Data models for Change Case #1 under hyper normalization.

ENABLING EVOLUTION OF EXISTING EDW COMPONENTS

The estimates offered previously in Table 14.2 suggested that hyper normalization could save an EDW team two-thirds of the development effort when creating the tables for a new warehouse or subject area. However, the effort of creating Version 1 of an EDW pales in comparison to the cost of adapting a data warehouse's structure and data for new requirements once its tables are loaded. Fortunately, hyper normalized data models prove to be resilient in the face of changing business requirements as well, as revisiting the change cases introduced in Chapter 12 will demonstrate.

Change Case 1: Splitting Out Entities

The first change case addressed the cost of splitting attributes out of an entity when it became clear that they had a separate life of their own and needed to be modeled as independent tables. Figure 12.15 illustrated this change case via an entity relationship diagram, showing the tables AD_MANAGER, AD_SITE, and PROMO being split out from the SALES_CHANNEL table. Table 12.7 calculated that this work would consume more than 1100 labor hours and cost nearly $150,000 (at a fully loaded labor cost of $125 per hour).

Figure 14.27 shows how the same functional update would manifest itself in the integration layer of a hyper normalized data warehouse. At first, the Ad Site and Promo columns are found in the attribute table of the sales channel, as shown in the detail to the right. In the second model, business key tables and dedicated attribute tables have been created for both of them. Linking tables have been created to maintain the relationships needed between the existing BK_SALES_ORDER_HEADER and the new business key tables for the ad manager, ad site, and promotion entities. The net impact is three new business key tables, five new link tables, and three new attribute tables. After the data in the original BK_SALES_CHANNEL and its linking and attribute tables have been moved into these new tables, they can be dropped. The sales order entity is still valid, so it will remain. By virtue of the data vault modeling rules, it is free of any foreign keys that would have to be adjusted given the new tables, so its structure and the rest of the model that links to the new tables through it can remain unchanged.

The modeling change under consideration involves many tables, but fortunately the labor needed to populate the new structures will remain quite modest. Figure 14.27 illustrates the modeling change this change case will require. The join pattern illustrated on the far right illustrate where the EDW team can source data elements from the original

TABLE 14.3 Hyper Normalization's Impact Upon EDW Re-Engineering Change Cases

Calculated at a blended hourly rate for all roles of: $125

| | Standard Normal Form (From Chapter 13) | | | | | | | | Hyper Normalized Form | | | | | | | |
| | Per Table Estimates | | #1: 4NF Fix | | | #2: Party Model | | | Per Table Estimates | | #1: 4NF Fix | | | #2: Party Model | | |
IT Activities	Effort	Expense	Tables	Effort	Expense	Tables	Effort	Expense	Effort	Expense	Tables	Effort	Expense	Tables	Effort	Expense
Once Per Conversion	68 hrs	$8,500		68 hrs	$8,500		68 hrs	$8,500	27 hrs	$3,390		27 hrs	$3,390		27 hrs	$3,390
Per New Table	181 hrs	$22,625	6	1,086 hrs	$135,750	8	1,448 hrs	$181,000	65 hrs	$8,178	11	720 hrs	$89,953	12	785 hrs	$98,130
Total				1,154 hrs	$1,44,250		1,516 hrs	$1,89,500				747 hrs	$89,953		812 hrs	$98,130
HNF-Generated Savings													38 percent			48 percent

tables. The new tables comply with the insert-only paradigm discussed previously, so populating these columns will require only copying information from the original tables rather than changing values in place. Such migration will be easy to accomplish—we need only to employ the parameter-driven ETL modules already built to insert the necessary records, using the existing tables as a data source. To load BK_Ad_Site, for example, the developers will only need to employ the business key loader to scan A_SALES_CHANNEL for unique instances of ad site names. To load L_AD_SITE_SO_HEADER, they will call the link-table loader and instruct it to scan a temporary join of the existing tables shown on the right side of Figure 14.27, creating new link records for each unique occurrence of sales order number and ad site manager. After using their parameter-driven ETL modules to place the existing data into the new tables, the developers will drop the three original tables because they are no longer needed, as indicated on the left of the figure.

Table 14.3 uses the estimated effort for new and updated tables calculated in Table 14.2 to identify the impact that hyper normalization will have on this change case. Because the hyper normalization requires more entities to store the same data, the number of new tables involved in this change case actually increased from 6 to 11. With the reusable, parameter-driven ETL at their disposal, however, even this increased number of tables will require the EDW team to invest only two-thirds as much effort as required under the standard approach. Instead of writing a special-purpose conversion script to transform existing data for each new table, the developers can simply call their reusable ETL widgets on the tables of the old model in order to populate the tables of the new. After converting the data, they then drop the tables or columns that are no longer needed. We will see far greater savings in the next change case, which requires a more complicated model revision.

Change Case 2: Upgrading to a Party Model

The second change case addressed the cost of converting the EDW's integration layer to a party model when it became clear that the development team would be constantly adding new entities for people and organizations if it did not "bite the bullet" and generalize them all into *parties*. The change in logical models can be quickly discerned by comparing the starting point shown in Figure 14.10 to the new model required, as depicted in Figure 14.28. This transition drops the entities for Customer, Agent, Installer, and Manufacturer, consolidating them all in BK_PARTIES. Separate attributes tables are maintained for each party type, and a new attribute for shared qualifiers has been added in ATTRIB_PARTY_CORPORATE. The "corporate" component of this new table's name reflects the fact that the Marketing and Sales departments have decided to collaborate on providing the EDW team with a list of corporate identifiers for all parties. The link between the four old entities is replaced by four new linking tables to the business keys for orders or packages. True to the Level 3 generalization approach to parties that we considered in Chapter 12, this new model has a rollup link table associated with the PARTY table so that the organization can track such notions as subsidiary ownership, trade associations, and purchasing collectives. In fact, the LINK_DEALERSHIP table in the old model has been subsumed by this LINK_PARTY_ROLLUP, becoming just another set of records in this new entity, distinguishable by a Rollup_Type column on the rollup entity's attribute table.

All told, the extent of this modification would be simply the effort to build and populate a new hyper normalized table for each of the 12 entities shown in the "New Tables" section of Figure 14.28. The effort of creating these tables is shown in the last section of Table 14.3 and amounts to roughly half of what a team would need to invest if it had built the EDW with a standard normal form data model.

Again, it is important to note that much of this savings comes from the ability to employ the reusable ETL modules to not only load new records into the revised model but also convert the existing records. The conversions required for this change case utilized temporary views between old and new tables to feed the team's already programmed data transforms,

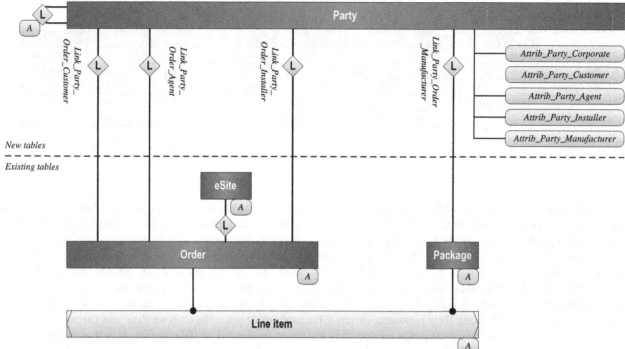

FIGURE 14.28   Hyper normalized model needed to solve Change Case 2.

much as was done in Change Case 1. ATTRIB_PARTY_INSTALLER, for example, has nearly the same structure as the old ATTRIB_INSTALLER table, only it has acquired the Installer_Number column that formerly served as the business key for the BK_INSTALLER table in the original model. In order to properly load some of the linking tables, the developers will have to run the reusable ETL module against some temporary joins between the original tables, as was necessary in the previous change case. For example, to load the linking table for installers between PARTY and ORDER, they will need to run the link loading module against a join of original LINK_INSTALLER_ORDER to the BK_ORDER (which will be retained) and BK_INSTALLER (soon to be dropped), as shown in Figure 14.29. This join will provide the order number and installer number combinations that the link loading module will scan for unique occurrences.

Loading the new LINK_PARTY_ROLLUP using records from the old LINK_DEALERSHIP table will require an even more extensive temporary join, as shown in Figure 14.30. The three tables in the middle of the join shown in the top of this diagram provide the necessary information from the previous model. The two party attribute tables joined on both sides will translate name attributes for these parties into business key elements that the link loading module will scan in order to detect unique combinations of installers and manufacturers. For each new combination, the load module will create a party rollup record, and once this load is complete and validated, the developers can drop the old LINK_DEALERSHIP table.

HNF-POWERED AGILE SOLUTIONS

The previous discussion presented many advantages of hyper normalized data models that, when combined, offer EDW team leaders a variety of attractive options for agile delivery of large data integration applications. We have seen that hyper normalization allows an EDW's integration layer to be

- modeled quickly with far more repeatable results than standard normal forms;
- constructed one small piece at a time;
- re-engineered in small pieces when confronted with new or changing requirements;
- loaded using only a few reusable ETL modules;
- adapted using the same reusable modules; and
- loaded quickly using high parallelization across inexpensive servers.

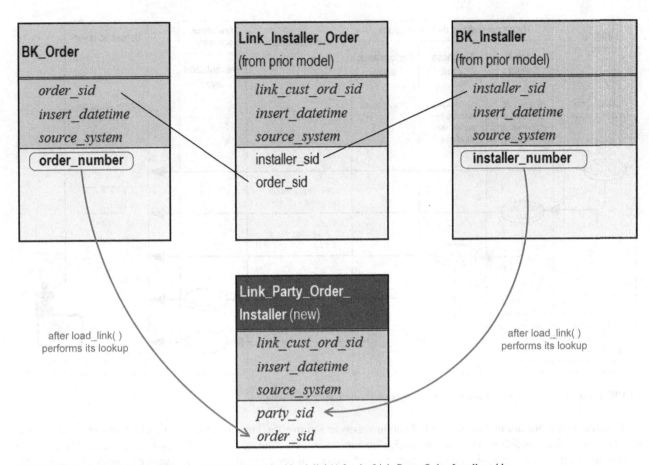

FIGURE 14.29 Joins of existing and new tables needed to feed load_link( ) for the Link_Party_Order_Installer table.

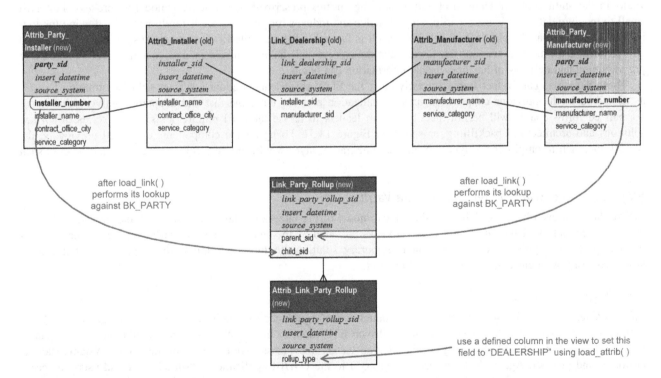

FIGURE 14.30 Joins of existing and new tables needed to feed load_link( ) for the Link_Party_Rollup table of dealership relationships.

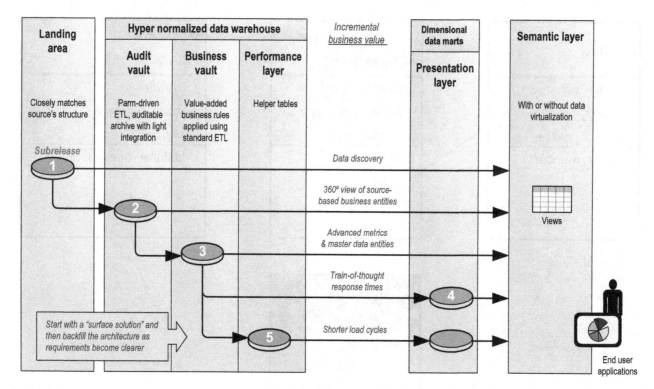

FIGURE 14.31   Surface solution patterns employing a hyper normalized integration layer.

I should also point out that hyper normalization seems to remove the large gulf between logical and physical modeling. During logical modeling, the team identifies business keys, then links, and finally attribute entities. The attribute entities are then logically partitioned to support distinct sources of operational data and change cadences among the elements provided by those sources. In practice, the tables of the physical models of at least the source vaults and staging vaults in the audit sublayer seem to closely match the entities prescribed by the logical modeling process. For most small to medium data warehouses, partitioning of tables and indexes for performance is rarely needed, allowing the logical model to serve as the physical model. This result is favorable for the agile EDW team because the more the logical and physical data models overlap, the fewer days developers will have to invest in data modeling before the EDW programming and delivery of business-usable information can begin.

These deliveries can in fact start very early on if the EDW team leaders adopt a surface-solution strategy. Exactly as described in the previous chapters on data virtualization and big data, the fast and adaptable delivery that hyper normalized forms enable will permit the EDW team leaders to tackle large BI requirements with a series of surface solutions and architectural backfilling, as shown in Figure 14.31. Using all the components examined previously, the typical approach to employing a hyper normalized integration layer would progress following a five-step process such as follows.

Step 1: Surface Solution with Raw Data Vault

Before the team even begins considering the logical model of the integration layer, it first must land the data and offer end users access to it. This access can come via views provided by the database or a data virtualization server, and it is intended only to support data discovery and temporary solutions to those burning business questions that can be answered easily with current, unintegrated information.

Step 2: Audit Sublayer

The EDW team leaders iterate quickly under a product owner's guidance to identify business keys, links, and attributes within the sources system data. Using parameter-driven ETL models, the EDW developers populate a staging vault a few tables at a time, steadily building out 360-degree views of business entities found in the source systems such as customer and product. Again, these features are brought to the DW/BI application's "surface" for end users to access via views or virtual star schemas.

Step 3: Value-Added Sublayer

Building on the insights into data sources and requirements uncovered by end-user reactions to staging vault data, the EDW team next switches to its standard ETL tools to apply business rules to the lightly integrated information in the audit sublayer. Here, the team must slow down as it performs the difficult work of cleaning and harmonizing data, as well as generating master data elements and derived metrics. The team places the results of value-added entities into the business vault sublayer and asks the end users to evaluate the new tables. If the team makes a mistake in design, the separation of business keys, links, and attributes will still allow it to correct its designs work fairly quickly and repeat the evaluation until it delivers true value for the business.

Step 4: Fully Managed Data Delivery Chain

With a sound integration layer assembled and a detailed notion of the analyses end users require from the new information, the EDW team can now project the integration-layer data into star schemas to give the business fast, multidimensional analytics.

Step 5: Performance Sublayer

The operations team may struggle to make some of the projections of hyper normalized data into star schemas run quickly enough to meet the company's desired refresh schedule. At this point, the EDW developers can add a few point-in-time and bridging tables to shorten the delivery times so that data transform processing fits comfortably into the data warehouse's load window.

EVIDENCE OF SUCCESS

The theory presented above may offer enough abstract reasons to inspire early adopters to begin experimenting with hyper normalized forms, but most enterprise data warehousing team leaders will need evidence of any modeling technique's success at reasonably large companies before they will be willing to stake the success of their next project on such a novel data modeling approach. Fortunately, we are more than 10 years past Dan Linstedt's 2003 "Data Vault Overview" in *The Data Administration Newsletter* [Linstedt 2003], and evidence is now quite easy to come by.

I began regularly hearing about data vaulting for enterprise data warehousing in 2011. In that year, EDW team leaders from Sydney, Australia, to Stockholm, Sweden, asked me how this new data modeling technique might augment the agile delivery of large analytic systems. Some online research revealed a large and active data vaulting community in The Netherlands. Before I began adding hyper normalized concepts to the agile data engineering classes I taught for The Data Warehousing Institute (TDWI), I traveled to Amsterdam to meet with a few thought leaders from this community and interview some of their customers for case studies that could illustrate the technique's success.

Data vaulting got started in The Netherlands when the government's internal revenue agency hired Dan Linstedt to teach its data warehousing team the Data Vault 1.0 standard. After several successful projects there, the members of that technical team relayed this new technique to private companies and nonprofit organizations so that now the Dutch data vaulting community can point to more than 600 completed data vault projects in their country alone. Many thanks go to Ron Damhof and Tom Breur for introducing me to the Dutch school of hyper normalized data modeling and facilitating the case studies described next. These gentlemen have been thought leaders in the rapid data warehousing movement there, and they estimate that approximately 80 percent of the new data warehousing projects in The Netherlands are now designed using data vaulting standards.

For a while, North America definitely seemed to be falling behind Europe in adaptable EDW designs, but I have recently seen rapidly growing interest in hyper normalized designs in North America. When I now teach agile data engineering at TDWI's world conferences, usually two or three people in the audience will share with the class that they have switched to either data vaulting or anchor modeling, adding that these techniques have greatly accelerated their EDW delivery speeds. At the time of this writing, Canada in particular seems to be in the lead on this continent. The largest financial services company, the largest semipublic pension fund, and the largest aircraft maker in Canada have all shared with me the tremendous success they have had with ensemble data modeling. To finish this chapter, I share with readers the highlights of two case studies I was able to complete while researching hyper normalization in The Netherlands.

Online Financial Services

One case study, a financial company offering online services for private and professional investors, demonstrated the power of data vaulting. BinckBank N.V. is one of the most successful young players in the Dutch financial landscape. It offers clients fast, low-cost access to the leading financial markets throughout the world, extensive market information, and accurate administrative processing of securities and cash transactions [BinckBank 2014]. During my interview with BinckBank, I met with the manager of BI and the technical lead on the company's data warehousing project. They explained that they employ data vaulting in the "enhanced style" described previously in this chapter using a code generator to create the target tables and ETL to build a 500-GB integration layer with 10 years of history based on Microsoft's SQL server.

When I was introduced to BinckBank, it was growing quickly through acquisitions. It had recently attempted to update an 80-user, Kimball-style warehouse—an experience that proved to the company that the enterprise data bus approach was never going to allow the EDW team to keep up with the company's steady stream of new requirements and acquisitions. Data vaulting gave the EDW team the ability to add new data sources and expand analytical services for end users at an incredibly quick pace. As an example, the technical lead related a recent situation in which he had to add all the data from an Oracle-brand customer relationship manager to the existing CRM subject area, which was based largely on a PeopleSoft application. "How long did that much additional data modeling take you?" I asked him. "Including getting coffee? All of about one morning." I looked to the BI manager for validation. "He's not kidding," was the response. "He was adding the new company's data to our warehouse by the end of the day." Needless to say, such rapid turnaround hinged upon having a good data model of the source available that made primary and foreign keys easy to discern. Such a case history makes the savings I have estimated for data vaulting in the previously presented change cases look very conservative indeed, suggesting that in practice EDW teams can expect to achieve incredible agility with hyper normalized data models.

The Free University

A second case study the Dutch data vaulting practitioners were kind enough to arrange on that same trip was with the Vrije Universiteit Amsterdam (known as "VU," the Free University, with "free" meaning "liberated"). VU is composed of 12 colleges with a total of 22,000 students and 4000 employees. There, I met with the data warehousing program manager, project leader, and lead engineer. This team had recently built a first release of an analytics system using Oracle and Business Objects that provided users with a large book of key performance indicators. The data for these KPIs originated from a wide variety of sources, including multiple registration systems, a newly marketed Student Life Cycle Management application from SAP, and other legacy systems for finance, human resources, housing, and research publications.

The project architects had chosen to build a classic-style integration layer in which the data vault provided a persistent staging area of lightly integrated source data that was then projected into the star schemas of their presentation layer. The first release of the warehouse contained 30 business keys, 70 links, 140 attribute tables, and 100 reference tables. Because the student life cycle application was new and still being changed regularly by the vendor, the VU data warehousing developers were particularly grateful that the data vaulting approach allowed them to update their integration layer as the table structures in that source continued to change. They found that the decoupling of business keys from links and attribute tables allowed them to create target tables and ETL before the source specification was finalized and adapt to any surprises with only a small amount of rework. Based on this ability to model fairly accurately in the abstract and quickly adapt to specifics, their team was able to make the first set of data available to end users only a month after a new sources system went online.

The VU team relied heavily on reusable ETL modules, which contributed greatly to the team's rapid deliveries of new features. Staging and integration programming was facilitated by template files. To create new features, the developers needed only to enter some parameters, such as the names of the staging target tables, and the ETL was generated for them. With programming largely automated, the data modeling became the most difficult part of providing new information services because it required investigating the source data and deciding how to structure the integration layer accordingly. They estimated that with their parameter-driven ETL, staging work consumed 10 percent of the effort, data modeling 65 percent, and ETL development only 25 percent.

The attribute tables team underscored the many ways that hyper normalized data models allowed it to be far more agile. Because the team was using a classic-style approach, its data warehousing activity focused on quickly capturing source data, leaving the value-added activities for the front-end programmers to implement when they created new dashboard features. The team estimated that the division of labor for adding new data elements to the warehouse was

10% for the data vaulting work and 90% for the BI layer. This allocation worked well for the team's analytics program because it minimized the effort invested in the non-value-added portions of the work, such as basic ETL coding, allowing the EDW leaders to reallocate staff to those portions in which the team was closely collaborating with the end users.

SUMMARY

To speed up both design and ETL coding for an enterprise data warehousing program, EDW team leaders should consider ensemble data modeling. This style of modeling dictates separate data tables for business keys, the relationships between them, and their attributes. There are three schools of ensemble modeling, all of them resulting in *hyper normalized* data models that have more tables than equivalent repositories designed using standard normal forms. Fortunately, these larger models contain only three or four kinds of tables, depending on the school of ensemble modeling a team decides to use. The table types are business keys, links, attributes, and optionally references—all of which can be populated using one parameter-driven ETL module for each table type. This approach allows EDW teams to not only begin capturing data after programming just a few reusable data transform modules but also employ these modules to quickly reload the data should the target data model need to change.

Hyper normalized data designs strongly support agility by removing the risk involved in building large integration layers for business analytics. By separating business keys, the foreign keys that model relationships, and the many qualifiers that provide context for those keys and relationships, modeling mistakes and new requirements tend to affect only one or two small tables and are therefore fast to correct. Accordingly, agile EDW teams can start their integration layers with only small set of tables and safely add on additional tables as further requirements become clear.

There are several architectural styles for employing hyper normalized data repositories. They differ in whether the EDW team chooses to combine or separate primary data capture and light integration from the application of value-added business rules. The style that first stages lightly integrated data and then populates a value-added layer using business-rules supports well agile data warehousing's notion of delivering surface solutions with steadily richer capabilities provided through later backfilling of the reference architecture.

Hyper normalization offers EDW team leaders many options for constantly delivering value to the end customers. However, all these advantages focus only on streamlining the creation and maintenance of the integration layer of the reference architecture. To extend this speed and labor savings to the remaining layers, EDW teams will need to consider *hyper generalized* design techniques, which are the subject of the next chapter.

Chapter 15

Fully Agile EDW with Hyper Generalization

The hyper normalized approach to enterprise data warehousing (EDW) integration layers described in Chapter 14 is popular with many agile data warehousing teams because of the advantages it offers over traditionally modeled data warehouses. Hyper normalized forms (HNFs) allow developers to build out the business intelligence applications in small pieces and then employ reusable data transform modules to load the warehouse, saving significant labor on extract, transform, and load (ETL) coding. More important, many of the HNF modeling rules make it easier for an EDW team to evolve the structure of an integration layer even after the company's operational data has been loaded. For other EDW teams, however, the thought of employing a hyper normalized form only creates concern. These teams are disquieted by the fact that HNF addresses only the integration layer of the data warehouse, that it doubles the number of tables of a standard normal form model, and that it makes data considerably more difficult to retrieve. They see the performance workarounds such as seeding null records and materializing point-in-time tables as kluges and wish there was a more widely supported means of generating a far more complete enterprise data warehouse.

A more complete solution does exist, and it lies in the opposite direction along the hyper modeling spectrum. Instead of hyper normalizing an EDW model into more tables, the development team should *hyper generalize* the integration layer down to just a handful of entities. Such hyper generalized forms (HGFs) enable EDW teams to generate and evolve nearly all of a data warehouse and its basic data management functions using a commercially available tool.

Although HGF involves fewer tables, it makes the details of the integration layer ironically more complex to understand. This chapter introduces the three main components of the hyper generalized data store: an associative repository for business entities and links, a stack of name-value pairs for attributes, and barely transformed relational structure for transaction records. The reader should remember that in practice, teams that utilize hyper generalization in their EDW programs invariably acquire a data warehouse automation tool to perform all the difficult work. This automation tool makes the complexity of the integration layer moot because it generates new and updated data warehouses according to the developer's instructions, communicated through data models and data flows expressed at the business level.

Because EDW team leaders should understand how hyper-generalized repositories permit such extensive model-driven development, this chapter begins by introducing HGF's inner workings. The reader should keep in mind that, given the automation tool, most of this complexity remains hidden from even the EDW programmers. The later sections of this chapter illustrate how the model-driven development enabled by an HGF repository eliminates more than 90% of the labor formerly required to create and modify a production data warehouse, including its presentation and semantic layers. With that level of acceleration and support, hyper-generalized integration layers represent the pinnacle of agile data warehousing and should be carefully considered at the beginning of any significant data warehousing project.

HYPER GENERALIZATION INVOLVES A MIX OF MODELING STRATEGIES

Chapter 14 demonstrated how ensemble modeling instills flexibility and resilience into hyper normalized integration layers. The warehouse decomposes source information into very small pieces that can be reassembled in a myriad of ways to meet a wide range of business needs. The hyper generalized data store obtains its advantages from ensemble modeling as well. However, where the HNF technique uses a single approach to modeling the integration layer (business keys, links, and attributes), the HGF repository employs three different styles of data storage.

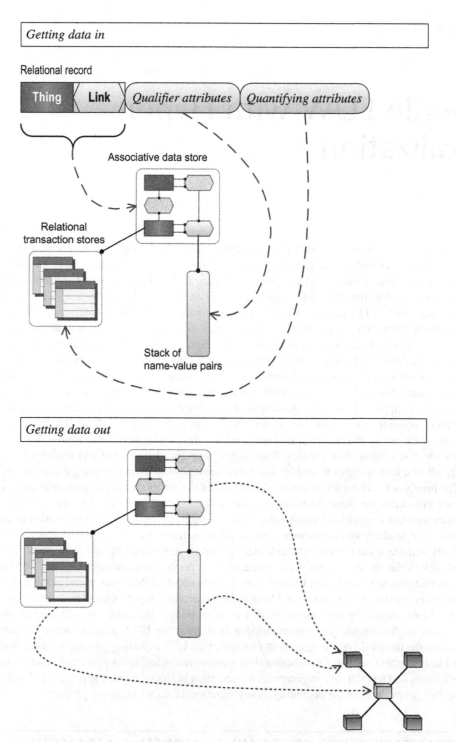

FIGURE 15.1   Decomposing data into a hyper generalized data store and then projecting it to a star schema.

As shown in Figure 15.1, the hyper generalized warehouse decomposes and stores an input record into multiple logical targets. The elements within the single source information record are decomposed into four categories:

- Things: All business entities (not just major "business keys" as in the hyper normalized approach)
- Links: Relationships between things
- Qualifying attributes: Analogous to the attributes in HNF
- Quantifying attributes: The measures occurring within transactions and events

Things and links are stored in an associative data model. The qualifying attributes are placed in a tall and skinny stack of name-value pairs. Quantifying attributes are recorded in dimensionalized fact structures with the foreign keys necessary to link them to things and links.

As with the HNF approach, the purpose of the hyper generalized data stores is to retain information in an elemental format that can be re-projected into a wide variety of star schemas as needed to meet specific analytical requirements. The bottom of Figure 15.1 depicts how the multiple storage areas within the HGF integration layer support the creation of presentation layer objects:

- The associative data store provides the core entities and rollup hierarchies for the dimensions.
- The name-value pair table enriches those dimensions with attributes.
- Information in the dimensionalized transaction store becomes the fact tables.

Readers who think that this data management strategy involves too many gymnastics should keep in mind that this exotic blend of data structures will enable the bulk of a data warehouse's design and operations to be controlled from business-level diagrams, eliminating three-fourths or more of the work that building an enterprise data warehouse used to require.

Extreme Generalization

Of the three storage areas for the HGF warehouse, the associative data store is the hardest to comprehend at first. Its nature is much easier to understand if we see it derived from hyper normalized model considered in Chapter 14. Such a theoretical transformation requires five conceptual steps, as shown in Figures 15.2–15.7.

Figure 15.2 depicts our starting point, a portion of an enterprise data warehouse already in hyper normalized form. This model fragment shows customer linked to sales orders, both with attribute tables. True to HNF's guidelines, these two business key tables contain nothing but a string representing each business entity's natural key(s), a surrogate key, plus the metadata columns for record source and insert timestamp. Aside from any differences in the size or data type of the natural key columns, the only aspect of these tables that makes them distinct is simply that they have been declared as separate objects with unique names. Would it not be easier just to store the records for both of these entities in a single business key table? We would need to record some metadata to indicate record type so that we could later distinguish between records describing customers from those documenting sales orders. Such a generalization would certainly reduce the number of tables within an HNF integration layer.

Figure 15.3 shows this change put into effect. CUSTOMER and ORDER have now been consolidated into a table called THING. Each THING table has a foreign key pointing to a record in another new table called THING_TYPE, which will remember which THINGs are customers and which are orders.

Similarly, the links shown in our starting model are structured all the same. They have only some foreign keys pointing to the business entities they link and then the same metadata columns we listed a moment ago. So why not collate all the link records into a single table and use a metadata column to document the type of relationship each describes?

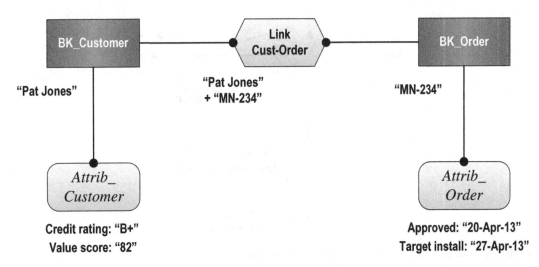

FIGURE 15.2 Hyper generalizing a HNF data model – starting point.

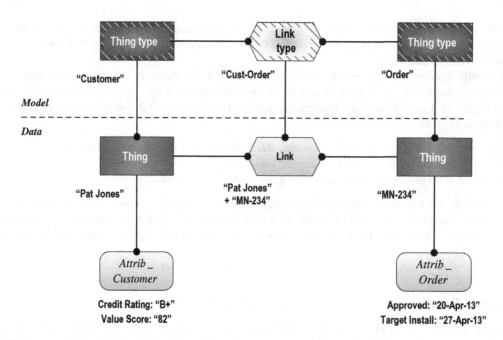

FIGURE 15.3   Hyper generalization Step 1 — add metadata tables.

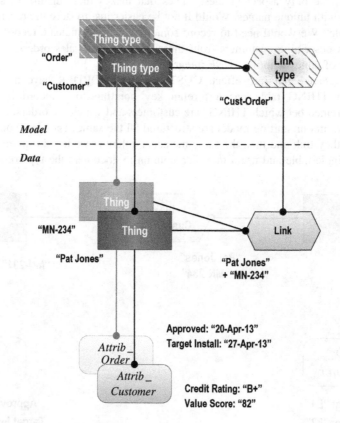

FIGURE 15.4   Hyper generalization Step 2 — simplify to one table per function.

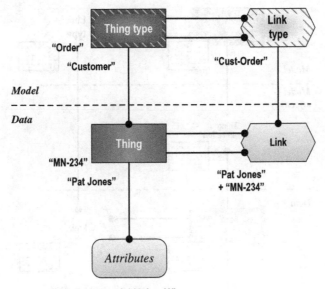

FIGURE 15.5   Hyper generalization Step 3 — "shred" attributes into name-value pairs.

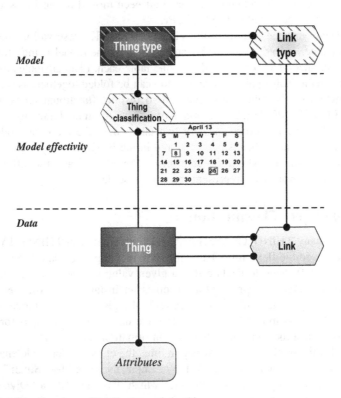

FIGURE 15.6   Hyper generalization Step 4 — temporalize thing type relationships.

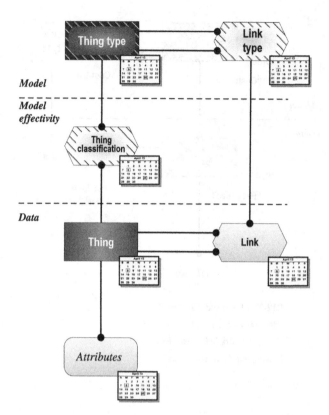

FIGURE 15.7   Hyper normalization Step 5 — temporalize the remaining entities.

Such a design change would further reduce the number of tables within the HNF model considerably. This generalization is also shown in Figure 15.3, in which the relationships have all been moved to the LINK table, and meta data records denoting the type of each have been collected in LINK_TYPE.

With the metadata now identifying the records in the THING and LINK, these various instances of those two entities no longer need to be kept separate. Indeed, Figures 15.4 and 15.5 show the model being "folded" upon itself so that the THINGs and LINKs become aligned and then merged into one table each. (The attributes associated with business keys and links must be converted to name-value pairs before they too can be folded together, as we will discuss in a moment.)

Note that this transformation of the tables has created two distinct functional areas within this integration-layer model. THING_TYPE and LINK_TYPE define what kinds of objects the model can store and the relationship that we expect to see between them. The records stored in these two tables describe the data model of the warehouse. Those records determine what kinds of business objects can be stored in the integration layer and the ways they can be joined together to create meaningful information about the enterprise. The THING and the LINK tables, on the other hand, store the actual values of the warehouse. They represent the enterprise data.

Adding Time-Oriented Object Classification

Figure 15.6 inserts a many-to-many THING_CLASSIFICATION table between THING_TYPE and THING, giving the hyper generalized data store incredible flexibility. This table provides a pair of date time values, "effective from" and "effective until," allowing the EDW team to declare that a given value is considered an instance of a particular thing type until a certain date, after which that same value becomes an instance of a different business class altogether. In other words, this classification table determines the effectivity of a given business model to the business data that the warehouse contains. Because business models now have effective dates, the HGF data store allows the EDW team to apply a series of data models against the company's business information across time.

By adding the constraint that the models cannot overlap in time, the classification table enables the agile EDW team to evolve the data warehouse as business conditions change. For example, the record for "Small Trucks" could be a "Business Unit" of a large automobile company up until June 30, after which it is linked to a "Division" THING_TYPE record, indicating that Small Trucks is now a fully independent business concern responsible for its own profit and loss statement.

By connecting Small Trucks to a new THING_TYPE record, the classification table causes that business object to be governed by a new set of the LINK_TYPE records after the effective date. The new LINK_TYPE records may well give Small Trucks a new place in a given rollup scheme or cause it to participate in several completely different types of rollups altogether.

This THING_CLASSIFICATION table lends great agility to the EDW team. Using the effectivity dates on the classification records, the developers can create a new model using THINGS and LINK and then declare that it takes effect sometime in the future. Such capability enables them to respond to upcoming requirements changes with a new pattern of classifications and hierarchies on the already existing data records. They are able to manage complex requirements changes such as a new rollup by simply inserting a few additional records in the model portion of the integration layer that represent the new relationships between entities. When the data is next projected out of the integration layer into the presentation layer, the data warehouse administrator makes a choice between the following:

1. Use the relationships that existed at the time of the transactions, in which case retrieval queries will follow the previous set of THINGS and LINKS records.
2. Use the relationships belonging to the current model, in which case the retrieval queries follow the new set of THINGS and LINKS records.

This inherent flexibility of the HGF repository allows the EDW team to steadily refine the data model without having to reload the existing production data—very agile indeed.

Given the power that effectivity in the classification table provides, many people would naturally suggest that such a strategy be employed throughout the rest of the data warehouse. Figure 15.7 depicts the final step in hyper generalizing a starting data model, which adds effectivity metadata columns to all the remaining entities in our integration layer's logical model. When records are added that represent the current business situation, the business date is placed in the effective-from column, and an "end of time" (EOT) value is placed in the effective-until field. By placing effective-from and effective-until dates on every entity, the HGF integration layer can depict a change in both the data and the data model of the warehouse by simply incrementing the image held in the data repository. When the source system next contains a change of fact, the load process retires the old image of the appropriate records by placing a non-EOT value in the effective-until column, and it creates a new image with current data in the repository, placing an EOT timestamp in the effective-until column.

Managing Things and Links with an Associative Data Model

The most exotic portion of an HGF warehouse manages the data for the backbone of an enterprise data model. We called the components of this backbone *business keys* and *links* when discussing the hyper normalized form in Chapter 14. As with the HNF approach, the company's notion of its major business entities and how they relate to one another determines the core truths that the hyper generalized warehouse will record and later express about the organization. The qualifying attributes, on the other hand, only provide a series of details or context about that larger truth. The hyper generalized repository manages things and links differently from qualifying attributes because when fundamental business conditions occur in the enterprise, it is usually the collection of business keys in the data warehouse and the relationships declared between that must change radically. The attributes already recorded about those things and links can often remain largely unchanged. The similar revision to the data warehouse is necessary when a team must correct a major misunderstanding regarding business requirements. By allowing the team to quickly adjust the backbone of the data warehouse, HGF data warehouses offer the ultimate in fail fast and fix quickly.

To provide flexible management of things and links, hyper generalized warehouse applications store business keys and links in an extremely flexible format called an *associative data model*. Associative databases store all different types of data together in a single consistent structure that never changes, no matter how many types of data are stored [Williams 2002]. The associative data model employed in hyper generalized data warehouses allows the five logical tables representing the things and links to be stored in a single physical table. Figure 15.8 shows a small portion of a business model that an EDW team wishes to implement using hyper generalization. The two entities, products and product types, have a many-to-one relationship. To capture this modeling fact, we need two entities in the THING_TYPE table, and their relationship must be then recorded in the LINK_TYPE table.

Figure 15.9 shows how the records inserted into the warehouse's business metadata table would be structured. Each record is given an object identifier (OID) when inserted in the repository. OID 1001 records that Product Category exists as an entity in the data model starting 8-April. OID 1002 records that Product also exists as an entity with the

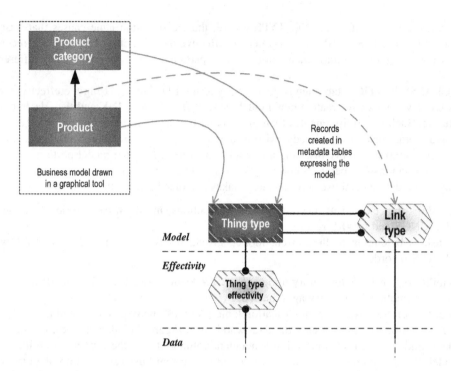

FIGURE 15.8 Business models are machine readable.

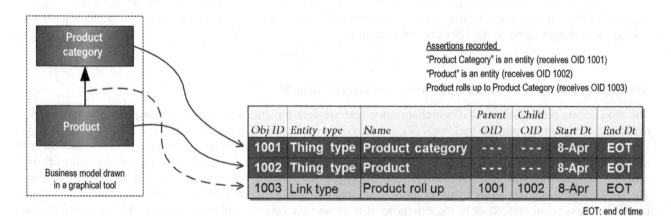

FIGURE 15.9 Dimensional objects from the business model translated to records in the associative data model.

same starting date. To express that product records will eventually roll up to product categories, OID 1003 asserts that OID 1001 (product category) is the parent of OID 1002 (product).

These records demonstrate the three parts of a record format called a *triple*. Triples consist of a subject, a predicate (all assertions beside the subject), and often an object (a portion of the predicate.) For OID 1001, the subject was product category, and the predicate was that this entity simply exists for a given data range. No object was needed for this assertion because associative data modeling treats existence as a root fact that stands alone, much the way that business keys are treated in the hyper normalized modeling paradigm. For record 1003, the triple structure is as follows:

- Subject: Parent OID 1001 ("product category")
- Predicate: Receives a rollup starting 8-April
- Object: Child OID 1002 ("product")

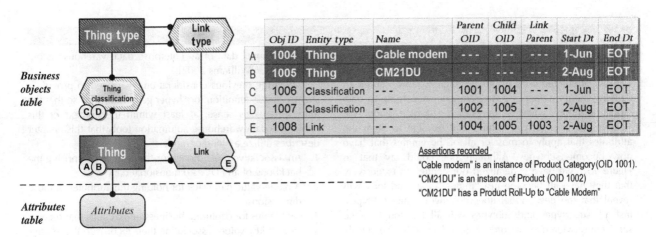

	Obj ID	Entity type	Name	Parent OID	Child OID	Link Parent	Start Dt	End Dt
A	1004	Thing	Cable modem	---	---	---	1-Jun	EOT
B	1005	Thing	CM21DU	---	---	---	2-Aug	EOT
C	1006	Classification	---	1001	1004	---	1-Jun	EOT
D	1007	Classification	---	1002	1005	---	2-Aug	EOT
E	1008	Link	---	1004	1005	1003	2-Aug	EOT

Assertions recorded

"Cable modem" is an instance of Product Category (OID 1001).

"CM21DU" is an instance of Product (OID 1002)

"CM21DU" has a Product Roll-Up to "Cable Modem"

FIGURE 15.10 Sample records for things and links in the associative data store.

The dimensional data governed by this model can be expressed as associative records as well, as shown in Figure 15.10. In this example, five data records express that a product known as "CM21DU" is considered to be a "cable modem" product type. Records for OIDs 1004 and 1005 provide the standalone assertions that "cable modem" and "CM21DU" exist. Logically, these records belong in the THING entity. OID 1006 registers that cable modem is a product type, utilizing the OID 1001 record shown in the previous diagram. Likewise, OID 1007 states that CM21DU is a product, referring to the OID 1002 record created previously. Both of these records belong to the THING_CLASSIFICATION entity. Finally, OID 1008 associates product CM21DU with the cable model product type by registering a parent–child relationship between OIDs 1004 and 1005. Logically, this record belongs to the LINK entity. Note that this entry also refers to OID 1003 as the "link parent," declaring that the actual rollup documented for data records here complies with a particular rollup already configured by the records depicting the data model.

The records registering the existing types and instances of both things and links are all expressed as triples. Because all the triples can be expressed using the eight columns shown in Figure 15.10, they can all be stored in the same physical table. "Hyper generalization," then, refers to not only the fact that an entire EDW model can be captured in a few logical tables but also that those logical tables can be further consolidated into even fewer physical tables.

Note that the term *hyper generalization* is a fairly loose concept that I coined for this book in order to contrast data warehouses based on associative data modeling with those utilizing the hyper normalization techniques discussed in Chapter 14. The sidebar explains how much of this approach is actually based on meta modeling and provides a more careful definition for the hyper generalization term. The crucial notion for EDW leaders to keep in mind is that they now have two new directions in data modeling to choose from besides the "Inmon versus Kimball" dichotomy established during the 1990s. When embarking upon a new project, the EDW architects can either (1) invest in a data model with more entities than standard normal forms would specify (hyper normalization) or (2) insist on extremely general data structures where only a handful of entities are necessary (hyper generalization). Either choice will enable teams to achieve considerable automation in the creation and maintenance of their enterprise data warehouses.

Hyper generalization's use of very few tables allows the EDW's underlying logical data model to be considerably simpler than a standard modeling approach, but it also makes the internal workings of the data warehouse more complex. The data capture operations shown in this section illustrate that many small records have to be perfectly coordinated to store a company's business information in the HGF's reduced number of tables. That introductory presentation left out many other details that the data warehouse will also have to manage, such as the following:

- Relationships between two entities can be optional.
- Multiple relationships might exist between two entities, in which case they need to be labeled for the various roles that the entities play.
- Name fields should be stored as references in case the name text changes over time.

Detailed technical requirements such as these were the primary obstacle keeping EDW teams from utilizing hyper generalization until the vendor community could offer reliable tools for managing all these internal operations.

Technically, the data modeling patterns described is this chapter go far beyond the traditionally recognized patterns of generalization, requiring us to be slightly more careful in defining the term "hyper generalization." According to data modeling theory, when we generalize a starting model, we steadily create supertype entities and reassign to them the attributes that apply to most or all of the entities that have now become subtypes. Although one could say that in Figure 15.7 we have generalized our entities so extensively that they have all become just "things," a second look will reveal that the new model does not involve any subtypes. Instead, supertypes and subtypes will all be stored in the same entity. Moreover, records in a model that has been truly generalized will still employ foreign keys or pointers within dependent tables for linking records of a dependent entity to records in its parent. The entity records in the hyper generalized data model we have been discussing no longer have foreign keys as part of their structures, given that the pointers between all the modeled objects have now been isolated to a single LINK entity.

Speaking precisely, then, the repository for the dimensional data of a warehouse described in this chapter is not an example of generalization but instead of *meta-modeling*. When people structure entities to capture a model of reality rather than reality itself, they have created a model for a model or, in other words, a meta model. The six logical entities in Figure 15.7 not only allow an EDW team to describe a data model as a series of assertions but also provide abstract storage for observed facts that comply with those model assertions. Creating meta models in computer science has a long history, and many patterns for meta models exist [West 2011]. The associative data model described here for holding the dimensional data of an enterprise data warehouse is but one example [Williams 2002].

Given the previous considerations, we need to provide a slightly larger definition for "hyper generalization" so that the term still makes sense, at least within the context of this book. The data warehouse automation tools that this chapter describes utilize a blend of models:

1. An associative meta model for the entities comprising the backbone of an EDW's dimensional data
2. A name-value pair stack for holding the attributes of those dimensions
3. Fact tables for capturing business transactions that receive foreign key values associating their records to the entities described by the associative meta model for dimensions

If one starts with a single record representation of EDW data, as we did in Figure 12.11, and then restructures it to reside comfortably in our data warehouse automation system, we will have abstracted that starting record in three ways:

- The dimensional entities will have become things and links.
- The dimensional attributes will have become key-value pairs with linked metadata records.
- Events and measures will have become an array of quantities with links to a wide variety of qualifiers that provide context information for each fact.

In this light, we have generalized business data to an extreme so that a computer can greatly assist us in creating, programming, and modifying an enterprise data warehouse. The term "hyper generalization," then, makes sense as long as we define it to include the three types of modeling abstractions listed here.

Storing Attributes as Name-Value Pairs

Astute readers will have noted that our generalization process hit a snag when it merged the THING and LINK tables in Figure 15.5. Combining these logical tables worked well for data and metadata tables belonging to THING and LINK because they had comparable structures to begin with. But what about the attribute tables tied to each business key and link table? In the HNF paradigm, many of those tables were closely modeled after the operational sources so that each will have a unique set of columns. Tables so structured cannot be simply combined because their column layouts do not match.

In theory, attributes could be treated as assertions and stored in the THING table along with the qualifier entities. However, vendors who have tried this approach have encountered performance challenges when trying to retrieve dimensional data from the associative data store. Automation tool makers have found that they can achieve far better performance without any loss in capability if they "shred" the attributes of dimensional entities into a stack of name-value pairs. As shown in Figure 15.11, each column in a given record can be converted to a record of its own, where one column provides the name of the element represented and the next column provides the value for that element. An additional column in the record holds the foreign keys necessary to link all the attributes back to the entity being described. Foreign key values stored in those columns will identify the parent object to which the name-value pair applies. In this example, the parent OID receives the values of the Line Item OID.

Because all tables arrive at the same structure when shredded in this way, their records can be directly combined. Such a transformation turns multiple short and wide tables into a single tall and skinny stack of information. Note that

Source records:

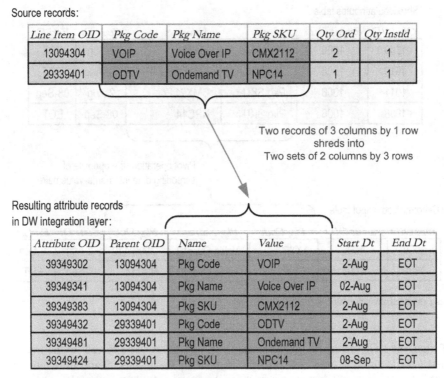

Line Item OID	Pkg Code	Pkg Name	Pkg SKU	Qty Ord	Qty Instld
13094304	VOIP	Voice Over IP	CMX2112	2	1
29339401	ODTV	Ondemand TV	NPC14	1	1

Two records of 3 columns by 1 row
shreds into
Two sets of 2 columns by 3 rows

Resulting attribute records
in DW integration layer:

Attribute OID	Parent OID	Name	Value	Start Dt	End Dt
39349302	13094304	Pkg Code	VOIP	2-Aug	EOT
39349341	13094304	Pkg Name	Voice Over IP	02-Aug	EOT
39349383	13094304	Pkg SKU	CMX2112	2-Aug	EOT
39349432	29339401	Pkg Code	ODTV	2-Aug	EOT
39349481	29339401	Pkg Name	Ondemand TV	2-Aug	EOT
39349424	29339401	Pkg SKU	NPC14	08-Sep	EOT

Note that the data warehouse automation system assigns the attribute records
surrogate keys (that point to parent records) and effectivity dates. EOT stands for
"end of time," i.e., no end date.

FIGURE 15.11   Shredding attributes into name-value pairs.

the hyper generalized form places effectivity columns on the shredded table as well so that the HGF integration layer can easily track the history of attribute values for any entity in the database by simply retiring old records with a defined end date and placing a new record in the table with an undefined end date.

When information needs to be retrieved from this stack, the data management system needs to *pivot* an appropriate set of name-value pairs back into a standard multicolumn format, as shown in Figure 15.12. The foreign key associated with each pair allows the reconstructed relational record to be linked to the appropriate parent entity. In the diagram, the shredded attributes table has three records providing a code, name, and stock keeping unit number for a package that a telecommunication company sells. The two records that pivot out of the name-value pairs for this package register that its SKU was CMX2112 until 8 September, at which point it changed to NPC14.

Storing Transaction Data in a Lightly Dimensionalized Format

The hyper generalized form transforms business entities and their relationships into triples and their attributes into shredded storage. All that remains to manage from the source data is the *transaction* information that depicts events in the life of the business. The hyper generalized form leaves this information in a relational structure that closely resembles how it is received from the source systems. When the HGF warehouse captures each transaction record, it simply replaces any natural foreign key values with new surrogate keys that relate it to the proper entities in the associative data store, arriving at a "lightly dimensionalized" format for facts.

In processing source information, HGF applications typically read through the input tables that represent the qualifiers first, identifying the business objects and storing them away with *object identifiers* or OIDs. When it later processes the transaction data (which may or may not be found in the same extracts just scanned for qualifier information), the HGF transform needs only to (1) identify the dimensional entities associated with each transaction and (2) save away the measures representing the transaction. The remaining qualifier information can be ignored during transaction capture because it was processed earlier and stored as things, links, and attributes. By identifying the

Shredded attributes table

Obj OID	Parent OID	Name	Value	Start Dt	End Dt
1009	1006	Pkg Code	VOIP	2-Aug	EOT
1010	1006	Pkg Name	Voice Over IP	02-Aug	EOT
1011	1006	Pkg SKU	CMX2112	2-Aug	08-Sep
1908	1006	Pkg SKU	NPC14	08-Sep	EOT

Pivot operation (the opposite of shredding data into name-value pairs)

Denormalized output table

Obj OID	Parent OID	Pkg Code	Pkg Name	Pkg SKU	Start Dt	End Dt
1009	1006	VOIP	Voice Over IP	CMX2112	2-Aug	8-Sep
1009	1006	VOIP	Voice Over IP	NPC14	8-Sep	EOT

FIGURE 15.12   Pivoting shredded attributes back to their original format.

qualifiers ahead of time, the HGF transform can translate them into OIDs to be stored on the transaction record so that they can be rejoined later to the measures and provide context for the events. Some transaction source data contain complex grains, so the developers will have to process those data sets multiple times, with each pass capturing the set of transactions for a particular level of granularity.

Transaction records do not need effectivity metadata. They will retain instead their event date. The HGF repository already maintains effectivity dates for everything that a transaction will be tied to, as well as its associated links and attributes. The effectivity dates on these other elements allow the context for an event to be re-created for any arbitrary point in time, so there is no need to treat a transaction extract as anything more than a stream of timestamped observations of business events.

Managing Hyper Generalized Data in HGF Requires an Automation Tool

Looking over the examples of how simple business notions require many records in an associative database, one realizes how difficult it would be to manage enterprise data in this format by hand. It is true that the transaction data is left in a relational form that most data warehousing staff members will understand and that most traditional ETL tools can support. Expressing things and links in triples, however, will force the EDW team to create dozens of records for even simple business assertions and to store them using a complex pattern of interlocking object identifiers. Building the ETL to perform these functions would be a complex undertaking that would consume the development team with creating the underlying data automation system and leave little time to construct the actual enterprise data warehouse. Similarly, storing the many millions of attribute values in name-value pairs would obligate the EDW developers to program shredding and pivot routines just to store data replicated from the sources system, seriously detracting from implementing the business rules that create new derived information that adds value to the organization.

For these reasons, hyper generalization cannot follow a build-it-yourself approach. Whereas hyper normalization requires only that the EDW team build a few reusable ETL modules before it can begin warehousing corporate information, hyper generalization will necessitate the EDW department to acquire a tool already built and validated to manage the triple stores and name-value pairs that HGF requires. Fortunately, such tools exist and have supported hundreds of successful EDW programs during the past decade. These tools perform multiple functions. They build the warehouse and load data into the new structures. When requirements or designs change, the admin tool allows the EDW team to update the data model and automatically convert much of the data between an old business model and the new. The tool also retrieves the data from this flexible integration layer, creating the desired presentation layer and appropriate semantic layer objects so that the data is ready for end-user analytics.

By doing far more than just creating the integration layer or loading it with information, these tools greatly acceler-ate the many services an EDW team must provide its customers, allowing the team to easily reach high levels of agility in a very short time. Because they do far more than just extract, transform, and load, I refer to these tools as *data ware-house automation systems*, in line with The Data Warehousing Institute's categorization of these products [Wells 2014]. This is a new term in the DW/BI industry, one that has not yet been properly recognized by the analyst industry [Pace 2013], a fact that will make simply identifying the products in this space challenging for the next few years. However, the features and performance demonstrated to date by the tools utilizing the hyper generalization should cause analysts to eventually categorize these products properly and give them the attention they deserve.

HGF ENABLES MODEL-DRIVEN DEVELOPMENT AND FAST DELIVERIES

If we focus on just the creation of new enterprise data warehouses or at least adding new subject areas to an existing EDW, we can see that hyper generalization accelerates DW/BI deliveries in multiple ways, including the following:

- Eliminating most of the logical and physical artifacts that other data modeling paradigms require
- Allowing teams to build integration layers directly from a graphical business model
- Enabling teams to update an existing data warehouse by making changes to the EDW's graphical model

Eliminating Most Logical and Physical Data Modeling

Consider the logical data model for data integration layers that the hyper generalized paradigm utilizes, as shown in the top portion of Figure 15.1. That diagram depicts the logical data model for any enterprise data warehouse built using this approach, so for any DW/BI team building an enterprise data warehouse, the logical data modeling work is com-plete the minute they select their warehouse automation tool. The fact that data for the dimensional entities will be stored in either a table of associative triples or a table of name-value pairs means the physical data model for the non-transactional data is also already defined. Transaction tables will receive a structure that closely matches the format in which event data arrive to the data warehouse. For that reason, the physical data modeling for the EDW is also largely complete once the team has selected its automation tool. With the logical and physical data modeling reduced to a mini-mum, the development team can redirect its efforts elsewhere.

Controlling the EDW Design from a Business Model Diagram

The logical and physical models for a hyper generalized integration layer may be already set, but the records expressing the conceptual nature of the company's information must still be entered into the model portion of the HGF repository. Where does the knowledge needed to make the correct entries into those entities come from? The answer is the business model for the EDW. The multiple forms that the hyper generalized data modeling paradigms use for storing things, links, and attributes makes it possible for the computer to read a graphical depiction of a business model and translate it into metadata entries in the model portion of the HGF repository. Moreover, once the EDW team supplements the busi-ness model with some business-level source-to-target column mappings, the data warehouse automation system can generate the ETL needed to capture the business data and translate it into instances of things, links, and attributes.

Figure 15.9 demonstrated how a simple entity diagram translates directly into records for the THING and LINK entities of an HGF data warehouse. Figure 15.13 depicts the diagram that a team would employ to define a larger portion of an enterprise data warehouse. This business model has been drawn using the business information modeler of the data warehouse automation system. The particular entities in the figure represent the standard normal form model shown in Figure 12.14 that serves as the starting point for the change cases I have been using to demonstrate the advan-tages of hyper modeled forms. The fifth normal form solution for dealerships has been included, but the fourth normal form violation still needs to be corrected. We will see how that violation is resolved using the HGF automation tool when we return to the four change cases later.

In Figure 15.13, 12 entities represent qualifier information the team wishes to capture, organized into six dimen-sions. The dark arrows point to the entities that hold the parent objects that dependent entities require and thus can be interpreted as equivalent of the foreign-key constraints used in relational database management system (DBMS) schemas. Two transaction data sets have been defined for the Sales Fact, one for sales made directly through the company's own web and the other for sales made through partner sites. These transaction sets have slightly different but overlapping fields for measures defined—in particular, there are no discounts allowed for sales made through

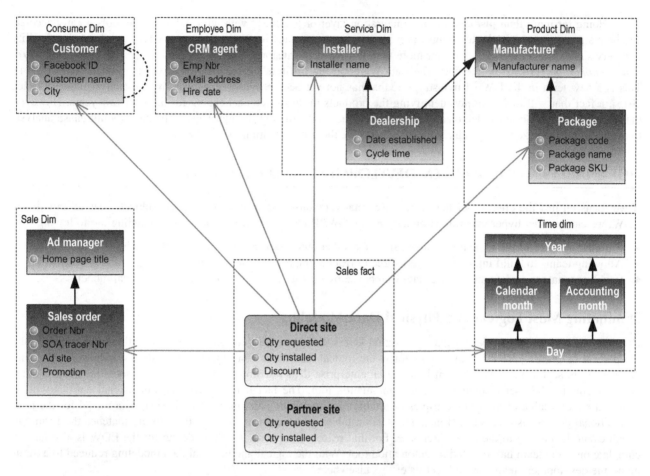

FIGURE 15.13   Data warehouse business model used for the change cases.

partner websites. The light arrows represent how these transaction records will connect to the dimensional information once the warehouse is loaded. For clarity, these links are shown for only one of the transaction data sets.

In this model, the developers have organized the qualifier entities into the dimensions they wish the final presentation layer to possess. The Sales Order and Ad Site entities will be denormalized into the Sales Dimension, for example, and the four components for dates will be consolidated into a Time Dimension. The company also desires to track subsidiary relationships between its customers, so the developers have declared a recursive relationship on the customer entity, with the dotted line indicating that some CUSTOMER instances may not have a parent record.

The entities show the attributes that the operational data will be able to provide. Similar to the examples in previous chapters, all customers will have values for names, social networking IDs, and their cities. The transactions data sets will both have quantities requested and installed, but only direct sales will have a measure for a discount on a sale.

Note that this model is expressed in business concepts. Every entity, attribute, and relationship drawn is a fact that the business subject matter experts working with the EDW developers can confirm or dispute as they review the diagram. This model, once drawn using the business modeling interface, can also be reviewed and interpreted by the HGF automation system. If the automation tool finds the business model complete and consistent, it will insert the records necessary to express that model into the logical entities shown in Figure 15.7. Once those configuration records have been inserted into the EDW's physical repository, it is ready to receive qualifier data. The team can then build data loading routines to capture the data for the dimensions using extracts from the operational systems.

The fact that this model can be interpreted by both business partners and the DW/BI development tool takes enterprise data warehousing to a much higher level of IT-business alignment. Business assertions can be translated directly by the machine into a data store that will behave as the subject matter experts desire. Such direct translation of business knowledge not only eliminates logical and physical data modeling chores for the EDW developers but also prevents many time-consuming mistakes they can easily commit when following traditional development practices.

Driving Design Changes Using a Business Model

Perhaps more important, the HGF automation system allows the EDW developers to change the data warehouse's structure by updating the very same business model they used to create the warehouse in the first place. When requirements change, the data warehouse administrators update the model and then publish the new version when they wish for it to take effect. The automation system will first retire and insert into the hyper generalized repository the new records needed to express the updated model. It will then adjust the dimensional data so that existing entities will comply with the newly declared relationship patterns from that date forward. When the presentation layer objects are refreshed, the EDW team can choose whether to portray the business dimensions as they were through the past or as they are now, given the new data model.

Figure 15.14 shows the details of how an updated diagram of the EDW's business model alters the entries made in the HGF things and link repository. The EDW team decided that, as of 7-October, the company should be able to categorize orders into electronic commerce segments without regard to which website they originated from. Until then, the originating website determined which market segment an order represented. In the business modeler, this change requires removing the arrow between AD SITE and eSEGMENT and replacing it with a direct link between orders and segments. In the model entities of the repository, the automation tool should retire the LINK_TYPE record that rolls up AD SITE and eSEGMENT and insert another relating ORDER directly to eSEGMENT. The bottom of the diagram shows how the automation system will interpret this request into actual data management actions. The record with OID 6014 (linking 6012 Ad Sites to 6011 eSegments) is given an end date of 7-October, and a record 10071 linking 6013 Orders directly to 6011 eSegments is inserted to take effect from that date onward.

Again, this update was accomplished without any logical and physical modeling, saving the development team a tremendous amount of time and effort. This direct link between the business model and the data warehouse's capabilities allows the EDW team to fluidly respond to new realization regarding requirements, thus dramatically improving the DW/BI department's agility. With the ability to fix quickly, a tremendous amount of EDW project risk has been eliminated. The business model no longer has to be perfect before the team can begin building the data warehouse, allowing teams to safely start the data warehouse with a modest subrelease and add on small increments with each development iteration.

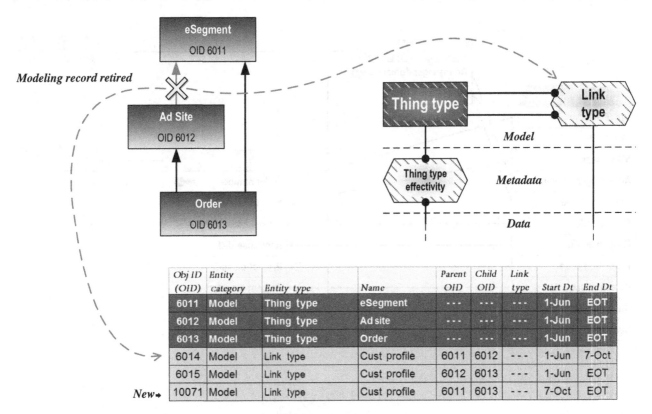

Obj ID (OID)	Entity category	Entity type	Name	Parent OID	Child OID	Link type	Start Dt	End Dt
6011	Model	Thing type	eSegment	---	---	---	1-Jun	EOT
6012	Model	Thing type	Ad site	---	---	---	1-Jun	EOT
6013	Model	Thing type	Order	---	---	---	1-Jun	EOT
6014	Model	Link type	Cust profile	6011	6012	- - -	1-Jun	7-Oct
6015	Model	Link type	Cust profile	6012	6013	- - -	1-Jun	EOT
10071	Model	Link type	Cust profile	6011	6013	- - -	7-Oct	EOT

FIGURE 15.14 Example of how graphical model changes impact the associative data store.

LOADING DATA INTO THE HYPER GENERALIZED INTEGRATION LAYER

Hyper generalization not only allows the EDW team to create the data warehouse's integration layer from a business model but also enables the team to build the data transforms using business concepts. Using the data warehouse automation tool, the team must configure two types of ETL modules to load the warehouse—one for populating the qualifier objects and another for loading transactions.

Loading the Dimensional Objects

The dimensional data transforms naturally must be executed before the transactional ETL modules. Figure 15.15 depicts the ETL that a team might create to load the Sales Dimension from Figure 15.13. The team has created this data flow mapping using a graphical user interface contained in the hyper generalized data warehouse automation system.

Of course, the actual configuration required for each data transform module will depend on the nature of the source extract employed. Here, the extract file contains the header information of the sales orders. The goal for this ETL module is to create instances of ad site and sales order objects from sales header input. Accordingly, the targets of this data flow mapping are the AD MANAGER and SALES ORDER objects. As determined by the business model, ad manager instances will be independent, but each eSegment instance will need an object identifier to associate it with a parent ad site.

The key functional widget comprising this mapping is the *add–modify instance* unit. It represents a reusable, parameter-driven ETL module, much like those that teams using hyper normalized integration layers must build. However, the HGF add–modify instance widget is provided by the automation tool. It is designed so that EDW teams can easily specify a data transform using a graphical drawing rather than calling hand-coded modules in a script using parameters to achieve different functionalities.

By considering the downstream objects to which it is connected, each add-mod instance widget drawn in an ETL module decides for itself much of what it will do during load time. Consider the widget connected to the Ad Manager object, for example. At run time, it will receive two fields from the data source—the domain of the ad manager serving

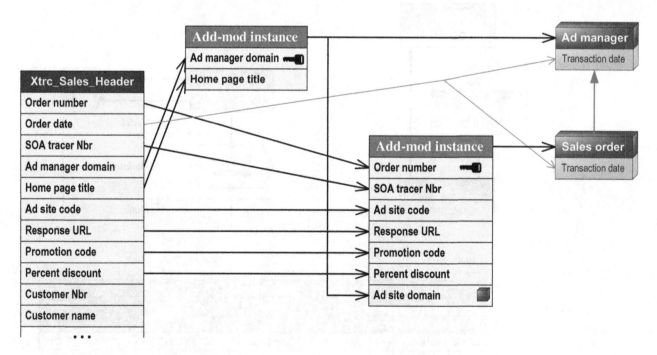

——▶ Data flow (all but elements loaded into transaction dates)

——▶ Data flow for transaction dates, shown in light color only to aid clarity.

FIGURE 15.15   Change Case 1's data transform for dimensions before the business model is updated.

the promotion through which a purchase was made and the title off of that service's Internet home page. To complete its role, it will take this information and do the following:

- Employ the fields declared as natural keys for creating unique occurrences of AD MANAGER instances
- Look up that value to determine whether the warehouse has encountered that particular ad manager before
- If no, create a new instance in AD MANAGER
- If yes, check whether the existing instance has a matching value for the home page title
- If that value differs from the source record, (1) retire the appropriate name-value pair for home page title in the attributes table, and (2) insert a new name-value pair with the updated value

Recall that every instance and attribute value in the hyper generalized integration layer is timestamped with effectivity dates. Accordingly, this ETL module contains a data flow that takes the order date to the Transaction Date element for each target object.

Note that the team was able to keep this mapping fairly simple because it did not need to specify any special processing for the source fields or target columns providing primary key values for the target objects. Because they had already declared the natural key using the business modeler, the developers only had to route the output of the add−modify instance widget to the target object. The automation tool automatically identified the natural key fields and provided the logic of creating object identifiers from them. All that design has been provided by the programming of the Add-Mod Instance widget by the publisher of the HGF automation system tool, making data transformation modules very fast to create and modify. This and other built-in functionalities provided by the HGF automation tool keep ETL modules very streamlined and intelligible, greatly amplifying EDW developers' ability to do impact analysis when the data warehouse must later be maintained or enhanced.

The add-mod instance widget feeding the SALES ORDER object must perform very similar tasks as described for Ad Manager, but it will need to store the appropriate object identifier for each sale's parent ad manager object. In fact, it will need to consider whether a particular sales order should be associated with an ad manager by comparing the transaction date to the effective date of the various models stored in the HGF repository. If the relationship is effective for a given transaction date, the information will be loaded with the proper object identifiers. If not, the automation system will refuse to load the record, keeping the warehouse data aligned with the company's sequence of business models.

Loading the Transactional Objects

Referring back to the business model for this example contained in Figure 15.13, we can see that the transaction records will be associated with six dimensions. After the HGF automation system has acquired the information for those six dimensions, it can then load the transaction data using a data transform such as the one depicted in Figure 15.16. Here, the source is a listing of sales order line items. This extract has many fields, but the mapping only draws upon a subset of them. Two of the measures available represent magnitudes for the business events that the EDW developers wish to capture, namely Quantity Ordered and Unit Price. Several others provide foreign key values they can use to link events to the data warehouse's dimensional objects, such as Ad Manager and Package.

In this mapping, Order Number performs a dual role, identifying a parent Order object and combining with the line item number to form a unique identifier for the transaction. Order Date also feeds two targets, identifying a parent Day object and providing value for the transaction date. Note the behind-the-scenes translation that the data warehouse automation tool performs in this module. The Package Code column in the extract, for example, is diagrammatically connected to the Package object reference in the target structure. The automation tool can clearly infer that this code should be used to link each transaction record to the appropriate package instance already stored in the dimensional data of the warehouse. Rather than trying to insert the Package Code value, it will search for an existing Package instance and insert the object ID instead.

Thus, the EDW developers can describe the data transform they desire at a business level: "I want that source column to be stored in this attribute of the target entity. Automation system, you perform the proper value-to-object identifier translations for me." By allowing teams to work using diagram-driven, business-level data transform programming and business-level repository creation, the hyper generalized approach dramatically accelerates the delivery speed of an enterprise data warehouse. Such capabilities explain why business executives regularly share comments with me such as "We got more done in 5 days using the data warehouse automation tool than two of the world's largest systems integrators were able to accomplish in the past 5 years."

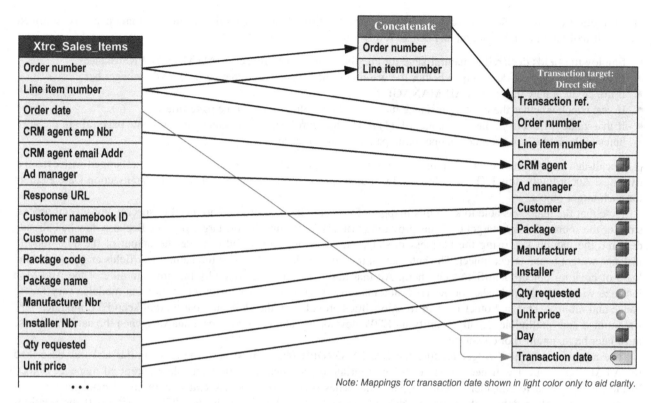

Note: Mappings for transaction date shown in light color only to aid clarity.

FIGURE 15.16   Starting data transform for the transaction data of Change Case 1.

RETRIEVING INFORMATION FROM A HYPER GENERALIZED EDW

The hyper generalized approach further accelerates DW/BI deliveries by automatically maintaining a performance sublayer within the EDW and automating the creation and refresh of presentation-layer objects. It was shown in Chapter 14 that hyper normalized data modeling techniques make data more difficult to retrieve from the EDW's integration layer. To compensate, the EDW team needed to selectively build helper objects such as point-in-time and bridging tables, locating them in a performance sublayer of the reference architecture. Although the hyper generalized strategy reduces the number of integration-layer tables required, the associative and shredded storage formats result in data warehouse records with a far greater level of interdependency. A careful observer would be concerned that this approach might require even more hand-crafted helper objects than the hyper normalized paradigm. Whereas the hyper generalized integration layer does include performance sublayer, fortunately, the HGF automation system automatically creates and maintains the objects required there—another reason why this approach allows for high productivity among agile EDW teams. In addition, the HGF toolset includes a query writer that allows the developers to define data retrieval modules using business-level concepts, much in the same way that they created the data warehouse structure and defined data transforms to load it.

HGF Systems Maintain a Performance Sublayer

Figure 15.17 depicts how data moves across the entire reference architecture in a hyper generalized approach. Source extracts arrive first in the landing area, where the data structures closely mirror how data appeared when taken from the source systems. The HGF automation tool then employs the business-level depictions of the repository and transform logic to move dimensional data into the core of the integration layer. Although an HGF warehouse employs a relational DBMS to hold the associative data records and name-value pairs of the integration layer's core repository, the hyper generalized formats used are extremely difficult to read, given that each source record can become hundreds of small HGF records, all linked together with object identifiers. With this design, the database engine must perform a high number of joins to reassemble the business information once placed in the core, so hyper generalized repositories need to consider performance problems.

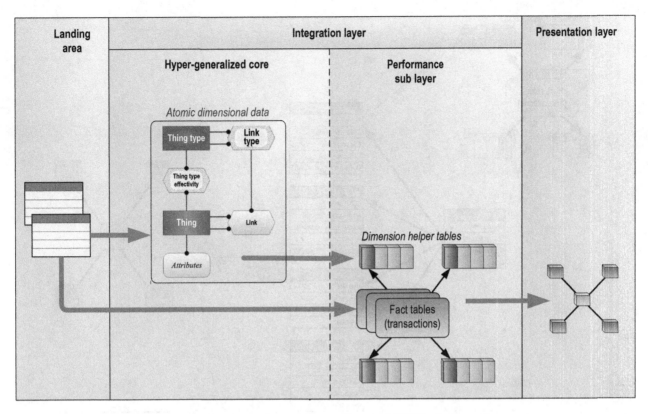

FIGURE 15.17   Hyper generalized data warehouse automation systems can address the full EDW reference architecture.

The HGF automation tool takes the same solution to this challenge that the hyper normalized data warehouse builders must resort to: It maintains a performance sublayer. In this layer, the atomic dimensional data are reassembled and pivoted until they appear very much like the enterprise-level dimensional tables. All the things and link records are connected together by following the object identifiers, and the attributes for each business object are pivoted out from the shredded records stored as name-value pairs. These reconstituted dimensional records will then link to the warehouse's fact tables, in which the company's transaction and events have been loaded.

These dimension helper tables are refreshed each time the data warehouse receives a load of operational data. Because this transformation operates only upon the increment of data acquired during the last load from source, it occurs fairly quickly for most of the dimensions in the warehouse. Readers who refer back to Figure 15.13 will see the dotted line boxes around qualifier entities and transaction data sets that mark each with the dimension or fact table of the performance sublayer into which they will be placed. Following this simple guidance from the application's business model, the HGF automation system knows what performance sublayer objects to update after each load of the warehouse. When it comes time to output a full data set to the presentation layer, the preprocessing will have already been accomplished, allowing fully dimensionalized information to be retrieved from the performance sublayer without extra delay.

Performance Layer Objects Enable Business-Intelligible Data Retrieval

Beyond providing fast creation of presentation layer objects, the helper tables in the performance sublayer allow EDW users to retrieve information using a graphical interface referencing business-level objects instead of using a technical query language such as SQL and pulling data from physical tables.

Figure 15.18 shows how this capability is possible. The process begins with the performance sublayer's preprocessed objects, as shown in the upper left. Here, the qualifiers have been assembled into dimensions as instructed by the business model that the team used to create and update the data warehouse. The automation system also provides fact tables from which to retrieve measures, each consolidated from the perhaps multiple transaction data sets grouped together by the EDW's business model, as Figure 15.13 illustrated for Direct Site and Partner Site.

On the query writer utility's graphical interface, the automation system depicts each dimension as a denormalized table. EDW teammates desiring to retrieve or refresh a data mart into the presentation layer need only to select which

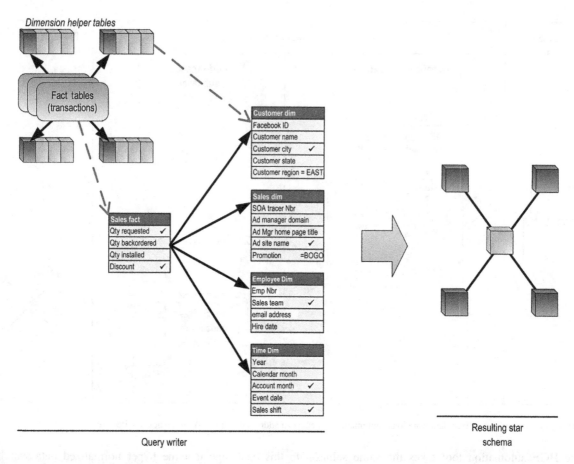

FIGURE 15.18   Helper tables allow EDW admins to write queries against business objects.

fields they wish to have placed in an output data set. They can also set constraints that will filter the result set down to the subset of data warehouse records they wish to retrieve.

Specifying a result set is thus very much like defining a query using any of the popular business intelligence front ends available today. The primary difference is the extent of actions that EDW teams can control using this utility of the automation system. At a minimum, they can simply run a query to create a data mart in the data warehouse's presentation layer. Small data marts can be sent to spreadsheets and even mailed to end users, larger data marts can be written to a relational database. When that desired data mart grows beyond what a typical database server can support, the EDW team can instruct the automation system to send the data mart to a data warehouse appliance, without having to do any more work than selecting the appropriate database connect to write through. All this migration takes place with a change in connect string rather than hand-crafted ETL objects—again making the EDW team very agile.

Moreover, the EDW developers can choose whether to send just the data to these targets or to deliver them complete with a semantic layer describing the data mart created. The business modeler allowed the EDW developers to enter business metadata while designing the warehouse. As long as the team entered this descriptive information, the automation tool can create semantic layers that include standardized business definitions for all the elements, making them much easier for the end users to understand and utilize for reporting.

The query writing utility represents a key advantage of a hyper generalized toolset over the hyper normalized approach we considered in Chapter 14. The HNF strategy certainly allowed EDW teams to create and maintain the integration layer with far less labor, but retrieving data involved difficult SQL programming or hand-crafted helper object in the performance sublayer. Some query writing tools are available from the HNF community, but finding, selecting, and implementing one is still a major undertaking the team must accomplish before the EDW will be fully operational. For that reason, one could consider hyper normalization a three-fourths solution for the integration layer only.

The hyper generalized approach, in contrast, consists of acquiring a tool from a commercial vendor. Especially with the more established vendors, such a tool will come complete with not only the business modeler but also the graphical data transform programmer and the query writer. Because this toolset allows the EDW team to build and maintain integration, presentation, and semantic layers, the hyper generalized approach represents a full solution with three times the scope of the hyper normalized strategy.

MODEL-DRIVEN EVOLUTION AND FAST ADAPTATION

So far, this chapter has focused on how hyper generalization can accelerate the design and implementation of a new data warehouse. As discussed in the previous few chapters, the agility of a given approach has far more to do with how readily an EDW team can change a data warehouse once it is in operation and loaded with an enormous number of records. The hyper normalized approach of Chapter 14 represented a significant improvement for managing the integration layer over standard normal forms. In the HNF context, most new business requirements will demand only that the EDW team add some tables and reuse the parameter-driven ETL modules to load them. Business keys or existing attributes are rarely affected, so conversion scripts for integration layer objects are rarely called for, saving significant time and money.

However, new business requirements can impact not only the integration layer but also objects in the dimensional presentation layer. As explored in the previous section, a hyper generalized warehouse automation system extends the reach of agile DW/BI into the presentation and semantic layers as well. Furthermore, it provides tools for re-specifying and re-generating the objects in all three layers using a graphical user interface rather than hand-code scripts. These two considerations make the hyper generalized strategy considerably more agile than even the HNF approach. This section will examine how the hyper generalized toolset supports model changes without requiring expensive data conversion efforts. It will then tally the savings in EDW maintenance labor that such a capability makes possible.

Impact of Model Changes on Existing Data

A major new business requirement can easily require restructuring the backbone of an existing data warehouse. Such a change will require an update to both the business model that controls the structure of the EDW and the data that the data warehouse contains. The hyper generalized toolset makes both of the modifications easy to accomplish. First, we discuss how to effect the necessary changes in terms of the records stored within the associative data model. We then consider how to use the business-level controls of the warehouse automation system to achieve these record changes.

Consider, for example, the modeling change illustrated in Figure 15.14. In this figure, a new business requirement necessitated the EDW team flatten the rollup pattern between the Order, Ad Site, and eSegment entities of the SALES dimension. When viewed in terms of the business model, the required change is easy to describe: Draw an arrow from the ORDER to the eSEGMENT entity to declare a new child–parent dependency, and then drop the arrow from AD SITE to eSEGMENT. When the team publishes this result, all data loaded henceforth will need to comply with this new hierarchy.

Such a modeling change will manifest as entries in the THING_TYPE and LINK_TYPE entities of our associative data model. When the developers update the business model, the HGF automation tool will read the new diagram and mark one LINK_TYPE record with a retirement date and insert another record with the proper value in Start Date. Of course, updating the model is not enough because the entities affected are metadata for real data records contained in the entities THING and LINK. Having a link with an end date that does not comply with the retirement of its reigning LINK_TYPE, for example, will cause data disparities within the associative data repository that would be very difficult for EDW analysts to identify and resolve. For this reason, the developers will have to use the automation system to adjust existing data records so that model and data remain aligned. Before we discuss how they will use the business model to make the change, we must first consider the changes in the existing records in the associative data tables that will represent the new hierarchal pattern.

Figure 15.19 shows the records impacted by flattening the rollup from Orders to eSegment. Records with OIDs 6011 through 8025 represent the information in the physical associative data table before the model change. (Note the records have been grouped by their HGF entity type and are not in perfect OID order.) The model change impacts only two of the existing records, which are marked as "retired" on the left edge of the table. They are superseded by two new records, 10071 and 10072, the first one for logical LINK_TYPE modeling entity and the second for the LINK data entity. The model change retired the LINK_TYPE record connecting Ad Site to eSegment (OID 6014), so the LINK between Ad Site and eSegment instances (OID 6018) had to be retired as well. Similarly, the new LINK_TYPE modeling record (OID 10071) needed a new LINK data record to provide the new direct association between Order and eSegment instances. Inserting record OID 10072 represents this new relationship.

Obj ID (OID)	Entity Category	Entity Type	Name	Parent OID	Child OID	Link Type	Start Dt	End Dt
6011	Model	Thing Type	eSegment	- - -	- - -	- - -	01-Jun	EOT
6012	Model	Thing Type	Ad Site	- - -	- - -	- - -	01-Jun	EOT
6013	Model	Thing Type	Order	- - -	- - -	- - -	01-Jun	EOT
6014	Model	Link Type	Cust Profile	6011	6012	- - -	1-Jun	07-Oct
6015	Model	Link Type	Cust Profile	6012	6013	- - -	1-Jun	EOT
10071	Model	Link Type	Cust Profile	6011	6013	- - -	7-Oct	EOT
6016	Data	Thing	Tech Warriors	- - -	- - -	- - -	01-Jun	EOT
8022	Data	Thing	Online Depot	- - -	- - -	- - -	2-Aug	EOT
9041	Data	Thing	CF904-A	- - -	- - -	- - -	4-Sep	EOT
6017	Metadata	Thing Classification	- - -	6011	6106	- - -	1-Jun	EOT
8023	Metadata	Thing Classification	- - -	6012	8022	- - -	2-Aug	EOT
8024	Metadata	Thing Classification	- - -	6013	9041	- - -	2-Aug	EOT
6018	Data	Link	- - -	6016	8022	6014	1-Jun	07-Oct
8025	Data	Link	- - -	8022	9041	6015	2-Aug	EOT
10072	Data	Link	- - -	6016	9041	10071	7-Oct	EOT

Retired ➡ (points to row 6014)
New ➡ (points to row 10071)
Retired ➡ (points to row 6018)
New ➡ (points to row 10072)

FIGURE 15.19   Records impacted by flattening the hierarchy between Orders and eSegment

The fact that some readers will find it demanding to follow the logic for resolving all the OIDs and associations involved with this update illustrates why an automation system is required by the hyper generalized approach. EDW teams should not attempt to manually maintain records stored in the hyper generalized data store because with so many dependencies between the records in the associative data store, it would be too easy to omit a connection and thereby corrupt the data within the warehouse. Indeed, maintaining the integrity of a hyper generalized integration layer is so complex that EDW teams should not even consider programming their own administration system but, rather, purchase a mature and proven tool instead.

Hyper Generalization Tools Facilitate Data Conversions

Updating the EDW business model is not enough when the warehouse already contains business data, however. This example restructured a Sales Dimension hierarchy. Now that ORDER instances should have a direct relationship to eSEGMENT records, the team will need to place the right foreign key values in the existing ORDER instances. Fortunately, this can be accomplished while still working at a business level, using the warehouse automation toolset.

Figure 15.20 shows how the developers would work with both the graphical business modeler and the data transform authoring tool in order to achieve the data conversion this example will require. The figure illustrates the progression that the data model will take, as shown in panels A–C. The team's strategy is to create new direct associations between ORDER and eSEGMENT by using a query of the existing indirect associations as a source for a data load.

This work is accomplished using the following steps:

Step 1: Use the query writer to define a module that will retrieve the business identifiers of existing orders and e-segments that are currently linked via a child–grandparent relationship.
Step 2: Create an optional relationship between ORDER and eSEGMENT—it must be optional because instances of both objects already exist, before any relationships between them have been loaded.
Step 3: Use the data transform authoring tool to create and run a simple loader that will create link instances between ORDER and eSEGMENT. This load module will look very much like the transform depicted in Figure 15.15. In this case, it will send business identifiers for associated eSegments and Orders to an Add-Modify Instance widget that loads Orders. When the developers run the load module using the query definition from Step 1 as a source, every unique combination of identifiers for eSegment and Order will create an association record in the HGF repository.

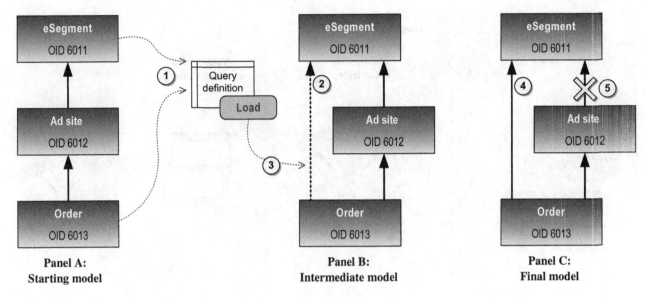

FIGURE 15.20   Steps to updating a hyper generalized EDW's dimensional entities and their data.

Step 4: Return to the business modeler to update the link between ORDER and eSEGMENT to be mandatory. Now that linking records have been loaded for this relationship, it no longer needs to be optional.

Step 5: Drop the link between ORDER and eSEGMENT.

Taking stock of all the assistance that the data warehouse automation tool provides the EDW team, we can appreciate that hyper generalization allows a dramatically different and less labor-intensive means for building and maintaining data warehouses. We have seen how the development team can create and modify the structure of the data warehouse by providing a business model of the next version of the data repository it wants. We have seen how that business model allows the team to then specify data transforms by referencing elements defined by that business model. Given that the bulk of an EDW can now be declared and updated while working with business-level objects and diagrams, we can reasonably predict that the business analysts and data modelers will be the ETL programmers of the future [Breur 2015], which will move the DW/BI profession dramatically closer to our desired goal of full IT-business alignment.

SUPPORTING DERIVED ELEMENTS

The capture and transformation of raw operational data is a primary function of a data warehouse, but most companies also need business rules applied and master data elements established. In the hyper generalized context, EDW teams achieve both of these objectives using *value added loops*, although the master data elements are typically achieved more easily by employing utilities provided by the warehouse automation system.

Value-Added Loops

Hyper generalized data warehouse automation systems can derive new values either during or after capturing the company's operational data. The graphical design tool for data transforms provides several additional controls than just the add−modify instance widget, including field parsing, time calculations, and decision points. However, EDW professionals who compare this toolset to today's traditional ETL tools and even the capabilities of the SQL engines of the typical RDBMS will consider the HGF offering quite rudimentary. The fact that HGF tools offer only the basics is not an issue, however, because the hyper generalized automation system operates on top of a database engine. The SQL command set of the underlying database will always be available, and many companies large enough to build a data warehouse will also have an ETL package available. The EDW team needs only to pull the data as captured from the operational systems out of the data warehouse, add derived values, and then insert the results back into the warehouse. This pattern represents extract, load, and transform (ELT) rather than the traditional extract, transform, and load (ETL).

Figure 15.21 depicts the overall processing pattern the HGF automation systems comfortably support. The core of the integration layer has captured the company's operational data and preprocessed it into performance sublayer objects,

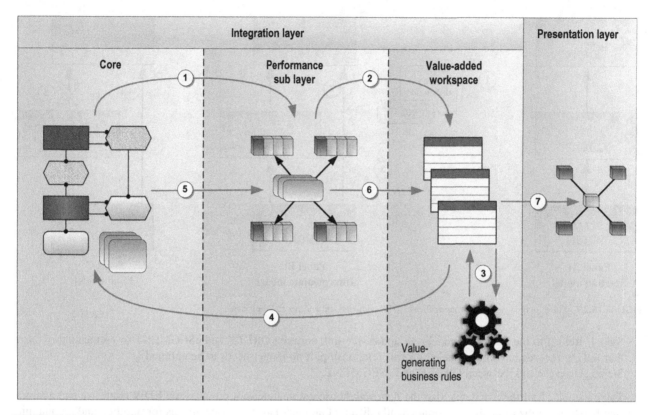

FIGURE 15.21   Creating derived columns and master data elements using value-added loops.

as discussed previously. The EDW developers next create a value-added loop. In a value-added loop, a query writer pushes an appropriate subset of data into one or more relational tables that have been created in a workspace maintained by the data warehouse's systems underlying database. The EDW developers then use a traditional ETL package or advanced SQL commands to apply business rules to this temporary data set, storing the values derived back into the temporary working tables. In practice, value-added loops can apply these business rules via many means, such as database views, stored procedures or other built-in functions offered by the database, or third-party statistical packages such as R. In order to bring the enriched data back into the data warehouse, the developers will need to define new objects and attributes in the HGF warehouse and then configure a data transform that loads the new values into the integration layer, as if the derived elements were just another operational data source. Having accomplished this step, the EDW team then defines a new result set that is projected all the way to the DW/BI presentation and semantic layers.

Following this work pattern, the team certainly accelerated its delivery of a complete analytic solution. The team accomplish all but Step 3 in the diagram using the graphical design utilities of the HGF automation system. They must still pursue some hand-coded data transforms, but at least creating and evolving the "basic plumbing" that makes up the bulk of a data warehouse's programming has been automated for them. These basic data management functions often represent 70–80% of the labor required to build a data warehouse. With HGF tools, this work typically requires only 10% of the effort it formerly consumed, as will be demonstrated with the change cases discussed later. By accelerating the development of the basic portion of the warehouse, the team can reallocate three or four times as many resources to programming the business-rule-driven features of the data warehouse. Consequently, the customer will see the team creating value-added features three or four times faster than when it relied on a standard approach. With faster turnaround from the DW/BI team, the business stakeholders will be able to work far more closely with the EDW developers, thus greatly increasing the company's overall DW/BI agility.

Model-Driven Master Data Components

Building on the notion of the preprogrammed *add–modify instance* widget, the leading data warehouse administrative package based on hyper generalization also provides an adaptable architectural component that development teams

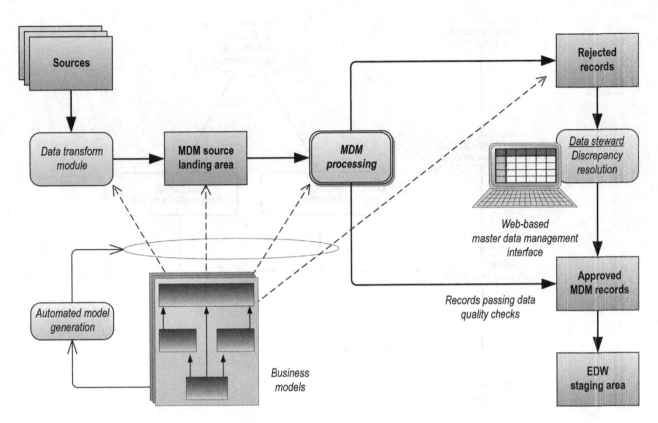

FIGURE 15.22   Using the master data management utility of the data warehouse automation tool.

can easily incorporate in order to quickly establish robust master data management (MDM) for their company's EDW applications.

Figure 15.22 shows how these packages enable EDW teams to generate key MDM elements from their business models and then draw upon an adaptable web-based master data administration tool to arrive at canonical records for key business entities such as customer, product, and location. Using the hyper generalized warehouse administration package, the EDW developers employ machine-driven development to create four components based on the business models they have created:

- The database tables of the landing area
- The ETL for processing the master data elements
- The master data repository for validated records, and another for rejected records

The data transform module for processing master data elements automatically assembles candidate master data records from the landing area according to the logic provided by the developer's business model. This process then decides whether to accept or reject each candidate record. Candidate records are evaluated using multiple tests, such as regular-expression parsing for acceptable formats, valid domains screening for legal values, and parent record lookup for implied foreign keys. Records passing these tests are sent to a staging area from which the data warehouse can load them into the EDW. The master data processing component also employs "fuzzy logic" to discern whether or not the candidate records are already in the master data repository. Fuzzy logic relies on cascading matching events to quantify how well candidate data resemble existing master data records. Candidates with many matching components will pass a threshold value that the master data managers have set for each entity, causing the MDM process to consider them already included in the master data, dropping them from any further processing.

The MDM process places records failing to meet the required threshold values for each master data element type into a work-in-progress area. The company's data stewards and data administrators then collaborate on manually processing the rejected records using a web-based user interface provided with the master data management utility. The web-based interface automatically adapts to the structure of each master data element and allows developers to customize the processing workflow for each entity. Figure 15.23 illustrates some of the details of a typical workflow. Data stewards selected from the departmental business staff review the rejected records, searching for defects in

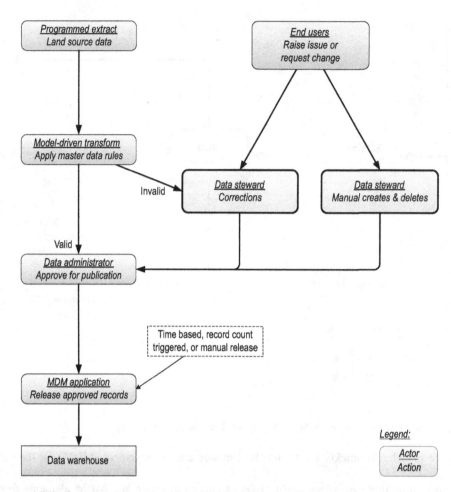

FIGURE 15.23 Sample workflow for master data processing, highlighting the role of the data stewards.

formatting or semantics that they can correct in order to make a candidate record acceptable for the master data collection. Later, a data administrator reviews the corrected records and releases those that he or she accepts to a pending-records pool.

MDM tools provide considerable flexibility, supporting other approval workflows besides the example discussed here. Data steward approval can be required even for new records that pass the data quality tests. These records can be distributed to data stewards as they arrive from source systems or queued for bulk authorization. No matter the path records take among the data stewards, when the pending pool of approved records reaches a preset limit, such as a time-based event or a particular number of pending records, the MDM applications release the accepted records to the data warehouse. The model-driven ETL will then treat the released master data records as simply a trusted source for dimensional entities and load them into the data warehouse.

The end users can search and browse the approved master data using another adaptable web-based interface included in the hyper generalized EDW automation system, making the MDM repository an important component to the company's BI data dictionary. Should end users spot records or values that they question, know must change, or believe are missing altogether, they can submit a change request via the MDM interface. The data stewards will process these requests, again using their web-based management tool, correcting the values or creating records as appropriate, all of which then flow to the master data administrator for approval and release to the warehouse.

Figure 15.24 provides a schematic notion of the management interface that the data stewards and administrators use. The middle of the top panel provides a summary of the candidate records waiting in the working area for the data stewards to correct. The right side shows the number of records now in *pending* status after data administrator review, as well as counts of records published for the data warehouse to incorporate in its subject areas.

The stewards and administrators can click into any one of the values displayed to enter a searchable list of the records for a given entity in any state within the master data repository. These users can open up any one of the values

Entity	Sub entity	Working area			Pending	Published
		Total	Rejected	Correct		
Customer	Marketing	556	128	428	3,971	397,143
Customer	Sales	463	102	361	7,717	6,619,048
Customer	Service	598	126	472	14,950	7,148,571
Customer	Warranty	537	64	473	4,131	7,648,971
Location	City	490	15	475	467	481
Location	Country	0	0	0	2	113
Location	County	516	15	501	491	523
Location	Postal code	500	20	480	549	585
Location	State	2	0	2	0	867
Phone	Area code	1	1	0	1	482
Phone	Number	527	11	516	493	553

Drill down to individual records

Entity	**Customer**			
Sub entity	**Service**			
Identifier		100283403		
Name		Westwood Rec Center		
Location	City	Westwood		
Location	Country	USA		
Location	County	LA	Error	Value not found in domain Location-County
Location	Postal code	99999	Error	Value invalid for entity Location-City

FIGURE 15.24 Master data management front end showing single-record correction screen.

shown in the resulting list to view and edit any record in particular. The bottom panel of Figure 15.24 shows a single rejected record for a service customer. The two errors displayed reveal that (1) this record has defective value for county (it should have been expressed as "Los Angeles," not "LA") and (2) it also has a postal code not found among those known for the customer's city. At this point, the data steward can click on both the county and the postal code to receive a searchable list of acceptable values for these fields. Once correct values have been selected, the error flags will be cleared and the record will be sent by the application's workflow to the data administrator for approval and release to the warehouse.

With the addition of a machine-driven master data management processing and a few adaptable web interfaces, the hyper generalized data warehouse automation tool eliminates a large number of value-added loops that the EDW team would have had to construct in order to derive clean dimensional data for the company's key business entities. By eliminating the need for so much programming, the MDM features represent a crucial element that EDW team leaders need to add to their reference architecture. They should consider the machine-driven master data facility as a preprocessing layer just before the data warehouse and add it to their reference architectural diagram. As shown in Figure 15.25, the MDM facility takes data from the landing area to a sublayer of published master data elements. Objects in the published sublayer will then be incorporated as trusted dimension tables into the integration layer and later the star schemas when warehouse data is projected into the presentation layer.

In this overall system, the hyper generalized data model allows the development team to deliver both master data management and regular data transforms using business-model-driven application generation and modification. Because it offers machine-assisted tools for both master data and subject area development, it is no surprise that teams opting for hyper generalization can achieve 3−10 times the delivery speed as teams using traditional EDW methods and technologies. The dollar value of the human toil that these tools eliminate alone will justify the purchase and implementation costs

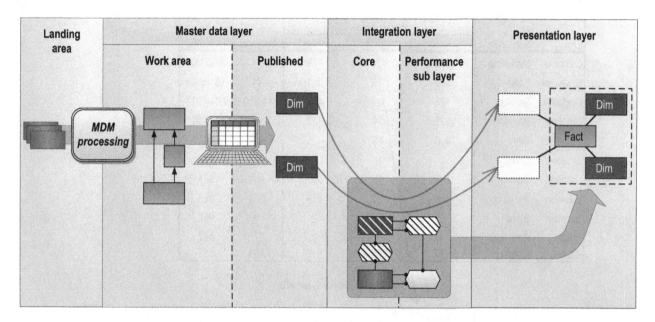

FIGURE 15.25   EDW reference architecture updated to include master data management layers.

of the hyper generalized data warehouse automation package. Far surpassing those savings, however, will be the value of the additional business opportunities from which companies will be able to profit because their EDW teams can now deliver and adapt a data warehouse—including its master data—with an order of magnitude greater agility.

ADDRESSING PERFORMANCE CONCERNS

When traditionally trained DW/BI architects look upon the "things and links" design of a hyper generalized data warehouse, they invariably suggest that this approach will have performance problems. Although HGF repositories do follow many more logical steps to retrieve data from their hyper generalized data stores than a traditionally modeled data warehouse, there are several countervailing factors with regard to overall performance.

First, the HGF architecture isolates any performance issues away from end users. The nonstandard data repositories lie within the integration layer of the warehouse. Data is projected out of these exotically designed data stores into the familiar star schemas regularly found in a data warehouse's presentation layer. End users will experience the desired train-of-thought level of performance, limited only by the capabilities of the resources of the presentation-layer host.

Second, the records in both the associative and the name-value pair data stores are very skinny records, so an impressive number of them are processed with every I/O cycle of the database engine's CPU. For this reason, integration-layer performance issues typically do not appear in hyper generalized data warehouses until they reach data volumes that would also give a relational data warehouse a challenge, somewhere in the neighborhood of tens of terabytes given today's hardware.

Third, HGF databases respond quite well to the same solution that DW/BI teams employ when their standard-approach EDWs begin to respond too slowly: The company should re-platform the application upon a data warehouse appliance. The HGF tool vendors are not hardware providers. Instead, they collaborate extensively with hardware makers and DBMS publishers, so their automation systems function well on the data warehouse appliances from all the major providers. Because of this collaboration between vendors, the performance limits experienced with hyper generalized data warehouses originate from the underlying platform and not from the nontraditional data stores that the HGF repositories employ.

Figure 15.26 provides a compilation of benchmarks based on the collaboration between the publisher of a leading HGF data warehouse automation system and one of the more popular providers of data warehouse appliances. Unlike most benchmarks that are compiled using machines in a vendor lab, these figures represent actual customer implementations. These statistics depict customer experiences in terms of several important "ceiling" considerations, such as the number of entities in the warehouse, the number of integrated sources, and the amount of data being managed. In terms of the number of entities within a business model, the HGF vendors have come very close to the maximum that a

	DW/BI	Hyper generalized data warehouse	
	Industry Max	Max	Industry
Entities	2,707	2,426	Consumer packaged goods
Integrated sources	n/a	240	Oil & gas
Number of users	33,000	6,000	Oil & gas
Records in largest table (billions)	2,000	14	Retail
Peak transactions per hour (billions)	n/a	2	Pharmaceuticals
Minimum reported data latency* (minutes)	n/a	15	Insurance

Courtesy of Kalido, 2012

* Time required to re-project data from integration to presentation layer, as reported by the owners of these systems. Users then queried presentation-layer star schemas as if working with a traditional data warehouse.

FIGURE 15.26   Hyper generalized data warehouse performance benchmarks.

documented data warehouse has ever managed. Although I have not found a documented maximum for the number of integrated sources ever consolidated by a data warehouse, the HGF implementations have incorporated well over 200 separate system feeds. In terms of the maximum number of concurrent users and records in the largest table, the HGF warehouses have not had customers coming anywhere near the DW/BI industry's maximum of 33,000 connections and 2 trillion records, but the 6000 concurrent users and 14 billion records they have achieved to date represent a very respectable performance. These numbers provide solid evidence that the HGF data modeling paradigm introduces no appreciable limitation that should cause an EDW team to steer away from this new approach for performance considerations.

DEMONSTRATING AGILITY THROUGH FOUR CHANGE CASES

The greatest advantage that hyper modeling in general offers to agile EDW leaders is that it allows a development team to start small and continually build out the data warehouse in small slices as requirements become clear. To make this possible, this data modeling paradigm must either (1) insulate existing data from change so that the team can move forward without writing expensive data conversion scripts or (2) make data conversions easy. Although the hyper normalized approach from Chapter 14 does allow teams to respond to requirements change by adding a few tables and converting data once with the help of some temporary views, the updates do require hands-on work applied to the warehouse's physical data objects.

Data warehouses built with a hyper generalized repository enjoy a much higher degree of machine-supported data conversion, as demonstrated by the example previously presented. Of course, certain modifications will require new or dramatically relocated objects so that no chain of OIDs will exist for EDW teams to leverage during a data conversion. However, in those cases, the developers can use business-level query writers and data transforms to populate the new objects and associations. This hands-on data conversion work can be achieved through a graphical interface operating on business-level objects only, not physical ones.

By allowing the EDW team to make most of the changes to existing warehouses using business-level modifications, the hyper generalized approach saves far more labor than even the hyper normalized form can save. This advantage is illustrated next as we use the HGF tools to accomplish the four change cases introduced in Chapter 12.

We must keep in mind that the hyper normalized approach can address only half the number of change cases that the hyper generalized toolset will be able to solve. Hyper normalized techniques only simplify changes to the integration layer. Regenerating presentation and semantic layer objects after a model change still require hands-on labor from the HNF-powered team. In contrast, the hyper generalized automation tools manage objects for the full arc of layers within the reference architecture—integration, presentation, and semantic—so we will see the highest labor savings for HGF in all four change cases.

Change Case 1: Upgrading Attributes to Entities

Change Case 1 addressed the cost of splitting attributes out of entities when it became clear that they needed to be managed separately in order to support newly discovered many-to-many relationships and varying change cadences.

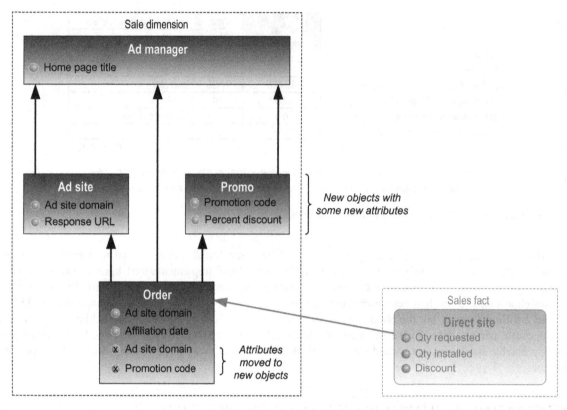

FIGURE 15.27 Business model changes needed to accomplish Change Case 1.

Figure 12.15 illustrated how a team would affect this change when working with standard normal forms. It showed the tables AD SITE and PROMO being split out from the Sales Channel table. Estimates in Chapters 12 suggested that making this relatively simple modification to a data warehouse loaded with production data would consume 1100 total hours from the many IT roles required to update the programmed components, convert the data, migrate the code, and validate the results. As analyzed in Chapter 14, teams working with a hyper normalized integration layer would save nearly 40 percent of this labor.

Figure 15.27 shows how the same functional update would manifest itself in the integration layer of a hyper generalized data warehouse. Using the graphical business modeler, the developers would create the AD SITE and PROMO objects within the SALE DIMENSION group. They would move the attribute for ad site domain to the AD SITE entity and add a new attribute, Response URL, which has just become available through the source systems. Similarly, they would move the promotion code field to the PROMO entity and add the newly available percent discount attribute. The developers would draw associations from ORDER to the two new objects, and from them to AD MANAGER. When the developers publish this new model, the HGF automation system will begin to update the entities in the modeling layer of the EDW's associative data store.

A change in data transforms must accompany the new objects in the business model. Figure 15.28 shows the updated ETL that the data warehouse will need in order to properly process sales dimension data after the business model changes. The starting version of this ETL was shown in Figure 15.15. In Figure 15.28, the added elements have been labeled as "new." Because a sales order will now have three parents instead of just one, the developers have had to add an object reference for Ad Site Domain and Promotion Code to the add-mod instance widget for the Order object.

This change case provides an example of where the team will have to provide hand-crafted data transforms because automatic data conversion is not possible. Because the Ad Site and Promotion objects are new, there are no existing OIDs that can be utilized to provide the association for Order records, so the team will need to explicitly generate and load those. Fortunately, this work is very easy to accomplish using the business-level ETL design tool provided by the HGF automation system. The team simply creates ETL mappings with add-mod instances widgets to process the source elements that will be sent to each new object. The output of these widgets will be inserts or updates to the appropriate object instances where needed, creating the new object identifiers that the existing ORDER records will need to reference.

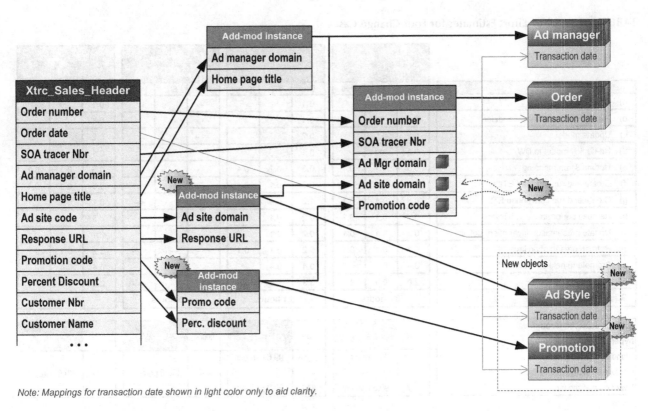

Note: Mappings for transaction date shown in light color only to aid clarity.

FIGURE 15.28   Data transform needed for Change Case 1 after modifications are made.

Returning to the updated ETL that will load records on a daily basis, note there are now data flows that take the results from the new Add-Modify Instance widgets to the new ad site and promotion objects shown at the lower right of Figure 15.28. Another pair of data flows takes the results from the new add-mod instance widgets for ad sites and promotions to the new parent object references just added to the ORDER entity. These latter two flows insert or update parent instances of orders as needed. The add-mod instance widgets automatically perform a tremendous amount of decision making, so this new ETL is very simple to draw using the graphical tool. They take care of creating OIDs when a new image of a given ad site or promotion is encountered. They also detect that changes have occurred to parents, retiring existing instances of AD SITE and PROMOTION and their associations whenever needed, replacing them with new ones.

The ETL shown in Figure 15.28 is appropriate for future feeds from the source system. We must still convert the existing Order records with transaction dates occurring after the new business model's effective date so that they become linked to the new Ad Site and Promotion instances. We can achieve this data conversion using the same type of ETL logic, only we need to pull the information to be converted from records already stored in the warehouse. To achieve this, the team needs only to use the query writer to retrieve the appropriate information from the warehouse and use that query as the source for a copy of the ETL shown in the figure. Although the team will run this ETL only once, it was at least very easy to create.

In fact, the overall labor required to fulfill this change chase is remarkably low. Table 15.1 shows the effort for the work described previously. Because an HGF automation tool makes such evolutions so straightforward, the times reported in the tables are not estimates but instead actual times that it took me to perform this work on a live system. Nine steps were required. The results were executed in both development and system integration test environments and then promoted to production. As shown in the figure, the graphical, business-level tools allow a data warehouse to be adapted for new requirements very quickly. Change Case 1 was accomplished in only a few hours rather than the multiple days required by data warehouses built using either standard or hyper normalized approaches.

We should consider the impact of the modifications made in this change case on the end user's reports, especially those for which the effective date of the modeling change occurs in the middle of the data being retrieved. Records in the result set occurring before the model change will not have objects for Ad Site and Promotion, but those occurring afterward will. The hyper generalized data warehouse automation system is intelligent enough to elegantly apply model

TABLE 15.1 Level-of-Effort Estimates for Four Change Cases

Task	Change case 1: 4NF correction			Change case 2: Party generalization			Change case 3: Change SCD trigger			Change case 4: Change of grain		
	Dev	SIT	Prod	Dev	SIT	Prod	Dev	SIT	Prod	Dev	SIT	Prod
a) Create restore point	0.1			0.1			- - -			0.1		
b) Fetch DW into business modeler	0.1			0.1			- - -			0.1		
c) Update model	0.2			0.2			- - -			0.2		
d) Re-deploy model to DW	0.1			0.1			- - -			0.1		
e) Update & run mapping	0.3	0.1	0.1	0.3	0.1	0.4	- - -	- - -	- - -	0.3	0.1	0.1
f) Create and run pre-load ETL	- - -	- - -	- - -	0.3	0.1	0.4	- - -	- - -	- - -	0.3	0.1	0.1
g) Create and run conversion ETL	0.3	0.1	0.1	1.2	0.4	0.4	- - -	- - -	- - -	0.1	0.1	0.1
h) Re-build performance sub layer	0.2	0.1	0.1	0.2	0.1	0.1	- - -	- - -	- - -	0.3	0.1	0.1
i) Update presentation layer query definition	0.2	0.1	0.1	0.2	0.1	0.1	- - -	- - -	- - -	0.1	0.1	0.1
j) Refresh presentation layer	0.1	0.1	0.1	0.2	0.1	0.1	- - -	- - -	- - -	0.2	0.1	0.1
k) Promote to next environment	0.4	0.4		0.4	0.4		- - -	- - -		0.4	0.4	
Total by environment	**2.0**	**0.9**	**0.5**	**3.3**	**1.3**	**1.5**	**- - -**	**- - -**	**- - -**	**2.2**	**1.0**	**0.6**
Grand total	**3.4 hours**			**6.1 hours**			**0.0 hours**			**3.8 hours**		

Savings achieved through hyper generalization	hours	HGF savings	hours	HGF savings	hours*	HGF savings	hours*	HGF savings
Standard normal forms	1,154	99.7 percent	1,516	99.6 percent	430	100.0 percent	792	99.5 percent
Conformed dimensional form								
Hyper normalized form	747	99.5 percent	812	99.2 percent				

* Hours for conformed dimensional form assume only one affected fact table. In practice, multiple fact tables would need to be updated, making the actual labor hours much higher.

changes to the presentation-layer data set that will be consumed by end users. Figure 15.29 illustrates the impact that Change Case 1 will have on the presentation data once it is regenerated. In this example, the EDW team published the new model to take effect on September 30, 2013. Reports for the last two quarters of that year, like the one shown, will span across the model change. Before the change, the orders for a given ad manager have attribute values for the ad site and promotion associated with each order. The AD SITE and PROMOTION objects, shown on the left side of the report, did not exist for those time points, so the data warehouse reports them as "unknown" values. After the modeling change, the ad site and promotion attributes are no longer populated and are therefore listed with unknown values, whereas the AD SITE and PROMOTION objects are now supported by the new ETL and thus have values shown.

Change Case 2: Consolidating Entities into the Party Model

Change Case 2 demonstrates the effort required to generalize a data warehouse from discrete entities for customers, agents, installers, and manufacturers into a shared Party entity. Figure 12.21 illustrated the modifications required by this case for a data warehouse in standard normal form. Figure 15.30 shows the comparable modification that the EDW team would employ when making this change with a hyper generalized integration layer. Using the graphical business modeler, a developer takes the four entities representing the parties participating in a sales order and drags them into a new entity called Corporate Party. This new entity has an attribute for Party Type (person or organization) and another for Corporate Party ID. In this scenario, several departments in the company have collaborated on a master data application that will apply a unique identifier across all the parties involved in a sale so that henceforth they can retrieve from the warehouse a single view of all activity for a given partner whether they play a combination of customer, agent, installer, and/or manufacturer roles.

By placing these four entities inside a shared entity, the hyper generalized HGF automation system will understand that an instance of a corporate party ID should be associated with each of the party subtypes from that day forward. The repository will not require us to have a parent party instance for existing customers, agents, etc. because they were loaded before the new data model was placed into force. Of course, the customer will want all existing party instances to have a Corporate Party ID, but we will have the luxury of running a data transform after the model change to provide those identifiers.

				Order			
Qtr	Ad manager	Ad site	Promotion	Nbr	Ad Site	Promo	Amount
3Q13	Google	UNK	UNK	21037	BigBuy.com	BOGO	$161,649
				21047	BigBuy.com	BOGO	$178,153
				21067	BigBuy.com	1st Free	$214,436
				21078	BigBuy.com	1st Free	$217,500
				21091	MobToys.com	BOGO	$197,518
				21105	MobToys.com	BOGO	$129,323
				21115	MobToys.com	1st Free	$110,784
				21127	MobToys.com	1st Free	$117,592
4Q13	Google	BigBuy.com	BOGO	21037	UNK	UNK	$212,029
				21054	UNK	UNK	$140,015
			1st Free	21068	UNK	UNK	$170,691
				21082	UNK	UNK	$158,673
		MobToys.com	BOGO	21092	UNK	UNK	$189,867
				21104	UNK	UNK	$145,533
			1st Free	21122	UNK	UNK	$210,236
				21134	UNK	UNK	$228,196

Model Change

FIGURE 15.29 Hyper generalized reporting can successfully span a change in business models

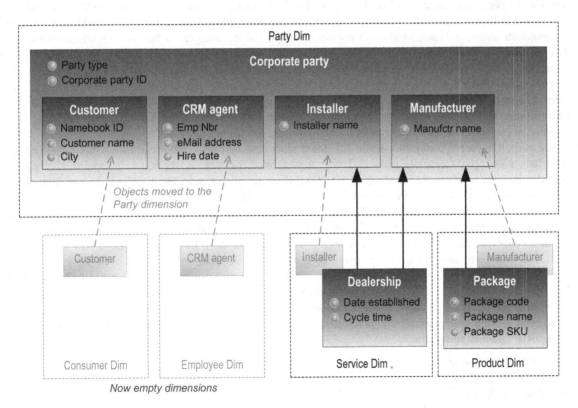

FIGURE 15.30 Business model changes needed to accomplish Change Case 2.

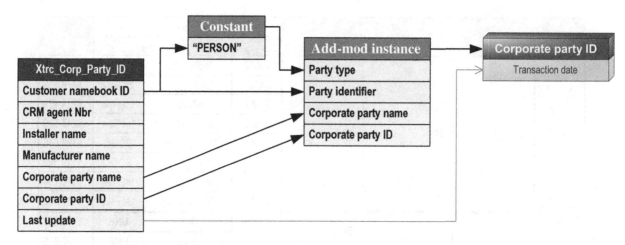

FIGURE 15.31   Pre-loading the Corporate Party objects for customers in Change Case 2.

Before the modeling change, the transaction data sets were visually linked in the modeler to the party entities such as CUSTOMER, as previously shown in Figure 15.13. When the developers drag the four party subtypes into the new CORPORATE PARTY entity, those links will stay attached. The existing instances for the four party subtypes will continue to exist in the repository, so the OIDs connecting sales transactions to them will remain valid, and no data conversion ETL for the transaction records will be necessary. Similarly, when Installer and Manufacturer were dragged into the Party Dim, the associations to Dealership and Package remained in effect, so they will not need conversion ETL development either.

We will need data transform modules to create the new CORPORATE PARTY instances and to associate the four party subtypes to them. The hyper generalized toolset makes these transforms very simple to create. First, the developers will need to preload the master data information into the warehouse so that the Corporate Party ID entities will have object identifiers that the party sub-entities can later reference. The ETL needed to load one set of those OIDs, for the Customer entities, is shown in Figure 15.31. The warehouse will need three more ETLs such as this one to backload Corporate Party OIDs for agents, installers, and manufacturers. The only new aspect of this mapping is the constant widget that will provide the add–mod instance widget with a "PERSON" value to place in the Party Type attribute of CORPORATE PARTY. I have diagrammed the easy case here, in which all customers are people. In practice, the data transform would have more sophistication to examine a few values in the incoming data and set the party type to "person" or "organization" appropriately. Once designed, the data transforms for these four party types need to be added to the regular processing regimen ahead of transforms that load the four party objects so that the latter set will find CORPORATE PARTY OIDs waiting for each customer, agent, manufacturer, and installer found in the source system extracts.

With the corporate party ID objects created, the team must next revise the data transforms that load the party subtypes to include a lookup of Corporate Party ID before the add-mod instance widget that will populate each party entity. The updated transform mapping that loads the CUSTOMER object is shown in Figure 15.32. The widgets that had to be added from the ETL existing before the model change are marked as "New." This transform will create or update the subtype customers with corporate party IDs when they occur in the operational data after the model change is put into effect, and the others will take care of the remaining three subtypes similarly. To get those corporate party IDs linked to those subtype records that do not appear in new operational data, however, the team will have to provide a conversion data transform and run all the existing records for the subtypes through it. Given the hyper generalized context, those conversion transforms will be easy to construct. The one for customers, for example, will look very much like the one in Figure 15.32, except that for its data source it will use a query definition that pulls all the existing customer records out of the warehouse for a quick update.

All told, this change case required the developers to complete the following steps using the business-level design tools of the HGF automation system:

- Update the business model
- Create four preload ETLs
- Update four load ETLs
- Use copies of the four load ETLs to perform data conversions

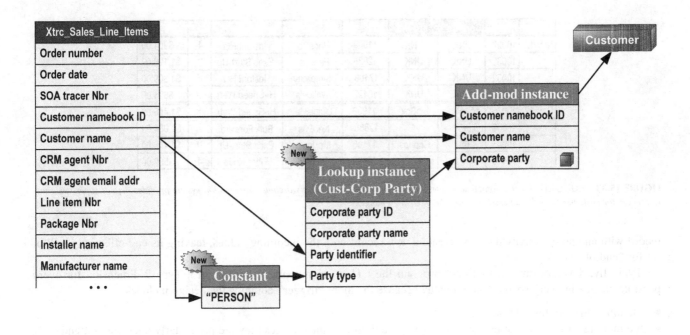

Note: Mappings for transaction date omitted for clarity.

FIGURE 15.32   Data transform needed for Change Case 2 after modifications are made.

Table 15.1 shows the actual labor times required to perform these changes for Change Case 2. The amounts for items e) through g) are four times larger than they were for Change Case 1, given that those tasks had to be repeated for each of the four party types. Despite the larger number of objects affected, Change Case 2 was also accomplished in hours instead of the multiple days needed to achieve the same result with a data warehouse in standard or hyper normalized form. Here again, the ability to accomplish all this work using business-level design tools saves more than 90 percent of the labor required by the baseline case defined in Chapter 12.

This change case included the data transforms to backfill corporate party IDs for all the subtypes already stored in the data warehouse, but not all sub type instances will have received standard identifiers from the upstream master data application. As with Change Case 1, the HGF automation system will elegantly manage data gaps caused by model changes when it refreshes the result sets in the presentation layer. Assume for the moment that the upstream systems provide corporate IDs for only parties involved in new sales. Figure 15.33 shows how the hyper generalized toolset will handle the fact that the model change left all the existing parties without a standard ID attribute. In this case, the model change was published to be effective on 30-Nov-2012. Before that time point, the customers in the data mart created by the HGF automation system are listed with "unknown" corporate party ID and name. After the model and ETL are changed, the customers in the data mart have both a corporate party ID and the name of their shared parent company.

Change Case 3: New Trigger for a Slowly Changing Dimension

Change Cases 3 and 4 focus on modifications typically required for data warehouses built using the conformed dimensional form—that is, EDWs that take data "straight to the star schema" without first placing it in an integration layer designed with standard norm forms. I believe these change cases are necessary for a full consideration of hyper generalization because many people believe that the enterprise data bus strategy accelerates EDW deliveries enough that no other solutions need be considered. Change Case 3 examines the cost of expanding the set of update triggers in a Type 2 slowly changing dimension. These dimensions track the history of the entities they reflect. EDW developers program the ETL for a Type 2 dimension to update the history recorded for a particular natural key value each time one of a particular set of "trigger" attributes changes value. The standard pattern for such an update is to mark the existing

Date	SO	Corp Cd	Corp Nm	Cust Cd	Cust name	Package	Qty	Unit Pr
Nov-12	10027	UNK	UNK	11909	PriceCo	Instant HQ	4	$904.00
	10030	UNK	UNK	12886	Pangea	Exec Start-Up	7	$1,196.00
	10032	UNK	UNK	17108	Simplicity	Instant HQ	8	$1,309.00
	10034	UNK	UNK	16492	Walton's	Hi-Speed Web	9	$894.00
Dec-12	10036	548	BigBox	11909	Quigley's	Hi-Speed Web	9	$1,456.00
	10038	"	"	12886	NeoPJs	Bulk Forward	7	$1,054.00
	10043	684	Chapps	17108	Morton's	Exec Start-Up	9	$1,448.00
	10045	"	"	16492	ProMix	Fiber Node	4	$589.00

FIGURE 15.33 HGF query writer automatically spans modeling changes. *The data warehouse automation system provides default supertype entity references for customer records that existed before the modeling change.*

record with an end-effectivity date and create a new record with the incoming values, leaving its end-effectivity null or set for "end of time."

Typically, development teams do not program the ETL to increment the history in a Type 2 dimension for every possible change in every source column value because the more "trigger" columns the design includes,

- the more difficult the ETL is to code;
- the more records the end users have to wade through to find the changes they are particularly interested in; and
- the more storage the dimension with all its history will consume.

Unfortunately, teams that let the customer specify a subset of columns to serve as a history trigger risk having the business change their mind and demand that a few more triggers be added to the list after the data warehouse enters production usage. As the estimates in Chapter 12 revealed, such maintenance on a production warehouse is an expensive proposition. Assuming that the organization has retained the source data from which at least some past history can be loaded, the change in history-tracking triggers will cause some existing records to become two or more records. The fact tables linking to any dimension receiving new history will then have to be rekeyed so that its records can be properly linked to the new history data. We saw that if only one fact table needs to be rekeyed, the effort will require more than 430 hours of labor. If 10 fact tables are affected, to take a more reasonable number, this effort will grow past five times that amount. With the re-engineering labor necessary to make this simple change running so high, many DW/BI professionals have difficulty calling the conformed dimensional form "agile."

The hyper generalized solution to this particular challenge is amazingly more efficient. In fact, the fundamentals of HGF data warehouses make this particular change case disappear. Consider again the structure of the logical data model for the hyper generalized integration layer, which was shown in Figure 15.1. The backbone of the dimensional data is stored in a set of associative entities, and its attributes are stored in a stack of name-value pairs. All of these tables carry effectivity dates so that every dimensional entity *and attribute* in the data warehouse is timestamped, with full history tracked automatically. With that configuration, customers cannot surprise the EDW team with a new set of columns for which they now want history. History is already being collected in every aspect of the data in the warehouse. The only question is, where would the customers prefer to have all that history masked out?

The query writer included with the HGF automation system allows the development team to create a result set with either current information only or the values from the time of transaction. For situations requiring history, the team will select the latter so that the downstream data mart will be loaded with dimensional values as they existed at the time of the transactions to which they are linked. The business intelligence front-end tool can be employed from that point on to summarize to current values those columns where end users do not want to see the history of the dimensional data.

Given that the HGF data warehouse is designed to maintain history on all elements, Change Case 3 becomes moot—history is always tracked. The team needs only to decide whether to display it. Table 15.1 lists the time required to make the requested adaptation for this change case zero, which translates to a 100 percent savings on the labor required to achieve the same result using a data warehouse modeled in conformed dimensional form.

Change Case 4: Increasing the Grain of a Fact Table

Change Case 4 addresses another common predicament confronting EDW teams that have based their data warehouse on the conformed dimensional form. Either new capabilities in the source systems or changing business requirements

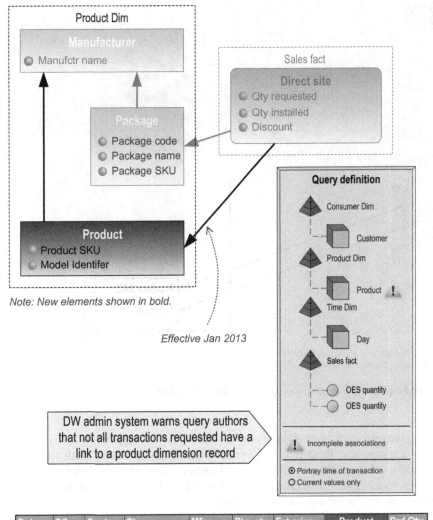

FIGURE 15.34   Business model update and resulting reporting for Change Case 4.

can suddenly necessitate adding a dimension to the star schema. Unfortunately, such a request requires that all impacted fact tables and their ETL modules be re-engineered to include another foreign key. Because the existing fact records may now need to be linked to a new set of dimensional records, the entire fact table will need to be rekeyed as well, thus requiring a conversion script. Figure 12.25 illustrated the case for our sales order analytics system. Here, the company's website has been retrofitted to begin providing information for the products included with each telecommunication package sold. Accordingly, the EDW's star schema needed to add a PRODUCT dimension table and include links to it in every sales transaction fact table.

Figure 15.34 depicts the changes that the EDW team working with a hyper generalized automation system would have to make to the business model that governs its warehouse in order to accommodate this change case. The team must draw a new product entity, shown in dark shading, and associate it with the manufacturer entity that will serve as

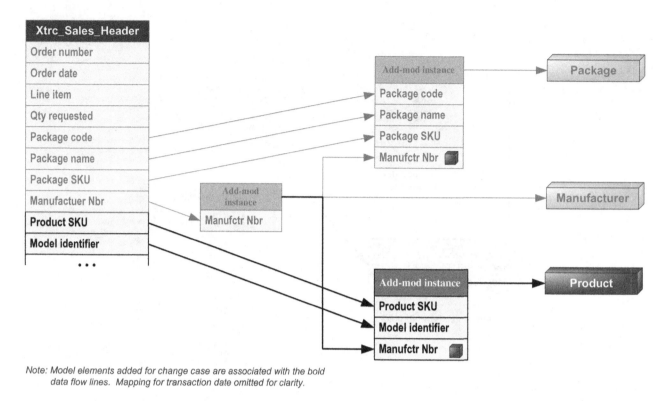

Note: Model elements added for change case are associated with the bold
data flow lines. Mapping for transaction date omitted for clarity.

FIGURE 15.35   Dimensional data transform changes needed to accomplish Change Case 4.

its parent. Because a given product from a particular manufacturer can appear in many of the packages that this company provides, the Package and Product entities remain unassociated so they both can vary independently. The developers must also add a link from the fact tables to the Product entity. The developers will declare an effective date so that both of the new associations will affect only information flowing into the warehouse from that point on. Existing records will remain untouched and linked as before.

Given the HGF repository's ability to maintain multiple models, the query writer will help the developers work effectively with this modeling change. As shown in the right half of Figure 15.34, the query writer's interface gives the developers the choice of seeing the data model in its current configuration or as appropriate for "time of transaction." The latter choice leads to a more complicated display that must hide the impact of modeling changes. The HGF automation system will warn developers that a newly added object such as product has an incomplete association to the transaction data.

The data warehouse's ETL logic will need to be updated to support the new Product object. Figure 15.35 shows the main ETL after developers updated it to support the new Product object in the business model. The components added to this data transform for this purpose are depicted more darkly. They include

- a redefined extract description that now includes product information;
- another add-mod instance to load the Product object; and
- a flow of Manufacturer OIDs to the Product entity so that product records will be linked to their parents.

If this model change is entered into the HGF automation system before the new source data is available, then no conversion of existing information will be necessary. If the model change is made after the product information becomes available, then the developers will need to make a special run of this ETL, feeding it the history file that now has product information in it. This special run will backfill any products or product to manufacturer associations that had been missed.

The developers will need to update the ETL for loading sales order transactions data as well. Figure 15.36 shows the simple upgrade required, which consists of adding only a data flow for the new product number field that is now available through the source. Note that no special widgets for looking up the product OID associated with a given product number are required. The HGF transaction loader is smart enough to perform that lookup for a data flow that delivers a product number to the product object referenced in the target structure for transactions.

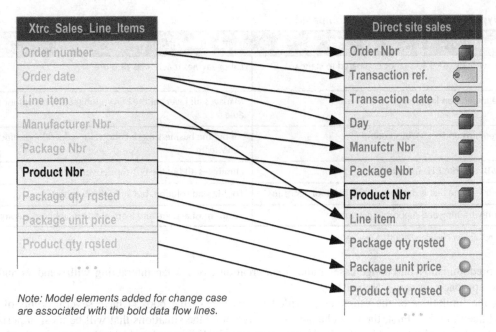

FIGURE 15.36 Transaction data transform changes needed to accomplish Change Case 4.

All told, this change case required the developers to complete the following steps using the business-level design tools of the HGF automation system:

- Update the business model
- Update the dimensional ETL module
- Conduct a special run of the dimensional ETL to backload some object IDs
- Update the transaction ETL module

Table 15.1 shows the actual labor times required to perform these changes. As can be seen from the tallies, the work for this change case was accomplished in hours instead of the multiple days needed to achieve the same result with a data warehouse in a conformed dimensional form. Again, the ability to complete all this work using business-level design tools saved more than 95 percent of the labor required by the baseline case defined in Chapter 12.

As with the previous change cases, the lack or existence of the new data elements will be managed elegantly by the HGF automation system when it refreshes the result sets in the presentation layer. Figure 15.34 included a sample report from the data mart that the HGF automation system would create, assuming that the model change described took effect on 01-Jan-2013. Before that time point, the source systems provided package information without listing the component products, and the HGF automation system populated the data mart with "unknown" product names up until that point. Afterward, the HGF automatically placed the product information on each record.

Recap of Change Case Findings

The previous three chapters have provided estimated and actual hours for achieving four change cases in order to gauge, however roughly, the degree to which the hyper modeled forms can accelerate enterprise data warehousing teams. The findings produced through this comparison are impressive: Hyper normalization saves between 40 and 50% of the labor needed to evolve a data warehouse, depending on the particular challenge confronting the team. Hyper generalization offers an even greater impact, saving 95 percent of that labor or more. Because these numbers are more than a little astonishing, I summarize here the context and limitations of the estimation process generating them so that readers can use my findings appropriately when deciding between data modeling paradigms.

With regard to context, these estimates are for change cases—that is, situations in which the business requirements governing an existing data warehouse changed, requiring the EDW team to evolve the analytics system after it had already been placed into production. Such change cases are in many ways more important than the use cases that guide initial EDW construction because the time and money that data warehousing teams spend maintaining, extending, and redesigning data warehouses far exceeds the investment required to build them in the first place. For that reason, readers

TABLE 15.2 Hyper Modeling Approaches Compared

Hyper Normalization	Hyper Generalization
EDWs evolve with 35–65% less labor compared to standard normal forms[a]	Labor savings reach 98% or more[a]
Addresses the integration layer only	Manages all layers of the EDW architecture except for the landing area
Data model remains under DW/BI's control	All but the business model and value-added loops hidden from the EDW team
Requires DW/BI to write ETL and queries	Eliminates all but the ELT for derived columns
Only a technique—one that is data based and ETL tool agnostic	Tool-bound solution, but still DBMS agnostic
Teams need only training and support to get going	Teams must acquire and learn a data warehouse automation tool

[a]Labor savings based on four common DW/BI change cases.

should focus predominantly on change cases rather than creation cases when interacting with vendors and consultants offering a new approach for data warehousing.

Regarding the limitations of the estimates provided in this part of the book, I have several points of caution that readers should keep in mind. First, the four change cases may not be the situations that will be most important for every EDW team. The team leaders should author and estimate the particular scenarios that make up the bulk of their particular DW/BI change cases.

Second, my forecast for the hours required for these change cases will not match the labor hours other EDW practitioners will provide. My estimates should be used as an illustration about how a team deciding between data modeling paradigms should derive labor estimates of its own. Different people forecast wildly different amounts for a given hypothetical situation. Generally, my estimates usually lie somewhere in the middle of those of my teammates when I am working on a development project, so many people will find the numbers I have used here within reason. However, readers should definitely prepare their own estimates, even if they use my four change cases as a template.

Third, my treatment of hyper normalization was missing an important piece required to fully compare it to the hyper generalized approach. I did not include the cost of refreshing presentation- and semantic-layer data marts while using the HNF approach. Because HNF is largely a technique, and one that does little to streamline the portion of the warehouse beyond the integration layer, these steps may well consume a considerable amount of additional labor. The HGF automation tool provides both of these services, making them quick to accomplish and speeding up data warehouse evolution all that much more. Teams that are having trouble deciding between the two hyper modeled paradigms should take the time to expand the estimates provided in Chapter 14 by the time it would take to refresh data marts and semantic layers.

The contrast between HNF and HGF approaches deserves more attention. Table 15.2 provides several points of comparison between the two styles of hyper modeling. Most of them favor the hyper generalized paradigm, as long as the EDW program can afford the cost of acquiring the necessary data warehouse automation tools. Usually, when one monetizes the value of delivering several times faster and evolving a data warehouse almost as fast as customers can refine their requirements, the cost of tools seems very small indeed.

Because the choice of data modeling paradigms is an important and early milestone in any DW/BI project, every team needs to explore the power of the hyper modeling paradigms for itself rather than taking another party's word for it. I have provided enough background on how I compiled my numbers that it should be a straightforward exercise to decide whether my estimates cover all the considerations that should be included, such as the time required from supporting teammates and the effort required to promote builds between applications.

HGF-POWERED AGILE SOLUTIONS

Although hyper generalization seems to offer the greatest potential for accelerating EDW teams, that fact does not necessarily mean that it is the best for agile data warehousing. Agility is more than just delivering fast. It has more to do with failing fast and cheaply and then fixing quickly. In previous chapters, the practice of surface solutions and architectural backfilling was key to providing a series of subreleases that allow customers to participate fully in refining the vision for a data warehousing application. Increased customer participation was key to uncovering errors and oversights committed by the EDW team. Hyper generalized data warehouses truly excel in supporting the surface-solution process and keeping IT aligned with the business as stakeholders discover what it is they truly need.

Easier Backfills for Surface Solutions

Figure 15.37 depicts an EDW reference architecture adapted for a hyper generalized data modeling approach. The integration layer has been renamed the "data warehouse automation system" because that tool appears to place much of the warehouse in a black box when viewed from the perspective of the EDW developers who will be working with it. Within the HGF automation system, the developers will find the core storage, the value-added workspace, and the performance sublayer as described previously. Separate from the HGF automation system will be the database area that receives the departmental data marts that the HGF automation tool will create and refresh after each load of source data.

When confronted with a new, large requirement, the first step the EDW team should take with its business partners is the same as the action suggested for all other paradigms: Provide a Subrelease 1 by placing as much operational data in a landing area as possible and then surfacing that raw data to the subject matter experts in the business. This simple step will allow the team to employ a nimble data visualization tool to collaboratively explore source data with the end users, investigate whether it offers any value, and research the data transforms needed to solve the business problem.

For Subrelease 2, the team should begin populating the core of the data warehouse, using the HGF business modeler to quickly create a repository for a first subject area or even a topic-oriented subset within that subject area. The focus should be simply acquiring the source data and integrating it in obvious ways. This data can then be projected to a beginning departmental data mart with the humble ambition of providing only items that can be replicated from the source. This subrelease will also offer light integration using the business entities clearly present in the source data. Here, the EDW leaders can promise the business only a 360-degree view of the "things you can count and sum." They will be able to slice and dice these simple metrics by qualifiers taken directly from the operational systems. Subrelease 2 may in fact involve several versions of this simple data warehouse because it will take customers some time to learn enough about their source systems and their true business needs to provide a "final" collection of requirements. However, the team will be using a hyper generalized data repository that gives it a 10-fold increase in delivery speed, even after the warehouse is loaded with information, so that such fast iterations will be possible.

Once the customer begins to exhaust the value that a quick warehouse of straight operational data can provide, the team can begin to add value-added loops and offer its business partners Subrelease 3. Because the derived columns making up the new features in this subrelease require hand programming, the iterations between builds may well slow

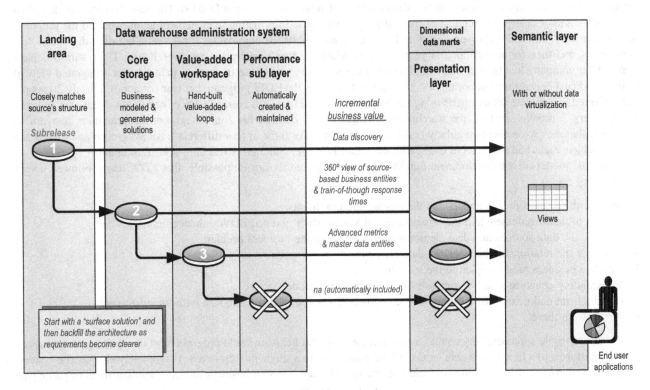

FIGURE 15.37 Surface solution patterns employing a hyper generalized integration layer.

down. However, the fact that the previous subrelease allowed the team to look deeply at the source data and reflect at length about the requirements, EDW's oversights and mistakes with Subrelease 3 should be rather small, making slightly longer iterations perhaps unnoticeable to the customer.

Note that Subrelease 3 is an end point in this process. With hyper normalization, we had another step in which the team addressed data latency issues by building objects in the performance sublayer. The hyper generalized approach addresses integration layer performance issues with both hardware and by projecting data into star schemas, so no further objects need to be developed. For this reason, the HGF data warehouse eliminates an entire step in the backfilling process and thus appears all the more agile to the end users.

EVIDENCE OF SUCCESS

For all the benefits that hyper generalization offers, I have been surprised to learn that only a few hundred companies utilize this technique worldwide. Although the products making this approach possible were first published more than 15 years ago, most enterprise data warehousing professionals are unfamiliar with it. My efforts to introduce this technology to companies needing a quick and inexpensive means of providing integrated analysis and reporting have at times met with considerable skepticism and resistance from the DW/BI directors and the EDW staff. Perhaps hyper generalization is just slightly ahead of its time, in which case DW/BI departments simply need evidence that this approach is effective and reduces project risk before they will begin considering it as a viable solution to the common challenges of enterprise data warehousing. To that end, I offer the following two case histories in which fairly large companies with serious business challenges found that a hyper generalized toolkit and model-driven development performed quite well for both the EDW team and their project sponsors. The first case history illustrates that a hyper generalized data warehouse automation system enables rapid interactions with business customers, leading to agile EDW delivery in the pharmaceutical industry. The second case history demonstrates the sheer ease of delivery that model-driven development brought to enterprise data warehousing for a specialty retailer, enabling analysts to ask more penetrating questions of their data and thereby attain greater competitive capabilities with less development expense.

Case History 1: Model-Driven Development in Pharmaceuticals

The first case history regarding the impact that hyper generalized tools can make on an agile EDW program took place at a Fortune 100 pharmaceutical company in the Midwest in the United States starting in 2006. This case history was described to me by the senior enterprise architect of the company's enterprise information management team, who led the program. At this company, she had employed a leading hyper generalized DW/BI automation for 4 years, building divisional data warehouses, and then for an additional 4 years while building the firm's enterprise data warehouse. The business departments at her company had been steadily funding the enterprise data warehouse in order to gain a better, integrated view of revenue and cost containment opportunities. During her 4 years on the EDW program, her team of approximately 20 people had delivered 25 separate subject areas using the hyper generalized tool—an average pace of one new subject area approximately every 2 months. In fact, the warehouse automation tool allowed her four integration programmers to work so efficiently that they were able to regularly build out subject areas for three or four different business groups at a time. Each of these subject areas had hundreds of users, with the total EDW user community reaching several thousand.

Using the model-driven development that the hyper generalized tool made possible, this EDW team followed a very fast delivery cycle:

1. Meet with the customer to understand the business requirements.
2. Draft a problem statement and the business objectives for their planned EDW enhancement.
3. Identify the data sources and data elements needed to solve the business problem.
4. Discover the relationship between the data elements.
5. Create a business model depicting the solution.
6. Immediately generate a data warehouse from that business model.
7. Build a front end using a BI tool, and validate this first version of the warehouse with the customer.
8. Iterate from there.

"It's a very agile approach," my contact assured me, adding that her team could progress from the opening conversations with the customer to a first, reviewable version of the warehouse in a single month—even if completely new source systems were involved. Many of her customers would become quickly familiar with business models, enabling them to participate extensively in the design process directly. Once they understood that *entities* represented dimensions and *transactions sets* depicted facts, they began to discuss business scenarios using the warehouse business model, which they could review directly using the design screen of the automation tool. For these customers, the development cycles quickly accelerated to the point where they could discuss a new set of requirements, increment the EDW's data repository, and review it via an updated front end in 2 or 3 days. With this fast-paced innovation and the power of the hyper generalized warehouse automation tool, her team was able to push a new EDW subrelease into production twice a month.

Frequently, a business group would need only a couple of cycles with the development team before it would say, "Yes! I know exactly what business actions I have to take" or "Now I know what decision I have to make." The tool's business model allowed these customers to take full ownership of the enterprise data warehouse. These business customers often "put the business model … on their office wall and reference it. They use it during discussions with their other business partners, especially the ones who are becoming the consumers of *their* integrated data."

I asked my contact if she had any evidence whether the business sponsors of the EDW were pleased with what her team had been able to accomplish using this process. "My four years with the EDW team have been very successful." She explained the difference that her fast, agile approach had made in her work. "We have dozens of data warehouses here besides the EDW, but ours provides the most widely adopted groups of reports within the company." The value that her customers found in the fast EDW delivery process translated into tangible, business-partner enthusiasm for the development process her team had devised. Often, when her team began a new project for one department, "other business groups would jump in" because they wanted to collaborate on the new subject area as well.

She could also measure success by repeat business. "My team is an enterprise information management group. We help the business groups to manage their information, making sure it is logically all part of an enterprise business model, and that it follows the company's master data foundation." In other companies, business groups often view the enterprise data warehousing team as an obstacle to creating business intelligence applications, providing nothing but hoops to jump through before it will allow department staff members to build the data mart they have in mind. However, her team's ability to quickly deliver basic data management and then steadily improve the solution for the customer turned the business partner's impression completely around. Many of her customers would start off warehousing their data without integration but then request that their information be upgraded to use the company's master data elements. "Through the business evolution of the project, we helped them understand the value of enterprise master data and how we could transform their one-off dimensions into an enterprise data model."

Perhaps her greatest measure of success lies in the fact that her team had been able to build an extensive enterprise data warehouse despite the fact that all of her projects had to be funded by the business groups, not out of a corporate IT budget. The business sponsors were so pleased with the speed and effectiveness of the model-driven development approach that the "funding has kept coming in steadily over the past 4 years."

This EDW team was able to achieve its high delivery speed and responsiveness to customers by driving development completely off a business model, except for the value-added loops, which they constructed using a typical ETL tool. I asked her if her team members ever felt hand-tied by the fact that they never got to see or touch the data model at work within the hyper generalized data warehouse automation system. On the contrary, "that is one of the most valuable aspects" of the tool. "Because, face it, if someone had a choice, who would want to have to create the logical and physical models that the automation tool hides? What would be the value to the business?" She pointed to how much additional maintenance is required to maintain a traditional EDW project's logical and physical models. "If you change one, you have to change it in three places. To be honest, I'm pretty technical, but I would never want to take the time and the energy required to create needless models. They're just an IT artifact. They don't add any value to the business. Let the software take care of it."

So, no frustration with the fact that the heart of the enterprise data warehouse is sealed up inside a black box? "A black box has its own beauty. If you think about the IT industry in general and the business we're in, my EDW team is not planning on being a software development firm. We want to be a business partner."

Case History 2: Hyper Generalized Data Warehousing in Specialty Retail

The second case history for the hyper generalized approach comes from Nik Green, a director of business intelligence working in the Charlotte, North Carolina, area. With more than 15 years of experience in enterprise reporting and advanced analytics for publicly traded firms, he now directs business intelligence and data management departments in providing enterprise data architecture, governance, master data management, and enterprise application integration. He has incrementally delivered enterprise data warehouses using short iterations in a diverse set of industries from consumer health products to specialty retail. His preferred tool employs the "things and links" associative data repository featured in this chapter. He recently used this technology to build enterprise data warehouses at two companies, including a Fortune 100 pharmaceuticals maker. The last of these projects resulted in a 3-terabyte business intelligence system for a women's apparel chain with $5 billion of annualized sales, more than 20,000 employees, and 12 million customers, with fact tables containing a billion records representing 5 years of transactions.

When I interviewed him for this book, the features of a hyper generalized tool were all too easy for him to enumerate. He had recently joined an international food retailer that had standardized on a database that ruled out his favorite model-driven development tool. Without access to this tool, he had to direct his new team in constructing an EDW using traditional software engineering, with ETL modules programmed by hand, one widget at a time. Having downshifted back to building data warehouses "the hard way," he was able to list the benefits of the hyper generalized approach that matter most to him in the past, namely

- a better way to work;
- mitigating risk;
- more effective use of development labor; and
- delivering a better warehouse.

Hyper Generalized Tools Offer a Better Way to Work

At his new company, Nik's challenge is to combine a merchandising data mart and a customer analysis data mart while his employer switches out the enterprise resource planning system that will serve as primary data source for the new warehouse. He sorely misses working with a hyper generalized tool that would have allowed his developers to generate each slice of the EDW directly from a business model. Using traditional methods, his team must first design a data integration area in third normal form, then employ a graphical tool to draft a business model, next build a logical model for the presentation layer, which can be finally used while hand coding the ETL. With all the additional layers of design work, Nik was very aware that it is "very easy for our business models and logical models and physical models to get out of synch," whereas with a hyper generalized toolkit "they're never out of synch because your business model drives [the application's hidden] logical and physical model."

Because his current company has not invested in a data warehouse automation tool, the team there must follow a standard approach with traditional tools. He has had to allocate 13 developers who have taken 6 months to get just the first subrelease to the end users. At his previous company where he had a hyper generalized data warehouse automation tool, he was able to merge two data warehouses while responding to a major source system upgrade with only a team of four or five people, delivering a new set of features every 6 weeks. The hyper generalized tool allowed his team to "continuously adapt to changes in our source systems while combining data marts into a single business model that gave users a holistic view of the company, even as a new ERP system was being rolled out." With HGF, "you're talking about going from model to report in 5 days," he assured me. "Modeling exclusively at the business model is definitely the better way to go."

Hyper Generalized Tools Mitigate Risk

Another advantage of the hyper generalized tools can be described in terms of the risk posed by uncertain or changing business requirements. Nik noted the advantages of working with a data warehouse automation tool rather than a product that is only a DW/BI code generator. "Most data warehousing generators are built to get a data warehouse up, but change is the tricky part." Using data warehouse automation products, on the other hand, "allows you to adapt to the changing business landscape in a way that would have been impossible using traditional tools." The EDW automation tools based on a hyper generalized integration layer allow a team to iterate through the business requirements one subject area at a time. "You just create a model, and run the data through it" to determine whether the team got the requirements and design correct. If not, the team needs only to correct the model and re-project a star schema that will now provide a better fit to purpose.

The traditional methods he had to use for his current company, in contrast, force the developers to get the design correct the first time. When a team must employ a long chain of data modeling and ETL coding, mistakes require a significant number of person hours to investigate and correct. "You have to investigate about 10 different areas to find out where the assumptions went wrong—maybe it was my model, maybe it wasn't." Given how long it takes to find and correct a design mistake, traditional EDW teams experience a lot of pressure to get the atomic level data correct first, which causes them to move slowly through design and coding activities of the project.

"It doesn't leave a lot of room for error," Nik summarized. With model-driven development, on the other hand, "you can make mistakes and then adapt [the application] to resolve those errors really quickly. I can build the next portion of a business model, load data, and validate that model in an hour or two instead of days or longer."

Hyper Generalized Tools Allow Better Use of Resources

Downshifting back to a traditional development clearly illustrated to Nik how much more effective model-driven development can be with labor resources. For a new increment of the warehouse, his previous team could use its model-driven data warehouse automation tool to complete both a conceptual model and an end-user review of the application's new features in 5 days. With only four or five developers, the team was able to offer its project stakeholders a new subrelease approximately every 6 weeks. In contrast, his current team of 13 developers, with their traditional methods, needed 6 months to deliver the first subrelease. The implied efficiency of the hyper generalized approach, then, incorporates an acceleration factor of four as delivery times improve from 6 months to 6 weeks, and a 2.5-fold improvement on labor productivity as staffing decreases from 13 to 4 or 5 developers. This case study, then, indicates that hyper generalized tools allow DW/BI directors to get a total of 10 times the productivity out of their development resources, "especially if you're using a good business intelligence [front-end] tool that [the data warehouse automation tool] can build out the meta data for." DW/BI directors, then, can have both smaller head counts and rapid turnaround, all at once. The hyper generalized approach "is tremendously faster," Nik emphasized. " I mean, it is *ridiculously* faster."

Hyper Generalized Tools Deliver a Better Warehouse

Nik pointed out that in addition to better resource utilization, the hyper generalized tools lead to far greater customer satisfaction. Of course, project stakeholders notice that the team is delivering with greater speed, but more important, they appreciate that this speed allows the DW/BI developers to tackle an entire class of business questions that are far more important.

He provided a simple example from his work with the specialty retailer. "If you look at a data mart in a retail company you're going to see point-of-sale transactions occurring at the store level. That's all you'll have because [the DW/BI team] can't spend the time needed to really understand the business." Switch to a model-driven toolkit, however, and the team will have the power to build applications enabling their business stakeholders to "look at a store and think about the detail of how it behaves, the dynamics actually happening at a cash register level." A cashier register sits within a particular lane at a specific store. Multiple cashiers cycle through that station every day, creating many nuances that the company needs to detect and explore.

The advanced capabilities that model-driven tools put within a team's reach "may not be a big deal when you're looking at the sales subject area," he explained, "but when you start to do investigations around fraud and looking for training opportunities, the ability to ask enterprise-level questions all the way down to where the true action occurs becomes a real game-changer." With traditional DW/BI development, EDW teams never have the time to provide this level of insights. With hyper generalized tools, however, a team can shift the hours it would have been spending on the logical modeling, physical modeling, and hand coding of the ETL to deeply learning about the business and adapting the BI applications as everyone learns more. In this case, his team was able to invest the effort needed to take the analysis down to the next level of detail and reveal inefficiencies and patterns of theft centered on the individual cash registers and cashiers. DW/BI customers see and appreciate the greater insight that teams utilizing model-driven development can achieve for them.

Barriers to Wider Adoption

With all the advantages that Nik was able to illustrate for his preferred approach, I asked him why no more than a few hundred companies have switched to the hyper generalized technology for enterprise data warehousing. In his appraisal, it is difficult to convince people to consider the model-driven approach because they do not compare "apples to apples." "You can join many [DW/BI departments] and the team doesn't even know what a slowly changing dimension is, even though they have claimed to have already built a data warehouse. Teams that do not build advanced data warehousing features such as slowly changing dimensions and suspended source record management won't have an appreciation of how the HGF tools can accomplish all that functionality and more, right out of the package with just a click of a check box." The hyper generalized tools create a world-class data warehouse for their users, he explained. If the agile data warehousing proponent does not establish up-front that such a high-quality data warehouse is necessary, then all the features offered by the hyper generalized tool will seem superfluous.

I asked Nik about a criticism of HG packages that I commonly hear from EDW architects and managers—that the integration layer's design and its ETL are essentially hidden from the development team. Aside from the documentation, one has to allow the product to work without knowing the details of the data transformation it employs.

"I loved the fact that it was a black box and automated," answered Nik. Of course, he and his team spent a lot of time at first learning how the product was built, especially the way the associative data store for dimensional information was structured. Once they achieved that level of insight, however, it proved unnecessary for any developer to actually examine the contents or inner workings of the hyper generalized data store. "We never looked at it and never touched it," he said as he summarized his last model-driven project. The hyper generalized tool "may be a black box, but what I care about is what it is producing. If what it produces mirrors back to my business model, what do I care what it did in between?"

That said, why do so many teams still pursue EDW projects using manually written ETL routines, I asked, when they could just generate 80% of an application from a business model? Nik pointed to the fact that system integrators still build many of the world's larger data warehouses, and that those companies benefit from following labor-intensive approaches when building the integration layer that sits in between source systems and the end user's presentation layer. "You know a lot of people make a lot of money doing that non-value-added work in the middle."

SUMMARY

Whereas hyper normalization provides important flexibility in the EDW integration layer by increasing the number of tables beyond the traditionally modeled approach, HGF takes the data model in the opposite direction. By generalizing to an extreme the components of a typical source data record, the EDW can store a company's information in just three data stores: a collection of associative records for dimensional data, a stack of name-value pairs for the qualifying attributes, and lightly dimensionalized event records for transaction data. Although the details of saving and retrieving data into the hyper generalized data stores are rather involved, that complexity is moot. Teams wishing to build a hyper generalized data warehouse need to invest in a data warehouse automation tool, and this tool will then hide most of the complexity from everyone, developers included.

With the HGF automation system, the development team can employ graphical design tools to create and manage most of the objects for an enterprise data warehouse by working with only business-level concepts. Data structures, data transforms, and retrieval queries for creating star schemas can all be authored directly from the application's business model. Moreover, these data warehouse components can be analyzed and updated while still working with only business-level designs. When used to update an existing data warehouse for new or overlooked requirements, the HGF automation system makes converting the remaining information relatively easy to accomplish because it employs fairly simple data transforms, designed using business concepts and run against data already stored in the data warehouse.

By eliminating the work of logical and physical data modeling, hyper generalized data warehousing tools remove 90 percent or more of the labor DW/BI teams used to invest in building and maintaining "the basic plumbing" of an enterprise data warehouse. The ability to quickly change the layout and data within a production data warehouse also enables the EDW team to provide a steady stream of new features to its customers—a hallmark of an agile team. EDW team leaders can now focus their resources on creating the "value-added loops" necessary to derive new information, thus greatly increasing the value DW/BI can add to the business. Because the hyper generalized toolset allows EDW developers to work at a business level, the team can include business partners in the requirements and design discussion. Requirements and design become far easier to discern, increasing the likelihood that the business intelligence applications will remain tightly aligned with current business needs. Case studies demonstrate that the new speed and flexibility that HGF tools permit allow EDW teams to start small, build out incrementally, and revise existing versions of the warehouse without lengthy and expensive re-engineering. In this way, hyper generalization nearly eliminates the risk that large enterprise data warehouse projects used to entail. Given the power of both hyper normalization and hyper generalization, EDW team leaders need to consider hyper modeling options carefully whenever starting a new data warehousing development effort.

Part IV References

Chapter 12

Becker, B., 2007, March 26. Think Critically When Applying Best Practices. Kimball Group (blog). <http://www.kimballgroup.com/2007/03/think-critically-when-applying-best-practices> (accessed September 2014).

Date, C.J., 2012. Database Design and Relational Theory. O'Reilly Media, Cambridge, MA.

Earley, S., 2011. The DAMA Dictionary of Data Management, second ed. Technic, Bradley Beach, NJ.

Inmon, W.H., Imhoff, C., Sousa, R., 2001. Corporate Information Factory, second ed. Wiley, New York.

Kimball, R., Ross, M., 2013. The Data Warehouse Toolkit, third ed. Wiley, New York.

Silverston, L, Agnew, P., 2008. The data model resource book, Universal Patterns for Data Modeling, vol. 3. Wiley, New York.

Singh, S.K., 2011. Database Systems: Concepts, Design and Applications, second ed. Pearson, India.

U.S. Department of Defense 2002, February 12. Defense.gov news transcript: DoD news briefing (news transcript). Defense.gov (blog). <http://www.defense.gov/transcripts/transcript.aspx?transcriptid = 2636>.

Wyllys, R.E., 2003. Overview of normalization. Database Management Principles and Applications. The University of Texas at Austin, Austin, TX, <https://www.ischool.utexas.edu/ ~ wyllys/DMPAMaterials/normover.html>.

Chapter 13

Altior, Inc., 2012, December 18. Altior's AltraSTAR—Hadoop storage accelerator and optimizer now certified on CDH4 (press release). Eatontown, NJ: Altior, Inc. Apache Foundation (2014). Apache Hive. <http://hive.apache.org> (accessed August 2014).

Babcock, C. 2012, June 15. Yahoo and Hadoop: In it for the long term. InformationWeek. <http://www.informationweek.com/database/yahoo-and-hadoop-in-it-for-the-long-term/d/d-id/1104866?>.

Borthakur, D., 2010, May 9. Facebook has the world's largest Hadoop cluster! HDFS (blog). <http://hadoopblog.blogspot.com/2010/05/facebook-has-worlds-largest-hadoop.html>.

DeWitt, D., Stonebraker, M., 2008, January 17. MapReduce: A major step backwards. Database Column. <http://www.databasecolumn.com/2008/01/mapreduce-a-major-step-back.html> or <http://homes.cs.washington.edu/ ~ billhowe/mapreduce_a_major_step_backwards.html> (accessed July 2013).

Douglas, L., 2001, February 6. 3D data management: Controlling data volume, velocity and variety. <blogs.Gartner.com>.

Du Preez, D., 2014, April 25. A big data reality check: What the hell is the use case? Diginomica. <http://diginomica.com/2014/04/25/big-data-reality-check-hell-case> (accessed July 2014).

Facebook, 2012, November 8. Under the hood: Scheduling MapReduce jobs more efficiently with Corona. Notes by Facebook Engineering. <https://www.facebook.com/notes/facebook-engineering/under-the-hood-scheduling-mapreduce-jobs-more-efficiently-with-corona/10151142560538920>.

Feinleib, D., 2012, July 9. The 3 I's of Big Data. Forbes. <http://www.forbes.com/sites/davefeinleib/2012/07/09/the-3-is-of-big-data> (accessed September 2012).

Finley, K., 2014, May 19. Why tech's best minds are very worried about the Internet of things. Wired. <http://www.wired.com/tag/internet-of-things/page/2>.

Finnegan, M., 2013, March 6. Boeing 787s to create half a terabyte of data per flight, says Virgin Atlantic. Computerworld UK. <http://www.computerworlduk.com/news/infrastructure/3433595>.

Henschen, D., 2012, October 24. Why Sears is going all-in on Hadoop. InformationWeek. <http://www.informationweek.com/it-leadership/why-sears-is-going-all-inonhadoop/d/d-id/1107038?> (accessed July 2014).

Henschen, D., 2013, March 22. Big data debate: Will Hadoop become dominant platform? InformationWeek. <http://www.informationweek.com/big-data/big-data-analytics/big-data-debate-will-hadoop-become-dominant-platform/d/d-id/1109226?> (accessed August 2014).

King, R., 2012, April 30. Sears hopes big data can generate big revenue. Wall Street Journal. <http://mobile.blogs.wsj.com/cio/2012/04/30/sears-hopes-big-data-can-generate-big-revenue>.

Kumar, V., 2013, May 7. Will Hadoop replace or augment your enterprise data warehouse? The Big Data & Analytics Hub, IBM. <http://www.ibmbigdatahub.com/blog/will-hadoop-replace-or-augment-your-enterprise-data-warehouse>.

Lohr, S., 2013, September 17. Improving the big data toolkit. New York Times. <http://bits.blogs.nytimes.com/2013/09/17/improving-the-big-data-toolkit/?_php = true&_type = blogs&_r = 0>.

Maguire, J., 2014, May 22. Big data survey: Big data growing quickly. Datamation. <http://www.datamation.com/data-center/big-data-survey-big-data-growing-quickly.html>.

Marr, B., 2014, February 28. Big data—The 5 Vs everyone must know. <http://www.slideshare.net/BernardMarr/140228-big-data-volume-velocity-variety-varacity-value> (accessed July 2014).

Press, G., 2013, December 12. $16.1 Billion big data market: 2014 predictions from IDC and IIA. Forbes. <http://www.forbes.com/sites/gilpress/2013/12/12/16-1-billion-big-data-market-2014-predictions-from-idc-and-iia>.

QuinStreet Enterprise Research, 2014. Big data outlook, 2014. <http://www.enterpriseappstoday.com/ebooks/184585110/97360/>.

Ryan, A., 2012, June 13. Under the hood: Hadoop distributed filesystem reliability with Namenode and Avatarnode. Facebook. <https://www.facebook.com/notes/facebook-engineering/under-the-hood-

hadoop-distributed-filesystem-reliability-with-namenode-and-avata/
10150888759153920>.

Shao, Z., 2008, October. Hive: Data warehousing & analytics on Hadoop.
SlideShare.net. <http://www.slideshare.net/zshao/hive-data-ware-
housing-analyticsonhadoop-presentation> (accessed May 2014).

Turck, M., 2014, May 11. The state of big data in 2014. Venture Beat.
<http://venturebeat.com/2014/05/11/the-state-of-big-data-in-2014-chart>
(accessed May 2014).

van der Lans, R., 2012. Data Virtualization for Business Intelligence
Systems. Morgan Kaufmann, Waltham, MA.

White, T., 2012. Hadoop: The Definitive Guide, third ed. O'Reilly Med,
Sebastopol, CA.

Chapter 14

BinckBank, 2014. BinckBank for Investors (website). <https://www.
binck.com/nl/corporate> (accessed September 2014).

Boyina, B., Breur, T., 2013, April 17. Adapting data warehouse architecture
to benefit from agile methodologies. Slideshare (website). <http://
www.slideshare.net/bboyina/adapting-data-warehouse-architecture-
to-benefit-from-agile-methodologies> (accessed February 2015).

Damhof, R., 2011a, January 29. Data vault schools. Data Management &
Decision Support (blog). <http://prudenza.typepad.com/dwh/2011/
01/data-vault-schools.html> (accessed September 2014).

Damhof, R., 2011b, February 17. Dan Linstedt & Ronald Damhof; Let's
be clear about the raw data vault. Data Management & Decision
Support (blog). <http://prudenza.typepad.com/dwh/2011/02/dan-
linstedt-ronald-damhof-lets-be-clear-about-the-raw-data-vault.html>
(accessed September 2014).

Data Vault Discussion Group, 2014, November. Barry McConnell (original post), "Load end dates and historical rewrites. Data Vault
Discussions (LinkedIn discussion group). <https://www.linkedin.
com/groups?home = &gid = 44926&trk = anet_ug_hm&goback = %
2Egna_44926>.

Date, C.J., Darwen, H., Lorentzos, N., 2002. Temporal Data & The
Relational Model. Morgan Kaufmann, Waltham, MA.

Hultgren, H., 2012. Modeling the Agile Data Warehouse with Data
Vault. New Hamilton.

Linstedt, D., 2003, January 1. Data Vault overview. The Data
Administration Newsletter (online). <http://www.tdan.com/view-
articles/5155> (accessed September 2014).

Linstedt, D., 2010a, May 13. Data Vault loading specification v1.2. DV
Standards (blog). <http://danlinstedt.com/datavaultcat/standards/
data-vault-loading-specification-v1-2> (accessed September 2014).

Linstedt, D., 2010b, May 13. DV modeling specification v1.0.9. DV
Standards (blog). <http://danlinstedt.com/datavaultcat/standards/dv-
modeling-specification-v1-0-8> (accessed September 2014).

Linstedt, D., 2014a, March 16. 2014 is the year of #DataVault 2.0. Dan
Linstedt (blog). <http://danlinstedt.com/datavaultcat/2014-is-the-
year-of-datavault-2-0> (accessed September 2014).

Linstedt, D., 2014b, June 30. Data Vault 1.0 and Data Vault 2.0 do NOT
compete. Dan Linstedt (blog). <http://danlinstedt.com/datavaultcat/
datavault-1-0-and-data-vault-2-0-do-not-compete> (accessed
September 2014).

Linstedt, D., 2015. Quotes. Dan.Linstedt.com (website). <http://
danlinstedt.com/solutions-2/quotes>.

Linstedt, D., Graziano, D., 2011. Super Charge Your Data Warehouse:
Invaluable Data Modeling Rules to Implement Your Data Vault.
CreateSpace Independent Publishing.

Regardt, O., Rönnbäck, L., Bergholtz, M., Johannesson, P., Wohed, P.,
2009. Anchor Modeling. In: Proceedings of the 28th International
Conference on Conceptual Modeling, ER '09 (Gramado, Brazil).
New York, Springer-Verlag, pp. 234–250.

Rönnbäck, L., Regardt, O., Johannesson, P., Bergholtz, M., Wohed, P.,
2013. Anchor Modeling and Data Vault comparison chart. Anchor
(blog). <http://www.anchormodeling.com/wp-content/uploads/2013/
06/AM-and-DV-comparison-chart.pdf> (accessed September 2014).

Vos, R., 2014a, June 12. A brief history of time in Data Vault. An
Expert View on Agile Data Warehousing (blog). <http://roelantvos.
com/blog/?p = 1174> (accessed February 2015).

Vos, R., 2014b, June 12. Integration layer. An Expert View on Agile
Data Warehousing (blog). <http://roelantvos.com/blog/?p = 57>
(accessed February 2015).

Chapter 15

Breur, T., 2015. Comments on this book's review manuscript. In:
Breur, T (Ed.), Vice President of Data Analytics. Cengage Learning,
Boston, MA.

Pace, S., 2013, October 8. Where's my magic quadrant? Kalido
Conversations (website). <http://blog.kalido.com/wheres-magic-
quadrant> (accessed February 2015).

Wells, D., 2014, April 15. Relieving the pain of the BI back room with
data warehouse automation. The Data Warehousing Institute
(website). <http://tdwi.org/articles/2014/04/15/data-warehouse-
automation.aspx> (accessed October 2014).

West, M., 2011. Developing High Quality Data Models. Morgan
Kaufmann, Waltham, MA.

Williams, S., 2002. The Associative Model of Data, second ed. Lazy
Software; <http://www.sentences.com/docs/other_docs/AMD.pdf>
(accessed May 2013).

Part V

Agile EDW Quality Management Planning

Chapter 16

Why We Test and What Tests to Run

Enterprise data warehousing (EDW) team leaders who implement the many suggestions in the prior four parts of this book may experience a strong resonance with the old Chinese proverb, "Be careful what you wish for." On the one hand, agile data warehousing techniques unleash data warehousing/business intelligence (DW/BI) developers to define and program extract, transform, and load (ETL) and BI modules as fast as humanly possible. On the other hand, if these agile techniques generate a flood of new modules and subsystems, how can EDW team leader know that this torrent of deliverables have been designed and programmed well enough to actually achieve meaningful customer objectives? What assures them that the programmers have not been cutting a thousand corners in order to meet Scrum's incessant deadlines and that the resulting application will not fail miserably once placed into production usage? These leaders could insist that the team's developers and testers validate every small piece of code in every conceivable way, but such a policy would consume so much labor and time that the project would completely lose its speed and responsiveness to the customer.

Similar to how agile requirements management focuses on providing "just enough" project definition and design to enable programming to get started, the agile quality assurance (QA) for data warehousing aims to provide just enough validation of deliverables to ensure the team is building the right thing in the right way. This agile approach to QA blends the same ingredients employed for risk mitigation, requirements management, and data engineering. Instead of overinvesting in detailed plans before the team has any real results to evaluate, agile QA relies on

- employing a lightweight analytical framework so the team asks the right questions;
- visualizing the challenges uncovered so everyone can participate in their solution;
- providing just enough definition that teammates can begin to self-organize toward a goal; and
- initiating programming as soon as possible and delivering in small increments so that feedback on real results can focus the team on what truly matters.

In that spirit, this and the following two chapters do not attempt to list every last test that a DW/BI team should throw against its enterprise data warehouse, nor the deep theory behind the practice and methods of QA in general. Readers interested in such an exhaustive discussion of those topics can start with the works referenced in this chapter. Instead, I provide an easy-to-express QA planning approach for EDW team leaders to following as part of their agile development approach. The work patterns offered here will allow them to structure the core elements of an effective QA program during the early portions of their DW/BI projects and then rely on the team to fill in the necessary details as development iterations progress. This approach employs a framework organized around the six basic interrogatives, ordered so that defining an effective EDW quality assurance plan is as straightforward as possible:

- *Why* should our teammates care about testing?
- *What* tests should they be running?
- *Who* should be writing the test cases?
- *When* should we be executing each type of test?
- *Where* should these tests be occurring?
- *How* should we be getting these tests to run?

Questions regarding why and what focus on identifying the tests that will occur, and these serve as the theme for this chapter. The questions of who, when, and where provide guidance to the EDW teammates while planning their individual roles in QA, and those are the topic of Chapter 17. Finally, the question of how pertains to execution details, which is addressed in Chapter 18.

Teams that follow this six-question framework to QA will find that they can define a good-enough set of test types quickly, get development and validation activities started, and then fluidly fine-tune the team's quality efforts as the project's delivery work steadily reveals the strengths and weaknesses of their testing plan.

WHY TEST?

Quality has received many definitions during the past few decades. The International Standards Organization defines quality as the totality of features and characteristics of a product or service that bears on its ability to satisfy stated or implied needs [Charantimath 2010, Chapter 1]. Genichi Taguchi, director of the Japanese Academy of Quality in the late 1970s, defined quality as a product's ability to maintain its value to society after taking into account the adverse results from quality inspections, customer complaints, added warranty costs, damage to company reputation, and loss of market share [Zairi 2010, Section 1.4.7]. The Six Sigma school of quality assurance suggests that quality is the result of managing a process until it achieves less than 4 defects per 1 million [Ramu 2010].

I prefer to define "quality" for an application such as an EDW as the system's *fit to purpose*, judged by the customer organization as it considers an application's features, behavior, and total cost of ownership. For now, we can define the related term of "testing" as the act of assessing an application's quality, although we will put a much finer point on this notion later in this chapter. These definitions take into account that both the *fit* and the *purpose* have to be perceived by the people receiving the application. It incorporates some notions of agility because it allows for that perception to change as a project unfolds and as everyone involved learns more about the problem space that the application should address. My working definition also suggests that quality is a product of how the system addresses both the customers functional and nonfunctional requirements, leaving the relative mix of the two for the organization to determine.

With these definitions in place, one could answer "Why should we test?" with the simple statement, "To measure whether the EDW is fit for purpose." However, the question has other possible answers, both obvious and subtle. To start with the simplest, we can point out that testing catches mistakes before they can impinge upon team velocity. The challenge of EDW projects is not only that these systems are big and complicated but also that software programming is an imperfect process that consumes inordinate resources and calendar time. Every EDW project will therefore involve some requirements oversights and many programming errors. The QA process needs to ferret out the flaws in application definition, design, and coding that have steadily crept into the product over the many months of the project. Without adequate testing, these errors will go undetected during development, only to be forced onto the customer as production-system defects. In practice, customers will tolerate a small level of imperfection in the application, but above a certain threshold, product flaws will cause the sponsor to label the application a disappointment or a failure, amounting to a career-limiting waste of time and effort for the information technology (IT) professionals involved.

Testing Keeps Agile Teams from Cutting Corners

A more subtle answer to "Why test?" revolves around the notion that software validation does more than catch programming mistakes—it instills a greater level of discipline and clarity of mind upon the team as it creates the software to test, leading to better execution of the software development process. Better execution of the software engineering process leads to a work product that is easier to manage as it is taking shape, which in turn makes QA easier to accomplish. Given their preference for self-organization, agile teams benefit in particular from this positive feedback loop.

One of the driving forces behind the move to agile development techniques is the need for speed, and veteran agile teams do in fact deliver new application modules very quickly. The Scrum method that lies at the heart of the agile data warehousing approach described in this book organizes work in "sprints," denoting speed in its name. The method keeps steady deadline pressure on the development teams so that they get the application programmed sooner. With all the pressure to deliver quickly, programmers can understandably emphasize "getting it done" rather than "getting it done right." The danger, of course, is that haste will make waste.

Gerry Weinberg's *zeroth law of quality* states that "if the software doesn't have to work, you can always meet any other requirement" [Weinberg 1993, p. 111]. The fact that a software application must work correctly and solve the right problem imposes a fundamental limitation on how fast and how inexpensively developers can accomplish their goals. If quality is the limitation, testing is how that limitation actually connects to the activities in the project room. The objective of every Scrum iteration is not the creation of a software prototype but, rather, the delivery of shippable or "consumable" work products. Testing reveals whether the delivered product is sound—that is, whether it is truly shippable code. It keeps us from fooling ourselves into thinking that fast deliveries necessarily equal effective programming. By revealing where we rushed through requirements, designed in haste, or programmed too simplistically, testing shows us where the team is cutting too many corners in its work habits and falling victim to the zeroth law of quality. In essence, testing allows agile EDW teams to work with discipline. Install an effective QA program for a project, and the need to monitor and cajole developers to work "in the right way" will largely disappear.

Testing Keeps Root Cause Analysis Manageable

Given the emphasis on fast deliveries established by the iterative development approach itself, agile EDW team leaders sometimes find it difficult to convince programmers to undertake a robust testing effort. Here, some theory can tip the balance toward more vigorous support for QA among the programmers.

Good, persistent testing keeps defects from compounding to the point where they undermine the team's ability to make any progress on building new features. Consider Figure 16.1, which depicts the process a team must go through to find the root cause for a given set of software defects. The first defect is depicted with a bold line. When a defect suddenly appears in isolation, it is easy to resolve given that the likely cause of the visible defect is the one and only change that was just made to the software. However, add more changes before the defects are noticed and the situation becomes far more complex. With just two more faulty changes, the total combinations of cause and effect that the team must consider has increased to nine, not just three, revealing that the effort to identify the root cause for a given set of defects grows exponentially with the number of coding changes made.

Accordingly, another answer to "Why do we test?" is to keep root cause analysis from becoming exponentially more difficult. Persistent, aggressive testing will detect defects as they occur, before the team throws further coding changes on the heap of possible causes that must be evaluated. Often, when my firm's agile consultants perform project rescues for our customers, we encounter teams that have had very weak testing plans and that are losing three-fourths or more of their bandwidth to resolving errors in the application's data. Because these teams have allowed defects to accumulate, the exponential increase in analysis has led to paralysis. Continuous testing keeps root cause analysis to a minimum, preserving the bulk of a team's resources for building new features. For this reason, programmers should be

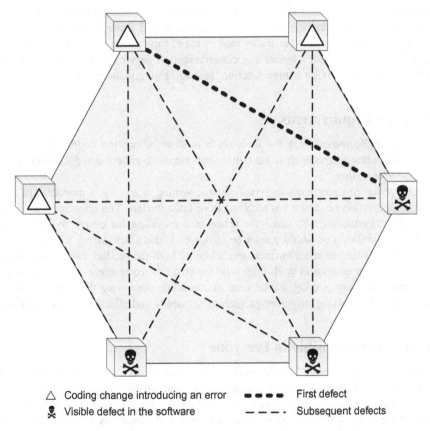

△ Coding change introducing an error   ▬ ▬ ▬ ▬ First defect

☠ Visible defect in the software   ─ ─ ─ ─ Subsequent defects

FIGURE 16.1 The level-of-effort needed to determine the root-cause of a defect increases exponentially with the number of defects that exist.

inspired to invest significantly into quality procedures because strong testing equals delivery speed. EDW team leaders should therefore set their sights on an *aggressive* QA effort—one that tests all modules and tests them continuously. The secret is knowing how much to test each object, a topic we will consider in a moment.

Testing Integrates Teamwork Across the Pipeline

As a further benefit, an aggressive testing campaign will increase team cohesion. Even projects that can collocate the developers will see silos of specialization occurring, a trend that only gets worse with remote teammates. Persistent, aggressive testing will greatly reduce this natural partitioning of the team that threatens to undermine its ability to self-organize and swarm problems in an agile manner.

As discussed in my prior books, agile DW/BI teams requires many skills that do not easily flow between teammates. For example, business analysts are good at capturing business rules, data modelers excel at database design, ETL leads can quickly draft processing flows, and BI programmers understand the front-end tool. Very few of these specialists can work adroitly outside of these specialties. Although specialization allows people to work in their "sweet spots" where they make the fastest progress, it also creates the need for work to be handed off between specialties. Errors in communication frequently occur during these handoffs when the receiver of a message believes he understands the direction provided by his upstream teammate but has not actually asked the right questions to fully comprehend the request. Testing provides feedback to the sender and receiver across these handoffs, highlighting communication gaps.

For example, when a programmer claims he has completed a module with exhaustive edge testing, the business analyst may well notice that no reconciliation tests have been performed. She realizes she forgot to mention that a set of aggregated control files exist, against which the data transform results can be validated. After mentioning these files to the programmer, she agrees with his suggestion that the module should automatically perform this reconciliation; hence an informal conversation about testing uncovers a further technical requirement. Without steady and effective testing, EDW teams will need to invest far more in careful, up-front design work and formal communication between specialties, perhaps resorting to written, detailed specifications. At some point, however, copious, written communications will become an inventory of technical requirements, and lean software development principles warn us that such inventories will frequently result in wasted effort. Teams that pursue aggressive testing find that the tests themselves convey a tremendous amount of information regarding requirements and design. The structure of their tests ends up replacing much of the communication that other teams must achieve through written specifications, and the instances in which those tests fail effectively highlight whether any communication gaps exist. By allowing an EDW to reduce specifications to where it provides just enough communication, testing again equals speed.

Testing Leads to Better Requirements

As will be discussed later, agile teams write the tests for a module before the coding begins. One pronounced by-product of this test-led development approach is far better requirements, underscoring another reason why agile EDW teams benefit from aggressive testing.

Given agile's preference for just-good-enough specifications, writing a test for a module will strain a programmer's understanding of the sparse direction he or she has received from team leaders. The questions the programmer must ask to fill the gaps in his or her understanding will cause the teammates providing the design to better articulate the technical requirements. Often, the programmer's questions cannot be answered without first asking for clarification on the functional purpose for a module, leading in turn to better business requirements from the product owner. Teams that pursue persistent, aggressive testing find that their programmers work from a far better set of requirements, even if most of those notions were delivered in a verbal format. Because nothing wastes time like building the wrong thing, better requirements results in a faster path to project success. By avoiding misguided programming, steady and effective testing again equals speed.

Testing Makes Real Progress Visible to Everyone

As a final answer to "Why do we test?", agile EDW teams can answer that we do so because it provides all stakeholders with far clearer evidence of team progress. Teams that invest in significant testing from the beginning of their project provide themselves with real, meaningful events for measuring the work completed. This depiction provides evidence-based trend lines that all teammates and project stakeholders can monitor in order to understand the project's accomplishments, eliminating much of the mystery that surrounds traditionally managed DW/BI projects.

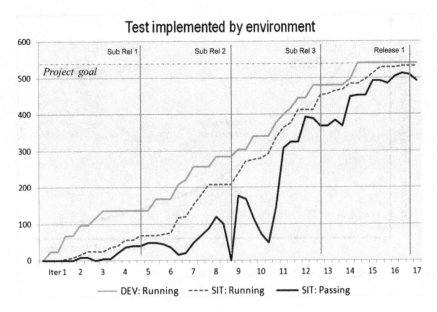

FIGURE 16.2 Visualizing quality via the number of tests executing or passing by environment.

Consider Figure 16.2, which we will discuss in greater depth in Chapter 18. This graph shows the number of tests executing in multiple DW/BI environments across time. The top line shows the number of tests defined and executing in the development environment. The middle line represents the number of tests defined and running in the system integration testing (SIT) environment. The bottom line reveals the number of those SIT tests that are passing.

The middle line in particular represents modules that have been designed, programmed, and integrated to the point where they undergo nightly testing. These modules provide substantial evidence that the EDW teams are diligently creating new system components. The bottom line indicates whether those efforts are effective. When the bottom line touches the middle line, it indicates that the EDW version running in SIT works and the team has achieved agile's goal of "shippable code."

This graphic can even portray whether the team has achieved enough. When applied to SIT, the test-led development technique mentioned previously can enable the team to forecast the number of SIT tests it will need to execute by the time the project is complete. That number represents a project goal, one that can be drawn on the test implementation chart, as shown in Figure 16.2. When the line for SIT tests running reaches the goal line, the programming has been roughly completed, and when the line for SIT tests passing touches the goal, that application is now polished enough to deliver. Persistent and aggressive testing provides the events and goals that are depicted on this graph and therefore makes real project progress visible to everyone involved.

AN AGILE APPROACH TO QUALITY ASSURANCE

Although the previous discussion provides plenty of motivation for investing significantly in a QA effort, one naturally wonders what such an effort would look like for an *agile* EDW project. The QA plans advocated in this book have three notable features:

- They emphasize the notion of balance.
- They translate many incremental techniques for programming into the realm of software testing.
- They extend the notion of *test-led development* far above the level of unit testing where it was originally defined.

Striving for Balance

Perhaps the most notable aspect of an agile QA plan is that it explicitly elevates the notion of balance to be a primary planning objective. Agile EDW teams do not have the funding, staffing, or calendar time to conduct every conceivable test for their applications. Even if we had the resources to test everything, we would still choose to reduce testing to just good enough, in order to divert more resources to programming, so that the customer receives as much value from the project as possible.

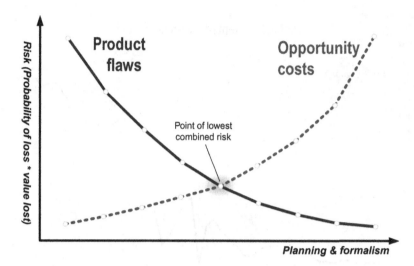

FIGURE 16.3   The optimal level of testing is a balance between two types of risks.

Judging how much QA a team should undertake and which tests to forego is a subjective decision, but it helps to visualize the optimal solution. Consider Figure 16.3, which shows the countervailing risks that a development team needs to manage as it sets its target level for application testing. The horizontal axis depicts how much time and effort a team chooses to invest in QA. The vertical axis represents the risk of adverse event, defined as the impact of the event multiplied by the likelihood that it will occur. Descending from the upper left is the risk of letting product flaws of any kind slip through and enter into a production application. Teams can drive this particular risk toward zero if they decide to invest to an extreme degree in QA.

Unfortunately, any decrease in the risk of product flaws achieved through extensive testing must be weighed against the concomitant increase in opportunity cost incurred. Companies that delay releasing business intelligence features so that they can complete exhaustive testing risk losing altogether the business benefit that the application was intended to capture. The project's sponsor commissioned the DW/BI application to address a pressing business challenge. Teams that take too long to deliver—for any reason—risk letting that opportunity to profit from solving that challenge disappear. The art of agile QA is finding the sweet spot depicted in the middle of Figure 16.3, where the intensity of testing is balanced against opportunity costs, and the sum of the two risk curves falls to a minimum.

Previously, this chapter identified the need for an aggressive QA program—one that tests all modules continuously. Figure 16.3 illustrates that the QA program must be *balanced* as well—that is, testing each module just enough to ensure that it's fit for purpose but not so much as to put the value of the entire application at risk. The mission for EDW project leaders, then, is to provide a plan for their teammates that identifies a small number of test types for each module type that will be just good enough to validate the next product release. The chapters in this part of the book offer a straightforward process for identifying a balanced QA program that involves the following set of action steps:

- Authoring a top-down testing plan that includes the interest of stakeholders outside the development team
- Negotiating a bottom-up testing plan to which the programmers will adhere
- Confirming that the two plans meet in the middle by implementing categorized event reporting
- Trimming the plan until it fits within budget
- Monitoring and adjusting the plan to maintain the maximum affordable test coverage

Keeping Quality Assurance "Agile"

I illustrate how EDW leaders can accomplish the planning objectives listed previously by progressing through the five remaining interrogatives—the what, who, when, where, and how of testing. The resulting plan will embody the agile principles and techniques utilized previously in this book for risk mitigation, requirements management, and data engineering. The agile notions built into the recommend quality process can be summarized as follows.

It is Collaborative, with High Customer Involvement

The entire team participates in writing test cases rather than leaving it for the project's system tester role. The team even requests test cases and product validation from its embedded business partner, the product owner.

It is Iterative and Incremental

Test execution starts with Iteration 1 and builds steadily throughout the project. This practice assures business stakeholders that all developed components will receive their fair share of QA efforts. In waterfall projects, testing is planned throughout development, but execution begins only as the application coding nears completion, risking that too little time and resources have been reserved to validate all the assembled features.

It Embodies the 80/20 Rule

The agile quality plan to be presented covers only the high and medium planning levels. Developers defer specifying the test details for a given module until it is time to develop it. In this way, the team follows "just-in-time test planning," investing only 20% of the predevelopment planning effort one typically sees in waterfall projects, but achieving up front 80% of the definition needed to execute an effective application testing campaign.

It Relies on Self-Organization

The system test role on an agile DW/BI team focuses much less on writing test cases and far more on mentoring his or her teammates in the art of testing and inspiring them to incorporate quality practices as part of their everyday work. The system tester and the remaining EDW team leaders provide their teammates with some easy-to-follow quality techniques and encouragement but from there on must rely on each developer to identify challenges as they arise and take the initiative in solving them.

It is Highly Transparent

The artifacts employed to represent and execute the plan are simple and highly intelligible so that anyone interested can quickly understand the intended process and hold the team accountable for following it. Moreover, this multistrand effort will resolve to a single *quality dashboard* displayed in the team room. With daily updates to the graphs displayed there, the status of quality for the current iteration, the current subrelease, and the application as a whole can be easily perceived, empowering stakeholders or IT management to take corrective action if necessary.

Its Artifacts are Lightweight

Quality assurance planning for agile EDW projects requires considerable thought and collaboration, but once the team has decided on a course, the entire plan can be expressed in only a few single-page artifacts. The advantage of this lightweight documentation is twofold. First, these artifacts can be readily understood by any interested party, including the programmers. For that reason, these artifacts should be displayed on the project room wall in order to keep the QA efforts of all teammates aligned with their leaders' balanced plan for testing. Second, because the team invests very little in the documentation, it will be willing to update the artifacts whenever the QA needs to change. Practices providing little value can be dropped, with new policies adopted and documented, without the high cost of updating artifacts causing the team to regret the change.

It is Stereoscopic

Agile EDW teams use two value chains during requirements management to ensure they arrive at a robust project description (see Part III). They also employ two units of measure during iteration planning to ensure that their estimates are accurate. Similarly, in planning QA, agile EDW teams take two approaches: top-down and bottom-up. They work their QA plan until both of these action plans meet in the middle, assuring them that they have not overlooked anything important.

It Retains QA Practices Already Included in the Base Agile Method

Many aspects of the Scrum method incorporate QA into the very act of defining, designing, and programming software applications, as discussed earlier in this and my previous two books. The following are examples of these practices:

- Teams ask the product owner for validation criteria as they discuss each user story during iteration planning.
- When a developer takes ownership of a work assignment from the task board, he or she must write out the tests that will be applied to the software module before programming begins.
- When the coder has completed his programming, he must ask a peer to validate the module according to the previously written tests before he can place the task card in the *Ready to Demo* column of the task board.
- At the end of the iteration, the current application is assembled and loaded with data, and the product owner performs a test drive through the information, determining whether or not she can perform the user stories that defined the sprint just completed.
- Afterward, the product owner may well take a few days to carefully validate the data in the warehouse and even reconcile it back to the source systems.
- At the retrospective, the team discusses policies and practices that did not work so well during the sprint. Often, these challenges include testing practices so that the agile team is constantly improving its approach to QA.

Extending Test-Led Development Far Above Unit Testing

One agile practice in particular serves as the backbone of the QA approach advocated here. Scrum already incorporates *test-led development* in the development method, as hinted at previously. Agile EDW teams take this practice of planning the test before creating an object to a much higher level—to the point where it sets the tone and shapes the QA efforts for the project as a whole.

Test-led development is a well-defined staple for the programming activities of agile teams, even those using a method other than Scrum. Figure 16.4 enumerates the five steps that programmers follow when utilizing this practice. In essence, before coding a module, the developer must write the tests that the module should pass when it is programmed correctly. He or she then executes the test harness to prove that the test will fail without the planned programming. By writing the test before coding, the programmer must think through the requirements and design

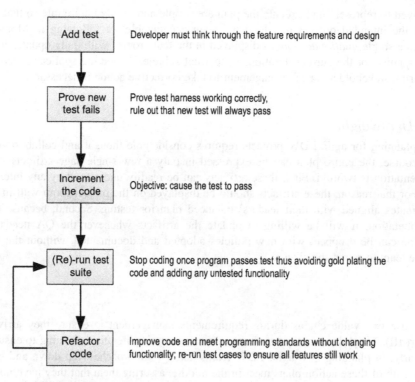

FIGURE 16.4 Steps in the test-led development approach.

guidance his or her team leaders provided. This second look is a major reason why agile teams build applications with far higher quality than their waterfall counterparts—they double think each module's requirements and design.

When the programmer begins development, he re-executes the test harness as needed until the module passes the tests, at which point he ceases adding new features. This policy prevents him from "gold plating" the code—that is, investing any more into a module than what is required to make it work. It also prevents him from adding additional features that are not addressed by the tests, allowing the agile team to maintain near 100% test coverage (the proportion of source code or features validated by the current test suite).

After the module passes the tests, the programmer cannot add new features, but he can "refactor" the code—that is, improve its quality without changing its behavior. Refactoring allows the developers to ensure that the module's algorithms are optimal and that the source code complies with the team's coding and naming standards. Each time a programmer refactors the code, however, he must re-execute the test suite in order to ensure that all the features still work.

This definition of test-led development that we receive from the agile community is a power technique, but it is limited in its original definition to only the realm of application units and components. Agile EDW teams elevate test-led development to where it bolsters a team's approach to the higher-level aspects of the software engineering process. They plan out QA in advance for integration, system, and user acceptance testing, anticipating that a second look at requirements and design will allow everyone to improve the definition of the project. In fact, agile EDW team leads strive to envision testing at the highest levels by asking themselves which tests the stakeholders and project sponsors will need to see before they believe that the money and effort invested in the project have achieved something valuable for the company. This write-the-test-first approach will be clearly visible in the next section, which describes how teams determine the types of tests they wish to execute.

"WHAT TO TEST?" ANSWERED WITH TOP-DOWN PLANNING

Armed now with the motivations for an aggressive and balanced testing program and the factors that will keep that effort agile, the EDW team leaders must start the difficult work of choosing the types of tests to place in their QA plan. Agile EDW teams make this selection working from two directions—top-down and bottom-up. Team leaders should iterate between these two approaches until they have drafted a coherent set of tests. Ultimately, we will assess whether the resulting plan is coherent by considering whether a single set of reporting categories allows a stakeholder to drill down from the top-level QA metrics all the way to the bottom, demonstrating that there are no gaps in the middle. The top-down process for selecting test types proceeds in three steps:

- Understanding six fundamental dimensions of testing
- Selecting from the universe of all possible test types the best set that the project can afford to implement
- Organizing those selected types in a two-by-two matrix in order to assess the plan's balance

The Six Dimensions of DW/BI Testing

Often, EDW team leaders first realize the enormity of the planning effort that QA requires when they consider just how many types of tests exist. Table 16.1 provides a list of the more common test types that I have encountered during my 30 years in DW/BI, although I seem to hear of yet another test type nearly every time I teach a QA class. The impact of this number becomes very clear when we use it to estimate how many actual *tests* a team will need to define if it plans to execute every *test type* on every module in an EDW. Table 16.2 calculates the size of the permutations involved for just the data integration portion of a medium-sized enterprise data warehouse with a dozen subject areas. This calculation assumes conservatively that each subject area workflow averages only a dozen data transforms, which in turn are validated using the few dozen test types listed in Table 16.1. Taking the product of these factors reveals that an EDW team would have to implement more than 24,000 test packages in order to exhaustively quality assure this medium-sized data warehouse.

Unfortunately, little can be done about the number of items in the first three components of this calculation because they are all a function of the application's design scope. The only degree of freedom that team leaders have here is to reduce the number of test types included in the quality plan so that the proposed level of testing remains feasible. Fortunately, they can whittle down the list of required test types by first realizing that the test types listed involve a considerable degree of overlap. Some of them describe a testing style or an intent rather than the actual type of assertion that a validation step will make. Moreover, one can define assertions that belong to several of these test types at once, so it should be possible to pick a subset from this list that actually addresses a large number of types at once. In order to pick the best subset, then, we need to understand the multiple *dimensions* of testing at work in Table 16.1. Six dimensions of

TABLE 16.1 Partial List of Tests Types for EDW Teams to Choose From

ID	Test Name	Dimension						Added by Agile
		System	Polarity	Time Frame	Planning	Functional	P.O.V	
1	Alpha test				Assurance		Validate	
2	Basis path test				Control			
3	Beta test				Assurance		Validate	
4	Black box test						Validate	
5	Code walkthrough				Control		Verify	
6	Component test	✓			Control			
7	Corner test				Management	Func.	Verify	
8	Domain test				Control	Func.	Validate	
9	End-to-end test	✓			Management		Validate	
10	Epic test				Management		Validate	✓
11	Exploratory test						Validate	
12	Gray box text					Func.		
13	GUI test					Func.	Validate	
14	Installation test				Assurance	Non-Func.		
15	Integration test	✓			Assurance			
16	Knock-out tests				Assurance			
17	Load test				Assurance	Non-Func.	Validate	
18	Statistical moment test				Control	Func.	Validate	
19	Monkey test					Func.	Validate	
20	Negative test		✓					
21	Performance test				Assurance	Non-Func.	Validate	
22	Positive test		✓					
23	Progression test			✓				
24	Recovery test				Assurance	Non-Func.		
25	Referential integrity test				Assurance	Func.	Validate	
26	Regression test			✓				
27	Sanity test				Assurance	Func.	Validate	
28	Scenario test						Validate	
29	Security test				Management		Validate	
30	Session-based test						Validate	
31	Smoke test				Assurance	Non-Func.		
32	Soak test				Assurance	Func.	Validate	
33	Soap opera test				Assurance	Func.	Validate	
34	Story test				Assurance		Validate	✓
35	Stress test					Non-Func.	Validate	
36	System test	✓			Management			
37	Theme test				Assurance		Validate	✓
38	Unit test	✓			Control			
39	Usability test					Func.	Validate	
40	User acceptance test				Management	Func.	Validate	
41	Variance test				Control	Func.	Validate	
42	White box test						Verify	

TABLE 16.2 Number of Test Packages Needed to Test Everything in Every Way for a Medium-Sized Data Warehouse

Estimating Factor	Items Per Factor	Cumulative Number
Subject Areas	12	12
Architectural Layers	4	48
Data Transforms	12	576
Test Types	42	24,192

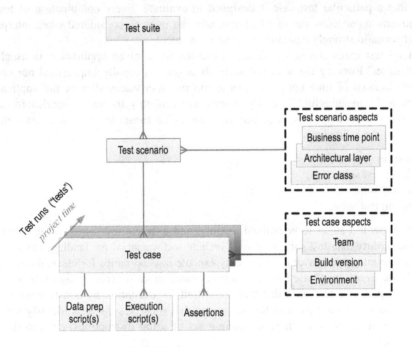

FIGURE 16.5   Relationships between test terms as used in this book.

testing can be found among the universe of test types offered previously: planning, system, functional, polarity, time frame, and perspective. Before we can discuss them effectively, however, we have to better define our terms.

Preliminary Definitions

We need a stronger definition of the noun "test" in order to adequately explain the dimensions of quality mentioned above. Unfortunately, this word is overloaded by the DW/BI profession. It can refer to something as simple as an observation of a single output value or something as large as a month-long run validation of an entire EDW involving thousands of assertions. The word *test* also qualifies a plethora of other terms, including test case, test script, test run, and test suite. Frequently, this mass of terminology leads to tremendous confusion during the planning and execution of a quality plan. EDW team leaders will need to be clear about how they use these terms if they are to avoid confusion in their test plans.

To bring clarity to these chapters on quality planning, Figure 16.5 outlines how I use these terms, with crow-feet connectors showing how atomic terms pack into larger notions. At the bottom are listed three crucial components in any EDW validation activity:

- The preparation one must take before she can run a test
- The call she will make to execute the necessary ETL or BI module
- The assertions she will make regarding the results

An "assertion" is a single statement that resolves to either true or false, an outcome that is typically interpreted as a "pass" or a "fail." Assertions come in many flavors, from simple ones such as "the target column contains no null values" to complex notions such as "the sum of the dollar values just added to Column X in either the target table or the suspense table must match the sum of the values taken from the source table's Column Y."

Because a single assertion frequently means very little by itself, validating even the smallest object within an application often requires packaging several assertions together into a "test case." When it comes to validating EDW data integration work, a test case typically marshals together the three components listed previously. By altering either the preparation or the ETL call, a tester can reuse the remaining test case components, including the assertions, under a variety of different contexts. These contexts can be understood as a combination of several "test aspects." Test aspects are characteristics that testers can use to identify important subsets among the test cases and the resources they require. For an EDW project, the test aspects can include the particular architectural layer, business time point, and type of error such as "dirty data" that a particular test case is designed to evaluate. Every combination of test aspects defines the "test scenario" that governs a particular run of a test case and that must be considered when interpreting its results. The aspects defining a test scenario strongly describe the scenario's intent.

The collection of all test cases run under all test scenarios for a given application is usually referred to as the application "total test suite." Running the total test suite all at once is usually impractical not only because it usually requires a considerable amount of time but also because too many characteristics of the application get evaluated at once to allow the run to be meaningful. Typically, teams will run only the test scenarios for a given set of values assigned to a couple of test aspects. Teams frequently refer to such a subset as "test suite" as well, but they can give it a qualifying name such as the following:

- The dirty-data test suite
- The presentation-layer test suite
- The end-of-quarter test suite
- The system-integration test suite

The testing aspects allow test suites to be defined flexibly, and different test suites end up sharing many of the same test cases. For example, a dirty-data test suite may well include test scenarios for landing, integration, and presentation-layer modules, whereas the integration-layer test suite may execute tests scenarios for clean, dirty, and missing data sets.

In this framework, the word "test" used in isolation becomes more precise. It signifies a particular run of a test case, usually invoked as part of a test suite that was identified for execution by constraining some or all of the test aspects for the component test scenarios. The test scenarios that those test aspects identify will generally cause the test cases within the chosen test suite to share a coherent set of setup instructions, calls to the ETL, and assertions applied to the resulting data.

With these terms clarified, the six dimensions of testing will be easier to describe. Note that an EDW team will probably use each of these dimensions as a test aspect and employ them frequently to define the test scenarios that should run together in a test suite.

Dimension 1: Planning

An EDW team must plan its software validation efforts to address three distinct realms: quality control, quality assurance, and quality management. These three realms differ in the degree of direct hands-on activity or control that the team has on the objects being tested. Each realm requires a different approach and often very different types of tests.

Figure 16.6 illustrates how these three concepts nest within each other. Starting with the inner realm, a team's work directly touches the object needing validation. A vast number of those objects are the modules programmed during an iteration. The programmers must demonstrate that they now meet their intended purpose. Because the developers are actively hands-on and can control the modules they are validating, we call this testing work "quality control."

Moving outwards, the team must also validate the overall application that will contain the new or altered modules the team has just finished touching. The project stakeholders want to be assured that the overall application will meet requirements, not just the few modules that were just altered. When developers provide this kind of assurance by assessing an entire application regardless of what components they have changed, they are performing "quality assurance."

At the highest level, the developers must validate that the new version of their application will behave properly when combined with other applications and technologies in the company's computer operations center. This level of

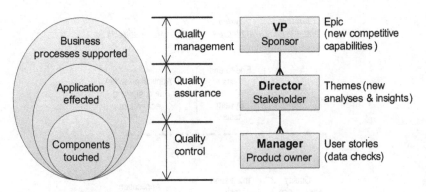

FIGURE 16.6 The difference between QC, QA, and QM.

validation may well require collaborating with IT teams over which the developers have no direct control. Often, these external teams own the source systems for a data warehouse, the downstream data marts, or the processing and data communications resources the warehouse relies on. The EDW teammates can only manage their collaboration with the parties that own these resources, so when they validate that their new application properly supports the overall business process, we call this work "quality management."

Although quality control, assurance, and management are separate concepts, it is cumbersome to continually distinguish between them. IT professionals often refer to them collectively as *quality assurance* (QA), although this term can be used more precisely, as described previously. In general, I use the broader definition when I refer to quality assurance, but will be careful to invoke the more narrow definition when it is necessary to distinguish it from quality control and quality management.

EDW teams naturally favor quality control over the other two realms because the tighter scope of that work makes it something that can be addressed directly with less effort. However, the team leaders should explicitly budget some of their quality efforts to address the other two realms. I once consulted with a firm at which the vice president of sales wanted the director of data warehousing replaced because the company's premier information product had a data latency of 30 seconds or more. When showing off the service to prospective customers, the sales representatives would push the "submit" button on the web page and then wait more than half a minute for a simple query to complete. The DW/BI director insisted that the warehouse was working fine because the developers could demonstrate subsecond response times when measured at corporate headquarters. When I pointed out that the data latency was upsetting the sales reps in the field, he answered simply "that means its Networking's problem." It was true that the networking group actually owned the products causing the data latency, but it was the total data warehousing system as viewed from the field that the vice president of sales was considering. By dismissing a quality problem caused by a team outside the DW/BI project room, the data warehousing team was pursuing only quality assurance and ignoring quality management, even though quality assurance concerns were about to get their director fired. The lesson here is that a balanced EDW quality plan may focus most of the team's effort on quality control and quality assurance but should still allocate some time to quality management as well.

Dimension 2: System

The system dimension pertains to the scope of the object a team is planning to test within the technical architecture— that is, whether the team is validating a part of a system, the whole system, or the overall ecosystem in which a new application will function. The traditional test-type choices from this dimension are unit, component, integration, system, and end-to-end. Many development teams actively plan to test only a couple of these levels. Because the levels in this dimension that get overlooked have a nasty habit of blindsiding the developers with grievously embarrassing defects, the more successful teams have learned to include at least a few tests for each of these layers.

Figure 16.7 illustrates how the various levels of the system dimension stack together and also how they link to the planning dimension described previously. Starting at the bottom, a "unit test case" provides the definition for tests that validate an application unit. A program unit is usually the smallest, independently executable object. It is also the most numerous item type that is independently managed using the project's source control utility. For procedural languages such as SQL scripting, the unit is typically contained in a single source code file. For ETL packages, the unit is usually a mapping, which is the smallest independently executable item displayed in the programming tool's object tree.

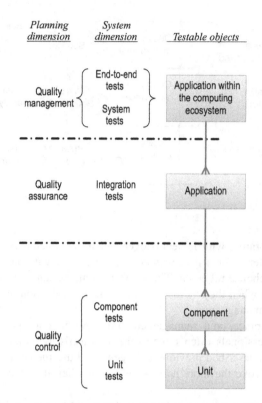

FIGURE 16.7 Relationships between two testing dimensions and physical objects.

Some programming tools make units slightly more difficult to distinguish. When working with a BI tool, for example, a single disk file housed in the source control utility can contain dozens of menus, scores of reports, and hundreds of display objects. In situations such as these, teams will need to take a moment to explicitly define what they mean by the word *unit* so that they can then define unit tests. These discussions will be easier if the team keeps in mind that each version of a unit is usually the work of a single programmer.

A "component test case" defines the context for tests that validate an application component. Components are assemblies of two or more units that still have a narrow functional purpose, such as "load source data into the customer tables of the landing area." For ETL packages, the components include many mappings and are often called "workflows" or "sequences." Components can include modules created by different developers, and determining whether these programmers communicated effectively while independently programming their separate modules is often a major objective of a component test.

As shown in Figure 16.7, many components assemble into an *application*. DW/BI applications provide many-faceted data services and usually provide the focus for an entire project. Validating applications requires "integration test cases" during which developers confirm that the many new and existing components that make up the product can be assembled together. Integration test cases also prove that any new or updated components interact as expected with any components that have not been touched during the current work effort. Like components, applications involve the work of many developers, so confirming that the proper "handshakes" occur between the components when the application executes is a major objective of the integration test. Because faulty handshakes of core components can cripple an entire application, agile teams run integration tests of the product's current build frequently rather than waiting to validate just the final build before a subrelease.

"System test cases" are similar to integration tests in that they execute the entire application. However, instead of confirming that the components within the application interact as expected, system tests validate interactions occurring outside the application. These tests confirm that the application behaves well enough when run as a system within the company's larger computational ecosystem.

The immediate audience of the system test is the operations team—the IT professionals who must keep the application running once it enters production usage. Their primary question will be whether the new build of the application will make their lives a living nightmare as they strive to coax it and a hundred other applications to share the same information resources. They will want to know that the application can successfully repeat its integration test cases once it has been installed in a test platform in the machine room. More importantly, however, they will want to see that the application responds elegantly to common system-level challenges. To prove this, they will ask the development team to validate a subrelease candidate using a variety of "knockout tests." These tests should demonstrate that an application can recover from events serious enough to knock it out. Their questions here will be similar to the following:

- What does the application do when it runs out of disk space for its target tables?
- What happens if the FTP node feeding it source data fails?
- If the application crashes and we re-feed it the same data set when it restarts, will it duplicate the information it contains?
- If a particular data load goes horribly wrong, how easy is it to roll the warehouse back to a known time point and re-run the ETL?

Finally, "end-to-end tests" involve the widest scope. Rather than focusing on the subrelease candidate for a given application, end-to-end tests validate that data flows successfully across the entire computing ecosystem in which the new application build will participate. In a DW/BI end-to-end test, someone typically updates information in the warehouse's source systems, and the validation team searches for the expected changes in the data delivered to the end users' reports and dashboards. Especially in companies with complex cloud or ERP applications serving as sources, end-to-end tests can be extremely expensive to conduct. Therefore, DW/BI teams typically include this type of test sparingly in the quality plans for their projects.

We can relate the notions from the planning dimension to those in the system dimension, as illustrated in Figure 16.7. Unit and component tests address modules that the team has modified, so they fall into the realm of quality control. Integration tests validate that the requested functionality can be gained from the entire application, including portions not recently touched by the development team, and therefore they lie in the realm of quality assurance. System and end-to-end testing will involve many applications, not just the one that the EDW team owns. Because it involves working with people beyond the immediate control of the EDW team leaders, these tests will require quality management.

Dimension 3: Functional

Aside from planning realms and system levels, individual tests can focus on either the actions the DW/BI application can take or the more abstract qualities of a system that determine the end users' overall experience and the system's total cost of ownership. The functional dimension speaks to this dichotomy by distinguishing between *functional* and *nonfunctional* tests.

Functional tests validate the application behavior that business stakeholders expect to find in the end product, both its end user interface and the data it contains. For DW/BI, functional tests touch a wide domain of objects, including:

- The source systems from which the data warehouse should pull data
- Whether the derived columns have been calculated properly
- The choices in the pull-down menus found in the front end's query definition screens
- The layout of reports and dashboard widgets
- The information revealed when end users drill down from an aggregate display

Nonfunctional tests validate the remaining characteristics of the application. Chapter 7 presented many of these characteristics, such as security, recoverability, and data latency. Nonfunctional requirements such as manageability, scalability, and extensibility can greatly impact the application's total cost of ownership—that is, how much the business will need to continue investing in the data warehouse long after its initial version has gone into production. Although nonfunctional requirements do not affect the prompts and results end users see on the front-end screens, they still greatly impact the business community's overall satisfaction with the end product. That overall impression may take weeks or months to materialize, but EDW leaders will still want to test for quality in the nonfunctional dimension so that they can be assured that the project is considered a success over the long term.

Dimension 4: Polarity

With the polarity dimension, quality planners distinguish between *positive* and *negative* testing. For both these test types, the team establishes some starting conditions and invokes the application. For positive tests, the team searches for specific responses from the application. For negative tests, the team confirms that nothing happened, or at least nothing undesired. In other words, negative tests prove that the application can respond elegantly to adverse conditions, such as data values and other parameters that are outside an expected range.

The polarity dimension is important for EDW team leaders to manage because most developers naturally gravitate toward positive tests. Positive tests are easier to imagine because one result is directly implied by starting conditions. For example, if the product owner stated that the warehouse should integrate work orders from the California offices with the existing Western Region sales orders, most developers can think of what to look for in the target tables to confirm that a proper linkage between sales and work orders has taken place. On the other hand, if the product owner said, "Don't close sales orders that have missing work orders," the developers must think deeper into the application's design, asking questions such as the following:

- How do I know what work orders are missing?
- If a work order does not exist, how do I find the sales order that should have linked to it?
- I know we should not close a sales order that is a missing work, but what other possible changes to the sales order should we make once we realize that the downstream events are incomplete?

The possibilities for such questions can seem endless to a developer who just wants to prove that he finished coding an ETL module, so many programmers find negative tests annoying in principle and tend to give them less attention than they deserve. However, because many exception cases typically exist for every positive specification, negative tests should actually outnumber positive tests in a well-conceived QA plan. To keep the investment in negative testing within reason for the unit and component levels, many teams adopt a rule of thumb such as two negative assertions for every positive validation in a unit test case unless circumstances clearly call for more. With regard to system testing, the knockout tests that the operations team expects frequently focus on whether the wrong starting condition will make the application malfunction, so system tests may well be predominantly negative testing.

Dimension 5: Time Frame

The time frame dimension addresses whether a test is looking forward or backward in time. For agile EDW, the number of new features added to an application during an iteration usually pales in comparison to the number of features that already exist. For an agile team adding 50 story points of new capability to an application with every iteration, by the time it delivers upon Sprint 10, the current build will consist of 450 story points of pre-existing features. *Progression testing* validates the new features just added—that is, those that the next version of the application should highlight. *Regression testing* demonstrates that, given the recent programming, the features added during the past iterations still work, despite the new programming.

EDW team leaders need to strive for the right mix of tests along the time frame dimension as vigorously as those in the polarity dimension. Like positive assertions, progression tests are easy for developers to imagine because they pertain to the features they are currently programming. In contrast, regression tests dwell on work that has already been completed and seems to have no new value to contribute now. On fast-moving projects, developers can find it difficult to accurately recall much about what they built in the past, even the previous iteration. If the quality plan does not balance difficult-to-author regression tests against the easier progression validations, the QA plan may miss the fact that new programming just undermined the 10 most important features in the subrelease candidate currently taking shape and the 20 most crucial capabilities of the version that is currently in production. Fortunately, teams that implement test automation find it very easy to maintain a robust regression test suite, a topic discussed in Chapter 18, which explores *how* to execute the planned test cases.

Dimension 6: Point-of-View

The point-of-view dimension considers whether the test cases were written standing outside the system or looking from within. If one writes a test from an outside point of view, one cannot see the code within a module. The system is an opaque "black box" and can only be judged by its externally observable behavior and how that changes with different starting conditions. If one could see inside the application, the system would be a "glass box." A tester could consider how to cause a module to malfunction by considering the algorithms employed and thus author a very different set of test cases.

Another closely related distinction involving one's point of view is that between validation and verification. When looking within the application and considering a module's actual programming, notions such as adherence to coding

TABLE 16.3 Validation Compared to Verification

Validation	Verification
Viewed externally	Viewed internally
Black box testing	Glass (white) box testing
Built the right thing	Built it the right way
Complete	Correct
Functional requirements	Technical requirements
Nonfunctional requirements	Coding standards

standards and the strength of the algorithms can be judged. Testers usually call such an examination of internals "verification" because the reviewer verifies that the application was written in "the right way."

Conversely, black box tests can only consider externally visible system behavior. They are limited to assessing whether or not the team has built "the right thing"—that is, whether the application is complete in its features. When speaking precisely, testers will call such a black box assessment of behavior a "validation." Because verification involves reading through an applications code, it is painstaking work and highly manual, so the bulk of the quality assessments on an EDW project will be validations, which are easier to accomplish. Because verification can represent a small portion of the overall quality effort, people often use the term *validation* to include tests from both points of view, so one has to be careful sometimes in conversations to ask what exact sense of the word is being employed.

Table 16.3 compares validation to verification and adds a few new terms to the mix. When the team validates an application from a black box perspective, it is asking, "Is the application complete?"—that is, are all the features we expected working? When an ETL technical lead evaluates newly coded modules from a glass box perspective, he or she is asking, "Is the coding of the application *correct*?"—that is, did the programmer build it according to standards and specs? Because they judge quality based on behavior, functional and many nonfunctional requirements fall within the category of validation tests. Verification tests often appear as part of code walkthroughs and tend to concern themselves with design and coding patterns in addition to technical requirements such as data precision and metadata management.

A 2 × 2 PLANNING MATRIX FOR TOP-DOWN TEST SELECTION

At a minimum, EDW project leaders can employ the categories described previously to ensure their quality plan incorporates at least some testing from both poles of each of the six dimensions. Unfortunately, some of those dimensions will require more planning than simply adding some tests from both ends of the spectrum for each test type. As Table 16.1 reveals, just the quality assurance and validation dimensions alone involve so many test types that this strategy will yield a QA plan larger than most EDW teams can afford to execute. To assist team leaders in planning quality with greater selectivity, the agile community has devised a useful two-by-two matrix for visualizing and evaluating the balance of a given test plan. Not only will this matrix assist in a top-down selection of test types but also it will allow a team to tie its QA plan back to the enterprise requirements management framework presented in Chapter 8. Moreover, we employ this matrix to record the decisions regarding the remaining interrogatives that QA plans must answer, namely *who, when, where,* and *how.*

A Framework for Assessing a QA Plan's Coverage

Figure 16.8 provides an example of the agile 2 × 2 QA planning matrix filled out for a typical EDW team. Here, the team decided it had the funds and time to pursue only 14 of the more than 40 test types listed in Table 16.1. By reflecting on the distribution of those tests on the 2 × 2 matrix, the team can judge whether it has planned on the correct blend of quality assessments for its project.

The notions defining the rows and columns of this 2 × 2 matrix originated with Brian Marick, one of the original signatories of the agile manifesto [Marick 2003]. The matrix itself was further refined and popularized by Lisa Crispin and Janet Gregory in their book *Agile Testing.* The rows of this matrix distinguish between tests that are business or technology facing. Business-facing tests can be understood by nontechnical stakeholders and speak to the capabilities

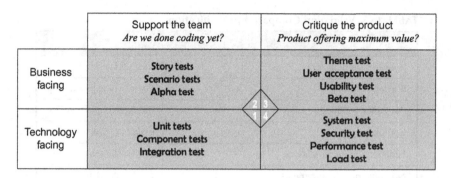

	Support the team *Are we done coding yet?*	Critique the product *Product offering maximum value?*
Business facing	Story tests Scenario tests Alpha test	Theme test User acceptance test Usability test Beta test
Technology facing	Unit tests Component tests Integration test	System test Security test Performance test Load test

FIGURE 16.8   Using the agile 2 × 2 QA planning matrix to visualize a team's choice of test types.

they wish to find in the application when they receive it. Technology-facing tests address concerns that the developers or other IT stakeholders may have about a module or a system and are expressed in programming terms and jargon [Crispin & Gregory 2009, p. 5].

With rows defined in those terms, this matrix suggests that a quality plan should have a reasonable mix between test types that speak to business and technical concerns. If the plan contained only technology-facing tests, the development team would obtain a good understanding of the system it has built, but business customers will have seen nothing reassuring them that the application is complete. Conversely, if all the test types in a plan speak to business stakeholder concerns, the customers might well be eager for the system to go online, but the development team will be left with grave doubts whether the application will be sustainable once placed into production. Business users have to approve of the development completed and developers have to know the application is sound, so a balance between the rows of this matrix is absolutely necessary.

The columns of this matrix distinguish between tests that support the team and those that critique the product. Tests that support the team inform the developers whether they have completed the coding they committed to deliver. Tests that critique the product demonstrate that the end users will receive compelling value from the application once it goes online. The column on the right can be viewed in terms of the epic stack, interpreting it to mean "What epics, themes, and user stories does this product fulfill and what additional user requirements need to be captured on a story card?"

Again, a development team wants to balance between the choices represented by these two columns. If all the test types focused on assessing whether the project's coding tasks have been completed, the team might well deliver an application that embodies what the product owner requested but is nowhere near what the business actually needs. Conversely, if all the test types focused on the value of the application, the programmers would be unable to declare their programming tasks "done," and no one would be able to state when the project was finished.

I have found that the fastest path to a good QA plan is to ask my teams to pick a dozen or so test types from Table 16.1 and place them on these quadrants. Frequently, the first collection of tests land mostly in Quadrant 1, technology-facing tests that will indicate when the development is complete. This initial distribution is predictable because programmers outnumber the other roles on the team. They are technical professionals and have anxiety over whether they have time enough to code all the modules that a project as large as an EDW will require. Quadrant 1 testing addresses that anxiety.

The product owner, who is facing budget and time constraints of his own, will quickly step in and insist on some tests that he and his stakeholders will be able to understand. The team then removes a few test types from Quadrant 1 and adds others that clearly belong to Quadrant 2.

At this point, the EDW team leaders need to ask the product owner a few questions, such as "How will you know whether . . ."

- the application is what your stakeholders require rather than just what you alone have asked for?
- the staff members who will use the application will be able to effectively operate the user interface?
- the company's directors will be able to properly interpret what this system's BI analyses are showing them?

These questions query whether the application will generate enough value for the development investment it will require, and they should lead the product owners to see the need for test types rooted in Quadrant 3.

Finally, the EDW project leaders need to ask their teammates how they will know that the application will meet the many nonfunctional requirements, such as performance, recoverability, and security. These characteristics will contribute importantly to whether the organization widely adopts the system and can maintain it over the long term. So that the quality plan will provide this type of insight as well, the EDW team will need to trim a few of the planned tests and replace them with test types appropriate for Quadrant 4.

Of course, the initial allocation of only a dozen tests at the start of this group exercise was arbitrary. The team is free to increase that limit, but the project architect needs to remind everyone that each additional test type added to the matrix will cost money and delay the delivery of the application. If a team begins adding tests without any concern for cost, I usually have its members take a moment to update the *definition of done* cards for the various module types that will make up the EDW. If they add tasks for completing the proposed level of testing and estimate the labor hours that those tasks will generally require, they will be able to quantify the impact of an overly ambitious quality plan for themselves. Once the teammates see the additional work that each test type creates for them, they usually find the motivation they need to trim back on the goals documented by the 2×2 top-down planning grid.

Linking Test Planning to Requirements and Risk Management

Quality is the flip side of requirements. When the product owner requests a feature, his team needs to not only build that feature but also validate that the feature answers the end users' needs in a dependable way. Quality is also risk mitigation under a different name. When team leaders identify an adverse event that could undermine the project, they should author a test case to demonstrate that the adverse event has not yet occurred. With those connections in mind, EDW teams can align their top-down QA planning matrices with the requirements management and risk management work described previously in this book.

Starting with requirements management, the reader may recall from Part III that agile EDW teams derive an overall project definition via two intersecting efforts:

- A generic agile value chain in which the product owner authors epics, themes, and user stories for the project
- An enterprise-capable value chain in which the team leaders ask the sponsors and directors of the company to briefly articulate the business challenges that they require the data warehouse to solve

We saw that if the project sponsor, directors, and product owners share a coherent concept for the data warehouse project, then not only will the epic and theme stories derived from these two value chains match but also every user story will trace back to a theme and every theme to an epic. Once the team has an initial draft of a 2×2 top-down QA planning matrix, the project architect should ask her teammates to double-check that it contains test types that support both the requirements value chains.

In the framework developed in Part III, the sponsor's epics describe new competitive capabilities that management wants the company to achieve. Because those capabilities may take a long time to visibly impact the business, the team will typically ask about leading indicators that will demonstrate that those business outcomes are taking shape. By including those leading indicators in the EDW's design, the team is in effect adding a test for whether the new business capabilities are being achieved. That is test-led development applied at the epic level.

Assessing these leading indicators may require business inquiries rather than data analysis, so the team has to be flexible in the modes it considers for running a test. For example, an EDW team may believe at first that all its testing will require examination of data but then realize that testing the sponsor's epic may require speaking to sales agents to find out if they believe that the call lists and prospective customer backgrounds provided by the data warehouse make their prospecting work more effective. Similarly, directors were interviewed for themes, which focused on the analyses necessary to change the behavior of the company's business staff. Accordingly, the EDW project's "theme tests" may have to be interviews focusing on departmental effectiveness rather than an SQL query against the presentation layer tables.

With regard to testing whether the EDW team has fulfilled the requirements of stakeholders above the product owner, the team leaders will need to think outside the data warehouse and use nontechnical assessments where necessary. If these crucial tests are overlooked by the plan, epics and themes will not be validated, and the sponsor and directors will not receive the feedback they need to believe the EDW project is addressing their requirements. These powerful executives could easily decide the company is not getting the value it needs from the DW/BI project and cancel it simply due to lack of information.

Testing epics and themes is truly challenging. Quality assessments become easier as we move down the epic stack to user and developer stories. User stories can be validated easily using story tests during the product demo for each iteration. Developer stories can be validated using unit, component, and integration testing.

Turning now to risk mitigation, Part II of this book suggested that the team needs to watch for possible errors in the concepts controlling the definition and design of the project. When teams first fill out the top-down quality planning matrix, the developers usually select multiple test types in Quadrants 1 and 2 that will reveal errors in the bottom layer depicted in Figure 6.3, application coding concepts. During quality planning, team leaders need to also ask about the next two layers if they remain unaddressed. Does the plan include test types that will expose solution-concept errors—for example, gaps in features that leave crucial stakeholders' needs unaddressed? Similarly, does the plan stipulate testing that will reveal errors in the business concept behind the project? A small portion of the QA budget needs to be allocated to seeking out reasons why end users might not utilize the application once it is delivered or why the information provided will cause directors to make the wrong decisions.

Quality revolves around "fit to purpose." Both fit and purpose for business intelligence applications are often very abstract or nuanced, so the quality assurance plan cannot consist entirely of tests that demonstrate simply that the data is correct. It must also include elements that speak to these less tangible aspects that will determine how extensive users will work with the end product and the business value they will receive from that interaction.

"WHAT TO TEST?" ANSWERED BOTTOM-UP

The 2×2 matrix previously employed approaches the challenge of EDW quality assurance from the team leader's point of view. The top-down plan it produces will surely contain unit and component testing—elements that must be translated into detailed guidance for developers. In very much the same way that they employ two viewpoints during requirements management and iteration planning, agile EDW team leaders examine QA from a second, bottom-up perspective, determining if the resulting action plan connects well with the top-down action plan provided by the 2×2 matrix.

The bottom-up approach we employ has several appealing features, namely:

- It draws upon techniques specific to data warehousing.
- It augments those techniques with several practices from traditional software testing.
- It organizes the results into an easy-to-follow matrix that developers can use as they build out each module.
- It identifies a set of reusable test widgets that the team can create to dramatically reduce their test coding time.

This section presents each of these elements in turn.

Data Warehousing Testing Techniques

Much of bottom-up quality planning revolves around test techniques that help testers author test cases. In their excellent book on testing applications at Microsoft, Alan Page et al. define a *test technique* as a systematic procedure that simply provides one approach to solve one type of complex problem, often relying on well-established heuristics [Page et al. 2009, p. 78]. Although many people criticize test techniques as gimmicks, my experience in DW/BI has shown me that EDW teams that adopt a dozen or so standard test techniques generate far more test cases in a shorter time with much less effort than teams that attempt to author test cases from scratch each time they build an application module. Moreover, teams that employ test techniques such as the ones presented here take a consistent approach to test case generation. As a result, they arrive at test suites that are far less likely to suffer from any serious gaps, especially on agile projects in which they can steadily tune their initial set of techniques until they provide the correct coverage for the given project.

Of course, team leaders need to watch that the developers do not over-rely on test techniques to the point that they stop thinking about the code they are writing. Test techniques seem to contribute well to the writing of the easiest 80% of the tests the average module requires. Accelerating that first 80% frees up the developers' energy and imagination for the remaining 20%. That last 20% will still require a solid understanding of requirements and design, in addition to much hard thinking. EDW team leaders should watch the development work during each iteration to ensure that the necessary hard thinking is taking place.

The following list of techniques is not intended to amaze anyone, because none of the ones shown are particularly insightful. Employ them all together, however, and EDW project leaders will find that they produce a good starting collection of unit tests for the agile EDW development team. The list will come in handy for team leaders particularly when they begin working with a developer or tester who does not seem to know where to start with unit testing DW/BI modules. By requesting such a tester to simply "go write one test case using each technique on this list and for every layer of the reference architecture," team leaders can get their new assistant oriented and writing tests right away.

The first set of test techniques that everyone on the team should be familiar with are listed in Table 16.4 and are simple. The remaining DW/BI-oriented test techniques require more explanation.

TABLE 16.4 Simple Tests for a Given Data Warehouse Table

Test Technique	Assertion Made
Unique values	A particular column is free of repeated values.
Valid range	The values in a particular field all fall between an acceptable minimum and maximum.
Count distinct	The number of elements within the set of distinct values for a column is as expected—for example, it matches the same type of count found in the source data set.
Group counts	When grouped by an expression, the counts of column values within each group are as expected—for example, they match the same counts by group made upon the source data set. Example: Ensure that the numbers of customers for both a source extract and records just added to the target system are distributed identically when grouped by first letter of the last name.
Sums, averages, medians	The calculation made upon the column values is as expected—for example, it matches the same calculation made against the source data set. Sums and averages require numeric or date fields. Medians work with text data.
"Diffs"	Especially for landing extract files, the team can output the loaded data to a text file and use Unix *diff* commands to ensure input and output are identical.

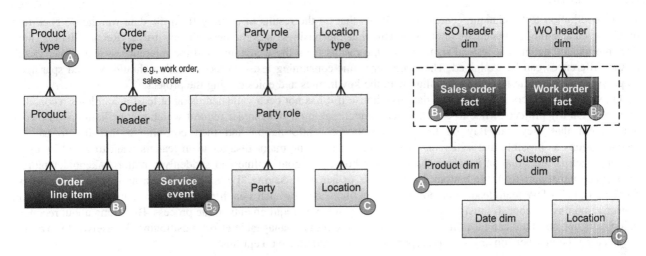

FIGURE 16.9 "Data corners" test technique for models in standard normal form and conformed dimensional form.

Referential Integrity Test

A referential integrity test asserts that all the foreign keys in a given column link to a correct record in the parent table. Such a test will be moot for a target database that has referential integrity constraints in effect because the database engine will ensure that this assertion is true each time it loads a record into the data warehouse. Many teams turn off referential integrity constraints, however, so that the data will load more quickly. They trust the logic of the data transform modules to achieve referential integrity. Any time the team designs ETL to implement an important business rule, it is wise to test that it has been implemented correctly. If referential integrity constraints in the database are turned off, then the project's QA effort should plan on explicitly testing that the foreign keys resolve without error.

Data Corners

A data corner test or "corner test" is a more advanced version of a referential integrity test. It tests that all the joins needed to traverse from one corner of the data model to the other are working properly. Figure 16.9 shows the integration layer schema and dimensional schemas that a particular EDW team plans to load from a set of operational sources. By querying the transactions in the source data, the team is able to create a count of sales by product types and postal codes. Once the data warehouse has been loaded, the team should be able to re-create that list using both the integration layer and the presentation layer. In other words, the team should be able to join the target tables of both layers from one corner of the model to the other and retrieve the same results despite all the joins these queries must make across the tables in the middle.

For the integration layer, shown on the left side of Figure 16.9, the team should be able to retrieve the expected results with a query that goes from Corner A (product type) to Corner C (location). This query will have to pass through five other tables—product, order line item, order header, service event, and party role—so it will in fact validate the collective referential integrity of six separate sets of foreign keys at once, making it a very demanding test.

When we get to the presentation layer, the integration layer information involves significantly fewer tables. The same corner test will require not only linking the dimensions for product (A) and location (B) to the fact tables but also drilling across from sales orders (B_1) to work orders (B_2), making it an extensive test of the information in the star schema.

Because one can mix and match the tables in a target schema thousands of ways, a team can go too far with this test technique, ending up with more test cases than the team has funds to implement. The teams I lead usually employ the two- or three-way combinatorial reduction technique described later to generate a representative set of tables for which to write corner tests. Perhaps even more insightful is the practice of authoring corner tests that mirror the data queries representing the key business questions that the end users plan on submitting to the data warehouse once it is online.

Reconciliation

The reconciliation test technique generates test cases that tie the results of a query from the data warehouse back to a report or data listing provided by another system that the business stakeholders already trust. "Reconciliation" here does not mean "match" but instead signifies that the results from the warehouse and the reference system either match or the differences can be explained. These are very time-consuming tests, so reconciliation should be used sparingly, employed only to create test cases that align with the key themes and epics driving the project.

Often, business users will not trust a data warehouse if it has not been validated using at least a couple of reconciliation tests. On my projects, I like to ask each department making a stakeholder request which reconciliation would convince them that they can rely on the data warehouse's information and then consolidate that list to as few reconciliations as possible that will satisfy all the requestors. The major disaster team leaders want to avoid by using this approach is the situation in which the data warehouse has gone online and suddenly a major stakeholder pulls a thick green bar report from the bottom drawer of his or her desk, saying "Let's see if the dashboard has gotten these numbers right." EDW team leaders do not want to be blindsided by such stealth reconciliation requirements, which can consume months of labor to satisfy, and often uncover many new requirements in the process. By asking about reconciliation tests upfront, they can turn this black hole of testing into a manageable effort, positioning themselves to say "no" to matching the numbers on any surprise reports that stakeholders have kept hidden.

Examples and Expected Results

For business rules that are very complicated, it is impossible to validate the data warehouse's information with analytical comparisons of source to target using the techniques discussed previously. Take the situation depicted in Figure 16.10, for example. Here, the values in nine particular source records are supposed to boil down to a set of completely different values in three target records along with two records in an associated suspense table. With the expected results technique, the business stakeholders provide the DW/BI team with a set of examples that include both specific source records and target records they expect the business rules to generate. During validation, the team or an automated script can repeatedly search for this exact pattern in the target data every time the test source data is transformed. These tests are expensive to set up not only because the examples have to be well documented but also because they require that the team maintain a repository of expected results records. However, for complex business rules such as customer segmentation or vendor value scoring, an example is often all the guidance that the business users can provide for ETL validation.

Traditional Application Testing Techniques

The test techniques discussed previously are fairly obvious ways to test a data-centric application. Agile EDW teams can also generate test cases by utilizing a collection of techniques that general software application testers rely on when

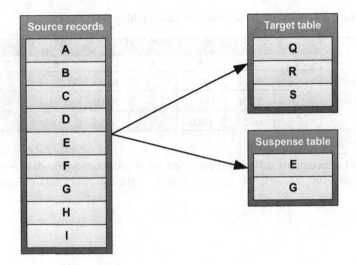

FIGURE 16.10 Typical situation requiring a team to use the "expected values" test technique.

they create non-DW/BI systems. Although each of the following test techniques provides a handy means of creating test cases, their emphasis is actually on helping testers to understand the minimum number of test cases necessary to validate a given feature and thereby reduce the burden of testing to an affordable level.

Equivalence Class Partitioning

Equivalence class partitioning is an extremely common technique for reducing the number of test cases that a team needs to execute in order to validate a particular aspect of the system the team is building. With equivalence class partitioning, test writers decompose and model the variable data for each input and/or output parameter for a given business rule into discrete subsets of valid and invalid classes [Page et al. 2009, p. 78]. They write their test cases utilizing only a few representative values from each class, feeling confident that the resulting small set will adequately qualify the system for the entire set.

For example, the customer last names often need to be cleansed when moving from source systems to data warehouse. Instead of writing a test case for every last name in the world—and every possible way of formatting those names—the team decides to create test cases only for a few distinct classes of last name, such as names with the following:

- Only a single letter
- 15 characters (the average length in the source data)
- 35 characters (the target column's maximum length)
- Names beginning with small letters, such as "diCicco"
- Names with spaces in them, such as "Del Monte" and "van der Waal"
- Names with hyphens, such as "Meyer-Jones"
- Names with single letter conjunctions, such as "Garcia y Viega"

If the ETL can manage these seven cases, the team believes it will be proof enough that the module has been programmed correctly for that target column.

Boundary Value Analysis ("Edge Testing")

Boundary value analysis guides teams in writing test cases that validate a module's ability to correctly operate with values at the extreme edges of an independent input variable or output column, as well as at the edges of the classes identified through equivalence class partitioning [Page et al. 2009, p. 90]. Because of its focus on the edges of input and output spaces, this technique generates what many people refer to as "edge testing."

In practice, edge testing requires teammates to understand where a given business rule inflects its logic given the inputs it will receive or the outputs it will produce. They next write test cases that approach and then cross those inflection points, otherwise known as edges. For example, if the business rules for a *current balance* column in the data

TABLE 16.5 The Combinatorial Reduction Test Case Writing Technique

Parameters	Cases							
	1	**2**	**3**	**4**	**5**	**6**	**7**	**8**
Valid customer	TRUE	TRUE	TRUE	TRUE	FALSE	FALSE	FALSE	FALSE
Valid sales agent	TRUE	TRUE	FALSE	FALSE	TRUE	TRUE	FALSE	FALSE
End of year	TRUE	FALSE	TRUE	FALSE	TRUE	FALSE	TRUE	FALSE

warehouse's Finance subject area employ different logic when the source transaction date progresses into a new month, the team might well use edge testing to write test cases that validate the following data points:

- June 29
- June 30
- July 1
- July 2
- December 30
- December 31
- January 1
- January 2

Note that this team suspected there may be an important difference between a time point representing a regular end-of-month versus the end of the year, so they chose to cover both types of edges. They also chose to test both one and two days on either side of the logical boundary. Because writing tests requires knowledge of each business rule and a good deal of intuition, another team may well have chosen to test only one day on each side of an edge.

Combinatorial Reduction

Often, a given ETL process or business rule combines multiple input variables in deciding what action to perform or values to output. Whereas one might argue that the results from all possible combinations of inputs should be tested, the possible combinations for a dozen parameters can multiply out to the millions or more, far exceeding what the team can afford to test. For this situation, test writers frequently employ a technique called *combinatorial reduction*, which methodically analyzes the dependent and semi-coupled parameter interactions in a complex feature set to systematically select an effective subset of tests from the universe of all possible combinations [Page et al. 2009, p. 100].

Consider Table 16.5, which lists combinations of input values for three input parameters of a particular business rule. The possible values for each of these parameters are either true or false so that the set of possible combinations that a team could test is indicated by the eight test cases in the table. However, the team realizes that for this module, testing every possible value combination for just the pairs of parameters (rather than all three at a time) would be enough. Through combinatorial analysis, they realized that Cases 1, 4, 6, and 7 (shaded) cover all the possible input values for the parameters when those possible parameter values are considered only two at a time. The other cases touched upon pairs of input values that are already represented by the four chosen cases and are therefore superfluous. By eliminating the redundant input value combinations, the team was able to reduce the number of test cases required to validate this feature by 50%.

Of course, module input parameters do not have to be Boolean. Table 16.6 shows the result of combinatorial reduction for three parameters that provide string inputs to a module. The parameters for sales order status, work order status, and promotion all take three or more text values. The total combinations possible number 64, but an online combination generator set for two-way analysis reduced the necessary test cases by 75% to just 16 input combinations. In general, the greater the number of parameters or values that each parameter takes, the greater the percentage of savings combinatorial reduction will offer.

Teams need to use their judgment while employing this technique, of course. If a particular combination of parameter values, such as "maximum values for every parameter," represents a special business case, that case needs to be included in the test plan, whether or not it was identified by the combination generator. Similarly, some combinations, such as "all nulls," will be ruled out by constraints somewhere else in the system and do not need to be tested, so they can be removed from the test cases generated.

Moreover, in many situations involving a dozen or more parameters, the team may well decide that two-way combinations will not provide enough test cases to reasonably identify the defects that could occur. These teams will

TABLE 16.6 Combinatorial Reduction Example

Parameters / Domain of Values
Sales Order Status: Accepted, Credit Hold, Credit Rejected, Changed Mind
Work Order Status: Submitted, Back Ordered, Parts Stocked, Installed
Promotion: BOGO, 1st Free, Baker's Dozen, 3 for 2

64 possible combinations

One possible set of test cases, covering all two-way combinations

Prepared using http://alarcosj.esi.uclm.es/CombTestWeb/combinatorial.jsp

Case #	Selected cases from the full set of 64 combinations
1	Accepted, Submitted, BOGO
2	Accepted, Back Ordered, 1st Free
3	Accepted, Parts Stocked, Baker's Dozen
4	Accepted, Installed, 3 for 2
5	Credit Hold, Submitted, 1st Free
6	Credit Hold, Back Ordered, BOGO
7	Credit Hold, Parts Stocked, 3 for 2
8	Credit Hold, Installed, Baker's Dozen
9	Credit Rejected, Submitted, Baker's Dozen
10	Credit Rejected, Back Ordered, 3 for 2
11	Credit Rejected, Parts Stocked, BOGO
12	Credit Rejected, Installed, 1st Free
13	Changed Mind, Submitted, 3 for 2
14	Changed Mind, Back Ordered, Baker's Dozen
15	Changed Mind, Parts Stocked, 1st Free
16	Changed Mind, Installed, BOGO

16 recommended combinations, 75 percent reduction in test cases

want to increase the combination algorithm to consider three or four parameters at once, although the number of new test cases will grow rapidly with these adjustments. If an analysis of the system reveals that crucial combinations of four parameters, for example, occur frequently, then a series of four-way combinations is a reasonable approach for the module in question. However, absent any particular insight such as that, many professional testers recommend starting with edge testing and pairwise combinations and then moving to three- and four-way testing if there is time and funding for these more exhaustive levels of system validation. Empirically, testing utilizing five-way combinations or more seems to offer too little additional defect detection power to warrant the expense. Team leaders can peruse the papers collected at Jacek Czerwonka's website (http://www.pairwise.org/papers.asp) should they wish to research this topic further.

Agile-Specific Test Techniques

Crispin and Gregory provide a thorough orientation to QA from an agile perspective. Rather than attempting to reproduce their work here, I only point out two notions from their books that agile data warehousing projects utilize frequently and that should be part of any team's bottom-up QA plan: the story-to-epic test stack and exploratory testing [Crispin and Gregory 2009].

Epic Stack Testing

Testers rely on repeatable patterns to help them plan validations and author test suites with less effort. "Stacks" serve as one useful pattern, and we have already seen two test stacks: the "quality control, quality assurance, and quality management" stack that makes up the planning dimension and the "unit, component, integration, and system test" stack that comprises the system dimension. Those two stacks are commonly found in the QA plans for traditionally managed projects. Agile teams add one further stack to their collection of planning techniques so that they remind themselves to always push a little farther on quality and make their test suites that much more complete and robust. On agile projects, we frequently speak in terms of testing the full epic stack—that is, validating stories from the backlog, then scenarios, themes, and, finally, the parent epic as a complete package rather than treating those multiple levels as stand-alone pursuits.

Starting from the bottom of the stack, story testing is of course the evaluation that product owners make during the iteration demo to determine whether a given user story has been fulfilled by new programming just completed by the developers. In agile data warehousing, the product owner would evaluate *developer stories* first and the parent user story later, after all of its developer stories had been delivered. Referring back to Chapter 8's recommended epic stack, we can see that evaluating developer and user stories will be insufficient, however, because user stories trace up to a theme, and a theme to an epic. Accordingly, after a complete set of user stories has been accepted, the agile team will continue validating all the way up the epic stack.

The first step above user story testing is an activity called "scenario testing," defined by Crispin and Gregory as validating the software's ability to support plausible business workflows that mimic end-user behavior [Crispin and Gregory 2009, Chapter 10]. As the resident expert on how end users will eventually employ the data warehouse to support business processes, the team's product owner should take the lead in identifying which scenarios need to be tested and even create the test cases for them.

For each major business process supported by the project, the team should create a couple of scenarios that reflect the extremes in operating context that the system will encounter during production. These edge-case scenarios can then be grouped together into various "soap opera tests," compound cases that can demonstrate how the system will respond under the very worst of conditions. For example, a team building an EDW based on an enterprise resource management system could review dashboards for the shipping dock receipts and returns for not just an ordinary month but also a period that stretches over two major holidays during which one of the company's major shipping vendors was on strike.

Theme-level testing represents the next level up from scenario validations. Following the structure of the recommended epic stack, user stories represent the business-level investigations that managers employ to determine that the analysis of the parent theme provides trustworthy insights. The theme tests will therefore start with a scenario test of the user stories making up the theme but then add a validation that asks the directors to confirm they can understand and benefit from the analysis provided by the theme.

Finally, because themes roll up to epics, the full chain of tests identified using this particular stack will end with an epic test that asks sponsors to confirm that the actions enabled by the themes will add up to the new competitive capabilities that their parent epic promised to deliver. Epic tests are frequently more involved than just reviewing the analysis of component themes with the sponsors. As discussed in the chapters on requirements management, new competitive capabilities require many months or years to manifest. When researching requirements for an EDW project, teams need to inquire about the "leading indicators" that executives will rely on to know whether the company has changed its behavior and is competing more vigorously. Consequently, a particular epic test not only needs to demonstrate that the component themes are functional but also must ask executives whether their preferred leading indicators are sufficiently supported.

Exploratory Testing

In classic software testing, "exploratory testing" is defined as the act of testing and designing tests at the same time. It is usually a "manual approach to testing where every step of testing influences the subsequent [validation] step" [Page et al. 2008, Chapter 4, pg. 71]. During exploratory testing, testers essentially write and execute a test, and the results of that test make them think of the next test they should run. Although it sounds undisciplined, exploratory testing uncovers a considerable number of defects in an application because it demands that testers get to know the product they are testing and allows them to author tests when their minds are most engaged with the application under review. Crispin and Gregory are careful to point out that exploratory testing is not as undisciplined as it sounds because, unlike ad hoc testing, exploratory testing starts with a charter that defines the application aspects to be validated and adds planning artifacts such as risk analyses, process and data models, collected comments from the programmers, and the tester's past experience [Crispin & Gregory 2009, Chapter 10].

Agile teams extend the notion of exploratory testing so that it is no longer a technique just for testers. During iteration demos, the programmers, team leaders, and product owners actively look past the surface of a given story test to think of additional validations the team should perform to guarantee that the application is not only complete and correct but also generating as much value for the company as possible. In this context, exploratory testing does not

TABLE 16.7 QA Planning Grid Showing Test Type by Target Column Type

Object Type: Presentation Layer, Type-2 Slowly Changing Dimension

	Unique Values*	Valid Range*	Equivalent Class	Edge Testing	Comb Reduction	Count Distinct*	Group Counts*	Sums or Averages*	Reconciliation	Expected Values*
Scope:		Whole Table					Load Delta			BR Specific
Surrogate Keys	✓									
Natural Keys	✓									
Foreign Keys						✓				
Replicated, Enumerated						✓				
... Continuous		✓	✓				✓	✓	✓	Imp.
Aggregated		✓								
Derived, Enumerated				✓	✓	✓				
... Continuous		✓	✓	✓					✓	✓
Source Metadata		✓								
EDW Metadata		✓						✓		

Techniques amenable to re-usable widget support   *Imp. : Impractical*

focus only on whether the programmers have completed their assigned work (Quadrant 1 in Figure 16.8). It has become instead a valuable business-facing test that critiques the product (Quadrant 3). As an example of exploratory testing at work, consider that teammates on an agile EDW project are reviewing whether they have fulfilled a user story for a standard costing data mart. The project architect might ask the product owner, "Have you considered linking this data mart to the revenue fact tables? Wouldn't that allow you to do analysis on product margins?" Because it put the team on the lookout for new ways to employ existing data assets, exploratory testing led these developers to uncover far more value for the company than if they had narrowed their thinking to simply whether the team had finished programming a particular user story from the backlog.

An Easy-to-Follow Test Technique Matrix for Low-Level Validations

At this point, the collection of test techniques discussed previously is just a long list of ideas for a project's quality control efforts. Agile EDW teams employ test-led development, so it is only appropriate to preprocess that list into a detailed plan for unit and component testing.

Table 16.7 depicts a likely result from such planning for a team preparing for the data integration work on a EDW project. Here, the test techniques have been arrayed along the top of the grid. The rows list the types of columns that the developers expect to find in most of their data warehouse target tables. In the body of the grid, the team has placed a check mark where the developers agree they should try authoring test cases using the indicated test technique for the given type of column. Where the developers believed a test technique had little or nothing to contribute for a given column type, they simply left the cell blank. If a particular test technique would be difficult to utilize for a certain column type, they marked the cell with "Imp." ("impractical"), as can be seen for the intersection of one type of replicated columns and expected results.

The matrix shown in Table 16.7 applies to Type 2 slowly changing dimensions. Note that the techniques have varying data scopes, as marked at the top of the table. Some of the implied assertions will pertain to an entire target table. The check mark in the upper left, for example, represents the statement, "All surrogate key values within the target table should be unique." Such a test is necessary for EDW projects that chose to speed up their data loads by turning off their database constraints.

Other test techniques assume that the test will focus only on the records just loaded into a target table, and they compare those values to the source delta file fed to ETL modules. Any greater scope for these tests would be infeasible,

TABLE 16.8 Sample Function Prototypes for Reusable Test Widgets

check_valid_range(target_table.target_column, min_value_allowed, max_value_allowed)
match_sum(source_table.source_column, target_table.target_column, load_process_id)
match_count_distinct(source_table.source_column, target_table.target_column, load_process_id)
match_group_counts(source_table.source_column, target_table.target_column, load_process_id, group_by_expr)
match_to_expected_values(target_table.target_column, load_process_id, reference_table.reference_column, expected_value_set_id)

which will be the case if the delta extract is the only source information available because landing data typically gets discarded after a successful ETL run. Evaluating the entire loaded column may well encounter a value that was not contained in the delta extract.

The data scope for the remaining test techniques can vary wildly and is therefore considered context specific. Whether one can reconcile a given column's values for just the recently loaded records or the entire table, for example, will depend on the business rules that govern a given column.

Because the appropriate combination of test techniques for each column type will vary somewhat with the type of system object being created, a team may well need one of the previous matrices for each major type of object it expects to build during the project. For the back end of the DW/BI system, the objects were all structures populated by ETL, such as landing tables, integration layer tables, and presentation layer tables including slowly changing dimensions and fact tables. For the front end of the system, the team will have to create test technique planning matrices for the set of objects appropriate for the BI tool employed. These objects include such notions as cross-module menus, query definition screens and their standardized lists of values for filtering criteria, as well as the individual display components that make up the reports and dashboards.

EDW team leads should be sure to involve the programmers when they fill out this grid of test types. Because the leaders are driving the QA planning process, they might be tempted to decide for themselves where the check marks will go. However, each check mark represents additional unit testing work that the team will expect programmers to complete for every module of a given type. If the collection of check marks adds up to more work than the programmers will reliably perform, the entire exercise will be counterproductive because it will position the leaders to believe modules are receiving far more careful testing than is truly the case. For this reason, team leaders can achieve more predictable results if they ask the programmers to collaborate on or even take the lead in completing this unit test planning grid.

Reusable Test Widgets

Once the teammates complete the unit test planning grids, they will have their detailed, technical testing requirements well documented. With one small step, they can translate these requirements into the specification of a set of reusable "test widgets" that will save them a tremendous amount of unit testing time.

First, many of the test techniques contained in these planning grids represent easily repeatable validations. Matching the distinct values or sums between source and target deltas, for example, involves applying the same logic to the inputs, no matter how many records exist in a column or which target tables are involved. Tests that will be heavily used and that execute the same algorithm in all contexts do not have to be hand-crafted each time they are employed. The team can develop some short, reusable, parameter-driven scripts or test widgets to perform the necessary calculations and comparisons. These test widgets can be called easily en masse from a driver script created for each target table.

The asterisks in the column headers of Table 16.7 indicate the test techniques that can be converted to reusable scripts with little effort. Table 16.8 shows a few of the function prototypes for these parameter-driven routines. For example, the technique "valid range" would become a "check_valid_range( )" widget and would need the programmer to call it with parameters for the target table and column to be validated plus the minimum and maximum values allowed. Since match_sum( ) is scoped to cover just the extract delta, it will require a parameter to indicate what value to search for in the target table's column of load timestamps or process identifiers so that only the records just created will be considered. The match_group_counts( ) compares the counts of records falling into user-defined "buckets" in both the source and the target data sets. Naturally, this function will include a parameter that passes an expression defining the desired buckets, such as one identifying the first letter of each string value.

Match_to_expected_values( ) ensures that a given set of source records exactly produces a set of predefined target results. This test can only be run against "canned" source data sets in which the team controls the input records and outputs completely, making the outputs entirely predictable once the transform logic is programmed correctly. For this test, the developers will need to add parameters for the target table and columns they want evaluated and another set for identifying the transformed values they expect to match. Because the developers will probably want to store more than one set of expected values in that table, they will have to provide a parameter identifying the specific comparison set for each call of this widget as well.

Note that many ETL modules place unloadable records into a suspense table rather than rejecting the input altogether. In that situation, the team will need to add parameters to many of the reusable widgets to identify the suspense tables so that the comparisons will execute against the union of all target objects.

Because of their simplicity, these reusable test widgets cannot catch all the defects a data warehouse will experience. However, experience has shown that by creating driver scripts that employ reusable widgets against target tables dozens of times after every ETL run, a great many defects can automatically be revealed, freeing up the team's time to invest in more complicated and value-added testing elsewhere.

Test Cases Roll Forward Along the System Dimension

Although the previous discussion focused largely on unit testing, we do not want to leave the higher level validations in the system dimension unsupported. Teams will find they have already completed much of the work necessary for integration and system testing if they plan on transferring unit and component tests to the higher-level test scripts.

In general, unit testing validates the objects that a single programmer modifies and that result in an atomic object in the team's change control utility. Component tests validate objects that multiple units assemble into, but they often evaluate very different qualities than the unit test. For many data warehousing projects, an ETL unit is a *mapping*, and thus ETL unit tests consider whether the business rules specified on a source-to-target map were properly programmed. A *workflow* or sequence of mappings represents the component, and component tests usually consider whether the component successfully executed the proper number of maps, not the business rules inside the maps.

Integration testing, however, is not entirely unlike the combination of unit and component testing. Integration testing will run ETL routines that may well invoke dozens of components. To ensure that all component processing completed as expected, the developers will in fact want to determine whether the correct number of maps executed and whether some key business rules were properly applied. In other words, they will want the integration test to repeat many of the unit and component tests.

Similarly, system testing tends to repeat much of an integration test. The goal that the operations team has for systems testing is to ensure that the application will run as predicted in the machine room with a reasonable amount of operator involvement. The system will be promoted into a near-production environment such as user acceptance testing (UAT) for validation. Operations team members will naturally focus on the knockout tests described previously, but they will also want to see that the application successfully completes its integration test in the new environment.

Thus, many unit and component tests will need to "roll forward" into the integration test suite, as illustrated in Figure 16.11, which also shows that much of the integration test cases will roll into the system test suite. Knowing that these test scripts need to consolidate in this way will give the team further incentive to implement as much of the unit and component testing as possible using parameter-driven test widgets because they make it particularly easy to collate driver scripts in the next higher level of testing. Teams can, in fact, configure an integration test by simply creating a super driver script that calls the driver scripts for unit and component testing, as shown in the diagram. At each progressively higher level, the new hand-crafted test steps will be the few additional tests that the scripts of the previous level did not entail.

Testing for Convergence

Once EDW teams have completed formulating both a top-down and a bottom-up EDW QA plan, they should consider whether the two concepts converge well into a single concept. If gaps appear when they try to connect these two plans, one or both of the plans have overlooked or misconstrued a significant validation concept. The gap provides a team with the opportunity to search the two plans for weak spots and augment the components until an overall approach emerges that contains a complete set of accurately targeted validation activities.

Figure 16.12 portrays the stereoscopic style of quality planning that teams employing the elements described in this chapter can achieve. On the left are the planning realms of quality management, assurance, and control. These link to the elements of the system dimension, such as unit and integration tests, in the manner indicated by the dashed lines.

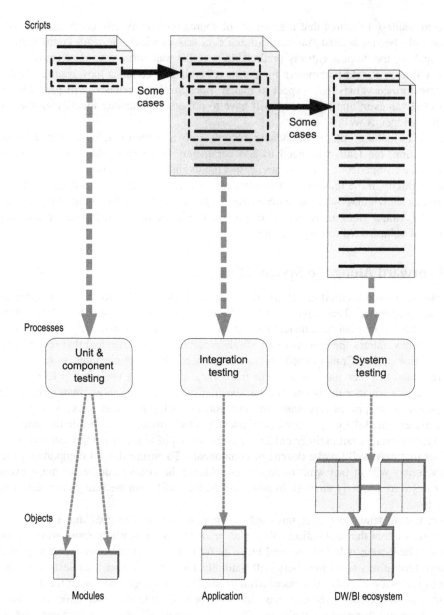

FIGURE 16.11 Many unit tests roll forward into the applications integration test suite.

The system dimension items link in turn to the output of the agile EDW requirements management value chains, as shown on the right.

The 2×2 planning matrix allowed the team to define these components from the top down. Starting from the top, Figure 16.12 shows that issues of quality management need to be found in the system test plan. Next, QA objectives have to be supported by the integration test, which should in turn validate the product owner's themes and user stories.

Regarding unit tests, the team has to resort to very granular test techniques and then consider how those would roll up to integration and system tests. At this point, team leaders can ask some demanding questions that will reveal whether they have a coherent quality plan:

- How well do the integration tests (created by rolling up unit tests) support the validations we planned for user- and theme-level stories?
- How well do the system tests (created by rolling up the integration tests) support the quality management objectives we set out for project?

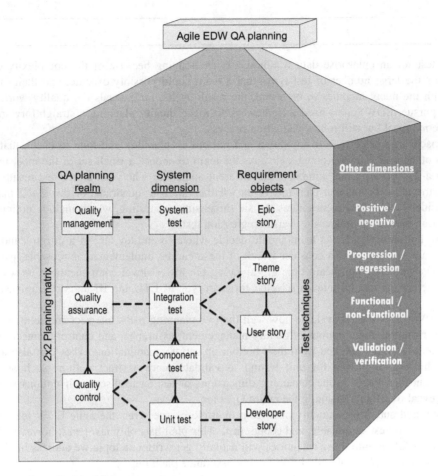

FIGURE 16.12 Overview of an agile QA planning approach.

Once they have resolved any gaps that appeared with these questions, they can further deepen the top-to-bottom alignment by trying to extend the unit test techniques upward along the system and planning dimensions by asking questions such as the following:

- How can we use expected results and reconciliations to ensure we are providing accurate information at the theme and epic level and not just for the actions envisioned by the user stories?
- How do the values we use for edge testing mappings (units) and workflows (components) translate into the boundaries we should be testing at for themes and epics?
- Do we need to expand or contract the data set we derived via combinatorial reduction for unit and integration testing so that we can use it also for themes and epics?

There is, in fact, a third approach visible in Figure 16.12 that the team can tap to further polish its quality plan. Notice the remaining validation factors listed on the right side of the cube. The team can explore concepts such as polarity, functionality, and regression testing to judge whether the validation actions identified at each level on the face of the cube form a truly complete set of tests. Such considerations apply notions such as negativity, regression, and nonfunctional requirements against the tests already defined and give rise to further questions, such as the following:

- We have planned for negative tests at the unit level, but can we define some negative tests for our themes and epics as well? What kind of extreme business situations might the executives and directors face that could possibly destroy the value provided by the data warehouse?
- The current system test plan focuses on restartability for only the modules we have added for the next subrelease. Shouldn't we be regression testing restart logic for the subject areas added during past subreleases to ensure they have not been adversely impacted by our new programming?
- We have plenty of user acceptance test cases for the subject area we just added, but once we have it running on the UAT host, shouldn't we validate nonfunctional aspects such as performance and security aspects as well?

SUMMARY

Deciding *what* to test for an enterprise data warehouse is challenging because of the complexity of the application. When one considers the large number of test types that a team could possibly execute, and then the combinations of those test types with the many modules to be tested, the resulting list far exceeds the quality work that the team has time or money to pursue. EDW teams need a framework to make quality planning a straightforward process and one that results in an economical but still robust validation process.

The agile approach is to perform both top-down and bottom-up planning and then to check that the two resulting plans support each other well. The top-down style asks the team to choose a small set of the most important test types and place them on a 2×2 matrix that combines the different audiences who wish to see test results versus the fundamental purpose of the tests. Teams can then reflect on whether the four quadrants of this 2×2 matrix are balanced. They can also consider how well it incorporates the six dimensions of testing, which include notions such as positive versus negative testing as well as progression versus regression tests.

Switching to the bottom-up path, the team should decide where to employ any of a dozen standard techniques for authoring unit test cases. It should also consider which of these can be implemented as reusable, parameter-driven test widgets that will save the team significant time in validating the lowest-level components of its warehouse. The team can also explore whether the test techniques selected for each type of ETL and BI units roll up easily into integration and system tests.

Finally, agile EDW teams should evaluate how well the two planning paths intersect and reinforce each other. They can consider whether the top-down notions of quality management, assurance, and control connect effectively with the integration and system tests that resulted from their bottom-up script consolidations. They can also ask where they can extend the test techniques employed for unit testing to validate more abstract notions such as epic- and theme-level stories. They can then factor in the remaining dimensions of testing to discover if notions such as negative and regression testing reveal oversights spanning the entire QA plan.

By understanding and authoring a quality plan from multiple perspectives, the agile EDW team can be reasonably assured that their plan is robust, actionable, and economical. This plan lists only *test types*, however. The next step is to plan how the *test cases* falling into those categories will actually get written, a topic we address in Chapter 17 when we consider the *who*, *when*, and *where* of agile EDW quality assurance planning.

Chapter 17

Designating Who, When, and Where

The stereoscopic view of quality assurance (QA) presented in Chapter 16 provides agile enterprise data warehousing (EDW) team leaders with a handy framework for choosing a reasonable set of tests for validating the application they have under development. Although they have answered, "What types of tests shall we use?" they are still far from having a full QA plan. Given that their team will need to assess the fit-to-purpose of many hundred facets of the product under construction, the next major question they will need to answer is, "*Who* will write all the tests we will need?" In answering this question, agile EDW leaders take a very different approach than that followed with traditional projects. They spread the responsibility for writing tests across the entire team rather than placing it all on the shoulders of the project's system tester. This chapter considers the best allocation of quality duties within an agile EDW team. With the responsibility for writing test cases distributed across many people, two further questions immediately emerge, namely "*When* do team leaders expect their teammates to complete each of their duties?" and, given that they are sharing physical resources, "*Where* should they perform their work?" This chapter suggests how team leaders can answer these three central planning questions, leaving only "*How* should they get that work done?" to be answered in Chapter 18.

WHO SHALL WRITE THE TESTS?

Traditional, waterfall projects place a tremendous burden on the role of system tester. Testing usually gets started toward the end of the project when a large inventory of programmed modules and possibly loaded data exist so that a considerable portion of the product can be validated. At that point, the system tester(s) begins working with the team. She examines the design specifications in order to write test cases that will demonstrate whether the application will dependably fulfill its intended purpose. Whether she will succeed in this effort will depend on her ability to glean intent as well as detailed technical requirements from the large collection of requirements and design documents the designers provide. This work is difficult because the artifacts she will work from are typically incomplete, poorly written, and, by the end of the project, considerably out of date. On top of these disadvantages, the system tester will probably receive too little support from the designers and programmers as she struggles with this insufficient documentation. She joined late, so she does not seem truly part of the team. Moreover, the others largely view testing as a necessary evil that does not help anyone finish programming the application by the time the looming deadline arrives. Every minute they spend explaining context and coding details to the system tester is another minute they will have to work during late nights and weekends in order to get their programming assignments finished.

As challenging as it is to write test cases from specifications during a waterfall project, it is completely impossible to accomplish in an agile setting. Because detailed specifications do not exist until programmers finish building a module, the agile system tester will not find to-be specifications to guide him in writing test cases. As it sprints through its development cycles, the team's goal is to deliver shippable code with each iteration if possible and certainly with each subrelease. Programmers work from 80/20 specifications (see Part III), so the team does not even pretend there are detailed specifications for most of the features it is actively adding to the current build. Detailed requirements are provided eye-to-eye in real time when a module is programmed.

As outlined in Chapter 16, agile teams need to test modules as they emerge from the programming process in order to keep defects from compounding and consuming developer time and energy that are better invested in creating additional features for the organization. Unfortunately, the system tester cannot write test cases with all the crucial information needed for understanding the modules, as built, locked away in the heads of so many other people:

- The product owner provided the intent for a large collection of modules taken altogether.
- The project architect coordinated how that purpose was distributed across subsystems and components.
- The data modeler chose how the target tables would interconnect.

- The system analysts supplied guidance on the business rules that should shape the information loaded into each target column.
- The programmers decided on the logical boundaries between units as they coded each module.

If the agile team is going to steadily execute complete and effective testing on the EDW application as modules emerge from programming, all of these parties will have to collaborate in writing the test cases, each providing validation objectives from his or her perspective. The role of the agile system tester, then, is no longer to author the validation events but instead to orchestrate all his teammates in writing their test scripts. The system tester will need to guide them and collate the results so that this decentralized test writing eventually amounts to an organized set of test suites that can be executed and re-executed with reasonable ease.

A Framework for Understanding Who Must Do What

In order to orchestrate distributed test writing, the system tester will need an organizational framework so that she can clearly express to each teammate his or her role and objectives in creating test cases. To some extent, she needs only to remind her teammates of the QA activities built into the agile method they are following. Higher levels of testing will be required, however, and to understand and communicate those responsibilities, she can use two simple tools: the "V-model" and an updated version of the 2 × 2 quality planning matrix.

The agile approach has instilled solid quality practices into the software development process that occurs with every programming iteration. Examples we have seen in this book so far include

- the validation sentence added to user story cards;
- the five-step test-led development pattern;
- code walkthroughs included in a task's definition of done; and
- the product owner test driving real extract, transform, and load (ETL) results at the end of every iteration.

Although these practices serve as a strong foundation for the quality efforts of an agile team, they focus largely on unit testing. The project will also need validations from higher-level perspectives such as epics, themes, the whole application, and the application functioning in its operational environment. The system tester will need to elicit a full gamut of test cases from his teammates by guiding them across the arch of the six dimensions of testing explored in Chapter 16.

Test writing must begin with Sprint 1 so that the team will have a successful subrelease candidate during the first few months of a project. Accordingly, the system tester needs to be part of the team from the very beginning. In fact, much of the quality planning described in Chapter 16 and in the following section need to be completed during Sprint 0. To coordinate activities of 10 people or more from the very start of the project, the system tester must arrive with ready-to-go guidelines defining the roles for each member of the team. In my experience, completing two simple artifacts will provide the necessary guidance:

- Analyze the responsibilities using the classic V-model for QA.
- Document and communicate the conclusions using the 2 × 2 top-down QA planning matrix from Chapter 16.

Using the Classic V-Model for Analyzing QA Responsibilities

The V-model is a classic analysis linking requirement artifacts to testing activities used for decades to plan QA for traditionally managed projects. Figure 17.1 depicts the V-model one can find in many QA textbooks [Hull et al. 2011, pp. 10–11]. Although it is drawn for a general software development project, we can adapt this diagram to understand how quality should serve as the flip side of requirements management within an agile EDW project.

In the traditional rendering, the major categories of QA work are dictated by the progressive elaboration of the project's system requirements. The vertical axis of Figure 17.1 represents the varying levels of abstraction at which the team works as it analyzes requirements, and the horizontal axis signifies project time.

We can see the requirements management work on the left side of the V. The team begins at the top with stakeholder requirements and then drops down a level to translate stakeholder requirements into a set of system requirements. From there, the project definition work continues dropping down, each time to a finer level of abstraction. The team progresses through subsystem requirements, component requirements, and, finally, detailed design, which we can think of as the technical requirements for individual modules.

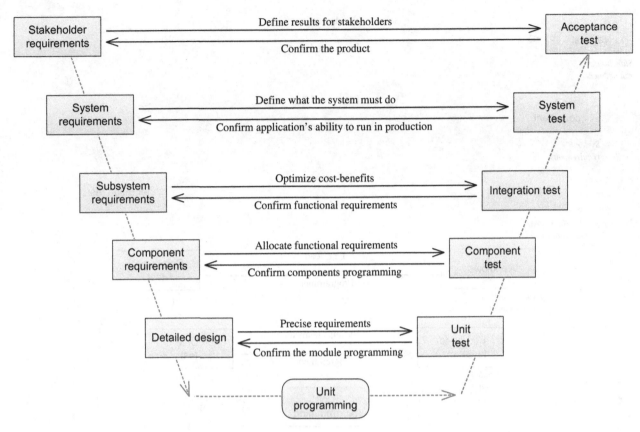

FIGURE 17.1 V-Model showing quality assurance as the flip side of requirements work. *(Adapted from Elizabeth Hull, et al, Requirements Engineering, 3 ed, Springer, London, 2011)*

Once the team has arrived at a detailed design at the bottom of the V, a coder can program the unit. At that point, QA work begins. According to this model, the tester must "dig himself out of the hole" that the tall stack of requirements management work created. He must perform a unit test to confirm that detailed design has been successfully expressed in the module's programming. Component testing confirms that the team has successfully implemented the functional requirements allocated to a closely related set of modules. Integration testing confirms that the subsystem meets the functional requirements set out for it, and system test confirms that application-level requirements have been fulfilled. Finally, the team returns to the top of the V to conduct an acceptance test, which confirms that the stakeholder requirements articulated at the start of the entire undertaking have been answered.

Adapted V-Model for Agile DW/BI Test Cases

Figure 17.2 depicts how EDW team leaders, guided by their system tester, can adapt the classic V-model to allocate test writing responsibilities across the members of the development team. I have kept the same set of testing labels on the right side of the model, but on the left I have replaced the textbook's list of requirements artifacts with the ones that agile EDW teams typically employ. Also, to better support the planning of responsibilities, I have redefined the arrows connecting each side of the V to document the parties performing the author and consumer roles involved at each level of abstraction.

Starting with the stakeholder requests, this artifact may have been originally compiled by the project architect, but at some point it became the "property" of the product owner because he or she is the team's authority on the services the business must receive from the data warehouse. From that point on, the project architect is the consumer of the stakeholder requests, treating the requirements within them as given facts with which she can create or update the project's vision document. To see the implications for QA, we must note that the acceptance test confirms that the

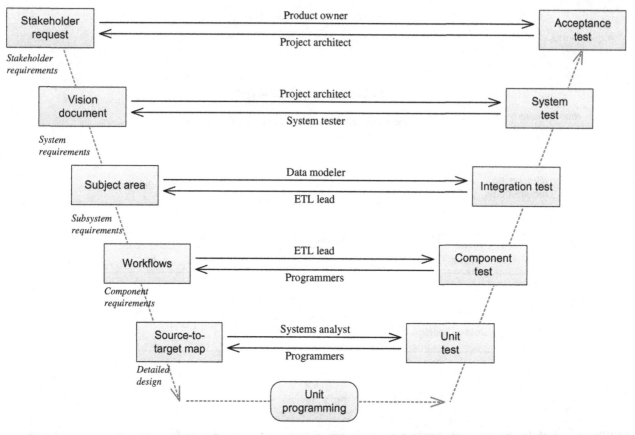

FIGURE 17.2   V-Model adapted for agile data warehousing and showing the authors and consumers of requirements and specifications.

stakeholder requests have been fulfilled. Which team roles could best write the test cases for the user acceptance process? The author and consumer of the stakeholder requests will have the greatest familiarity with this document, and thus the product owner and project architect will be in the best position to author test cases at this level.

At the next level down, the vision document is a sketch of the system that the team will develop. It provides the major organizational concepts of the application that system test must assess once it is operating in a near-production environment. Accordingly, the project architect and system tester, as the respective author and consumer of the vision document, will be the teammates most familiar with the guidance at this level of abstraction and thus are best positioned to write system tests. Data warehouses divide their systems into subject areas, which serve as the natural scope for integration tests. The data modeler defines the subject areas, and the ETL lead decides how to best populate them with data, making these two roles the author and consumers at this level of abstraction. Consequently, this pair is the most capable of writing the test cases for the subject area. At the next level down, the ETL lead designs the workflows and the programmers implement those designs, so these roles are best positioned to write cases for the component tests that confirm the application's workflows are properly constructed. Finally, the system analyst authors the source-to-target mappings that the programmers follow while programming individual modules; thus, as author and consumers of these mappings, these roles will be the best authors for the unit test cases.

Communicating the QA Assignments

Test writing consumes a tremendous amount of energy, at least until everyone on the team settles into their new QA responsibilities. EDW team leaders will be wise to record the conclusions derived from the V-model analysis so that the teammates can hold each other accountable for getting the quality work completed. For communicating the QA at a high level, the 2 × 2 top-down planning matrix we built in Chapter 16 will document those decisions well. For the projects I lead, we display the "who" version of this matrix prominently on the project room wall and update it frequently as the development iterations show us where we must fine-tune the roles assigned to the various areas of quality work.

		Support the team *Are we done coding yet?*		Critique the product *Product offering maximum value?*	
Business facing	**Story tests** **Scenario tests** **Alpha test**	*Product owner* *Product owner* *Business analyst*		**Theme test** **Acceptance test** **Usability test** **Beta test**	*Product owner* *Product owner* *System tester* *System tester*
Technology facing	**Unit tests** **Component tests** **Integration test**	*Developer* *ETL lead* *Project architect*		**System test** **Security test** **Performance test** **Load test**	*Operations team* *Ops. security* *DW architect* *DW architect*

FIGURE 17.3 Using the 2 × 2 QA planning matrix updated to communicate test writing responsibilities.

Using the 2 × 2 Top-Down Matrix

Figure 17.3 illustrates how the planning matrix from Chapter 16 would appear once it is updated for the conclusions from the V-model analysis. Of course, there are many types of tests that are not explicitly listed on the V-model, so EDW team leaders need to invest a further increment of thinking in order to make this update. Story and theme tests, for example, were not on the V-model, but it is clear with a moment's reflection that they are directly traceable to stakeholder requests. Because the product owner is the owner of stakeholder requests, he or she will have the best knowledge for authoring tests for the project's theme and users stories. Other tests will require a judgment call, but the V-model analysis will be a good anchor for the thinking required.

A good example can be found in alpha tests, in which the developers will try out the system before a subrelease, working with the front end as if they were the end users. This test should demonstrate that the system features will properly support the new business process that the stakeholders desire for their departmental staff members. Business processes fit somewhere in between the topics discussed in the vision documents and the data transforms documented on the source-to-target mapping. Thus, alpha test cases should be created by the authors of these two artifacts, namely the project architect and the systems analyst. Even better, the team's business analyst, if one has been assigned, is a role falling between project architect and systems analyst that focuses explicitly on re-engineering a business process to utilize a new information system. For these reasons, the system tester might well suggest that alpha test cases be authored by the business analyst, too.

Using a More Detailed Grid

Listing the responsible roles on the 2 × 2 quality planning matrix is fine for initial planning, but as the project progresses, the team will develop a more detailed notion of who should perform quality duties, including those beyond testing. Table 17.1 shows a more detailed grid for planning out quality roles on an agile EDW team. The quality work items are listed in the rows, and the roles on the team provide the column headings. The team will borrow many of the elements for this grid from the 2 × 2 summary matrix. Check marks indicate for each category of testing who is responsible for authoring the test cases and even ensuring that they get properly executed.

This grid portrays some of the detail that would not fit on the 2 × 2 planning matrix, especially those test categories for which more than one teammate is expected to help in writing the test cases. For example, the team preparing this grid believed that integration tests on Line 4 should result from a collaboration between the project architect, the systems analyst, and the system tester.

This grid also lists a few additional QA activities that involve some roles outside of the team room. Responsibility for preparing test data for the integration test data needed by each iteration has been assigned to the project architect, systems analyst, and system tester on Line 1, for example. The duty of presenting a subrelease candidate and leading operational readiness reviews has been given to other roles, including some IT support groups, on Lines 15 and 16. Agile EDW teams usually feel the need for this grid soon after their first. Once drafted, this grid also makes a good reference artifact to display on the team room wall.

One-Up, One-Down Validation Can Save Time

Focusing on the roles of author and consumer by abstraction level and test cases provides the foundation for a further important quality practice for agile teams called "one-up, one down validation." By design, agile teams should be

TABLE 17.1 Quality Assurance Responsibilities Documented by Roles and by Test Type

Ln	Type / Who ➡	Product Owner	Project Architect	Business Analyst	Data Modeler	Systems Analyst	Programmer	System Tester	IT Support Team
1	Iteration Integration Test Data Prep		✓			✓		✓	
2	Unit Tests					✓	✓		
3	Component Tests					✓	✓		
4	Integration Tests		✓	✓	✓				
5	Story Tests	✓	✓	✓					
6	Scenario Tests	✓		✓					
7	Alpha Tests	✓		✓					
8	Theme Tests	✓		✓	✓				
9	Acceptance Tests	✓	✓	✓					
10	Usability Tests	✓		✓					
11	Beta Tests	✓		✓					
12	System Tests		✓		✓	✓			✓
13	Performance Tests		✓						✓
14	Load Tests		✓				✓		✓
15	Subrelease Candidate Presentations	✓	✓						
16	Operational Readiness Reviews							✓	✓

collaborative, but many teams take collaboration to an extreme. They "socialize" *every* decision regarding requirements, design, and programming. Such extensive involvement in defining work tasks obviously leaves the teammates mired in never-ending meetings and slows deliveries to a snail's pace. To preserve the team's velocity, agile teammates need a way to enable individuals to work rapidly on their own and still validate their output. One-up, one-down validation will allow them to immediately escape the ineffective nature of oversocialization.

When I join a team that is mired in too many review meetings, I suggest they attempt to depict their team using a diagram such as Figure 17.4. This diagram uses rows to signify the levels of abstraction comprising the software engineering process and columns to indicate the engineering roles on the team. The lozenge shapes drawn in each column indicate the engineering areas in which each role participates. The thicker the lozenge for a given role, the more that role naturally understands and cares about the type of work in question.

The wide arrows in Figure 17.4 indicate the handoffs of work between engineering steps, thereby indicating the author—consumer roles between teammates. For each of these handoffs, the work being transmitted should be validated as part of the team's overall quality assurance plan.

These validations need not involve every member of the team, but they can be quite effectively performed by just three people: the author of the work, the person serving as the subject matter expert, and the other person who will have to consume the artifact created. In other words, when a teammate completes an artifact, he should validate it with the person one level up and the individual one level down from his position in the engineering value chain.

Consider, for example, an increment of the data model. The data modeler takes guidance from the project architect concerning the major changes needed within the warehouse's data repository to support the next subrelease. He or she then translates those directions into a data model that will support the desired system functionality. That data model next serves as the starting point for the systems analyst in writing business rules for the source-to-target maps. The project architect is one-up from the data modeler, and the systems analyst is one-down, so these two individuals should be all that is necessary to provide "just good enough" validation for the changes to the data model. These two reviewers will be able to confirm that the data modeler not only understood the assignment but also expressed himself clearly for the next person in the value chain. Given how many person-hours large meetings cost a team, the data modeler will keep the project moving far more quickly by leaving everyone else out of the review.

If this approach often seems too Spartan to many agile practitioners, I encourage them to keep in mind several considerations. First, meetings that serve only to communicate general information to teammates are usually very wasteful. At large meetings, the Scrum master should always multiply the time spent by the number of people involved by

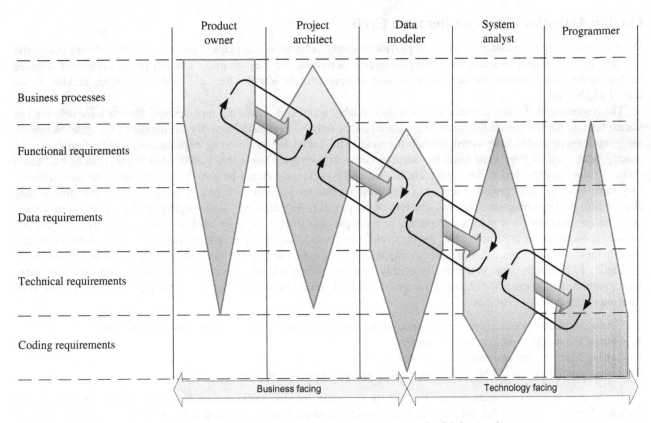

FIGURE 17.4 Teams can avoid "over socializing" decisions by employing a "one-up, one-down" validation practice.

a representative wage rate for the team. Ten people costing an average $150 per hour in wages and facilities spending just 90 minutes in a meeting consumes more than $2,000 of project funds. If most of the people involved with that meeting have very little to say during the session, the Scrum master should ask, "Isn't there a way to communicate this information just as well that doesn't cost $2,000? How about using the team wiki board included in our document repository application?"

Second, to maintain their velocity, effective agile teams rely on just-in-time communication to guide detailed work. When starting work on a module, upstream roles should provide a teammate only an 80/20 artifact to get her started. When she finds herself stuck, she can call for support in real time across the project room table. She can also announce at the next daily stand-up meeting that she needs to meet with whomever understands the artifact that is troubling her. In the same way that upstream roles do not need to provide detailed specifications for the next teammate who will work on an item, they also do not need to keep everyone completely informed on every detail of the project. As long as the team has some high-level artifacts to keep all teammates aligned, it is far more efficient to let each team member request further background and details when they start working on an item.

Third, if a particular type of artifact regularly needs more input than one-up, one-down validation can provide, this fact can be discussed and resolved at the next iteration retrospective. In this way, the team establishes wider review processes only where necessary, leaving the bulk of their handoffs occurring with the least labor consumed as possible.

WHEN SHOULD TEAMMATES PERFORM THEIR QA DUTIES?

The core of QA is writing and executing test cases for all the necessary aspects of a system under development. There are also some higher-level activities that need to be wrapped around this core of testing. When a project begins, agile EDW teams experience considerable confusion regarding when each role should execute this large collection of activities. They become significantly more effective at their quality work once they map out the proper sequence and timing for each event.

Quality Activities Within an Iteration Cycle

Parallel to the way programming iterations provide a strong order in which major development steps should occur, the iteration cycle can also structure the timing of quality activities. As they progress through the development steps of each programming iteration, the developers should be cognizant of whether they are in the beginning, middle, or the end of a QA cycle.

The beginning of the development step is understandably a stressful, confusing time because the clock for delivery has started ticking, but the objects that must be programmed are only 80 percent defined. By the middle of the sprint, however, the programmers should have sorted through the unknowns, called for any missing explanations, and be fairly clear on exactly what each of them must build by the time demo day arrives. During that middle stretch, they should be "heads down," coding quickly, and as they approach the end of the cycle they should be getting ready to demo the new software they have created. EDW project leaders can help their teammates perform their quality work far more smoothly if they align it with the beginning—middle—end structure of the programming iteration. At the beginning of the cycle, some uncertainty in the iteration's test plan is acceptable, so a simple sketch of the quality work to come will suffice. During the middle, however, more actionable plans for the cycle's final validation should be taking shape. On demo, the team should execute on the quality plans it has prepared during the past few weeks and get the new software validated and approved.

Figure 17.5 depicts some of the major quality functions found within a development iteration and organizes them into a pattern that supports the changing nature of the work during the sprint. The rows group activities by the focus of four important types of activities:

- Getting modules specifications correct enough so that errors do not occur from poor communication
- Getting the modules programmed correctly
- Getting ready for the upcoming product demo
- Re-demonstrating the last build delivered with a more realistic set of data

Because agile EDW projects require that the quality work for one iteration stretch somewhat into the next, I have depicted Iterations 3 and 4 for this hypothetical project and shaded the activities that belong to Sprint 3. For clarity, I drew this figure for a team using 4-week iterations, but readers can simply list days of the sprint if it must be adjusted for a differently sized time box. Similarly, they should add rows when their projects encounter aspects of quality work needing management within an iteration that are not mentioned here.

Regarding Row 1, we can acknowledge that providing clear guidance for programmers on requirements and design will be an important consideration having direct impact on the quality of the team's end product. When the iteration starts, the programmers will receive an orientation from their EDW leaders including a data model, ETL programming patterns for the modules they will be coding, and a source-to-target map. The team's first look at these artifacts occurs during an

QA focus	Iteration 3				Iteration 4			
	Wk 1	Wk 2	Wk 3	Wk 4	Wk 1	Wk 2	Wk 3	Wk 4
Correct technical requirements	Initial presentation	Churn allowed	Changes negotiated	Locked	Initial presentation	Churn allowed	Changes negotiated	Locked
Accurate coding	Pay off tech debt	Code & unit test	Code & unit test	Focus on load for demo	Pay off tech debt	Code & unit test	Code & unit test	Focus on load for demo
Next user demo	Sketch next demo	Draft next demo script	Update next demo script	Alpha test next demo	Sketch next demo	Draft next demo script	Update next demo script	Alpha test next demo
Re-demo prior iteration	Iteration 2 Small-volume demo	Iteration 2 Full-volume load	Iteration 2 Full-volume alpha test	Iteration 2 Full-volume demo	Iteration 3 Small-volume demo	Iteration 3 Full-volume load	Iteration 3 Full-volume alpha test	Iteration 3 Full-volume demo

Work depicted for Iterations 3 and 4, by which time the team should largely understand the structure of a programming iteration.
Shaded items represent the complete set of actions belonging to Iteration 3

FIGURE 17.5 Sequencing QA work within an iteration.

"initial presentation" from their technical leaders, as listed in the first week in row 1. The initial presentation of a module design will probably include discussions during iteration planning on Day 1 plus design briefings by the system analysts on a module-by-module basis when a programmer later takes responsibility for creating a particular system object.

The artifacts reviewed during these initial presentation will be 80/20 specifications, so they will only address the most important aspects of the module to be programmed. As the programmers begin work on a module, questions regarding the remaining 20 percent of the design will arise, some of them requiring several hours or several days to answer. The agile work pattern for technical requirements shown in Figure 17.5 indicates that the EDW leaders may well churn on the specifications originally provided to the programmers during first part of an iteration. I chose the word "churn" because the project architect, data modeler, and systems analyst may well go back and forth on a few details as they strive to clarify their thinking and communicate it to the programmer. A bit of churn at the beginning of the iteration is healthy because everyone needs the details to be correct. Prolonged churn on technical requirements, however, will seriously undermine the programmer's ability to build a quality module within the time box allowed.

Accordingly, by Week 3, the leaders need to let the programmers refuse to change their specs if the new guidance is going to be too disruptive, because the day of product demo is growing close. By Week 4, the specifications need to be considered "locked" because the priority has shifted to getting whatever can be completed ready to demonstrate. If, during these last 2 weeks, the specifications are irrecoverably wrong, the EDW leaders should simply pull the developer story in question from the iteration backlog and substitute one of the iteration's stretch goals if possible. In cases in which an appropriate stretch does not exist or cannot be completed in time, then the product demonstration will simply have a gap in it. Either way, the team will discuss this misfire during the retrospective and create some new work patterns that will prevent it from happening again.

Viewed from the programmers' point of view, their focus on quality changes throughout the iteration, as shown in row 2 of Figure 17.5. During the first week, they should be intent on paying off any "tech debt"—that is, the little corrections they promised the product owner they would make in exchange for him or her accepting a not-quite complete story during the prior iteration's product demo. During Weeks 2 and 3, the focus should be on coding, unit testing, and code walkthroughs so that the maximum number of task cards on the task board land in the "ready to demo" column. For the last week of an EDW development iteration, the coding should be essentially complete because the team needs to use that time to load the target tables so that the product owner will have data to review during the upcoming product demo.

Row 3 pertains to that upcoming product demonstration and recognizes that it will not just spontaneously occur. Many folks will be attending this ceremony, including the team leaders, often the programmers, and sometimes the projects' near stakeholders. Accordingly, the product owner needs to be prepared to conduct his or her test drive efficiently, so the EDW team leaders would do well to do some light planning for this event. The centerpiece of Week 1 is iteration planning, and the team leaders should use the information surfaced during that session to lightly sketch the items they hope to evaluate at the demonstration that will occur a few weeks later. Sometime during the next week the product owner or project architect should take a closer look at the planned demonstration and add details about what queries the product owner will issue against the warehouse data at each point in the test drive. As the programmers start completing modules during the second half of the iteration, these two leaders may well hear of capabilities added or dropped that will make them want to update their script for the product demo during Week 3. In Week 4, once the build is complete and the data for the demonstration is being loaded, the development team should determine if they can execute the product owner's demonstration script by conducting a mini-alpha test so that the demo will be free of any nasty surprises.

Row 4 of the "when" grid focuses on re-demonstrating the build from the prior iteration. This aspect of agile QA is unique to agile data warehousing/business intelligence (DW/BI) projects that include significant data integration. Throughout the years of trying to build data warehouses in short iterations, teams have learned that it is physically impossible to prepare 80/20 specs for a module, program the business rules, integrate the code, and load the warehouse with near-production data all in 3 or 4 weeks. Just loading a realistic slice of operational data can take 3 or 4 days alone. The workaround that all agile data warehousing teams seem to adopt is executing the iteration's product demo using a small, managed data set that can adequately demonstrate the new, functional aspects of the application. This data set is relatively *small* so that it loads quickly—for example, in less than 1 hour. It is *managed* so that it contains a good illustration of every business rule the product owner needs to review. With this data set in hand, agile EDW teams typically run the product demo at the end of the iteration using the small data set and then ask the system tester to load the new build with near-production data sometime during the next iteration.

Our "when" grid reflects this practice. Starting with the last day of Iteration 3, the small-data demo begins. It is shown stretching into the first week of Iteration 4 because frequently a product owner will take a few days to approve all the work, even if looking at the small, managed data set. The product owner may want to study the transformed data more closely, working offline from the rest of the team.

In a perfect world, the small-data demo would be enough for the product owner to accept the work of the iteration just completed. Unfortunately, he or she knows that just one or two records out of a million can cause a data transform to fail, so the prior iteration's build must also be evaluated with the data that represents the size and content of a real production data set. Only a data set very much like a full snapshot of the production source systems can ferret out a full set of design and programming defects. For this reason, once the team has concluded the product demonstration on Row 3 of Figure 17.5, the system test spends the following iteration working in the remaining boxes in Row 4. After the small-data product demo concludes, the system tester moves the current build to a separate host, which will free up the development platform so that programmers can start working on the next iteration's developer stories. He can then begin loading the prior iteration's build with full volume data during Week 2. In Week 3, he can repeat the product demo on his own, searching for any new defects engendered by this larger data set. If the new build seems acceptable to him, he will then arrange for the product owner to repeat the prior iteration's demonstration with the full data set during Week 4.

As the previous discussion highlights, the quality work within an agile iteration changes considerably as the weeks of a sprint go by. In order to avoid confusion, missed cues, and wasted effort, the team leaders should ensure that a grid such as that shown in Figure 17.5 gets filled out and displayed on the project room wall. Such guidance will allow all the roles of the team to properly direct their own efforts as the iteration time box progresses. Rather than drafting it on their own, however, these leaders should invite the programmers to participate in defining the different combinations of quality efforts occurring with each week, using Figure 17.5 as a starting suggestion. After programmers have a chance to define a "when" grid of their own, they will feel they own the plan and will follow it, requiring much less monitoring and nagging by the team leaders. A new team may need to wait a few iterations before the components illustrated previously will make sense. However, the grid controls an important aspect of development work and can always be revisited later, so team leaders should probably plan to hold a collaborative session to draft a first version of this planning grid no later than the end of Iteration 2.

Quality Duties at the End of a Release Cycle

In Part II, we discussed wrapping development iterations within a set larger risk mitigation cycle. In defining when teammates should perform their QA work, some thought should be given to these larger cycles as well.

Figure 17.6 repeats a portion of the risk mitigation strategy diagram from Chapter 6. There, I suggested that IT staff members, because they work in and around software engineering projects, tend to focus largely on errors originating from application coding concepts. However, by the time coding begins, the stakeholders and business analysts, as well as the team's project architect, could all have committed errors with far greater impact regarding the project's solution and business concepts. To know that an application is entirely correct, the agile EDW team needs to extend their validation efforts upward, to the levels involving solution and business concepts. Unfortunately, the agile teammates cannot touch much of these higher levels during a development iteration, so a robust quality plan will have to arrange for additional testing efforts when the team presents a subrelease candidate and when a subrelease enters production usage.

The first of these higher-level ceremonies will be the release candidate review, as listed in the middle layer of Figure 17.6. Although called a "review," the team should consider this event as a very important test that the application's current build must pass. During this review, the product owner will present the current build to the project's near stakeholders, asking them a question such as, "Does this build have enough new features to warrant the $50,000 it will take to promote it into production usage?" As noted in Table 17.1, the product owner and project architect are frequently the team members who prepare the script for this type of review. We can consider the elements on that script as test cases for the subrelease candidate review. If the stakeholders agree that the new features merit the expense, effort, and distraction of a new subrelease, the team will have passed this very important quality assessment.

The next larger cycle test will be the operational readiness review, during which the operations team will evaluate whether the subrelease candidate will behave well enough as a member of the company's IT ecosystem to be installed into the company's production computing environment. The operations staff members will want to review not only the design of the application but also the way that the application was tested, so all of the QA activities leading up to this review will need to be organized for a summary presentation. As noted in Table 17.1, the system tester and any collaborators she can find among the operations team should take the lead in defining the items for this presentation. Those items will be test cases for the system test represented by the operational readiness review.

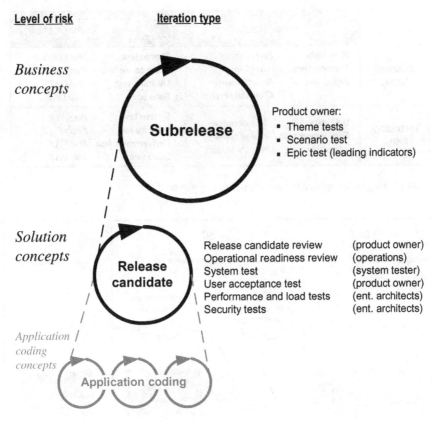

FIGURE 17.6   Quality assurance work linked to the larger project cycles surrounding development iterations.

If the application passes the readiness review, operation staff members will move the build into the user acceptance testing (UAT) environment, where they will insist on completing a system test before allowing the business staff to start acceptance testing. During this system test, the operations team will utilize many of the test cases provided by the system tester in addition to many from a standard list that they maintain.

Should the application pass system testing, the next validation will be user acceptance testing, where the business departments waiting for the system will validate the application using a script they authored earlier and then conduct longer-term reviews that often include beta tests and soak testing. The EDW team leaders should also plan on performing the additional tests from Quadrant 4, discussed in Chapter 16. These tests include suites such as performance, load tests, and security tests and usually occur after acceptance testing because they must take place on a near-production host holding near-production data.

When the subrelease candidate passes user acceptance tests, IT will promote that build into production, placing the application into the top cycle listed in Figure 17.6, the subrelease. This event will allow the organization to conduct an even higher class of tests that are essential to determining the success of the EDW project. Only here can the product owners and business stakeholders validate that the project's business concepts are correct. To investigate and document this level of fit-to-purpose, they need to conduct tests such as theme, scenario, and epic tests. The epic tests in particular will revolve around the leading indicators of business success identified by the project sponsor during the interview for the sponsor's concept briefing, as discussed in Part III. These all-important tests need to be placed on the *when* portion of the EDW team's QA plan, with the appropriate role for authoring the test cases indicated as well. These twin considerations of when and who for the larger cycle tests are illustrated in Figure 17.6.

If a team has successfully thought through all of the higher-level testing described previously, the EDW leaders should be able to summarize the timing of major quality events using the 2×2 top-down planning matrix started in Chapter 16. Figure 17.7 illustrates a version of that grid updated to display *when* the tests selected will occur. Eventually, the agile EDW quality assurance approach will provide *where* and *how* versions of this chart as well. Taken together, the multiple versions of the 2×2 matrix that the agile EDW validation planning process will generate will provide a set of easily comprehended artifacts for the project room wall that will express a crisp, complete, and easily comprehendible overview of the team's quality plan.

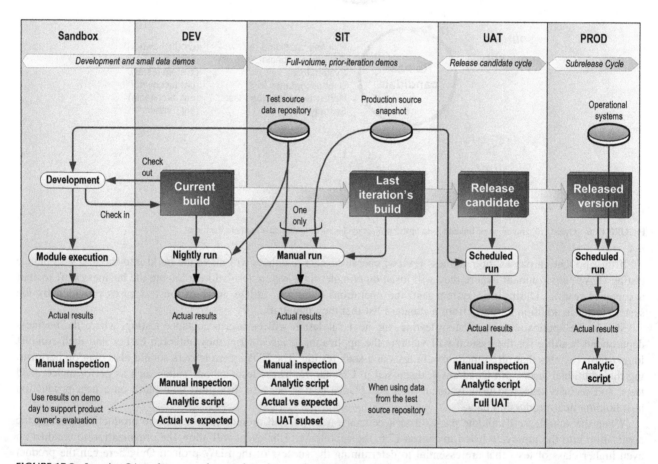

	Support the team *Are we done coding yet?*		Critique the product *Product offering maximum value?*	
Business facing	**Story tests** **Scenario tests** **Alpha test**	*End of sprint* *...week later* *Before release* *Candidate review*	**Theme test** **Acceptance test** **Usability test** **Beta test**	*Mid iteration* *Early UAT* *Mid UAT* *Late UAT*
Technology facing	**Unit tests** **Component tests** **Integration test**	*Mid-iteration* *End of sprint* *Nightly build*	**System test** **Security test** **Performance test** **Load test**	*Pre-ORR* *Early UAT* *Mid UAT* *Mid UAT*

FIGURE 17.7   The 2 × 2 QA planning matrix updated to show when test cases will run.

FIGURE 17.8   Locating QA work among a data warehouse's execution environments.

WHERE SHOULD TEAMMATES PERFORM THEIR QA DUTIES?

The agile EDW team may adroitly plan the what, who, and when of its QA work, but if it makes no effort to provide the computing environments necessary, no system validation work will occur. The developers will need multiple workspaces for conducting their quality activities, and the considerations regarding *where* testing need to be coordinated with the *when* aspects explored previously. We can provide the EDW team leaders with a simple artifact that should make planning where quality assessments will happen fairly straightforward.

Distributing Test Activities Across Environments

Figure 17.8 is a simple artifact that EDW team leaders can use to analyze not only how many host environments their project requires but also where major types of quality work will occur on the servers they do have. The question of how many servers is important to address early in a project. I know of some teams that are forced to complete development, testing, and production services using only two environments. The time-consuming gyrations they must execute in order to swap different builds and data sets on and off this restricted number of servers essentially kills any hope of appearing "agile" to their business customers.

Figure 17.8 shows five environments, which is more than most teams can procure but is hardly excessive given the demanding product validation cycles that an agile team must follow. The diagram also lists the portions of the development process that will most heavily use these environments, taken from the *when* discussion in the previous section. The combinations of where and when illustrated here begin with a *sandbox*, where individual programmers can code the module required to fulfill a developer story. Typically, a developer checks out the module he will modify so that no one else can simultaneously alter that program. When he has finished, he checks the module back into the development build. DEV (development) is the environment where the programmers can perform integration tests on the current build and later conduct a product demo at the end of an iteration using a small, managed data set. In system integration test (SIT), the system tester places the prior iteration's build on a server where she can load it with full-volume data, so that she and the product owner can repeat the previous product demo. When this version accumulates a critical mass of new features, it is moved into UAT, where the team leaders and selected end users conduct the planned acceptance tests. From there, the build is promoted into PROD (production), where the business staff can use it to improve company performance and the EDW team leaders can simultaneously test for business-concept errors.

Figure 17.8 also suggests the class of data and the type of execution that each instance of the application will utilize, a topic we consider further in Chapter 18. In brief, the team will execute modules in isolation in the sandbox but put the entire build through a full integration test suite every night in DEV. The system tester will execute manual runs as needed in SIT, but the application will be driven by a scheduler once it arrives in UAT and PROD.

Figure 17.8 illustrates well the headaches a team can suffer when budgets or IT policies force them to operate with fewer environments:

- How does a programmer work after hours without a sandbox when DEV is occupied with a nightly testing run?
- If the developers must place DEV and SIT on the same host, how do they demo a build from both the current and the prior iterations?
- If the developers must use UAT for SIT, how will they demo the next build to the product owner when the business departments fall behind on user acceptance testing and want the prior subrelease left running undisturbed in the UAT environment for the next two months?

Platform architects actually have many clever ways of implementing multiple logical servers on one physical host, but setting up such protean resources requires a good deal of lead time and a high level of testing of its own. For that reason, EDW team leaders are wise to draft a diagram such as Figure 17.8 during Iteration 0 and send to IT management the appropriate request for resources so that the necessary environments are present when the team starts its development iterations. Once IT has provisioned the environments, a diagram such as Figure 17.8 should be updated with machine names and data schema information and then displayed prominently as a planning reference on the project room wall.

Distributing Test Techniques Across Environments

Figure 17.8 also displays some important information regarding the styles of test evaluations that the team will employ to validate each type of build. This topic is considered in greater detail in Chapter 18 when we discuss planning *how* tests cases will be executed, but to finish describing this diagram we can summarize that information here. The unit tests occurring in the sandbox will be evaluated via manual inspection until the programmer believes the module is ready for integration. The integration tests in the DEV environment will be driven by the automated data warehouse test engine, if the team has invested in one. Those results will be validated not only through manual inspections but also through analytical scripts that compare sources to targets, perhaps using the parameter-driven test widgets described in Chapter 16. They may also be evaluated by comparing actual data output to an expected-results data set.

These same evaluation techniques will be used on the results generated by the manual integration test runs in SIT, but there the system tester can also employ a subset of the cases planned for acceptance testing, especially just before that build is promoted into UAT. For builds in UAT, the business staff will employ manual inspection and the full UAT test suite. Some of those test cases may well involve analytical scripts to automatically compare the release candidate to information found on the operational source systems. Finally, for subreleases promoted to PROD, the company might wish to continue running analytical scripts to validate production loads. Often, these scripts perform reconciliations

	Support the team *Are we done coding yet?*		Critique the product *Product offering maximum value?*	
Business facing	Story tests	SIT	Theme test	SIT
	Scenario tests	SIT	Acceptance test	early UAT
	Alpha test	SIT	Usability test	mid UAT
			Beta test	late UAT
Technology facing	Unit test	DEV	System test	early UAT
	Component test	DEV	Security test	early UAT
	Integration test	SIT	Performance test	mid UAT
			Load test	mid UAT

FIGURE 17.9   2 × 2 QA planning matrix updated to show where test cases should execute.

back to operational sources and also evaluate whether the number of records or sums of numeric columns have varied excessively compared to the previous load.

When fully detailed, the Test Build by Environment diagram becomes a useful reference for the team, but it does not list the types of tests that will be executed in each environment. To close the loop with the top-down planning of Chapter 16, EDW team leaders might take a moment to create a *where* version of the 2 × 2 planning matrix, as shown in Figure 17.9.

KEY QUALITY RESPONSIBILITIES BY TEAM ROLE

Placing test-writing responsibilities on the 2 × 2 matrix communicates the team's QA responsibilities at a high level. Getting that artifact completed in the early days of a project will certainly ensure that the QA planning is underway and that everyone on the team is participating. Over the long run of the project, however, teammates will need greater details regarding the precise activities for which they are responsible. In order to fully internalize his or her role in application quality, each teammate will need a list of the duties required of him or her at every point throughout the development process.

With that need in mind, we can see that the key responsibilities for the system tester should include the following:

1. Maintaining an organized list of the QA duties by role so teammates know what to do
2. Stepping teammates through the quality process while they are learning their roles
3. Monitoring and supporting teammates as they struggle to perform those roles correctly

The agile nature of iterative development may greatly assist the system tester in performing these responsibilities. Agile teams are collaborative, self-organized groups, so the system tester does not need a perfect or comprehensive list by which to steer the team. If the system tester can get a conversation regarding roles and responsibilities started and provide enough ideas to seed the discussion, his teammates should be able to fill in the missing details. This discussion will go a long way to achieve the team learning mentioned in Step 2, and it will provide the material that should comprise the list of duties cited in Step 1. This section provides the system tester with a starting notion of how to structure an initial quality conversation with his or her teammates and the types of duties that should emerge from that discussion.

Guiding the Team to Self-Organized Quality Planning

When the consultants from my company and I introduce agile QA to EDW teams, we first set the context using the artifacts discussed so far in these chapters, including the 2 × 2 top-down planning matrices and the bottom-up test-by-column-type grid considered in Chapter 16. At that point, we need to get the teammates to start taking ownership of the quality process, which is best accomplished if they assign themselves to the validation work that needs to be done. A general sense of ownership works better than having them self-assign detailed duties because then members will continue searching for the small quality chores that were overlooked during the initial planning rather than ignoring neglected activities because they were never specifically expected of them.

To get a team started on this habit of "continually scanning for quality plan gaps and taking responsibility to fill them," our consultants typically meet with the team and ask the participants to complete the last column in Table 17.2. This table lists the general aspects of a DW/BI application and its mission, and then it asks who should be responsible for assuring quality for each aspect. I have listed those considerations here with suggested answers, but the most

TABLE 17.2 Quality Assurance Responsibilities by Key DW/BI Aspect
Who on this team should ensure that the data warehouse and its front end are correct in the following ways?

Things to Get Right	Who Will Be Responsible
The bit and the bytes	Programmers
The values in the columns	System analyst
The rows in the tables	Data modeler and systems analyst
The number and types of tables	Data modeler
The way end users see those tables	Product owner and project architect
The meaning of the data	Product owner and data modeler
What customer can learn from the data	Product owner and business analyst
The limitations of the system	Project architect and ETL lead
The flexibility of the system	Project architect
The exceptional circumstances it must handle	Product owner
New business situations it should support in the future	Product owner

important aspect of this exercise is that the team members must collectively select the assignments in the last column for themselves. Note that the right column focuses on who is responsible for the results being correct, not who needs to design or program a given component.

Many of the notions listed on the left in Table 17.2 are fairly abstract, so one would think that results from this exercise would quickly be discarded in favor of all the other more precise artifacts offered previously in this chapter. However, on many of the projects I have led, teammates debating a quality issue have drawn upon the conclusions from this grid far more frequently than any other part of the quality plan. It seems to provide the big picture for EDW quality assurance in a more immediate way than any other artifact.

The assignments shown above are only suggestions, but they are typical of what most teams decide upon. A few aspects of this typical result are notable. First, these topics reach a long way beyond unit testing. True to the agile mindset, the focus is predominantly on the value that the warehouse provides the organization. Such an orientation demands that the team start viewing quality as a goal that emerges out of collaboration across many roles, thus requiring the team to consider far more than just testing.

Second, the product owner is listed frequently. Product owners often struggle to see their role when they first join an agile development team. They often ask why they need to allocate as much as half their time to the project. That uncertainty seems to dissipate quickly once they participate with the team on this exercise.

Third, the system tester is nowhere on this grid. Some teams begin this exercise by nominating the system tester on every row but quickly rethink that approach when the system tester begins asking, "Without detailed specs to work from, how am I going to know that a particular item was done right?" The system tester will not have the expertise needed to perform such assessments. His teammates will have to continue thinking about quality in the categories listed above. The system tester's role will focus instead on regularly asking whether this table needs to be updated and then supporting the individuals assigned to each category.

Suggested Quality Duties by Role

The previous exercise will instill in the agile EDW teammates a high-level notion of who is responsible for quality on their project. It will move the teammates into the right mindset, but they will need to translate the abstract responsibilities assigned during the exercise into a checklist of QA responsibilities that each person can refer to as he or she works. The system tester should follow up the exercise by conferencing with the teammates fulfilling each role to define such checklists. The following lists should help get those follow-up conversations started. They are not complete by any means, but they focus instead on the core quality responsibilities of each role. A system tester should expect his or her teammates to reshuffle these suggestions between the roles to better match the personalities on their team, their particular skill sets, and other project circumstances.

Product Owner

- Participate in defining pro-forma product demos by module type
- As modules begin development, brainstorm specific product demo items
- During each iteration's product demonstration
  - Consider quality when deciding whether to accept or reject each module
  - Ask "How do I know I can trust the information this system provides?"
- During the full-data demonstration that follows an iteration demo day
  - Validate the data loaded for proper applications of business rules, completeness, and overall reasonableness
- Direct the product demonstration to cover the full functional needs implied by user stories, themes, and epics
- Gather product demo items into a user acceptance test script for the next subrelease
- Prepare and conduct subrelease candidate reviews with the project's near stakeholders

Project Architect

- Drive quality assurance planning until it is sufficient and correct
- Participate in defining
  - Pro-forma unit, component, and integration tests
  - Pro-forma product demos by module type
- During development iterations, participate in
  - Tech requirements walkthrough, especially discussions of business rules
  - Brainstorming integration testing for each iteration's application build
  - Brainstorming specific product demo items
- Facilitate the product demo
- Ensure product owner fulfills his or her quality responsibilities, fill in the gaps as necessary
- For each subrelease candidate, certify that it has the functionality and quality needed to solve the focal business problems

Data Modeler

- Participate in defining
  - Pro-forma integration tests
  - Coding patterns for module types, especially metadata and key columns
- During development iterations, participate in
  - Tech requirements walkthrough, focusing on referential integrity topics
  - Brainstorm integration testing for modules
  - Prepare the SQL or BI modules for product demos reviewing the deeper layers of the reference architecture
- Before both small-data and large-data product demos, validate data loaded for referential integrity and overall reasonableness
- Serve as a steward for test data including
  - The scripts that create and re-create test data sets
  - The bulk data records in the test source repository
  - The data records for test cases requested by others on the team
  - Records of expected results, where appropriate

Systems Analyst

- Participate in
  - Pro-forma definitions of unit and component tests
  - Coding patterns for each module type
  - Defining subsetting logic for generating records for the small-data product demo data set
- As modules begin development, participate in
  - Tech requirements walkthrough with coders, focusing on source-to-target maps (STMs)
  - Brainstorming unit and component testing for modules
  - Brainstorming integration testing for each iteration's application build
- Attend code walkthroughs, focusing on implementation of STM business rules

- Before both small-data and large-data product demos
    - Validate that the business rules listed in the STM were properly implemented
    - Double-check that unit and component tests were executed properly
    - Prepare explanations for defects that will be visible during the product demo

Programmers and Programming Leads

- Project start
    - Draft pro-forma unit and component tests for each module type
    - Draft coding patterns for each module type
- During development iterations
    - Put resolving tech debt ahead of new development
    - Draft unit and component test for each module to be built
    - Conduct unit and component tests
    - Ensure that unit and component tests are repeatable, to support maintenance programming later
- Conduct code walkthroughs to ensure
    - Programming meets project standards
    - Unit and component tests meet the team's standards
- Load tables for each small-data product demo
    - Determine if the data loaded has high enough quality to demonstrate to the product owner

Scrum Master

- Ensure quality work exists in the team's definition of "done"
- During development iterations, ensure that teammates
    - Include quality tasks in their estimation
    - Work off tech debt before turning to new programming
    - Remind teammates to follow new quality policies adopted during last retrospective
- During the product demonstrations, ensure
    - System tester certifies the demo
    - The team reviews the tech debt items before examining the results of new work
    - The product owner considers quality before accepting or rejecting work
- During iteration retrospectives, ensure team considers which of its quality practices are working well and which need to be improved
- Ensure the team invests in automation where it will save time or improve results
- At subrelease candidate reviews, ensure the project architect addresses both features and quality when he or she certifies the current build as a solution to the company's business problem

THE OVERARCHING DUTIES OF THE SYSTEM TESTER

Now that we have the quality activities of the other team members in focus, we can turn to the responsibilities of the system tester. Stated briefly, the system tester's primary responsibilities are to

- drive the QA planning until everyone understands their duties;
- organize the testing infrastructure;
- mentor and support the team as it pursues those duties;
- visualize progress; and
- attend to the quality activities not assigned or performed by other teammates.

Because of the agile approach to requirements and design, the system tester cannot author or execute the unit and component tests himself, so his role evolves to where he guides those who can specify and perform the detailed level of validations necessary. He can build upon the work performed by others, however, collating the low-level tests as appropriate into higher-level integration and system test suites.

The system tester will use the integration test in particular as a regular "moment of truth" that both teammates and business stakeholders can understand. If the project has only five test cases defined for the integration test by the end of Iteration 10, everyone can see that the team is not fulfilling its commitment to deliver a quality application. Similarly, if the 900 out of 1,000 integration test cases are failing by the end of Iteration 15, both IT and business will know that although the developers have certainly defined quality for the project, they have not yet committed to achieving it.

Table 17.3 provides a typical list of duties for the system tester. Readers will certainly think of additional items they would like to add, so EDW team leaders should consider this list as a starting point to begin the conversation with whomever is assigned to be their team's system tester.

TABLE 17.3 Key Responsibilities for the Agile EDW System Tester Role

- Drive the initial draft and ongoing revisions of the project's quality assurance plan
- Ensure the validations are balanced between
  - Customer- and technology-facing tests
  - Supporting the development team and critiquing the product
- Ensure the validations are balanced along the six dimensions of testing, including
  - Positive and negative testing
  - Progression and regression testing
  - Functional and nonfunctional testing
- Ensure the validations address the three domains of project risk, namely
  - Application coding concepts
  - Solutions concepts
  - Business concepts
- Guide team in defining quality duties and activities using top-down and bottom-up planning devices
- Document the current quality plan with easy-to-comprehend artifacts and display them prominently for frequent reference during development
- Support the data modeler and system analyst in the definition, derivation, and categorization of the test source data and any necessary collection of expected result records
- For each iteration planning session, provide an outline of
  - The integration testing plan
  - The test source data and expected results to be used
- Mentor and support teammates on test case writing
- Attend design sessions during the iterations to ask, "How do you plan to test that object?"
- Attend code walkthroughs to review the effectiveness of unit and component testing
- Implement nightly integration testing
  - Report findings at the team's daily stand-up meeting
  - Track defects discovered and defects resolved for the current build
- Certify the data considered at each iteration's product demo, assuring the product owner that the application was loaded
  - From a reasonable collection of source data
  - Using a single, successful run of the data transforms
  - Contains no manual edits during or after ETL runs
- Repeat each iteration's small-data demo for the product owner using full-volume, near-production data
- Add tests for departmental standards regarding
  - System installation
  - Operations and help desk
  - Metadata
  - Enterprise architecture
- Plan and prepare formal system test runs for each subrelease
- Represent team and the current build of the application at the operational readiness review
- Support product owner in planning and preparing for
  - Release candidate reviews with business stakeholders
  - User acceptance testing
- Drive execution of formal systems test for each release candidate
- Propose improvements to the quality plan and activities during iteration retrospectives

Certifying the User Demo's Data

EDW teams frequently wonder why I suggest in the previous list that the system tester certify the data loaded in the current build just before the product owner reviews it during an iteration's product demo. Most of the EDW professionals I have had the pleasure to work with have been highly principled individuals. That said, there are also scoundrels present in our profession. The developers on a few of the teams I have led have responded to the steady deadline pressure imposed by the iteration time box by cobbling together a set of source data that steers around the defects they knew were in the code. In other situations, the ETL was so flimsy that they had to resurrect it a half dozen times in order to complete a single data load, signaling that the application was not yet truly integrated. Worse yet, a few have actually hand-edited the output data in order to mask the records that would cause the product owner to reject the current build.

To safeguard against such dubious practices, the system tester needs to watch developer activity toward the end of an iteration to the point that she can state with conviction that no one is attempting to spoof the product owner. She must assure the product owner that the integrity of the data presented for the product demo warrants the time it will take to review it.

With the duties envisioned in the previous list, the system tester role clearly changes from the "doer," as it exists on waterfall projects, to one consumed more with planning, mentoring, preparing, collating, watching, and certifying. On an agile EDW project, then, the system test role is a leadership position, one that demands that the person taking this responsibility not only have a clear idea of what good quality practices are but also can persuasively communicate that notion to his or her teammates and inspire them to complete the difficult work that quality requires.

HOW MANY TESTERS ARE NEEDED?

Quality assurance costs money. Done right, it will consume a very tangible proportion of a project's budget. EDW team leaders will need to request a reasonable level of testing resources, and the most important of those will be system testers. Estimating how many system testers a project will need is difficult, especially before the development iterations begin. To assist readers in formulating such an estimate, Table 17.4 offers the ratios of testers to programmers with which most of my company's projects have been able to succeed. Keep in mind that the number of testers required should increase with the level of risk involved in the project, as illustrated by the line at the bottom for chip-embedded software, which I included for comparison. When the software is very difficult to change or small errors can cause a large amount of harm, more testers should be added to the project, to the point where they will outnumber the programmers, if that is what it takes.

Many of my colleagues on waterfall projects use the 1:3 ratio as a rule of thumb for their projects. Because agile projects drive teams hard with time-boxed iterations and proceed with just-in-time specifications, iterative delivery projects require an even higher ratio of 1:2 if the QA duties are not distributed as described previously. Note that as the quality responsibilities become distributed across the team, the ratio of system testers to programmers improves. That trend reflects the fact that several EDW team leaders will be writing the test cases. Test automation, which is discussed in Chapter 18, helps improve the ratio by 50 percent, but it is not a panacea for the high cost of quality because test cases still have to be authored by the human mind.

Finally, we can see in Table 17.4 one measure of the cost of poor-quality practices. In my experience, a team that fails to plan its QA efforts and distribute the test-authoring roles will find it needs a 1:2 tester-to-programmer ratio, equivalent to that of a new team in which the system tester is performing all the quality duties. Compared to the 1:4 or 1:6 ratio of a team that has invested in planning, that first team will need two or three times the labor from system testers to achieve the same level of quality. In other words, agile EDW teams that want to dump responsibility for QA on some poor tester should expect to triple their testing budget if they want to get the system right. Such a bump in head count is an expensive proposition, usually costing enough to convince IT management to support the approach to quality advocated here.

TABLE 17.4 Typical Tester-to-Programmer Ratios for Agile Enterprise Data Warehousing Projects

Situation	Reasonable Tester-to-Programmer Ratio
New teams with system tester performing all the QA duties	1:2
Newer teams with distributed QA duties	1:3
Established teams without test automation	1:4
Established teams with test automation	1:6
Test automation with automatic use of parameter-driven unit tests	1:7
Significant coordination between multiple projects	Add one tester for cross-system integration
Chip-embedded software (for comparison)	3:1

SUMMARY

The techniques discussed in Chapter 16 for identifying the type of tests developers should execute address only part of the QA planning a team should perform. Agile teams need to consider the *who*, *when*, and *where* of testing as well. The agile development approach requires team leaders to distribute test writing responsibilities across all the members of the development team. The V-model technique for matching the author and consumer of specifications provides a handy way to begin planning who should write which kind of tests. Although quality is essential to any data warehousing project, agile teams need to be careful not to lose velocity by oversocializing design and testing decisions. Following a one-up, one-down validation technique can save a tremendous amount of time.

Answering who should assume various quality responsibilities immediately leads to needing to specify when they should perform their duties. Listing quality activities by iteration week will allow the team to discuss how to organize validation work so that it meshes well with the changing demands placed on each team role throughout the development iteration's time box. Revisiting the way that application coding iterations roll up into release candidates, and how those in turn flow into release cycles, gives the team a second perspective on timing—one that accommodates many of the higher-level test types that do not fit within an iteration.

Once all teammates understand their responsibilities for QA, they will want to know where they should perform each type of work. The build-type by environment chart provides a good way for developers to envision and document the distinct testing areas they need, providing ammunition for requesting additional environments if the analysis shows they have too few. The findings from the discussions regarding who, when, and where can all be added to the 2×2 quality planning matrix we started in Chapter 16 to provide a quick summary of the project's system validation plan that teammates can follow as they pursue design and programming work during the remainder of the project. The agile context transforms the system test role from a "doer" into a leadership position—one that provides the planning, guiding, mentoring, collation, support, and review services necessary to ensure that the QA work captured on the many planning artifacts described here actually occurs.

Now that the why, what, who, when, and where of quality work have been addressed, it should be clear that an effective plan for agile EDW projects will involve a tremendous number of tests. The remaining challenge will naturally be, "How will we get all these tests executed?"—a question that Chapter 18 will strive to answer.

Chapter 18

Deciding How to Execute the Test Cases

The framework presented in the past two chapters will provide an enterprise data warehousing (EDW) team with nearly a complete quality assurance (QA) plan that lists what types of tests to execute, who will write the test cases, when they will perform their validations, and where those assessments will run. Such a solid test plan will allow teams to perform some important calculations regarding the level of effort the QA plan will require. For example, the plan will show how many *types* of tests the team desires per module. Multiplying by an estimated number of modules will forecast the number of test *cases* their quality plan will entail. Many EDW teams will be impressed to see this number exceeds 10,000. Multiplying that number again by the number of workdays in an iteration, and most agile EDW teams are truly alarmed to see the estimated number of test case *executions* approach 1 million, a fact that brings them to one last, crucial question regarding their quality plan: "How on Earth are we going to get that many test cases to actually run given our limited time and resources?"

This final chapter on agile QA planning for EDW suggests answering that question with the following 11 action steps:

1. Update the top-down plan with decisions about manual and automated test execution.
2. Start building the parameter-driven widgets.
3. Plan out the test data sets.
4. Implement the engine, whether manual or automated.
5. Define the project's set of testing aspects.
6. Build and populate the test data repository.
7. Quantify the testing objectives.
8. Begin creating test cases.
9. Start up the test engine.
10. Visualize the team's progress with quality assurance.
11. Document the team's success.

If the resulting plan proves larger than the team or the organization can sustain, then this last step of quality planning has revealed an important gap in the business concept driving the project. Revealing that the business concept calls for an application that is far larger than the overall organization can or is willing to test gives sponsors and the EDW development team the opportunity to realign expectations and resources. After perhaps a couple of iterations with the stakeholders, a team following the execution planning steps listed here will arrive at an appropriately sized project with a well-organized and actionable quality plan. This last bit of planning will have positioned them to quickly deliver a trustworthy information system that will make an important and positive impact on their company's competitive capabilities.

GOOD AGILE QUALITY PLANS INVOLVE NUMEROUS TEST EXECUTIONS

In order to build a realistic notion regarding *how* an agile team will execute its EDW testing plan, team leaders need to first estimate the size of the challenge. Table 18.1 provides a "back of the envelope" estimate of the number of test cases for a medium-sized data warehouse. The top half of the table views the project in terms of requirements objects such as epics and themes, and the bottom focuses on the physical objects the EDW will need, such as units and components. For the hypothetical project portrayed here, the team promised to deliver the six new competitive capabilities (epics) requested by the sponsor over the span of 1 year. The left side of the table focuses on estimating the number of objects, and the right side translates those estimates into the number of required test types.

TABLE 18.1 Estimating the Number of Test Cases Needed for a Modest Level of EDW Testing

Looking from the Requirements Side / Mostly Manual Executions

Requirements Object [1]	Items Per Level [2]	Cumulative Number [3]	Typical Deliverable [4]	Planned Test Type* [5]	Test Cases per Test Type [6]	Total Test Cases [7]	Execution Frequency [8]
Epics	6	6	Subreleases	User Acceptance Test	12	72	once before promotion to UAT once while in UAT
				Usability Test	12	72	
				Beta Test	12	72	
				Performance Test	1	6	
				Load Test	1	6	
				Alpha Test	48	288	
				Scenario Test	12	72	
				System Test	12	72	
				Security Test	?	?	
Themes	6	36	Analyses, Dashboards, Report Packages	Theme Test	4	144	once in mid iteration then repeated along with epic testing
User Stories	6	216	Data Checks	Story Tests	2	432	once during product demos then repeated with epic testing

Subtotal for Manually Executed Test Cases   1,236

Looking from the ETL Design Side / Mostly Automatable

Requirements Object [1]	Items Per Level [2]	Cumulative Number [3]	Typical Deliverable [4]	Planned Test Type* [5]	Test Case per Test Type [6]	Total Test Cases [7]	Execution Frequency [8]
Subject Areas	12	12	n/a	Consolidated Integration Test	6	72	Nightly regression testing
Architectural Layers	3	36	Workflows / Sequences	Integration Test	6	216	Nightly regression testing
Data Transforms	12	432	Mappings	Component Test	6	2,592	Nightly regression testing
Modules	3	1,296	Initial loads, incremental loads, archiving routines	Unit Test	6	7,776	Nightly regression testing

Subtotal for Automatable Test Cases   12,468

Taken from example outlined in Figure 16.8

Starting from the top, each epic decomposed into six analyses for directors (themes), each of which broke down further into six business-level data checks for the managers and financial analysts (user stories), for a total of 216 user stories. Translating this into programmed modules began by noting that the six epics would require a data warehouse with 12 subject areas. Each subject area needed modules in at least three architectural layers: landing, integration, and presentation. The architectural layers averaged a dozen data transforms, each of which required three extract, transform, and load (ETL) modules for the initial and incremental data loads plus an archiving routine to roll off data that has outlived its usefulness. Multiplying out these parameters revealed that the warehouse will require the team to build nearly 1300 objects, each of which needs to be quality assured.

The right half of Table 18.1 calculates the number of test cases that will be needed to validate this collection of objects. This modest plan employs the 14 test types listed in the 2 × 2 planning matrix of Figure 16.8. Column 5 groups

TABLE 18.2 Estimating the Number of Low-Level Test Case Executions for Four Subreleases

Iteration	Iteration Type	Progression Test Cases			Regression Tests			Total Cases			Total Test Cases	Regression Testing Percent	Nightly Test Runs per Iteration	Total Nightly Executions
		Unit	Comp.	Integ.	Unit	Comp.	Integ.	Unit	Comp.	Integ.				
1	Dev.	648	216	24	0	0	0	648	216	24	888	0.0%	13	11,544
2	Dev.	648	216	24	648	216	24	1,296	432	48	1,776	50.0%	13	23,088
3	Dev.	648	216	24	1,296	432	48	1,944	648	72	2,664	66.7%	13	34,632
4	Sub Rel. 1	648	216	24	1,296	432	48	1,944	648	72	2,664	66.7%	13	34,632
5	Dev.	648	216	24	1,944	648	72	2,592	864	96	3,552	75.0%	13	46,176
6	Dev.	648	216	24	2,592	864	96	3,240	1,080	120	4,440	80.0%	13	57,720
7	Dev.	648	216	24	3,240	1,080	120	3,888	1,296	144	5,328	83.3%	13	69,264
8	Sub Rel. 2	648	216	24	3,240	1,080	120	3,888	1,296	144	5,328	83.3%	13	69,264
9	Dev.	648	216	24	3,888	1,296	144	4,536	1,512	168	6,216	85.7%	13	80,808
10	Dev.	648	216	24	4,536	1,512	168	5,184	1,728	192	7,104	87.5%	13	92,352
11	Dev.	648	216	24	5,184	1,728	192	5,832	1,944	216	7,992	88.9%	13	103,896
12	Sub Rel. 3	648	216	24	5,184	1,728	192	5,832	1,944	216	7,992	88.9%	13	103,896
13	Dev.	648	216	24	5,832	1,944	216	6,480	2,160	240	8,880	90.0%	13	115,440
14	Dev.	648	216	24	6,480	2,160	240	7,128	2,376	264	9,768	90.9%	13	126,984
15	Dev.	648	216	24	7,128	2,376	264	7,776	2,592	288	10,656	91.7%	13	138,528
16	Sub Rel. 4	648	216	24	7,128	2,376	264	**7,776**	**2,592**	288	10,656	91.7%	13	138,528

Total Executions During the Project: **1,246,752**

these test types with the appropriate object, Column 6 provides reasonable counts for the number of test cases per object, and Column 7 multiplies that value by the number of objects calculated earlier in Column 3. The resulting estimates for the number of test cases might be surprising. For this modestly sized data warehouse, the team will need to conduct more than 1000 tests for the major requirement items (the first subtotal) and over 12,000 test cases for design objects (the second subtotal).

Surprise may turn into alarm when EDW team leaders realize that the previous calculations estimate only test cases. Only when we consider test case *executions* does the enormity of the QA work needed for enterprise data warehousing become truly visible. Most test cases are executed numerous times during the long arch of an EDW project. As discussed in Chapter 16, continuous testing enables teams to minimize the effort lost to root cause analysis of defects, preserving the bulk of their resources for building new features. With their fast pace of programming, most agile EDW teams implement this continuous testing as nightly, full regression testing so that new defects can be detected and resolved within a daily work cycle. Table 18.2 reveals what daily testing implies for test case execution counts. It extends the bottom half of Table 18.1 by the number of workdays in a 3-week iteration and then tallies the total number of executions for the 16 iterations that would make up a development project lasting 1 year. One can see the number of unit, component, and integration test cases is growing steadily toward the upper limits identified in Table 18.1 as the iterations progress (see bolded numbers in the last row). These numbers hold steady at four points throughout the project when the team promotes a subrelease iteration into production and therefore does not create a new code needing progression testing.

With these assumptions, the number of test case executions begins at slightly less than 900 for the first iteration. By the time the project concludes 16 iterations later, the number of executions has grown to more than 130,000 per iteration, with more than 90% of that amount representing regression testing of features from previous development sprints. By totaling the numbers in the last column of Table 18.2, we can see that a robust QA plan for even a modestly sized enterprise data warehousing project will entail more than 1 million test executions. Readers are invited to re-draft the previous estimates using the particulars of their own projects. Their results will certainly differ, but because of the multipliers, the order of magnitudes will be approximately the same. Clearly, one of the major challenges in the entire QA planning process will be for agile EDW team leaders to devise a strategy for conducting such a large number of test events with the labor resources they have and recording that many results in an intelligible manner.

Alternatives to Sufficient Testing Unattractive

When first confronted with the magnitude of QA effort before them, many EDW team leaders try to argue with fate, claiming they simply do not want to invest in such an intensive level of testing. Certainly, many data warehouses have been promoted into production usage during the past few decades with far less testing than suggested here. Such practices may well be the reason that our industry has been plagued with project failure rates of 50% or higher, depending on the size of the project [Ericson 2006]. As discussed in Chapter 16, choosing the correct level of QA for a project should be a question of economics, balancing costs against benefits. What if a team wanted to proceed with a level of testing far less than implied by the estimate sketched above? The compromises its leaders might consider would include the following.

Test Fewer Items

Perhaps not every aspect of the programmed units and components have to be tested. Using the vernacular of quality engineers, they could reduce the level of their plan's "test coverage." Of course this option always exists, but the team leaders should first consult project sponsors and other business stakeholders, letting them know that the developers believe robust QA is too expensive and that they are going to only test a quarter or so of the application. The stakeholders should rightly respond by asking what will happen if the application goes into production usage and the end users find some significant defects that undermine the value of the project. The implied answer is that members of the EDW team will probably be fired. Do the EDW team leaders want to stake their careers on how serious the defects that will slip into production might be? The answer is usually no.

Test Only a Few Times

The previous estimate assumes that many of the lower-level tests will be executed nightly in order to support the fast development pattern of agile teams. EDW leaders could decide that nightly tests are excessive and switch to executing the lower-level test suites just before a product demo. To accurately appraise this proposal, teammates should ask themselves what will happen when they execute those tests at the end of an iteration and find so many defects that demonstrating the current build would be pointless. It is true that they will have only lost one iteration's worth of work, but if they maintain this policy the next iteration may be scuttled by product flaws, too. Moreover, teams that rarely test lose considerable time as they are forced to program around the defects they have not analyzed or resolved. The software engineering profession has extensively documented that keeping a project code clean equals faster delivery.

Further reflection reveals that testing only once in a while would do little to relieve the burden of QA. Say the team only executed its lower-level test suites once per iteration. As can be seen in Table 18.2, this policy would only reduce the amount of test executions by a factor of approximately 10. The resulting number would still be in the hundreds of thousands. If the team needs to gear up for 100,000 executions, it might as well plan for 1 million and capture the benefit of daily defect summaries so that the programmers can keep their code defect-free.

Build a Smaller Scope

As a third option, EDW team leaders could present their estimate of the testing required by the project plan and propose that the sponsor and business stakeholders reduce the scope of the project. Frankly, this is the most appealing of three bad options. Because they will base crucial business decisions on the information provided by the data warehouse, companies should not invest in building more analytical features than they can afford to quality assure.

In a sense, the estimate outlined in the previous tables is a good example of test-led development applied to the higher planning levels of a project. When the business stakeholders ask for a given scope and the EDW team responds with an estimate of the labor it will take to quality assure the implied application, the team is actually testing whether all the features requested by the business are truly necessary. If the stakeholders stick by their request, the entire project may well be as important as they say. If instead they reconsider and reduce the scope of the project, the EDW team's test of the requirements just uncovered the project's first error. Given that the project leaders are speaking with executives during this early planning, the flaw uncovered probably resides in the business-concept level, which contains some of the most expensive mistakes possible, as discussed in Part II.

Facing Up to Test Automation

At this point in the planning process, EDW team leaders have realized that the number of test executions required by their project is worrisomely large and that alternatives to full testing are unattractive. When confronting this dual reality, agile data warehousing teams usually come to the same conclusion: Their project needs to invest in test automation in order to make the required level of system validation affordable. With that realization, the project leaders should discuss where automation can help.

The team can use the top-down planning matrix from the previous chapters to record its conclusions regarding automation, as shown in Figure 18.1, which labels each test type with the degree that it can be automated. Quadrant 1 focuses on the test types suggested by the system dimension identified in Chapter 16. Note that the entries here make a distinction between the degree of automation possible for progression testing versus regression testing. In general, unit test cases lend themselves to reusable, parameter-driven test widgets, so they can be automated fairly easily. Moreover, many unit tests roll up into component and integration tests, so a predominant portion of the tests found in the systems dimension can be automated.

The only nuance will concern the new features that a team creates during a development iteration. Trying to simultaneously program a module and automate its testing ends up doubling the number of technical items that a coder has to keep aligned. Most programmers prefer to build and unit test a module by hand until the module has been accepted and they know the code will no longer be changing. After the module is accepted, of course, programmers never want to think about its unit testing again, so they are happy to add that module to the regression test driver then. The system tester has a different outlook because he is receiving rather than programming modules. His goal is to build a repeatable integration testing script so his preference will be to automate every test case sent his way. As keeper of the regression test script, he will automate as many of those test cases as possible so that he can configure each one once and not have to think about it again for the rest of the project. For that reason, Quadrant 1 labels the progression testing conduct by programmers as manual and the remaining test cases, executed by the system tester, as automated.

In practice, many of the story and scenario tests listed in Quadrant 2 can be automated for regression testing as well. For example, the product owner will naturally want to conduct a story test manually when deciding whether to accept a newly programmed module. The system tester can watch how the product owner evaluates that story during the product demo and then create a script that closely approximates that same evaluation for the regression testing suite. For this reason, many test items landing in Quadrant 2 will be labeled "manual" for progression testing and "automated" for the regression test suite.

Quadrant 3 tests will have to remain manual because they involve presenting a new subrelease to the business stakeholders and collecting their impressions. Referring back to Figure 17.7, we can see that these tests are run only during subrelease evaluations and acceptance testing cycle, and therefore would not benefit from automation much even if it were possible.

Lastly, some of the tests in Quadrant 4 will have some manual testing, but many will be tool driven. As discussed previously, the first item listed in our sample matrix, system test, has two components. The first repeats integration testing in a near-production environment, so that portion can be automated. The other portion is driven by the operations

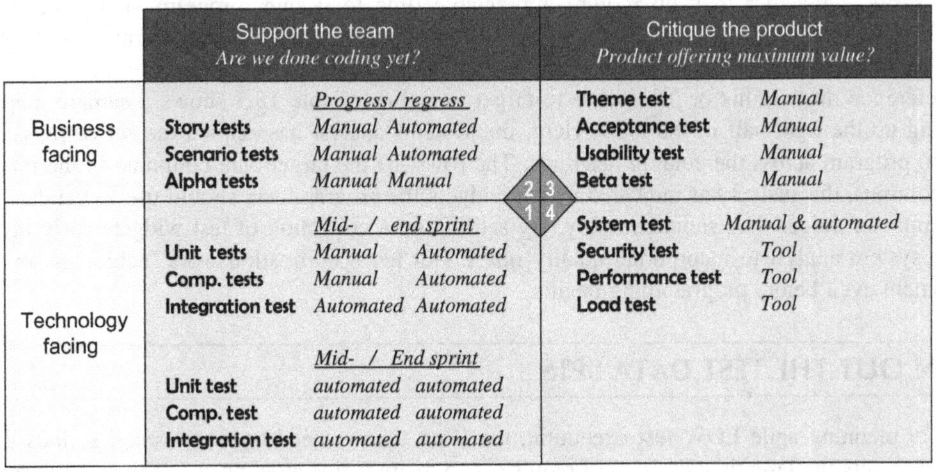

FIGURE 18.1   2 × 2 QA planning matrix communicating how team will execute test cases.

team, which can think up new validation criteria at any time. Moreover, this team's evaluations occur only once per subrelease cycle, so automating this spontaneous and occasional validation will yield little benefit. Many of the remaining tests in this quadrant, however, concern nonfunctional requirements that nearly every application, whether front-end or data warehousing/business intelligence (DW/BI), must meet. For decades now, the information technology (IT) industry has provided utilities for validating these nonfunctional requirements, such as security and performance. Security tests, for example, can be tool-assisted using widely available, open-source tools available from associations of system administrators. (See, for example, the list provided on http://sectools.org.) Similarly, utilities called "emulators" can simulate the processing loads that thousands of users and ETL routines will impose on a host server. For these reasons, many of the tests falling into Quadrant 4 can be labeled as "tool assisted," and whether that results in full automation will depend on the tool that the company chooses for each validation.

All told, test automation is highly desirable for agile EDW projects, and many of the tests will lend themselves to a machine-driven approach. Fortunately, rudimentary test automation scripts are fairly straightforward to write, as will be shown later, and even better, ready-made test automation engines for DW/BI applications exist in the marketplace today. Still, we should be careful not to let the question of whether to automate testing derail the conversation concerning *how* to execute a validation plan. Even manual testing has to be organized so that it is a repeatable process. EDW leaders who do not want to automate can still plan and manually execute their validation scheme by following the same step-by-step approach suggested in the remainder of this chapter.

STEP 1: UPDATE THE TOP-DOWN PLAN

As a first step in planning how to fulfill a quality plan, agile EDW teams need to arrive at a working decision about how they will execute the tests they need to conduct. Updating their 2×2 top-down planning matrix for "manual" or "automated" as done in Figure 18.1 often provides the visual focus a team needs to structure the conversation they must have. (EDW teams choosing not to automate testing can record their decisions in terms of "occasional execution" and "constant repetition" instead.) The portions of the execution plans slated for manual execution will need the system tester to write out an execution plan that a human can follow. The portions destined for automation will need a driver script, one that calls the reusable test widgets discussed previously.

STEP 2: START BUILDING THE PARAMETER-DRIVEN WIDGETS

While discussing what types of tests to run for an EDW project in Chapter 16, I noted that EDW teams will find themselves repeating a handful of common assertions thousands of times throughout the long arc of their development project. I suggested that teams convert these assertions into reusable, parameter-driven "test widgets"—such as match_count( ), match_sum( ), and match_expected_values( )—and provided function prototypes for them in Table 16.8.

As a second step in implementing a testing plan, agile EDW teams will need to begin programming these reusable test widgets. Getting an early start on these assets will provide two important benefits. First, although each widget is a short, simple script, altogether they do require appreciable time to design, program, and validate. Getting them programmed during Iteration 0 would ensure they will exist to provide valuable services throughout the entire project.

Second, the act of getting them coded will provide a clear list of available test widgets to the team's system analyst, who can then reference them in his or her source-to-target mappings. Table 18.3 shows a sample mapping with such references making up the right half of the table. Here, the systems analyst has echoed the set of reusable widgets that the team plans to program across the column headings. The rows list the target data columns. In the intersection of test types and data columns, the analyst has indicated which widgets the programmers should use to validate each transform and even the parameter values they should employ. By settling on a collection of test widgets early in the project, the team allows the system analyst to incorporate quality into his or her specification work, achieving an important level test-led development even before programming begins.

STEP 3: PLAN OUT THE TEST DATA SETS

As a third step in planning agile EDW test execution, the team leaders need to invest some serious thought into the types of source data sets the tests they desire will require. Too many teams attempt to test their applications with just a few data sets when the true number they need is more like two or three dozen.

TABLE 18.3 Sample Source-to-Target Mapping Referencing Reusable Test Widgets

Source Table	Source Field	Target Table	Target Field	Target Column Category	no_empties( )	all_unique( )	within_range( )	match_uniques( )	match_group_counts( )	match_sum( )	match_median( )	valid_codes( )	match_results( )
n/a	n/a	STG_ISSUED	POLICY_ISS_SID	Surrogate Keys	Y	Y							
IP_COMMON	POL_NBR	STG_ISSUED	ISSUED_PRODUCT_ID	Natural Keys	Y	Y	Y						
IP_COMMON	IN_FORCE_DT	STG_ISSUED	COVERAGE_START_DT	Natural Keys	Y	Y	Y						
IP_HSHOLD	IP_HSHOLD_NBR	STG_ISSUED	PARTY_SID	Foreign Keys	Y				Y				
IP_HSHOLD	BILL_POST_CD	STG_ISSUED	BILLING_POSTAL_CODE	Replicated, Enumerated	Y				Y		Y		
IP_COMMON	RCLSS_CD	STG_ISSUED	RATING_CLASS_CODE	Replicated, Enumerated					Y				
n/a	n/a	STG_ISSUED	POLICY_MAX	…Continuous			10000, 9999999			Y	Y		
IP_DEPOSIT	FIRST_PRMN_APPIED	STG_ISSUED	BINDING_DEPOSIT	Aggregated			0, 10000		Y		Y		
n/a	n/a	STG_ISSUED	STATUS_CD	Derived, Enumerated								master_code, corp_party_status, code	
n/a	n/a	STG_ISSUED	MONTHLY_RESERVE_ACCR	…Continuous			0, 50000						view_test_reserve_calc
IP_COMMON	LAST_UPDATE	STG_ISSUED	SOURCE_UPDATE_DTM	Source Metadata	Y		parm_bus_date - 1, parm_bus_date						
n/a	n/a	STG_ISSUED	EDW_PROCESS_SID	EDW Metadata	Y					Y			

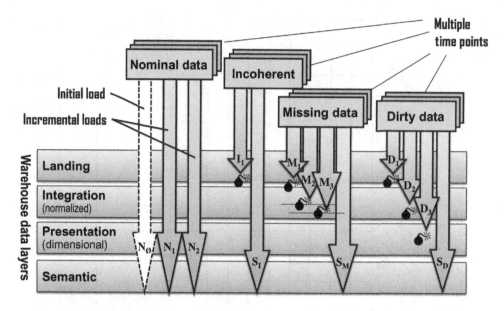

FIGURE 18.2 Full regression testing for an EDW requires many data sets.

Identifying How Many Data Sets are Required

The need for so many data sets becomes clear when one considers Figure 18.2, which shows how test data will progress across the layers of the EDW reference architecture. All teams validate their coding with at least a set of *nominal data*, which is a collection of data records that should load without errors once the application's ETL is programmed correctly. Interestingly, most teams need at least three data sets for nominal test cases. A "Day 0" data set will simulate the initial load the team plans for the data warehouse. Initial-load source records often come from entirely different systems than those that will provide the data warehouse's incremental-load data. Initial sources are often archive tapes or legacy data marts that will be retired after the new warehouse goes online. A Day 1 data set will simulate the first incremental load with a structure appropriate for the ongoing source systems that will feed the warehouse. A Day 2 data set will provide a second incremental load. We need two incremental data sets because data warehouses regrettably encounter a very different set of error conditions when applying an incremental load on top of a previous incremental load than they do when attempting an incremental load against an initial load.

Unfortunately, nominal loads are not enough to validate a data warehouse. The EDW leaders must ask themselves how they will prove that their ETL can handle situations in which the data extracts arrive in the wrong order (incoherent data). Similarly, they must demonstrate the application's ability to respond gracefully when entire tables, essential records, and crucial column values are absent from the source extracts (missing data). Moreover, the ETL must be able to manage extracts that contain human-intelligible formatting and semantic errors (dirty data). In fact, there are several additional classes of source data errors beyond the three shown in Figure 18.2. Table 18.4 provides a full listing of the error classes my company's consultants typically include in their QA plans. The data warehouse must be able to transcend errors from all of these classes.

Each class of error can require multiple data sets in order to validate that the ETL is programmed correctly. Consider the dirty data case, for example. The formatting errors it submits to the ETL may well be caught when the data set is landed or at least during integration, but there will be other errors that will not be apparent until the data is moved to the presentation layer and meshed with reference information provided by the business departments. Assume for the moment that the ETL is coded to simply halt when it encounters such a data defect. Each layer of the architecture will then need its own data set because errors halting the ETL in one layer will prevent the warehouse from ever seeing the errors that were meant to be caught in the next layer down. If the ETL is designed to check for missing data in three locations, as shown in Figure 18.2, then the team will need one data set for each location. These may be very small data sets with very few records besides those that will trigger the intended error condition, but they will still have to be separately loaded and transformed, with the results individually evaluated. Moreover, each class of error will need a "sweeper" data set to demonstrate that the ETL can be restarted and finish normally once the data defects that caused the abnormal ends of previous runs have been corrected. These sweeper data sets are shown in Figure 18.2, labeled as S_I, S_M, and S_D.

TABLE 18.4 Typical Test Data Sets for Agile EDW Projects

Data Set Type	Situation Addressed
Classes of Errors	
Nominal ("happy path")	Normal loading when data is error-free
Incoherent Data	Data arriving in the wrong order
Missing Data	Insufficient tables, files, and column values
Dirty Data	Human-visible syntax and formatting flaws
Corrupted Data	Machine-detectable formatting flaws
Duplicate Data	Same data with different wrappers
Other Data-Based Testing Scenarios	
End-of-Period	Time points for end of month, quarter, year
Archiving	Data past expiry that should be removed
Catch-Up	Loading higher volumes to make up for a system outage
Performance Modeling	Representative subset with enough records to reveal if ETL is too slow

Many teams design their ETL to respond to challenges such as missing information and faulty semantics by placing the offending records into a suspense table. This approach envisions that when the ETL later encounters an extract that has the data errors corrected, the suspended records will be located and flagged as "loaded." Such an approach can slightly reduce the number of data sets required, but each class of errors will need to be represented by a distinct set of records within the combined data set. Flagging and maintaining many records that speak to different error situations when they are all located in a single data set creates a management challenge. Teams trying this approach will discover it requires carefully tracking and jiggling record type indicators within that shared data set. Most teams eventually realize that these record type indicators are more work than they are worth, and they decide it is far easier just to place each major type of defect in its own source table.

Regardless of which approach they take, the teammates will need either many or "many, many" extracts to address all of the class of errors required to fully evaluate a data warehousing application. Moreover, this number will further increase when the team considers the demands of special time points. End-of-month processing often involves significantly different business rules than do mid-month data loads, as do time points for the end of quarters and the end of years. Often, the testing plan will call for a separate data set for each time point that must be evaluated. Considering just the four error classes illustrated in Figure 18.2, the developers will need 13 data sets to cover the intended error detection points. When they factor in special time points, that number could easily grow past three dozen. Extend that calculation by the additional data set types listed in Table 18.4 and fully regression testing an enterprise data warehouse may require close to 100 data sets.

Planning to Create Dozens of Data Sets

EDW team leaders need to plan carefully for managing and processing such a large number of test data sets. A few of the data sets will be large, such as those needed for nominal loads and those modeling application performance under high data volumes. The rest can contain only a few hundred records each, so teams will be investing in filtering and subsetting data from the source systems and then adding in records to test special circumstances by hand. These data sets must be carefully created. Simply grabbing a random set of records from the production system as the foundation for each data set will be counterproductive. Instead, the EDW team will have to invest in building repeatable subsetting routines that it can apply against the production source systems.

Must Subset Production Data

Most of the test data sets need only a few hundred records, so the first choice a team must make is whether to create the test data records by hand or derive them from a production data source using a subsetting script. Source systems are complex with many nuances hidden within the data, so, in practice, synthesizing the records by hand usually requires too much time and leads to poor results. Most EDW teams decide to subset the production data instead.

Common techniques for subsetting production data are to first filter the master data elements such as customer and product and then extract the records from the remaining source tables that join to these "driver records." These extracts can be re-executed once for each time point the team desires to have in its source test data sets.

Often, the test data must have source records that represent a complete set of business situations that the ETL is designed to handle. These business cases are indicated by a combination of flags and code values found in the source. In order to minimize the number of records in each test source subset, teams can use the combinatorial reduction technique introduced in Chapter 16 to generate a representative set of these flags and codes to search for when subsetting source data.

Data Will Need to be Re-Created

Although it is tempting the think that each data set needs to be created only once, agile EDW teams would be wise to design their subsetting routines as a repeatable processes. In the agile context, the team proceeds with 80/20 requirements, meaning it has only a mid-level notion of the overall application design at the start of the project. Moreover, business requirements can change for any project, necessitating the team to update the design in order to include data from new source systems. Either way, the data sets created at the beginning of the project will need to be expanded later.

Most teams find it difficult to simply add selected records from the newly required source tables to the existing data sets and still maintain referential integrity. They will achieve more coherent data sets by rerunning the subsetting script against the entire production source, identifying a full complement of related records at a single time. When the data has to be updated for new requirements, the developers simply add more queries to the script and re-execute it to generate in one stroke a new subset from which to work.

Once the source data has been subsetted, the defects that the test cases are designed to catch need to be introduced into the resulting records by such actions as dropping necessary records or mangling crucial column values. The defects injected into each data set will be different, of course, because each data set pertains to a different class of errors. These alterations should be added to the data preparation scripts so that they too become repeatable actions. Without scripting, it is too easy to forget to insert a few of these deliberate defects, and when these defects disappear, it can make the ETL appear to be running better than it is in reality.

The Refresh Must Leave the Data Set Unchanged as Much as Possible

Repeatability must be achieved for record identifiers and key column values as well in order to avoid developer frustration. Developers get to know their test data, memorizing such items as order numbers, customers' personal identifiers, and product numbers. If the subsetting routine reloads the test repository's source data tables based on a new set of driver records, a completely different cohort of records will land in the test data set. The programmers will be forced to start re-memorizing their landmarks, leading to frustration, mistakes, and lost time. Similarly, the defects injected into the test data sets by the subsetting routine must each land on the same record as before in order to maintain the developers' familiarity with error triggers for which they are programming a response.

All told, the team needs to design a subsetting facility that generates with each run the same records and the same defects, except for additional records the new tables that prompted rerunning the script.

Must Use Repeatable Masking

We must add one further degree of constancy to the subsetting routine so that it provides repeatable masking for sensitive information. Many data sets contain protected information for customers and employees and sometimes trade secrets belonging to vendors. These values need to be masked out of the test data somehow so that the protected information is no longer visible. The subsetting routine should be designed to utilize repeatable masking so that the key values that developers use to locate their favorite test records no longer represent sensitive information but also do not change with each refresh of the test data. If this constancy of masked key values is not achieved, each refresh will force the team members to begin rememorizing the landmarks of their favorite test records. All told, the data creation routines will have to be elegantly programmed modules in their own right, making it important for the EDW teams to begin planning and developing them early in the project.

Planning Storage for Dozens of Data Sets

As each testing data set emerges from the subsetting routine, the team will need to place it in a test data repository. This data repository will need some design effort as well. First, the team will need to choose the physical format in which the test source data will be stored. A successful approach can involve a mix of data tables, XML files, SQL "INSERT" commands, and simple text. Data stored outside of a database frequently needs to have loader routines created that will place it in the landing tables from which the ETL will pull it.

For test data that will be stored using a database, the team must decide whether to store each data set in a separate data schema or place all of them in a shared set of tables. The latter case has the advantage of keeping the number of objects in the test data repository to a reasonable number, but it requires metadata tags to allow the separate cohorts of records belonging to each data set to be identified.

If the team opts for placing the data in a shared set of tables, these tables will be structured very much like the sources from which the data is pulled. As new tables are needed from source, corresponding tables must be added to the test data repository. These tables will be slightly different than the operational tables they are modeled after, however, because they will need some metadata columns. The typical metadata columns record where data was gathered from and when, as well as probably a serial number so that successive instances of each test record can be distinguished. Metadata columns that record the particular runs of the subsetting routines will allow the developers to store record sets from different extract sessions so that they can simultaneously test the ETL belonging to different builds. This feature will be crucial for flexible regression testing of past subreleases.

The metadata columns added will also need to support the many ways that the test data will need to be fetched from the repository. Chapter 16 touched on these "testing aspects" that allow EDW teams to distinguish between parameters that define test scenarios such as error class, time point, and layers of the reference architecture. Table 18.5 lists these aspects of data subsetting along with several others that agile EDW projects have found useful for managing and retrieving test data during test execution. This table organizes the testing aspects into hierarchies that offer a progressive decomposition path. These testing aspects will also play a crucial role in the execution of tests, the management of expected values, and the analysis of actual results, so that we will revisit this table later.

Planning also for Expected Results

When previously discussing what test types an EDW project will need, we saw that many test assertions cannot be evaluated with analytical approaches. They require instead that the test consider whether a particular business rule produced the exact set of expected records. EDW team leaders can use much of the planning steps discussed so far to also specify how to properly create and store the data representing these expected results. Expected results will need to be accurately refreshed each time the team re-runs the source subsetting routines so that source and expected records stay aligned. To what extent expected results can be refreshed via scripts or table lookups rather than by hand will depend on the exact business rules being employed. In either case, the refresh mechanism needs to be added to the test data management plan.

Usually, expected values are stored in a separate repository from test source data. As we saw with source data, the expected value repository will need to simultaneously hold multiple version of the data, necessitating the same metadata tags, so that the various cohorts of records can be distinguished, managed, and retrieved independently.

In summary, test data for validating agile DW/BI has to be well derived, flexible, and dynamic. EDW teams are wise to invest a good deal of thought early in the project regarding the test data they will need, the means by which they will obtain it, and the repository in which they will keep it.

STEP 4: IMPLEMENT THE ENGINE, WHETHER MANUAL OR AUTOMATED

As a fourth step in implementing the EDW testing plan, the team needs to implement an engine, whether manual or automated. A manual engine is nothing more than a documented pattern that teammates will follow in executing by hand a test of a given type. Automation simply translates most of such patterns into machine-executable pieces, although the highest layer of the procedure will remain manual.

As illustrated by Figure 18.3, every test involves five major steps, as follows. Note that the use of the word *scenario* here is independent of its use in the term "scenario test" from Chapter 16.

- Discern the test scenario that should be executed.
- Locate the test source data and place it where the ETL process being validated can access it.

TABLE 18.5 Commonly Employed Testing Aspects

Aspect	Comments
Test Scenario Aspects	
Structural Hierarchy	
Project	e.g. Finance External Reporting Warehouse, Revenue Assurance Data Mart
Subject Area	e.g. Customer, Product, Sales, Standardize Cost, Fulfillment
Architectural Layer	e.g. Landing, Integration, Presentation, Semantic, Front-End
Requirements Hierarchy	
Epic	Identifiers often taken from the agile project management software package team employs to provide task boards and burndown charts, e.g. Ep 6, Th 6.12, US 6.12.4, DS 6.12.4.9
Theme	
User Story	
Developer Story	
Business Rule	e.g. Customers with receivables aged greater than 120 days will lose 25 percent of their value score
Data Type	e.g. Replicated, Derived, EDW Metadata, Business Metadata, Process Metadata
QA Dimensions	
Data Error Class	e.g. Nominal, Dirty, Missing, Incoherent
Polarity	e.g. Positive, Negative
Functionality	e.g. Functional, Non-Functional
Test Case Aspects	
Project Hierarchy	
First Subrelease	Target subrelease when test case first defined, e.g. 1, 2, 3, …
First Iteration	Project iteration when test case first defined, e.g. 1, 2, 3, …
First Usage	Category from system dimension when first authored, e.g. Unit, Integration
Author Role	Teammate who understands derivation of test and the data required to execute it, e.g. Data Modeler / ABaker, System Analyst / CDaniels
Author Name	

- Execute a script of actions that accomplishes the data transform.
- Evaluate the actual results of the data transforms against expectations.
- Record the findings from that evaluation.

Manual engines consist of instructions for the team to follow in order to complete this cycle. It will include mechanisms for coordinating the actions of multiple teammates so that they can run their individual tests simultaneously with shared resources without undermining each other's efforts. It will also require writing up a "definition of done" cards for each type of test so that the team can be assured that all the test runs included comparable steps for preparation, execution, and evaluation. A manual process will also include instructions about where to find expected results and how to record the findings of the evaluations so that the system tester can review which tests are passing and assess the application's current level of quality.

Automated engines encapsulate much of the above. Their configuration tables have pointers to the source data and expected results that the team leaders have prepared, making these resources easy for reviewers to locate. They also record all test runs and outcomes in a repository of their own, making it possible to use a business intelligence tool to present aggregate test results, which can then be sliced and diced by testing aspects to identify the application's problem areas. The best of these automated test engines provide the ability to define data staging, script execution, and results evaluations as reusable actions so that the EDW team members mix and match these components into a plethora of test cases.

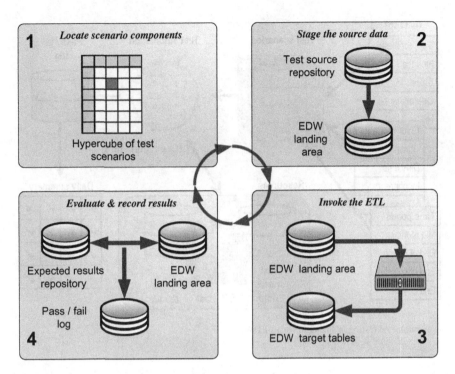

FIGURE 18.3 Automated testing cycle for a single testing scenario.

Teams that opt for a manual approach will need some lead time to get their testing standards defined and instructions written up. Teams that invest in an automated test engine may need even more lead time to select, install, and train on the tool they will be using. In either case, this work is best accomplished before Iteration 1 so that the team can start using a single pattern for QA from the moment that development begins.

Defining Test Scenarios

Most EDW projects are so large and complicated that manual approaches usually cannot scale enough to meet the team's QA objectives. Thus, the remainder of this chapter focuses on projects employing automated test engines. Figure 18.4 depicts the main algorithm that an automated EDW test engine needs to follow. It also provides a visible definition for the very important concept of a *test scenario*.

A test scenario is a combination of test aspects that controls the particular source data, ETL calls, and results evaluations a given test case will include. In Figure 18.4, various testing aspects such as subject area, error class, and data time point combine into a hyper cube representing all the test scenarios that must be executed in order to completely quality assure an EDW application. The figure shows only three aspects, but my company has clients that have employed 50 or more for categorizing the test cases they run.

When performing QA, the automated engine iterates through a user-selected subset of the test-scenario hyper cube. For each scenario, the engine executes the four steps shown in Figure 18.3 by staging the correct data, calling the proper components of the ETL, evaluating assertions concerning the actual results, and logging the defects found. The team can then use its BI tools against the engine's repository to learn whether the test cases detected a defect and then to research the conditions that made the ETL application fail.

STEP 5: DEFINE THE PROJECT'S SET OF TESTING ASPECTS

Once the test engine is in place, the EDW team needs to configure it for the testing aspects that will define the scenarios. This configuration involves entering into reference tables the actual values the team wants to employ for each aspect.

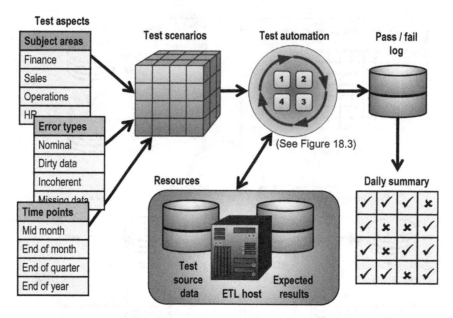

FIGURE 18.4   Overview of automated testing by scenario for an EDW.

Table 18.5 provides a starter set of aspects for the team leaders to consider, along with examples of the values that each aspect will take. As can be seen from the examples, this collection of testing aspects would allow the team members to define test runs that execute all the validations in the test engine's repository for very specific test suites. For instance, they could request a full regression test for the integration layer of the Revenue Assurance data warehouse's finance subject area, executing only the functional tests using the data set containing dirty data. Programmers could request this test for just a particular developer story of the current build that they are working on, whereas the system tester could run the same test suite for the entire build that the product owner evaluated at the last product demo.

In Step 3 discussed previously, the leaders planned which aspects the test source data and expected results will require. Once they configure the test engine to support the desired aspects, the test results it will generate will also be tagged with the same metadata values so that programmers will be able to examine their test outcomes without getting them confused with those belonging to others on the team.

STEP 6: BUILD AND POPULATE THE TEST DATA REPOSITORY

Now that the EDW team members have decided on the structure of the test data repository and the testing aspects that will tag the records it will hold, it is time for them to build the repository and populate it with the data generated by the subsetting scripts created in Step 3. Table 18.6 lists the structure of a source data table that employs the testing aspects identified in Table 18.5. Note that the columns for testing aspects have all been prefixed with "TMD_" (testing metadata). One can instruct the test engine to omit transferring values for all columns with a given prefix when staging data for a test run, making it possible to simply use a SQL command similar to "select * from PROPERTY.INFORCE_POLICY where...." If the test engine did not have this omit-prefix feature, teammates configuring staging steps would have to name every column required from the repository table rather than simply using an asterisk to indicate "all source table columns."

While populating the repository for the test scenarios, the team will frequently need to decide on the scope of each test case. A given test case will utilize a specific cohort of source records from the repository that will support a specific set of assertions when evaluating the results. At this point, the developers need to decide how large to make their test cases. At one extreme, they could create a test case that contains all the assertions to be used in evaluating a given scenario. At the other extreme, they could choose to place only one assertion in each test case, which will require many more test cases to achieve the full evaluation.

The right compromise between these two extremes will vary from scenario to scenario. For example, the developers may decide to combine the assertions for both positive and negative tests into one test case for the customer master data subject area but break out positive and negative tests into separate cases for the revenue-assurance ETL.

TABLE 18.6 Sample Test Source Data Structure

Data Center.System.Table: Western.Property.Inforce_Policy

COLUMN_NAME*	TYPE	LEN	NULLABLE	COMMENT
TMD_ARCH_LAYER	CHAR	48	N	Test metadata: Architectural Layer
TMD_SUBJ_AREA	CHAR	48	N	Test metadata: Subject Area
TMD_ERR_CLASS	CHAR	48	N	Test metadata: Error Class
TMD_POLARITY	CHAR	48	N	Test metadata: Polarity
TMD_FUNCTION	CHAR	48	N	Test metadata: Functionality
TMD_1ST_SUB_REL	CHAR	48	N	Test metadata: First Subrelease
TMD_1ST_ITERATION	CHAR	48	N	Test metadata: First Iteration
TMD_PROJECT	CHAR	48	N	Test metadata: Project
TMD_PROGRAMMER	CHAR	48	N	Test metadata: Programmer
TMD_REQUIREMENT	CHAR	48	N	Test metadata: Requirement
TMD_BUS_TIME_POINT	DATE-TIME		N	Test metadata: identifies different collections of records subsetted from source
POL_NBR	CHAR	12	N	Source system data column
IN_FORCE_DT	DATE		N	Source system data column
IP_HSHOLD_NBR	NUMERIC	12	N	Source system data column
BILL_POST_CD	CHAR	2	N	Source system data column
RCLSS_CD	CHAR	2	N	Source system data column
FIRST_PRMN_APPIED	NUMERIC	12	N	Source system data column
LAST_UPDATE	DATE		N	Source system data column
META_SID	NUMERIC	24	N	Test repository row-level metadata: record's unique identifier
META_INSERT_DATE	DATE-TIME		N	Test repository row-level metadata: record's creation timestamp
META_SOURCE_SYSTEM	CHAR	48	N	Test repository row-level metadata: source system providing the record

* TMD = "test metadata"

The correct answer usually depends on the size of the data needed and the complexity of the business rules. The team's system tester needs to be ready to advise the developers on which factors favor more granular test cases.

As illustrated in Figure 18.5, there is a dividing line between where a given set of assertions manifests itself as simply different sets of records employed during a test case and where they should be relegated to a separate test case of their own. In this diagram, the multiple considerations involved in splitting a given validation idea into separate test cases are ranked by the number of instances involved in each. In the figure, the split between one versus many single test cases is as high up in the stack as is usually possible. Teams naturally need to define separate scripts for restart points because the first defects in the test source data set will cause the data transformation to stop, preventing process from reaching the remaining defects. Whether or not a given set of business rules or ETL logic points justify separate scripts will be a case-by-case decision.

STEP 7: QUANTIFY THE TESTING OBJECTIVES

By the time a team reaches this step, the test engine is configured with data ready to employ. We want to use the test engine to constantly inform the developers and business stakeholders regarding the progress of the project. Thus, before diving into creating tests for the next iteration, the team leaders should take a moment to define the quality objective for the sprint (and later for the subrelease) so that every morning queries against the test engine's repository can show how close the team has come to achieving its QA objectives.

Teams following the planning framework provided by this part of the book will have invested time in not only QA planning but also in estimating how many tests the team will need to execute. With one small additional effort at the

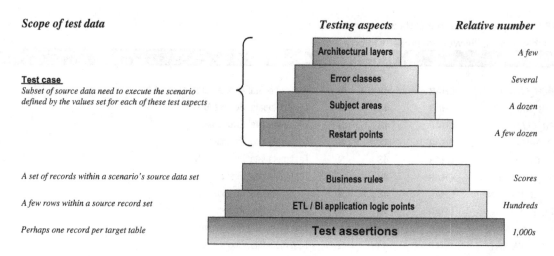

FIGURE 18.5 Relationship between test case, test assertions, and the data required for each.

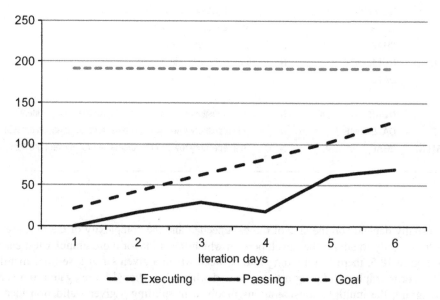

FIGURE 18.6 Test case build-up chart for a single iteration.

beginning of each iteration, the team leaders can use that existing information to forecast how many tests of each type will be needed to evaluate the modules listed on the current iteration backlog. With that number in hand, the leaders will be able to use a BI tool against the test engine's data repository to create buildup charts such as shown in Figure 18.6, illustrating how close the integration tests for the current iteration have come to the desired level of testing.

The graph in Figure 18.6 depicts exactly this idea, with the horizontal line at the top representing the agreed upon goal. The first buildup line represents the number of tests defined and executing in the test engine, which is a good indicator of how hard the team is trying to reach its quality goal. The bottom line shows the number of tests that are actually passing, an accurate measure of the quality that the team has actually achieved. This graph makes a good companion to the team's burndown chart, providing an evidence-based measure of progress for all stakeholders to review at the developer's daily stand-up meeting. Similar buildup charts can be created for visualizing progress for the current subrelease and the project as a whole, although the forecasts for the number of tests that teams should achieve will not be as accurate.

STEP 8: BEGIN CREATING TEST CASES

At this point, the testing infrastructure is in place and an objective for an iteration has been set. The team should begin development work, using the test engine not only to validate its programming but also to measure and display its progress within the iteration.

As a developer completes programming each module, she can enter its unit and component test cases into the test engine, tagging them with her name, the developer story she is working on, the project's current iteration number, and the other testing aspects that her teammates have agreed on. As each test case is added, the engine will be able to provide not only an increasingly comprehensive regression test for the current build but also a quality buildup chart that illustrates the team's progress toward its goal. The metadata values added to the test cases will allow the team to constrain the reports generated by the test engine's repository so that it shows the success of test cases for individual programmers, allowing each to demonstrate when she has completed his programming assignments for the iteration.

As they create ETL and reporting modules, the programmers should find the system analyst's suggestions for reusable test widgets in the source-to-target maps they are following. They can call those widgets using the validation scripts they enter into the test engine. These activities will be complex at first, so the system tester will be busy instructing programmers and supporting them as they create the test cases. When not supporting the programmers in this way, however, the system tester can enter integration test cases for the current and previous application builds into the test engine so that the team can demonstrate success when measuring the quality of the application as an assembled whole.

The best test engines allow test cases to be defined with reusable staging statements, test scripts, and evaluations. As the iterations progress, then, both the system tester and the programmers will be able to draw upon steadily more test components that are already defined, making the work of this step progressively easy to accomplish.

STEP 9: START UP THE ENGINE

At this point, the programmers can invoke the test engine during the day to execute unit and component tests. The system tester should also connect the test engine to a scheduling package so that the combined systems can execute a full integration test on the team's current build during the evening hours. This latter test run will provide important feedback to the developers on a daily basis, helping them keep their code extremely clean.

Figure 18.7 depicts the type of summary information that automated, nightly integration test runs can provide. In this figure, each row represents a different subject area in the data warehouse. The components of the reference architecture are listed along the top of the columns in bold, arranged in the order that data for each subject area will follow during the loading process. Listed in the column heading for each reference architecture area are the error classes that the EDW team has decided to employ in its QA program. For clarity, this figure lists only a few that a typical team would employ, namely those for nominal, missing, and dirty data. In the graph, happy faces indicate test suites that are

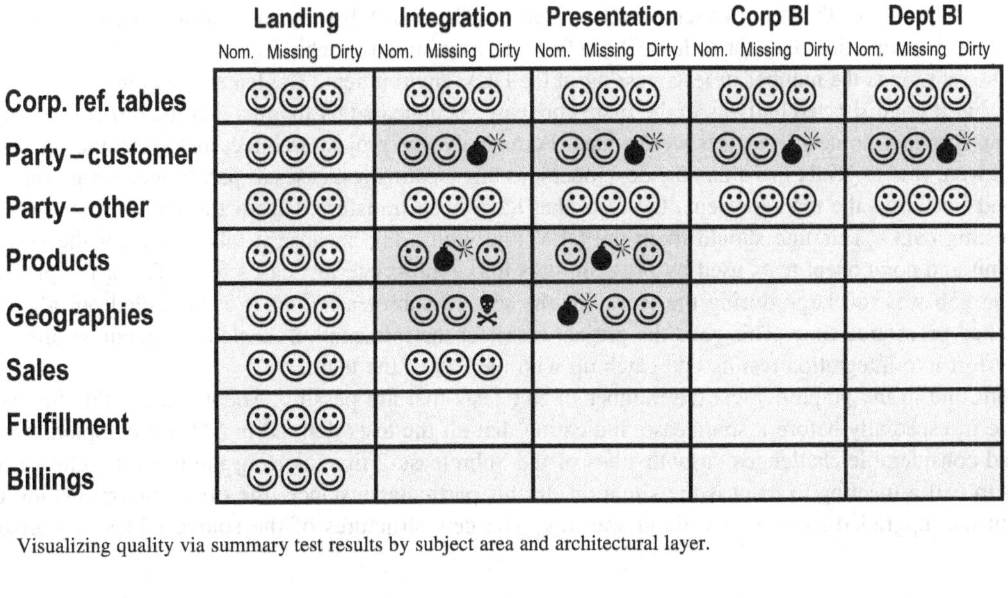

FIGURE 18.7   Visualizing quality via summary test results by subject area and architectural layer.

passing without error. Bombs label test suites for which actual results do not match expectations, and the skull and crossbones symbol shows where the test script itself had an execution error.

The system tester would employ a BI tool to display this graphic daily at the team's stand-up meeting. With this particular display, the system tester could provide the following summary during his or her check in:

- "Today all the landing area jobs are completing successfully, so 'Yay, Team.'
- In the integration layer, the Party subject area is failing on the dirty data set, which is causing that same data set to fail for the remainder of the subject area.
- That's a new bug. ... It was working fine yesterday morning.
- Who did anything yesterday that might have possibly caused the Party subject area to start failing?? Raise your hands. OK, looks like Terry and Pat. Could you two conference after our check in and see if you can figure out what caused these ETLs to start to fail?
- Product is still failing when it comes to missing data. Sam's working on that one. We'll see it switch to happy face once he gets it done.
- Here's a new one: The scripts for geographies are so messed up they can't even execute. Who was working those scripts yesterday? Sandy? OK, looks like you've got to track down what's making that test case so unhappy."

Being able to supply the team with this level of insight on a daily basis enables the system tester to provide the team with real leadership. With steady feedback of this caliber, the team can easily keep its code extremely free of defects, leading to better product demos, less time wasted coding around programming flaws, and fewer defects sneaking through subrelease testing into the production instances with which end users will work.

STEP 10: VISUALIZE PROJECT PROGRESS WITH QUALITY ASSURANCE

At this point, the team is fully executing on the QA plan, and the automated test engine is providing a large amount of useful information on what the team has achieved. The system tester needs to assemble that feedback into a dashboard that depicts the team's progress for the project sponsor and the other business stakeholders to monitor. EDW team leaders can use this same display to detect when and where the team might be struggling, empowering it to better keep development effort on track.

Tests Implemented by Environment

Figure 18.8 shows a *project quality dashboard* that is easy to assemble using the information already being tracked by the team's Scrum master and its automated test engine. The table in the upper left is the same as the one just discussed. The graph in the upper right provides an aggregate look at the same test events, this time in a trending format. We saw this graph in a larger format in Figure 16.2. This *Tests Implemented by Environment* graph depicts the state of testing across the weeks and iterations of the project. The horizontal time line is divided into four areas representing the next few incremental subreleases the team leaders have decided on. One can tell from this particular chart that the project is just past the expect completion date for Release 1, so they are running a bit behind.

The top line represents the number of tests passing in the DEV environment. The team was doing well at the beginning of the project, but it got distracted halfway to the first subrelease, as indicated by the fact that the *test cases running in DEV* line stayed flat, meaning no new test cases were added. Fortunately, the project architect and system tester were watching this graph and were able to gently insist that the developers resume creating test cases as part of their programming work.

The second line from the top represents the tests that have been transferred from the DEV environment to system integration testing (SIT). This line should track the DEV line with a lag because it takes time for the system tester to convert the unit and component tests used by programmers into appropriate test cases for SIT. For the project shown in this graph, the gap was too large during the work for the second subrelease, and it even stalled out altogether as the team approached promotion time. This gave the project architect the information needed to encourage the system tester to put more effort into integration testing and catch up with the rest of the team.

The bottom line in the graph depicts the number of SIT tests that are passing. Theoretically, this line should touch the line above it, especially before a subrelease, indicating that all the tests defined in SIT are completing successfully. This team had considerable challenges on both sides of the Subrelease 2 line, alerting the project architect and even IT management to call a meeting to discuss the situation. In this particular instance, the organization owning the primary source system had upgraded its system without warning. The new structures of the source tables had broken the data

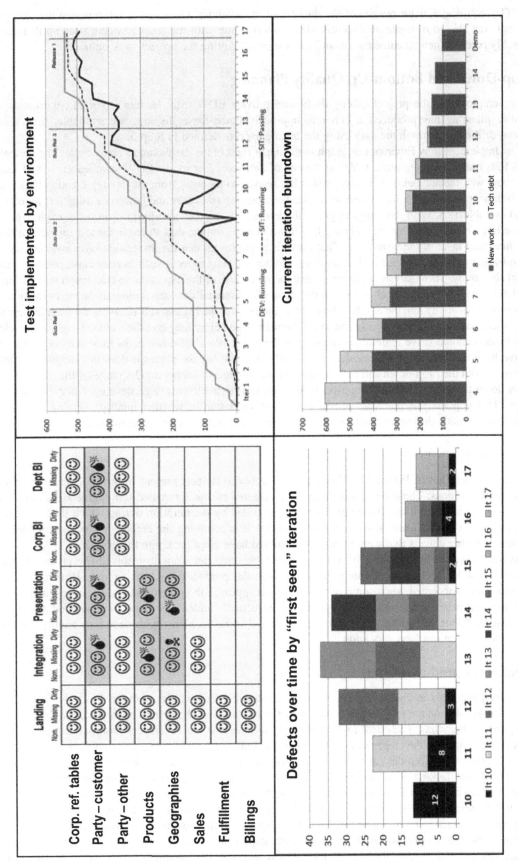

FIGURE 18.8 A sample project quality dashboard showing four measures of quality achieved by a development team.

warehouse's ETL, requiring a major rewrite of the data transform modules. Once this graph revealed the disruption, the EDW department was able to instigate an executive-level intervention with the source system team so that the DW/BI developers quickly received new documentation and extra support, getting the project back on track.

Connect Top-Down and Bottom-Up Quality Planning

The BI graphics employed in the project quality dashboard provide EDW team leaders a perfect opportunity to prove that their quality planning has produced a coherent approach. Once these displays are available, they should test whether they can drill down through the data using the testing aspects defined in Step 5.

Take the Test Implemented by Environment graph in the upper right of the dashboard as an example. The normal display would show all tests runs for a given project. Yet, at the end of Iteration 13 or so, the EDW team leaders would surely want to know more about why the number of SIT tests passing has strayed so far away from the line representing the tests executing in that environment. Fortunately, the system tester has been tagging test cases and outcomes using test aspects, such as those suggested in Table 18.5. With those tags in place, the leaders will be able to drill down into the graph—for example, right click on the line for SIT Tests Passing and have it redrawn to break out the data stored in the test engine's repository for a particular architectural layer of the warehouse. That analysis might reveal that the integration layer is where the numbers start to dip. The leaders can then continue to drill down by additional testing aspects, such as error class, polarity, author role, and requirements hierarchy. This analysis could reveal that the root cause of the gap in the overall graph stems from the fact that the tests defined by the systems analyst for running Epic #3's nominal data are failing all of the negative test cases. Testing aspects provide visibility into the numbers behind the numbers for quality assurance, giving the team leaders the guidance needed to detect quality problems quickly and to get them resolved before they cost the team any significant velocity.

EDW team leaders should strive to define at the start of the project the drill-down paths they will need. Once the testing aspects have been defined, team leaders should carefully scan the list for places it does not support the drill-down paths they desire. If both their top-down and bottom-up planning produced a coherent QA strategy, they should be able to drill all the way down from the highest testing aspects (e.g., project) to the lowest (e.g., developer story) without encountering any gaps. This gap analysis therefore provides a robust validation of whether quality planning is complete and should be repeated frequently during the early portions of the project until the team's current quality plan passes this test.

Defects Over Time

The bar chart in the lower left of Figure 18.8 displays the number of defects present in the application's current build over the past several iterations. These defects include those detected by the automated test engine and those discovered by other, manual validation activities. These defects are color coded by the iteration during which they were first seen. Such a format allows the team to not only discern how quickly it is resolving the defects uncovered for each iteration but also determine whether defects that were previously resolved have crept back into the system.

The defects uncovered during Iteration 10, for example, took three iterations to resolve. The project architect was somewhat concerned about the fact that cleaning up those particular product flaws took so long. However, everyone on the team was extremely concerned when some of those flaws reappeared three iterations later, suggesting that someone had either undermined earlier work with new programming or actually added new logic to those modules even though they were supposedly "done." In either case, this chart revealed some problems with design or coding discipline that the team leaders need to get resolved very soon.

Current Iteration Burndown Chart

The bar chart in the lower right in Figure 18.8 is a standard iteration burndown chart, with the dark color showing the total number of hours-to-go listed on the task cards for the current iteration. Here, the system tester has added the tech debt left over from the previous iterations. Tech debt represents the little fixes that the developers promised to make in exchange for the product owner accepting developer stories that were not quite done at the time of the previous product demo. The developers should work off the tech debt at the beginning of every iteration so that the new programming is not applied to a faulty code base. Teams lacking good discipline often move on to new coding first because often those tasks are more interesting than cleaning up the last iteration's mistakes, so tech debt is an important quality measurement that EDW team leaders should watch assiduously. Here, the team did not resolve all of the tech debt until Day 13 of the three-week sprint, revealing an important issue in team discipline that should be discussed at the next iteration retrospective.

Taken together, the four charts on this dashboard clearly depict the real events occurring in the project room. The task board and regular burndown charts that agile teams employ to communicate progress to themselves and stakeholders are good first looks at the current state of an iteration, but EDW team leaders should keep in mind that both of those artifacts reflect the tasks that developers *say* they have completed. The information displayed on the QA dashboard in Figure 18.8 is derived from the testing process, representing the work that the programmers have both completed and gotten to pass quality assurance. Such information is *evidence-based* and is not vulnerable to the oversights or spin that the developers might insert into the status information they report, making the quality dashboard a far more dependable measure of the team's true progress toward stakeholder goals.

STEP 11: DOCUMENT THE TEAM'S SUCCESS

To succeed at quality assurance, an EDW development team must do more than get its application to pass all the tests thrown at it. It must document that the application has fulfilled its QA plan, especially the benefit of stakeholders such as the project sponsor and the operations team. The test engine previously envisioned can greatly assist with this final effort, but making that effort easily manageable may well require a further adjustment to the EDW team's quality platform.

Figure 18.9 depicts the process that meets the quality-fulfillment documentation required in many large organizations. This pattern focuses on the communication between a quality management system and the automated test engine.

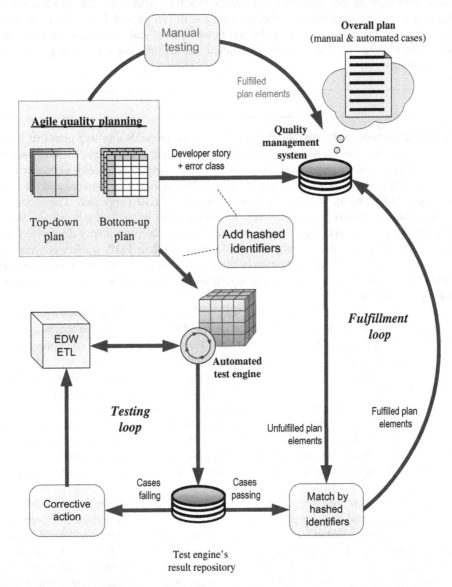

FIGURE 18.9 Supporting quality fulfillment documentation with an automated test engine.

The process begins with the agile quality assurance planning, as outlined in this and the previous two chapters. This planning results in top-down and bottom-up planning artifacts that represent the overall quality plan. This plan encompasses both the automated lower-level testing and the higher-level validations such as theme tests that will have to be executed manually. Both of these categories of testing are then entered into the quality management system (QMS), which is essentially a database that holds a validation plan and a log of events that demonstrate each plan element has been fulfilled.

When manual testing elements are successfully completed, the team records that fact in the QMS database. For the automated test elements, the team can configure the test engine to automatically update the QMS, which is extremely convenient given how many automated test elements an EDW quality plan usually entails.

One extra step is required to enable this integration. The team needs to add hash identifiers in the QMS for the quality elements that will be validated through the automated test engine. These identifiers are typically MD5 hashes on the aspects of each test case that make it unique. Combining the developer story number and the architectural layer is often a good candidate for such an identifier.

As the EDW's ETL is validated by the automated testing engine, some tests pass and others fail. The tests that fail lead to corrective updates to the EDW application, as shown on the left side of Figure 18.9. For the tests that pass, an extra process in the test engine calculates the hash identifiers for each case and then attempts to find them among the records still marked as unfulfilled in the QMS. When it finds a matching hash value, this process updates the attributes of the QMS's image of the test, documenting that the test case has in fact passed. Later, the team can retrieve a report from the QMS that documents the degree to which the combined manual and automated test elements have been fulfilled. When enough of the plan has been sufficiently completed, the organization can opt to promote the application to the next operating environment.

SUMMARY

The intensive QA planning outlined in this and the previous two chapters yields a testing plan that is very ambitious. In fact, even medium-sized data warehouses with a modest quality plan will require tens of thousands of test cases and hundreds of thousands of test case executions. Because of the large number of quality events involved, EDW team leaders need to seriously plan for how such a large number of test case runs can be invoked and tracked.

For this last segment of QA planning, EDW practitioners employ an 11-step approach. These steps start with revisiting the 2×2 top-down planning matrix to record where test automation might assist in getting the validations completed. It next calls for the team to get started programming the reusable, parameter-driven test widgets identified previously when they decided on the types of tests that would make up their EDW quality program. The planning for how to execute tests next includes enumerating the two or three dozen data sets that an EDW team will require to fully validate its application. The following step considers how to arrange for these data sets to be generated from the production systems in a repeatable manner.

Next, the team should specify and implement the test "engine" it will use, whether the engine will be a completely manual process or include substantial automation. With the engine defined, the team leaders will need to articulate the values they wish to employ for the multiple testing aspects their teammates will use to categorize test data, test scripts, and test results. At that point, the leaders can define the likely number of test cases that the next iteration will involve, allowing them to display for their teammates charts of tests executing and passing that build up toward this known goal.

With all the previously mentioned preparation, the team's coders can now begin entering test cases into the test engine and invoke that engine to validate the ETL modules they are programming. The results can be displayed via several graphs that not only allow the programmers to keep their code defect-free but also enable the leaders to provide evidence-based progress reporting to the developers and project stakeholders. By adding hash identifiers to the tests identified in the quality plan, the team can configure the automated test engine to programmatically register successful lower-level testing cases in the quality management system that IT is using to document the fulfillment of the EDW application's overall QA plan.

The planning described in this and the past two chapters provides a sound platform for measuring the quality of data warehouse objects. By organizing and tracking product quality so aggressively, the agile EDW team can move forward, rapidly coding in increments, assured that any mistakes undermining product integrity will quickly come to the surface so that the team can get them resolved. As discussed in the next and final chapter of this book, a sound quality assurance platform is absolutely necessary to interconnect the work that agile EDW teams perform in all three software engineering arenas we have discussed: iterative risk mitigation, just-in-time requirements, and incremental data engineering.

Part V References

Chapter 16

Charantimath, P.M., 2011. Total Quality Management, second ed. Pearson India, Chennai, India.

Crispin, L., Gregory, J., 2009. Agile Testing. Addison-Wesley, Waltham, MA.

Marick, B., 2003, August 21. My Agile testing project. Exploration by Example (blog). <http://www.exampler.com/old-blog/2003/08/21/#agile-testing-project-1>.

Page, A., Johnston, K., Rollison, B.J., 2009. How we Test Software at Microsoft. Microsoft Press, Redmond, WA.

Ramu, G., 2010, April. Introduction to Six Sigma. Presentation before the Silicon Valley chapter of the American Society for Quality. <http://www.slideshare.net/Sixsigmacentral/introduction-to-sixsigma> (accessed November 2014).

Weinberg, G., 1993. Quality Software Management, vol. 2. Dorset House, New York.

Zairi, M., 2010. Benchmarking for Best Practice. Routledge, New York.

Chapter 17

Hull, E., Jackson, K., Dick, J., 2011. Requirements Engineering, third ed. Springer-Verlag, London.

Chapter 18

Ericson, J., 2006, April 1. A simple plan. Information Management. <http://www.information-management.com/issues/20060401/1051182-1.html>.

Part VI

Integrating the Pieces
of the Agile EDW Method

Chapter 19

The Agile EDW Subrelease Cycle

I began this book with what was perhaps a brazen claim—that agile techniques have solved the fundamental problem of enterprise data warehousing (EDW). I suggested that our profession's fundamental problem is that enterprise data warehouses take so long to deliver and cost so much to build that they end up providing too little value to the businesses to justify their construction. The root cause for this lamentable state of affairs was the risk that even a simple mistake in requirements or design would obviate months of data transform programming and system implementation. The four practice elements that solve this fundamental problem are

- agile coding techniques;
- agile requirements management;
- agile data engineering; and
- agile quality assurance.

My previous books presented the first element in detail, showing how the development team can work with the business staff in small increments, regularly validating the project's accomplishments one small piece at a time. This book provided new iterative approaches to the remaining practice elements, showing how EDW teams can quickly define a project, deliver data repositories that can be readily adapted to new business requirements even after they have been loaded with operational information, and repeatedly validate a fast stream of data warehousing/business intelligence (DW/BI) deliverables with a reasonable amount of labor.

Implementing four new practice elements while simultaneously managing the frenetic engineering activities that make up an EDW development project is a tough assignment. EDW team leaders new to agile will need an overarching approach that allows them to evenly pursue the four agile practices despite the chaos occurring in the project room. At the start of this book, I offered the subrelease cycle as a convenient means of managing project risk. We can augment the notion of the subrelease cycle in order to make it a single, repeatable process that forges together the four practice elements of agile EDW. This chapter presents the agile EDW subrelease cycle as a continuing series of eight major steps that can be centered around the crucial concepts of data governance and application quality assurance. The resulting development process will be extremely transparent and responsive to the EDW team's business customers, so this chapter will build upon the integrative subrelease cycle by presenting an EDW customer's bill of rights that describes the dramatically improved service levels that DW/BI departments can offer their project sponsors once they convert to agile methods. In order to succinctly express how DW/BI professionals can achieve the lofty goal set forth by this customer's bill of rights, I close this book with an extended version of the agile manifesto—one that accommodates the many innovations discussed in previous chapters.

MAKING THE RELEASE CYCLE A REPEATABLE PROCESS

Chapter 1 suggested that EDW projects are slow and expensive because their leaders fear making a mistake in requirements or design that will wipe out months of extract, transform, and load (ETL) programming. Non-agile DW/BI teams believe they should mitigate this risk by compiling a complete set of requirements and design specifications up front, before any coding commences. Unfortunately, this "big-spec up-front" approach causes a long delay between the day the business staff members describe what they need and the moment they can begin solving their pressing problems with a business intelligence application. Big specifications up front also prevent frequent business reviews of completed work so that mistakes in application coding, solution mapping, and business concepts creep into the application, letting development teams invest months into building an inadequately designed application.

We have seen in the preceding chapters that agile versions of requirements management, data modeling, and quality assurance can eliminate the risks that call for big specifications up front. However, we have discussed the agile EDW practice elements only one at a time, each in isolation. New agile EDW team leaders will benefit from a step-by-step list of actions that places all these techniques into a single, repeatable process, making them easier to deploy evenly during their first several projects. For me, the best packaging for such a step-by-step approach has always been the subrelease cycle.

Why package the agile EDW practice areas into the cycle for a subrelease rather than for a complete release or perhaps something shorter, such as an iteration? The cycle for building a complete application release is too lengthy—it transpires only once per project and thus does not provide team leaders with frequent enough checkpoints to dependably validate developer progress. At the other extreme, the development iterations are so small in scope that they would force the team to overlook data management issues that play out across the multimonth arc of an EDW project.

Occurring three or four times per year, the agile EDW subrelease cycle fits well between these two extremes and will provide the development team with just enough feedback to fine-tune its implementation of the agile practices to match the situation at hand.

In Chapter 6, we explored how the development teams can employ the subrelease cycle to drive adverse risk out of EDW development projects. After every few development iterations, the team should present the application's current build as a release candidate to the project's near stakeholders in order to get vital, constructive criticism of the product from the company's departmental directors. Should these directors accept the candidate, the team can promote it into production usage and then receive further feedback from the all-important end users.

Throughout the years, I have found that subrelease cycles are more effective if, during the months that they take to complete, teams pursue them through a particular set of steps:

1. Workflow-driven data governance and prototyping
2. Associative data discovery
3. Collaborative source-to-target mapping
4. Live data prototyping
5. Hyper-modeled key integration points
6. Enriched hyper-modeled solution
7. Collaborative analytics
8. Model-driven solutions

This recommended progression of topics guides the team in steadily answering some major questions concerning the subrelease as a whole—questions that do not fit comfortably within a single development iteration, such as the following:

- What are the company-wide definitions for the data elements that the data warehouse will provide?
- How will company staff members interact with the data warehouse in order to maintain the proper encodings for fundamental data items?
- What should be the key integration points between the diverse subject areas within the data warehouse?
- How will the users actually use the information that the EDW team has proposed to supply them?
- Which of the business rules creating new data elements should be implemented in the warehouse, the business intelligence application, or left to the end users to calculate for themselves?

The subrelease cycle described previously provides a structured means for teams to derive just good enough answers to these questions—which revolve around issues of data governance, data integration, and data derivations—to allow the next several development iterations to proceed without getting waylaid by major, unanswered questions.

In practice, many EDW teams must center their development practices on both data governance and application quality. Data governance enables them to deliver information sufficiently standardized so that all business departments can use it, and quality assurance allows them to confirm that they have followed those guidelines. Though we explored quality assurance extensively in Part V, we should take a moment to clarify what we mean by data governance so that we can properly define a subrelease cycle to support it as well.

TRADITIONAL NOTIONS OF DATA GOVERNANCE

Throughout the years I have spent presenting agile data warehousing techniques to DW/BI managers, many of them have scoffed at the agile approach, claiming that an incremental method will crash and burn upon the rocks of data governance. These skeptics do not believe a data warehousing team can appropriately plan a company-wide information management process working one small piece at a time, and they therefore dismiss agile data warehousing completely.

I certainly understand their concerns, but I believe they are misinterpreting the concept of data governance so that it is an impossible task to begin with. By reframing the notion of data governance so that it matches the best practices of enterprise information management, I believe we can easily craft an incremental approach that will support it.

For the large enterprise, standardized metrics and master data are essential for understanding the relative performance of the business units and reallocating resources between them as they struggle to meet market threats and opportunities. Standardized metrics are typically numerical quantities that all business departments understand and will acknowledge as honest representations of their situation and performance. Master data elements are standard labels and categorizations of crucial corporate entities, such as customers, locations, and product, that allow the business departments to analyze and aggregate standardized metrics in a way that others will readily understand and accept. "Data governance" is the overarching efforts within a company to achieve high-quality master data and link it to standardized business metrics. More precisely, we can define it as the exercise of decision making and authority to ensure the availability, usability, integrity, and security of the data employed in an enterprise (a consolidation of definitions taken from [Rouse 2007] and [Thomas 2014]).

Without effective data governance, standardized metrics and master data are impossible to achieve. Poor data governance leads to data disparities—that is, situations in which comparable questions generate conflicting answers depending on where and how a person retrieved the information used to answer them. Data disparities can severely disrupt corporate decision making in at least three ways. First, executives will struggle to agree on simple facts such as how well certain products are selling or how many customers the company has gained and lost. With data disparities, meetings can degenerate into arguments about whose spreadsheets are correct. Second, departments will maintain their own data marts because they cannot understand or trust the information in the enterprise data warehouse. Third, changing the data warehouse for a new requirement takes months just to research and plan because the impact on master data elements cannot be readily assessed [Eckerson 2001].

Note that these definitions imply an enormous undertaking for the company's staff members. A sound data governance program requires a governing body or council, a defined set of procedures, and a plan to execute those procedures [Rouse 2007]. To achieve high data quality within master data and standardize metrics, the business departments must not only harmonize the definitions they employ for the hundreds of data elements they wish to share but also adopt complementary business processes for populating their information systems with values that comply with these definitions. With data quality so dependent on the thinking and actions of the business staff, data governance must be a business-led endeavor. With data governance requiring such a widescale change in business work patterns, it should be no surprise that only 1 out of 10 companies have implemented an enterprise data strategy [Fisher 2009]. IT in general and an EDW team in particular are not in a position to dictate to the business that they will undertake a data governance program. Instead, they can only be facilitators of data governance, aligning the information systems they manage with the data governance policies the business staff has decided it wants to follow. Formulating a data governance program as an IT-led effort invariably leads to failure because if the business staff are not enthused and dedicated to standardizing their thoughts and actions as they create operational data, IT will not be able to force them to maintain the quality of the company's information.

For these reasons, rejecting agile data warehousing because one cannot imagine how the EDW team will achieve effective data governance is unreasonable. This dismissal assumes that IT could drive the data quality effort within a company. With business involvement absolutely essential and business enthusiasm for data governance so limited, EDW development teams cannot pursue data governance on its own, whether or not they use incremental delivery methods to construct the enterprise data warehouse. A far more realistic goal would be to require agile EDW techniques to effectively support those data governance activities that the business side of the company has decided to pursue. Fortunately, that goal is easily achieved.

A Life Cycle for Data Governance

Data governance is actually just one component of a larger discipline called *enterprise information management* (EIM), which was introduced in Chapter 11 when considering how agile EDW teams can best support nonfunctional requirements coming from the company's enterprise architecture group. EIM is the disciplined activities a company must take to manage its data and all other types of enterprise information as an asset [Ladley 2010]. EIM is comprised to two complementary practices: data governance and information management.

As shown in Figure 19.1, an informal way to describe the division of labor between these two practices is that "data governance is defining and planning the right things to do, information management is actually doing those things

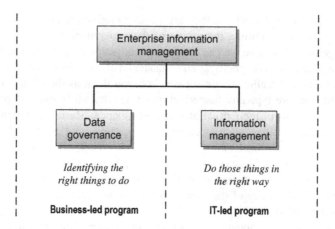

FIGURE 19.1   Enterprise information management includes a business-led data governannce program and an IT-led information managment program.

right" [Ladley 2013]. Data governance is the business-led portion of the EIM effort. Information management comprises the systems design and implementation work that IT must provide to achieve the data governance the business has defined.

In his 2010 book, John Ladley provides an iterative approach for the business side of a company to pursue when it decides to invest in EIM [Ladley 2010]. I believe this cycle provides a reliable, step-by-step process that companies should follow in order to achieve effective data governance. During the previous chapters on requirements management, this book described an enterprise-capable requirements management (ERM) process for defining the application an agile EDW team intends to build. This project definition process started with sponsor concept briefings, included a vision document, and resulted in a current estimate. Not only does this ERM value chain of artifacts enable a team to move smoothly into the development iterations of a subrelease cycle but also it links quite well with the EIM process Ladley proposes, as shown in Figure 19.2. Because this linkage is so extensive, the agile EDM project startup process provides a strong sequencing for the information management activities needed to support a company's data governance program, should one exist. I summarize the complementary nature of these two processes level by level, as each progresses through its own particular form of planning, approaching the moment when a team can execute upon those plans. The dividing line between steps 5 and 6 in Figure 19.2 indicates where both of these linked cycles transition from planning activities to putting their plans into action.

The EIM cycle begins with *alignment*, which Ladley describes as an effort to understand the goals and objectives needed to articulate a direction for enterprise information management within a company [Ladley 2010]. Alignment includes a discovery process to uncover the primary drivers that determine the performance of the business. Examples of these drivers are the executives' desire to improve market share, increase customer interactions, or achieve faster product innovation. This discovery process will identify the same high-level goals and objectives that the agile EDW team leaders uncover when they draft their *sponsor's concept briefing* and *stakeholder requests*, artifacts created as part of Iteration −1 of the ERM project-definition process.

The next level in the EIM cycle is *vision*, during which the data governance team proposes information management goals in terms that the business staff can understand so that they can achieve buy-in for particular area of the enterprise where the EIM program has decided to improve the company's management of information assets. The EIM vision artifacts include business cases for the proposed policy changes, a preliminary set of information requirements, and an initial business model. These elements closely match the solution statements, feature and benefits listing, and target business model called for by the agile EDW project definition process's *vision document*.

Level 3 of the EIM process is an increasingly detailed business model. This model consists of a more complete expression of the company's conceptual data model, information requirements, usage scenarios, and information taxonomy. These elements align very well with the work product that the EDW team leaders will deliver as part of their Iteration 0 startup work, which includes a 80/20 logical data model for the warehouse, a supporting data dictionary, ETL design patterns, and the first set of source-to-target mappings.

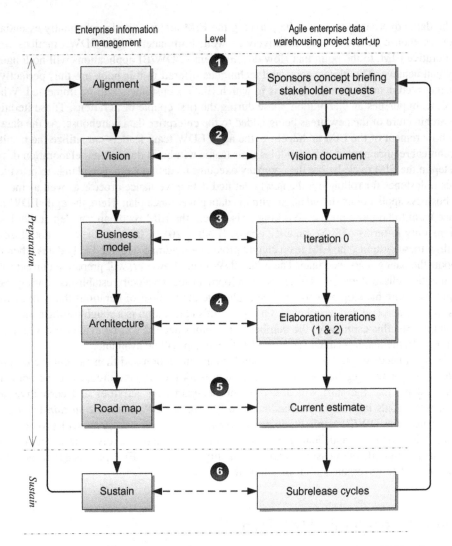

FIGURE 19.2   Agile EDW project start-up aligns well with the data governance cycle. *Adapted from [Ladley 2013].*

Next, the data governance team invests in an *architecture*, during which the team drafts the following artifacts in a business-intelligible format [Ladley 2013]:

- Enterprise metric architecture
- Information application framework
- Business data management architecture
- Data governance architecture
- Data quality architecture
- Information value chain architecture
- Community social network architecture
- Detailed taxonomy

Many of these components will provide crucial requirements for the data warehousing applications that the EDW team has been asked to develop. The previous list is daunting if one views it as a set of artifacts that must be complete and perfect before the data governance team moves on to the next level of the EIM process. Providing 100% complete versions of these artifacts is counter to EIM best practices, however. Ladley urges EIM teams to never implement more data governance than they can sustain [Ladley 2013]. He defined the EIM cycle so that companies can approach information management iteratively, implementing with each effort only the policies that the business staff will be able to support with the changes in their thinking and daily work actions.

The fact that the data governance team will be pursuing the EIM architecture incrementally essentially mandates that the enterprise data warehouse be constructed iteratively as well. Fortunately, agile EDW practices will accelerate IT's ability to support iterative EIM, to the point that slow development of DW/BI applications will no longer limit how much EIM the company can achieve. The philosophies and techniques offered in this book are thus perfectly aligned with the realities of the business-led data governance process in which EDW's customers will be immersed. When starting a project, the agile EDW team pursues an elaboration phase during the first couple of iterations. Those iterations are dedicated to proving out the architecture of the new areas being added to the enterprise data warehouse. As the data governance team works through each increment of the EIM architecture, the agile EDW team leaders can utilize the resulting EIM artifacts as business and technical requirements for the modules their teams will build during their elaboration development work.

The last prep step in the EIM cycle before the company executes its data governance plan is to provide a *roadmap*. This roadmap prescribes milestones for rolling out the newly defined data governance process as well as the order in which the company's major business applications should align with the data governance plan. Here, the agile EDW method can enable the data governance team to be more precise. Working in isolation, the EIM roadmap can depict the desired alignment of business applications only in terms of EIM maturity phases [Ladley 2013]. Because they are not close enough to the IT work required to align these systems, the EIM team cannot provide a roadmap with the likely dates when these systems will be adapted to support the data governance plan. The agile EDW team, however, will prepare a current estimate once it has completed the elaboration-phase iterations. Using the development team velocity established during these iterations, the team can story point the entire backlog of work and then calculate the number of iterations that will be required to achieve the target changes in the enterprise data warehouse. Of course, this calculation is a rough estimate, and the team's velocity can later change, but at least this estimate of the number of iterations needed will be evidence-based and can thus provide meaningful dates for when the features called for by the EIM roadmap will be available.

Finally, the EIM team needs to put the data governance plan into action and then *sustain* the corporate data quality. The sustain activities include training business staff in the new work patterns required, the development or modification of the information systems that the staff will use, plus metrics-gathering activities and corrective actions when data quality does not meet the goals laid out in the roadmap. For the agile EDW team, the *sustain* level of the EIM process translates directly to iterative DW/BI *application development*. The subrelease cycle will provide the small doses of requirements, design, development, and quality assurance work necessary to evolve the corporate data warehouse to support the master data, standardized measures, and data quality metrics the EIM plan needs in order to track business-unit compliance with the data governance policies adopted.

Data Governance Actions for the EDW Team

The agility of the EDW team to deliver evolving business analytics systems will translate directly into fast feedback loops for the data governance team, making the EIM process all the more effective at detecting and correcting data quality issues. To this end, the agile EDW team leaders can support the EIM program as they work with the company's various business units to develop the enterprise-level data integration and reporting applications:

- They can familiarize themselves with the standards defined by the current version of data governance regulations, notify data governance when they encounter source systems that do not comply, and ensure that new EDW designs do align with those standards.
- Because they are working closely with many business staff members, they can collect end-user opinions regarding the effectiveness and accuracy of the data governance regulations.
- They can document cross-business-unit data elements encountered within their work on individual projects and bring them to the data governance board for inclusion in the EIM standards.
- They can provide the repositories and data transformations needed to implement the data governance decisions in existing or new portions of the enterprise data warehouse.
- The can prototype proposed EDW features in a way that allows business staff to see and evaluate each element's impact on data fields included in the data governance plan.
- When application prototypes are approved, they can implement those enhancements to the EDW in a business-reasonable time frame.

In essence, the EDW team can provide an important service for detecting discrepancies between the corporate data as it exists and EIM's data governance standards. When those gaps reside in the enterprise data warehouse, the EDW team can work quickly to resolve them.

Machine-Assisted Data Governance for the Subrelease Cycle

So that the agile EDW team can provide the invaluable services outlined above, I have defined Step 1 on the subrelease delivery cycle proposed below to support data governance. The EDW team can execute this step manually, but my experience shows that the development team will be far more effective if it leverages its efforts with a workflow-driven data governance and prototyping tool. Whether manual or machine-assisted, the four actions within this data governance step will be as follows:

1. Seek out and define shareable data elements while working with subject matter experts.
2. Model standardized BI metrics and qualifiers for business staff review.
3. Assemble some sample data that can illustrate these shared elements.
4. Load sample data into the data model proposed for the BI solutions so that end users can review a prototype of the requested capabilities.
5. Adjust that prototype until subject matter experts approve of proposed features for the warehouse.

Products currently on the marketplace enable agile EDW teams to pursue this work with many times the productivity compared to manual techniques [Balanced Insight 2011].

Consider Action 1, for example. EDW teams defining data elements manually would call for large meetings of staff members from multiple business units at the beginning of a project, asking them to agree on common definitions for a long list of potentially shareable data items. Often, these meetings would consume days of the participants' time because marketing, sales, fulfillment, billing, and warranty all have inherently different definitions for common business concepts such as customer, product, and cost. For example, "Customer" to the marketing staff is any head of household in the company's service area because marketing is most interested in contacting potential buyers. For sales, a customer is anyone who has inquired about the company's goods and services, whereas fulfillment and billing consider a customer as a person who has placed an order. These differences become ever more extreme when considering the contrasting perspectives of the business units dedicated to unique segments of the marketplace, such as commercial, consumer, and wholesale merchandising. Ironing out shared definitions for the company's master data elements often takes weeks of meetings, generating a large collection of notes created by the EDW staff, not all of which will be processed, reviewed, and correctly incorporated into the design of the conformed dimensions included in the next application release.

Workflow-driven data governance products make this business-input gathering work far easier, faster, and more effective. Instead of calling for long meetings, the business analyst on the EDW team can interview one or two subject matter experts, type their definition for a master data element or standardized metric into a data governance repository, and then submit that definition for approval by the other stakeholders within the company. The workflow engine alerts these stakeholders to the new definitions waiting for their review and then regularly reminds them of any waiting items until they process each submitted definition. To review a submission, the stakeholder clicks on the URL in the email to see that particular term in the tool's user interface, reads the proposed definition of the shared item, and then either approves the definition or types in how one could improve upon it. Later, the business analyst can review the comments from all respondents in the data governance repository and update the candidate definition using the input from the stakeholders. He or she can then resubmit each element to the workflow engine for recirculation and review among the stakeholders.

Eventually, the stakeholders will either arrive at a consensus on a definition or suggest that an element be divided into two or more parallel definitions in order to allow for variations by business unit. By utilizing a workflow-driven data governance utility, the entire company has (1) avoided many hours of expensive meetings, (2) arrived at a set of usable definitions and stored them in an online corporate data dictionary, and (3) documented the evolution and approvals of each definition in that dictionary.

With approved items in the repository, the EDW team can begin modeling standardized BI qualifiers and metrics (Action 2) by using this data governance tool to visually stack the defined items into hierarchies, combine the hierarchies into proposed dimensions, and connect those dimensions to the standardized metric definitions also residing in the repository. Using the same workflow engine, the team would send out this candidate dimensional model to the business stakeholders, again letting them approve or send back comments until they reach a consensus on the proposed design.

Once the organization has a working business design for standard metrics and dimensions, the EDW leaders can then collaborate with their product owner to search through source systems for good examples of the data to place in this new dimensional model (Action 3). Once they have identified a modest number of usable data records, the EDW team would use the tool to load the sample data into the dimensional prototype. Using the workflow engine again, they would send out the URL to the stakeholders so that they can see the hierarchies they agreed on previously, this time with representative data displayed within them. Based on the comments fetched by the workflow engine on this data-enriched prototype, the EDW team leaders will evolve the proposed dimensional solution until the stakeholders decide whether it is worth building.

At this point, the EDW developers possess

- a rock-solid, tangible expression of business requirements for those upcoming aspects of the next EDW subrelease that will support data elements under data governance;
- approved definitions for the entities and attributes involved; and
- sample data that the company can use for testing and demonstrations once the necessary data transform modules have been programmed.

All this was accomplished via asynchronous workflow with little time spent in meetings listening to the business staff argue over definitions and little or no time spent performing ETL programming.

THE AGILE EDW SUBRELEASE VALUE CYCLE

With the proper role for an DW/BI team in data governance outlined previously, we can now assemble a repeatable value cycle for an agile EDW team that will guide it in defining, coding, and validating the multiple subreleases needed to build an application. Figure 19.3 presents the eight steps that my colleagues and I typically employ once we reach Level 6 of the startup process illustrated in Figure 19.2. With this cycle, the team steadily adds value to either the company's understanding of the application it wants to build or the current subrelease candidate of that application.

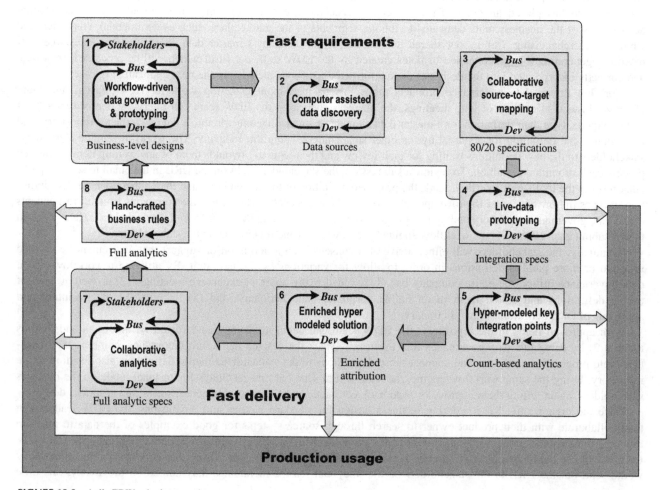

FIGURE 19.3   Agile EDW subrelease cycle.

This cycle naturally divides into two sets of steps: (1) those that allow the team to quickly gather the requirements needed to guide the programming of the next subrelease and (2) those that allow them to rapidly deliver upon those requirements. Each of the steps in these two groups can be iterative, allowing the team to make more than one pass as needed to accomplish the objectives for each of them. For most, the iterations will involve expressing information gathered from business subject matter experts and then validating it with them. The fact that the team may need to iterate on many of these steps makes it difficult to portray how this cycle progresses across time because the activities may actually split and recombine multiple times as the team works its way around the process. For example, the product owner and the project architect may accomplish enough data governance during the first step to enable the systems analyst to start working on Step 2 while they return to invest more time in the field definitions called for by Step 1. In this case, two streams of work will be making their way around the cycle and may not resynchronize until the moment the programmers begin coding complex business rules in Step 8.

The point of the subrelease cycle is to provide EDW project leaders with a clear notion of a value chain of activities that will allow their teams to repeatedly define and create new subrelease candidates, saving time through accuracy and well-timed precision. As long as the team leaders can derive from this cycle a handful of well-articulated developer stories for the programmers to code every iteration, no one will care whether the project leaders have one or many cycle steps simultaneously active.

When seeing the subrelease cycle for the first time, some agile practitioners have been disquieted that I describe many of its steps in terms of both the human activities involved and the productivity tools the developers would use. These practitioners believe that methodological steps should be defined purely with activities because each team may employ a very different tool for a given work activity. Fortunately, a team could perform the steps of the recommended value cycle nearly as described, even if its developers want to conduct all the suggested work by hand, so mentioning a tool type for each step will not weaken the presentation. Although mentioning tools makes the descriptions a tad less theoretical, I still identified the appropriate tool type(s) for each step because developers do in fact work somewhat differently (usually better) when they employ a productivity tool for a given task.

The Fast Requirements Portion of the Subrelease Cycle

Steps 1–4 of this subrelease cycle allow the team to progressively define the data elements that the target subrelease will deliver and the business rules required to properly load them.

Step 1: Workflow-Driven Data Governance and Prototyping

As described in the previous section, one or two business analysts can perform the data governance and prototyping step using a workflow-driven tool. They repeatedly send out candidate definitions of key business terms for comment and approval by the members of various data governance committees. The business staff members may have to iterate a bit on their own as they consult with others in the company in order to decide how each business unit wants to define the requested terms.

After defining the business terms, the EDW analysts assemble them into hierarchies, dimensions, and facts and then use the workflow engine again to elicit stakeholder comments and approvals for these modeled constructs. The analysts next provide sample data matching the proposed star schemas, which the tool then places in a sample semantic layer it has generated for the company's preferred business intelligence front-end tool. Finally, after building a few illustrative graphs and pivot tables on this data-enriched semantic layer, the analysts can once more employ the workflow engine to circulate these dashboard components among the end users. With just this first step of the agile value cycle complete, DW/BI arrives at an approved concept of the subrelease it proposes to build over the next few programming iterations. Without consuming any funds for programmer time, the EDW team leaders were able to visualize for end users the entire increment of the data warehouse's design, from the business terms to be used to a good sample of what the end-user dashboard will contain.

Step 2: Associative Data Discovery

With the basic target structures now defined and approved, the EDW leaders can deploy the *data cowboy* discussed in Chapter 11. The data cowboy's objectives will be two-fold: (1) Vet the data in the source systems from which the project architect proposes to feed the data warehouse, and (2) work with the product owner to further elaborate the business rules that the programmers should follow while transforming that source data. Here, the data cowboy will proceed fastest if he or she uses a BI visualization tool such as an associative query engine that will provides machine-assisted join discovery when fed a large number of source records. These engines allow the team to easily build candidate joins between source tables and try out proposed transformation rules, quickly zeroing in on the precise logic that the ETL modules should utilize.

Step 3: Collaborative Source-to-Target Mapping

Guided by the findings of the computer-assisted discovery work, the team's product owner and system analysts can now begin spelling out the source-to-target maps (STMs) that the developers should follow when they program the data warehouse's ETL modules. This work can be performed by hand if the effort is small enough for one or two systems analysts to finish. When many analysts are required and/or this step will entail a steady, high volume of STM entries, my colleagues and I have found that we produce far more useful mappings using a collaborative source-to-target authoring tool. These tools are multiuser and provide good version tracking, enabling EDW teams to easily resolve those moments of high confusion that occasionally beset enterprise-scale projects. Moreover, these tools streamline the STM authoring process so that analysts can redirect their energy into developing more accurate and precise mapping specifications, sometime to the point where they are machine actionable and can be transferred directly to the ETL and automated test engines, saving considerable development time [Norris 2012]. The STM authoring tool also provides a permanent repository of detailed to-be specifications that the current team can later use for code walkthroughs and future teams can use for impact analysis when the data warehouse's design must be updated.

Step 4: Live Data Prototyping

Armed with a good notion of how the source data must be joined and transformed to create value for the company, the EDW team can now configure a trial integration of the source objects using one of the data virtualization servers (DVSs) discussed in the agile data engineering section of this book. As described in Chapter 13, a DVS will allow the developers to simultaneously join a wide variety of relational and nonrelational data across many brands of database management systems. These DVS-performed joins will allow the team to validate many of the integration and transformation rules identified in the previous steps using operational data or replicas of them, thus providing a "live-data prototype." The team leaders should vet this prototype with not only the product owner but also the project's near stakeholders so that this step results in a validated, fairly detailed design ready to program. The team will not be able to confirm all of the business rules and integration points using this virtual star schema because the DVS tools have some performance and transformation limitations. They will be able to validate the core of the subrelease's solution concept, however, making the output of this step and the entire fast requirements portion of the value cycle a very strong 80/20 specification.

The Fast Delivery Portion of the Subrelease Cycle

At this point, the team now understands well the nature of the next subrelease and can pivot to the labor-intensive portion of the value cycle in which it has to program the data transforms identified by the fast requirements steps. The first part of the cycle has made the risk that a major requirement or design point has been overlooked exceedingly small. The programmers will be able to resolve the remaining 20 percent of the specification by working in real time, eye-to-eye with the team leaders and the product owner.

The next four steps steadily work their way through the remaining unknowns, each time chipping away at the uncertainties and risks. They start with the core of the desired data integration and then drape details and derived columns over that backbone, with the team validating the results of each step with the product owner. Notice that at any point during the remaining steps, the product owner can declare the existing build "good enough" and request that it be presented as a subrelease candidate to the project's near stakeholders and then promoted into production usage if approved. Not every set of features has to be programmed if, for example, a touch of data integration augmented by a large dose of data virtualization will suffice. In this way, many subrelease cycles end in success far earlier than anyone imagined, a fact that makes the agile EDW team appear to be delivering value to the customer all that much faster.

Step 5: Hyper-Modeled Key Integration Points

In this step, the team employs either a hyper normalized data modeling technique or a hyper generalized data warehouse generator to quickly implement the major entities and the key integration points specified by the first half of the subrelease cycle. Seeing the backbone of the proposed target data often enables the product owner to point out major conceptual mistakes before the developers have invested a large amount of time into a particular solution concept. This step focuses on linking together the primary and foreign keys between the target entities. For attributes, the developers can replicate many of them straight from source. Because the data warehouse's fact tables will have only basic dimensional qualifiers attached, the end users may be limited to only rudimentary analyses, perhaps only "things you can count and sum, sliced and diced by text values taken straight from the source systems." Even with this basic functionality, the product owner should be able to address many of the user stories from the project backlog and even perform some of the theme-level actions the department directors have requested.

Step 6: Enriched Hyper-Modeled Solution

Once the business has validated the key integration points utilized in the previous step, the EDW can leverage the hyper-modeled technology to quickly enrich the warehouse's data repository with the easier business rules found in the project backlog. The hyper-modeled data repository allows the EDW team to deliver these enhancements without expensive re-engineering of tables, even if the business had opted to put the results of the last release candidate into production usage. During this step, the team typically adds the derived values whose formulas are well understood and therefore represent little risk. If the source systems offer competing versions of key business entities such as customer, product, and location, this step can begin to resolve those conflicts by creating "golden records" in those areas in which the business rules are clear. With this step in the value cycle, the team will add a far richer set of "slice and dice" capabilities to the previous build, often augmenting the basic counts and sums with some beginning master data elements and the easier derived metrics the business has asked for.

Step 7: Collaborative Analytics

Now that the end users have moderately rich analytics to work with, the EDW team leaders should place a version of the subrelease into production (or at least the user acceptance environment) and step back for a while. They need to let the business departments work on their own with the real data in the warehouse to determine if the information and insights it provides are substantive and accurate. This temporary version of the warehouse will contain only replicated columns and the easier portion of the requested derived values and master data elements. It will still serve to let the product owner and business users finish researching the exact logic needed for the remaining, complex data transformations required.

A good set of productivity tools exist for this step of the release cycle. *Collaborative analytics* environments allow end users to query the warehouse; then filter, sort, and combine results sets; and finally communicate with each other about what they have found in the data [Devlin 2009]. These environments provide a web-based interface for working with the warehouse data so that they can build their own derived columns using any of the basic and advanced commands found in mainstream spreadsheet packages. With this level of capability, the end users can build the analyses they need to get real work done using this preliminary version of the warehouse and thus pursue a good deal of the theme- and epic-level stories from the project backlog. Moreover, these tools provide a social-networking environment that allows end users to share their results, polling each other and rating the analyses they have built on top of the data warehouse information.

Best of all, when the end users finally inform the EDW team that they have identified the full solution to the business problems, the developers do not need to ask them to explain what they have done. The collaborative analytic environment recorded every query, derivation, and discussion that the end users had while working with the temporary data warehouse so that the specifications for the last set of user-requested features are now largely documented in the tool's event repository.

Step 8: Model-Driven Solutions

With this last step in the subrelease cycle, the EDW team needs to build the value-added loops discussed in the chapters on agile data engineering. This value-added processing will deliver on the specifications discovered and documented during the previous steps of the subrelease cycle. There may be a few specifications still requiring discussions with the product owner, but the preceding steps of this agile value cycle will ensure that their scope will be small. On the rare occasion that a new specification emerges during this step that requires a major modification to the structure of the data warehouse, the hyper-modeled technology employed by the agile EDW team will in nearly all cases keep the impact of the changes localized. In fact, teams using a hyper generalized EDW generator and management tool will be able to accomplish most of those structural changes and the data conversion required by working solely with the project's business model rather than having to interpret the changes at the logical and physical level, too.

All told, the combination of agile work methods, techniques, and tools described previously allows the EDW team to follow this iterative subrelease cycle while collaborating closely with the business, vetting designs before investing expensive programming resources, and thereby steadily chipping away at the unknowns that could undermine an enterprise data warehousing project.

CENTERING THE VALUE CYCLE ON DATA GOVERNANCE AND QUALITY

The version of the subrelease value cycle previously presented focused on accelerating the team and mitigating the risk of the project. We can extend this diagram by placing additional concepts at its center, allowing it to provide guidance regarding the data governance and quality assurance goals that the team must also achieve.

Deepening the Support for Data Governance

Figure 19.4 enhances the previous value cycle diagram to address the needs of the company's EIM program by placing data governance at the center of the EDW subrelease development process. By doing so, we will guide the EDW team in focusing its contribution to the business-side of EIM, especially the data definition aspects of data governance.

In Figure 19.4, the dotted arrows pointing toward the center represent contributions that EDW team leaders can make during each step of the value cycle to a company's data governance process. Taken together, these flows will

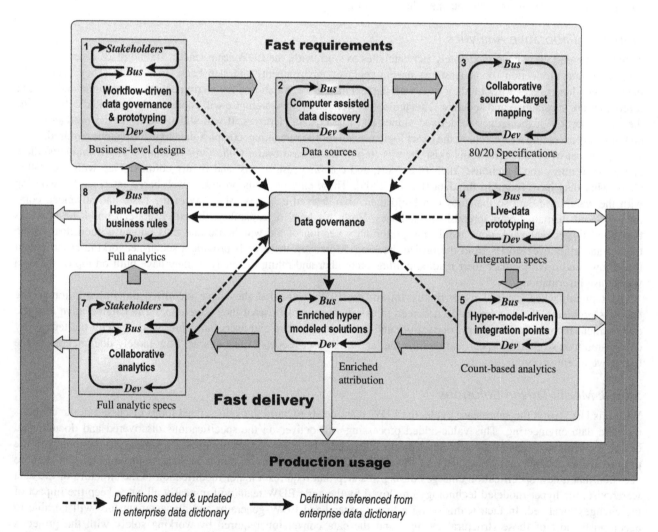

FIGURE 19.4   Agile EDW subrelease cycle showing support for data governance.

contribute a rich collection of target column definitions, which will be extremely reliable given the multiple validations they will receive from both business and the EDW developers during the many steps of the value cycle. The solid arrows indicate areas where referencing the data governance information collected during early steps of the subrelease assists either business or EDW team members in completing their work. These flows consist of the following:

Step 1: Column and star schema object definitions vetted by the business while examining the data governance prototype

Step 2: Further target column definitions and initial business rules stemming from the data cowboy's discovery work

Step 3: Detailed business rules and target column definitions gleaned from the system analyst's source-to-target mappings

Step 4: Additional details on the meaning, usefulness, and limitations of the proposed analytical application's components (e.g., a star schema's metrics and dimensions) given the stakeholder's review of the live data prototype

Step 5: Further documentation regarding the basic set of metrics and dimensional attributes the business considered while reviewing the backbone of the proposed data solution

Step 6: End-user refinements on the meaning and usefulness of the derived columns defined during previous steps

Step 7, outflow from center: The data definitions for data warehouse elements to date, which will guide the end users as they utilize the candidate version of the data warehouse to solve business problems

Step 7, inflow to center: Refined definitions for both existing and newly requested features of the analytic application, based on the innovations that end user created while using the candidate version of the warehouse

Step 8, outflow: Data governance definitions that will guide the EDW developers as they build the remaining components requested by end users

Step 8, inflow: Definitions for the last set of derived columns just programmed into the subrelease candidate

Achieving World-Class Quality Assurance

We can also extend the original version of the agile subrelease value cycle diagram to emphasize the quality assurance aspects of the EDW team's development work. Figure 19.5 places quality assurance at the center of the cycle and uses inflow arrows to indicate the steps at which the team should be contributing test cases to the test suites for the subrelease. Similarly, the outflow arrows document where the EDW team should be heavily utilizing the integration test suites to detect coding and design errors. Steps 1−5 focus on subrelease requirements and an initial design. By and large, these activities define the next version of the application. The diagram encourages the team leaders to generate validation cases for the test engine during each fast requirement step so that when the second half of the cycle focuses on delivery, the team can use those test cases for test-led development. If they keep quality assurance in mind during the first half of the cycle, the EDW developers will indeed find the test repository full of test cases for their modules when they begin development in earnest during steps 5−8. Generic agile textbooks define test-led development for the programming iterations. This diagram instills the practice for the next higher delivery process—that of an entire subrelease. In my experience, teams that conscientiously pursue test-led quality assurance at both these levels will find themselves delivering applications that are nearly defect-free.

GUIDING THE AGILE EDW TRANSITION

Now that we have defined a step-by-step process for the subrelease cycle, we can reflect on the overall impact that agile thinking and development techniques should have on the craft of enterprise data warehousing. With the eight steps presented above, I believe the agile EDW practitioner's toolkit is now complete enough to solve the fundamental problem of enterprise data warehousing, as set forth in the introduction of this book. To the basic notions of Scrum and Kanban that one can find in the average agile textbook, we have added some adapted coding techniques, advanced requirements management, agile data modeling, and iterative quality assurance planning. Transitioning simultaneously to all four of these agile EDW practices will indeed represent an enormous change for DW/BI departments currently employing traditional development methods. It can easily take a waterfall-oriented DW/BI department 2 years or more to incorporate the full extent of these practices and tools into its delivery methods. When embarking upon such an extensive voyage, it is good to have a polar star by which to steer. I offer two such guides to assist the readers' journey. The first is a "EDW customer's bill of rights" that approximates the world-class level of service that project sponsors and business stakeholders should receive from their DW/BI departments once the developers have acclimated to an agile delivery approach. The second is an EDW-specific extension of the agile manifesto that will allow teams to remind themselves of the philosophical tenets that will empower them to achieve the speed and transparency called for by the customer's bill of rights.

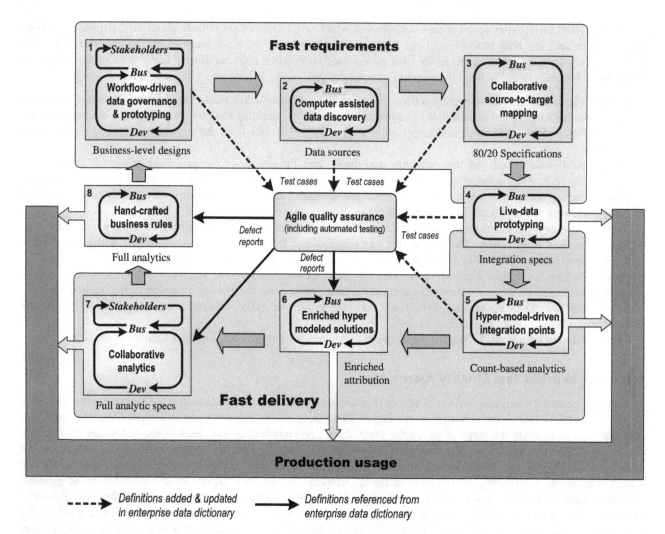

FIGURE 19.5   Agile EDW subrelease cycle showing support for quality assurance.

The DW/BI customer's Bill of Rights

In the chapter on risk management, I listed some of the horror stories of failed DW/BI projects related to my colleagues and I by companies seeking our help in turning around those challenged data warehousing programs. Whether out of incompetence or ill intent, these customers were, in my opinion, abused by their previous systems integrators. It should go without saying that every DW/BI customer has the right to be treated honorably, but now that books exist that explain how to implement an agile EDW delivery effort step-by-step, customers should be able to demand more than just fairness. I believe they have the right to expect the speed, quality, and lower expense that iterative development methods can offer. With agile EDW techniques in hand, the outside vendors and internal development teams with which companies contract should offer their customers a bill of rights. My company shares the following statement with our prospective clients:

> As a data warehousing/business intelligence application development customer, you have a right to work with a vendor that provides:
> - Intelligible solutions
> - Continuous benefits realization
> - Adaptable designs
> - World-class quality assurance

Taking these points in order, we can point out first that agile EDW requirements management revolves around single-sentence statements of business needs, all expressed in the language of end users. There is no reason, then, that 80% or more of a project backlog should not be readily intelligible to the business people who will be paying and waiting for the data warehouse to be built.

Second, iterative, time-boxed development methods and the agile EDW subrelease cycle provide a straightforward means for both coding and validating an application one small piece at a time. Therefore, there is no reason the customer should not see a steady stream of compelling accomplishments pouring out of the project room.

Third, agile data engineering removed the last hurdle to incremental EDW delivery by making it possible to design and populate an enterprise data warehouse a few tables at a time without risking large re-engineering tasks or ruinously expensive data conversations when confronted with new business requirements. For this reason, customers should be able to incrementally refine the information service they request from their BI applications and change directions altogether when the business they are running must suddenly change.

Finally, automated test engines exist, enabling teams to economically collect and run extensive, detailed test suites that will achieve full regression testing on a nightly basis. With that level of testing power available, there is no reason why a production release should not be free from all but the most insignificant defects when it is received by a customer.

The Need for a Business-Side Project Architect

Listing a bill of rights for DW/BI customers raises several challenging questions. An agile EDW toolkit, such as the one outlined in this book, is complex, with many interlocking components. How does a project sponsor know whether or not the development team with which he or she is working understands the toolkit well enough to be able to follow its precepts? If the development team pays only lip service to the method and neglects to honor crucial portions of its guidance, its business partners may be unaware that the project is heading toward slow deliveries, high costs, and unacceptable levels of risk—until it is too late to save the development effort from failure. How can the business sponsor and his or her staff acquire enough clarity on what the developers are actually doing so that they can be assured that the project in on track to succeed?

I witnessed the advent of the certified Project Management Professional (PMP) in the IT industry starting in the mid-1980s. Although business partners seemed happy at first that the IT project managers were now following a baseline concept of how projects should be run, they also found all the new language and diagramming techniques PMPs employed to be fairly opaque. Although they might have felt some assurance that their projects were under better control, they also experienced that control belonged entirely to IT, and many of them did not care for that state of affairs. The business sponsors realized they needed someone on their side who understood both the baseline method and whether the IT team was following it. Many business units now employ project managers of their own, not to run the development effort but, rather, to work alongside of IT, tracking events and communicating a project's intent and performance to the business sponsors in a language they can understand.

If agile EDW has become more complicated as it establishes a baseline approach, perhaps the customer needs to employ a similar strategy. IT provides a *project architect* to lead development projects—someone who can certify that the money being spent will solve the intended business problem. The business unit footing the bill for the development effort would be completely in its rights to hire a project architect of its own and insist that he or she be able to work alongside the IT's lead architect. The business project architect must have built a data warehouse before using an iterative method so that he or she will understand what the IT side of the project should be doing, when IT should have done it, and whether IT really got it done.

The IT project architect must certify the solution built by the team, giving him the responsibility to drive requirements, design, and quality assurance. The business project architect would not be responsible for driving these functions but would need to be active enough in the project's high-level planning and reviews functions to know that requirements, design, and testing were all pursued in a manner that ensures they produced solid, 80/20-level artifacts. Because he would be observing rather than driving the process, the business-side project architect would have the band width to monitor two or more projects, so the additional cost of this safeguard for the business sponsor would be relatively small compared to the size of the EDW development budget.

With a business-side project architect in place, the business sponsor will have two independent voices informing her that the development team is spending the project's funds effectively—one from IT and one reporting directly to her. When these two voices cannot jointly certify that the project was defined, designed, and validated following the agile EDW baseline, the sponsor will know that something in the project room has gone very wrong. As we have seen throughout this book, early detection is the key to positioning oneself to overcome a challenge. Adding a second project architect reporting to the business is an effective way to ensure that problems in project execution get pushed to the surface early and often.

Toward an Agile EDW Manifesto

Of course, the flip side of offering a higher level of service is delivering on the promise, a goal that will require a new mindset on the part of the developers on the EDW team. The mindset for generic agile delivery was encapsulated by the agile manifesto, posted to the Internet in 2001. Agile EDW teams will need their own version of that proclamation, one that extends the original in a style that accommodates the ways DW/BI is different from general application development. I therefore conclude this book by offering a set of four philosophical tenets that I posted to the Internet on the 10th anniversary of the agile manifesto. They form an "agile data warehousing manifesto" for readers to consider as they examine the techniques described in my books and begin applying them to projects of their own.

Offering the DW/BI customer a bill of rights will engender a very high level of customer expectations. Setting lofty expectations can be constructive because it requires the EDW team to be serious and disciplined about building business intelligence solutions. However, the team may not be emotionally ready to redouble the ardor with which it pursues development projects. How can EDW team leaders be assured that their teammates will rise to the occasion?

If a few lines spoken to the customer can create the challenge, then perhaps another short statement spoken to the developers will instill in them the attitude for success. The agile manifesto encapsulated the new mindset that programmers should adopt for iterative and incremental delivery of general software applications. Its four philosophical tenets, listed in Chapter 2, still readily apply to business intelligence projects. However, the data integration aspects of EDW applications make data warehousing considerably different from general application development. For this reason, I have long believed that EDW developers need a few agile tenets of their own that will properly orient them to the big ideas needed to overcome the difficulties involved in iterative data integration.

Throughout the years, I have offered the extension of the agile manifesto listed in the sidebar below to my customers, teammates, and students. These four bullets always seem to encourage the high level of open-mindedness, courage, and innovation that agile EDW requires. Because they incorporate the spirit of the method's new solutions for risks, requirements, data design, and quality, I believe they will provide readers a handy way to illustrate the new outlook that EDW development teams will need when they transition to iterative delivery. I provide some explanation for each of these tenets, expressing the ideas in the same way that my colleagues and I introduce them to the new teams that we start coaching. Of course, these four short maxims do not convey the entirety of the agile EDW approach, but they should communicate to new teammates what is different about the agile approach and give team leaders the stage needed to present the remaining elements of the incremental delivery method they have chosen.

Prompt, Sponsor-Appreciated Results Over Technical Perfection

The original manifesto's four tenets advocated software developers to concentrate on customer collaboration, working software, the interactions between individuals, and responding to change as a means to accelerating the delivering of working software. Whereas these maxims certainly point to a better alternative than process-heavy approaches based on comprehensive documentation, contract negotiation, and slavishly following a plan, they omit the unifying goal of agile development and are therefore too weak to depict the new way EDW developers must pursue their projects. What is the benefit in the abstract notion of "working software"? The challenge facing EDW teams is that data warehousing consumes months and years of time before providing any new competitive capabilities to the company, so our first extension to the agile manifesto must focus squarely on remedying that predicament. As agile EDW practitioners, we will provide fast deliveries that delight the people paying for these inordinately expensive projects. In other words, our team will drive hard toward prompt, sponsor-appreciated results.

Sidebar: The Agile DW/BI Manifesto

A Supplement to the Four Tenets of the Agile Manifesto (http://www.agilemanifesto.org)
Using Agile techniques, we are finding ways to break through the problems which used to make data warehousing projects frequently fail: high cost, slow delivery, and excessive risk. Through this work we have come to value the following notions in addition to the tenets of the Agile manifesto:

- Prompt, sponsor-appreciated results over technical perfection
- Evolving data over iterating on application code
- Managing risk over eliminating uncertainty
- Appropriate technology over maintaining an infrastructural monoculture

Given that today agile techniques have been well pioneered, what is the anti-pattern that DW/BI teams follow that keeps them from achieving this goal? It is still the desire for a big design up front, particularly a perfect data model. Today's development tools for front-end and back-end programming make those portions of an EDW project fairly predictable. The data model, however, instills our team leaders with great fear because small changes there can undermine months of BI and ETL programming. The traditional EDW mindset will not allow our developers to start programming until the data model is perfect.

We can no longer ask our sponsors to wait months and years while we slowly fine-tune the target data schema until it obtains a bullet-proof, third normal form. Our customers need business intelligence now, so we must let go of this notion of the technically perfect data model. The value of the opportunities lost far exceeds the cost of the applications we are building. If we can deliver in the next few weeks only the most important 5 percent of our customers' business needs by patching together landed data with a data virtualization tool and a small bit of data transform programming, we are going to do it. We will then move on to deliver the next most valuable increment until eventually the customer has received the business intelligence necessary to enable the company to compete and thrive in its particular industry.

Evolving Data Over Iterating on Application Code

Veteran DW/BI professionals will instantly ask what our team will do if our series of small data warehouse increments adds up to an unsupportable mess. We will prevent this undesirable outcome by refusing to layer data on top of data without a plan. Instead, we will utilize the agile hyper modeling techniques that allow us to progressively elaborate our EDW's data model.

For the most part, these new data modeling techniques enable us to add the next subject area to a warehouse without having to restructure or convert existing tables and their already loaded data records. Our front-end tools are already incredibly nimble enough with regard to providing new visualizations or adapting to new sources. The hyper modeling techniques bring that same adaptability to the back-end portions of the warehouse. The hyper normalized or hyper generalized data models they support eliminate the majority of the programming required to create the basic data warehouse transformations, so throughout the project we will be able to focus on getting the data right instead of coding the ETL.

On the rare occasions when new requirements make some of our existing EDW structures obsolete, these hyper modeling paradigms greatly constrain the impact that the necessary design changes will have, thereby keeping the labor required to re-engineer and reload data to a minimum. Whereas in the past an EDW project would start with a long-delayed, perfect data model and then spend months trying to get the ETL code correct, agile EDW teams employ techniques that allow us to (1) focus on meeting immediate needs with our best guess regarding table design and then (2) progressively update data structures and content so that the warehouse supports the shifting needs of our sponsors. We can indeed achieve our goal of fast, sponsor-appreciated deliverables because the agile data modeling paradigms allow us to continuously evolve the data rather than fuss with the ETL code.

Managing Risk Over Eliminating Uncertainty

Veteran DW/BI professionals will scoff at the notion of evolving data structures that will not need constant widescale re-engineering. Our agile EDW team will counter this skepticism by following the original manifesto's counsel to emphasize customer collaboration. Every few iterations, we will present the current build to project stakeholders as a ready-to-consume business intelligence application and ask for permission to put that build into production usage. These stakeholders can evaluate the release candidate in all the ways that matter, including functional capabilities, aesthetics, and nonfunctional quality such as security and performance.

Of course, they may reject this release candidate because we have misunderstood the design and capabilities they require, but we do not fear this uncertainty because, in our method, stakeholder review is either a success or an opportunity to resolve shortcomings. If the business stakeholders agree to promote the build, we will know that we have correctly perceived the important aspects regarding requirements. If they refuse the build, we will have identified misunderstandings and deficiencies in our work, and we will be in a position to fix them. Within another subrelease cycle or two, we will have a new EDW version that the business will want. And with another subrelease or two, our DW/BI colleagues who doubt that enterprise data warehouses can evolve one step at a time will see that indeed adaptive data modeling truly works.

Each of these release candidates will steadily reduce the potential that our team has either misunderstood the customer or tackled a design that exceeds our programming capabilities or the source data available. Instead of fearing the uncertainty about what to build for customers, we will follow a strategy of "fail fast and fix quickly." Instead of trying to eliminate uncertainty with a perfect up-front design, we will manage the risk of failure with a steady stream of release candidates, each one zeroing in on the application that the business needs.

Appropriate Technology Over Maintaining an Infrastructural Monoculture

In order to steadily evolve the business intelligence solutions we offer, the agile EDW team will need an expanded toolkit. Various combinations of products, such as fast data visualization tools, hyper modeling utilities, data virtualization servers, data warehouse generators, and big data repositories, will allow us to move fast and adapt quickly. This may well conflict with a strategy of traditional IT management to maintain an infrastructural monoculture—that is, the smallest feasible technical platform. Small technical platforms minimize software licensing and support costs, as well as the expense of hiring and training staff. Those concerns have merit, so our EDW team will not be extreme in its requests for non-standard tooling. Instead, we will build a solid business case for each product we wish to use, but be aware that we will be estimating the opportunity cost of delivering business intelligence solutions 3–10 times more slowly when evaluating scenarios in which the agile team is forced to use the traditional toolset. Because these opportunity costs will include the impact of losing crucial business opportunities, the business case for the agile toolset will be far more compelling than many people might first assume. We will also distinguish between tools that we will use for production applications and the tools we need for discovery and prototyping because the latter category has much lower costs for licensing, support, and training. A rational balancing of costs and benefits will lead IT to an expanded toolset for DW/BI development that includes a set of technologies that are appropriate for the company's business situation, and one that steadily evolves as that situation changes, rather than clinging to a static infrastructural monoculture.

SUMMARY

The many innovative techniques introduced in this book can be assembled into an easy-to-follow and repeatable value chain that fits perfectly inside the subrelease cycle that previous chapters identified as a robust risk mitigation strategy. This value chain provides eight steps that EDW teams should follow as they define and program each subrelease. The overall agile EDW project startup process aligns well with the enterprise information management (EIM) work patterns that many companies follow. Moreover, the subrelease cycle, once structured to include all eight steps, delivers the IT support needed to sustain a company's EIM initiative. In fact, EDW teams can embed the data governance portion of an EIM program in the center of the subrelease value cycle so that the process will feed the data governance program with a steady stream of definitions and also alert data governance stewards to unaligned business applications and harmful departmental data practices. Moreover, the agile EDW team can embed system validation in the center of the value cycle in order to generate a similar stream of test cases that will then form the heart of a world-class quality assurance effort.

All told, agile techniques for enterprise data warehousing offer many ways to accelerate and improve the delivery of crucial business intelligence applications. DW/BI service providers need to offer their customers the full benefits of these agile approaches. They need to offer them an EDW customer's bill of rights so that project sponsors will know what they can reasonably demand from their DW/BI development teams. In turn, the development teams will need to acquire a new mindset that will guide them in meeting the expectations nurtured by the customer's bill of rights. They need to adopt a version of the agile manifesto updated for DW/BI so that everyone on the delivery team will have a concise strategy statement to follow. This agile DW/BI manifesto emphasizes several philosophies and techniques that allow a team to work in ways that are faster, better, and cheaper, enabling them to better service their business partners and deliver to their companies far greater value than ever before.

Do the new approaches to risk, requirements, data modeling, programming, and quality assurance espoused in this book combine effectively into a workable solution to the fundamental problem of enterprise data warehousing? Readers will have to decide for themselves, but I have formed an opinion based on the EDW projects my colleagues and I have supported during the past 15 years: Agile EDW techniques work amazingly well. If a team transitioning from a waterfall method is not delivering EDW modules two or three times faster after implementing all of these practice elements, then the call for help should go out to other agile EDW practitioners. We will need to rally around this challenged program to identify which incremental EDW practices have been overlooked or misapplied, because if a team of developers has not at least tripled its effectiveness over traditional methods within 6 months of switching to iterative and incremental delivery, there is surely another powerful technique waiting for them in the agile enterprise data warehousing toolkit.

Part VI References

Chapter 19

Balanced Insight, 2011, June. Transforming BI: Subway IPC turns to balanced insight consensus. Balanced Insight Case Studies (website). <http://www.balancedinsight.com/wp-content/uploads/2011/06/Balanced-Insight-Inc-IPC-Subway-Case-Study.pdf> (accessed January 2015).

Devlin, B., 2009. Collaborative Analytics: Sharing and Harvesting Analytic Insights Across the Business (white paper). 9sight Consulting, Cape Town, South Africa, <http://www.9sight.com/collaborative_analytics_white_paper.pdf> (accessed January 2015).

Eckerson, W., 2011. Creating an Enterprise Data Strategy (white paper). Business Applications and Architecture Group, TechTarget, Newton, MA.

Fisher, T., 2009. The Data Asset: How Smart Companies Govern Their Data for Business Success. Wiley, New York.

Ladley, J., 2010. Making Enterprise Information Management (EIM) Work for Business. Morgan Kaufmann, Waltham, MA.

Ladley, J., 2013. Planning Your Enterprise Data Strategy (course book). DataVersity, Studio City, CA, <www.dataversity.net>.

Norris, D., 2012, June. AnalytiX Mapping Manager: The missing link in moving data around. Bloor (website). <http://www.bloorresearch.com/analysis/analytix-mapping-manager-missing-link-moving-data> (accessed January 2015).

Rouse, M., 2007. Essential guide. TechTarget (website). <http://search-datamanagement.techtarget.com/definition/data-governance> (accessed December 2014).

Thomas, G., 2014. Definitions of data governance. The Data Governance Institute (website). <http://www.datagovernance.com/adg_data_governance_definition> (accessed December 2014).

Index

Note: Page numbers followed by "*b*," "*f*," and "*t*" refer to boxes, figures, and tables, respectively.

2 × 2 planning matrix, 481−482, 481*f*
  for top-down test selection, 441−444
    framework for assessing QA plan's
      coverage, 441−443
    linking test planning to requirements and
      risk management, 443−444
3NF data model, hyper normalizing, 332*f*
80/20 specifications, 90−92, 142, 148−149
231 swamps
  derive from command and control strategy,
    110−111
  enterprise data warehouse slip into, 109−111

A

Accuracy, 137−138, 143
  vs. precision, 137*f*, 138*t*
Add-mod instance widget, 391, 404
Administrative metadata, 65−66
Agile data engineering, 8, 257, 286−287, 517
Agile DW/BI project
  cost impacts, investigating, 106−107, 106*t*
  evidence-based service level agreements,
    102−104, 103*f*
  proof for working, 104−107
Agile EDW transition, guiding, 515−520
  agile DW/BI manifesto, 518*b*
  agile EDW manifesto, 518−520
    appropriate technology over maintaining
      infrastructural monoculture, 520
    evolving data over iterating on application
      code, 519
    managing risk over eliminating
      uncertainty, 519−520
    prompt, sponsor-appreciated results over
      technical perfection, 518−519
  DW/BI customer's bill of rights, 516−517
    business-side project architect, need for, 517
Agile manifesto, 9, 13−15, 15*f*, 17*f*, 18*f*,
    19−20, 24, 26, 29, 31−33, 49−51, 85,
    89, 111, 145*t*, 242, 441−442, 503, 515,
    518, 520
  revised for agile EDW. *See* Agile EDW
    transition, guiding
Agile methods, 14−15, 17*f*, 31
  definition of, 13−19
  elements by origin, 16*t*
  Extreme Programming. *See* Extreme
    Programming (XP)
  Scrum. *See* Scrum method
  values and principles of, 18*f*, 19−20

Agile notions and quality assurance, 430−432
Agile practices, 3−7, 20, 432, 503−504
Agile principles, 6, 18*f*, 19−21, 24, 26, 47, 49,
    53, 88, 430
Agile quality assurance, 8, 516*f*
Agile quality planning, 477−482
  alternatives, 480
  test automation, 481−482
Agile requirements gathering, 63, 149, 174
Agile software development
  fundamental problem of, 1
  in nutshell, 1−3
Agile teams, quality assurance and, 426−427
Agile values, 19−20, 243*t*, 321, 443, 511, 513
Alternative to agile EDW, 5
Analysis, 173
Analysis paralysis, 235
Analytical systems, 13, 63*t*, 66, 77−78, 279, 371
Anchor modeling, 331, 343−344
Apache Hive, 321
Apache Software Foundation, 317
Application Builds, 70
Application coding (AC), 3, 4*f*, 66
Application coding concept errors, 115−116
  examples, 115*t*
  risk mitigation of, 116
Architectural frameworks, 76−79
  Zachman enterprise, 76
  DAMA functional framework, 76−77
  Hammergren DW planning matrix, 77−79
Architectural review, clearing, 361
Architectural uncertainties, 229
Architecture. *See also specific types of*
    architectures
  data, 71−74
  enterprise, 75−76
  reference, 74−75
  system, 70−71
Artifacts. *See specific types*
Association for Computing Machinery (ACM),
    68−69
Associative data model, 381−383
Attribute tables and agility, 340−342
Automated engines, 488−489
Automation, 389, 481−482, 487
  requirement of, 386−387

B

Balancing between two extremes, 123
Baseline method for agile EDW, 5−7

Big data technologies, 308−327
  to enhance EDW agility, 325−327
  Hadoop, 311−313
    Hadoop MapReduce, 312−313
  and Hive, 324−325
  Hive, making MapReduce look like SQL
    with, 317−324
    tempered view of Hive, 320−324
  need for, 309−310
  "schema-on-read", 310−311
  SQL and MapReduce, notable contrasts
    between, 314−317, 317*t*
  surface solutions leveraging big data, 326*f*
  and traditional RDBMSs, 325*f*
Big spec up front approach, 130−131
Blivit factor, 129
Boehm multiplier, 128−129
Bottom-up quality planning, 444−455
  agile-specific test techniques, 449−451
    epic stack testing, 449−450
    exploratory testing, 450−451
  data warehousing testing techniques,
    444−446
    data corners, 445−446
    examples and expected results,
      446
    reconciliation, 446
    referential integrity test, 445
  low-level validations, easy-to-follow test
    technique matrix for, 451−452
  reusable test widgets, 452−453
  test cases roll forward along system
    dimension, 453
  testing for convergence, 453−455
  top-down planning and, 496
  traditional application testing techniques,
    446−449
    boundary value analysis, 447−448
    combinatorial reduction, 448−449
    equivalence class partitioning, 447
Boundary value analysis, 447−448
Bridging tables, 359−360
Broader architectural activities, agile EDW
    supporting, 219−221
Business analysts, 189
  implicit in two project lead roles, 149
Business application, 66
Business concept errors, 115−116
  examples of, 115*t*
  risk mitigation of, 119−120

Business conceptual model, 71, 72*f*, 258–259
Business department, 64, 172–173
Business intelligence (BI), 7, 61, 293, 520
   hierarchy of needs, 172–174, 172*f*
   iterative coding improving, 85–86
Business key tables and agility, 339
Business models, 52*t*, 71–72, 258–259, 381,
      382*f*, 386–391, 390*f*, 393, 397, 399*f*,
      404*f*, 407*f*, 411*f*, 417–418, 506, 513.
      See also Target business model
Business partners, adverse to traditional
      requirements efforts, 138–139
Business process reengineering (BPR), 131,
      135–136, 135*f*, 136*f*
Business process supported, 202–207
   business-level data validation steps,
      205–207
   sample business queries, 207
   use case model, 202–203
   Venn diagram, 203–205
Business professionals, 64–65
Business queries, sample, 207
Business rules, 65, 237, 446
   complex business rules, conquering,
      235–239
   discovery, 238–239
Business solution, 190, 194*f*
Business unit, 63–64
Business value, 159, 228
Business vault, 339
Business-intelligible data retrieval, enabling,
      393–395
Business-level data validation steps, 205–207
Business-side project architect, need for, 517

C
CAGE code, 289
Case history, lessons from, 296
Certified Business Intelligence Professional
      (CBIP) certification program, 60
Certified Data Management Professionals
      (CDMP), 60
Change cases, 281
   for appraising data modeling paradigm,
      286–291
   case 1, 287, 366–368, 390*f*, 392*f*, 403–406,
      404*f*, 405*f*, 406*t*, 409
   case 2, 287–289, 367–368, 368*f*, 406–409,
      406*t*, 407*f*, 408*f*, 409*f*
   case 3, 289–290, 406*t*, 409–410
   case 4, 290–291, 406*t*, 410–413, 411*f*, 412*f*,
      413*f*
Chaos Report, 13–14
Close stakeholders, meaning of, 69*t*
CM21DU, 383
Collaborative analytics, 513
Collaborative source-to-target mapping, 512
Combinatorial reduction, 448–449
Commercial, off-the-shelf software (COTS), 66
Commercial Marketing business unit, 179–180
Communication gaps, 428
Competency centers, 67
Complex business rules, conquering
   with embedded method, 235–239

Complex integration layers, standard normal
      forms leading to, 251–253, 252*f*
Complex presentation layers, conformed
      dimensions leading to, 253–255, 254*f*
Components, definition of, 69–70
Computer programming, 66
Conceptual data model, 196
Configuration items, 69–70
Configuration management, 70
Conformed dimensional form (CDF), 250
Conformed dimensions. *See* Conformed
      dimensional form (CDF)
Construction phase, 221
Context diagram, 194–195, 263*f*
Continuous flow, 15*f*, 16*t*, 29, 31–32, 34,
      41–44, 47
Continuous flow work management approach,
      42–43
   visualizing and maintaining, 43–44, 43*f*
Contracting Party, 283
Convergence, testing for, 453–455
Corner test. *See* Data corners test
Corporate information factory (CIF), 82
Corporate Party, 406
Corporate-level planning functions that
      generate architectural requirements,
      218*f*
Count distinct, 445*t*
Cowboy role. *See* Data cowboy role
Cross-Industry Standard Process for
      Data Mining (CRISP-DM), 237, 237*f*,
      238*t*
Current estimate, 95–97, 96*f*, 144
Current record indicators, 356
Customer experience, 188
Customer's Bill of Rights, 9
Cycle-time analysis
   cumulative time in learning cycles, 324*f*
   cumulative time in usage cycles, 324*f*
   fundamentals, 322*f*

D
Data, definition of, 65
Data access, 172–173
Data architect, 258
Data architecture, 71–74, 257–258, 257*f*
Data caches, of DVS, 300
Data conversions, hyper generalization tools
      and, 396–397
Data corners test, 445–446, 445*f*
Data cowboy role, 235–236, 511–512
   modified data mining method, 236–238
   placing business rules discovery and analysis
      into the effort curves, 238–239
   special skills and tools required, 236
Data dictionary, 81
Data engineering (DE), 3, 4*f*, 8
Data governance (DG), 217–218
   for EDW team, 508
   life cycle for, 505–508
   machine-assisted data governance for
      subrelease cycle, 509–510
   support for, 514–515, 514*f*
   traditional notions of, 504–510

Data Governance and Stewardship
      Professionals (DGSP), 60
Data integration, 61, 85–86
Data loads, 80
Data Management Association (DAMA), 60,
      62*t*
   functional framework, 76–77, 78*f*
Data management paradigms, relative strengths
      of, 318*t*
Data mart, 82
Data model, 257*f*, 258–259
   associative, 381–383
   conceptual, 196
   dimensional, 82
   hyper generalized, 256, 256*f*
   hyper normalized, 255–256, 255*f*
   logical, 72
   normalized, 81–82
   physical, 72–74, 259
Data modeler (DM), 258, 472
   role for DW/BI, 88
Data modeling paradigms, 247
Data modeling techniques, 2–3, 8
Data modeling vs. architecture, 259–260
Data normalization, 261, 262*t*, 280
Data schema, 81
Data services, 200–201
Data sets, planning storage for dozens of, 487
"Data spanker", 235
Data transform specification analyst, 235
Data validation steps for subrelease
      description, 206*f*
Data vaulting, 330, 334, 343–344, 371
   blending styles to achieve agility, 365
   case study, 372
   classic style, 330
   enhanced style, 330, 363–364
   raw vault style, 364–365
   reference tables in, 343
   simple style, 362–363
   source vault style, 364
Data virtualization server (DVS), 81, 296–307,
      301*f*, 353, 512
   basic use case, 297–299, 298*f*
   data virtualization, defining, 297
   dynamic delivery approach using, 304–305
   EDW's reference architecture becoming
      dynamic, 303*f*, 306–307
   performance features, 299–300
   surface solutions, and progressive
      deployment, 302–304, 304*f*, 307*f*
   value proposition, 305–306, 306*f*
   virtual solutions, economics of, 300–302,
      301*f*
Data warehouse, definition of, 61
Data Warehouse Appliance, 82
Data warehouse automation systems, 387
Data warehousing/business intelligence (DW/
      BI), 7, 35
   current estimates, 95–97
   customer's bill of rights, 516–517
   developer stories in, 92–95, 92*f*, 94*f*
   modules, 169
   new roles for, 86–90

primary source for standards, 60–62
Rational Unified Process (RUP) for, 52–53
Scrum method for, 85–86. *See also* Agile DW/BI project
testing, six dimensions of, 433–436, 441, 456, 458
  functional dimension, 439
  planning dimension, 436–437
  point-of-view dimension, 440–441
  polarity dimension, 439–440
  system dimension, 437–439
  time frame dimension, 440
Database management system (DBMS), 79, 297, 359
DEV (development), 469
Developer stories, 92–95, 156
  business-valued, 159
  demonstrable, 156–158
  estimateable, 159
  in data warehousing/business intelligence, 92*f*, 93–94, 94*f*
  independent, 158
  layered, 158
  primary technique for decomposing user stories into, 158*f*
  refinable for, 159
  testable for, 159
  testing of, 156–159
  and values, 94–95
Developers. *See also* Developer stories
  meaning of, 69*t*
  work-in-progress limits for, 100
Development iterations, 23
Development team, meaning of, 69*t*
Diffs, 445*t*
DILBERT'S test, 156, 158*f*
Dimensional data model, 82
Dimensional objects, loading, 390–391
Dimensions, of DW/BI testing, 433–435
"Dimensions of value" diagram, 200
  front-end dimensions of value diagram, subrelease plan summary on, 201*f*
  subrelease scope drawn on, 201*f*
Documentation of team's success, 497–498
Dollar value at risk, 140, 141*f*
Dummy attribute records, 356
Dutch school of data vaulting, 330–331

E

Edge testing, 447–448
Effort curves, placing business rules discovery and analysis into, 238–239
Elaboration phase, 221, 226–228
  choosing developer stories for, 226–227
  "steel thread", proving out architectures using, 227–228
Embedded method, conquering complex business rules with, 235–239
End users, 66, 400
  business intelligence applications, 75
  and data virtualization servers, 307
  hierarchy of needs, 171–174, 176
    analysis, 173
    data access, 172–173

prediction, 173
reporting, 173
research, 173
End-to-end tests, 439
Engine implementation, 487–489
  test scenarios, defining, 489
Enhanced vault style, 363–364
Enriched hyper-modeled solution, 513
Ensemble modeling
  and hyper normalization, 329–331, 330*f*
  light integration and agility, 339–342
    attribute tables, 340–342
    business key tables, 339
    linking tables, 339–340
Enterprise, definition of, 63
Enterprise architecture (EA), 75–76, 217–218
Enterprise data bus (EDB), 82
Enterprise data warehouse planning, hierarchy of, 220*t*
Enterprise data warehousing (EDW), definition of, 61–62
Enterprise information management (EIM), 217–218, 505–508, 506*f*
Enterprise requirements management, 147–148, 150*f*
  vs. generic requirements management, 183*t*
Enterprise requirements value chain, artifacts for, 181
  ERM as a flexible RM approach, 183–184
  generic value chain, 181–183
  identifying project objectives stakeholder's requests, 189–191
    business system challenges, 189
    current manual solution, 189–190
    dependent systems, 190–191
    desired business solution, 190
    volume requirements and end-user census, 190
  module use cases, providing developer guidance with, 209–212
    alternative flow of events, 210–212
    goal, 209
    nonfunctional requirements as supplemental specifications, 212
    source-to-target mappings as supplemental specifications, 212
    special requirements, 212
    standard flow of events, 209–210
  project requirements, enterprise aspects of, 184–186
    functionality dimension, 184–185
    orientation dimension, 185–186
    polarity dimension, 185
    streamlined ERM templates, 186
  sketching the solution with a vision document, 191–198
    context diagram, 194–195
    features and benefits list, 191–194
    high-level data flow, 197
    nonfunctional requirements, 197–198
    solutions statements, 191, 193*f*
    target business model, 196–197
  sponsor's concept briefing (SCB), 186–189
    customer experience impacts, 188

functional area impacts assessments, 188
    justification type, 187–188
    program success metrics, 189
    value of the program, 188
  subrelease overview, segmenting the project with, 198–209
    business process supported, 202–207
    nonfunctional requirements, 208–209
    subrelease identifier, 200
    subrelease scope, 200–202
    technical description, 207–208
Enterprise resource planning (ERP) system, 66, 94
Enterprise-capable requirements management, 144–149, 183, 186, 506
Entrepreneurs and venture capitalists, 309
Epic and theme, testing, 443
Epic decomposition framework, 151–156, 152*f*
  aligning the epic stack to the company's hierarchy, 152–154
  backlog hierarchy's structure, defining, 151–152
  clearly defining each level within epic stack, 154–156
Epic stack, 151
  aligning company's hierarchy, 152–154, 153*f*
  defining levels, 154–156, 155*t*
  revenue assurance example, 157*t*
  testing, 449–450
Epic trees, 151–152, 156, 163–165
Epics, allocating value to, 164
Equivalence class partitioning, 447
Error management logic, 211
Estimating project value, 164
Evidence, 7, 29, 44–45, 97, 102–104, 179, 189, 191, 281–282, 371–373, 402–403, 416–420, 428–429, 492, 496–498, 508
Expected results (testing), 446, 451, 455, 469, 472, 487–488, 490
Exploratory testing, 450–451
Extract, load, and transform (ELT), 397
  programming, 79–80
Extract, transform, and load (ETL) module, 79–80, 190, 253, 330, 339, 348–350
  parameter-driven ETL module prototypes, 346–347
  process, 235
  programming, 79–80
  self-validating, 350–352
Extreme Programming (XP), 3, 32
  contributions from, 26–29
  principles of, 18*f*, 27–29
  values of, 18*f*, 27–29

F

Facebook Hive data warehousing example, solution architecture for, 320*f*
Fact qualifier matrix (FQM), 202
  for a subrelease description, 203*t*
Fishbone diagrams, 174–176
Five-step collaborative effort, example of, 294–296
Five-step delivery iteration, 23–26

Flow, 27–29, 243*t*, 260
Flow of events
    alternative, 210–212
    standard, 209–210
Foreign key, 80
Formal document control, 241
Fortune 500, 109
Free University (case study), 372–373
Freeze–fridge–countertop metaphor, 242
Fulfillment Channel code, 265
Fulfillment Channel Management System, 263
Fulfillment Channel table, 271
Functional dimension, 439
Functional tests, 439
Functionality dimension, 184–185
"Funding waypoints", 229
Fuzzy logic, 399

G
Generalization, 260, 271–279
    advantages and disadvantages of, 271–274
    of sales table for the party entity (example),
        274–279
Generic requirements management (GRM) value
        chain, 144, 147–149, 169, 170*t*, 183, 215
    business intelligence (BI) hierarchy of needs,
        173–174
    end users' hierarchy of needs, 171–174
        analysis, 173
        data access, 172–173
        prediction, 173
        reporting, 173
        research, 173
    and enterprise requirements management
        value chains, contrast between, 183*t*
    mind maps and fishbone diagrams,
        174–176, 175*f*
    product roadmaps, 178–180, 178*f*, 179*f*
    requirements churn, 169–170
    user modeling/personas, 170–171
    vision boxes, 176, 177*f*
    vision statements, 176–178, 177*f*
Generic Scrum, 86
Generic value chain, 181–183
Google Ngram, 52, 53*f*
Grain of fact table, increasing, 410–413
"Green team estimating problem", 223
Group counts, 445*t*

H
Hadoop, 309, 311–313
Hadoop distributed file system (HDFS), 309,
        311–312
Hadoop MapReduce, 312–313
Hammergren DW planning matrix, 77–79, 79*f*
Helper tables, 393, 394*f*
High-level data flow, 197
Hints, of DVS, 300
Hive, 321, 323
    big data and, 324–325
    making MapReduce look like SQL with,
        317–324
    tempered view of, 320–324

Hyper generalized data modeling, 256, 256*f*, 375
    demonstrating agility, 403–414
        change case findings, recap of, 413–414
        consolidating entities into the party model,
            406–409
        increasing the grain of a fact table,
            410–413
        new trigger for a slowly changing
            dimension, 409–410
        upgrading attributes to entities, 403–406
    derived elements, supporting, 397–402
        model-driven master data components,
            398–402
        value-added loops, 397–398
    evidence of success, 416–420
        hyper generalized data warehousing in
            specialty retail, 417–420
        model-driven development in
            pharmaceuticals, 416–417
    HGF-powered agile solutions, 414–416
        surface solutions, easier backfills for,
            415–416
    hyper generalized integration layer, loading
        data into, 390–391
        dimensional objects, 390–391
        transactional objects, 391
    mix of modeling strategies, 375–387
        adding time-oriented object classification,
            380–381
        automation tool, requirement of, 386–387
        extreme generalization, 377–380
        leaving transactions data in
            dimensionalized format, 385–386
        managing things and links with
            associative data model, 381–383
        storing attributes as name–value pairs,
            384–385
    model-driven development and fast
        deliveries, enabling, 387–389
        controlling EDW design from business
            model diagram, 387–388
        driving design changes using business
            model, 389
        eliminating most logical and physical data
            modeling, 387
    model-driven evolution and fast adaptation,
        395–397
        data conversions, facilitating, 396–397
        impact of model changes on existing data,
            395–396
    performance concerns, addressing, 402–403
    retrieving information from hyper
        generalized EDW, 391
        business-intelligible data retrieval,
            enabling, 393–395
        performance sublayer maintenance,
            392–393
Hyper generalized form (HGF), 250, 385–386,
        397
    HGF-powered agile solutions, 414–416
    hyper generalized data management in,
        386–387
    maintenance of performance sublayer,
        392–393

Hyper modeled forms (HMF), 250–251
Hyper normalization, 329–344, 336*f*, 338*f*, 353
Hyper normalization modeling, 255–256, 255*f*,
        260, 274, 329
    common data retrieval challenges, 352–361
        architectural review, clearing, 361
        audit layer's goal, 354
        integration layer, addressing, 353–354
        retrieving data from HNF repository
            doubly difficult, 354–356
        Solution 0: Focus on Presentation Layer
            Objects, 356
        Solution 1: Dummy Attribute Records,
            356
        Solution 2: Current Record Indicators, 356
        Solution 3: Point-in-Time Tables, 356–357
        Solution 4: Table Pruning, 358–359
        Solution 5: Bridging Tables, 359–360
        Solution 6: Retrieval Query Writers,
            360–361
    concepts, 331–344
        attribute entities, 335–337
        business key entities, 333–334
        ensemble modeling components allow
            light integration and agility, 339–342
        insert-only paradigm, 342–343
        lightly integrated, persistent staging area,
            337–339
        linking entities, 334–335
        Swedish variation, 343–344
    EDW reference architecture, 362*f*
    enabling evolution of existing EDW
            components, 366–368
        splitting out entities, 366–367
        upgrading to a party model, 367–368
    ensemble modeling, 329–331
    evidence of success, 371–373
        Free University, 372–373
        online financial services, 372
    HNF-powered agile solutions, 368–371
    re-architecting EDW for, 361–365
        blending styles to achieve agility, 365
        enhanced vault style, 363–364
        raw vault style, 364–365
        simple vault style, 362–363
        source vault style, 364
    reusable ETL modules accelerating new
            development, 344–352
        calling the reusable ETL modules, 348–350
        comparative development effort, 352
        parameter-driven ETL module prototypes,
            346–348
        self-validating reusable ETL Modules,
            350–352
    varieties of, 330–331
Hyper normalized data model, 255*f*, 331–344
Hyper normalized form (HNF), 250, 361, 375
    aiding leading edge of the integration layer
        only, 353–354
    HNF-powered agile solutions, 368–371
    hyper generalization, 377, 377*f*
    repository, retrieving data from, 354–356
Hyper-modeled key integration points,
        512–513

I

Inception phase, 221
  iterations −1 and 0 fitting into, 221−222
Incremental delivery methods. *See* Agile
    software development
Incremental precision, managing, 229−232
  freezer, fridge, counter metaphor, 230−232
  progressive requirements, framework for
    visualizing, 230
Indexes, on database tables, 80
Information, definition of, 65
Information management (IM), 217−218
Information technology (IT), 66
Initial load of data, 210−211
Inmon, William, 82, 279, 361
"Inmon vs. Kimball" debate, 286, 383
Insert-only paradigm, 342−343
Integration layer, 82, 251, 280
  hyper generalized, 390−391
  with hyper normalization, 329
  traditional, 281−285
Integration testing, 68, 453
Interproject milestones, meeting, 229
INVEST test, 156, 158*f*
Ishikawa fishbone diagram, 176
IT project architect, 517
Iteration −1 and 0, 100−101, 221−222
Iteration burndown chart, 496−497
Iteration product review, 25
Iteration retrospective, 23, 26
Iterations, smoothing out, 229
Iterative delivery, 114

K

Kanban, 3, 6−8, 31−32, 41−47
  adding techniques from, 97−101
  comparison with Scrum, 45−47, 46*t*
  cycle time distribution analysis for team,
    44*f*
  evidence-based service levels, 44−45
  sketch of, 41−43
  transition from Scrum to, 48*f*
  work board, 42*f*
Key performance indicators (KPIs), 105*f*, 173
Kimball, Ralph, 82, 207−208, 286, 289−291
Kimball group, 286
Knockout tests, 438−440

L

Landing area, 156−158, 227, 286, 289, 295,
    295*f*, 302−303, 306−307, 334, 370*f*,
    392, 393*f*, 399, 399*f*, 401, 415−416,
    438, 489*f*, 494
Leading indicators, 189
Lean
  principles, 33−41, 33*f*
  tools (techniques), 32−41, 33*f*
  values, 33*f*
Lean software development, 31−41
  as long-term destination, 32−33
  origins, 31−32
  principles, 33−41, 33*f*
  tools, 33−41, 33*f*

Learning Cycles, 323
"Level 0" data flow diagrams. *See* Context
    diagram
Lightly integrated area, 337−339
Lightweight programming techniques, 14−15
Line Item Number, 333
Line Item table, 264−265
Linking tables and agility, 339−340
Live data prototyping, 512
Logical and physical data modeling,
    eliminating, 387
Logical data model (LDM), 72, 72*f*, 259, 387

M

Machine-assisted data governance, 509−510
Manual engines, 487−488
Many-to-many (M−M) relationships,
    334−335, 336*f*
Map/Reduce join operation, 314*f*, 316*f*
MapReduce, 309, 311−313
  and SQL, 314−324, 317*t*
Massively parallel processing (MPP), 308
Master data management (MDM), 399−401
Metadata, definition of, 65−66
Mind maps and fishbone diagrams, 174−176,
    175*f*
Minimal viable products (MVPs), 119−120
Model-driven evolution and fast adaptation,
    395−397
  data conversions, facilitating, 396−397
  impact of model changes on existing data,
    395−396
Model-driven master data components,
    398−402
Module, definition of, 70
Module use cases, providing developer
    guidance with, 209−212
  flow of events
    alternative, 210−212
    standard, 209−210
  goal, 209
  special requirements, 212
  supplemental specifications
    nonfunctional requirements as, 212
    source-to-target mappings as, 212
Motivation, 39
  to take requirements seriously, 128−130
  through value buildups by environment,
    165−166
Motivation to agile EDW, 5−7
Multivalued dependencies, 266−267, 270−271

N

Name−value pairs, attributes storage as, 377,
    379*f*, 384−385
Natural keys, 80, 346−347, 391
Negative feedback loop, 1−2, 2*f*
Negative test, 439−440
Net income, 196−197
Nonfunctional requirements, 40, 74, 78,
    126−127, 182, 184−186, 197−198,
    232, 481−482, 505
  addressing, 217−221

broader architectural activities, agile EDW
    supporting, 219−221
  proper problem domain for agile EDW,
    217−219
  allocating time for, 234−235
  as supplemental specifications, 212
Nonfunctional tests, 439
Normalization, 260−271, 261*f*
  context diagram for, 263*f*
  data normalization, history of, 262*t*
  designing databases to eliminate update
    anomalies, 260−262
  first to fifth normal form (example),
    262−271
  hyper normalization, 329−344, 336*f*, 338*f*,
    353
  re-architecting the EDW for, 361−365
Normalized data model, 81−82
Notabe Apache Hadoop software components,
    312*f*

O

Object identifiers (OIDs), 381−382, 385−386,
    391
Online analytical processing (OLAP)
    applications. *See* Analytical systems
Online financial services (case study), 372
Online transaction processing (OLTP)
    applications. *See* Operational systems
Open source software (OSS) projects, 66,
    308−309
Operational systems, 66, 83
Order Number, 60, 333, 363−364, 391
Orientation dimension, 185−186

P

Paradigm. *See also* Data modeling paradigm
  vs. data modeling, 259−260
Parameter-driven widgets, building, 482
Party model, 274, 275*f*, 276*f*, 277*f*, 367−368
  consolidating entities into, 281−282
  generalizing to, 287−289
  upgrading to, 367−368
Performance concerns, addressing, 402−403
Persistent staging area, 331−332, 337−339
Personal protected information (PPI), of
    customers, 198
Personas, 170−171
Physical data model (PDM), 72−74, 259
Pipelined delivery approach, 98−100, 99*f*
Planning dimension, 436−437
Point-in-time tables, 356−357, 358*f*
Point-of-view dimension, 440−441
Polarity dimension, 185, 439−440
Portfolio, of programs, 83
Positive test, 439−440
Precision, 137−138, 138*t*
Predecessor/successor dependencies, 228
Pre-development estimate
  managing, 225−226
  preparing, 224*f*
Pre-development iterations, fitting RM artifacts
    into, 223*f*

Predevelopment project estimate, arriving at, 223–225
Prediction, 173
Presentation layer, 280–281, 286, 295
Presentation layer objects, 355–356
Primary key, 80
Principles, 19
Problem statements, 191
Product owner, 20–22, 25–26, 116–117, 119–120, 142, 148–149, 153, 161, 169–170, 174, 182–183, 185, 207, 216, 450, 465–466, 472
   meaning of, 69t
   proxy product owner, 89–90
Product roadmaps, 178–180, 178f, 179f
Production data, subsetting, 485–486
Production environments, 165–166
Program vs. project manager, 84
Programmers, 5, 25, 68–69, 92, 222, 427–428, 433, 465, 493
   meaning of, 69t
   and programming leads, 473
Programming leads, 473
Programs, 83
Progression testing, 440, 481
Progressive elaboration, 230–232, 235, 242
Progressive requirements
   elaboration pattern, 231t
   framework for visualizing, 230
Project, definition of, 83
Project architect (PA), 100–101, 120, 149, 160, 164, 183, 188–189, 191, 194, 196–200, 202, 207–209, 213, 215, 230–232, 372, 472, 517
   role of, 87–88, 149
Project backlog, 95, 171, 176, 228–229
   architectural uncertainties, 229
   business value, 228
   "funding waypoints", 229
   interproject milestones, meeting, 229
   predecessor/successor dependencies, 228
   prioritizing, 228–229
   resource scheduling, 229
   smoothing out iterations, 229
Project charter, 84
Project governance, 164, 225
   interfacing with, 239–241, 240f
Project leaders, 111, 114, 127–130, 136–137, 143–144, 151, 161–164, 185–186, 190, 194, 199, 217, 221, 225–229, 232, 235–237, 242, 261–262, 274, 281, 296, 321, 442–443
Project Management Institute (PMI), 186
Project management office (PMO), 84, 162
Project portfolio management, 83
Project quality dashboard, 494, 495f, 496
Project requirements, enterprise aspects of, 184–186
   functionality dimension, 184–185
   orientation dimension, 185–186
   polarity dimension, 185
   streamlined ERM templates, 186
Project value, 164
Proper problem domain for agile EDW, 217–219

Proxy product owner (PPO), role for DW/BI, 89–90
Pull-based system, 37–38, 42–43
Pushdown processing, of DVS, 299–300

Q
Quality, definition of, 426
Quality activities within an iteration cycle, 464–466, 464f
Quality assurance (QA), 3, 4f, 8, 425
   agile approach to, 429–433
      agile notions, 430–432
         striving for balance, 429–430
         test-led development, 432–433
   bottom-up quality planning, 444–455
      agile-specific test techniques, 449–451
      data warehousing testing techniques, 444–446
      low-level validations, easy-to-follow test technique matrix for, 451–452
      traditional application testing techniques, 446–449
   "fit to purpose", 444
   plan, 477
   top-down planning, 433–441
      functional dimension, 439
      planning dimension, 436–437
      point-of-view dimension, 440–441
      polarity dimension, 439–440
      preliminary definitions, 435–436
      six dimensions of DW/BI testing, 433–435
      system dimension, 437–439
      time frame dimension, 440
   top-down test selection, 2 × 2 planning matrix for, 441–444
Quality control, 436–437
Quality duties at the end of a release cycle, 466–467, 467f
Quality fulfillment documentation, 497–498, 497f
Quality management, 436–437
Quality management system (QMS), 497–498
Quality responsibilities, by team role, 470–473
   self-organized quality planning, guiding the team to, 470–471
   suggested quality duties by role, 471–473
      data modeler, 472
      product owner, 472
      programmers and programming leads, 473
      project architect, 472
      scrum master, 473
      systems analyst, 472–473
Query injection, of DVS, 300
Query substitution, of DVS, 300
Query writers, 360–361, 410

R
RASCI chart, 284
Rational Unified Process (RUP), 3, 67–68, 144–146, 181, 183, 221
   for data warehousing/business intelligence, 52–53
   Google Ngram of, 52, 53f

overview of, 49–51
phases borrowed from, 221
principles, 50f
techniques, 49–50, 221, 226
templates used with, 52t
values, 50f
values and principles of, 50f
whale chart, 51f
Raw vault style, 364–365
Reconciliation test, 446
Reference architecture, 73f, 74–75, 75f, 249–251, 306–307, 326f, 354, 362f
Reference Model for Open Distributed Processing (RM-ODP), 70–71
Referential integrity, 81
Referential integrity test, 445
Regression testing, 89, 440
Relational database management system (RDBMS) servers, 299–300, 308, 311, 325, 325f, 397
Release cycle, 221–226, 466–467, 503–504
Release cycle of organization, supporting, 221–226, 222f
   iterations −1 and 0 fitting into inception phase, 221–222
   predevelopment estimate, managing, 225–226
   predevelopment project estimate, arriving at, 223–225
   rational unified process, phases borrowed from, 221
   release cycle, completing, 226
Repeatability, 486
Repeatable masking, 486
Reporting, 173
Requirements churn, 169–170
Requirements management (RM), 3, 4f, 125, 130–136. See also specific types
   for agile enterprise data warehousing, 126–130, 127f
   agile objectives for, 141–143, 145t
   disadvantages to traditional, 139, 139t
   easy to overinvest in, 130–136
   effective, building the case for, 126–130
   enterprise-capable requirements management (ERM), 183–184, 186
   formal definition of, 130
   generic requirements management (GRM) value chain, 183
   inherently complex, 132–134, 132t, 133f, 134t
   process, 174
   process agile, 144
   RM demands, visualizing with effort curves, 232–234, 233f, 234f
   team motivation to, 128–130
   two intersecting value chains, 144–149
   waterfall-style, 131f
Requirements specification document (RSD), 130–131
Requirements traceability, agile EDW's version of, 215–217
Research capabilities, 173
Residential Marketing, 179–180
Resource scheduling, 229

Retrieval query writers, 360–361
Reusable ETL modules, 348–350
    accelerating new development, 344–352
    calling, 348–350
    comparative development effort, 352
    parameter-driven ETL module prototypes,
        346–348
    self-validating, 350–352
Reusable test widgets, 351f, 352, 444,
    452–453, 452t, 482, 483t, 493
Risk calculation framework, 233f
Risk management, 519–520
Risk mitigation, 111–113
    application coding concept errors, 116
    of business concept errors, 119–120
    extended, for agile enterprise data
        warehouse, 114–120
    fundamental, for agile enterprise data
        warehouse, 111–114
    solution concept errors, 116–119
    value accounting, 162
Root cause analysis, 427–428

S

Sales Channel Monitoring System, 263
Sales Fact, 387–388
Sales Order, 263
Sales Order Header table, 264–265, 287
Sandbox, 70, 469
Scenario testing, 450
"Schema-on-read", 310–311
Scrum
    principles, 20
    techniqes, 27, 32, 45
    values, 20
Scrum master, 6, 21, 24–26, 86, 90, 95, 104,
    462–463, 473
Scrum method, 3, 6–8, 20, 31–32, 34, 52–53,
    86t, 426–427
    burndown chart, 25f
    for data warehousing/business intelligence,
        85–86
    essence of, 21f
    five-step delivery iteration, 23–26
    Google Ngram of, 53f
    in nutshell, 20–26, 22f
    steps in transition from, to Kanban, 48f
    task board, 24, 24f
Scrum's collaboration model, 181–182
Scrumban approach, 47–49
    comparison with Kanban, 45–47, 46t
    two-tiered task board, 48f
Scrum-But, 6
Security tests, 481–482
Self-organized quality planning, guiding the
    team to, 470–471
Self-service BI, 173, 202, 296–297
Shadow IT, 67
    leveraging, 294–296, 295f
        case history, lessons from, 296
        five-step collaborative effort, example of,
            294–296
    Ship joins, of DVS, 300
Simple vault style, 362–363

Slowly changing dimension, new trigger for,
    289–290, 409–410
Small Trucks, 380–381
Soap opera tests, 450
Software, 66
Software development life cycle (SDLC),
    67–68
Software engineering, 23, 47, 67–70
Software release cycle, 221–226
Solution concept errors, 115–116
    examples of, 115t
    risk mitigation of, 116–119
Solutions architect. See Project architect
Solutions statements, in vision document, 191,
    193f
Sort-merge joins, of DVS, 300
Source vault style, 364
Source-to-target map (STMs), 89, 185, 212,
    461–462, 512
    example of, 213f
    as supplemental specifications, 212
Sponsor's concept briefing (SCB), 186–189,
    187f
    customer experience, 188
    functional area impacting assessments, 188
    justification type, 187–188
    program success metrics, 189
    project goals and, 186–189
    value of the program, 188
Sponsor-appreciated results, 518–519
Sprints iterations, 23
Stakeholder requests (SHRs), 146, 186, 189,
    213, 216
Stakeholder's requests, project objectives,
    189–191
    business system challenges, 189
    current manual solution, 189–190
    dependent systems, 190–191
    desired business solution, 190
    volume requirements and end-user census,
        190
Stakeholders, 83
    meaning of, 69t
Standard normal form (SNF) data model, 250,
    252f, 283f, 361
    leading to complex integration layers,
        251–253
Standard risk analysis, 140f
Standish Group's analysis, 13–14
Star schemas, 174, 286, 410–411
Statistical data, of DVS, 300
"Steel thread", proving out architectures using,
    227–228
Story cards, 22–23
Story conference, 23
Story points, 23–24, 95, 225
Story testing, 450
"Straight-to-star" as a controversial alternative,
    286
Streamlined ERM templates, 186
Streamlined Stakeholder Request (SHR),
    template for, 190f
Streamlined Vision Document (VDoc),
    template for, 192f

Structured query language (SQL), 79, 236, 299,
    315–317, 394, 397
    and MapReduce, notable contrasts between,
        314–317, 317t
    override, of DVS, 300
Subrelease candidate reviews, 117, 118b
Subrelease description
    data validation steps for, 206f
    use case model for, 202–203
    Venn diagram for, 203–205
Subrelease overview (SRO), streamlined
    template for, 205f
Subject matter experts, 142, 149, 196, 212,
    236–237, 271
    meaning of, 69t
Subrelease cycle, 481–482, 501
    agile EDW transition, guiding, 515–520
        agile DW/BI manifesto, 518b
        DW/BI customer's bill of rights, 516–517
        toward an agile EDW manifesto, 518–520
    centering the value cycle on data governance
        and quality, 514–515
        deepening the support for data
            governance, 514–515
        world-class quality assurance, achieving,
            515
    data governance, traditional notions of,
        504–510
        data governance actions for the EDW
            team, 508
        life cycle for data governance, 505–508
        machine-assisted data governance for the
            subrelease cycle, 509–510
    fast delivery portion of, 512–514
    "fast requirements" portion of, 511–512
    making the release cycles a
        repeatable process, 503–504
    value cycle, 510–514
Subrelease overview, segmenting the project
    with, 198–209
    business process supported, 202–207
        business-level data validation steps,
            205–207
        sample business queries, 207
        use case model, 202–203
        Venn diagram, 203–205
    nonfunctional requirements, 208–209
    subrelease identifier, 200
    subrelease scope, 200–202
        data services, expressed as, 200–201
        fact qualifier matrix (FQM), expressed
            using, 202
        target business model, expressed as, 202
    technical description, 207–208
        data sourcing details, 208
        non-reusable target dimensions details,
            208
        reusable target dimensions details,
            207–208
        target fact tables details, 207
Subthemes, 176
Sums, averages, medians, 445t
Superoptimizer, 297
Superthemes, 176

Supplemental specifications
  nonfunctional requirements as, 212
  source-to-target mappings as, 212
Surface solution patterns, 370f, 415–416, 415f
Surface solutions, 293, 365, 370f
  big data technologies, 308–327
    to enhance EDW agility, 325–327
    Hadoop, 311–313
    and Hive, 324–325
    Hive, making MapReduce look like SQL
      with, 317–324
    need for, 309–310
    "schema-on-read", 310–311
    SQL and MapReduce, notable contrasts
      between, 314–317, 317t
  data virtualization server (DVS), 296–307
    basic use case, 297–299, 298f
    defining data virtualization, 297
    dynamic delivery approach using,
      304–305
    EDW's reference architecture becoming
      dynamic, 306–307
    performance features, 299–300
    surface solutions, and progressive
      deployment, 302–304
    value proposition, 305–306
    virtual solutions, economics of, 300–302,
      301f
  Shadow IT, leveraging, 294–296, 295f
    case history, lessons from, 296
    five-step collaborative effort, example of,
      294–296
  with raw data vault, 370
  using shadow IT vs. data virtualization
    servers, contrast between, 305t
Surrogate ID (SID), 334, 336
Surrogate keys, 80
Swedish anchor modeling technique, 343–344
System architecture, 70–71
System dimension, 437–439
System integration test (SIT), 70, 165–166,
    429, 469, 494–496
System test cases, 438
System tester(s), 5, 9, 68, 70, 89–90, 91f, 98,
    100–101, 107–108, 221, 233–234,
    234f, 431, 457–463, 481–482, 488,
    490–491, 493–494, 496
  organizational framework, 458–463
    adapted V-model for agile DW/BI test
      cases, 459–460
    classic V-model for analyzing QA
      responsibilities, 458–459
    communicating the QA assignments,
      460–461
    one-up, one-down validation, 461–463
  overarching duties of, 473–475
  role for DW/BI, 89
System testing, 43, 68, 100, 453
Systems analyst (SA), 88–89, 129–130, 212,
    233–234, 242, 472–473

T

Table pruning, 358–359
Taiichi Ohno, 31–33

Tao Teh Ching, 32
Target business model, 196–197, 196f, 199,
    202–203, 208
  for subrelease description, 199f
Task planning, 23–24
Team leaders, 69t, 188–189, 194, 216–217,
    249, 253
Team motivation, 128–130
Team roles, effort levels by, 232–235
  nonfunctional requirements, allocating time
    for, 234–235
  visualizing requirements management
    demands with effort curves, 232–234,
    233f, 234f
Team's progress, visualizing, 494–497
  defects over time, 496
  iteration burndown chart, 496–497
  tests implemented by environment,
    494–496
  top-down and bottom-up quality planning,
    connecting, 496
Team's success, documentation
    of, 497–498
Technical platforms, 520
Test activities distribution across environments,
    468–469
Test assertions, 487, 492f
Test automation, 481–482
Test case, 436, 440, 443–444, 446–448, 447f,
    448t, 449t, 453, 459–460, 468f, 477,
    516f
Test cases, execution of, 477
  agile quality planning, 477–482
    alternatives to sufficient testing, 480
    automation, 481–482
  beginning of creating test cases, 493
  documentation of team's success, 497–498
  engine, starting up, 493–494
  engine implementation, 487–489
    test scenarios, defining, 489
  parameter-driven widgets, building, 482
  team's progress, visualizing, 494–497
    defects over time, 496
    iteration burndown chart, 496–497
    tests implemented by environment,
      494–496
    top-down and bottom-up quality planning,
      connecting, 496
  test data repository, building and populating,
    490–491
  test data sets, 472, 477, 482–487, 485t
    identifying required data sets, 484–485
    planning for expected results, 487
    planning storage for dozens of data sets,
      487
    planning to create dozens of data sets,
      485–486
  testing aspects, configuring, 489–490
  testing objectives, quantifying, 491–492
  top-down plan, updating, 482
Test executions, 431, 477–482, 487
Test scenario, 89, 435f, 436, 487, 488t,
    489–490, 490f
  defining, 489

Test suite, 98, 433, 435–436, 435f, 440, 444,
    449–450, 453, 454f, 458, 469–470,
    473, 480–481, 490, 493–494, 515, 517
Test techniques, 429, 444, 445f, 445t,
    446–447, 451–452, 454–456, 455f,
    469–470
Test widgets, 351–352, 453, 456, 469,
    481–482, 498
  reusable, 452–453
Testing
  and agile teams, 426–427
  and better requirements, 428
  integration of teamwork across pipeline, 428
  need of, 426–429
  progress, visibility of, 428–429
  root cause analysis, 427–428
Testing techniques, 444–446, 445t
  data corners, 445–446
  distribution, across environments, 469–470
  examples and expected results, 446
  reconciliation, 446
  referential integrity test, 445
Test-led development, 24, 432–433
The Data Warehousing Institute (TDWI), 60, 62t
Theme-level testing, 450
Themes, 176
  allocating value to, 164–165
Time frame dimension, 440
Time-boxed iteration, 23
Time-oriented object classification, adding,
    380–381
Top-down planning, 433–441
  and bottom-up quality planning, connecting,
    496
  DW/BI testing, six dimensions of, 433–435
  functional dimension, 439
  planning dimension, 436–437
  point-of-view dimension, 440–441
  polarity dimension, 439–440
  preliminary definitions, 435–436
  system dimension, 437–439
  time frame dimension, 440
  updating, 482
Total test suite, 436
Toyota Production System, 31–32
Traditional data modeling paradigms and their
    discontents, 247
  change cases, for appraising a data modeling
    paradigm, 286–291
  data architecture, 257–258, 257f
  data model, 257f, 258–259
  data modeling paradigm, 257f, 259–260
  enterprise data warehouse (EDW), 249–257
    agile alternatives, 255–257
    conformed dimensions leading to complex
      presentation layers, 253–255, 254f
    reference architecture, reviewing, 249–251
    standard normal forms (SNF) leading to
      complex integration layers, 251–253,
      252f
  generalization, 260, 271–279
    advantages and disadvantages of, 271–274
    of sales table for the party entity
      (example), 274–279, 275f, 276f, 277f

normalization, 260–271, 261*f*
  designing databases to eliminate update
    anomalies, 260–262
  first to fifth normal form (example),
    262–271
  standard approach and its data modeling
    paradigms, 279–281
  "straight-to-star" as a controversial
    alternative, 286
  traditional integration layer as a challenged
    concept, 281–285
    entailing high maintenance conversion
      costs, 283–285
    expensive hidden layer, involving,
      281–282
    results, understanding, 282–283
Traditional project management, 82–84, 239
"Traditionally modeled forms" (TMF),
  250
Transaction capture systems. *See* Operational
  systems
Transactional objects, loading, 391
Transition phase, 51, 221
Transitive dependencies, 265
Triples, 382–383
Two-pass testing, 101

U

Uncertainty
  architectural, 229
  eliminating, 519–520
Unified Anchor Model, 332
Unified Modeling Language (UML), 50
Unique values, 445*t*
Unit testing, 453–455
Units, definition of, 69–70
Usage Cycles, 323
Use case model, 202–203, 205*f*
Use cases, 16*t*, 53, 202–203, 209–212,
  323–324, 327, 413–414. *See also*
  Rational Unified Process (RUP)
User acceptance testing (UAT), 43, 68, 70,
  165–166, 453
User demo, 23, 25–26, 474–475
User modeling, 170–171, 171*f*
User stories, 21–22
  allocating value to, 164–165
  hiding data integration work, 92–93

V

Valid range, 445*t*
Value, project, 164
Value accounting, 151, 159–162, 160*f*
  basics of, 160–161
  making effective developers, 161–162
  risk mitigation, 162
Value chains intersection for stereoscopic
  project definition, 215
  conquering complex business rules with
    embedded method, 235–239
  data cowboy role, adding, 235–236

effort curves, placing business rules
    discovery and analysis into, 238–239
  modified data mining method, 236–238
  special skills and tools required, 236
elaboration phase, 226–228
  choosing developer stories for, 226–227
  "steel thread", proving out architectures
    using, 227–228
incremental precision, managing, 229–232
  freezer, fridge, counter metaphor, 230–232
  progressive requirements, framework for
    visualizing, 230
nonfunctional requirements, addressing,
  217–221
  agile EDW supports broader architectural
    activities, 219–221
  proper problem domain for agile EDW,
    217–219
project backlogs, prioritizing, 228–229
  architectural uncertainties, 229
  business value, 228
  "funding waypoints", 229
  meeting interproject milestones, 229
  predecessor/successor dependencies, 228
  resource scheduling, 229
  smoothing out iterations, 229
project governance, interfacing with,
  239–241, 240*f*
supporting the organization's software
  release cycle, 221–226
  arriving at predevelopment project
    estimate, 223–225
  iterations –1 and 0 fitting into the
    inception phase, 221–222
  phases borrowed from rational unified
    process, 221
  predevelopment estimate, managing,
    225–226
  release cycle, completing, 226
team roles, effort levels by, 232–235
  nonfunctional requirements, allocating
    time for, 234–235
  visualizing requirements management
    demands with effort curves, 232–234,
    233*f*, 234*f*
two value chains, intersecting, 215–217
  requirements traceability, agile EDW's
    version of, 215–217
  waterfall approach, 242
Value cycle (VC), productivity-tool driven, 3,
  4*f*, 8–9
Value cycle for agile EDW team, 510–514
  data governance and quality, centering the
    value cycle on, 514–515
  deepening the support for data
    governance, 514–515
  world-class quality assurance, achieving,
    515
  fast delivery portion of, 512–514
  Step 1: Workflow-Driven Data Governance
    and Prototyping, 511

Step 2: Associative Data Discovery,
  511–512
Step 3: Collaborative Source-to-Target
  Mapping, 512
Step 4: Live Data Prototyping, 512
Step 5: Hyper-Modeled Key Integration
  Points, 512–513
Step 6: Enriched Hyper-Modeled Solution,
  513
Step 7: Collaborative Analytics, 513
Step 8: Model-Driven Solutions, 513–514
Value proposition, of data virtualization,
  305–306
Value stream mapping, 34–35, 34*f*
Value-added loops, 397–398
Values, definition of, 19
Venn diagram, 203–205
  for subrelease description, 206*f*
Views, definition of, 81
Virtual solutions, economics of, 300–302, 301*f*
Vision boxes, 176, 177*f*
Vision document
  sample context diagram for, 195*f*
  sample high level architecture diagram for,
    198*f*
  sample target business model for, 196*f*
  sketching the solution with, 191–198
    context diagram, 194–195
    features and benefits list, 191–194
    high-level data flow, 197
    nonfunctional requirements, 197–198
    solutions statements, 191, 193*f*
    target business model, 196–197
Vision statements, 176–178, 177*f*
V-model, 459*f*, 460*f*
  for agile DW/BI test cases, 459–460
  for analyzing QA responsibilities, 458–459
Vrije Universiteit Amsterdam (VU), 372–373

W

Waterfall method, 13, 17–19, 17*f*, 242
Waterfall projects, 457
Westwood Rec Center, 264
Whale chart, 51, 90, 91*f*
Workflow-driven data governance and
  prototyping, 511
Workflow-driven data governance products,
  509
World-class quality assurance, achieving, 515

X

XP
  principles, 27–29
  techniqes, 27, 32
  values, 27–29

Z

Zachman enterprise architectural framework,
  76
Zeroth law of quality, 426–427

Printed in the United States
By Bookmasters